Theorizing Multiculturalism

For *Lori Jo Willett*
and *Leslie Anita Chiang*

Theorizing Multiculturalism
A Guide to the Current Debate

Edited by
Cynthia Willett

BLACKWELL
Publishers

Copyright © Blackwell Publishers Ltd, 1998

First published 1998

2 4 6 8 10 9 7 5 3 1

Blackwell Publishers Inc.
350 Main Street
Malden, Massachusetts 02148
USA

Blackwell Publishers Ltd
108 Cowley Road
Oxford OX4 1JF
UK

Library of Congress Cataloging-in-Publication Data

Theorizing multiculturalism: a guide to the current debate/edited
by Cynthia Willett.
    p.   cm.
Includes bibliographical references and index.
ISBN 0–631–20341–9 — ISBN 0–631–20342–7 (pbk.)
    1. Multiculturalism.   2. Pluralism (Social sciences)   I. Willett,
Cynthia, 1956– .
HM276.T49   1998
306—dc21   97–37878
                                                                        CIP

British Library Cataloguing in Publication Data
A CIP catalogue record for this book is available from the British Library.

Typeset in 10 on 12½pt Sabon
by York House Typographic Ltd
Printed in Great Britain by T. J. International, Padstow, Cornwall

This book is printed on acid-free paper

Contents

List of Contributors   viii
Acknowledgments   x
Introduction   1

1   **Post-Hegelian Dialectics of Recognition and
    Communication**   17
    1   From Redistribution to Recognition? Dilemmas of
        Justice in a "Post-Socialist" Age   19
        Nancy Fraser
    2   Unruly Categories: A Critique of Nancy Fraser's Dual
        Systems Theory   50
        Iris Marion Young
    3   A Rejoinder to Iris Young   68
        Nancy Fraser
    4   Recognition, Value, and Equality: A Critique of Charles
        Taylor's and Nancy Fraser's Accounts of
        Multiculturalism   73
        Lawrence Blum
    5   Ludic, Corporate, and Imperial Multiculturalism:
        Impostors of Democracy and Cartographers of the New
        World Order   100
        Martin J. Beck Matuštík

II   Post-Marxism and Issues of Class   119
     6   Multiculturalism: Consumerist or Transformational?   121
         Bill Martin
     7   Post-Marxist Political Economy and the Culture of the
         Left   151
         Donald C. Hodges

III Continental and Analytical Feminism   167
     8   Identity, Difference, and Abjection   169
         Kelly Oliver
     9   Psychological Explanations of Oppression   187
         Ann E. Cudd

IV   Corporeal Logic and Sexuate Being   217
    10   Toward the Domain of Freedom: Interview with
         Drucilla Cornell by Penny Florence   219
         Drucilla Cornell
    11   Morphing the Body: Irigaray and Butler on Sexual
         Difference   234
         Tamsin Lorraine

V   Critical Race Theory   257
    12   Alienation and the African–American Experience   259
         Howard McGary
    13   "Stuck Inside of Mobile with the Memphis Blues
         Again": Interculturalism and the Conversation of Races   276
         Robert Bernasconi

VI   Postcolonialism and Ethnicity   299
    14   Fanon and the Subject of Experience   301
         Ronald A. T. Judy
    15   White Studies: The Intellectual Imperialism of US
         Higher Education   334
         Ward Churchill

VII Liberalism   357
    16   Moral Deference   359
         Laurence M. Thomas
    17   "Multiculturalism," Citizenship, Education, and
         American Liberal Democracy   382
         Lucius Outlaw, Jr.

VIII Pragmatism 399
18 Ceremony and Rationality in the Haudenosaunee
Tradition 401
Scott L. Pratt
19 Educational Multiculturalism, Critical Pluralism, and
Deep Democracy 422
Judith M. Green
20 Universal Human Liberation: Community and
Multiculturalism 449
Leonard Harris

Index 458

Contributors

Robert Bernasconi, Department of Philosophy, University of Memphis, Memphis.
Lawrence Blum, Columbia University, New York.
Ward Churchill, University of Colorado, Boulder.
Drucilla Cornell, School of Law, Rutgers University, Newark.
Ann E. Cudd, Department of Philosophy, University of Kansas, Lawrence.
Nancy Fraser, Department of Political Science, The New School Graduate Faculty, New York.
Judith M. Green, Department of Philosophy, Fordham University, New York.
Leonard Harris, Department of Philosophy, Purdue University, West Lafayette.
Donald C. Hodges, Department of Philosophy, Florida State University, Tallahassee.
Ronald A. T. Judy, Department of English, University of Pittsburgh.
Tamsin Lorraine, Department of Philosophy, Swarthmore College, Swarthmore.
Howard McGary, Department of Philosophy, Rutgers University, Newark.
Bill Martin, Department of Philosophy, De Paul University, Chicago.
Martin J. Beck Matuštík, Department of Philosophy, Purdue University, West Lafayette.
Kelly Oliver, Department of Philosophy, University of Texas, Austin.

Lucius Outlaw, Jr, Department of Philosophy, Haverford College, Haverford.
Scott L. Pratt, Department of Philosophy, University of Oregon, Eugene.
Laurence M. Thomas, Department of Philosophy, Syracuse University, Syracuse.
Iris Young, Graduate School of Public and International Affairs, University of Pittsburgh.

Acknowledgments

Lewis Gordon, Tommy Lott, Pamela Hall, Tom Flynn, David Carr, Jason Wirth, Sōraya Mékerta, Robert McCauley, Deepika Bahri, Patricia Huntington, Darrell Moore, Alison Brown, Felicia Kruse, Carola Dudzik, Cheryl Lester, Barry Shank, Philip Barnard, Julie Maybee, Tom Tuozzo, Kae Chatman, Dawn Jakubowski, Amy Coplan, John McClendon, Rex Martin, Richard De George, Stefan Boettcher, Julie Willett, and Randy McBee are among some of the many who helped me envision the aim, scope, and organization of this anthology. Thanks also to Dawn Jakubowski for excellent assistance with the manuscript. Steve Smith at Blackwell Publishers offered exceptional guidance throughout the stages of planning, writing, and production. Mary Riso and Jack Messenger provided excellent assistance with tasks of production. My contributors are an exciting group of philosophers and theorists to work with, and produced profound essays for the volume. I owe deeply felt thanks to each one of you.

The editor and publishers are grateful for permission to reproduce the following copyright material:

The New Left Review for Nancy Fraser's "From Redistribution to Recognition? Dilemmas of Justice in a 'Post-Socialist' Age" (no. 212, July/August 1995, pp. 68–93); Iris Marion Young's "Unruly Categories: A Critique of Nancy Fraser's Dual Systems Theory" (no. 222, March/April 1997, pp. 147–60); and Nancy Fraser's "A Rejoinder to Iris Young" (no. 223, May/June 1997).

Routledge for Howard McGary's "Alienation and the African–American Experience" and Laurence M. Thomas's "Moral Deference" in John P. Pittman (ed.), *African–American Perspectives and Philosophical Traditions* (1997); the latter essay was revised for this anthology.

Ward Churchill for permission to reprint his essay "White Studies: The Intellectual Imperialism of US Higher Education."

Christine Battersby and Penny Florence for permission to reprint "Toward the Domain of Freedom: Interview with Drucilla Cornell by Penny Florence." from *Women's Philosophy Review*.

The publishers apologize for any errors or omissions in the above list and would be grateful to be notified of any corrections that should be incorporated in the next edition or reprint of this book.

Introduction

Multiculturalism has not yet been fully theorized. In part, the lack of a unifying theory stems from the fact that multiculturalism as a political, social, and cultural movement has aimed to respect a multiplicity of diverging perspectives outside of dominant traditions. The task of theorizing these divergent subject positions does not easily accommodate the traditional genre of the philosophical treatise penned by some single great mind. On the contrary, if these divergent perspectives demand to be theorized by those who have lived through or otherwise participated in the experiences that they represent, then the theorizing of multiculturalism demands a coalition of authors, and is especially well suited to the genre of the anthology.

The essays in this volume reflect some of the multiplicity of perspectives that should contribute towards any contemporary theoretical formulation of the issues of race, ethnicity, gender, class, and sexuality. The issues and concerns discussed stem from distinct social, cultural, and historical experiences, so it should not be surprising that some essays put forth assumptions or claims that are antithetical to positions adopted in other essays. The anthology opens up a range of perspectives for a kind of theorizing that does not readily conform to systematic philosophy's assimilationist demands for unity, consistency, or coherence. On the contrary, as Bill Martin explains in his contribution (chapter 8), "the whole issue of multiculturalism raises the question of difference in a way that would seem to run against inherited forms of philosophical or social theoretical system building." For example, Martin notes, the Marxist "idea that all practices aim toward a single practice recapitulates Kant's argument that all thought intends a system." A totalizing mode of thinking constitutes a problem, not a solution, for the essays in the collection. Therefore they adhere neither to a materialist nor an idealist logic of identity. They do not seek to ground all conflict in a single source (class, race, etc.) nor define history in accordance with a single meaning. At the same time, the diverse perspectives in the collection also carefully avoid fragmenting into a divisive politics of identity, or, alternatively, into what Martin diagnoses as a multiculturalism that is "consumerist." A multiculturalism that is not "consumerist" but "transformational" requires, as Martin argues, a framework.[1] Some of the significant elements for such a framework are what this volume aims to lay out. While the represented views diverge on many aspects of theory-building, including issues of method and the relative importance and specific significance of class, race, gender, sexuality, and ethnicity (for Martin, the more deep-rooted variable is class), the views correspond with one another in terms of a basic concern for overcoming oppression through social, political, and cultural conflict and the need to articulate this multifaceted concern for oppression from discordant positions. It is this correspondence, or affinity, between the essays that orients the diverse views towards a collective vision of social change and towards what Martin terms a "transformative multiculturalism."[2]

Many of the essays borrow tools of critique or analysis from post-modernist philosophies. However, taken as a group, the essays also move beyond much of the fragmentation, disorientation, and stoic paralysis that has been associated with postmodernism and towards the more productive task of reconceptualizing the central components for social, political, and ethical theory. Still it often seems that the multicultural movement has taken over from postmodernism a strong dislike for normative theorizing of any kind. It is true that multiculturalism has inherited many of its more radical claims from postmodernism. From postmodernism, multiculturalism has learned to distrust the universalism and foundationalism of traditional theory-construction and the exclu-sionary and hierarchical impulses of normitivity. In its more productive moments, however, multiculturalism marks a progressive stage beyond the negativism of postmodern critique.

One of the more significant differences between multiculturalism and postmodernism has been associated with deconstruction. Classic decon-struction consists in part of textual strategies for undermining the dualistic and hierarchical values that control the production of linguistic meaning. These strategies expose double binds that disrupt the social and political forces of control in the production of meaning and value. The result is linguistic equivocation and moral indeterminism. Like post-modernists generally, multicultural writers also aim to unsettle dominant systems of meaning and moral authority. However, while the post-modernist may argue that linguistic dissonance and moral ambiguity are unsurpassable resources in themselves for attacking hierarchical construc-tions of knowledge and power, transformative multiculturalists aim to establish in the margins of hegemonic systems alternative sources of meaning and moral authority.

Martin Matuštík argues along these lines in his essay (chapter 5). Matuštík warns against those "ludic multiculturalists" who "focus almost exclusively on the undecidability of texts." The ludic multi-culturalist tends "to regard both politics and play in terms of intertextual transgressions of existing cultural discourses." The problem with ludic multiculturalism is that its playful strategies for displacing dominant signifiers and disrupting existing hierarchies risk leaving the center intact. As Matuštík argues, "decentering practices [can] offer salutary micro-politics [only] if cultural workers become cognizant of the oppressed identities and occluded differences in ways that grand narratives of modernity were not." Listening attentively to the voices of the oppressed and embracing a "foundationless foundation" for a concrete social ethics sets the stage for a new mode of theorizing. For Matuštík, "this realization announces a *new multicultural enlightenment*. Overcoming abstract lib-eral, monogenealogically communitarian, and ludic multiculturalist phases, resistance postmodern multiculturalists join liberation struggles of concrete peoples."

But, as Leonard Harris warns in chapter 20, the struggles of a concrete people cannot be reduced and simplified to the "definitive interests and modes of agency" of "an undifferentiated entity." Harris argues that "contrary to the doxastic picture of social entities – a picture in which social entities invariably embody stable interests and essences – it is the adversarial features of social entities that may be the most important arguable sources for liberation." Harris concludes that "a radical trans-formation of misery, exploitation, starvation, the homelessness of immigrants, racial stereotyping and ethnocentrism may well depend on our achieving, through the aegis of our multiple locations, conditions for the possibility of liberation."

While what Matuštík has identified as a new and emergent mode of multicultural theorizing lacks any widely accepted name or model, many writers of the last decade or so borrow jointly from both deconstruc-tive postmodernism as well as its arch-rival, dialectic.[3] The models of thinking or strategies of negotiation that emerge from this or other hybrid methodologies are sometimes (but not always) rather loosely referred to as moral pragmatism.[4] Only a few of the substantial number of contemporary writers who associate themselves with themes of a moral pragmatism trace their roots back to the particular tradition called "pragmatism" in American philosophy. In fact the elements for a multicultural "moral pragmatism" grow out of diverse if not clearly differentiated philosophical sources, including Post-Hegelian theories of recognition and communication, Post-Marxism and issues of class, postcolonialism and ethnicity, Continental and analytical feminism, corporeal logic and sexuate being, critical race theory, liberalism, and pragmatism proper. Clearly, each of these theoretical orientations provides paradigmatic examples, generalizations, or styles of inquiry and interrogation that conflict with some of the more basic assumptions or working principles of other orientations. However, these various orientations also work constructively and pragmatically together, forming a multivalent critique of oppressive cultural and social practices while projecting the major elements for social change.

The renewal of theoretical activity is anchored in transformative conceptions of ethical subjectivity. One reoccurring claim, resurrected from critical theory, is that oppression can in part be measured through repression. Multicultural writers may acknowledge some of the concerns articulated by Foucault in his critique of the repressive hypothesis, but as a consequence these writers have developed a more multifaceted understanding of the social and psychological causes of repression.[5] According to Foucault, sexuality and other shadowy dimensions of the self are not primarily primitive drives, impulses, or desires that have been repressed by society. Rather, sexuality and other expressions of embodiment take shape through the matrices of knowledge and power. In other words, the subject with his or her needs and desires is socially and discursively constructed. Of course, if the subject is socially constructed all the way down, it is difficult to explain "psychological death," trauma, and other socio-psychological effects of repression. Multicultural writers borrow from psychoanalytic theory (Lacan, Zizek) and postmodern ethical theory (Derrida, Levinas) an interest in the effects of trauma and repression on the constitution of the socially responsible subject. However, multiculturalists differ from Lacanians and various postmodernists in that they do not assume that either trauma or repression are structurally necessary for the production of the subject. As Ronald Judy suggests in chapter 6, trauma and other forms of anxiety result from social and psychological forces of oppression that are based on specific if sometimes global histories of racism, sexism, homophobia, etc. Nor do multiculturalists assume *à la* Freud that sexuality or various other desires are primitive and therefore entirely separable from either discursive and historical forces or from core issues of personal identity, ego formation, or a culture-bound process of individuation. Judy argues that according to Fanon, "repression is a constitutive function of the colonial economy." After carefully locating his own reading of Fanon by way of Said, Gates, Spivak, and Bhabha among others, Judy explains in detail the traumatic process by which the Antillean "ego identifies with the master discourse of Europe."

"Fanon's agenda," Judy observes, "is to correct the situation so that the Black has ontological resistance in the eyes of the White." But if, for Fanon, it is not clear how this resistance can occur other than by means of a violence that repeats the trauma, still Fanon – like so many multicultural writers – seeks social processes of healing and models of subjectivity that "work through" abject, traumatic, or other unidealized and embodied dimensions of experience.

Kelly Oliver (chapter 10) treats a related concern in her essay "Identity, Difference, and Abjection." Oliver examines the postmodernist claim that subjectivity emerges through a "process of abjection." She argues that postmodern theorists are wrong to assume that abjection or other violent psychological processes of rejection or exclusion are normally constitutive of the self. Abjection is not a necessary condition of subjectivity but the contingent consequence of patriarchy, racial terror, or other social and psychological forms of political oppression. These consequences can be countered with effective political or social action.

In chapter 13, Tamsin Lorraine introduces the pair of terms "corporeal logics" and "conceptual logics" in order to articulate the conditions for a non-repressive interaction between cerebral and corporeal levels of the self. Lorraine develops, critiques, and expands Irigaray's conception of sexual difference and Butler's analysis of the lesbian phallus. Her conclusion is that "Instead of leaving us in a poststructuralist and relativistic void, [Butler's] analysis [of the lesbian phallus] suggests that there is a material basis for innovation in identity and social practices. If to be an embodied subject means to have already achieved a kind of corporeal coherence then listening to the wisdom of the body with a discriminating intellect might present new possibilities for being and acting."

But then if we are to free our "corporeal logics," or as Drucilla Cornell argues, "the imaginary domain," from patriarchal propagation of heterosexual norms, then we must define and protect rights for "sexuate beings." In an interview (chapter 12), Cornell explains the key concepts of her own contributions to the debate: "The imaginary domain is a philosophical concept in the sense that it tries to articulate the conditions that any theory of justice or ethics as social arrangements has to have as a starting place: the equivalent evaluation of each of us as a sexuate being."

A second major claim surrounding the issue of ethical subjectivity arises out of the attack on the social atomism and hyper-individualism of the modern tradition. According to this claim as it is developed in various multiculturalist writers, the social psychology of oppression, including the phenomenon of "social death," can be explained only if one assumes that the subject emerges through a socially and historically embedded dialectic of alienation and recognition. While multiculturalists are wary of reestablishing nineteenth-century dialectical norms of integration, assimilation, or synthesis, they nonetheless borrow from dialectical philosophies the idea that individuality emerges through the encounter with the Other. Oliver explains these constitutive relationships by revisiting Hegel's account of the development of self-consciousness in *Phenomenology of Spirit*. She argues that Hegel is right to define the subject in terms of the desire for the Other, but that Hegel is wrong to construe this desire as a search for a mirror-like reflection of the Self in the Other. Hegel's conception of desire as narcissistic means that those who are different are perceived as oppositional and as a threat. Oliver suggests that the Hegelian account of desire should be diagnosed as an illusion of mastery, an illusion that "kills the possibility of desire. Desire requires a fluidity and openness that charges and electrifies the space between two people. ... Relationships require identification across and through difference, identification that does not reduce the other to the same, identification as compassion and communion." Oliver also points out that conceptions of the subject that normalize either asocial or agonistic relations with the Other usually assume that the primordial asocial or agonistic relation is with the mother. If the relation between the mother and the child is not treated as asocial but as cooperative, then individualization can be viewed as a process that does not require abjection but reciprocity.

While Oliver focuses on the ways in which social compassion and communion begin in overcoming alienating models of mothering, Howard McGary in his classic essay "Alienation and the African–American Experience" (chapter 14) examines the social effects and philosophical implications of a race-based alienation. McGary argues that classic liberal conceptions of autonomy and Marxist notions of economic alienation cannot fully address the socio-psychological sources of alienation that African Americans have to confront in a racist society. According to McGary, while there are significant resources in ethnic communities for dealing with the forms of alienation caused by racism, and while the lack of recognition does not always lead to alienation, race-based alienation is a reality and must be central in any social theory.

In chapter 15 Robert Bernasconi argues that "everyone should learn more about a number of cultures in addition to their own, including ... how those cultures see one's own culture. ... The greatest contribution of multiculturalism in the fullest sense will be the change that it could bring about within the dominant group, thereby making the conversation of the races less one-sided." Bernasconi develops his concerns by examining the history of the Blues as a source from which European Americans might come to understand how African Americans deal with racism. The "intercultural" exchange that takes place via the Blues also demonstrates how incommensurable cultures might communicate "without limiting the analysis to formal encounters." Bernasconi argues that "the Blues provides a ... test case with which to explore in concrete terms the complex range of issues posed by multiculturalism. ... The Blues ... exhibits very clearly the phenomenon of intercultural borrowings ... and in such a way that the plurality of cultures is not compromised in the direction of hybridism."

Multiculturalism's focus on socially based differences can be at odds with theories that emphasize the economic basis for alienation and oppression. Those theorists who focus on economic forces of exploitation may find their roots in Marxist and Neo-Marxist critiques of capitalism. However, in chapter 9 Donald Hodges argues that traditional Marxist theories of political economy fail to distinguish a "political economy of labor" from a "a political economy of the working class, a 'class' that includes a new crop of exploiters consisting of professional workers." These more traditional Marxists also fail to account for how the new economic order supplements capitalist exploitation with bureaucratic exploitation. Hodges points out that Leftists in general tend to think of social tension as fueled by an opposition between workers and capitalists. In the post-capitalist era, however, "capitalists are in the rumble seat and ... the private sector plays second fiddle to the quasi-public or corporate sector." For Hodges, the elimination of surplus labor in various forms of capital requires that the Post-Marxist unmask as illusion the "vain hope that making the pie bigger will eventually provide relief for everyone." There are fundamental limits for any system of political economy, Hodges argues, and this means accepting scarcity as a condition for human cooperation. Hodges concludes that the bourgeois liberal notions of labor and value that find their way into the core of traditional Marxist thought should give way to a new asceticism.

In chapter 1 Nancy Fraser notes the political and ideological tensions between "a socialist imaginary centered on terms such as 'interest,' 'exploitation,' and 'redistribution'" and "the rise of a new political imaginary centered on notions of 'identity,' 'difference,' 'cultural domination,' and 'recognition.'" Her aim is to locate a basis for a "critical theory of recognition, one which identifies and defends only those versions of the cultural politics of difference that can be coherently combined with the social politics of equality." Fraser argues that identity-based theories of recognition conflict with a transformative politics of redistribution because the former promote group differentiation, while the latter calls "for abolishing economic arrangements that underpin group specificity." She concludes that only a transformative politics of recognition, specifically one that would deconstruct group identities, can work together with a transformative politics of redistribution in order to secure the goal of universal recognition. Her primary example of a transformative politics of recognition is queer theory, whose aim is not to solidify a gay identity, but "to deconstruct the homo–hetero dichotomy so as to destabilize all fixed sexual identities."

Some of those who affirm group identities, however, may aim to affirm these identities in ways that are transformative – both of the group identity and of the basic, orienting values of society as a whole. Mothers may not want to subscribe to any of the traditional expectations for the overly sentimentalized and undervalued caretaking of children. However, they may take mothering as a more powerful and richer social force than can be acknowledged or understood by any of the prevailing models of social relations, and one that can lead towards the radical transformation of underlying social and political frameworks.

In chapter 2 Iris Young touches upon the complex issue of compensating women for their work as primary caretakers. In opposition to Fraser, Young argues that theorists should not separate cultural and material forms of oppression, not even for purposes of analysis. Young believes that the cultural recognition of specific group identities provides a necessary means towards material, social, and economic equality. Young also contends that "New Left theorizing has insisted that the material effects of political economy are inextricably bound with culture," and she offers her own five-fold classification of oppression as an example.

In chapter 4 Lawrence Blum argues that Fraser is right to critique theorists such as Taylor for overemphasizing the cultural at the expense of material components of justice. In addition, according to Blum, Taylor confuses the concept of culture with that of cultural group, and then mistakenly identifies multiculturalism with the recognition of the equality of cultures rather than the equality of cultural groups. Because of this mistake, Blum argues, Taylor's vision of multiculturalism leads to unintelligible, unnecessary, and counterproductive comparisons of the "value" of different cultures. Moreover, according to Blum, Fraser's emphasis on the goal of equality leads her to undervalue the need for groups to be recognized for their distinctiveness. While Fraser's essay urges a double focus on the material and cultural values of multiculturalism, and Young's essay urges that the recognition of distinct groups serves as a means to the end of material equality, Blum argues that multiculturalism requires a double focus on equality and distinctiveness.

While multicultural writers may appropriate central concepts or tools from psychoanalytic theory or from dialectical philosophies of recognition in order to account for the psychology of oppression, Ann Cudd (chapter 11) offers an alternative explanation based on the scientific evidence of social cognitive theory and the methodology of analytical feminism. She demonstrates how oppression originates in the cognitive process of stereotyping. This cognitive process is biased to favor "in-groups" over "out-groups." Interesting findings include the fact that "it takes very little information or basis for identification for people to establish an in-group/out-group distinction," and that "stereotyping cannot be seen as an unbiased information-processing phenomenon, but one that is creatively manipulated by persons to serve their interest in a coherent rationalization of . . . social roles." As Cudd explains, "the social cognitive description of [the desire for recognition] would be that we have the desire to categorize ourselves as members of in-groups and then make those groups distinctive, and insofar as possible, positive. Thus, this psychological theory can explain the desire for recognition as a part of our cognitive functioning in a social world." Cudd goes on to demonstrate the economic incentives for members of both oppressed and dominant groups to behave according to the stereotypes for their groups. One of her conclusions is that "these stereotypes begin to change when material incentives change."

If the subject emerges through a dialectic of recognition or, alternatively, through processes of stereotyping, in the encounter with the Other, this "other" is not only the personal Other but also larger forces of society, history, and nature. Some of these forces may haunt intersubjective encounters and yet act in part behind the back of the individuals involved in those relationships. These forces of oppression or sources of trauma may not be fully open to historical documentation or discursive analysis. In other words, to appropriate from Lacanian critiques of dialectic, misrecognition may be an unavoidable aspect of subjectivity and intersubjectivity. However, the acknowledgment of the role of non-rational forces from history or nature or social interaction should not be taken to imply that life-denying or otherwise oppressive forces cannot be redressed by human hands. On the contrary, major writers in the multi-cultural movement have strong views regarding the moral difference between the better and the worse, and the need for some strong and guiding conception of social progress. Multiculturalists may attempt to offer, through specific examples, compelling images, or broken narratives, philosophical models for the measure of this progress. Because the histor-ical, social, and corporeal forces that shape subjectivity are not necessarily available for discursive analysis or coherent narrative representation, social and ethical conceptions of freedom and justice may at times find their most suitable theorizing in, for example, the medium of music, dance, or poetry. And because the denounced subjects of history may not have the resources to respond to a philosophical call for moral resolve or correct reasoning, writers may use their poetic gifts to summon spiritual forces, including the healing power of love (Toni Morrison, Gayatri Spivak, bell hooks).⁶ The result is a methodology that can turn any European form of dialectical mediation, not only *à la* Marx, "right side up," but also inside out.

European dialectical philosophy mediates Reason and the Other of Reason through (European) Reason. For Hegel, this mediation occurs in a cultural life that begins in art and religion and that culminates in the Absolute Idea of European philosophy. The multiculturalist, like the Hegelian, also tends to locate some of the more fundamental sources of conflict and mediation in the social values and institutional practices of culture. Indeed, the change of focus in much contemporary philosophy from an analysis of problems in language to issues of culture has promp-ted Julie Maybee to argue that the "linguistic turn" has given way to the "cultural turn."⁷ For the multicultural critic, the Other that is known by Eurocentric Reason or other cultural components of dominant traditions (in other words, the Other that could be caught in the narratives, logics, and imaginative constructs of a hegemonic culture) is not the Other of the Other but the Other of the Same. Therefore, the multiculturalist may begin the search for the forces of mediation between Europe and its Other in the reason and culture, as well as the economic concerns, of the Other.

Hegel's discussion of the "African Spirit" exemplifies the blindness of the European dialectic. In the Introduction to *The Philosophy of History*, Hegel constructs the major poles of his dialectical narrative through the opposition between the "sensual Negro" and the "rational free spirit of the European," and then argues that the rational mediation between the Negro and the European is slavery:

> "Viewed in the light of such facts [i.e. that the construct of the 'Negro' was, for the European, the alterity of European rationality], we may conclude *slavery* to have been the occasion of the increase of human feeling among the Negroes . . . . Every intermediate grade between this [i.e. the 'Natural condition' of the 'Negro'] and the realization of a rational State retains – as might be expected – elements and aspects of injustice; therefore we find slavery even in the Greek and Roman States, as we do serfdom down to the latest times. But thus existing in a State, slavery is itself a phase of advance from the merely isolated sensual existence – a phase of education – a mode of becoming participant in a higher morality and . . . culture."[8]

While Hegel's *Phenomenology* aligns itself with a project of emancipation, and proceeds to trace the concept of freedom from its source in the culture of the European slave of antiquity, Hegel's *History* relegates modern slavery to an anomaly and a necessary condition for a race fixed in the "Natural Condition." In both earlier and later works, Hegel narrates the origins of the idea of freedom from the Greek or Roman slave to the master of the modern European household and bourgeois citizen of the state. Meanwhile, the African who was enslaved by the European and transported to America did not experience dialectical mediation – the middle passage through European morality and culture – as an education. The black slave experienced the mediation of European reason and culture as unmediated terror.

While some multicultural writers may borrow from the postmodern critics of European reason literary and philosophical strategies for accentuating disjunction and difference over logics of identity and literary techniques for narrative unity, they often also search for healing forces that mediate and, in so doing, take us beyond some of the differences that divide us. These writers may draw upon non-European cultural traditions in order to open paths that overturn some of the dualisms, or level some of the hierarchical values, of Western culture, and that prepare for an authentic mediation between European and non-European cultures – i.e. one that is not based on trauma or terror, one that is not a form of "slavery." For example, in chapter 7 Ward Churchill argues that the native world view known as the "Hoop" or "Wheel" or "Circle" of Life provides a basis for interrelating what Westerners have "compartmentalized as distinct 'spheres of knowledge'." Moreover, according to Churchill, the "organic rather than synthesizing or synthetic view" of native thought is "inherently anti-hierarchical" and therefore provides the basis for an alliance with, for example, both deconstructionists and dialectical thinkers from the Marxist tradition.

In chapter 18 Scott Pratt connects the tradition of rationality of the Iroquois with pragmatist and feminist conceptions of rationality as a communal process. He argues that "in contrast to European conceptions of rationality as a process of acquisition ... rationality from within the Haudenosaunee tradition may be understood as a process of conversation and responsive action." This is a form of reason that is found in the "dream-guessing rite" and other healing ceremonies, and that is expressed not in fixed laws but in "a song or expression of an individual which needs interpretation and an active response." These songs can be heard not only from human beings but throughout nature. While communication between human beings and our "animal brothers" is known by the Iroquois to be difficult, "human beings and animals [are portrayed] as part of the same community, sharing knowledge, ceremonies, and resources."

As Judith Green argues in chapter 19, the implications of these kinds of concerns is that

> in societies like America that are formally but not deeply democratic and that are increasingly dominated by a powerful and pervasive transnational capitalist economic sector, the culturally and existentially unsustaining and unsustainable character of such a limited instantiation of democracy has become visible in the last years of the twentieth century in the form of two primary, interactive social pathologies: existential nihilism and ontological rootlessness."

For "those who fully grasp the contingent, processive metaphysics of deep democracy," Green argues, "persons, life-enhancing relations, our ecosystem and its constitutive elements, and nature as a whole are regarded as awe-inspiring – holy." Green proceeds to recommend a direction for a strong multicultural education. As she argues, "in the emergent, braided American tradition of resemblant commonalities across diversities in geopolitical location and cultural roots, education has been regarded from our beginning as the most desirable and effective mode of personal formation and social transformation."

Yet, as Lucius Outlaw argues in chapter 17, education in the past in America has "produced a hegemonic 'monoculturalism' devoted to assimilating various ethnics of European descent to a unified America resting on each person's appropriating and living out suitable identities and loyalties given his or her place in racialized and gendered social (political, economic, cultural) hierarchies." Such efforts have been "legitimated by appeals to the grounding of these knowledges in the universality of a singular rationality unfolding in the historical telos of the leading nations of the white race." What is needed is

> the formulation of an epistemology and a pedagogy that facilitates the translation of local knowledges and their interconnections of particular cultural groups so as to allow them to be shared by others as a major factor in the continuous process of nation-building that no longer requires total assimilation on the way to unity, but strives for unity in and through diversity.

While postmodern movements may develop deconstructive or other transgressive strategies for the disruption of hierarchies, these strategies tend to preempt any effort to find new sources of meaning and value, or of what Outlaw terms "the ties that bind." For the hard-core deconstructionist, any effort to construct large or small-scale structures, or to weave local or grand narratives, does not challenge but only redraws the lines and circles that define insider and outsider. Meanwhile, some of the more compelling voices in multiculturalism celebrate the forces of mediation – as long as these forces replace the logic of identity and difference with healing ceremonies and other social and revolutionary practices of connection and resistance. Like American pragmatism, multiculturalism borrows from dialectical philosophy its moral impulse and its aim to heal the social wounds of dualistic and exclusionary thinking. However, multiculturalism's "moral deference" to the voices of the "slaves" of history undercuts any easy, consumerist universalism, and points in the direction of a more productive critique of the "master narratives" of Western culture, along with an enlightened transformation of the universals embedded in our cultures. These less abstract and more mediating universals would have to come, not from the top down, but from the ground up – from the experiences, practices, and thought of those who create culture in the shadows of power.

The notion of moral deference as it is developed by Laurence Thomas (chapter 16) is especially useful in countering one of the more easy temptations of the universalist liberal who thinks that he or she pays due respect to the Other and yet interprets, judges, and experiences the meaning of respect through a language, a logic, or an imaginative weave of associations that belongs to a dominant and oppressive culture. As Thomas argues, neither reason, imagination, nor sympathy can give one "adequate insight into the weal and woe of others," at least not in a world that is divided by "diminished social-categories groups" and "privileged social-category groups." "Moral deference is owed to persons of good will when they speak in an informed way regarding experiences specific to their diminished social category from the standpoint of an emotional category configuration to which others do not have access," Thomas writes. "The attitude of moral deference is, as it were, a prelude to bearing witness to another's pain with that person's authorization. To bear witness to the moral pain of another . . . is to have won her confidence that one can speak informedly and with conviction on her behalf." Finally, then, multiculturalism solicits moral deference, not towards those who occupy positions of power but towards those who suffer from the lack of power. If human beings (including the philosophers among us) have an amoral tendency to respect power, then Thomas's notion of moral deference serves as a much-needed corrective. This corrective may be multiculturalism's most deeply moral gesture. It certainly demands that the multicultural movement always remains receptive to new voices and should never be fully theorized.

Notes

1 Tommy L. Lott argues this point quite forcefully in "Black Vernacular Representation and Cultural Malpractice," *Multiculturalism: A Critical Reader*, ed. David Theo Goldberg (Oxford: Blackwell Publishers, 1994), pp. 230–58.

2 For a fuller treatment of my use of "correspondence," see Cynthia Willett, *Maternal Ethics and Other Slave Moralities* (New York: Routledge, 1995), pp. 92–4.

3 Homi Bhabha is one prominent example of a theorist who mixes dialectic and poststructuralist elements into his analysis of a space that lies between "the master and the slave, . . . overcomes the given grounds of opposition and opens up a space of translation: a place of hybridity." See "The Commitment to Theory" in Bhabha's *The Location of Culture* (New York: Routledge, 1994), pp. 19–39.

4 For a theoretical discussion of the significance of pragmatism with respect to issues of race, see "Taking Race Pragmatically," in David Theo Goldberg, *Racist Culture: Philosophy and the Politics of Meaning* (Cambridge, Mass. and Oxford: Blackwell Publishers, 1993), pp. 206–73.

5 See "We 'Other Victorians'" in Michel Foucault, *The History of Sexuality Volume I: An Introduction*, Robert Hurley, trans. (New York: Vintage Books, 1980), pp. 3–13. For an insightful critique of the risks of this aspect of multiculturalism, see Andrew Cutrofello's "Multiculturalism's Repressive Hypothesis" (paper presented at the annual meeting of the Association for the Psychoanalysis of Culture and Society at George Washington University, November, 1996).

6 On the significance of love as a healing force, see Toni Morrison's novel

Beloved (New York: Penguin, 1987) as well as Pamela M. Hall's discussion of Morrison's work in the context of virtue ethics and tragedy, *Ethics and Tragedy* (work in progress); "Translator's Preface" and "Afterword" in *Imaginary Maps: Three Stories by Mahasweta Devi*, translated and introduced by Gayatri Chakravorty Spivak (New York: Routledge, 1995); and "Love as the Practice of Freedom," in bell hook's *Outlaw Culture: Resisting Representations* (New York: Routledge, 1994).

7 Julie Maybee, "Who Am I? The Limits of Shared Culture as a Criterion of Group Solidarity and Individual Identity" (paper presented at the African Studies Program, University of Kansas, spring, 1996).

8 Georg Wilhelm Friedrich Hegel, *The Philosophy of History*, trans. J. Sibree (New York: Dover, 1956), pp. 98–9.

Part I

Post-Hegelian Dialectics of
Recognition and Communication

1

From Redistribution to Recognition? Dilemmas of Justice in a "Post-Socialist" Age

Nancy Fraser

The "struggle for recognition" is fast becoming the paradigmatic form of political conflict in the late twentieth century. Demands for "recognition of difference" fuel struggles of groups mobilized under the banners of nationality, ethnicity, "race," gender, and sexuality. In these "post-socialist" conflicts, group identity supplants class interest as the chief medium of political mobilization. Cultural domination supplants exploitation as the fundamental injustice. And cultural recognition displaces socioeconomic redistribution as the remedy for injustice and the goal of political struggle.

That, of course, is not the whole story. Struggles for recognition occur in a world of exacerbated material inequality – in income and property ownership; in access to paid work, education, healthcare and leisure time; but also more starkly in caloric intake and exposure to environmental toxicity, hence in life expectancy and rates of morbidity. Material inequality is on the rise in most of the world's countries – in the United States and in Haiti, in Sweden and in India, in Russia and in Brazil. It is also increasing globally, most dramatically across the line that divides North from South. How, then, should we view the eclipse of a socialist imaginary centered on terms such as "interest," "exploitation," and "redistribution"? And what should we make of the rise of a new political imaginary centered on notions of "identity," "difference," "cultural domination," and "recognition?" Does this shift represent a lapse into "false consciousness?" Or does it, rather, redress the culture-blindness of a materialist paradigm rightfully discredited by the collapse of Soviet Communism?

Neither of those two stances is adequate, in my view. Both are too wholesale and un-nuanced. Instead of simply endorsing or rejecting all of identity politics *simpliciter*, we should see ourselves as presented with a new intellectual and practical task: that of developing a *critical* theory of recognition, one which identifies and defends only those versions of the cultural politics of difference that can be coherently combined with the social politics of equality.

In formulating this project, I assume that justice today requires *both* redistribution *and* recognition. And I propose to examine the relation between them. In part, this means figuring out how to conceptualize cultural recognition and social equality in forms that support rather than undermine one another. (For there are many competing conceptions of both!) It also means theorizing the ways in which economic disadvantage and cultural disrespect are currently entwined with and support one another. Then, too, it requires clarifying the political dilemmas that arise when we try to combat both those injustices simultaneously.

My larger aim is to connect two political problematics that are currently dissociated from one another. For only by articulating recognition and redistribution can we arrive at a critical-theoretical framework that is adequate to the demands of our age. That, however, is far too much to take on here. In what follows, I shall consider only one aspect of the problem. Under what circumstances can a politics of recognition help support a politics of redistribution? And when is it more likely to undermine it? Which of the many varieties of identity politics best synergize with struggles for social equality? And which tend to interfere with the latter?

In addressing these questions, I shall focus on axes of injustice that are simultaneously cultural and socioeconomic, paradigmatically gender and "race." (I shall not say much, in contrast, about ethnicity or nationality.)[1] And I must enter one crucial preliminary caveat: in proposing to assess recognition claims from the standpoint of social equality, I assume that varieties of recognition politics that fail to respect human rights are unacceptable even if they promote social equality.[2]

Finally, a word about method: in what follows, I shall propose a set of analytical distinctions, for example, cultural injustices versus economic injustices, recognition versus redistribution. In the real world, of course, culture and political economy are always imbricated with one another; and virtually every struggle against injustice, when properly understood, implies demands for both redistribution and recognition. Nevertheless, for heuristic purposes, analytical distinctions are indispensable. Only by abstracting from the complexities of the real world can we devise a conceptual schema that can illuminate it. Thus, by distinguishing redistribution and recognition analytically, and by exposing their distinctive logics, I aim to clarify – and begin to resolve – some of the central political dilemmas of our age.

My discussion proceeds in four parts. In section one, I conceptualize redistribution and recognition as two analytically distinct paradigms of justice, and I formulate "the redistribution–recognition dilemma." In section two, I distinguish three ideal-typical modes of social collectivity in order to identify those vulnerable to the dilemma. In section three, I distinguish between "affirmative" and "transformative" remedies for injustice, and I examine their respective logics of collectivity. Lastly, I use these distinctions, in section four, to propose a political strategy for integrating recognition claims with redistribution claims with a minimum of mutual interference.

1 The Redistribution–Recognition Dilemma

Let me begin by noting some complexities of contemporary "post-socialist" political life. With the decentering of class, diverse social movements are mobilized around cross-cutting axes of difference. Contesting a range of injustices, their claims overlap and at times conflict. Demands for cultural change intermingle with demands for economic change, both within and among social movements. Increasingly, however, identity-based claims tend to predominate, as prospects for redistribution appear to recede. The result is a complex political field with little pro-grammatic coherence.

To help clarify this situation and the political prospects it presents, I propose to distinguish two broadly conceived, analytically distinct under-standings of injustice. The first is socioeconomic injustice, which is rooted in the political–economic structure of society. Examples include exploita-tion (having the fruits of one's labor appropriated for the benefit of others); economic marginalization (being confined to undesirable or poorly paid work or being denied access to income-generating labor altogether); and deprivation (being denied an adequate material standard of living).

Egalitarian theorists have long sought to conceptualize the nature of these socioeconomic injustices. Their accounts include Marx's theory of capitalist exploitation, John Rawls's account of justice as fairness in the distribution of "primary goods," Amartya Sen's view that justice requires ensuring that people have equal "capabilities to function," and Ronald Dworkin's view that it requires "equality of resources."[3] For my purposes here, however, we need not commit ourselves to any one particular theoretical account. We need only subscribe to a rough and general understanding of socioeconomic injustice informed by a commitment to egalitarianism.

The second kind of injustice is cultural or symbolic. It is rooted in social patterns of representation, interpretation, and communication. Examples include cultural domination (being subjected to patterns of interpretation and communication that are associated with another culture and are alien and/or hostile to one's own); nonrecognition (being rendered invisible via the authoritative representational, communicative, and interpretative practices of one's culture); and disrespect (being routinely maligned or disparaged in stereotypic public cultural representations and/or in every-day life interactions).

Some political theorists have recently sought to conceptualize the nature of these cultural or symbolic injustices. Charles Taylor, for example, has drawn on Hegelian notions to argue that:

> Nonrecognition or misrecognition ... can be a form of oppression, impris-oning someone in a false, distorted, reduced mode of being. Beyond simple lack of respect, it can inflict a grievous wound, saddling people with crippling self-hatred. Due recognition is not just a courtesy but a vital human need.[4]

Likewise, Axel Honneth has argued that:

> We owe our integrity ... to the receipt of approval or recognition from other persons. [Negative concepts such as "insult" or "degradation"] are related to forms of disrespect, to the denial of recognition. [They] are used to characterize a form of behaviour that does not represent an injustice solely because it constrains the subjects in their freedom for action or does them harm. Rather, such behaviour is injurious because it impairs these persons in their positive understanding of self – an understanding acquired by intersubjective means.[5]

Similar conceptions inform the work of many other critical theorists who do not use the term "recognition."[6] Once again, however, it is not necessary here to settle on a particular theoretical account. We need only subscribe to a general and rough understanding of cultural injustice, as distinct from socioeconomic injustice.

Despite the differences between them, both socioeconomic injustice and cultural injustice are pervasive in contemporary societies. Both are rooted in processes and practices that systematically disadvantage some groups of people vis-à-vis others. Both, consequently, should be remedied.[7]

Of course, this distinction between economic injustice and cultural injustice is analytical. In practice, the two are intertwined. Even the most material economic institutions have a constitutive, irreducible cultural dimension; they are shot through with significations and norms. Conversely, even the most discursive cultural practices have a constitutive, irreducible political–economic dimension; they are underpinned by material supports. Thus, far from occupying two airtight separate spheres, economic injustice and cultural injustice are usually interimbricated so as to reinforce one another dialectically. Cultural norms that are unfairly biased against some are institutionalized in the state and the economy; meanwhile, economic disadvantage impedes equal participation in the making of culture, in public spheres and in everyday life. The result is often a vicious circle of cultural and economic subordination.[8]

Despite these mutual entwinements, I shall continue to distinguish economic injustice and cultural injustice analytically. And I shall also distinguish two correspondingly distinct kinds of remedy. The remedy for economic injustice is political–economic restructuring of some sort. This might involve redistributing income, reorganizing the division of labor, subjecting investment to democratic decision-making, or transforming other basic economic structures. Although these various remedies differ importantly from one another, I shall henceforth refer to the whole group of them by the generic term "redistribution."[9] The remedy for cultural injustice, in contrast, is some sort of cultural or symbolic change. This could involve upwardly revaluing disrespected identities and the cultural products of maligned groups. It could also involve recognizing and positively valorizing cultural diversity. More radically still, it could involve the wholesale transformation of societal patterns of representation, interpretation and communication in ways that would change *everybody's* sense of self.[10] Although these remedies differ importantly from one another, I shall henceforth refer to the whole group of them by the generic term "recognition."

Once again, this distinction between redistributive remedies and recognition remedies is analytical. Redistributive remedies generally presuppose an underlying conception of recognition. For example, some proponents of egalitarian socioeconomic redistribution ground their claims on the "equal moral worth of persons"; thus, they treat economic redistribution as an expression of recognition.[11] Conversely, recognition remedies sometimes presuppose an underlying conception of redistribution. For example, some proponents of multicultural recognition ground their claims on the imperative of a just distribution of the "primary good" of an "intact cultural structure"; they therefore treat cultural recognition as a species of redistribution.[12] Such conceptual entwinements notwith-standing, I shall leave to one side questions such as, do redistribution and recognition constitute two distinct, irreducible, *sui generis* concepts of justice, or alternatively, can either one of them be reduced to the other?[13] Rather, I shall assume that however we account for it metatheoretically, it will be useful to maintain a working, first-order distinction between socioeconomic injustices and their remedies, on the one hand, and cultural injustices and their remedies, on the other.[14]

With these distinctions in place, I can now pose the following questions: What is the relation between claims for recognition, aimed at remedying cultural injustice, and claims for redistribution, aimed at redressing eco-nomic injustice? And what sorts of mutual interferences can arise when both kinds of claims are made simultaneously?

There are good reasons to worry about such mutual interferences. Recognition claims often take the form of calling attention to, if not performatively creating, the putative specificity of some group, and then of affirming the value of that specificity. Thus, they tend to promote group differentiation. Redistribution claims, in contrast, often call for abolish-ing economic arrangements that underpin group specificity. (An example would be feminist demands to abolish the gender division of labor.) Thus they tend to promote group de-differentiation. The upshot is that the politics of recognition and the politics of redistribution appear to have mutually contradictory aims. Whereas the first tends to promote group differentiation, the second tends to undermine it. The two kinds of claim thus stand in tension with each other; they can interfere with, or even work against, one another.

Here, then, is a difficult dilemma. I shall henceforth call it the redistribution–recognition dilemma. People who are subject to both cul-tural injustice and economic injustice need both recognition and redistribution. They need both to claim and to deny their specificity. How, if at all, is this possible?

Before taking up this question, let us consider precisely who faces the recognition–redistribution dilemma.

2 Exploited Classes, Despised Sexualities, and Bivalent Collectivities

Imagine a conceptual spectrum of different kinds of social collectivities. At one extreme are modes of collectivity that fit the redistribution model of justice. At the other extreme are modes of collectivity that fit the recognition model. In between are cases that prove difficult because they fit both models of justice simultaneously.

Consider, first, the redistribution end of the spectrum. At this end let us posit an ideal-typical mode of collectivity whose existence is rooted wholly in the political economy. It will be differentiated as a collectivity, in other words, by virtue of the economic structure, as opposed to the cultural order, of society. Thus, any structural injustices its members suffer will be traceable ultimately to the political economy. The root of the injustice, as well as its core, will be socioeconomic maldistribution, while any attendant cultural injustices will derive ultimately from that economic root. At bottom, therefore, the remedy required to redress the injustice will be political–economic redistribution, as opposed to cultural recognition.

In the real world, to be sure, political economy and culture are mutually intertwined, as are injustices of distribution and recognition. Thus we may doubt whether there exist any pure collectivities of this sort. For heuristic purposes, however, it is useful to examine their properties. To do so, let us consider a familiar example that can be interpreted as approximating the ideal type: the Marxian conception of the exploited class, understood in an orthodox and theoretical way.[15] And let us bracket the question of whether this view of class fits the actual historical collectivities that have struggled for justice in the real world in the name of the working class.[16]

In the conception assumed here, class is a mode of social differentiation that is rooted in the political–economic structure of society. A class only exists as a collectivity by virtue of its position in that structure and of its relation to other classes. Thus, the Marxian working class is the body of persons in a capitalist society who must sell their labor-power under arrangements that authorize the capitalist class to appropriate surplus productivity for its private benefit. The injustice of these arrangements, moreover, is quintessentially a matter of distribution. In the capitalist scheme of social reproduction, the proletariat receives an unjustly large share of the burdens and an unjustly small share of the rewards. To be sure, its members also suffer serious cultural injustices, the "hidden (and not so hidden) injuries of class." But far from being rooted directly in an autonomously unjust cultural structure, these derive from the political economy as ideologies of class inferiority proliferate to justify exploitation.[17] The remedy for the injustice, consequently, is redistribution, not recognition. Overcoming class exploitation requires restructuring the political economy so as to alter the class distribution of social burdens and social benefits. In the Marxian conception, such restructuring takes the radical form of abolishing the class structure as such. The task of the proletariat, therefore, is not simply to cut itself a better deal, but "to abolish itself as a class." The last thing it needs is recognition of its difference. On the contrary, the only way to remedy the injustice is to put the proletariat out of business as a group.

Now consider the other end of the conceptual spectrum. At this end we may posit an ideal-typical mode of collectivity that fits the recognition model of justice. A collectivity of this type is rooted wholly in culture, as opposed to in political economy. It only exists as a collectivity by virtue of the reigning social patterns of interpretation and evaluation, not by virtue of the division of labor. Thus, any structural injustices its members suffer will be traceable ultimately to the cultural-valuational structure. The root of the injustice, as well as its core, will be cultural misrecognition, while any attendant economic injustices will derive ultimately from that cultural root. At bottom, therefore, the remedy required to redress the injustice will be cultural recognition, as opposed to political–economic redistribution.

Once again, we may doubt whether there exist any pure collectivities of this sort, but it is useful to examine their properties for heuristic purposes. An example that can be interpreted as approximating the ideal type is the conception of a despised sexuality, understood in a specific stylized and theoretical way.[18] Let us consider this conception, while leaving aside the question of whether this view of sexuality fits the actual historical homosexual collectivities that are struggling for justice in the real world.

Sexuality in this conception is a mode of social differentiation whose roots do not lie in the political economy, as homosexuals are distributed throughout the entire class structure of capitalist society, occupy no distinctive position in the division of labor, and do not constitute an exploited class. Rather, their mode of collectivity is that of a despised sexuality, rooted in the cultural-valuational structure of society. From this perspective, the injustice they suffer is quintessentially a matter of recognition. Gays and lesbians suffer from heterosexism: the authoritative construction of norms that privilege heterosexuality. Along with this goes homophobia: the cultural devaluation of homosexuality. Their sexuality thus disparaged, homosexuals are subject to shaming, harassment, discrimination, and violence, while being denied legal rights and equal protections – all fundamentally denials of recognition. To be sure, gays and lesbians also suffer serious economic injustices; they can be summarily dismissed from work and are denied family-based social-welfare benefits. But far from being rooted directly in the economic structure, these derive instead from an unjust cultural-valuational structure.[19] The remedy for the injustice, consequently, is recognition, not redistribution.

Overcoming homophobia and heterosexism requires changing the cultural valuations (as well as their legal and practical expressions) that privilege heterosexuality, deny equal respect to gays and lesbians, and refuse to recognize homosexuality as a legitimate way of being sexual. It is to revalue a despised sexuality, to accord positive recognition to gay and lesbian sexual specificity.

Matters are thus fairly straightforward at the two extremes of our conceptual spectrum. When we deal with collectivities that approach the ideal type of the exploited working class, we face distributive injustices requiring redistributive remedies. When we deal with collectivities that approach the ideal type of the despised sexuality, in contrast, we face injustices of misrecognition requiring remedies of recognition. In the first case, the logic of the remedy is to put the group out of business as a group. In the second case, on the contrary, it is to valorize the group's "groupness" by recognizing its specificity.

Matters become murkier, however, once we move away from these extremes. When we consider collectivities located in the middle of the conceptual spectrum, we encounter hybrid modes that combine features of the exploited class with features of the despised sexuality. These collectivities are "bivalent." They are differentiated as collectivities by virtue of *both* the political–economic structure *and* the cultural-valuational structure of society. When disadvantaged, therefore, they may suffer injustices that are traceable to both political economy and culture simultaneously. Bivalent collectivities, in sum, may suffer both socio-economic maldistribution and cultural misrecognition in forms where neither of these injustices is an indirect effect of the other, but where both are primary and co-original. In that case, neither redistributive remedies alone nor recognition remedies alone will suffice. Bivalent collectivities need both.

Both gender and "race" are paradigmatic bivalent collectivities. Although each has peculiarities not shared by the other, both encompass political–economic dimensions and cultural-valuational dimensions. Gender and "race," therefore, implicate both redistribution and recognition.

Gender, for example, has political–economic dimensions. It is a basic structuring principle of the political economy. On the one hand, gender structures the fundamental division between paid "productive" labor and unpaid "reproductive" and domestic labor, assigning women primary responsibility for the latter. On the other hand, gender also structures the division within paid labor between higher-paid, male-dominated, manufacturing and professional occupations and lower-paid, female-dominated "pink-collar" and domestic-service occupations. The result is a political–economic structure that generates gender-specific modes of exploitation, marginalization, and deprivation. This structure constitutes gender as a political–economic differentiation endowed with certain class-like characteristics. When viewed under this aspect, gender injustice appears as a species of distributive injustice that cries out for redistributive redress. Much like class, gender justice requires transforming the political economy so as to eliminate its gender structuring. Eliminating gender-specific exploitation, marginalization, and deprivation requires abolishing the gender division of labor – both the gendered division between paid and unpaid labor and the gender division within paid labor. The logic of the remedy is akin to the logic with respect to class: it is to put gender out of business as such. If gender were nothing but a political–economic differentiation, in sum, justice would require its abolition.

That, however, is only half the story. In fact, gender is not only a political–economic differentiation, but a cultural-valuational differentiation as well. As such, it also encompasses elements that are more like sexuality than class and bring it squarely within the problematic of recognition. Certainly, a major feature of gender injustice is androcentrism: the authoritative construction of norms that privilege traits associated with masculinity. Along with this goes cultural sexism: the pervasive devaluation and disparagement of things coded as "feminine," paradigmatically – but not only – women.[20] This devaluation is expressed in a range of harms suffered by women, including sexual assault, sexual exploitation, and pervasive domestic violence; trivializing, objectifying, and demeaning stereotypical depictions in the media; harassment and disparagement in all spheres of everyday life; subjection to androcentric norms in relation to which women appear lesser or deviant and which work to disadvantage them, even in the absence of any intention to discriminate; attitudinal discrimination; exclusion or marginalization in public spheres and deliberative bodies; and denial of full legal rights and equal protections. These harms are injustices of recognition. They are relatively independent of political economy and are not merely "super-structural." Thus, they cannot be remedied by political–economic redistribution alone but require additional independent remedies of recognition. Overcoming androcentrism and sexism requires changing the cultural valuations (as well as their legal and practical expressions) that privilege masculinity and deny equal respect to women. It requires decentering androcentric norms and revaluing a despised gender. The logic of the remedy is akin to the logic with respect to sexuality: it is to accord positive recognition to a devalued group specificity.

Gender, in sum, is a bivalent mode of collectivity. It contains a political–economic face that brings it within the ambit of redistribution. Yet it also contains a cultural-valuational face that brings it simultaneously within the ambit of recognition. Of course, the two faces are not neatly separated from one another. Rather, they intertwine to reinforce one another dialectically, as sexist and androcentric cultural norms are institutionalized in the State and the economy, while women's economic disadvantage restricts women's "voice," impeding equal participation in the making of culture, in public spheres, and in everyday life. The result is a vicious circle of cultural and economic subordination. Redressing gender injustice, therefore, requires changing both political economy and culture.

But the bivalent character of gender is the source of a dilemma. Insofar as women suffer at least two analytically distinct kinds of injustice, they necessarily require at least two analytically distinct kinds of remedy – both redistribution and recognition. The two remedies pull in opposite directions, however. They are not easily pursued simultaneously. Whereas the logic of redistribution is to put gender out of business as such, the logic of recognition is to valorize gender specificity.[21] Here, then, is the feminist version of the redistribution–recognition dilemma: how can feminists fight simultaneously to abolish gender differentiation and to valorize gender specificity?

An analogous dilemma arises in the struggle against racism. "Race," like gender, is a bivalent mode of collectivity. On the one hand, it resembles class in being a structural principle of political economy. In this aspect, "race" structures the capitalist division of labor. It structures the division within paid work between low-paid, low-status, menial, dirty, and domestic occupations, held disproportionately by people of color, and higher-paid, higher-status, white-collar, professional, technical and managerial occupations, held disproportionately by "whites."[22] Today's racial division of paid labor is part of the historic legacy of colonialism and slavery, which elaborated racial categorization to justify brutal new forms of appropriation and exploitation, effectively constituting "blacks" as a political–economic caste. Currently, moreover, "race" also structures access to official labor markets, constituting large segments of the population of color as a "superfluous", degraded subproletariat or underclass, unworthy even of exploitation and excluded from the productive system altogether. The result is a political–economic structure that generates "race"-specific modes of exploitation, marginalization, and deprivation. This structure constitutes "race" as a political–economic differentiation endowed with certain class-like characteristics. When viewed under this aspect, racial injustice appears as a species of distributive injustice that cries out for redistributive redress. Much like class, racial justice requires transforming the political economy so as to eliminate its racialization. Eliminating "race"-specific exploitation, marginalization, and deprivation requires abolishing the racial division of labor – both the racial division between exploitable and superfluous labor and the racial division within paid labor. The logic of the remedy is like the logic with respect to class: it is to put "race" out of business as such. If "race" were nothing but a political–economic differentiation, in sum, justice would require its abolition.

However, "race," like gender, is not only political–economic. It also has cultural-valuational dimensions, which bring it into the universe of recognition. Thus, "race" too encompasses elements that are more like sexuality than class. A major aspect of racism is Eurocentrism: the authoritative construction of norms that privilege traits associated with "whiteness." Along with this goes cultural racism: the pervasive devaluation and disparagement[23] of things coded as "black," "brown," and "yellow," paradigmatically – but not only – people of colour.[24] This depreciation is expressed in a range of harms suffered by people of color, including demeaning stereotypical depictions in the media as criminal, bestial, primitive, stupid, and so on; violence, harassment, and "dissing" in all spheres of everyday life; subjection to Eurocentric norms in relation to which people of color appear lesser or deviant and which work to disadvantage them, even in the absence of any intention to discriminate; attitudinal discrimination; exclusion from and/or marginalization in public spheres and deliberative bodies; and denial of full legal rights and equal protections. As in the case of gender, these harms are injustices of recognition. Thus, the logic of their remedy, too, is to accord positive recognition to devalued group specificity.

"Race," too, therefore, is a bivalent mode of collectivity with both a political–economic and a cultural-valuational, face. Its two faces intertwine to reinforce one another dialectically, as racist and Eurocentric cultural norms are institutionalized in the state and the economy, while the economic disadvantage suffered by people of color restricts their "voice." Redressing racial injustice, therefore, requires changing both political economy and culture. And as with gender, the bivalent character of "race" is the source of a dilemma. Insofar as people of color suffer at least two analytically distinct kinds of injustice, they necessarily require at least two analytically distinct kinds of remedy, which are not easily pursued simultaneously. Whereas the logic of redistribution is to put "race" out of business as such, the logic of recognition is to valorize group specificity.[25] Here, then, is the anti-racist version of the redistribution–recognition dilemma: How can anti-racists fight simultaneously to abolish "race" and to valorize racialized group specificity?

Both gender and "race," in sum, are dilemmatic modes of collectivity. Unlike class, which occupies one end of the conceptual spectrum, and unlike sexuality, which occupies the other, gender and "race" are bivalent, implicated simultaneously in both the politics of redistribution and the politics of recognition. Both, consequently, face the redistribution–recognition dilemma. Feminists must pursue political–economic remedies that would undermine gender differentiation, while also pursuing cultural-valuational remedies that valorize the specificity of a despised collectivity. Anti-racists, likewise, must pursue political–economic remedies that would undermine "racial" differentiation, while also pursuing cultural-valuational remedies that valorize the specificity of despised collectivities. How can they do both things at once?

3 Affirmation or Transformation? Revisiting the Question of Remedy

So far I have posed the redistribution–recognition dilemma in a form that appears quite intractable. I have assumed that redistributive remedies for political–economic injustice always de-differentiate social groups. Likewise, I have assumed that recognition remedies for cultural-valuational injustice always enhance social group differentiation. Given these assumptions, it is difficult to see how feminists and anti-racists can pursue redistribution and recognition simultaneously.

Now, however, I want to complicate these assumptions. In this section, I shall examine alternative conceptions of redistribution, on the one hand, and alternative conceptions of recognition, on the other. My aim is to distinguish two broad approaches to remedying injustice that cut across the redistribution–recognition divide. I shall call them "affirmation" and "transformation" respectively. After sketching each of them generically, I shall show how each operates in regard to both redistribution and recognition. On this basis, finally, I shall reformulate the redistribution–recognition dilemma in a form that is more amenable to resolution.

Let me begin by briefly distinguishing affirmation and transformation. By affirmative remedies for injustice I mean remedies aimed at correcting inequitable outcomes of social arrangements without disturbing the underlying framework that generates them. By transformative remedies, in contrast, I mean remedies aimed at correcting inequitable outcomes precisely by restructuring the underlying generative framework. The nub of the contrast is end-state outcomes versus the processes that produce them. It is *not* gradual versus apocalyptic change.

This distinction can be applied, first of all, to remedies for cultural injustice. Affirmative remedies for such injustices are currently associated with mainstream multiculturalism.[26] This proposes to redress disrespect by revaluing unjustly devalued group identities, while leaving intact both the contents of those identities and the group differentiations that underlie them. Transformative remedies, by contrast, are currently associated with deconstruction. They would redress disrespect by transforming the under-lying cultural-valuational structure. By destabilizing existing group identities and differentiations, these remedies would not only raise the self-esteem of members of currently disrespected groups. They would change *everyone's* sense of belonging, affiliation, and self.

To illustrate the distinction, let us consider, once again, the case of the despised sexuality.[27] Affirmative remedies for homophobia and heterosex-ism are currently associated with gay-identity politics, which aims to revalue gay and lesbian identity.[28] Transformative remedies, in contrast, include the approach of "queer theory", which would deconstruct the homo–hetero dichotomy. Gay-identity politics treats homosexuality as a substantive, cultural, identificatory positivity, much like an ethnicity.[29] This positivity is assumed to subsist in and of itself and to need only additional recognition. "Queer theory", in contrast, treats homosexuality as the constructed and devalued correlate of heterosexuality; both are reifications of sexual ambiguity and are co-defined only in virtue of one another.[30] The transformative aim is not to solidify a gay identity, but to deconstruct the homo–hetero dichotomy so as to destabilize all fixed sexual identities. The point is not to dissolve all sexual difference in a single, universal human identity; it is rather to sustain a sexual field of multiple, debinarized, fluid, ever-shifting differences.

Both these approaches have considerable interest as remedies for mis-recognition. But there is one crucial difference between them. Whereas gay-identity politics tends to enhance existing sexual group differentia-tion, queer-theory politics tends to destabilize it – at least ostensibly and in the long run.[31] The point holds for recognition remedies more generally. Whereas affirmative recognition remedies tend to promote existing group differentiations, transformative recognition remedies tend, in the long run, to destabilize them so as to make room for future regroupments. I shall return to this point shortly.

Analogous distinctions hold for the remedies for economic injustice. Affirmative remedies for such injustices have been associated historically with the liberal welfare state.[32] They seek to redress end-state maldistribution, while leaving intact much of the underlying political–economic structure. Thus, they would increase the consumption share of economically disadvantaged groups, without otherwise restructuring the system of production. Transformative remedies, in contrast, have been historically associated with socialism. They would redress unjust distribution by transforming the underlying political–economic structure. By restructuring the relations of production, these remedies would not only alter the end-state distribution of consumption shares; they would also change the social division of labor and thus the conditions of existence for everyone.[33]

Let us consider, once again, the case of the exploited class.[34] Affirmative redistributive remedies for class injustices typically include income transfers of two distinct kinds: social-insurance programs share some of the costs of social reproduction for the stably employed, the so-called "primary sectors" of the working class; public-assistance programs provide means-tested, "targeted" aid to the "reserve army" of the unemployed and underemployed. Far from abolishing class differentiation per se, these affirmative remedies support it and shape it. Their general effect is to shift attention from the class division between workers and capitalists to the division between employed and nonemployed fractions of the working class. Public-assistance programs "target" the poor, not only for aid but for hostility. Such remedies, to be sure, provide needed material aid. But they also create strongly cathected, antagonistic group differentiations.

The logic here applies to affirmative redistribution in general. Although this approach aims to redress economic injustice, it leaves intact the deep structures that generate class disadvantage. Thus, it must make surface reallocations time and again. The result is to mark the most disadvantaged class as inherently deficient and insatiable, as always needing more and more. In time such a class can even come to appear privileged, the recipient of special treatment and undeserved largesse. An approach aimed at redressing injustices of distribution can thus end up creating injustices of recognition.

In a sense, this approach is self-contradictory. Affirmative redistribution generally presupposes a universalist conception of recognition, the equal moral worth of persons. Let us call this its "official recognition commitment." Yet the practice of affirmative redistribution, as iterated over time; tends to set in motion a second – stigmatizing – recognition dynamic, which contradicts universalism. This second dynamic can be understood as the "practical recognition-effect" of affirmative redistribution.[35] It conflicts with its official recognition commitment.[36]

Now contrast this logic with transformative remedies for distributive injustices of class. Transformative remedies typically combine universalist social-welfare programs, steeply progressive taxation, macro-economic policies aimed at creating full employment, a large nonmarket public sector, significant public and/or collective ownership, and democratic decision-making about basic socioeconomic priorities. They try to assure access to employment for all, while also tending to de-link basic consumption shares from employment. Hence their tendency is to undermine class differentiation. Transformative remedies reduce social inequality without, however, creating stigmatized classes of vulnerable people perceived as beneficiaries of special largesse.[37] They tend therefore to promote reciprocity and solidarity in the relations of recognition. Thus, an approach aimed at redressing injustices of distribution can help redress (some) injustices of recognition as well.[38]

This approach is self-consistent. Like affirmative redistribution, transformative redistribution generally presupposes a universalist conception of recognition, the equal moral worth of persons. Unlike affirmative redistribution, however, its practice tends not to undermine this conception. Thus, the two approaches generate different logics of group differentiation. Whereas affirmative remedies can have the perverse effect of promoting class differentiation, transformative remedies tend to blur it. In addition, the two approaches generate different subliminal dynamics of recognition. Affirmative redistribution can stigmatize the disadvantaged, adding the insult of misrecognition to the injury of deprivation. Transformative redistribution, in contrast, can promote solidarity, helping to redress some forms of misrecognition.

What, then, should we conclude from this discussion? In this section, we have considered only the "pure" ideal-typical cases at the two extremes of the conceptual spectrum. We have contrasted the divergent effects of affirmative and transformative remedies for the economically rooted distributive injustices of class, on the one hand, and for the culturally rooted recognition injustices of sexuality, on the other. We saw that affirmative remedies tend generally to promote group differentiation, while transformative remedies tend to destabilize or blur it. We also saw that affirmative redistribution remedies can generate a backlash of misrecognition, while transformative redistribution remedies can help redress some forms of misrecognition.

All this suggests a way of reformulating the redistribution–recognition dilemma. We might ask, for groups who are subject to injustices of both types, what combinations of remedies work best to minimize, if not altogether to eliminate, the mutual interferences that can arise when both redistribution and recognition are pursued simultaneously?

4 Finessing the Dilemma: Revisiting Gender and "Race"

Imagine a four-celled matrix (see table 1.1). The horizontal axis comprises the two general kinds of remedy we have just examined, namely, affirmation and transformation. The vertical axis comprises the two aspects of justice we have been considering, namely, redistribution and recognition. On this matrix we can locate the four political orientations just discussed. In the first cell, where redistribution and affirmation intersect, is the project of the liberal welfare state; centered on surface reallocations of distributive shares among existing groups, it tends to support group differentiation; it can also generate backlash misrecognition. In the second cell, where redistribution and transformation intersect, is the project of socialism; aimed at deep restructuring of the relations of production, it tends to blur group differentiation; it can also help redress some forms of misrecognition. In the third cell, where recognition and affirmation intersect, is the project of mainstream multiculturalism; focused on surface reallocations of respect among existing groups, it tends to support group differentiation. In the fourth cell, where recognition and transformation intersect, is the project of deconstruction; aimed at deep restructuring of the relations of recognition, it tends to destabilize group differentiations.

This matrix casts mainstream multiculturalism as the cultural analogue of the liberal welfare state, while casting deconstruction as the cultural

Table 1.1

	Affirmation	*Transformation*
Redistribution	*Liberal welfare state* Surface reallocations of existing goods to existing groups; supports group differentiation; can generate misrecognition.	*Socialism* Deep restructuring of relations of production; blurs group differentiation; can help remedy some forms of misrecognition.
Recognition	*Mainstream multiculturalism* Surface reallocations of respect to existing identities of existing groups; supports group differentiation.	*Deconstruction* Deep restructuring of relations of recognition; blurs group differentiation.

analogue of socialism. It thereby allows us to make some preliminary assessments of the mutual compatibility of various remedial strategies. We can gauge the extent to which pairs of remedies would work at cross-purposes with one another if they were pursued simultaneously. We can identify pairs that seem to land us squarely on the horns of the redistribution–recognition dilemma. We can also identify pairs that hold out the promise of enabling us to finesse it.

Prima facie at least, two pairs of remedies seem especially *un*promising. The affirmative redistribution politics of the liberal welfare state seems at odds with the transformative recognition politics of deconstruction; whereas the first tends to promote group differentiation, the second tends rather to destabilize it. Similarly, the transformative redistribution politics of socialism seems at odds with the affirmative recognition politics of mainstream multiculturalism; whereas the first tends to undermine group differentiation, the second tends rather to promote it.

Conversely, two pairs of remedies seem comparatively promising. The affirmative redistribution politics of the liberal welfare state seems compatible with the affirmative recognition politics of mainstream multiculturalism; both tend to promote group differentiation. Similarly, the transformative redistribution politics of socialism seems compatible with the transformative recognition politics of deconstruction; both tend to undermine existing group differentiations.

To test these hypotheses, let us revisit gender and "race." Recall that these are bivalent differentiations, axes of both economic and cultural injustice. Thus, people subordinated by gender and/or "race" need both redistribution and recognition. They are the paradigmatic subjects of the redistribution–recognition dilemma. What happens in their cases, then, when various pairs of injustice remedies are pursued simultaneously? Are there pairs of remedies that permit feminists and anti-racists to finesse, if not wholly to dispel, the redistribution–recognition dilemma?

Consider, first, the case of gender.[39] Recall that redressing gender injustice requires changing both political economy and culture, so as to undo the vicious circle of economic and cultural subordination. As we saw, the changes in question can take either of two forms, affirmation or transformation.[40] Let us consider, first, the *prima facie* promising case in which affirmative redistribution is combined with affirmative recognition. As the name suggests, affirmative redistribution to redress gender injustice in the economy includes affirmative action, the effort to assure women their fair share of existing jobs and educational places, while leaving unchanged the nature and number of those jobs and places. Affirmative recognition to redress gender injustice in the culture includes cultural feminism, the effort to assure women respect by revaluing femininity, while leaving unchanged the binary gender code that gives the latter its sense. Thus, the scenario in question combines the socioeconomic politics of liberal feminism with the cultural politics of cultural feminism. Does this combination really finesse the redistribution–recognition dilemma?

Despite its initial appearance of promise, this scenario is problematic. Affirmative redistribution fails to engage the deep level at which the political economy is gendered. Aimed primarily at combating attitudinal discrimination, it does not attack the gendered division of paid and unpaid labor, nor the gendered division of masculine and feminine occupations within paid labor. Leaving intact the deep structures that generate gender disadvantage, it must make surface reallocations again and again. The result is not only to underline gender differentiation. It is also to mark women as deficient and insatiable, as always needing more and more. In time women can even come to appear privileged, recipients of special treatment and undeserved largesse. Thus, an approach aimed at redressing injustices of distribution can end up fueling backlash injustices of recognition.

This problem is exacerbated when we add the affirmative recognition strategy of cultural feminism. That approach insistently calls attention to, if it does not performatively create, women's putative cultural specificity or difference. In some contexts, such an approach can make progress toward decentering androcentric norms. In this context, however, it is more likely to have the effect of pouring oil onto the flames of resentment against affirmative action. Read through that lens, the cultural politics of affirming women's difference appears as an affront to the liberal welfare state's official commitment to the equal moral worth of persons.

The other route with a *prima facie* promise is that which combines transformative redistribution with transformative recognition. Transformative redistribution to redress gender injustice in the economy consists in some form of socialist feminism or feminist social democracy. And transformative recognition to redress gender injustice in the culture consists in feminist deconstruction aimed at dismantling androcentrism by destabilizing gender dichotomies. Thus, the scenario in question combines the socioeconomic politics of socialist feminism with the cultural politics of deconstructive feminism. Does this combination really finesse the redistribution–recognition dilemma?

This scenario is far less problematic. The long-term goal of deconstructive feminism is a culture in which hierarchical gender dichotomies are replaced by networks of multiple intersecting differences that are demassified and shifting. This goal is consistent with transformative socialist–feminist redistribution. Deconstruction opposes the sort of sedimentation or congealing of gender difference that occurs in an unjustly gendered political economy. Its utopian image of a culture in which ever-new constructions of identity and difference are freely elaborated and then swiftly deconstructed is only possible, after all, on the basis of rough social equality.

As a transitional strategy, moreover, this combination avoids fanning the flames of resentment.[41] If it has a drawback, it is rather that both deconstructive–feminist cultural politics and socialist–feminist economic politics are far removed from the immediate interests and identities of most women, as these are currently culturally constructed.

Analogous results arise for "race," where the changes can again take either of two forms, affirmation or transformation.[42] In the first *prima facie* promising case, affirmative action is paired with affirmative recognition. Affirmative redistribution to redress racial injustice in the economy includes affirmative action, the effort to assure people of color their fair share of existing jobs and educational places, while leaving unchanged the nature and number of those jobs and places. And affirmative recognition to redress racial injustice in the culture includes cultural nationalism, the effort to assure people of color respect by revaluing "blackness," while leaving unchanged the binary black–white code that gives the latter its sense. The scenario in question thus combines the socioeconomic politics of liberal anti-racism with the cultural politics of black nationalism or black power. Does this combination really finesse the redistribution–recognition dilemma?

Such a scenario is again problematic. As in the case of gender, here affirmative redistribution fails to engage the deep level at which the political economy is racialized. It does not attack the racialized division of exploitable and surplus labor, nor the racialized division of menial and non-menial occupations within paid labor. Leaving intact the deep structures that generate racial disadvantage, it must make surface reallocations again and again. The result is not only to underline racial differentiation. It is also to mark people of color as deficient and insatiable, as always needing more and more. Thus, they too can be cast as privileged recipients of special treatment. The problem is exacerbated when we add the affirmative recognition strategy of cultural nationalism. In some contexts, such an approach can make progress toward decentering Eurocentric norms, but in this context the cultural politics of affirming black difference equally appears as an affront to the liberal welfare state. Fueling the resentment against affirmative action, it can elicit intense backlash misrecognition.

In the alternative route, transformative redistribution is combined with transformative recognition. Transformative redistribution to redress racial injustice in the economy consists in some form of anti-racist democratic socialism or anti-racist social democracy. And transformative recognition to redress racial injustice in the culture consists in anti-racist deconstruction aimed at dismantling Eurocentrism by destabilizing racial dichotomies. Thus, the scenario in question combines the socioeconomic politics of socialist anti-racism with the cultural politics of deconstructive anti-racism or critical "race" theory. As with the analogous approach to gender, this scenario is far less problematic. The long-term goal of deconstructive anti-racism is a culture in which hierarchical racial dichotomies are replaced by demassified and shifting networks of multiple intersecting differences. This goal, once again, is consistent with transformative socialist redistribution. Even as a transitional strategy, this combination avoids fanning the flames of resentment.[43] Its principal drawback, again, is that both deconstructive anti-racist cultural politics and socialist–anti-racist economic politics are far removed from the immediate interests and identities of most people of color, as these are currently culturally constructed.[44]

What, then, should we conclude from this discussion? For both gender and "race," the scenario that best finesses the redistribution–recognition dilemma is socialism in the economy plus deconstruction in the culture.[45] But for this scenario to be psychologically and politically feasible requires that people be weaned from their attachment to current cultural constructions of their interests and identities.[46]

5 Conclusion

The redistribution–recognition dilemma is real. There is no neat theoretical move by which it can be wholly dissolved or resolved. The best we can do is try to soften the dilemma by finding approaches that minimize conflicts between redistribution and recognition in cases where both must be pursued simultaneously.

I have argued here that socialist economics combined with deconstructive cultural politics works best to finesse the dilemma for the bivalent collectivities of gender and "race" – at least when they are considered separately. The next step would be to show that this combination also works for our larger sociocultural configuration. After all, gender and "race" are not neatly cordoned off from one another. Nor are they neatly cordoned off from sexuality and class. Rather, all these axes of injustice intersect one another in ways that affect everyone's interests and identities. No one is a member of only one such collectivity. And people who are subordinated along one axis of social division may well be dominant along another.[47]

The task then is to figure out how to finesse the redistribution–recognition dilemma when we situate the problem in this larger field of multiple, intersecting struggles against multiple, intersecting injustices. Although I cannot make the full argument task here, I will venture three reasons for expecting that the combination of socialism and deconstruction will again prove superior to the other alternatives.

First, the arguments pursued here for gender and "race" hold for all bivalent collectivities. Thus, insofar as real-world collectivities mobilized under the banners of sexuality and class turn out to be more bivalent than the ideal-typical constructs posited above, they too should prefer socialism plus deconstruction. And that doubly transformative approach should become the orientation of choice for a broad range of disadvantaged groups.

Second, the redistribution–recognition dilemma does not only arise endogenously, as it were, within a single bivalent collectivity. It also arises exogenously, so to speak, across intersecting collectivities. Thus, anyone who is both gay and working class will face a version of the dilemma, regardless of whether or not we interpret sexuality and class as bivalent. And anyone who is also female and black will encounter it in a multi-layered and acute form. In general, then, as soon as we acknowledge that axes of injustice cut across one another, we must acknowledge cross-cutting forms of the redistribution–recognition dilemma. And these forms are, if anything, even more resistant to resolution by combinations of affirmative remedies than the forms we considered above. For affirmative remedies work additively and are often at cross purposes with one another. Thus, the intersection of class, "race," gender, and sexuality intensifies the need for transformative solutions, making the combination of socialism and deconstruction more attractive still.

Third, that combination best promotes the task of coalition building. This task is especially pressing today, given the multiplication of social antagonisms, the fissuring of social movements, and the growing appeal of the Right in the United States. In this context, the project of transforming the deep structures of both political economy and culture appears to be the one over-arching programmatic orientation capable of doing justice to *all* current struggles against injustice. It alone does not assume a zero-sum game.

If that is right, then, we can begin to see how badly off track is the current US political scene. We are currently stuck in the vicious circles of mutually reinforcing cultural and economic subordination. Our best efforts to redress these injustices via the combination of the liberal welfare state plus mainstream multiculturalism are generating perverse effects. Only by looking to alternative conceptions of redistribution and recognition can we meet the requirements of justice for all.

Notes

This essay is a slightly revised version of a lecture presented at the University of Michigan in March 1991 at the Philosophy Department's symposium on "Political Liberalism." A longer version will appear in my forthcoming book, *Justice Interruptus: Rethinking Key Concepts of a "Postsocialist" Age*. For generous research support, I thank the Bohen Foundation, the Institut für die Wissenschaften vom Menschen in Vienna, the Humanities Research Institute of the University of California at Irvine, the Center for Urban Affairs and Policy Research at Northwestern University, and the Dean of the Graduate Faculty of the New School for Social Research. For helpful comments, I thank Robin Blackburn, Judith Butler, Angela Harris, Randall Kennedy, Ted Koditschek, Jane Mansbridge, Mika Manty, Linda Nicholson, Eli Zaretsky, and the members of the "Feminism and the Discourses of Power" work group at the Humanities Research Institute of the University of California, Irvine.

1 This omission is dictated by reasons of space. I believe that the framework elaborated below can fruitfully address both ethnicity and nationality. Insofar as groups mobilized on these lines do not define themselves as sharing a situation of socioeconomic disadvantage and do not make redistributive claims, they can be understood as struggling primarily for recognition. National struggles are peculiar, however, in that the form of recognition they seek is political autonomy, whether in the form of a sovereign state of their own (e.g. the Palestinians) or in the form of more limited provincial sovereignty within a multinational state (e.g. the majority of Québecois). Struggles for ethnic recognition, in contrast, often seek rights of cultural expression within polyethnic nation-states. These distinctions are insightfully discussed in Will Kymlicka, "Three Forms of Group. Differentiated Citizenship in Canada" (paper presented at the conference on "Democracy and Difference," Yale University, 1993).

2 My principal concern in this essay is the relation between the recognition of cultural difference and social equality. I am not directly concerned, therefore, with the relation between recognition of cultural difference and liberalism. However, I assume that no identity politics is acceptable that fails to respect fundamental human rights of the sort usually championed by left-wing liberals.

3 Karl Marx, *Capital*, volume 1; John Rawls, *A Theory of Justice* (Cambridge, Mass., 1971) and subsequent papers; Amartya Sen, *Commodities and Capabilities*, (North-Holland, 1985); and Ronald Dworkin, "What is Equality?

Part 2: Equality of Resources." *Philosophy and Public Affairs*, vol. 10, no. 4 (fall 1981). Although I here classify all these writers as theorists of distributive economic justice, it is also true that most of them have some resources for dealing with issues of cultural justice as well. Rawls, for example, treats "the social bases of self-respect" as a primary good to be fairly distributed, while Sen treats a "sense of self" as relevant to the capability to function. (I am indebted to Mika Manty for this point.) Nevertheless, as Iris Marion Young has suggested, the primary thrust of their thought leads in the direction of distributive economic justice. (See her *Justice and the Politics of Difference*, Princeton, 1990.)

4 Charles Taylor, *Multiculturalism and "The Politics of Recognition"* (Princeton, 1992), p. 25.

5 Axel Honneth, "Integrity and Disrespect: Principles of a Conception of Morality Based on the Theory of Recognition", *Political Theory*, vol. 20, no. 2 (May 1992), pp. 188–9. See also his *Kampfum Anarkennung* (Frankfurt, 1992; English translation forthcoming from The MIT Press under the title *Struggle for Recognition*). It is no accident that both of the major contemporary theorists of recognition, Honneth and Taylor, are Hegelians.

6 See, for example, Patricia J. Williams, *The Alchemy of Race and Rights* (Cambridge, Mass., 1991) and Young, *Justice and the Politics of Difference*.

7 Responding to an earlier draft of this essay Mika Manty posed the question of whether how a scheme focused on classifying justice issues as either cultural or political–economic could accommodate "primary political concerns" such as citizenship and political participation ("Comments on Fraser," unpublished typescript presented at the Michigan symposium on "Political Liberalism"). My inclination is to follow Jürgen Habermas in viewing such issues bifocally. From one perspective, political institutions (in state-regulated capitalist societies) belong with the economy as part of the "system" that produces distributive socioeconomic injustices; in Rawlsian terms, they are part of "the basic structure" of society. From another perspective, however, such institutions belong with "the lifeworld" as part of the cultural structure that produces injustices of recognition; for example, the array of citizenship entitlements and participation rights conveys powerful implicit and explicit messages about the relative moral worth of various persons. "Primary political concerns" could thus be treated as matters either of economic justice or cultural justice, depending on the context and perspective in play.

8 For the interimbrication of culture and political economy, see my "What's Critical About Critical Theory? The Case of Habermas and Gender" in Nancy Fraser, *Unruly Practices: Power, Discourse and Gender in Contemporary Social Theory* (Oxford, 1989); "Rethinking the Public Sphere" in Fraser, *Justice Interruptus*: Critical Reflections on the "Postsocialist" Condition, (Routledge, 1997), and Fraser, "Pragmatism, Feminism, and the Linguistic Turn", in Benhabib, Butler, Cornell and Fraser, *Feminist Contentions: A Philosophical Exchange* (New York, 1995). See also Pierre Bourdieu, *Out-*

line of a Theory of Practice (Cambridge, 1977). For critiques of the cultural meanings implicit in the current US political economy of work and social welfare, see the last two chapters of *Unruly Practices* and the essays in Part 3 of *Justice Interruptus.*

9   In fact, these remedies stand in some tension with one another, a problem I shall explore in a subsequent section of this essay.

10   These various cultural remedies stand in some tension with one another. It is one thing to accord recognition to existing identities that are currently undervalued; it is another to transform symbolic structures and thereby alter people's identities. I shall explore the tensions among the various remedies in a subsequent section of the essay.

11   For a good example of this approach, see Ronald Dworkin, "Liberalism," in his *A Matter of Principle* (Cambridge, Mass., 1985).

12   For a good example of this approach, see Will Kymlicka, *Liberalism, Community and Culture* (Oxford, 1989). The case of Kymlicka suggests that the distinction between socioeconomic justice and cultural justice need not always map onto the distinction between distributive justice and relational or communicative justice.

13   Axel Honneth's *Kampf um Anerkennung* represents the most thorough and sophisticated attempt at such a reduction. Honneth argues that recognition is the fundamental concept of justice and can encompass distribution.

14   Absent such a distinction, we foreclose the possibility of examining conflicts between them. We miss the chance to spot mutual interferences that could arise when redistribution claims and recognition claims are pursued simultaneously.

15   In what follows, I conceive class in a highly stylized, orthodox, and theoretical way in order to sharpen the contrast to the other ideal-typical kinds of collectivity discussed below. Of course, this is hardly the only interpretation of the Marxian conception of class. In other contexts and for other purposes, I myself would prefer a less economistic interpretation, one that gives more weight to the cultural, historical and discursive dimensions of class emphasized by such writers as E. P. Thompson and Joan Wallach Scott. See Thompson, *The Making of the English Working Class* (London, 1963); and Scott, *Gender and the Politics of History* (New York, 1988).

16   It is doubtful that any collectivities mobilized in the real world today correspond to the notion of class presented below. Certainly, the history of social movements mobilized under the banner of class is more complex than this conception would suggest. Those movements have elaborated class not only as a structural category of political economy but also as a cultural-valuational category of identity – often in forms problematic for women and blacks. Thus, most varieties of socialism have asserted the dignity of labor and the worth of working people, mingling demands for redistribution with demands for recognition. Sometimes, moreover, having failed to abolish capitalism, class movements have adopted reformist strategies of seeking recognition of their "difference" within the system in order to augment their

power and support demands for what I below call "affirmative redistribution." In general, then, historical class-based movements may be closer to
what I below call "bivalent modes of collectivity" than to the interpretation
of class sketched here.

17 This assumption does not require us to reject the view that distributive
deficits are often (perhaps even always) accompanied by recognition deficits.
But it does entail that the recognition deficits of class, in the sense elaborated
here, derive from the political economy. Later, I shall consider other sorts of
cases in which collectivities suffer from recognition deficits whose roots are
not directly political–economic in this way.

18 In what follows, I conceive sexuality in a highly stylized theoretical way in
order to sharpen the contrast to the other ideal-typical kinds of collectivity
discussed here. I treat sexual differentiation as rooted wholly in the cultural
structure, as opposed to in the political economy. Of course, this is not the
only interpretation of sexuality. Judith Butler (personal communication) has
suggested that one might hold that sexuality is inextricable from gender,
which, as I argue below, is as much a matter of the division of labor as of the
cultural-valuational structure. In that case, sexuality itself might be viewed as
a "bivalent" collectivity, rooted simultaneously in culture and political
economy. Then the economic harms encountered by homosexuals might
appear economically rooted rather than culturally rooted, as they are in the
account I offer here. While this bivalent analysis is certainly possible, to my
mind it has serious drawbacks. Yoking gender and sexuality together too
tightly, it covers over the important distinction between a group that occupies
a distinct position in the division of labor (and that owes its existence in large
part to this fact), on the one hand, and one that occupies no such distinct
position, on the other hand. I discuss this distinction below.

19 An example of an economic injustice rooted directly in the economic structure would be a division of labor that relegates homosexuals to a designated
disadvantaged position and exploits them as homosexuals. To deny that this
is the situation of homosexuals today is not to deny that they face economic
injustices. But it is to trace these to another root. In general, I assume that
recognition deficits are often (perhaps even always) accompanied by distribution deficits. But I nevertheless hold that the distribution deficits of sexuality,
in the sense elaborated here, derive ultimately from the cultural structure.
Later, I shall consider other sorts of cases in which collectivities suffer from
recognition deficits whose roots are not (only) directly cultural in this sense.
I can perhaps further clarify the point by invoking Oliver Cromwell Cox's
contrast between anti-Semitism and white supremacy. Cox suggested that for
the anti-Semite, the very existence of the Jew is an abomination; hence the
aim is not to exploit the Jew but to eliminate him/her as such, whether by
expulsion, forced conversion, or extermination. For the white supremacist, in
contrast, the "Negro" is just fine – in his/her place: as an exploitable supply
of cheap, menial labor power; here the preferred aim is exploitation, not
elimination. (See Cox's unjustly neglected masterwork, *Caste, Class, and
Race*, New York, 1970.) Contemporary homophobia appears in this respect

to be more like anti-Semitism than white supremacy: it seeks to eliminate, not exploit, homosexuals. Thus, the economic disadvantages of homosexuality are derived effects of the more fundamental denial of cultural recognition. This makes it the mirror image of class, as just discussed, where the "hidden (and not so hidden) injuries" of misrecognition are derived effects of the more fundamental injustice of exploitation. White supremacy, in contrast, as I shall suggest shortly, is "bivalent," rooted simultaneously in political economy and culture, inflicting co-original and equally fundamental injustices of distribution and recognition. (On this last point, incidentally, I differ from Cox, who treats white supremacy as effectively reducible to class.)

20 Gender disparagement can take many forms, of course, including conservative stereotypes that appear to celebrate, rather than demean, "femininity."

21 This helps explain why the history of women's movements records a pattern of oscillation between integrationist equal-rights feminisms and "difference" oriented "social" and "cultural" feminisms. It would be useful to specify the precise temporal logic that leads bivalent collectivities to shift their principal focus back and forth between redistribution and recognition. For a first attempt, see my "Rethinking Difference" in *Justice Interruptus*.

22 In addition, "race" is implicitly implicated in the gender division between paid and unpaid labor. That division relies on a normative contrast between a domestic sphere and a sphere of paid work, associated with women and men respectively. Yet the division in the United States (and elsewhere) has always also been racialized in that domesticity has been implicitly a "white" prerogative. African Americans especially were never permitted the privilege of domesticity either as a (male) private "haven" or a (female) primary or exclusive focus on nurturing one's own kin. See Jacqueline Jones, *Labor of Love, Labor of Sorrow: Black Women, Work, and the Family from Slavery to the Present* (New York, 1981) and Evelyn Nakano Glenn, "From Servitude to Service Work: Historical Continuities in the Racial Division of Reproductive Labor", *Signs: Journal of Women in Culture and Society*, vol. 18, no. 1 (autumn 1992).

23 In a previous draft of this essay I used the term "denigration." The ironic consequence was that I unintentionally perpetrated the exact sort of harm I aimed to criticize – in the very act of describing it. "Denigration," from the Latin *nigrare* (to blacken), figures disparagement as blackening, a racist valuation. I am grateful to the Saint Louis University student who called my attention to this point.

24 Racial disparagement can take many forms, of course, ranging from the stereotypical depiction of African Americans as intellectually inferior, but musically and athletically gifted, to the stereotypical depiction of Asian Americans as a "model minority."

25 This helps explain why the history of black liberation struggle in the United States records a pattern of oscillation between integration and separatism (or black nationalism). As with gender, it would be useful to specify the dynamics of these alternations.

26 Not all versions of multiculturalism fit the model I describe here. The latter is
an ideal-typical reconstruction of what I take to be the majority understanding of multiculturalism. It is also mainstream in the sense of being the
version that is usually debated in mainstream public spheres. Other versions
are discussed in Linda Nicholson, "To Be or Not To Be: Charles Taylor on
The Politics of Recognition", *Constellations* (forthcoming) and in Michael
Warner et al., "Critical Multiculturalism," *Critical Inquiry*, vol. 18, no. 3
(spring 1992).

27 Recall that sexuality is here assumed to be a collectivity rooted wholly in the
cultural-valuational structure of society; thus, the issues here are unclouded
by issues of political–economic structure, and the need is for recognition, not
redistribution.

28 An alternative affirmative approach is gay-rights humanism, which would
privatize existing sexualities. For reasons of space, I shall not discuss it
here.

29 For a critical discussion of the tendency in gay-identity politics to tacitly cast
sexuality in the mold of ethnicity, see Steven Epstein, "Gay Politics, Ethnic
Identity: The Limits of Social Constructionism", *Socialist Review*, no. 93/94
(May–August 1987).

30 The technical term for this in Jacques Derrida's deconstructive philosophy is
"supplement."

31 Despite its professed long-term deconstructive goal, queer theory's practical
effects may be more ambiguous. Like gay-identity politics, it too seems likely
to promote group solidarity in the here and now, even as it sets its sights on
the promised land of deconstruction. Perhaps, then, we should distinguish
what I below call its "official recognition commitment" of group de-
differentiation from its "practical recognition effect" of (transitional) group
solidarity and even group solidification. The queer-theory recognition strategy thus contains an internal tension: in order eventually to destabilize the
homo–hetero dichotomy, it must first mobilize "queers." Whether this
tension becomes fruitful or debilitating depends on factors too complex to
discuss here. In either case, however, the recognition politics of queer theory
remains distinct from that of gay identity. Whereas gay-identity politics
simply and straightforwardly underlines group differentiation, queer theory
does so only indirectly, in the undertow of its principal de-differentiating
thrust. Accordingly, the two approaches construct qualitatively different
kinds of groups. Whereas gay-identity politics mobilizes self-identified homosexuals *qua* homosexuals to vindicate a putatively determinate sexuality,
queer theory mobilizes "queers" to demand liberation from determinate
sexual identity. "Queers," of course, are not an identity group in the same
sense as gays; they are better understood as an anti-identity group, one that
can encompass the entire spectrum of sexual behaviors, from gay to straight
to bi. (For a hilarious – and insightful – account of the difference, as well as
for a sophisticated rendition of queer politics, see Lisa Duggan, "Queering
the State", *Social Text*, no. 39, summer 1994.) Complications aside, then, we
can and should distinguish the (directly) differentiating effects of affirmative

gay recognition from the (more) de-differentiating (albeit complex) effects of transformative queer recognition.

32 By "liberal welfare state," I mean the sort of regime established in the US in the aftermath of the New Deal. It has been usefully distinguished from the social-democratic welfare state and the conservative-corporatist welfare state by Gøsta Esping-Andersen in *The Three Worlds of Welfare Capitalism* (Princeton, 1990).

33 Today, of course, many specific features of socialism of the "really existing" variety appear problematic. Virtually no one continues to defend a pure "command" economy in which there is little place for markets. Nor is there agreement concerning the place and extent of public ownership in a democratic socialist society. For my purposes here, however, it is not necessary to assign a precise content to the socialist idea. It is sufficient, rather, to invoke the general conception of redressing distributive injustice by deep political–economic restructuring, as opposed to surface reallocations. In this light, incidentally, social democracy appears as a hybrid case that combines affirmative and transformative remedies; it can also be seen as a "middle position," which involves a moderate extent of economic restructuring, more than in the liberal welfare state but less than in socialism.

34 Recall that class, in the sense defined above, is a collectivity wholly rooted in the political–economic structure of society; the issues here are thus unclouded by issues of cultural-valuational structure; and the remedies required are those of redistribution, not recognition.

35 In some contexts, such as the United States today, the practical recognition-effect of affirmative redistribution can utterly swamp its official recognition commitment.

36 My terminology here is inspired by Pierre Bourdieu's distinction, in *Outline of a Theory of Practice*, between "official kinship" and "practical kinship."

37 I have deliberately sketched a picture that is ambiguous between socialism and robust social democracy. The classic account of the latter remains T. H. Marshall's "Citizenship and Social Class" in *Class, Citizenship, and Social Development: Essays by T. H. Marshall*, ed. Martin Lispet (Chicago, 1964). There Marshall argues that a universalist social-democratic regime of "social citizenship" undermines class differentiation, even in the absence of full-scale socialism.

38 To be more precise: transformative redistribution can help redress those forms of misrecognition that derive from the political–economic structure. Redressing misrecognition rooted in the cultural structure, in contrast, requires additional independent recognition remedies.

39 Recall that gender, *qua* political–economic differentiation, structures the division of labor in ways that give rise to gender-specific forms of exploitation, marginalization, and deprivation. Recall, moreover, that *qua* cultural-valuational differentiation, gender also structures the relations of recognition in ways that give rise to androcentrism and cultural sexism.

Recall, too, that for gender, as for all bivalent group differentiations, economic injustices and cultural injustices are not neatly separated from one
another; rather they intertwine to reinforce one another dialectically, as
sexist and androcentric cultural norms are institutionalized in the economy,
while economic disadvantage impedes equal participation in the making of
culture, both in everyday life and in public spheres.

40 I shall leave aside the *prima facie* unpromising cases. Let me simply stipulate
that a cultural–feminist recognition politics aimed at revaluing femininity is
hard to combine with a socialist–feminist redistributive politics aimed at
degendering the political economy. The incompatibility is overt when we
treat the recognition of "women's difference" as a long-term feminist goal.
Of course, some feminists conceive the struggle for such recognition not as an
end in itself but as a stage in a process they envision as leading eventually to
degenderization. Here, perhaps, there is no formal contradiction with socialism. At the same time, however, there remains a practical contradiction, or at
least a practical difficulty: can a stress on women's difference in the here and
now really end up dissolving gender difference in the by and by? The converse
argument holds for the case of the liberal–feminist welfare state plus deconstructive feminism. Affirmative action for women is usually seen as a
transitional remedy aimed at achieving the long-term goal of "a sex-blind
society." Here, again, there is perhaps no formal contradiction with deconstruction. But there remains nevertheless a practical contradiction, or at least
a practical difficulty: can liberal–feminist affirmative action in the here and
now really help lead us to the deconstruction of gender in the by and by?

41 Here I am assuming that the internal complexities of transformative recognition remedies, as discussed in note 31 above, do not generate perverse effects.
If, however, the practical recognition effect of deconstructive feminist cultural politics is strongly gender-differentiating, despite the latter's official
recognition commitment to gender de-differentiation, perverse effects could
indeed arise. In that case, there could be interferences between socialist–
feminist redistribution and deconstructive–feminist recognition. But these
would probably be less debilitating than those associated with the other
scenarios examined here.

42 The same can be said about "race" here as about gender in notes 39 and
40.

43 See note 31 above on the possible perverse effects of transformative recognition remedies.

44 Ted Koditschek (personal communication) has suggested to me that this
scenario may have another serious drawback: "The deconstructive option
may be less available to African-Americans in the current situation. Where
the structural exclusion of [many] black people from full economic citizenship pushes 'race' more and more into the forefront as a cultural category
through which one is attacked, self-respecting people cannot help but aggres-
sively affirm and embrace it as a source of pride." Koditschek goes on to
suggest that Jews, in contrast, "have much more elbow room for negotiating
a healthier balance between ethnic affirmation, self-criticism, and cosmopol-

itan universalism – not because we are better deconstructionists (or more inherently disposed toward socialism) but because we have more space to make these moves."

45 Whether this conclusion holds as well for nationality and ethnicity remains a question. Certainly bivalent collectivities of indigenous peoples do not seek to put themselves out of business as groups.

46 This has always been the problem with socialism. Although cognitively compelling, it is experientially remote. The addition of deconstruction seems to exacerbate the problem. It could turn out to be too negative and reactive, i.e. too *deconstructive*, to inspire struggles on behalf of subordinated collectivities attached to their existing identities.

47 Much recent work has been devoted to the "intersection" of the various axes of subordination that I have treated separately in this essay for heuristic purposes. A lot of this work concerns the dimension of recognition; it aims to demonstrate that various collective identifications and identity categories have been mutually co-constituted or co-constructed. Joan Scott, for example, has argued (in *Gender and the Politics of History*) that French working-class identities have been discursively constructed through gender-coded symbolization; and David R. Roediger has argued (in *The Wages of Whiteness: Race and the Making of the American Working Class*, Verso, London, 1991) that US working-class identities have been racially coded. Meanwhile, many feminists of color have argued both that gender identities have been racially coded and that racialized identities have been gender-coded. I myself have argued, with Linda Gordon, that gender, "race," and class ideologies have intersected to construct current US understandings of "welfare dependency" and "the underclass." (See Fraser and Gordon, "A Genealogy of 'Dependency': Tracing a keyword of the U.S. Welfare State", *Signs: Journal of Women in Culture and Society*, vol. 19, no. 2, winter 1994.)

2

Unruly Categories: A Critique of Nancy Fraser's Dual Systems Theory

Iris Marion Young

Have theorists of justice forgotten about political economy? Have we traced the most important injustices to cultural roots? Is it time for critical social theory to reassert a basic distinction between the material processes of political economy and the symbolic processes of culture? In two recent essays, Nancy Fraser answers these questions in the affirmative.[1] She claims that some recent political theory and practice privilege the recognition of social groups, and that they tend to ignore the distribution of goods and the division of labor.

> Demands for "recognition of difference" fuel struggles of groups mobilized under the banners of nationality, ethnicity, "race," gender, and sexuality. In these "post-socialist" conflicts, group identity supplants class interest as the chief medium of political mobilization. Cultural domination supplants exploitation as the fundamental injustice. And cultural recognition displaces socioeconomic redistribution as the remedy for injustice and the goal of political struggle.[2]

Fraser proposes to correct these problems by constructing an analytic framework that conceptually opposes culture and political economy, and then locates the oppressions of various groups on a continuum between them. With a clear distinction between those issues of justice that concern economic issues and those that concern cultural issues, she suggests, we can restore political economy to its rightful place in critical theory, and evaluate which politics of recognition are compatible with transformative responses to economically based injustice.

Fraser's essays call our attention to an important issue. Certain recent political theories of multiculturalism and nationalism do indeed highlight respect for distinct cultural values as primary questions of justice, and many seem to ignore questions of the distribution of wealth and resources and the organization of labor. Fraser cites Charles Taylor's much discussed work, *Multiculturalism and the Politics of Recognition*,[3] as an example of this one-sided attention to recognition at the expense of redistribution, and I think she is right. Even the paradigmatic theorist of distributive justice, John Rawls, now emphasizes cultural and value differences and plays down conflict over scarce resources.[4] Some activist expressions of multiculturalism, moreover, especially in schools and universities, tend to focus on the representation of groups in books and curricula as an end in itself, losing sight of the issues of equality and disadvantage that have generated these movements.[5] Some recent theoretical writing by feminists or gay men and lesbians has pondered questions of group identity abstracted from social relations of economic privilege and oppression.

Nevertheless, I think that Fraser, like some other recent Left critics of multiculturalism, exaggerates the degree to which a politics of recognition retreats from economic struggles. The so-called "culture wars" have been fought on the primarily cultural turf of schools and universities. I see little evidence, however, that feminist or anti-racist activists, as a rule, ignore issues of economic disadvantage and control. Many who promote the cultivation of African-American identity, for example, do so on the grounds that self-organization and solidarity in predominantly African-American neighborhoods will improve the material lives of those who live there by providing services and jobs.

To the degree they exist, Fraser is right to be critical of tendencies for a politics of recognition to supplant concerns for economic justice. But her proposed solution, namely to reassert a category of political economy entirely opposed to culture, is worse than the disease. Her dichotomy between political economy and culture leads her to misrepresent feminist, anti-racist and gay liberation movements as calling for recognition as an end in itself, when they are better understood as conceiving cultural recognition as a means to economic and political justice. She suggests that feminist and anti-racist movements in particular are caught in self-defeating dilemmas which I find to be a construction of her abstract framework rather than concrete problems of political strategies. The same framework makes working-class or queer politics appear more one-dimensional than they actually are.

Fraser's opposition of redistribution and recognition, moreover, constitutes a retreat from the New Left theorizing which has insisted that the material effects of political economy are inextricably bound to culture. Some of Nancy Fraser's own earlier essays stand as significant contributions to this insistence that Marxism is also cultural studies. Rather than oppose political economy to culture, I shall argue, it is both theoretically and politically more productive to pluralize categories and understand them as differently related to particular social groups and issues. Thus, the purpose of this essay is primarily to raise questions about what theoretical strategies are most useful to politics, and to criticize Fraser for adopting a polarizing strategy. The goal of strong coalitions of resistance to dominant economic forces and political rhetoric, I suggest, is not well served by an analysis that opposes cultural politics to economic politics. Specifying political struggles and issues in more fine-tuned and potentially compatible terms better identifies issues of possible conflict and alliance.

1 Redistribution Versus Recognition

According to Fraser, there are two primary kinds of injustice. The first, socioeconomic injustice, is "rooted" in the political and economic structure of society. Exploitation, economic marginalization, and deprivation of basic goods are the primary forms of such injustice. The second kind of injustice is cultural or symbolic. It is "rooted" in social patterns of representation, interpretation, and communication. Such injustice includes being subject to an alien culture, being rendered invisible in one's cultural specificity, and being subject to deprecating stereotypes and cultural representations. Corresponding to these two irreducible roots of injustice are two different remedies. Redistribution produces political and economic changes that result in greater economic equality. Recognition redresses the harms of disrespect, stereotyping and cultural imperialism.

Fraser asserts that in the real world the structures of political economy and the meanings of cultural representation are inseparable: "Even the most material economic institutions have a constitutive, irreducible cultural dimension; they are shot through with significations and norms. Conversely, even the most discursive cultural practices have a constitutive, irreducible political–economic dimension; they are underpinned by material supports."[6] The distinction between redistribution and recognition is, therefore, entirely theoretical, an analytical distinction necessary for the construction of an account. Fraser claims that this categorical opposition is useful and even necessary in order to understand how the political aims of oppressed groups are sometimes contradictory.

To demonstrate this tension, Fraser constructs a continuum for classifying the forms of injustice that groups suffer. At one end of the continuum are groups that suffer a "pure" form of political economic injustice. Since the redistribution–recognition distinction is ideal and not real, such a group must also be an ideal type. Class oppression considered by itself approximates this ideal type. On the other end of the continuum are groups that suffer "pure" cultural oppression. Injustice suffered by gay men and lesbians approximates this ideal type, inasmuch as their oppression, considered by itself, has its roots only in cultural values that despise their sexual practices.

Remedies for injustice at each of these extremes come in reformist and revolutionary varieties, which Fraser respectively terms "affirmative" and "transformative." The affirmative remedy for class oppression is a welfare-state liberalism that redistributes goods, services, and income while leaving the underlying economic structure undisturbed. A transformative remedy for class injustice, on the other hand, changes the basic economic structure and thereby eliminates the proletariat. An affirmative remedy for sexual oppression seeks to solidify a specific gay or lesbian identity in the face of deprecating stereotypes, whereas a transformative cultural politics deconstructs the very categories of sexual identity.

The main trouble comes with groups that lie in the middle of the continuum, subject both to political economic and cultural injustices. The oppressions of gender and race lie here, according to Fraser. As subject to two different and potentially opposing forms of injustice, the political struggles of women and people of color are also potentially contradictory. From the point of view of political economy, the radically transformative struggles of women and people of color ought to have the aim of eliminating the gender or racial group as a distinct position in the division of labor. This goal of eliminating the structured position of the group, however, comes into conflict with a "politics of identity." In the latter, women or people of color wish to affirm the group's specific values and affinity with one another in the face of deprecating stereotypes and cultural representation. Affirmative politics of recognition, according to Fraser, conflicts with transformative politics of redistribution because the latter requires eliminating the group as a group while the former affirms the group identity. This conflict shows the error of such an affirmative politics of recognition, and the need instead for a transformative cultural politics that deconstructs identities.

2 Why Theorize with a Dichotomy?

Fraser recommends a "deconstructive" approach to a politics of recognition, which unsettles clear and oppositional categories of identity. Yet her theorizing in these essays is brazenly dichotomous. Injustices to all groups are reducible to two, and only two, mutually exclusive categories. The remedies for these injustices also come in two mutually exclusive categories, with each further divisible into a reformist and radical version. All social processes that impact on oppression can be conceptualized on one or the other side of this dichotomy or as a product of their intersection. Thus, redistribution and recognition are not only exclusive categories, but together they comprehend everything relevant to oppression and justice.

As I have already noted, Fraser denies that this dichotomy describes reality. What, then, justifies its use in theory? Fraser answers that an analytical framework requires concepts through which to analyze reality, and it must be able to distinguish among these concepts. This is certainly true. Such a justification does not explain, however, why a critical social theory should rely on only two categories. Why adopt an analytical strategy, furthermore, that aims to reduce more plural categorizations of social phenomena to this "bifocal categorization."

In *Justice and the Politics of Difference*, I explicate a plural categorization of oppression. I distinguish five "faces" of oppression – exploitation, marginalization, powerlessness, cultural imperialism, and violence.[7] Many concrete instances of oppression should be described using several of these categories, though most descriptions will not use all. The purpose of elaborating a plural but limited categorization of oppression is to accommodate the variations in oppressive structures that position individuals and groups, and thus to resist the tendency to reduce oppression to one or two structures with "primacy."

In her essay criticizing this book, Fraser performs just such a reduction.[8] These five forms of oppression are "really" reducible to two: a political economic injustice of maldistribution (exploitation, marginalization, and powerlessness) and a cultural injustice of misrecognition (cultural imperialism and violence). Fraser neither justifies this reduction of five to two, nor does she notice that the description of at least one of the categories she allocates to the "redistributive" side – namely powerlessness – is explicitly described *both* in terms of the division of labor and in terms of norms of respect. My point is not to argue for the particular framework I have developed, but to ask why the imposition of two categories is not arbitrary.

In her later essay, "From Redistribution to Recognition," Fraser raises an objection to her claim that the categories of political economy and culture exhaust description of social structures and injustice: this categorization appears to have no place for a third, political, aspect to social reality, concerning institutions and practices of law, citizenship, administration, and political participation. Rather than taking this objection seriously, Fraser sets to work reducing these political phenomena to the dichotomous framework of political economy and culture. She appeals to Habermas to do so:

> My inclination is to follow Jürgen Habermas in viewing such issues bifocally. From one perspective, political institutions (in state-regulated capitalist societies) belong with the economy as part of the "system" that produces distributive socioeconomic injustices; in Rawlsian terms, they are part of the "basic structure" of society. From another perspective, however, such institutions belong with "the lifeworld" as part of the cultural structure that produces injustices of recognition; for example, the array of citizenship entitlements and participation rights conveys powerful implicit and explicit messages about the relative moral worth of various persons.[9]

In an earlier essay, "What's Critical about Critical Theory? The Case of Habermas and Gender,"[10] Fraser fashioned an important and persuasive critique of dichotomous thinking in general, and of this particular dichotomy between "system" and "lifeworld." She argued that Habermas's categorical opposition between system and lifeworld eclipses more nuanced concepts in his theory. She showed how this dichotomy obscures the contribution of women's domestic labor to a reproduction of state and economic systems, while reinforcing a gendered opposition between public (system) and private (the lifeworld in which people appear as cared-for individuals). She argued that Habermas's dichotomy wrongly separates cultural norms from the social processes that reproduce bureaucratic and corporate institutions. For this reason, she suggested, Habermas's dichotomous theory cannot ground the conditions for the possibility of communicative democratization within those state and corporate institutions. Contrary to her reduction of the political to system and lifeworld in the above quotation, in "What's Critical about Critical Theory?," Fraser invoked a category of political action and struggle as additional to, and upsetting, the neat dichotomy of system and lifeworld. While in that essay, Fraser suggested that dichotomous theorizing tends to devalue and obscure the phenomena that do not easily fit the categories, and to distort those that are conceptualized in its terms, I think a similar argument can be applied to her own theoretical strategy in these more recent essays.

2.1 Distinctions in theory and reality

Fraser's stated reason for constructing a dichotomy is that a mutually exclusive opposition best enables the theorist to identify contradictions in reality. With the dichotomy between political economy and culture, redistribution and recognition, Fraser wants to highlight the contradiction between various political goals. Feminist and anti-racist movements, she aims to show, cannot take as ends both the affirmation of their group identities and the elimination of their gender- or race-specific positions in the division of labor. Because she conceptualizes transformative redistribution as incompatible with affirmative recognition, Fraser succeeds in constructing an account in which the goals of feminist and anti-racist movements appear internally contradictory. If the dichotomous categorization of redistribution and recognition does not correspond to reality, however, but is merely heuristic, how do we know that the tension is not merely an artifact of the theoretical dichotomy? Why should we accept Fraser's claim that the dichotomy reveals a fundamental political tension, rather than a superficial or even imagined one? Shortly I will argue that this categorization fails to understand that, for most social movements, what Fraser calls "recognition" is a means to the economic and social equality and freedom that she brings under the category of redistribution.

The injustices of political economy, according to Fraser's account, include exploitation, marginalization and deprivation. The remedy for any economic injustice is some sort of political – economic restructuring: "This might involve redistributing income, reorganizing the division of labor, subjecting investment to democratic decision-making, or transforming other basic economic structures. Although these various remedies differ importantly from one another, I shall henceforth refer to the whole group of them by the generic term 'redistribution'."[11] But one can surely ask why such diverse social processes should all be categorized as redistribution, especially since Fraser herself wishes to reintroduce distinctions into that category. Fraser believes, and I agree with her, that redistributive remedies for economic injustice, typical of the public provision of goods and services for needy people, do not change the conditions that produce this injustice and, in some ways, tend to reinforce those conditions. She thus recommends those remedies which transform the basic economic structure: "By restructuring the relations of production, these remedies would not only alter the end-state distribution of consumption shares; they would also change the social division of labor and thus the conditions of existence for everyone."[12] Fraser calls these remedies "transformative redistribution," as distinct from the "affirmative redistributive" remedies which leave the basic structure intact. But why bring them both under the same general category at all? Why not choose plural categories to distinguish and reflect those issues of justice that concern the patterns of the distribution of goods from those that concern the division of labor or the organization of decision-making power?

In earlier work, I proposed just such distinctions in order to show that many theories of justice wrongly collapse all issues of justice into those of distribution, and thereby often wrongly identify the remedies for injustice with the redistribution of goods. I criticize this distributive paradigm for just the reasons that Fraser distinguishes affirmative and transformative redistributive remedies: to emphasize that end-state distributions are usually rooted in social and economic structures that organize the division of labor and decision-making power about investment, the organization of production, pricing, and so on. For evaluating the justice of social institutions, I propose a four-fold categorization. Societies and institutions should certainly be evaluated according to the patterns of distribution of resources and goods they exhibit; but, no less important, they should be evaluated according to their division of labor, the way they organize decision-making power, and whether their cultural meanings enhance the self-respect and self-expression of all society's members.[13] Structures of the division of labor and decision-making power are no more reducible to the distribution of goods than are cultural meanings. They both involve practices that condition actions and the relations among actors in different social locations; these serve as the context within which income, goods, services, and resources are distributed. If we begin with distinctions among distribution, division of labor, and decision-making power in our analytic framework, then we do not need later to uncover a confusion between remedies that "merely" redistribute and those that transform the basic structure.

Fraser's desire to dichotomize issues of justice between economy and culture produces categories that are too stark. A more plural categorization better guides action because it shows how struggles can be directed at different kinds of goals or policies. For example, distinguishing issues of justice about decision-making power from those concerning distribution can show that struggles about environmental justice cannot simply be about the placement of hazardous sites, a distributive issue, but must more importantly be about the processes through which such placements are decided.[14] Changes in the division of labor, furthermore, do not amount merely to "redistributing" tasks, as Fraser's dichotomy suggests, but often in redefining the cultural meaning and value of different kinds of work. The gender division of labor that allocates primary responsibility for care work to women outside the paid economy, for example, will not change without greater recognition of the nature and value of this work.

With a more plural categorization of issues of justice, furthermore, we can more clearly see the variables that must come together to constitute just institutions, as well as the tensions among them that can occur. Just as a plural categorization diffuses the starkness of redistribution, moreover, it demotes culture to one among several of such variables to be combined with others in analysis of social justice.

3 An Alternative: Fraser's Materialist Cultural Theorizing

Fraser introduces the dichotomy between redistribution and recognition to correct what she perceives as a tendency in multiculturalism and identity politics to ignore issues of political economy. While I agree that this characterization is sometimes accurate, the remedy for such a failing does not consist in setting up a category of political economy alongside, and in opposition to, culture. A more appropriate theoretical remedy would be to conceptualize issues of justice involving recognition and identity as having inevitably material economic sources and consequences, without thereby being reducible to market dynamics or economic exploitation and deprivation.

As I understand it, this has been the project of the best of what is called "cultural studies": to demonstrate that political economy, as Marxists think of it, is through and through cultural without ceasing to be material, and to demonstrate that what students of literature and art call "culture" is economic, not as base to superstructure, but in its production, distribution and effects, including effects on reproducing class relations. Political economy is cultural, and culture is economic.

The work of Pierre Bourdieu well exemplifies this mutual effect of culture and political economy. In several of his works, Bourdieu demonstrates that acquiring or maintaining positions in privileged economic strata depends partly on cultural factors of education, taste and social connection. Access to such enculturation processes, however, crucially depends on having economic resources and the relative leisure that accompanies economic comfort.[15] In his remarkable book, *Encountering Development*, Arturo Escobar similarly argues for the mutual effect of cultural and material survival issues of access to resources in the struggles of oppressed peasants. Many Latin American peasants, who often come from indigenous cultures which have been neither eliminated nor assimilated by the dominant Latin culture, are struggling against repressive governments and international finance giants to obtain a barely decent life. Such peasant resistance, says Escobar, "reflects more than the struggle for land and living conditions; it is above all a struggle for symbols and meaning, a cultural struggle."[16] Latin American peasants struggle with World Bank representatives, local government officials and well-intentioned NGO leaders over the cultural interpretation of the most basic terms of political economy: land, natural resources, property, tools, labor, health, food. We should not mistake this claim for a "reduction" of political economy to culture. On the contrary, in this case, struggle about cultural meaning and identity has life and death consequences.

> The struggle over representation and for cultural affirmation must be carried out in conjunction with the struggle against the exploitation and domination over the conditions of local, regional, and global political economies. The two projects are one and the same. Capitalist regimes undermine the reproduction of socially valued forms of identity; by destroying existing cultural practices, development projects destroy elements necessary for cultural affirmation.[17]

With such a materialist cultural–political theory one can, for example, problematize the apparently simple call for an economic system that meets needs. With Amartya Sen, we can ask just *what* is to be equalized when we call for equality.[18] A materialist cultural approach understands that needs are contextualized in political struggle over who gets to define whose needs for what purpose. This is the approach that Nancy Fraser herself takes in an earlier paper, "Struggle Over Needs," where she argues that needs are always subject to struggle and interpretation, and that the inequalities in the struggling parties are structured simultaneously by access to material resources and discursive resources: "Needs talk appears as a site of struggle where groups with unequal discursive and non-discursive resources compete to establish as hegemonic their respective interpretations of legitimate social needs."[19] With a materialist cultural analysis, we can notice that, under circumstances of unjust social and economic inequality, the mobilization of communication in official publics often reflects and reproduces social and economic inequalities. In another earlier essay, Nancy Fraser argues that the best recourse that economically subordinated groups have is to form subaltern counterpublics as "discursive arenas where members of subordinated social groups invent and circulate counter discourses to formulate oppositional interpretations of identities, interests and needs."[20] Any struggle against oppression, Fraser suggests in that essay, is simultaneously a struggle against cultural and economic domination, because the cultural styles of subordinated groups are devalued and silenced, and the political economy of the bourgeois public sphere ensures that subordinated groups lack equal access to the material means of equal participation.

Thus, the Nancy Fraser of "From Redistribution to Recognition?" appears as nearly the contrary of the Nancy Fraser of at least three earlier papers I have cited. Where the earlier Nancy Fraser theorized discursive cultural processes of group identification and of needs and interests from its own point of view, as a process of political context to produce change in economic structures, the more recent Fraser separates culture from economy, and argues that they tend to pull against each other in movements against injustice. I recommend the position of the earlier Fraser over the later. The earlier articles consider a politics of recognition as a means of struggle toward the end of material, social and economic equality and well-being. In the most recent work, however, Fraser takes recognition as an end in itself, politically disconnected from redistribution.

4 Recognition for the Sake of Redistribution

In her critique of multiculturalism and the politics of identity, Fraser writes as though the politics of recognition is an end in itself for movements of subordinated groups. Sometimes it is. The separatist movement of the Québecois, on which Taylor models his politics of difference, arguably takes recognition of the Québecois as a distinct people as a political end in itself, and the same is sometimes true of other nationalist movements. Interest in multiculturalism in education, to take a different sort of example, sometimes considers attention to and recognition of previously excluded groups as an end in itself.

When recognition is taken as a political end in itself, it is usually disconnected from economic issues of distribution and division of labor. I agree with Fraser that a political focus on recognition disconnected from injustices of exploitation, deprivation or control over work is a problem. The remedy, however, is to reconnect issues of political economy with issues of recognition. We should show how recognition is a means to, or an element in, economic and political equality.

In "From Redistribution to Recognition?" Fraser does just the reverse of this. She treats all instances of group-based claims to cultural specificity and recognition as though recognition is an end in itself. For the movements that Fraser is most concerned with, however – namely, women's movements, movements of people of color, gay and lesbian movements, movements of poor and working-class people – a politics of recognition functions more as a means to, or element in, broader ends of social and economic equality, rather than as a distinct goal of justice.

Fraser constructs gay and lesbian liberation as a "pure" case of the politics of recognition. In this ideal type, the "root" of injustice to gay men and lesbians is entirely cultural. Gays and lesbians suffer injustice because of the cultural construction of heterosexism and homophobia. Although the images of gays and lesbians as despicable and unnatural has distributive consequences, because the root of the oppression is culture, the remedy must also be cultural: the recognition of gay and lesbian life styles and practices as normal and valuable, and the giving of equal respect to persons identified with those practices.

Although arguments could be mounted that historically marriage is largely an economic institution, I will not quarrel here with the claim that heterosexism and homophobia are cultural. Nevertheless, the claim that, even as an ideal type, oppression through sexuality is purely cultural trivializes the politics of those oppressed because of sexuality. Whatever the "roots" of heterosexism, and I would theorize them as multiple, this harm matters because those on the wrong side of the heterosexual matrix experience systematic limits to their freedom, constant risk of abuse, violence and death, and unjustly limited access to resources and opportunities. Among the primary political goals of gay, lesbian, bisexual, transsexual or queer activists are material, economic and political equality: an end to discrimination in employment, housing, healthcare; equal protection by police and courts; equal freedom to partner and raise children. Precisely because the source of inequality in this case is cultural imagery that demonizes those who transgress heterosexual norms, a politics of difference is a crucial means for achieving the material goals of equal protection and equal opportunity. For example, positive and playful images of the possibilities of sexuality aim to undermine the monolithic construction of norm and deviant, which is a necessary condition of respect and freedom.

The polarization of political economy and culture, redistribution and recognition, I have argued, distorts the plurality and complexity of social reality and politics. Fraser's account of anti-racist and feminist politics reveals such distortions. Race and gender, Fraser argues, are "dilemmatic" modes of collectivity. The injustices of race and gender consist in a dialectical combination of two analytically distinct modes of oppression, distributive injustice and lack of recognition, for which there are two distinct kinds of remedy, redistribution and recognition. But these two forms of remedy are often contradictory, according to Fraser. The radical, transformative goal of redistributive justice for women or people of color should consist in eliminating the structures in the division of labor that allocate certain kinds of devalued work to white women and women of color, and which keep them – especially people of color – in a marginalized underclass "reserve army." Insofar as gender and race are defined by this division of labor and structural marginalization, the goal of redistribution should be to eliminate the oppressed gender or race as a group, just as the goal of working-class movements must be the elimination of the proletariat as a group.

According to Fraser, however, the politics of recognition when applied to gender or race pulls the other way. The goal of such cultural politics is to affirm the specific difference of women or African Americans or Chicanos or Navajos, to develop pride in women's relational orientation, or the moral qualities generated by musical, religious, and storytelling legacies. Thus, a politics of recognition seeks to affirm the group as a good, which contradicts and undermines the transformative goal of redistribution:

> Insofar as people of color suffer at least two analytically distinct kinds of injustice, they necessarily require at least two analytically distinct kinds of remedy, which are not easily pursued simultaneously. Whereas the logic of redistribution is to put "race" out of business as such, the logic of recognition is to valorize group specificity ... . How can anti-racists fight simultaneously to abolish "race" and to valorize racialized group specificity?[21]

Here Fraser imposes dichotomous categories on a more complex reality and, by doing so, finds contradiction where none exists. She suggests that culturally affirming movements of people of color aim to abolish "race" by affirming "race." But this is a distortion of, for example, most black cultural politics. The purpose of affirming the cultural and social specificity of African Americans or First Nations or North African Muslim immigrants is precisely to puncture the naturalized construction of these groups as "raced." These groups affirm cultural specificity in order to deny the essentialism of "race" and encourage the solidarity of the members of the group against deprecating stereotypes. Fraser's position seems similar to that of conservative opponents of anti-racist politics who refuse to distinguish the affirmation of specific economic, political and cultural institutions of solidarity and empowerment for oppressed people of color from the discriminatory and racist institutions of white exclusion.

4.1 The material and the cultural entwined

Fraser finds these movements internally contradictory, moreover, because she assumes that their politics of recognition is an end in itself. It may be true that some activities and writings of culturally affirming movements of people of color treat cultural empowerment and recognition as itself the substance of liberation. More often, however, those affirming cultural pride and identity for people of color understand such recognition as a means of economic justice and social equality. Most African Americans who support culturally based African-American schools and universities, for example, believe that the schools will best enable African-American young people to develop the skills and self-confidence to confront white society, and collectively help transform it to be more hospitable to African-American success.

Movements of indigenous peoples, to take another example, certainly consider recognition of their cultural distinctness an end in itself. They also see it as a crucial means to economic development. They assert claims to land for the sake of building an economic base for collective development and for achieving the effective redistribution of the fruits of white colonial exploitation. Many also believe that the recovery of traditional indigenous cultural values provides vision for forms of economic interaction and the protection of nature whose wider institutionalization would confront capitalism with transformative possibilities.

Fraser's claim of internal contradiction may have a bit more force in respect to struggles against gender oppression. The infamous "equality versus difference" debate poses a genuine dilemma for feminist politics. Ought feminists to affirm gender blindness in the policies of employers, for example, in the allocation of health benefits, leave, promotion criteria, and working hours? Or should they demand that employers explicitly take into account the position of many women as primary caretakers of children or elderly relatives in deliberations about just allocations? Opting for the latter strategy risks solidifying a sexual division of labor that most feminists agree is unjust and ought to be eliminated. Opting for the former, however, allows employers to continue privileging men under the banner of equality.

Notice, however, that this feminist dilemma is not between a redistributive strategy and a strategy of recognition, but rather between two different redistributive strategies. By Fraser's own criteria, moreover, it could be argued that the second strategy has more transformative possibilities, because it takes the gender division of labor explicitly into account, whereas the first ignores this basic structure. Be that as it may, it is difficult to see how a feminist politics of recognition "pulls against" a feminist politics of redistribution. To the extent that undermining the misogyny that makes women victims of violence and degradation entails affirming the specific gendered humanity of women, this would seem also to contribute to women's economic revaluation. To affirm the normative and human value of the work that women do outside the labor force, moreover, is to contribute to a redistributive restructuring that takes account of the hidden social costs of markets and social policies.

Feminists discuss these issues in counter-publics where they encourage one another to speak for themselves, from their own experience. In these counter-publics, they form images and interests with which to speak to a larger public that ignores or distorts women's concerns. Such solidarity-forming identity politics need not reduce women to some common culture or set of concerns. While some feminist discourse constructs and celebrates a "women's culture" for its own sake, more often claims to attention for gender-specific experience and position occur in the context of struggles about economic and political opportunity.

I conclude, then, that Fraser is wrong to conceptualize struggles for recognition of cultural specificity as contradicting struggles for radical transformation of economic structures. So long as the cultural denigration of groups produces or reinforces structural economic oppressions, the two struggles are continuous. If a politics of difference disconnects culture from its role in producing material oppressions and deprivations, and asserts cultural expression as an end in itself, then such politics may obscure complex social connections of oppression and liberation. If Muslims were to focus only on their freedom to send their girls to school in headscarves, or Native Americans were to limit their struggles to religious freedom and the recovery of cultural property, then their politics would be superficial. Set in the context of a larger claim that people should not suffer material disadvantage and deprivation because they are culturally different, however, even such issues as these become radical.

5 Conclusion

Fraser is right to insist that radicals renew attention to material issues of the division of labor, access to resources, the meeting of needs, and the social transformations required to bring about a society in which everyone can be free to develop and exercise their capacities, associate with others and express themselves under conditions of material comfort. Her polarization of redistribution versus recognition, however, leads her to exaggerate the extent to which some groups and movements claiming recognition ignore such issues. To the degree such a tendency exists, I have argued, the cure is to reconnect issues of symbols and discourse to their consequences in the material organization of labor, access to resources, and decision-making power, rather than to solidify a dichotomy between them. I have suggested that a better theoretical approach is to pluralize concepts of injustice and oppression so that culture becomes one of several sites of struggle interacting with others.

Despite Fraser's claim to value recognition as much as redistribution, her criticisms of what she calls an affirmative politics of recognition seem pragmatically similar to other recent Left critiques of the so-called politics of identity. On these accounts, the politics of difference influential among progressives in the last twenty years has been a big mistake. Feminist, gay and lesbian, African-American, Native-American, and other such movements have only produced divisiveness and backlash, and have diverted radical politics from confronting economic power.[22]

Yet, when capitalist hegemony is served by a discourse of "family values," when affirmative action, reproductive rights, voting rights for people of color, and indigenous sovereignty are all seriously under attack, suggesting that gender- or race-specific struggles are divisive or merely reformist does not promote solidarity. Instead, it helps fuel a right-wing agenda and further marginalizes some of the most economically disadvantaged people. A strong anti-capitalist progressive movement requires a coalition politics that recognizes the differing modalities of oppression that people experience and affirms their culturally specific networks and organizations.

The world of political ends and principles Fraser presents is eerily empty of action. She calls for a "deconstructive" rather than an "affirmative" approach to culture and identity, but I do not know what this means for the conduct of activism on the ground. From Zapatista challengers to the Mexican government, to Ojibwa defenders of fishing rights, to African-American leaders demanding that banks invest in their neighborhoods, to unions trying to organize a Labor Party, to those sheltering battered women, resistance has many sites and is often specific to a group without naming or affirming a group essence. Most of these struggles self-consciously involve issues of cultural recognition and economic deprivation, but not constituted as totalizing ends. None of them alone is "transformative," but, if linked together, they can be deeply subversive.

Coalition politics can only be built and sustained if each grouping recognizes and respects the specific perspective and circumstances of the others, and works with them in fluid counter-publics. I do not think that such a coalition politics is promoted by a theoretical framework that opposes culture and economy.

Notes

I am grateful to David Alexander, Robin Blackburn, Martin Matuštíck and Bill Scheuermann for comments on an earlier version of this essay.

1   Nancy Fraser, "Recognition or Redistribution? A Critical Reading of Iris Young's *Justice and the Politics of Difference*", *Journal of Political Philosophy*, vol. 3, no. 2, (1995), pp. 166–80; "From Redistribution to Recognition? Dilemmas of Justice in a 'Post-Socialist' Age". *NLR* 212, pp. 68–93.
2   Fraser, "From Redistribution to Recognition?"
3   Charles Taylor, *Multiculturalism and the Politics of Recognition* (Princeton, 1992).
4   See John Rawls, *Political Liberalism* (New York, 1995); I have commented on this shift in a review essay of this book in *Journal of Political Philosophy*, vol. 3, no. 2 (1995), pp. 181–90.
5   Todd Gitlin tells stories of such a focus on recognition as an end itself in school board battles in California. See *Twilight of Common Dream* (New York, 1997). I do not think that such stories of excess in the politics of difference warrant his blanket inference that all attention to group difference has been destructive of Left politics in the US.
6   Fraser, "From Redistribution to Recognition?" p. 23.
7   I. M. Young. *Justics and the Politics of Difference* (Princeton 1990), ch. 2.
8   Fraser, "Recognition or Redistribution?"
9   Fraser, "From Redistribution to Recognition." p. 42, n. 7.
10   In *Unruly Practices: Power, Discourse and Gender in Contemperory Social Theory* (Minneapolis, 1989).
11   Fraser, "From Redistribution to Recognition?" p. 23.
12   Ibid.
13   Young, *Justice and the Politics of Difference*, ch. 1.
14   Christian Hunold and Iris Marion Young, "Justice, Democracy and Hazardous Siting," paper submitted to *Political Studies*.
15   See Pierre Bourdieu, *Distinction: A Social Critique of the Judgement of Pure Taste* (Cambridge, Mass., 1979). Also "What makes a Social Class?" *Berkeley Journal of Sociology*, vol. 32, 1988, pp. 1–18; Craig Calhoun, *Critical Social Theory: Culture, History and the challenge of Difference* (Oxford, 1995), ch. 5.
16   Arturo Escobar, *Encountering Development* (Princeton, 1993), p. 168.
17   Ibid., pp. 170–1.
18   In "From Redistribution to Recognition?" Fraser Incorrectly identifies Sen as a pure theorist of political economy. In fact, Sen is acutely sensitive to

variations in cultural meaning and the implications of human needs and the cultural meaning of goods and social networks within which needs are to be met. See *Re-examining Inequality*, (Cambridge, Mass., 1992).

19 Fraser, "Struggle over Needs: Outline of a Socialist–Feminist Critical Theory of Late Capitalist Political Culture," in *Unruly Practices*, p. 116.

20 "Rethinking the Public Sphere: A Contribution to the Critique of Actually Existing Democracy," in Craig Calhoun (ed). *Habermas and the Public Sphere* (Cambridge, Mass, 1992) p. 123.

21 Fraser, From Redistribution to Recognition pp. 30–1.

22 See James Weinstein, report on independent politics. *In These Times*, February 18, 1996. pp. 18–21; Gitlin. *Twilight of Common Dreams*.

3

A Rejoinder to Iris Young

Nancy Fraser

Iris Young and I seem to inhabit different worlds. In her world, there are no divisions between the social Left and the cultural Left. Proponents of cultural politics work cooperatively with proponents of social politics, linking claims for the recognition of difference with claims for the redistribution of wealth. Virtually no practitioners of identity politics are essentialist, moreover, let alone authoritarian or chauvinist. Claims for the recognition of difference are only rarely advanced, finally, as ends in themselves; nearly all are put forward as transitional socialist demands. According to Young, therefore, the divisions that inspired my article are artifacts of my "dichotomous framework," figments of my imagination.

In fact, of course, it was not I but "post-socialist" political culture that has conjured up these divisions. I did not fantasize a march on Washington of a million black men in which not a single socioeconomic demand was raised. Nor did I imagine the widespread gloating on the US social Left over the *Social Text* hoax, which was thought to discredit the "phony leftism" of cultural studies. What I *did* do was construct a framework for analyzing existing splits between class politics and identity politics, socialist or social-democratic politics and multiculturalist politics. My aim was to show that these splits rest on false antitheses. "Post-socialist" ideology notwithstanding, we do not in reality face an either/or choice between social politics and cultural politics, redistribution and recognition. It is possible in principle to have both.

Recall the context my essay addressed: increased marketization and sharply rising inequality worldwide; the apparent delegitimation of socialist ideals; the growing salience of claims for the recognition of difference and the relative eclipse of claims for egalitarian redistribution; the decoupling of the cultural Left from the social Left; and the seeming absence of any credible vision of a comprehensive alternative to the present order. In my diagnosis, unlike that of Todd Gitlin and James Weinstein, and unlike that of Young, who is on this point their mirror opposite, the split in the Left is *not* between class struggles, on the one hand, and gender, "race," and sex struggles, on the other. Rather, it cuts across those movements, each of which is internally divided between cultural currents and social currents, between currents oriented to redistribution and currents oriented to recognition. In my diagnosis, moreover, the split does not reflect a genuine antithesis. Rather, it is possible in principle to combine an egalitarian politics of redistribution with an emancipatory politics of recognition.

Thus, far from dichotomizing culture and political economy, I diagnosed their current decoupling in "post-socialist" ideology. Far from championing class politics against identity politics, I refuted the view that we must make an either/or choice between them. Far from manufacturing nonexistent contradictions, I provided a framework for transcending political divisions that exist. Far from trashing movements against sexism, racism, and heterosexism, I distinguished affirmative from transformative currents within those movements in order to show how claims for redistribution and recognition could be integrated with one another in a comprehensive political project.

Young, however, systematically distorts my argument. In a discussion that is more tendentious than analytical, she conflates three different levels of analysis: the philosophical, the social-theoretical, and the political.

On the philosophical level, my starting point was the current dissociation of two distinct paradigms of justice. One of these, the distributive paradigm, has supplied the chief approach for analyzing justice claims for at least 150 years; in the 1970s and 1980s especially, it was subject to intense and often brilliant philosophical elaboration. The other paradigm is, in contrast, much newer; centered on the normative concept of recognition, it is currently being developed by philosophers such as Axel Honneth and Charles Taylor, largely in response to the recognition politics of the 1980s and 1990s. Both paradigms are normatively powerful; each succeeds in identifying an important set of justice claims and in accounting for their moral force. Yet the two paradigms of justice don't communicate. They are mutually dissociated in moral philosophy today and need to be articulated with one another.

Contra Young, I did not invent these paradigms, nor did I contrive their dissociation. Still less did I advocate a theory of justice divided into "two mutually exclusive categories." On the contrary, I posed the philosophical question of how we should understand their relation to one another. One possibility is that one of the paradigms can be conceptually reduced to the other; but no one has managed to do this, and I doubt that in fact it can be done. Short of that, the most philosophically satisfying approach is to develop a more general overarching conception of justice that can encompass both distribution and recognition. This is the approach pursued in my *NLR* essay.[1]

On the social-theoretical level, I did not describe the material processes of political economy as "entirely opposed" to the symbolic processes of culture. Rather, I began where capitalism has placed us, in a social formation that differentiates specialized economic arenas and institutions from other arenas and institutions, including some that are designated as cultural, and from the larger background that Karl Polanyi called "society." To illuminate this social formation, one must account both for the historical fact of capitalist economic/cultural differentiation and also for the underlying reality of their thorough interpenetration. To that end, I invoked the culture/economy distinction in a specific – analytical – guise. *Contra* Young, I did not mark out two substantive institutional domains, economy and culture, assigning redistribution to the first and recognition to the second. Rather, I distinguished two analytical perspectives that can be trained upon any domain. Refuting the view that culture and economy constitute two separate mutually insulated spheres, I revealed their interpenetration by tracing the unintended effects of cultural and economic claims. The entire thrust of my essay was to demonstrate that cultural claims have distributive implications, that economic claims carry recognition subtexts, and that we ignore their mutual impingement at our peril. Thus, what Young labels a "dichotomy" is actually a *perspectival duality*.[2]

This approach is consistent, moreover, with my earlier work, including my 1985 essay on Habermas. There, I took what had been presented as a substantive institutional distinction (system and lifeworld) and reinterpreted it as an analytical distinction of perspectives (the system perspective and the lifeworld perspective). *Contra* Young, I did not simply reject the distinction; nor did I criticize dichotomous thinking in general. Rather, I criticized the conflation of an important analytical methodological distinction with a substantive institutional distinction. (The identical perspectival dualist view is clearly stated, incidentally, in the passage on politics Young cites from page 72 of my *NLR* essay; there I claim that political phenomena can be viewed from both the lifeworld and the system perspectives.) Thus, the two Nancy Frasers are really one.

Throughout her discussion, Young erroneously assumes that to draw a two-fold distinction is to dichotomize. Hence her insistence, at odds with scientific parsimony, that five is better than two. (One is tempted to say that she is "brazenly" pentagonist, an ominously militarist stance.) The real issue, of course, is not the number of categories but their epistemic status and explanatory power.[3] But here Young's objections to my distinctions are unpersuasive. She gives us no good reasons to reject, for example, my contrast between affirmative and transformative remedies for injustice, a contrast that is illuminating in two respects. First, it permits us to preserve the formal essence of the idea of socialism, as distinct from the liberal welfare state, even when we are no longer clear about how to fill in socialism's substantive content. Second, it reveals otherwise hidden connections between socialism and deconstruction, on the one hand, and the liberal welfare state and mainstream multiculturalism, on the other.

This brings me, finally, to the level of politics. *Contra* Young, the existing splits between proponents of recognition and proponents of redistribution are not simply a matter of false consciousness. Rather, they give expression in distorted form to genuine tensions among multiple aims that must be pursued simultaneously in struggles for social justice. Theorists can help illuminate these tensions, provided that they eschew cheerleading and think critically about the social movements they support. To deny or minimize the difficulties is to bury one's head in the sand. Nor does it suffice to point out that some who press claims for the recognition of cultural differences hope thereby to promote economic restructuring; rather, one must go on to ask whether such hopes are well-founded or whether, rather, they are likely to run aground. Nor, finally, is it helpful to adopt the pollyanna-ish view that the tensions within and among progressive social movements will somehow be automatically resolved in some all-encompassing "coalition" whose basis and content need not be specified.

My essay defended the project of integrating the best of socialist politics with the best of multicultural politics, while frankly acknowledging its genuine difficulties. I did not claim, *contra* Young, that redistribution conflicts with recognition. I argued, rather, that in the current historical context, the tensions between various group-differentiating and group de-differentiating claims assume the guise of a single contradiction, which I called "the redistribution/recognition dilemma." In this context, demands for economic justice seem to conflict necessarily with demands for cultural justice. But the appearance, I sought to demonstrate, is misleading. Once we distinguish affirmative approaches from transformative approaches, what looked like an ineluctable contradiction gives way to a plurality of possible strategies from which we must reflectively choose. Some kinds of recognition claims, especially the "deconstructive" kind, are better suited than others to synergizing with claims for socioeconomic equality.

Young rejects this last conclusion, of course, having written what is in essence a brief for the politics of affirmative recognition. In the end, however, she offers no good reasons for thinking that such a politics can promote transformative redistribution. I continue to believe it cannot.

Notes

1 For a further elaboration of this approach, see my "Social Justice in the Age of Identity Politics," in *The Tanner Lectures on Human Values*, vol. 18 (University of Utah Press, 1997).
2 For further elaboration, see "Social Justice in the Age of Identity Politics."
3 Here Young's own approach is deficient. The five-fold "plural" schema she proposes to characterize "group oppressions" is ad hoc and undertheorized. Indiscriminately mixing items from different regions of conceptual space, it contains nothing that cannot be analyzed from the standpoints of redistribution, recognition, or both. See my "Culture, Political Economy, and Difference: On Iris Young's *Justice and the Politics of Difference*," in Nancy Fraser, *Justice Interruptus: Critical Reflections on the "Postsocialist" Condition* (Routledge, 1997).

4

Recognition, Value, and Equality: A Critique of Charles Taylor's and Nancy Fraser's Accounts of Multiculturalism

Lawrence Blum

Charles Taylor's influential essay, "The Politics of Recognition," has helped to solidify the view that *recognition* is central to multiculturalism. Taylor's lasting contribution is to provide a plausible philosophical underpinning for a human need to be recognized in one's *distinctness*, especially (as he focuses in his essay) on *cultural* distinctness. Taylor sometimes connects recognition to two other ideas – *value* and *equality*. I will argue that Taylor's account of these connections is confused, and especially that the concept of "equality" is misplaced in the realm of culture. It *is* appropriate, however, as a form of recognition directed toward human beings not in their distinctness but in their shared humanity and equal citizenship. While Taylor initially credits this form of recognition, by the end of the essay, recognition has lost its link to the equality of common humanity and has been confined to the domain of distinctiveness.

In her essay "From Redistribution to Recognition?", in this volume, Nancy Fraser never loses sight of equality as a primary goal of recognition as it is discussed within multiculturalist discourse; in this way she provides a vital antidote to Taylor's view. At the same time, Fraser, I will argue, loses sight of precisely what gives Taylor's essay its canonical place in the literature – the human need for a recognition of distinctness, *apart from* its connection to social and political equality.

"Multiculturalism" is a contested term. I will include within its reach opposition to racism, or an ideal of racial justice, though some discussions distinguish the latter from the former. The character of the groups we think of as "cultures" in the context of multiculturalism, especially within the United States – African Americans, Latinos, Asian Americans, and Native Americans – are intimately bound up with the *racial* history of the US and the racist treatment of these groups. In fact, these groups are often thought of *as* "racial" groups. (David Hollinger's felicitous term "ethno-racial groups" preserves this duality.)[1] Hence the grounds for a particularly intimate connection between culture and race within the ethical foundations of multiculturalism. To keep my discussion within a manageable purview, I will not focus on the wider range of groups and forms of discrimination – gender, age, sexual orientation, and the like – that are often also considered within "multiculturalism."

1 Opposition to Racism

Taylor himself is little concerned directly with racism, and with anti-racism or racial justice as a distinct element in his theoretical framework. Nevertheless, it plays some role in my critique of Taylor, and so requires at least a brief account. As I see it there are two fundamentally distinct kinds of racism, ethically speaking – superiority racism and bigotry racism. My concern here is with the former, which encompasses forms of racism in institutions and societies that involve the domination of one group by another, and the sorts of culturally shared and individual attitudes that directly rationalize such domination – that is, attitudes in which one regards some race as distinctly inferior (generally to one's own, though there can be internalized forms of racism in which one regards one's own race as inferior). Attitudinal superiority racism can exist outside racist structures; nor are racist structures always supported by superiority racist attitudes. So-called "institutional racism" can be perpe-tuated by attitudes that are fairly racially innocuous considered purely in their own right (a belief in "merit," in just doing one's job, in test scores as the primary criterion for selection for jobs and college admissions).

Superiority racism offends against familiar human and civic ideas of equality and equal dignity. All humans possess certain capacities – to reason, to guide one's life by principles, to suffer and to know one is suffering, to form human attachments whose loss causes pain and grief, to have a conscience, and the like. Different theories highlight different ones of these as the basis on which all human beings are said to have a common dignity. Racism offends against that dignity by declaring one group of persons humanly inferior in some basic and fundamental ways, or by keeping (racially) unjust structures in place whose justification and impli-cation seems to require that same sense of inferiority.[2]

I will explore Taylor's notion of recognition as the basis for an ethical injunction that it be accorded to persons. I will discuss the appropriate objects of recognition, and will explore its connection to the central value in opposition to racism, namely *equality*. Taylor initially clearly distinguishes *equality*-based from *recognition*-based values. However, as his argument progresses, he imports equality into the domain of culture, illegitimately putting forth an ideal of the "equal worth of cultures," about which he remains ambivalent but nevertheless defends in some form. I will argue that the "equal worth of cultures" is a meaningless notion that has crept into multiculturalist discourse (not only Taylor's), serving only to obfuscate, and that it should be discarded.

I argued in an earlier work that Taylor fails to articulate opposition to racism as a value distinct from cultural recognition or respect.[3] Thus, Taylor both imports an equality where it does not belong (in respect to cultures), and also fails to recognize it where it does (in the arena of racism). At the same time, while Taylor articulates a value of equality as equal rights for individuals – this being the value to which he contrasts recognition – he also endeavors to subsume a fuller, more group-based equality value *under* or *within* recognition. But, I argue, this attempt fails.

2 Recognition

Taylor sees the acknowledgment of recognition as a recent arrival in the articulation of human needs,[4] though he traces its genesis in Rousseau, Herder, and Hegel. Moreover, Taylor says that members of all societies need this recognition; he portrays it as an almost trans-historical human need. However, in societies with fixed social positions into which one is born and which one seldom leaves, the recognition can be taken for granted. It is only in the relatively more fluid societies of modern democracy that this need becomes clear.

Taylor articulates two basic forms of recognition. One is a democratic form, directed toward others in regard to their sameness with oneself – for example, as equal citizens of a shared polity, as equal human beings, or as equal creatures of God. "Equal dignity" is the most common form in which Taylor states the content of this form of recognition. Of the two forms of recognition, Taylor is less interested in this one; it is not what he has in mind in the title of his essay, "The Politics of Recognition." However, this particular idea of recognition has been developed further by Axel Honneth in his book, *The Struggle for Recognition: The Moral*

Grammar of Social Conflicts.[5] Honneth sees the attributing of equality to members of a polity as having a significance beyond the institutional (especially legal) conferring of certain liberties and immunities. The acknowledgment of fellow members of the polity as having equal rights with oneself is a manner of regard in which we hold those others. This seeing of others as equals to ourselves, as possessing the human requisites for equal participation, characterizes the moral culture of a society. It is not solely – though it is necessarily – a matter of institutional arrangements. Rather, it is a manner in which citizens in a democratic polity (should) *regard* and *treat* one another. This is how it constitutes *recognition*.

The second form of "recognition" – the one Taylor is more interested in – is recognition directed toward a person in her *distinctiveness*, that is, with regard to her distinct identity as an individual (in contrast to the sameness of being a fellow human being, having equal dignity, and the like). Taylor sees this form of recognition as the driving force behind contemporary multiculturalism. As does Herder, on whom Taylor draws, Taylor sees both a group and an individual object of this form of recognition. Cultural groups in their distinctiveness are to be recognized, as are individuals.

Taylor does not sustain a clear differentiation between the group and the individual as objects of recognition in his subsequent discussion; but I think it is essential to do so. While multiculturalism can be seen as resting, in part, on this need for recognition in *both* individual and group venues, the ethical principle plays out somewhat differently in the two cases.

In fact, we need to distinguish *three* distinct entities, all of which have been cited (though seldom clearly distinguished) as candidates for recognition: (a) the *individual* in light of her distinct cultural identity; (b) cultural, or culturally defined, *groups*; (c) *cultures* themselves. The form of culture we, and Taylor, are concerned with here is *ethno*-culture. Multiculturalism is not generally taken to embrace, for instance, professional cultures, regional cultures, institutional cultures, neighborhood cultures, family cultures (except insofar as the latter are forms of ethno-cultures), though each of these is a genuine type of "culture" and can be deeply important to particular individuals.

The difference between the three objects of recognition is this. The first is a single individual, in light of the particular relationship she holds to her own ethno-culture. A theory of recognition need not assume that a person's ethno-culture is *necessarily* deeply important to her. It says only that, *if it is*, it deserves recognition. A "cultural group" refers to the actual persons comprising a given cultural group – African Americans, Polish Americans, Poles, Québecois, Ethiopians. It is the group of which the individual is a member. Finally, "culture," that notoriously difficult concept, can be taken in this context to refer to the forms of cultural expression, folkways, ways of life, as well as the cultural "products" of a given cultural group. As we shall see, what recognition means varies depending on which is taken to be its object.

As I understand "recognition," it is properly directed only toward *persons* (including groups of persons). It is human beings who require recognition – of their distinctive identity(ies) – for their flourishing. This would exclude cultures themselves as appropriate objects of recognition. In the literature on multiculturalism, however, one does hear talk of "recognizing cultures," and Taylor is not entirely careful about his terminology on this point. But I take the latter locution to mean either "recognizing cultural groups" (that is, groups of persons), or to involve some other meaning of "recognition."

3 Recognition of the Individual, in Light of Her Culture

What are the appropriate forms that recognition of the individual should take? This very much depends on the context. Discussions of recognition are sometimes pitched at a level of generality that masks the fact that "recognition by whom? in what context? in what regard?" are questions that must be addressed in any theory of recognition that will give us actual guidance as to how to implement its prescriptions. For example, in normal circumstances one does not need, or want, one's cultural identity acknowledged by the subway rider next to you, or by your waiter in a restaurant. By contrast, if one's friends fail to accord a recognition of the importance of one's cultural identity to one, this would be a culpable failure or recognition. One may not be at all concerned, and may not even welcome, recognition from those whom one disrespects. As Honneth emphasizes, certain institutions can be important agents of recognition; but not all would be equally important.

Schools are an important venue for such recognition, as Taylor notes. This is so for several reasons – school curriculum implicates different ethno-racial groups, school social and interpersonal life is often organized along ethno-racial lines, pedagogical practice must be sensitive to ethno-cultural identities. Taylor also mentions that schools, and curricula, can reflect demeaning images of ethno-cultural groups. Partly because of its importance, and partly to pin down one particular venue for exploring issues of recognition, this essay will focus on schools. I will draw particularly on an ethnography concerning students' identities in schools,

Making and Molding Identity in Schools: Student Narratives on Race, Gender, and Academic Engagement by Ann Locke Davidson.[6]

Davidson provides numerous examples of recognition-related issues. She interviews a Mexican American student, a recent immigrant, whom she calls Marbella Sanchez. Recognition of her Mexican American cultural identity is very important to Marbella. In her "foods" class, Marbella speaks Spanish to her non-Spanish-speaking teacher, Mrs Everett. "We [meaning her small group of friends] have a rule. On Tuesdays and Thursdays we speak only Spanish" (p. 56). Marbella in no way resists the learning of English; on the contrary, she sees it as the path to opportunity. But she wants her Mexican-related identity to be recognized, as contrasting distinctly with those of the dominant Anglo group of students in the school, and Mrs Everett acknowledges it.

Davidson gives other examples of *lack* of recognition, this time directed toward the Spanish-speaking students in the school as a group. The school bulletin (always posted and occasionally read) is only in English, never in Spanish. Spanish-speaking students can not get into classes qualifying them for the honor society. An awards ceremony at the end of the year for high-achieving Spanish-speaking students is limited to them and their families, and is distinct from what is taken as the "regular" awards ceremony for the school as a whole. "The achievements of the immigrants were not made part of the public school discourse, keeping evidence of their existence hidden from European American and English-speaking Latino peers" (p. 69).

Taylor mentions a further, higher-profile, issue of curricular recognition of concern to the cultural group in question, for example Mexican Americans – their historical experiences. Such curriculum-based recognition must be bounded by an intellectual rationale for such inclusion. We cannot pretend that, for example, the experience of Cambodian Americans, almost all of whom have arrived since 1975, possesses the same historical significance as that of Mexican Americans.[7] As Taylor notes, the *educational* rationale – presenting all students (from varied ethno-cultural backgrounds) with a portrayal of their shared national history in which a particular group's experience is adequately and properly reflected – is distinct from the *recognition* rationale directed specifically at the cultural group in question.[8]

What does recognition consist in with regard to the individual as a member of a cultural group? The obvious feature is according explicit acknowledgement to the cultural marker or markers that the individual regards as indicating her distinctive cultural identity (for Marbella, this was speaking Spanish in a non-Spanish class). Cultural markers can be individualized; so recognition should take account of what the particular individual sees as signifying her distinct cultural identity. For example, speaking Spanish is *not* a cultural marker for non-Spanish-speaking Mexican Americans, and they may experience an expectation that they will speak or understand Spanish as non recognition and even insult. Yet this cultural identity may be important to them, and may be indicated, in particular cases, by foods, types of music (Mexican, "tejano"), dance, an interest in Mexico, features of Mexican-American youth culture, and the like.

Regarding cultural *groups*, individualized knowledge is of course not possible; and recognition will have to consist in what can reasonably be taken to be cultural markers and corresponding recognition – for example, inclusion in school-wide venues in which academic awards are presented, putting notices in Spanish, including Mexican-American historical experience in the curriculum.[9]

Who is it who does the recognizing? There are different appropriate agents of recognition – the larger institution itself (e.g. the school), particular teachers (e.g. Mrs Everett), fellow students in the school.

4 Recognition and Value

Recognition of the individual and cultural group is a way of acknowledging someone in her or their (here, cultural) distinctness. It does not, however, require that the identity component in question (ethno-culture) be accorded a distinct worth or value apart from its worth *to the individual or group in question*. It requires only an acceptance, a certain legitimacy within the context in question. When Marbella wants to assert herself as a Spanish-speaker, and wants her teacher to acknowledge the legitimacy of her speaking Spanish, this is not the same as wishing for a declaration that the Spanish language, or Mexican culture, *has value* in Taylor's sense, namely that it possesses a value that applies to those outside the culture, and can be appreciated from outside the culture. That type of value "has something to say to all human beings," as Taylor puts it ("The Politics of Recognition," p. 66). Marbella simply wants recognition of the value, importance, and meaningfulness of her Mexican-American cultural identity *to her*.

This point holds as well for broadcasting the daily bulletin in Spanish, or holding assemblies that showcase the immigrant students. The message in doing so (if the school were to do it) is not to declare that the Spanish language is a good language or that Mexican-American culture has a distinct value; it is merely to recognize the Spanish-speaking students as a distinct cultural group whose presence in the school warrants full acknowledgement along with the Anglo students.[10]

The idea that the agents of recognition ought to be constantly engaged in assessing the value of every cultural marker they find it appropriate to recognize is, in fact, a quite bizarre suggestion.

This point holds as well for curriculum inclusion. To study the experience of a *cultural group* within its national context is to *recognize* the cultural group. This does not require declaring the *culture* of that group to be *of* (Taylorian) *value*. Of course, one may also say that the culture has produced objects of value – either to the world at large (certain kinds of literature, or music, for example), or to the larger national life (Mexican-American leaders, inventors, and the like). In any concrete case of a major ethnic group, we will certainly have both reasons for portraying the group in question within the curriculum. But the point is that there are two distinct reasons: one is recognition of the cultural group as a distinct group of persons, the other an assessment of value in a culture itself.[11] (The issue of cultural value will be discussed further below.)

The historical experience of a *cultural group* that is appropriate for curricular inclusion, and that addresses the legitimate desire for recognition, is not always itself focused on the group's actual *culture*. Take African Americans as an example. If, for instance, a curriculum accords attention only to forms of African-American music, religion, art, and literature in the context of various historical developments within the African-American community, it would have omitted an important dimension of the historical experience of African Americans, namely their having been enslaved, segregated, and generally discriminated against in systemic ways for hundreds of years.

I am not making the obvious point that a responsible presentation of American history requires attention to the oppression of African Americans; but rather that the value of *recognition* as applied to African Americans as a group should encompass not just "cultural" matters strictly or narrowly defined, but issues of historical experience bound up with racist subordination. One does not give due recognition to African Americans without attending to this history of subordination and its concomitant experience.

It might be replied that in my initial breakdown of the objects of recognition, "cultural groups" was one of the items; but "African American" is, as it were, ambiguous as between a cultural group and a racial group; and in my argument here I am implicitly treating it as a racial group rather than a cultural group.

To this I have two responses. First, the cultural and the political/social cannot be so readily disentangled in the case of many groups, certainly including African Americans. So much of what I mentioned above as *cultural* expressions of black culture is bound up with resistance to, or otherwise coming to terms with, racist oppression. Black Christianity, to take another important example, was a racist and colonialist *imposition* on American blacks, part of a deliberate attempt to eradicate their indigenous African religions. On the other hand, Black Christianity very much bears the stamp of black creativity in giving this imposed religion a distinctive character; moreover, it became at various points a central locus for resistance to racist subordination. Various forms of black music – spirituals, blues, rap – are also deeply implicated in the experience of racist oppression. So there can be no clear separation between politics and culture in the case of African Americans. And this is true to *some* extent of *every* American group that has suffered discrimination or subordination (Latinos of various groups, Jews, Native Americans, Asian Americans).

Second, we must remember the distinction between a cultural group and a culture, for both of which the issue of acknowledgement of distinctiveness is raised. African Americans as a distinct group of persons are to be distinguished from the culture of African Americans. It is the former who warrant recognition, just as do the immigrant Mexican-American students at the school Ann Davidson studied. Part of doing so means giving due recognition to the *distinctive* historical and current experience of their group. But in *both* cases (though Davidson's example does not address this point directly) part of what is to be *recognized* is the group's historical experience of subordination, resistance and accommodation to it, and the like. As long as our concern is the "cultural group" and not the "culture" itself, then, even if one could draw a distinction between the "race-based" and the "culture-based" dimensions of that experience (which I have argued above one cannot, or mostly cannot), the race-based part would still have to be encompassed in what is to be taken into account in meeting the recognition need.[12]

Returning to the original point then, recognition need involve no evaluative judgment at all, nor is it particularly appropriate, or even natural, to engage in assessing the culture of the student or the cultural group, when all that is at stake is recognizing that forms of cultural expression, and historical experiences, of the cultural group are important to that student, and that in the context of a school, they warrant an institutional acknowledgment.

5 Taylor on Recognition and Equal Worth

Though recognition does not entail finding value (except to the group itself), Taylor's discussion ties recognition closely to the *assessment* of the individual or group's culture as having "equal worth." So, when Taylor shifts from special rights for the Québecois and Quebec grounded in a legitimate interest in cultural survival (in section IV of his essay), to *recognition* of, say, French-speaking residents of Quebec (in section V), he says, "the further demand we are looking at here is that we all *recognize* the equal value of different cultures; that we not only let them survive, but acknowledge their worth" (p. 64). And further on in his argument, discussing specifically education-based demands for recognition, Taylor says, "Although it is not often stated clearly, the logic behind some of these demands seems to depend on a premise that we owe equal respect to all cultures" (p. 66).

Why does Taylor think that the logic of the demand for recognition of the cultural group leads to requiring a judgment of equal value of the culture? Taylor never makes this clear; yet the thrust of his argument earlier in the essay provides a clue as to why he regards recognition of equal value of different cultures as a central prop of the politics of difference. For he wants to argue that the more familiar Enlightenment idea of *equal dignity* of individuals became wedded to and transformed into equal respect for distinct cultures (and for distinctness more generally), and this is only a short step to "equal respect to actually evolved cultures" (p. 42).

Yet in articulating a notion of recognition, we must reject at the outset "equal valuing of distinct cultures" as a legitimate, and even intelligible, expression of a defensible multiculturalism, and deny that it is entailed by recognition of distinct cultural identity of individuals and cultural groups.

The injunction to value all cultures equally runs into three insuperable obstacles. First, it presumes that every culture can be regarded as the sort of totality to which a measure of value can be assigned. But what is *the value* of Mexican culture, of Anglo-American culture, of Ethiopian culture, of Polish-American culture? (I am intentionally mixing ethno-cultures with national cultures here, as all of these have come in for the "equal respect" injunction.) What could be the basis of assigning one overall value to a way of life that includes rituals, beliefs, modes of personal interaction, artistic production, and the like?[13]

A second difficulty is that, even independent of the "total cultural value" assumption, the "equal value" assumption further presumes that cultures can be unproblematically *compared* with respect to the values they realize. One ground for rejecting this assumption is a thorough-going relativism according to which either (a) cultures can never be compared with respect to value in any way, as there can be no standards of value outside a given culture; or (b) even if common standards could not in theory be rejected, no one could ever be in a position to be certain that she is in possession of them; so no one would ever be in a position to make the requisite comparison. According to either scenario, we would never be justified in making comparisons of value between different cultures.

I would want to reject this thorough-going relativism. I agree with Taylor's view that different cultures produce things of value to human beings in general, and that persons from cultures other than the one in question can come to recognize that value. Often doing so involves an expansion of one's scheme of values that arises from gaining an extensive understanding of another culture and what it finds valuable, and thinking that perspective through in light of and in comparison with one's own scheme of values. Taylor borrows from Gadamer the expression "fusion of horizons" to express how this new value framework which allows appreciation of the value of cultures other than one's own arises.

Yet, even accepting these points and rejecting full-scale relativism, the assumption that the cultural products and forms of life of distinct cultures *can always* be compared as to their value is certainly questionable. Can traditional Thai forms of dance be compared with Irish ones as to their overall value? Can we be sure that the literary forms of West Africans, French, and Slavs can be evaluatively compared in any overall way? It seems unlikely. And if we cannot do so with forms of artistic production of roughly the same character, how much less can we do so with cultural products of diverse characters, and, even less, with the complex and amorphous "ways of life" dimension of all distinct cultures?[14]

The idea that we can either affirm or deny an overall evaluative ranking of cultures depends on a much more extensive evaluative comparison among cultures than could ever intelligibly be undertaken. Hence, the idea that cultures have "equal worth" remains barely intelligible, and is certainly unable to be operationalized, even independent of the first assumption, that overall expressions of value can be attached to cultures as a whole.

A third difficulty with the "equal value" position is that it cannot coherently provide the content for an injunction to accord recognition or respect to other cultures. As Thomas Sowell says, derisively commenting on the multiculturalist goal of respect:

> History cannot be prettified in the interests of promoting "acceptance" or "mutual respect" among peoples and cultures. There is much in the history of every people that does not deserve respect. Whether with individuals or with groups, respect is something earned, not a door prize handed out to all. It cannot be prescribed by third parties.... "Equal respect" is an internally contradictory evasion. If everything is respected equally, then the term respect has lost its meaning.[15]

Sowell overstates his point by presuming that respect must always be directed toward positive achievement and attainment; that is only *one kind* of respect. As we saw in our discussion of anti-racism, a notion of "equal dignity" *of individuals* underlies the moral wrong of superiority-based racism; respect for that equal dignity would be a kind of "equal respect." However, equal respect for *cultures* is a different matter, since while every individual human being can be presumed to possess whatever qualities ground equal dignity (for example, the capacity for reason or morality, as Kant thought), respect for *cultures* as Sowell implies, does require attributing distinctive positive characteristics to cultures or cultural products.

Taylor, too, is concerned with how cultural respect can be made an object of moral demand. Taylor heaps scorn on those (if there are any such) who would shun the idea of cultural value altogether, collapsing the demand for cultural respect into a mere assertion of a valueless (and, Taylor argues, insulting and patronizing) solidarity with previously devalued or excluded cultures (p. 78). Taylor recognizes that one must actually *apprehend* value in another culture in order to accord it genuine (as opposed to spurious) respect. Yet how can the apprehension of equivalent value be an object of moral demand? Apart from the earlier arguments that the notion of "equivalent value" is barely intelligible, even if it *did* make sense, people cannot be morally enjoined to find value in something.

Three difficulties, then, plague the attempt to make "equal respect" in the form of a finding or declaring of "equal value" in every culture an expression of multiculturalism as an ethical norm: (1) cultures cannot be assigned overall, summary values, such as could be compared with the values of other cultures; (2) even "portions" of cultures cannot always be compared to something like analogous "portions" of other cultures, as the finding of "equal value" requires; (3) even if, *per impossible*, two cultures did have equal value (that is, value to "the world," to those outside the culture), their apprehension could not be made an object of ethical demand.

6 Respect, Value, and Equal Value

Must we, then, abandon cultural value as a component of multiculturalism? Fortunately not. There remains a form of "cultural respect" that
survives the three criticisms above. This is the view that every ethnic or
national culture contains something of distinctive value "to the world" –
value that is able to be appreciated by those outside of that culture.

This form of cultural respect avoids the defects of the "equal respect"
view. It presumes no overall total value of a given culture, but only that it
contains *something* of value. It does not require *comparison* with other
cultures, but simply treats each culture in its own right. Finally, it does not
require a finding of *equal* value, such as could not be made an object of
ethical injunction – but only of *some* value (something of value). This does
not mean that the view declares cultures to be of *unequal* value, while
accepting *some* value as sufficient. Rather, it rejects the comparison
between or among cultures as meaningless. So cultures are seen neither as
equal nor as unequal. The whole dimension of equivalence and non-
equivalence of value drops out of the picture entirely.

Yet even the latter may seem to pose a problem, expressed in (3) above.
How can we ethically demand that an individual find value in a culture?
Taylor addresses this very point in a justly famous passage in which he
says that every culture should be accorded a presumption that it possesses
such value:

> Merely on the human level, one could argue that it is reasonable to suppose
> that cultures that have provided the horizon of meaning for large numbers
> of human beings, of diverse characters and temperaments, over a long
> period of time – that have, in other words, articulated their sense of the
> good, the holy, and the admirable – are almost certain to have something
> that deserves our admiration and respect, even if it is accompanied by much
> that we have to abhor and reject (pp. 72–3).

How does this presumption provide a foundation for a moral injunction? The moral injunction would seem to be "Take up a stance toward
other cultures in which one shows interest in those cultures and presumes
that further knowledge will reveal to one the value(s) they embody, and
which one is capable of appreciating." To put it another way, the
injunction is to avoid both ethnocentrism and an indifferent ignorance in
one's view of other cultures. These formulations construe the content of
the injunction as something that one engages in, rather than as the
adoption of a mental state of assessment that cannot be summoned
through personal agency.

Even while providing this important basis for the appreciation of value, Taylor confuses the matter by continuing his practice of conflating the issue of *equal* worth with that of *some* worth. So he prefaces the long passage quoted above by saying, "What there is is the presumption of equal worth I described above: a stance we take in embarking on a study of the other." (p. 72).

This linking of recognition or respect (not to equate these two) with equal valuing is not a mere idiosyncrasy of Taylor's. It shows up quite regularly in discussions of multiculturalism. One of its sources is a reaction to the ethnocentrism of Euro-Americans assuming that European civilization is the repository of all, or almost all, of what civilization has produced in the way of value. When a school district in Florida passed a resolution that "American" culture was superior to any other world culture (and also, by implication, to any of the non-white ethno-cultures *within* the US), many were rightly outraged at the arrogance of this position.[16] The idea that no culture is superior to any other – that all cultures are *equal* in value – might seem a reasonable statement of the view underlying this reaction.

My suggestion is that we resist countering assertions of superiority of cultures with assertions of equality. Rather, we should challenge the intelligibility of making the former assertions at all, and proceed to examine the specific bases the speaker proposes for having made the assertion of superiority:

1   Often, for example, the *practice* of a "third world" culture (e.g. female circumcision, or infibulation) will have been compared with an *ideal* that is part of the political culture of the speaker (e.g. gender equality).
2   The Florida district that originally passed the "superiority of American culture" directive had in mind "the free market system and Constitutional liberty" as part of its conception of American culture. Is it not misleading to subsume political and economic systems under an idea of "culture?"
3   Moreover, the district Board does *not* say that children need to be taught the extraordinary inequalities in wealth, income and life prospects among Americans, or our widespread poverty, among the worst of any industrialized nation. If the distinction between economy, polity, and culture *is* to be soft-pedaled, do not these matters have equal claim on curricular attention as part of "American culture?"

If we decouple "equality" and "culture," the former does have an important role to play in multiculturalism – in the anti-racist, or more generally, anti-discrimination, branch of multiculturalism discussed earlier, as well as in the idea that each individual is, equally, owed recognition in her distinctness. Taylor articulates the worry that women and students from previously (or currently) excluded groups have been given a demeaning picture of themselves (p. 65). They, and other such groups, have responded by saying that indeed they are the equals of those who devalue them. This is an assertion of *equality*, and it can become a political demand that that equality be respected. So the demand for equal respect gets taken up within the ethical injunctions of multiculturalism.[17]

Yet Taylor frames this concern for equal respect within the framework of "recognition of distinctiveness," by speaking of a group's wishing to avoid a demeaning image of themselves being reflected back to them, of the members' need to struggle for a form of recognition of their distinct identity that is not demeaning. (On page 65 Taylor cites Frantz Fanon as an earlier theorist of this concern). But it is misleading of Taylor to see the concern for respect as an equal as a type of "concern for recognition of distinctiveness." A concern not to be seen as inferior, that one's image in the larger culture or institution not be a degraded one, is not the same as the need for recognition of one's distinct identity in the first place – the need to be seen, to be acknowledged as who one is. The former concern is much more properly regarded as what Taylor calls "democratic recognition" than "distinctiveness recognition."[18]

As I mentioned above (p. 75), while Taylor's historical account of the genesis of the human need for recognition allows two importantly distinct strands, in fact as his essay proceeds the democratic/sameness-based recognition falls away *as a type of recognition*. The focus on democratic recognition recedes to the background. Recognition comes to be identified with "recognition of distinctness, or difference." While the issue of democratic sameness remains, it loses its deeper connection with forms of recognition – becoming, instead, an institutional structure that grants people *equal rights as individuals*, or, more generally, difference-blind norms for social policy.

This is clearest in Taylor's famous discussion of whether the Québecois should, for the purpose of protecting their distinct French-speaking culture, be accorded certain privileges and immunities not accorded to English-speaking Canadians. There, sameness-based liberalism is identified with granting all individuals the same rights (of which language schools to send their children, in what language to write commercial signs, and the like) with the implication of denying any special status to the Québecois cultural group.

But the desire to be acknowledged in one's cultural distinctiveness is not the same as the desire to be seen as an *equal*. Subordinated groups struggling for recognition retain this dual focus, of which Taylor loses sight; on the one hand they want their distinctive culture acknowledged, on the other they want to be seen as not-inferior. In think part of what throws Taylor off from sustaining this duality throughout the essay is his identification of equality with a purely *individualistic* basis – equal rights for individuals. This means that when he focuses on particular *groups* and their need for recognition, the sameness/equality dimension threatens to disappear.[19]

The form of equality that *is* pertinent to multiculturalism as it is applied to groups, then, is an acceptance of groups, and members of those groups, as equals. But we have to be clear in what sense these groups are seen as equals. It cannot be, as I have argued above, that their *cultures* are equal; this, I argued, was meaningless. It can only be that they are the kind of groups who, having been denied full human equality, are demanding to be granted it. The groups in question that Taylor mentions are gender and racial groups. I would add, as a usefully illustrative case, groups defined by sexual orientation. In these cases, the demand is that their distinguishing characteristic – "race," gender, sexual orientation – should *not* be taken as a badge of inferiority or deficiency. It is not that they wish to jettison the distinguishing characteristic. As I am envisioning these groups, their group identity as blacks, women, lesbians, is very important to their members' sense of individual identity. They wish this identity component to be recognized. But their concern here is that the identity component should not be taken to mark them as inferior.

There are two forms of equality then, not unrelated, which *are* appropriate to multiculturalism broadly construed (embracing anti-racism or anti-discrimination more generally). One is the purely individualistic notion of equal dignity – one which drives Taylor's discussion of the alternative conception to "recognition of difference" and which Sowell implicitly denies in his derisive criticism of a notion of "equal respect for cultures." A second, closely related, is a desire for groups as groups, or as members of groups, for their group membership not to be taken as a badge of inferiority.

The difference between the two could be put in this way: the first says, for example, "I am black and have no desire to deny this, nor would I wish to be anything other than black. I am a human being who happens to be black and it is as a *human being* that I declare myself the moral equal of any other human being." The second, by contrast, would say, "It is *as* black that I declare myself the moral equal of a person of any other race, especially white."[20] It is this second form that Taylor's account omits.

Yet if we abandon "equal cultural value" are we not still left with the problem that unless an *individual* student's own culture is seen as equal to that of her peers, she will herself feel unequal? No, we are not. As Taylor says, the problem arises when a student is presented with a demeaning picture of her culture. Such a demeaning picture is one that declares the culture unworthy, or paltry compared to other cultures on the scene. But if we accept Taylor's presumption of value, then no culture need be portrayed as wholly or largely unworthy or demeaning, even if it might contain practices that a student may come to feel are, in Taylor's words, "abhorrent," or at least shameful.

A pupil is not psychically damaged simply from the failure of her ethno-culture to be declared equal to that of other ethno-cultures, but only if it is distinctly portrayed in a demeaning light. Or, to modify this point, since multiculturalist discourse has sometimes encouraged the idea that cultures must be declared equal, some students, influenced by this, may actually feel (or feel as if they feel) demeaned unless their culture is declared to be, and portrayed as, the equal of that of any other. But, as I have argued, it is the task of educators to teach multiculturalism in a way that shows the kind of respect for cultures that is appropriate to them and does not push toward a meaningless comparison between different cultures in terms of their overall value.

To summarize the argument regarding Taylor, then:

1   Taylor powerfully articulates the need for recognition of one's distinct identity (its presence, and its distinctness), of which culture can be one important element.
2   People also desire to be recognized by (appropriate) others as equals. This recognition can take a purely individual form; but it can also take a group-based form, in which the desire is that a group characteristic should not be taken as a badge of inferiority. Taylor fails to articulate this group-based form of equality recognition.
3   Taylor is correct to say that we can presume every culture of sufficient longevity and extent to contain something of value not only to its members but to all of humanity. However, his frequent slide from this position into the idea that all cultures are of *equal* value is a tilt toward meaninglessness, and orients multiculturalism in a counterproductive direction.

7 Fraser on Recognition and Equality

Nancy Fraser's impressive attempt to synthesize a range of political and intellectual concerns in a postmodern, and what she calls "post-socialist" climate, contains an implicit critique of Taylor. Analogizing "cultural injustice," whose concern is the according of recognition to the political–economic injustice of maldistribution, Fraser is concerned that both forms of injustice be given their due. She criticizes theorists like Taylor whose concerns seem to have shifted entirely toward the cultural injustice side of the spectrum, as if either (1) we no longer have reason to be concerned with economic injustice; (2) cultural injustice is more important than economic injustice; or (3) cultural injustice provides significant leverage by itself to attack the structures of power that produce economic injustice. Fraser rejects all three of these positions, emphasizing the importance of addressing structures of economic injustice independently (though in concert with, and intertwined with, addressing cultural injustice, as the two systems of injustice reinforce one another).

This part of Fraser's argument is an important corrective to Taylor, and I agree with it fully. Fraser recognizes racism as a distinct justice concern, sees its political–economic dimension, and does not attempt to subsume it within recognition concerns. So Fraser's view corrects for two deficiencies in Taylor's account: first, his failure to articulate economic/political equality as a concern distinct from valuational equality; second, his collapsing of all recognition concerns into recognition of difference.

On the first point, Taylor could perhaps reply that he was simply not concerned in his essay with economic/political inequality in its own right, but only with its relation to recognition. However, his essay concerns, in addition, the ethical character of liberal polities as a whole, and thus *should* take account of other forms of inequality as well. As I argue in "Multiculturalism, Racial Justice, and Community,"[21] Taylor does take some note of racial inequalities, but his discussion of it is inadequate. So he is open to the charge that Fraser lodges against a family of theorists (of whom Taylor is one) that they have come to supplant concerns for material equality with recognitional equality.

On the second point I argued above that, despite an initial attention to equality as one of the two forms of recognition, as Taylor's essay proceeds, "recognition" comes to be applied only to recognition of *difference*, implying that equality concerns are limited to the area of political rights (though, as noted, Taylor does also import an unnecessary and diverting notion of equality in relation to *culture*, which Fraser's account neither involves nor requires). Fraser, by contrast, maintains equality as a central focus of her notion of recognition.

For Fraser, recognition in the context of her target groups – racial, gender, sexual minority groups – always concerns a group that is *devalued* within the larger society. And what recognition primarily comes to for Fraser is the *revaluing* toward a state of (valuational) equality with the corresponding currently privileged group (whites in the case of race, men in the case of gender, heterosexuals in the case of sexual orientation). Fraser distinguishes two approaches to this revaluing, affirmative and transformational. The former calls for a positive revaluing while leaving the current form of the identities in question in place, while the latter, more radical, alternative calls for an undermining of current forms of both the privileged and the undervalued forms of identity and the valuational structure underlying them. Despite the difference in approach and result, both directions aim at the same goal of equal valuing.

Yet while Fraser corrects for Taylor's failure to give the equality dimension of recognition the centrality it deserves, Fraser's view presents precisely the reverse problem – she almost entirely drops the "recognition of difference" as a matter *distinct* from equality. By this I do not mean to imply that Fraser is blind to the issue of difference; far from it. She is concerned about her target groups in their distinct identity. However, her overriding concern in *attending* to difference is how best to promote *equality*. "Which of the many varieties of identity politics best synergize with struggles for social equality? And which tend to interfere with the latter?" she asks.[22]

What is missing in Fraser's account is the very point on which Taylor is so convincing, and that is the need for recognition in one's individual identity as a need *distinct* from the need to be seen as an equal. The absence of concern or recognition of this point is bound up with Fraser's choice of target group. Her groups (race, gender, sexual orientation) are all *devalued* groups; their need is *no longer to be devalued*. Fraser's use of the term "cultural" to refer to the terrain in which these issues of group valuing are expressed and worked through conflates two different dimensions of the need for recognition – recognitional equality and recognitional distinctness. (Indeed, Fraser's overarching language of "justice" already tilts towards equality rather than recognitional concerns; the language of "recognitional injustice" is already a bit of a stretch.) For Fraser, cultural groups are really understood as devalued and discriminated-against identity groups.

In this regard it is significant that Fraser explicitly omits *ethnic* and *national* groups in her discussion of "identity politics". While suggesting in footnote 2 following upon this declaration of omission that some of her analysis might apply to these sorts of groups as well, I think it is revealing that she does not include them in her core analysis of identity groups. To do so would force acknowledgment of the "cultural difference" dimension of those groups. Taylor's Québecois, for example, are concerned with recognition of their interest in maintaining a culture distinct from Canadian anglophone culture. This is not a concern for *equality* (except, as Taylor says, equal recognition of distinctiveness).

The inattention to cultural distinctness is revealed also in the devalued groups Fraser does discuss. "Racial" groups are particularly pertinent to our concerns. Fraser sees such groups (gender is another) as "bivalent collectivities," by which she means that they suffer from *both* economic/political *and* recognition-based or cultural/valuational injustices. But when Fraser describes the character of the recognition-based injustices, they all take the form of the racial group being subject to various sorts of disparagement, devaluation, and discrimination.[23] Omitted here is another "bivalency" – that racial groups are often also ethno-cultural groups and, as such, are concerned not only to be seen as equal human beings, but also that their distinct culture be recognized within the larger cultural/social sphere. Regarding the small example of the Mexican-American students in the school studied by Ann Locke Davidson, their concern, as Davidson presents it, is not only to be equals in the school but also to have their distinct cultural identity acknowledged. Fraser's analysis omits one entire dimension of this duality.[24]

Fraser's analytical framework separates "distributional" issues from "recognitional" ones. Fraser states at the outset that this distinction is made for analytical purposes only, and should not be allowed to mask the fact that the two sorts of issues, or domains, are intertwined. Indeed, part of the point of Fraser's essay is to reveal the connections between these two domains.

But the framework itself is more misleading than Fraser recognizes. One could equally well structure a discussion of the morality of politics and culture around a *different* duality, one that cross-cuts Fraser's – between equality concerns (of either a recognitional or economic sort) and cultural distinctness (of either a recognitional or economy-related sort). In a sense, the duality that Fraser articulates in her "bivalent collectivities" such as race and gender are both manifestations of the same thing – the desire, need, or demand to be *treated as an equal*. Blacks deserve to be treated as equals; to do so involves economic, political, social, representational, and cultural spheres. Moreover, these spheres are not readily separable from one another, in a way that Fraser's analytical separation masks.

At the same time, recognition of distinctness has both an attitudinal dimension – a purely interpersonal dimension of recognition – and a material dimension, such as the provision of state resources for cultural preservation and expression or laws governing the language in which commercial activity is to be transacted (to advert to Taylor's discussion). *Both* the attitudinal and the material are, or can be seen as, expressive of an underlying unity, that of *recognizing cultural distinctness*; just as the many interpenetrating domains mentioned immediately prior can all be seen as forms expressing the underlying principle of *treating people as equals*.

Thus, Fraser's choice of an analytic framework framed by the polarities of material/distributional and recognitional has the effect of masking an equally significant "bivalency" – between equality and distinctness. It calls into question Fraser's claim that her two domains operate according to "distinctive logics" that it is the goal of her essay to delineate.

That Fraser's analytic division between distributional and recognitional is problematic can be seen by focusing on the particular domain of the *legal/political*. That domain does not fit very clearly into either Fraser's conception of "distribution" or that of "recognition." At first, Fraser refers to the former domain as "political–economic," and that nominal equation persists throughout the essay. Nevertheless, when Fraser spells out what she means by this domain, it is described almost entirely in economic terms, related to the market, the division of labor, and the material resources produced in the economic sphere. Indeed, the metaphor of "distribution" is much more naturally an economic than a political one, and Fraser's view of *class* as the fundamental group-based division of this sphere comports with the economic emphasis.

Of course, economics cannot be separated from politics; but each conveys a different emphasis, and Fraser clearly has the economic more strongly in mind. Moreover, when Fraser enumerates specific forms of "cultural-valuational" injustices suffered by racial groups, some of what she includes is straightforwardly political/legal ("denial of full legal rights and equal protections") or suggestive of the political ("exclusion from and/or marginalization in public spheres and deliberative bodies"). Other injustices mentioned by Fraser in this section (harassment, discrimination, violence) hardly seem paradigm cases of either "purely recognitional" injustices or "distributional" ones.

The domain of the political is an especially central one in which "recognition of equality" plays a part, as Honneth spells out in his book *The Struggle for Recognition* and which Habermas develops in his essay "Struggles for Recognition in the Democratic State" in Gutmann's

Multiculturalism. Yet Fraser's analysis gives it no comfortable home.[25] The lesson I suggest we draw from this, taken together with the other injustices that do not fit very well into either category of her dyad, is that there is something importantly misleading about an analytical framework organized around the concepts of "distributional" and "cultural/ valuational," because some important injustices do not fit comfortably into either one, the entire domain of the *political* being a prime example; because these omissions suggest something much closer to a continuum, or even a complex interdependence; and, finally, because, at another level, the injustices with which Fraser is concerned all reflect a fundamental concern with treating persons as equals.

Thus, in summary, I have argued that while Fraser's analysis corrects Taylor's undertheorizing of the equality dimension of group recognition, Fraser makes an error entirely complementary to Taylor's, masking the entire issue of recognition of cultural distinctness. This omission is linked to a larger problem in Fraser's entire analytic framework. What she sees as a fundamental duality can, in another framing, be seen as two expressions of one pole of *another* duality – equality, counterposed to the omitted concern for distinctness.[26]

Notes

1   David Hollinger, *PostEthnic America* (New York: Hill and Wang, 1995).
2   *Bigotry* racism is distinct from superiority racism and I will not be discussing it here. A person can be bigoted against a person of another race without thinking him inferior; Jews and Asians have often been targets of racial bigotry while being thought of as threats, and as in some important ways superior (thought, at the same time, both groups, and especially Jews, have also been thought of as *morally* inferior). Jorge Garcia's "The Heart of Racism," *Journal of Social Philosophy*, winter 1996, has convinced me that not all racism is concerned with superiority and inferiority. Laurence Thomas makes a similar distinction between hatred and superiority racisms ("The Evolution of Anti-Semitism," *Transition*, no 57, p. 107ff) and uses this framework to distinguish between racism against Jews (anti semitism) and racism against blacks. While I am in accord with his general analysis, there is a good deal of racial hatred against blacks, and not all contemporary forms of anti-black racism are tied up with beliefs in black inferiority.
3   L. Blum, "Multiculturalism, Racial Justice, and Community: Reflections on Charles Taylor's 'The Politics of Recognition'," in L. Foster and P. Herzog (eds), *Defending Diversity: Contemporary Philosophical Perspectives on Pluralism and Multiculturalism* (Amherst: University of Massachusetts Press, 1994).

4   Taylor ties the need for this recognition to a theory about how identity is formed, namely through interaction and recognition by others – a "dialogic" view of the self. But I wish to disaggregate these two strands. We can recognize that a person can be caused a kind of substantial harm through being seen as an inferior, or not seen at all – that is, through forms of failed recognition – and can acknowledge that this harm is caused in part through the individual's internalizing the other's view (or non-view) of her; we can accept this without buying into the larger idea that our entire identities are formed fully through dialogue with others. It is not that I definitively reject the latter view. But it seems to me to go substantially beyond what is actually required in the way of a theory of identity sufficient to ground the ethical principles with which I am concerned. I believe, moreover, that Taylor's view of the need for recognition is not itself as dependent on his theory of the dialogical self as he thinks it is.

5   Axel Honneth, *The Struggle for Recognition: The Moral Grammar of Social Conflicts* (Cambridge, Mass.: MIT Press, 1995).

6   Ann Locke Davidson, *Making and Molding Identities in Schools: Student Narratives on Race, Gender, and Academic Engagement* (Albany: SUNY Press, 1996).

7   Nevertheless, in a school with an appreciable contingent of Cambodian students, it would be appropriate to find some way to give curricular and/or non-curricular recognition to this group.

8   In this spirit, David Hollinger cautions us not to read the current ethno-racial demographics of a class, school, or society back into history. See Hollinger, *PostEthnic America*, p. 125.

9   Some literature on recognition implies that cultures are static and relatively unchanging. Indeed, Taylor's discussion of French Canadian culture in Quebec, and his general notion of cultural recognition, could be taken in this way, though other interpretations are possible. But the notion of a "cultural marker" more clearly suggests the changeable and variable character of cultures themselves, as well as the different significances they may have for individuals. The value of "cultural recognition" should not allow itself to be captured by cultural conservatives and traditionalists. As Will Kymlicka points out in *Liberalism, Community, and Culture* (New York: Oxford University Press, 1989), the values of cultural preservation, respect, and recognition can be framed so as to be neutral between more and less traditional understandings of the culture in question.

10 Of course, a material dimension is at stake here as well, bearing on an equality of opportunity value that has little to do with recognition. If the broadcasting of the messages is confined to English, some of the immigrant Spanish-speaking students will not have the same access to important information as the native English-speaking students. This matter is distinct from the more psychologically based "need for recognition" with which Taylor is concerned.

11 Susan Wolf makes something very close to this point in her "Comment" on

Taylor's essay in Gutmann, *Multiculturalism* (Princeton: Princeton University Press, 1994, pp. 80ff.); only she does not clearly distinguish the cultural group from the culture.

12   Favoring curricular recognition of different ethno-cultural racial groups need not commit us to any specific form of that recognition. In particular, it does not take sides on the important curricular dispute as to (a) whether this recognition is best accomplished through distinct "ethnic studies" programs, that offer courses focused as much as possible on particular ethno-racial-cultural groups, or that place modular units of that character within social studies or history courses; or (b) whether historical understanding and inclusion is better accomplished through a more integrated approach that weaves the ethnic history into its context in the larger history of the nation, of diasporic movements of that group, or world history. While I personally favor the latter approach, the argument presented in this essay does not engage this important curricular issue.

13   Suppose we abandon the "cardinal number" version of the view in question, and weaken the principle slightly to this: "I can't assign a distinct numerical value to Anglo-American culture, but I can say that Mexican culture is equal in value to it." This would barely be an improvement. What could be the basis for a claim of that sort?

14   This is not to deny that an individual deeply knowledgeable about two different cultures could make *some* judgments of comparative value regarding particular products of the two distinct cultures. Let us keep in mind, however, that frequently those who confidently assert the superiority of Western, or American, culture are not such knowledgeable persons, but are generally ignorant of the cultures whose inferiority they proclaim, knowing only, for example, that (some members) engage in objectionable practices such as infibulation, that their governments are too quick to jail dissidents, that some members have been known to burn brides whose dowries they deem insufficient, or that they have widespread poverty. The latter facts are hardly bases on which the total superiority of one entire culture to another could be asserted; and, as various commentators have pointed out, the focus on abhorrent and objectionable practices of some members of other cultures yields certain moral and intellectual dangers: (1) Generalizing from single practices to the moral character of a culture as a whole; (2) mistaking cultural for political practices, and (3) diverting attention from deficiencies in the social, political, or cultural systems of those making the invidious comparisons.

15   Thomas Sowell, *Migrations and Cultures: A World View* (New York: Basic Books, 1996), pp. ix–x.

16   See "Fla. Union Vows to Fight District's 'Americanism' Policy," *Education Week*, May 25, 1994.

17   We should recognize, however, that not everyone appears to be concerned about what images the wider culture has of them, *nor* about recognition of distinctness. While this may be a minority consciousness within any devalued group, some people gain their recognition and esteem from other reference

groups and are concerned only about equal, non-discriminatory access to opportunities such as housing, employment, education, public accommodations, and the like – not about how or whether others outside those groups see them. I think this fact does require some adjustment in Taylor's general thesis about the need for recognition; but it does not undermine it entirely, since those individuals perhaps still require recognition from *some* persons.

18 Beyond this point, but related to it, while Taylor closely links the need for recognition with the desire that the image of one's group not be portrayed in a demeaning fashion, the two things are distinct. A person could be concerned that *if* her group were portrayed in public venues, such as film, advertisements, and school curricula, these portrayals not be demeaning; yet the person may not care if the group were actually publicly represented in the first place. This would be a concern *not to be demeaned*, but not a concern *to be recognized*.

Moreover, Taylor overstates the degree to which members of devalued groups actually internalize the devaluing to which they may be subject. A person who is entirely secure in her own esteem and sense of worth could still be concerned that the larger culture portrays a negative view of her group. She need not feel devalued herself in order to object to demeaning public portrayals of her group. For more on this criticism of Taylor, see Blum, "Multiculturalism, Racial Justice, and Community."

19 The disappearance of group-based desires for recognition-as-equals can be seen in Taylor's discussion of affirmative action (p. 40). There, Taylor discusses attempts by the politics of equality/sameness to encompass the seemingly threatening politics of difference. One form of "difference recognizing" politics that Taylor agrees *can* be encompassed within standard universalistic liberal egalitarian sameness policies is affirmative action (which Taylor misleadingly calls "reverse discrimination"). It can be encompassed because such policies can be understood as temporary measures to compensate for historical group-based disadvantages and bring these groups to the same starting point where they can then compete *as individuals* in a color-blind fashion.

Absent in this discussion (though not inconsistent with what Taylor actually says) is a recognition that blacks and women may see affirmative action as consistent with, and an extension of, other anti-discrimination policies which do more than provide a "color-blind" level playing field for individuals independent of their race and gender. Rather, they see these policies as affirming the *equality* of blacks to whites, women to men, in the face of a culture which still does not fully accept that equality. That is, the policies can be seen as taking a group-based identity and conferring on it the recognition of democratic equality that Taylor speaks about in his early general discussion but loses once he begins focusing on group identities. Democratic measures (including affirmative action) are not about affirming distinctness in its own right; they are, however, about recognizing distinctness but claiming equality for it.

Ironically, in Taylor's later discussion of groups like blacks and women and their desires for recognition, he recognizes that these identities can be deeply significant, not mere way-stations to a color-blind level playing field. As we saw earlier, one of the ways that a cultural group gains an appropriate kind of recognition is through its distinct historical experience being recognized. African Americans and Latinos wish that experience to be recognized, and they see its acknowledgment as part of an appropriate exemplification of Taylor's notion of recognition. However, what makes that experience distinctive *is* that it is so deeply shaped by the denial of that group's human equality. Taylor misses this because he thinks of distinctiveness solely in terms of *cultural* distinctiveness, rather than a distinctiveness (of experience) that is intimately connected with *inequality*.

20   Cf. Appiah, "Identity, Authenticity, Survival: Multicultural Societies and Social Reproduction" in Gutmann, *Multiculturalism*, p. 161.

21   Blum, pages 191–5.

22   "From Redistribution to Recognition?" p. 20, this volume. Fraser echoes this concern as central to her general intellectual stance in the following quote from another essay, "Multiculturalism, Antiessentialism, and Radical Democracy" in *Justice Interruptus: Critical Reflections on the "Postsocialist" Condition* (Routledge, 1997), p. 186: "the crucial political questions of the day: Which identity claims are rooted in a defense of social relations of inequality and domination? And which are rooted in a challenge to such relations?" (186).

23   See p. 30: "This depreciation is expressed in a range of harms suffered by people of color, including demeaning stereotypical depictions in the media as criminal, bestial, primitive, stupid, and so on; ... subjection to Eurocentric norms in relation to which people of color appear lesser or deviant and that work to disadvantage them, even in the absence of any intention to discriminate."

24   Fraser certainly does sometimes use the language of "recognition of distinctiveness." Such language is especially prevalent in another essay in *Justice Interruptus*, "Multiculturalism, Antiessentialism, and Radical Democracy: A Genealogy of the Current Impasse in Feminist Theory." She provides a succinct historical account of the development of "difference feminism" (sometimes called "cultural feminism"). Yet Fraser (rightly I think, from a historical point of view) portrays this movement's goal as "[opposing] the undervaluing of women's worth by recognizing gender difference and revaluing femininity" (p. 176). That is, the goal is still one of *equal* valuing rather than valuing of distinctness as a good in its own right.

25   Fraser discusses "despised sexualities," groups whose state of oppression stems from cultural devaluing rather than political economic arrangements (pp. 26–7). She recognizes that gays and lesbians are discriminated against in the world of work, housing, and social benefits. But she says that since these inequalities stem from cultural devaluing, "The remedy for the injustice, consequently, is recognition, not redistribution" (p. 26). But it seems more accurate to say that the remedy is a *combination* of equal valuing and *civic equality*, the domain untheorized by Fraser. For a sustained attempt to

theorize civic equality for gays and lesbians, see Morris Kaplan, *Sexual Justice: Democratic Citizenship and the Politics of Desire* (New York: Routledge, 1997).

26 No doubt Fraser would reply to some of this argument that equality concerns are just *more important* than difference-recognition concerns (even allowing that the latter sometime take material forms). I agree with this position. In this sense, from a political point of view, Fraser's masking of difference concerns is less problematic than Taylor's masking of equality.

I would like to thank Rene Arcilla for crucial feedback on an earlier draft of this article.

5

Ludic, Corporate, and Imperial Multiculturalism: Impostors of Democracy and Cartographers of the New World Order

Martin J. Beck Matuštík

To theorize multiculturalism is to return in some respects to the conversations surrounding Plato's education and politics for liberation. His *Republic* not only provided a classical academic and political canon for the leaders of the ideal state, it became a guide to the ongoing debate on the pedagogy of the oppressed. Plato's aim in designing a suitable liberal arts curriculum as well as economic and political arrangements was to get the prisoners out of the Cave of ignorance. The publically sanctioned cultural myths serving this ideal would seem to be, some object today, *merely* 'philosophically correct.' More broadly viewed, the culturally and politically conservative yet thoughtful Plato, by way of his state's Noble Lie, attempted to define the cement of social cohesion necessary even in the polity run by good and wise philosopher–kings. In debating what form the canon of an ideal republic should take (tradition was never canonical of itself), Plato in effect inscribed the issue of 'political correctness' into the heart of liberal arts.

I am, however, less concerned with Plato and his discontents, than with the lasting insight that in the founding of a polis *we* inevitably invoke, along with sound philosophical reasons, some story. If even an idealized *we* cannot but employ a notion of what is politically or philosophically correct for *us* at this time and place, then the option may be neither enlightenment nor myth. Rather, the better question becomes, which or whose reasons and stories can be normative and meaningful now and which ones do *we* need to jettison as at best outlived and at worst invidious? Plato's questioning concerning what should and should not be in the curriculum, economics, and politics for liberation is of this thoughtful stock. Never mind his answers! Conservatives and liberals may still benefit from Plato's questions better than from the inane framework of the current debates on 'political correctness' or multiculturalism.[1]

All sides in the current debates on rethinking the western canon concede that the multicultural world is here to stay. The culture, political, and economic wars turn on how and through whom to tell the multicultural story. The charge against critical multiculturalists of *mere* 'political correctness' is a distracting flare. All partisanship is vying for a correctness of its myths. That the winning tale of our democratic diversity is no longer recognized as an even remotely 'Noble Lie' underscores Plato's insight into the function of myths in founding even rational states. I return to his lovers and impostors of justice in order to unmask founding myths among the cartographers of *our* New World Order (NWO): which, whose, reasons and stories are normative and meaningful? Which, whose, must we give up? What should fashion culture, economics, and politics for liberation?

1 Impostors

If multicultural reality is not going away, it could be hijacked. First, ludically, one may decenter it all yet emerge from the culture wars of identity and difference with one's center intact. Second, one may incorporate the game of diversity into the flexible accumulation of capital. Third, one may adopt diversity for imperial foreign policy or colonization by other means. If multicultural democracy envisions a more just polity, its impostors deal in tokens of diversity, and meanwhile they cleverly restructure the existing Cave.

1.1 Ludic multiculturalism

Ebert distinguishes 'ludic postmodernism' from 'resistance postmodernism.' As with multicultural movements, if postmodern sensibilities can be digested into the cultural ethos of our age, the pertinent question becomes which or whose story should matter. Ebert's distinction may likewise guide the current multicultural debate.[2]

The cultural Luddites focus almost exclusively on the undecidability of texts (production of signs). They tend to regard both politics and play in terms of intertextual transgressions of existing cultural discourses. On this view, the postmodern political game intervenes in power-contexts of signifiers, disrupts existing hierarchies, announces signifying possibilities.

Decentering practices offer salutary micropolitics if cultural workers become cognizant of the oppressed identities and occluded differences in ways that grand narratives of modernity were not.

Yet the emphatically 'ludic' character of these interventions poses a problem. Just as the "1779 half-witted Leicestershire workman"[3] and the nineteenth-century Luddites *misread* the source of their oppression – attacking in protest the labor-saving machines rather than transgressing exploitative production – so the twentieth-century postmodern inter-textualists may *misread* interventions in culture as bringing about genuine social change in concrete material existence. 'Ludic postmodern multi-culturalists' can live happily thereafter within intact dominant centers of power. Moreover, the ludic media and cultural intrusions need not ever leave hegemonic centers of power while traveling in imagined texts and across imagined borders to the projected margins. In the academy as well as in the cyberspaces both types of *kinesis* (decentering and traveling to the margins from intact centers of power) are possible without liberating any marginalized form of life. The ludic aspect of such intrusions betrays the fallacy of their misplaced concreteness: by celebrating the heterogene-ity of signs, by parading the cultural spectacle of difference, one imagines oneself as already free. The multicultural neo-Luddite, disconnected from the sources of real suffering and free-floating in textual spaces without the weight of body and face, might sketch but a masculinist, White, and economically privileged fiction. Multicultural impostors of radical demo-crats are (Sartre and Marcuse exposed certain liberals some time ago) just as pernicious to the marginalized as overt conservative bigots or oppres-sors.[4]

I argue in the concluding section that overcoming abstract humanism, i.e. modern patriarchy and racism, need not involve rejection of post-modern experiences of intertextual hegemonic struggles over signs. Nor need one reject the postmodern Luddite. To become a 'resistance post/ modern multiculturalist,' one would do well to learn how to decenter and transgress powers that be. Yet one should not mistake comic enunciations of textual undecidabilities (liberation of texts) with concrete human and institutional faces (liberation of peoples).

1.2 *Corporate multiculturalism*

Jameson links postmodernism to the cultural logic of flexible accumula-tion that, after 1989 more than ever before, defines globally regional late capitalism.[5] The fifty largest multinational corporations made it – either through an international division of labor or by takeovers – into the world's top one hundred national economies. Corporate image-makers and market strategists are well positioned either to supplement the mono-genealogical assimilation of nationalist integrations or to exploit nationalist conflicts and the fragmenting role of nation-states. With ethnic revivals raging in their backyards, corporate headquarters, ads, and logos worldwide are decked in fashionable pomo imagery. Corporate bodies have become racialized, gendered, and flexible enough to present both the local and global image, a place of belonging in diversity. One would suppose that Plato's just republic, Kant's perpetual peace, Hegel's mutual recognition, and the multiculturalist utopia are realized by corporate guardians in corporate heavens.

Giroux insightfully analyzes Benetton and Disney as two corporate bodies which successfully retell the story of multiculturalism to promote their 'goods.' We could name others. The key is that image makers and market strategists learn multicultural and Marxist lessons – to stealthily promote cultural recognition of corporations and for the sake of redis-tributing public wealth to corporations. At the time when ludic postmodernists sneer at grand narratives, corporations are busy at work chiseling lasting temples of themselves; in the 'post-socialist condition' when political proceduralist liberals and market-conservative neoliberals, almost in a Gregorian chant, intone the advent of democracy realized, corporations realize capital gains of globally unregulated economic kingdoms.[6]

My claim – that multicultural and Marxist lessons of recognition and redistribution are relearned by flexibly multicultural corporations – might sound less off the wall if one is positioned eastward of the old Cold War border. Fukuyama tried to convince us that 1989 signified the end of nationalist and other ideologies and victory for liberal democracy and neoliberal markets. This aim is part and parcel of the flexibly global logic of postmodern and multicultural capitalism. Yet we know who the domestic corporate victors are in the post-Communist East: *apparatchiki*, *nomenklatura*, former secret service agents, and various old (district and city Communist officials) and new mafias.[7]

Let us consider three types of examples. In its mildest forms, e.g. in the Czech Republic, the post-Communist redistribution to the corporations proceeds in stages of coupon privatization of publically owned com-panies: they are first democratically offered to nationals recognized by the state. Large accumulations of coupons end up then in a few 'invisible hands.' In more aggravated dramatizations, we find, e.g. in Slovakia, the former stasis taking a grip on the nationalist–paternalistic government and redistributing the state companies along nepotistic and nationalist–

party lines. While popular recognition is given a distinctly nationalist facade, the fight over redistribution is among in-group factions and becomes earmarked for the ascending state mafias. In the most tragicomic relief of the post-Communist capital gains, we encounter banking schemes, such as the pyramid one supported by the Albanian government. A comparison with the nineteenth-century Freedmen's Bank in the US post-Civil War era is not inappropriate: Du Bois describes how this bank "chartered by the Nation" to serve the purposes of democratic and economic transition from slavery to postwar reconstruction, abused the trust of the US Freedmen's Bureau. "Then in one sad day came the crash, – all the hard-earned dollars of the freedmen disappeared . . . all the faith in saving went too, and much of the faith in men." Likewise, the Albanian pyramid fraud, backed up with the prestige of its government, robbed the lifesavings of the entire population. In each case, public and private wealth was redistributed to the ruling cliques composed of the previous masters. Whether in the lure of free coupons in the sale of Communist state property, or in the pyramid lure of the quick capital gain, or in the broken "vision of 'forty acres and a mule' . . . which the [US] nation had all but categorically promised the freedmen," we find a false populism and a redistribution to the elites. That the government collapses with the scheme changes little in how lessons of deceit and redistribution are relearned and hijacked by the Communist-cum-capitalist corporate robber barons. The story in these three scenarios echoes Plato's political and psychological anatomy of a decaying republic. We need not accept aristocratic guardians as Plato's check on the Mutinous Crew; but we must unmask the impostor arguments for justice and the founding myths of corporate republics.[8]

Positioned westward of the old Cold War border, we run into the old line, in place invisibly yet firmly: in spite of AT&T's regionally global promise, "It's All Within Your Reach," flights to the 'East' are more costly, rental cars are not allowed across, and if driven anyway, they are likely to be stolen by the Russian car mafias; and populations in the East are both hungry for Western 'goods' and culturally offstandish to all foreigners. Multinationally flexible corporations adapt to both trends in order to reap profits: they hire local poets, philosophers, and computer designers to help them create regionally appealing ad campaigns. And then they link products and services to the double desire of cultural recognition and new 'goods.'

As an example, take the German Volkswagen's recent expansion to the East: VW appropriates more than 50 percent of the Czech Škoda car in exchange for the promise to renovate the production and employ Czech labor. VW carries the Škoda logo and name, yet the logo and name are owned (sold to) VW. When economic difficulties emerge, promises are broken, and labor strikes are imminent; VW threatens to move production to Mexico. Škoda with its Czech logo and ironical name, Favorit, now in foreign hands, can be expropriated multiculturally (recognition can withdraw and move across the Continent) and economically (redistribution means the beginning of corporate welfare as we have always known it). In a heightened comedy of all errors, the Levis corporation suggests with its TV ad that one can exchange Škoda for a pair of sexy jeans, while another car company promises *Infinity* (infinite meaning or desire) on Prague streets. What Hitler did not achieve in direct colonization (he did admire industrialists, like Porsche, and VW as the true *volkish*–people's car), the multicultural corporate handlers, multinational car producers, and circulating currency can achieve in the shadow of pan-European multicultural and economic integration.[9]

Meet the wild East with its joint ventures between corporate ex-Communists and western capitalist cowboys. Whatever we thought in 1989, at the end of the day the joint venture is clearly an impostor of democracy. Corporate multiculturalism – such as the impostor racial harmony of the United Colors of Benetton (e.g. in the ad with the White baby suckling milk from a Black woman), or the hollow decks of the home-sweet-home of Disneylandias (check the US fetish paraphernalia in your local amusement park or video arcade) – wages war games with flexible tokens of diversity for intracorporate profit sharing. The communitarians and liberals, along with the postmoderns of either confession, dispute virtues and vices of the western canon. Meanwhile, corporate strategists of symbolic crossdressing and marketing relearn how to join economy and culture (the base and superstructure of orthodox Marxism) to invent the most successful robbery of radical political and economic democracy.

I argue in conclusion for resistance post/modernism and multiculturalism. Marx gleaned a liberation path from insights of the political economists of his times; we would not fare badly by liberating the corporate mythologizing of multicultural recognition and economic redistribution from its impostor imaginary. Ad practices reveal what sells (Dostoyevsky's "Grand Inquisitor" reveals how to manipulate the desire and fear of radically egalitarian freedom); corporations disclose that what our age already rationally knows it needs, what it freely wants, is radical political and economic democracy.[10]

1.3 Imperial multiculturalism

S. Huntington argues that, first, cultural identity-formation, and not political ideologies or economic divisions, has become the defining factor of social dis/integration and conflict in the post-Cold War era; second, traditional aspiration to western cultural universalism must yield to strategic civilizational multicultural coexistence. Huntington, thus, adopts this multicultural narrative in two crucial aspects. He grasps that the politics of identity and difference and the struggles for mutual recognition mark the post/modern spirit of the times. No single agent or story of liberation unifies the playing field in the way that the East/West divide did. And he certifies the consequence of our multipolar world in the actual and the desirable decline of the cultural supremacy of the West. Since clashes likely occur in cultural–religious fault lines between eight core civilizations (this includes satellite states), giving up the messianic need to export cultural westernization offers the best policy advice for how to preserve the Kantian perpetual peace (in the league of civilizations) and the Hegelian mutual recognition (in a global, multicultural not western, world spirit) within the post-Cold War era.[11]

Yet Huntington proscribes multicultural life for domestic law and order even while, as a good Machiavellian auxiliary to the guardians of the US republic, he prescribes multiculturalism as a necessary 'Noble Lie' for foreign policy. There are two necessary 'Noble Lies' he counsels to adopt, and they parallel his seeming grasp of what multicultural revolutions are all about. The first necessary state myth stipulates that because civilizations are homogeneous units that tend to clash with other such units, we would weaken our chances of survival in this strategic theater of the politics of identity-in-difference if we did not enhance a cultural conservation of the West. It is assumed that *we* (who speaks here for whom?) always already know who *we* westerners are in our identities and what *we* should preserve (homogenize against intrusions by multicultural difference) in the Euro-American civilization. The second necessary state myth stipulates that because civilizations are homogeneous units, they not only tend to clash with other such units, but are inherently closed, hardened, stoic systems of identity-formation (whose gender and race formation is here sketched and universalized?) set off in radical difference from other civilizations. Nominally fashioned, no civilization would be capable of entering with others into intrinsically transformative leagues of perpetual peace, not to speak of mutual recognition (CC, pp. 125–30, 290ff., 305–21).

While Huntington rejects Fukuyama's neoliberal happy-end-of-ideology scenario (CC, pp. 31ff.), he presupposes it in other regards by claiming that the future world conflicts will not be economic ones between rich and poor worlds (p. 33). Indeed, given the post-1989 'perpetual peace' on *our* terms, his counsel to the US king offers an ethnocentrically conservative multiculturalism for a new imperial foreign policy. This is obvious when we sift through the sentimental pretend-humility (that Euro-American family values should not be imposed on the world) and reach the strategic salient point: economic self-adulation and the patriotic gore of plain old *pax Americana*.

> The West is and will remain for years to come the most powerful civilization. [p. 29] The futures of the United States and of the West depend upon Americans reaffirming their commitment to Western civilization. Domestically this means rejecting the divisive siren calls of multiculturalism. Internationally it means rejecting the elusive and illusory calls to identify the United States with Asia. [p. 307] If North America and Europe renew their moral life, build on their cultural commonality, and develop close forms of economic and political integration to supplement their security collaboration in NATO, they could generate a third Euroamerican phase [i.e. following the first modern European conquest since 1492 and the second phase in American industrial expansion in this century alone] of Western economic affluence and political influence. [p. 308]

We must not harbor doubts that 'ludic' and corporate dimensions of multiculturalism form the heart of this eclectically postmodern (West is no longer the center of a linear and progressivist paradigm of the end of history) yet symbolically conservative and neoliberally imperial multiculturalism. The most powerful *de facto* multicultural country homogenizes its territory, fashioning a univocal nation-state. (Pat Buchanan calls this "saving the American soul.") The empire crafted through assimilative marginalization of the 'un-American' elements deploys the economic multinationals as its beachheads. The NWO corporations must be flexible enough to provide the strategic defense at home. (IBM or GM are as 'American' as apple pie, but who knows, to mix the metaphor, in which 'sweatshop' the apples are harvested and crust produced?) Yet they must guide an unhindered expansion, exploit uncontrolled labor markets, and circulate profits globally. Greider warns against the manic logic of global capitalism where the overproduction by rich corporations using cheap labor in poor countries can no longer be absorbed by the buying power of rich countries. The warning echoes Derrida's description of a post-1989 melancholic logic of the NWO as well as Soros's warning against the threat to closed societies from "robber capitalism" and the "gangster state" (*CT*). Huntington (*CC*, p. 308) only cites a warning by Malaysia's Prime Minister Mahathir (one almost feels the lusting anticipatory approval): "With their trading clout the EU–NAFTA confederation could dictate terms to the rest of the world."[12]

From the Berlin Olympics of 1936 to the Atlanta Olympics of 1996 is but a half century. The filmic symbolics and the ad campaigns have been perfected since Leni Riefenstahl's *Triumph of the Will* became the lab for creating individual, corporate, and imperial demi-gods. True, Hitler's Olympics celebrated the Aryan race and used the gymnastic–national display to cover up the totalitarian nature of that German state; and none of this is *prima facie* true of the Atlanta event. Yet we would be amiss not to recognize the parallel use of 'cultural studies' and 'populist' rhetoric to market recognition and economic prosperity through an adherence to the dominant economic and political players in the state. The Atlanta games were manifestly multicultural, global, with open borders, equality, liberty, fraternity for all. The message revealed in the media coverage, in the advertising epiphany of Coca-Cola (the key sponsor of these and the next games) and others, targeted existing multicultural worlds to ascertain the symbolic and material hegemony of the host country. The US is and will be number one; other civilizations should buy, emulate, belong, submit, etc. to the US: that was the message in the presentation of the games, in commentaries, and in ads.

I argue in conclusion that by recognizing the many faces of oppression, we may empower broader coalitions and even more intimate solidarities. Coalitions and solidarities must be fashioned across existing or maliciously created homogeneities, disrupt fake multicultural belongings, and transgress symbolically as well as economically fortified, elite protectionist borders.

2 Cartographers

If multicultural reality is not going away, it could be carved into xenophobic and exploited segments. Against perceived multicultural dangers, the cartographers of the NWO invent a doubly inverted world. They pursue greater homogeneity at home by suppressing all internal countercultural and economic dissent and by fostering fragmentation and marginalization of the 'foreign' elements. And they promote the culturally segmented world orders by suppressing all interlocking of global dissent and solidarity, fostering instead fragmentation and marginalization of the 'foreign' elements in international strategic theaters. Broad coalitions or intimate solidarities both within and across civilizations become nil. I now revisit ludic, corporate, and imperial multiculturalism, this time focusing on their doubly inverted worlds.

2.1 Inverted 'Ludic' multiculturalism: backlash misrecognition

An inverted 'ludic' world becomes manifest in an all-out panic fear of any multiculturalism, i.e. in a conservative xenophobia of home cultures against all strangers. This 'ludic' performance may wear various masks. Among the milder are the attempts to defend cultural orthodoxies in both secular and religious forms. Forms are often mixed, as in the US civil religion of the pledge of allegiance, family–patriotic values, singing *America the Beautiful*, and trading in the religiousness inscribed on paper dollar bills. The more sinister inversions emerge in the culture wars. Phobias of symbols can hide an ignorance of the classical controversies about western canons. A maleducated raving xenophobe either does not tell or does not know: such a raging bull can appear on stage as *A Big Fat Idiot*, polluting media with nonsense about 'feminazis' or un-American multicultures, and contributing not an iota to the Socratic care for the soul. Lastly, the most invidious are the skinhead, the neo-Nazi, or FreeMen attacks on racial, gender, and any other 'Other.' The culture wars become party platforms – the right-wing agendas in France, Germany, Russia, or East Europe. Political planks fuel cleansings of bodies symbolized by their queer otherness.[13]

2.2 Inverted corporate multiculturalism: selective redistribution

A one-sided recognition goes in tandem with carving out selective redistribution channels for ascending groups. Balibar notes that racism and ethnocentrism function as symbolic supplements to nation-states. As supplements they entrench cycles of nationalisms within nationalism and allow for an economic exploitation of the newly marginalized.[14] With the inverted multiculturalism of multinationals, the political collapse of nation-state islands, as we know them, seems imminent. Long live corporate nationalism! The economic end of the welfare nation-state is already upon us. Long live corporate welfare for the rich! New rituals are invented in commercial campaigns. We pledge allegiance to this corporation, one country and creed under the god in whom we trust, *e pluribus unum* . . . .

Enter brave new multiculturally inverted corporate worlds: Telecom promises to enhance intimacy with concrete multicultural others; the socially responsible mutual funds entice us to help the poor and the environment by playing their stocks; The United Colors of Benetton usher us to the Promised Land of racial harmony and inclusive society; a local restaurant offers a progressive menu with a Green Party Wrap and a New Party Soup and a Healthy Boost; the health food megastore sells non-traumatized beef from cows who lived in luxuriant peaceful spaces and were sensitively killed; the major furniture producer features the next door gay and lesbian couples celebrating family values in their newly furnished homes; Calvin Klein's Obsession licenses socially prohibitive-charged sexual desires: miscegenation, transgender ecstasy, a boss dominatrix ....

When I lived in state-Communism, I was told that the Promised Land was almost upon us. That is why we did not have commercials. In heaven one has everything according to one's needs, one contributes in light of one's abilities. Competition is not needed in such a Land. Yet the Party slogans structured every visual map and saturated all audible spaces. The new symbolics of 'the heavens almost upon us' relandscaped the state socialist historical geography; it sculpted the future Man and Woman; and it poetized the homo- and hetero-erotics of socially redeemed nature, clean and exercised bodies, the love unto death of the guardian Party, the chosen Nation, or the goddess Revolution ....

Enter brave new multiculturally inverted corporate worlds – doubly inverted. Not much needs to be altered on the facades of the state Party to make over its face into a Corporation. The same old political and secret-agent cadres, their buildings and dirty money, can be laundered with the transition to democracy. A Party boss retools to become a new corporate CEO, a Party retreat house opens freshly as a resort hotel, the Party five-year planning adapts to the equally dogmatic IMF corporately controlled 'free markets,' old mafias transform into legitimately prospering companies or they perfect themselves as new mafias .... To illustrate, Havel warns that *nomenklatura* bosses laugh now at the same workers for whom the promised paradise has been lost, better robbed, twice. Yet he offers his half of the entertainment complex, Lucerna (restituted by the Havel family from the state), to Chemapol, a firm known for its shady ties with former state agents and now new mafias. To his critics, he retorts (ironically? in a strangely realistic–absurd drama of himself?), I act as a "market president."[15]

Marge Piercy fictionalizes the world of the twenty-first century after environmental disasters: the planet is carved into three types of social organization that cut across major civilizational fault lines. First, there are twenty-three heavily defended and environmentally secluded multi-enclaves. These Corporate Fortresses parcel out the continents and other space platforms among themselves, and hire technical specialists as well as day laborers to supplement services by robots. "Multis" enforce a pan-corporate perpetual peace. There are occasional business raids, assassinations, skirmishes, but after the last nuclear conflict, no all-out wars. Second, there exist multiple areas called the Glop, Piercy's invented slang for the megalopolis with the overcrowded, starved, diseased, violent conditions in which the bottom majority live on every continent. And third, there are the free urban–rural towns which have the technical as well as the traditional know-how for defense from the multis and the Glop. These new towns form environmentally and economically self-sustaining communities of free yet socially and multiculturally bonded, highly developed individuals. Piercy's fictional portrait, contrary to S. Huntington's paradigm of the world in a clash of civilizations, comes closer to what is becoming our waking reality.[16]

2.3 Inverted imperial multiculturalism: cannibalizing global diversity

"Simplified paradigms or maps are indispensable for human thought and action," writes S. Huntington (*CC*, p. 30). He approvingly cites Gaddis: "Cartography, like cognition itself, is a necessary simplification that allows us to see where we are, and where we may be going." Huntington's political advisory – monocultures at home and strategic multiculturalism for export (p. 307) – designs a "geopolitical cartography" to replace the landscapes of the Cold War era.[17]

Huntington perceives the US multicultural movement as a domestic threat to the ability of the Euro-American civilization to compete, withstand, and in the end prevail in the post-1990 world with eight other major civilizations (*CC*, map 1.3 and pp. 305–8, 318). "The idea of a multicultural country" (p. 290) is an *anathema* to him, yet the urge to cannibalize global diversity remains a tactical plan. The sin of "the American multiculturalists" is that "they wish to create a country of many civilizations, which is to say a country not belonging to any civilization and lacking a cultural core." This is the original sin of a cosmopolitan consciousness: "A multicivilizational United States will not be the United States; it will be the United Nations" (p. 306).

The advisory for US self-restraint appears to be enlighteningly anti-ethnocentric (Huntington rejects "Western belief in the universality of Western culture" as "false; ... immoral; ... [and] dangerous," p. 310). Yet in reality he weds US protectionism and self-interest (don't pour water on what does not burn you, such as "the affairs of other civilizations") with calculated economic aggression (assert "western technological and military superiority over other civilizations," p. 312). It becomes clear soon enough that not the love of one's fatherland and culture, not an admiration of the global multicultural diversity, but rather the yearning for new expansion drives the geopolitical cartography of imperial multi-culturalists. They hope to "generate a third Euroamerican phase of Western economic affluence and political influence" (p. 308) as the divining sign of "the uniqueness of Western culture" (p. 318).

The global neoliberal mania against which Greider warns is already harvesting the cannibalized bodies of global multicultural diversity for the next Euro-American century. The imperial multiculturalists advance their cartographies of the NWO ahead of the 'free' trade agreements such as NAFTA and GATT. Invoking the politics of recognition does not make much dent against this advance. Politically liberal proceduralism does not pose any threat to imperially charged monocultural platforms at home; western political liberalism allows NAFTA's economic neoliberalism to destroy, e.g. the Mayan economy of Chiapas. In homogenizing diversity at home and marketing it for profit globally, naively liberal politics and a conservatively neoliberal economy jointly facilitate eco-destructive border-crossings: new imperial maps are drawn and exploitative con-quests initiated under the name of liberal democracy and multicultural globalism. To challenge this western home rule with its formal political liberalism, monocultural conservatism, and imperial multiculturalism, as self-destructive of domestic and civilizational peace, could be liberat-ing.[18]

3　A New Multicultural Enlightenment

Conservative assumptions of the cultural monogenealogy of civilizations are just as counterintuitive as liberal assumptions of culture-escaping universalism.[19]

First, there are multiple traditions, multiplicities within traditions, and multiple modernities within those traditions to boot. Du Bois's analysis of 'double consciousness' in African-American cultures reveals that yearn-ings for a reunified Euro-American culture are at best driven by an insupportable myth about 'Europe' and at worst constitutive of the prevailing anti-Black racism inscribed into monocultural (mostly White, patriarchal) desire. West and Outlaw argue that African modernity com-plements the European and the new world modernity yet cannot be identified with it. One could conjecture about influences of Native American conceptions of tribal federations on the French Enlightenment and the Founding Fathers of the US. Critical traditionalists such as Nandy, Kothari, and Gandhi persuasively show that various traditions can undergo their modernizing–critical phases, learn from other traditions they meet, yet do so without needing to become absorbed, e.g. westernized. The Occidental enlightenment cannot be equated with every modernity or critical traditionality as such, since its universalism itself has been culturally laden, often in unenlightening ways.[20]

Second, critical multiculturalists can meet critical traditionalists half way: the latter thinkers reject westernization but accept elements of western modernization along with indigenous sober evaluations of inherited traditions (e.g. neither Gandhi in India's struggle against the British, nor Subcommander Marcos in the Mayan struggle in Chiapas against *la conquista*, are uncritical traditionalists or anti-modernists in their defense of local cultures). The former, then, develop a critical relation to western culture, or the idea of 'Europe,' without abstracting from it: this involves narrating multiple secular and religious traditions coexisting from time immemorial within the West (after all, Auschwitz, Gordoba and Granada, Haiti and Cuba, Istanbul and Jerusalem, Prague and Sarajevo, Wounded Knee ... are part of the West). Further, westerners must learn to root cultural critique within their own multiple traditions. Postmodern cultural eclecticism helps to shed abstract humanism, especially where the human mask harbors racism and patriarchy within the cherished liberal ideals of autonomy and the communitarian ones of community. Finally, one cannot become enlightened either alone (the Cartesian *cogito* as well as the Kantian 'I think' cannot suffice) or through an autoerotic play with textuality (although a liber/al/tarian individualist, undecidable ludic multiculturalist, or conservative monoculturalist ... could still get satisfied alone). This realization announces a *new multicultural enlightenment*. Overcoming abstract liberal, monogenealogically communitarian, and ludic multiculturalist phases, resistance post/modern multiculturalists join liberation struggles of concrete peoples.[21]

Thus, third, the body and cultural performatives that matter – to racial, gender, and socioeconomic justice – must empower agencies of the ongoing coalitions and communities in resistance. Marx learned from international capital markets because he was no ludic anti-capitalist. Instead, he capitalized on capitalism by seeking an international *labor-market* resistance to capital's anti-humanism. We must learn from corporations and multinationals today: one cannot be an anti-multiculturalist in the worlds of Benetton, Coca-Cola, Boeing,

Internet-providers, or S. Huntington. The academic culture wars are lagging behind the corporate war games where the new magic with multicultural signs is performed for real body and blood money. Resistance post/modern critical social theorists and multiculturalists need to address the corporate and imperial multinationals who harbor no sentimental needs 'to save the American soul.' The remaining grand religious narrative of the NWO has gone manically ahead to rethink the canon and redraw the maps in the last desperate dash for profit.[22]

The ubiquity of monetary and labor capital was for Marx a *step forward* from feudal relations: in promising universal democracy and egalitarian economic chances, capital's shapeshifting forms of life were to become its gravediggers. If the corporate promise of a multicultural and just social form of life masks an imposture, Marx's insight retains its untimely timeliness, no matter what political liberals and market neoliberals think of Marxism after 1989. In my wager, the viability of the multinationals, not of Marx, is what is in question: if the corporate multicultural promise, regionally and globally, is not an imposture, but rather an inconsistency with corporate practices, then multinationals already prepare the way for radical multicultural, political, and economic democracy. One could fare worse than with this wager.

Instead of biting my tongue, I submit that corporate, globally local multiculturalism is a *step forward* from nationalist monocultures and protectionist economic discontents. This seems to be so even though nation-states alone can still nowadays check global corporate raids. Multinational corporations pretend to be the new regionally global guardians of multicultural justice. In that pretense the multiculturally global conquests can become their own gravediggers. Indeed, advertised corporate lifeworlds fake the politically just and democratic forms of life. Yet we must still invent a *new multicultural enlightenment*. By introducing such inventions into existence (Fanon *BSWM*, p. 229, names this an existential–social 'leap'), we inhabit in resistance to the corporate impostor-imaginary, and nurture among ourselves hope for an existentially rich individuality, multiple coalitions, and even more intimate yet open, variegated, and unique communities.

Notes

1   Plato, *Republic*, central bks. 4–6. Cf. Plato's dialectic of 'Noble Lie' (myth) and philosophical rule (enlightenment) with the main thesis of Max Horkheimer and Theodor W. Adorno, *Dialectic of Enlightenment* (1944), trans. John Cumming (New York: Continuum, 1987), viz. every myth is already enlight-

enment, enlightenment inevitably falls back into myth (where 'enlightenment' refers both to the birth of conceptual thought and culture as such and to the Enlightenment).

2 Teresa L. Ebert, "Political Semiosis in/of American Cultural Studies" (pp. 113–35), *American Journal of Semiotics* 8, no. 1/2 (1991), p. 115; and *Ludic Feminism and After: Postmodernism, Desire, and Labor in Late Capitalism* (Ann Arbor: University of Michigan Press, 1996), chs 1 and 3. Cf. Henry A. Giroux and Peter McLaren (eds), *Between Borders: Pedagogy and the Politics of Cultural Studies* (London, New York: Routledge, 1994), pp. 198ff; Mas'ud Zavarzadeh and Donald Morton, *Theory as Resistance: Politics and Culture after (Post) Structuralism* (London, New York: Guilford Press, 1994).

3 *Webster's New Collegiate Dictionary* (Springfield, Mass.: Merriam, 1977), p. 683.

4 Jean-Paul Sartre, *Anti-Semite and Jew* (1946), trans. George J. Becker, preface by Michael Walzer (1995, pp. v–xxvi) (New York: Schocken Books, 1948, 1976). Herbert Marcuse, "Repressive Tolerance," in Herbert Marcuse, Robert Paul Wolff and Barrington Moore, Jr, *A Critique of Pure Tolerance* (Boston: Beacon Press, 1965), pp. 81–117; with a new Postscript by Marcuse (1968), pp. 117–23; *One-Dimensional Man: Studies in the Ideology of Advanced Industrial Society*, with a new introduction by Douglas Kellner (Boston: Beacon Press, 1964, 1991).

5 Fredric Jameson, *Postmodernism, or The Cultural Logic of Late Capitalism* (Durham: Duke University Press, 1991).

6 Henry A. Giroux, *Disturbing Pleasures: Learning Popular Culture* (London, New York: Routledge, 1994): on Benetton and Disney, see chs 1 and 2. Exceptions to my claim are, among critical social theorists, Nancy Fraser, *Justice Interruptus: Critical Reflections On the "Postsocialist" Condition* (New York, London: Routledge, 1997); among poststructuralists, Jacques Derrida's *Specters of Marx: The State of Debt, the Work of Mourning, and the New International*, trans. Peggy Kamuf (New York, London: Routledge, 1994) – hereafter cited as *SM* – and in critical post/modern social theory, Iris Marion Young, *Justice and the Politics of Difference* (Princeton: Princeton University Press, 1990) – hereafter cited as JPD; "Unruly Categories: A Critique of Nancy Fraser's Dual Systems Theory," ch. 2, this volume. In spite of the differences among the above thinkers, each of them theorizes the logic of cultural recognition along with the logic of flexible accumulation in late neoliberalism.

7 Francis Fukuyama, *The End of History and the Last Man* (New York: Free Press, 1992); Stephen Cohen, "It's Not a Transition in Russia – It's a Full-blown Disaster," *Pittsburgh Post-Gazette*, December 22, 1996, E, pp. 1, 4; Stephen Resnick and Richard Wolff, "Between State and Private Capitalism: What Was Soviet 'Socialism'?" *Rethinking Marxism* 7, No. 1 (spring 1994), pp. 9–30. Cf. George Soros, "The Capitalist Threat," *The Atlantic Monthly* 279, No. 2 (February 1997), pp. 45–58. Hereafter cited as CT.

8 See Burghardt W. E. Du Bois, *The Souls of Black Folk*, a new Introduction by

Randall Kenan (New York: Penguin Books, 1982, 1995), pp. 74ff. and 70, two citations above (hereafter cited as *SBF*). Plato, *Republic*, bks 8–9, describes the political and psychological pathology of a decaying ideal. The Mutinous Crew which throws the good Captain overboard exemplifies the plight of Socrates in the Athenian democracy: he is sentenced to death for rocking the economic boat (he was not a market-savvy Sophist) and certain cultural and state-religious canons.

9   See the essay by Mary Williams Walsh, "VW Falls Into a Publicity Pothole," *Los Angeles Times*, December 1, 1996, A, pp. 1, 16, and the published archival photo of Hitler admiring the new VW model.

10 See Fyodor Dostoyevsky, *Notes from the Underground and the Grand Inquisitor*, trans. Ralph E. Matlaw (New York: E. P. Dutton, 1960), pp. 119–41. Karl Marx and Friedrich Engels, *The Communist Manifesto* (1848), trans. Samuel Moore (New York: Washington Square Press, 1964).

11 Samuel P. Huntington, *The Clash of Civilizations and the Remaking of World Order* (New York: Simon and Schuster, 1996), pp. 19–39 (hereafter, cited as *CC*). *Hegel's Philosophy of Right*, trans. T. M. Knox (London: Oxford University Press, 1967); Immanuel Kant, "Perpetual Peace," *On History*, trans. Lewis White Beck, Robert E. Anchor and Emil L. Fackenheim (Indianapolis: Bobbs-Merrill, 1963).

12 See William Greider, *One World, Ready or Not: The Manic Logic of Global Capitalism* (New York: Simon and Schuster, 1997) (hereafter cited as *OW*). Mohammad Mahathir, *International Herald Tribune*, May 23, 1995, p. 13.

13 See Al Franken, *Rush Limbaugh Is a Big Fat Idiot* (New York: Delacorte, 1996). Rush Limbaugh, *The Way Things Ought to Be* (New York: Pocket Star Books, 1992), pp. 194–203, 205–14, 228, 278. Note western canonical debates: on the Nicean creed, Aquinas's use of Aristotle, the Reformation from Jan Hus to Martin Luther, the Jesuit inculturation of western values in China, Japan, and the Americas.

14 Etienne Balibar, *Masses, Classes, Ideas: Studies On Politics and Philosophy Before and After Marx*, trans. James Swenson (New York, London: Routledge, 1994); and Balibar and Immanuel Wallerstein, *Race, Nation, Class: Ambiguous Identities*, trans. Chris Turner (New York, London: Verso, 1991).

15 Václav Havel, *Letní přemítání* [Summer Meditations] (Prague: Odeon, 1991); on his warning, see pp. 44–95, on the Lucerna affair, see Czech daily press after February 1997. Cf. Derrida, *SM*, pp. 81–4; and Soros, *CT*.

16 Marge Piercy, *He, She and It* (New York: Fawcett Crest, 1991). I owe to Patricia Huntington my discovery of this utopian text.

17 S. Huntington, *CC*, p. 30, cites John Lewis Gaddis, "Towards the Post-Cold War World," *Foreign Affairs*, 70 (spring 1991), p. 101.

18 See Charles Taylor, "The Liberal–Communitarian Debate," in Nancy Rosenblum (ed.), *Liberalism and the Moral Life* (Cambridge, Mass.: Harvard University Press, 1989); and Taylor et al., *Multiculturalism: Examining The Politics of Recognition*, ed. Amy Gutmann (Princeton: Princeton University

Press, 1994, expanded 2nd ed). Jürgen Habermas, "Struggles for Recognition in the Democratic Constitutional State," trans. Shierry Weber Nicholsen, in Taylor et al., *Multiculturalism*, pp. 107–48. John Rawls, *A Theory of Justice* (Cambridge, Mass.: Harvard University Press, 1971) and *Political Liberalism* (New York: Columbia University Press, 1993).

19   Cf. Jacques Derrida, *The Other Heading: Reflections on Today's Europe*, trans. Pascale-Anne Brault and Michael B. Naas, intro. M. B. Nass (Bloomington: Indiana University Press, 1992) and Martin J. Beck Matuštík, *Specters of Liberation: Great Refusals in the New World Order* (Albany: SUNY, 1998), hereafter cited as *SL*.

20   Du Bois, *SBF*, pp. 45, 51; and "The Conservation of Races," in Howard Brotz (ed.), *African–American Social and Political Thought, 1850–1920* (New Brunswick, NJ: Transaction Publishers, 1992), pp. 483–92. M. K. Gandhi, *Non-Violent Resistance (Satyagraha)* (New York: Schocken Books, 1961). Ashis Nandy, "Cultural Frames for Social Transformation: A Credo," *Alternatives* 12, No. 1 (January 1987), pp. 113–23. Rajni Kothari, *Growing Amnesia: An Essay on Poverty and the Human Consciousness* (Delhi: Viking, 1993); *Transformation and Survival: In Search of a Humane World Order* (Delhi: Ajanta, 1988). Lucius Outlaw, Jr, *On Race and Philosophy* (London, New York: Routledge, 1996). Cornel West, *Keeping Faith: Philosophy and Race in America* (New York, London: Routledge, 1993).

21   I find support in Frantz Fanon, *Black Skin, White Masks* (New York: Grove Press, 1967) – hereafter cited as *BSWM*; and *The Wretched of the Earth*, trans. Constance Farrington (New York: Grove Press, 1963).

22   Judith Butler's *Bodies that Matter: On the Discursive Limits of "Sex"* (New York, London: Routledge, 1993) and *Excitable Speech: A Politics of the Performative* (New York, London: Routledge, 1997), two studies of the body-and-language performatives, will matter insofar as they are joined with the multiple faces of oppression. Cf. Young, JPD; "Asymmetrical Reciprocity: On Moral Respect, Wonder, and Enlarged Thought," *Constellations: An International Journal of Critical and Democratic Theory* 3, No. 3 (1997), pp. 340–63. Patricia J. Huntington elaborates the notion of asymmetrical reciprocity in *Ecstatic Subjects, Utopia, and Recognition: Kristeva, Heidegger, Irigaray* (Albany: SUNY, 1998). Gyan Prakash, "Postcolonial Criticism and Indian Historiography," *Social Text* 31–2 (1992), pp. 8–19. "Out of the Shadows: The Communities of Population in Resistance in Guatemala, A Struggle for Survival" (Washington: Epica/CHRLA Report, 1993); and Matuštík, *SL*, chs. 5, 6, 8, and 9.

Part II

Post-Marxism and Issues of Class

6

Multiculturalism: Consumerist or Transformational?

Bill Martin

The reflections presented here are not yet integrated into any kind of "system." In fact, I'm not sure that we are ready for that yet, and, in any case, the whole issue of multiculturalism raises the question of difference in a way that would seem to run against inherited forms of philosophical or social theoretical system building. The discussion that follows, then, consists in three parts that are only loosely related. In the opening part, I take up the issue of a possible Marxist perspective on multiculturalism, pointing especially to some perhaps unexpected sources. In the middle part I raise the issue of class and some worries about what I call "consumerist" multiculturalism. Finally, in a more personal vein, I stitch on to this already crazy quilt a few stories that I hope will be illustrative.

1 Beyond Diamat

I would like to open this discussion with a few remarks concerning the place that I have been assigned in this anthology. Professor Cynthia Willett, valued friend and colleague, and editor of this anthology, asked me to speak to the question of multiculturalism from a Marxist point of view. She even used the term, "dialectical materialism," which is not something one hears very often these days. Professor Willett did not just pull these things out of the air, of course. I am indeed a Marxist, of some sort – a sort that other Marxists, of what I would call a more "orthodox" cast, are often not comfortable with. In general, I subscribe to a "materialist" understanding of history and society, but a good deal of my work in the ontological aspects of Marxism has been concerned with overcoming reductivist and monological formulations of materialism.[1] While I am more comfortable with the term "historical materialism," I also accept that a dialectical or conflictual model is a good one for understanding *some* natural and *some* social phenomena. (Somewhere in the vicinities of quantum singularities and love, desire, and sexual attraction this model tends to run into problems.) *However....*

However: there are so many provisos that I would add to these statements. The collective effect of the provisos is that it is doubtful that my position could be called one of "dialectical materialism" in the sense in which this term has been used in the past century or so, and even my approach to Marxism is quite different to what people who actually know something about this subject would expect.

I would not go on at any length about my own approach to philosophical and social questions except for the fact that this approach has been formed, in large part, through the encounter with issues that fit very much under the heading of multiculturalism – such that what follows is just as much a multicultural reading of Marxism as it is a Marxist reading of multiculturalism.

"Dialectical materialism" is a term that came to the fore during the Stalin period, when this philosophy or "methodology" was put forward in a formulaic way as "diamat."[2] Unlike many on the academic Left, I do not think this period is so easily gotten around, and I think we ignore Stalin and the Stalin period at great cost. Indeed, I don't think we've really taken stock of the many lessons that this period might teach us.

Among the many difficulties of "diamat" is that it focused on questions of ontology and methodology, as though, if we could only get the ontology right, we could go on to have a "science" of society, history, and the natural world that would overcome all mysteries.[3] Of course, there are important historical factors involved in the congealing of Marxism into an ontology, factors not addressed by simply chanting some mantra about "Stalinism." At least in terms of the basic orientation, however, the key can be found in the references Marx makes, in the "Theses on Feuerbach" and thereafter (*The German Ideology* is an especially good source) on "sensuous human practice." In other words, Marx's materialism has first of all to do with the idea that the key to understanding human society, including human ways of knowing, is to look first at practices and the social frameworks (themselves the creation of practices) in which practices occur.

Perhaps it is the inattention to this question that has allowed Foucauldian discourse to somewhat monopolize the idea of practices in recent years. However, it is also the case that, whereas Foucault and some other contemporary thinkers such as Deleuze, Guattari, de Certeau, etc. (Canguilhem and Bachelard being the main precursors), tend to speak of *practices*, in the plural, the more monological trends in Marxism have labored under the assumption that all practices have an essential unity – as aspects of the grand march of the modes of production – and *telos*: all practices aim toward an eventual, single, unified form of practice.

One sees here at least two things. One is the way that Marxism is clearly the inheritor of German idealism. The idea that all practices aim toward a single practice recapitulates Kant's argument that all thought intends a system. The other is that the mainstream of Marxist thought, at least the part of it that has not become mere reformist social democracy and "Leftism" (that is, oriented toward the "Left" end of the existing political spectrum), has understood communism as, fundamentally, a mode of production.

These questions will be pursued further in a moment. However, I would like to interject here that I think it would be a very bad idea to let go of either Kant's insight regarding thought and totality (which really goes back to Aristotle's thinking on categories) or the idea of a "mode of production" – even if we find ourselves supplementing and transforming these ideas in various ways.

Still, the idea of a diversity of practices that not only cannot, but, from an ethical–political perspective, *should not* be too quickly brought into even a theoretical (much less practical) unity – this idea has eluded modern Western philosophy and Marxism thus far. One worry is that, if we give up on the project of bringing things into a theoretical unity, we will simply give reign to theoretical "eclecticism." And, as anyone who has been around orthodox Marxist discourse knows, eclecticism is petty-bourgeois. Continuing this line of reasoning, we find that "*multi*culturalism" is itself petty-bourgeois eclecticism; therefore, it is no surprise that we should find this ideology being propagated in the liberal academy.

There are unities and there are unities. There are also instances where there is more than a little truth to the more orthodox reading of multiculturalism, even if the alternative is not, at least in my view, monologism.

One of the aspects of "diamat" that is most problematic from the standpoint of thinking diverse practices and cultures is that this interpretation of materialism presumes that the study of society can be understood, ultimately, as a branch of the natural sciences. This is the old positivist dream (in my view, a nightmare) that holds with a concentric circles model, wherein the broadest category is physics,[4] and human psychology is a subset of this category. Something like this schema underlies all theories, even those purportedly resistant to positivism, that aim toward a unified theory of human practice.[5]

Working through at least some themes in Marxism, Jean-Paul Sartre proposed a quite different model, whereby the dialectic itself is an effect of the interaction of different human consciousnesses (especially in their resistance to what he called the practico-inert, the weight of practice congealed in things and institutions – what Marx called "dead labor").[6] The interaction gives rise to *praxis*, which, for Sartre, in no sense has to be singular. (Indeed, only the "praxis" of the God of classical Christian theology could be singular; but then, this God would have no need of praxis.) Meanwhile, Donald Davidson has given us a model of the mind that is at one and the same time "material," and yet not reducible to an understanding in terms of strict causal laws (this is Davidson's argument for "anomalous monism"). As he makes clear in "Mental Events," Davidson's arguments also reflect a Kantian inspiration, though taken in a different direction.[7] We might take a few pages from both Davidson and Sartre, therefore, and consider the possibility of an "anomalous materialism." (One would hope that the first term in this formulation would militate against the possibility of a dogmatic settling into "anomat.")

For the Soviet Union in the time of Lenin, and especially that of Stalin, multiculturalism was no idle academic question. Indeed, here we find a fairly elongated historical experience that we would do well to learn from. Readers may have forgotten, or not have known, that Stalin in fact had a long engagement with "multicultural" issues, both as a theorist and a primary shaper of policy (to say the least). Stalin's theoretical work on these issues spans at least the period from just before the First World War, when he wrote a pamphlet on the "nationalities question" (1913; scholars generally accept that the pamphlet reflected Lenin's views on the question), to some writing he did in the last year or so of his life, published under the title, "Marxism and Problems of Linguistics" (1954).[8] Obviously, the full dimensions of this experience cannot be addressed in an essay, but an important step forward could be made if we could agree to set aside the usual smirks and clichés and attempt to grapple with the issues presented by this theoretical and policy work.

We might remember, too, that many, perhaps even most, policy decisions and initiatives in the USSR during the Stalin period were carried out in a "crisis mode." Given the conservatism of much of Stalin's thinking, we might even find certain parallels with what conservatives in the United States see as a "crisis" caused by multiculturalism.

The model that Stalin worked with, though much less nuanced and subtle than Marx's, reflected the monologism that has continually come to the fore in Marxism. Ultimately, in Stalin's view, different nationalities will be assimilated to a single social formation, under the leadership of the proletariat. Broadly speaking, this social formation will have its foundation in the culture of Europe.

Perhaps the cultural policy for Soviet composers demonstrates this point as well as anything. Composers such as Shostakovich and Prokofiev were encouraged to create works in European classical forms (orchestral, chamber, etc.) that integrated folk music themes from the diverse nationalities of the Soviet Union. Ultimately, there was to be a blending into a common music, a synthesis if you will.

Now, despite the ways that composers such as those mentioned (they were the most famous, but also arguably the best) may have balked at the pressure of "Zhdanovism" (named for the Commisar of Culture in the 1930s), sometimes out of artistic or political integrity and sometimes out of the perhaps (here it comes again) petty-bourgeois idea that in no way should anyone tell artists what to do, the model did in fact yield some very good and important music.

Obviously the model was not an isolated phenomenon; "folk" themes had been incorporated into European "art" music since the time of Bach and before. In the later nineteenth century and the first part of the twentieth century, there was a general movement among composers from those European countries not included among the "great powers" to incorporate folk material. This "nationalist movement" included composers such as Dvorak, Smetana, Sibelius, Grieg, and perhaps most significantly, Bartok. Of course, any or all of these are candidates for being considered "great" and canonical composers of the European classical music tradition, as are, of course, Shostakovich and Prokofiev. In the language of that tradition, one would say that their art "transcends" what they were doing with material that was merely "local" (even if the "locality" is Finland, Hungary, Armenia, etc.). "Transcends" locality toward what? Toward "humanity," of course, but it turns out that the notion of humanity here is quite obviously and undeniably constructed on a European model.

Stalin tended to approach such questions in a geographically straitjacketed way: the buildup to universal humanity will occur as an add-on and assimilation to the European model and, in fact, to the Russian or Soviet model.[9] But again, setting sneers aside, it is not hard to see where Stalin got this model and why he thought it was a good one. For one thing, it was a model no different from that held to by other European philosophers, socialists, or political theorists from long before the time when Marx, much less Stalin, came on the scene. For sure, this model tended to be based on a Europe with Prussia or the Austro-Hungarian empire or France or England ("Rule Brittania!") at the core of both its "spirit" and its actual political, economic, and military power – *not* Russia. But, for another thing, Russia had proven its right, in Stalin's view, to carry forward the essence of Europe, the essence of humanity, and the essence of the proletariat, by having defeated the sham, rotted, and historically retrograde pretender to that essence, namely Nazi Germany, in the Great Patriotic War. Indeed, Stalin even claimed that the Western European ruling classes had thrown down the banners of democracy and humanism (even in their bourgeois forms), and that it was up to the international working class, with the Soviet Union and the Russian people in its lead, to pick up these banners.[10]

In light of (1) the sacrifice of the Soviet Union and Russian people in fighting the Nazi *Wehrmacht*, (2) the clearly rotten state that one of the great cultures of Europe–Germany – had descended to, and (3) the fact that the other "great powers" (France, Germany, and the United States) offered only token resistance to, at best, and sometimes outright collusion with, the spread of fascism and Nazism in Europe, who was to say that Stalin was wrong? And, after all, the Soviet Union was one-sixth of the Earth's land mass, a rather considerable piece of real estate. Wouldn't it have made perfect sense that the path forward was to geographically add on to this territory? Wouldn't it have made sense that the first area that needed to be added on to the land of universal humanity would be Central and Western Europe, where there was still the possibility of building on and assimilating the productive capacities and relations of advanced capitalism?[11]

It has become all too easy to dismiss this "perfect sense" as so much "Stalinism" or "totalitarianism."[12] After the war, however, this logic garnered tremendous prestige and sympathy, which led to the Marshall Plan, the full-tilt effort to develop the hydrogen bomb, and a rhetoric of notions such as "democracy" and "human rights" that, in countries such as Britain had never counted for very much and in the United States was increasingly integrated into the spectacles of the culture industry and consumerism ("It's not just your car, it's your freedom").[13]

Indeed, it was on the basis of this logic, or what might even be called the "sensus communis" of Soviet socialism, that Stalin was skeptical of models of revolutionary praxis that seemed to take a different approach to social transformation.[14]

In particular, Stalin was skeptical of Mao's leadership of the Chinese

communist movement, and even referred to Mao as a "margarine socialist." Mao, in turn, attempting to lead China beyond the orbit of the
capitalist powers that saw the land and people of China as nothing more
than a mere resource to be brutally exploited (the way it is again now,
with the restoration of the old order there under Deng Xiaoping and his
successors), sought an alternative to the "Soviet model" that had been
shaped under Stalin's leadership. But Mao's alternative, which included
rethinking questions of dialectics in a way that has some aspects in
common with recent philosophies of difference (by 1968, all of this for a
time became part of a common landscape of practice and theory, something we tend to forget nowadays), was generated in part by working
through the framework that Stalin had set out, and not in a sterile
academic vacuum.[15]

Leading a revolution in a country (or, in reality, a territory that was
barely unified and could not really be called a "country" in the European
sense) that was even much further removed from European civilization
and economic forms than was Russia in 1917, Mao forged another sense
of "communism," a sense in which the essence of communism is not its
economic form. For this, of course, more orthodox and Eurocentric
Marxists have called Mao an "idealist" and a "utopian."[16] And, it turns
out, one can still get away with a pretty straightforward Eurocentrism (at
least of a kind that remains unproblematized even in multiculturalist
critiques of Eurocentrism) with regard to this Maoist theory and practice.[17]

Of course, we see in science fiction that there can be many different
utopias – some those of multiculturalism, some just the opposite.

Well, there are obviously enormous difficulties in all of this that need to
be worked out. I avoided some of the more "forceful" aspects of Stalin's
leadership, not because I think we can forget about them – indeed, at the
heart of the multicultural issue is the question of what will allow *different*
possibilities for being human and different human possibilities to flourish
– but rather because the perpetual and monotonous bleat regarding the
"horrors" and "failures" of communism, both real and imagined, takes us
nowhere in terms of relating this historical experience to the present
possibilities for the encouragement of human flourishing. I hope that the
narrative of Marxist developments I have presented thus far shows that,
on the contrary, there is somewhere to go with this experience, something
to build on.

Let us now turn to the discussion around multiculturalism "proper";
some of the themes presented in this section will resurface in what
follows.

2 More than the Multicultural Career

This part of the discussion is based on a talk that I was asked to give to an undergraduate philosophy club at Loyola University of Chicago. Indeed, besides having friendly contacts with the philosophy department at Loyola, one reason I was invited to speak was that the members of the club were under the impression that I am "an expert on race." Beyond the fact that I was quite uncomfortable with this designation and felt that many others could better speak from this perspective (of course, as any social theorist ought to, I have thought a great deal about questions of race, ethnicity, nationality, color, etc., but I feel sure that I have not made any important contributions in this area), I was also interested in addressing an issue that I felt had been left out of many discussions of multiculturalism, namely that of class. In addition to the title of this essay, therefore, my talk included the subtitle, "Why class matters to discussions of race, gender, and sexuality." Taken as a whole, this rather cumbersome and infelicitous title is indicative of the very large range of issues that have to be gathered together in order to adequately address the question of multiculturalism. Indeed, most discussions of multiculturalism, including some that I have previously contributed to, have yet to really frame "the" question. Of course, there isn't simply one question, and, in fact, the challenge of multiculturalism is to explode all models that reduce the diverse forms of human existence to a unitary scheme. And yet, we need a framework and, I am convinced, however we proceed there will be some sort of framework at work, at least in the background of our discussions. I propose to move the framework to the foreground and to fill it out somewhat.

If multiculturalism, as a social and political agenda, is to be more than a banner under which diverse groups pursue their piece of the pie (a banner which is all too quickly assimilated to what I will call "consumerist" multiculturalism), then it must indeed be a matter of a "gathering," one that aims to, through the enactment of a radical diversity, bring together a radical confluence of possibilities for all humankind.[18] I think about multiculturalism, therefore, in terms of a rethinking of the possibilities of *communism*, of a global community of mutual flourishing. The question I want to pose for this rethinking is whether it is possible to imagine this community as made up of many, diverse cultures. This probably gets much too far ahead of the game, however, in a way that may be merely utopian; at the same time that we need to imagine a world in which the diverse possibilities of human being are given full play, we also need to work, in the here and now, for ways in which these possibilities may lay the groundwork for a future community.

Most likely, the terms that I have been speaking in thus far will seem unlike what is usual heard in discussions of multiculturalism. At least this is my hope, to shift the terms of discussion somewhat, even while recognizing the valid and significant contributions that have been made to the discussion by others. If our "theory" of multiculturalism is going to be oriented toward the creation of a future community, then both the theory and the community will necessarily be radically underdetermined, for we find ourselves working in the midst of a society that is, if anything, an anti-community. That is, we need to talk about possibilities that cannot be fully articulated in our present context.

By some of its detractors, as well as some of its enthusiasts, multiculturalism has been associated with some rather experimental trends in philosophy, for example with the work of Jacques Derrida. This is appropriate, for, in both cases, it is a matter of what Derrida calls an "experiment and experience of the impossible," an opening to the other, the other who does not exist and whose voice cannot be heard in the terms of the dominant culture.[19] The existing world is so at odds with this experiment that it will necessarily appear that someone who speaks of it does not know what she or he is talking about. Thus, the detractors of multiculturalism, and, it should be said, of the philosophy of Derrida, accuse the proponents of these trends of fuzzy, imprecise, and obfuscatory thinking. To be sure, each trend does have its share of proponents who, for whatever reason, seem overly and unjustifiably obscure. However, in the name of "precision," "rigor," "standards," "merit," many human possibilities are closed off, marginalized, violently crushed, for the sake of a kind of Eurocentric agenda that is insecure but well-armed.

At least in the academy, though, the silencing of other voices takes place through a simple gesture: the poker face, the throwing up of hands, saying "huh?" or "I just don't get it." This is what Roland Barthes called "blind and dumb criticism": "one believes oneself to have such sureness of intelligence that acknowledging an inability to understand calls in question the clarity of the author [or speaker] and not that of one's own mind."[20] One says, "I just don't get it," as though one has said something profound. On the question of listening to other voices, the blind and dumb critic "just doesn't know what you are talking about," and therefore there is no point to further discussion. But, of course, only in a situation of unequal power and access could one side of the failed dialogue get away with being so dismissive.

In the kind of academic discourse where such dismissiveness is often found, we might venture that the proponents of listening to other voices are not yet in a position of absolute enmity to those doing the dismissing.[21] The hope is that further attempts at discussion will bring some understanding. A comparison that I find useful here is with the relations that one has with one's family (the analogy is based more on the perspective of young people). There are some people who look forward to "going home for the holidays" (or some other significant family occasion), and others who dread it. The experience of family is so different for each group that the one really does not know what the other is talking about. The real tragedy occurs when neither group tries any longer to understand what the other is feeling. Something like the same tragic logic is at work when the person who is circling the wagons around Western civilization says that he or she does not know what the proponent of listening to other voices is talking about. If we are indeed about striving for a level of mutual human flourishing that has never yet existed, and that is qualitatively remote from our experience of society today (even if this community is significantly foreshadowed in some aspects and periods of human experience), then certainly and necessarily we will not know what we are talking about. Neither will the political theorist who attempts to give a systematic expression to this striving know what she or he is talking about. But, to surrender in the face of blind and dumb criticism, indeed, to see the attempt to give expression to these possibilities as anything less than absolutely necessary – even if our expressions will seem (and, indeed, will be) "fuzzy," inchoate, this is to give in to the logic of counter-possibility.[22]

Of course, the wagon-circlers are happy with this, and when they make their poker-faced gestures at (*necessarily*) flawed attempts to understand and work toward something beyond what already exists, they can be satisfied that, in the terms that they are comfortable with, they have "won" the intellectual game. But there is more at stake than this rather narrow and indeed stupid game.

There is another critique of multiculturalism that zeroes in on a feature of some multicultural agendas that is, unfortunately, known all too well. This is the case where multiculturalism has itself become caught up in playing the intellectual game which, in a market-centered society, often comes down to the finding or creation of an academic *niche*. (The very word, which comes to us from the French language, is indicative of the puniness of the undertaking.) Within academia, it is very difficult to not get caught up in such games. In this light, I'd like to present a few remarks concerning controversies such as the one that has flared up in the aca-

demic institution of philosophy in the past few years, played out in a series
of exchanges between Christina Hoff Summers and a number of feminist
philosophers in the *Proceedings of the American Philosophical Association*. Similar exchanges have taken place in the forums of other
disciplines, perhaps especially in the humanities.

For the sake of argument, let us imagine that both sides to such disputes
are truly interested in pursuing justice, or at least what is fair. (I realize
that this is stretching things a great deal; however, this assumption at least
serves as a useful heuristic.) If this is the case, then the problem within the
more narrowly circumscribed field of academia is that, in an attempt to be
fair, people are turning on each other. They are doing this in a period
when, it would seem, there is less to go around. What is more, the period
is one in which the radical movements and ideals of the 1960s, which still
motivate the pursuit of greater equality and diversity, seem a distant
memory. Indeed, a certain amount of cynical "realism" has set in. The
question is, where does multiculturalism fit into this period of seeming
historical impasse?

If multiculturalism, feminist interventions in the academy, affirmative
action, etc., are part of a general movement to create a whole new society,
one in which mutual flourishing without exploitation or domination is the
standard, *then* these trends make a great deal of sense according to a larger
liberatory logic. When, however, these movements get stuck in the rut of
having no discernible socially transformative aspect, then they tend to
turn into their opposite. That is, such movements simply become a
reinforcement of the existing social formation, especially its class relations. This last point needs to be understood, for one sees on the part of a
great deal of purely academic feminism or multiculturalism these days a
marked hostility to the question of class and especially to the idea of a
class that is systematically marginalized by the existing society, what
Marx called the proletariat. This is the case even if, more recently, it has
become *de rigueur* to mention that, most certainly and of course, we must
"attend to class." When anyone actually does attend to class in the vicinity
of such circles, however, it is amazing to see the hostility that comes out.
It is also very disturbing.

The academy is for the most part a very middle-class institution;[23] any
feminism or multiculturalism (I'm including gay studies under this heading also) that does not address itself to this fact will tend to be coopted by
the class system and eventually to reinforce (and conceivably even extend)
this system.[24] Really addressing this system would mean social transformation in general, not just in the academy. Although saying what I will
say next opens one up to the charge of reductivism, I find it absolutely

necessary to say: without such transformation, the emancipation of women, people of color, and other oppressed or dominated groups cannot ultimately be accomplished. As I have said many times in my work, I recognize that there really is such a thing as reductivism, including "class reductivism," but I find that the charge, leveled in this context, is often itself one version of hostility to the question of class. The point can be made from the other side: the marginal improvement in the situation of *some*, mostly middle-class women and people of color, gay people, etc., if it is largely accomplished under the "it's our turn" model of inclusion (I'm thinking of the rhetoric that some members of such groups used to justify support for Bill Clinton in 1992), *depends* on the non-transformation of the class system and, ultimately, the defense of the privileged spaces that open up in a dominant, wealthy, capitalist and imperialist country such as the United States.[25]

A few moments ago, I spoke of a "period of historical impasse." In a nutshell, what I mean by this is the fact that our society has been, for a long time, ripe for social transformation, but the social transformation hasn't come.[26] (This is not to say that there haven't been many significant developments.) As a result, first-world societies have become "overripe" – jaded and cynical. Indeed, cynicism has become something like the dominant ideology (more-so, I think, than outright jingoism).[27] Cynicism as the dominant ideology fits in well with a society where people are not *citizens*, in any significant sense, but instead primarily consumers, customers, and spectators. In a consumer society, what counts is what you can buy, what sort of buying power you have.[28] "Truth" equals what sells. The question I have been working up to is one of promoting a multiculturalism that is *not* fashioned on or coopted by a cynical, consumerist model.

To take one key example: if programs such as affirmative action, which is after all the model for reformist academic feminism and multiculturalism, are part of a merely reformist agenda, then they can have the effect of simply reinforcing what is one of the most disgusting aspects of capitalist society. Namely, this kind of agenda says that we only have so much room to employ and develop people's abilities; therefore, an implicit quota has to be set regarding who, at any given time, might develop their potential. "Affirmative action" in this case is simply a different *application* of the logic of counter-possibility. As part of a merely reformist agenda, it is an application that mirrors the implicit quotas that are already set by the dominant culture. This logic has it that people cannot consciously work together in a way that promotes mutual flourishing, but rather that consciousness must be subordinate to the instrumental reason of commodity production – in other words, we only need so many minds at work at any given time, and thus we implicitly accept the principle of the division of labor, especially the division between mental and manual labor. Marx argues that this principle is at work in all oppressive societies, most dramatically in capitalist society, and that the creation of a global community of mutual flourishing requires the transcendence of this narrow horizon. I think that he is absolutely right, and that this is an argument that we have to deal with in considering the question of multiculturalism.

The impasse makes a principle out of society's not being able to make fundamental transformations. Everything in our jaded and cynical society is increasingly premised on the supposed impossibility of such transformation – speak in any way about fundamental problems with existing social structures, the sort of problems that cannot be addressed with mere reforms and band-aids, and you will immediately be told that "you can't change the world," you are "unrealistic," "utopian," etc. The impasse gives rise to a situation where people turn on one another: on the one side, some feminists and multiculturalists (awkward category, I realize), who are now taking "their turn"; on the other side, resentful intellectuals, mostly white males to be sure, who have worked hard and who now find that this hard work does not mean anything.

Perhaps this is too quickly to leave aside the large group – one hopes it isn't the majority – of people in the academy, almost all white males (but also a few white women), who haven't really done much of anything, except take up their class privileges. These, of course, are the people who are now administering affirmative action, which is one of the great ironies. But it should be added that these academic equivalents of Rush Limbaugh, blowhards without substance, are also the people howling the loudest about "maintaining standards," "quotas," etc.

Of course the white males who have worked hard to become intellectuals of substance have targeted the wrong "enemy." Of course it is not feminism or multiculturalism that has set the terms of things such that, as far as the social system is concerned, whether your life means anything or not is completely irrelevant. And of course it is easier for the resentful white male to vent his resentment against the feminist down the hall rather than against the actual social system that is the real root of the problem. But it is also easier for the reformist academic feminist or multiculturalist to target the white male in academia rather than the actual social system. This is the case even if (1) it has not been all that "easy," and it is in fact still not easy, for women and people of color and gay people to enter the professoriate (the big lie is that these folks are getting all of the positions; anyone who opened their eyes for a minute would see that this isn't the case); and (2) it must be emphasized that the burden does not and has never fallen equally; historically, there is not even a scale on which to compare the fortunes of white males in the academy with everyone else, and the recent difficulties experienced by (mostly middle-class) white males in the academy are not much to write home about when compared with real oppression and suffering in this world.

Frankly, I cannot take the hysterical male who goes ballistic over having his penis insulted very seriously.

But the point is to find a way out of this impasse. The question of class tells us something, too, when we consider that most working-class people look upon the squabble among middle-class academics, whatever their color or gender or sexual orientation, as something completely irrelevant to their lives. To the extent that the controversy over feminism and multiculturalism in the academy degenerates into a squabble over whose turn it is to exercise middle-class privilege, this controversy *is* irrelevant to changing the world in such a way as to encourage mutual flourishing. As the fortunes of the US continue to decline, or as new imperialist schemes are put forward and enacted in order to keep the US on top (e.g. the Gulf War, or the "war on crime," which is almost entirely a war on black and Latino youths), to continue the "squabble" in this necessarily degenerating way is practically criminal.

Kathleen League has written a powerful essay concerning the way that the question of class has been marginalized in recent discussions of otherness. In "The New Invisibility of Class (in Discourses of Alterity and Marginality)," League infuses discussion of theoretical issues with her own experience growing up below the poverty line in a lower-working-class family, as well as her experience in the academy. I would like to quote one example from the latter category:

> Another example I'd like to relate comes from when I was in graduate school studying art history. I took a course on documentary photography. At one point the work shown was by a photographer who photographed working-class couples primly seated in their tidy little living rooms. The shots and poses were all alike and made the subjects look like specimens, as though they were bugs pinned into position in a box and then photographed. The presentation seemed clearly designed to invite a condescending and scornful attitude to the people depicted, as though the viewers are supposed to think "these little people in their little living rooms with their little horizons and lives." Sure enough, that's the reaction it elicited. All of these supposedly sophisticated art history graduate students started snickering at these photographs and referring to the people in them as "lunch box joes." It was all very insulting.[29]

But what to do? – do we need to add class to the list of issues already grouped under multiculturalism, make sure that some classes are taught on this issue, etc? I don't think that's a bad idea, necessarily. Do we need to break down class barriers to access to academia at all levels, from the first year of college to the professoriate? Pursue this question and you'll see why the earlier question, about bringing issues of class into discussions of multiculturalism, hasn't been well-received. *Up to a point*, as long as no real structural issues are addressed, the system can absorb *a certain number* of middle-class women and people of color and gay people into *some* of the basic institutions of this society. I am careful to qualify this statement, indeed, to qualify it substantially: I have no doubt, and I want to be absolutely clear on this, that for the basic institutions of this society to absorb, *as full and real participants*, truly substantial numbers of women and people of color and gay people would require a radical remaking of society, even if the class question was not raised as such. Of course, this is simply not possible on a whole other level, in that *most* women and people of color are in fact from the working class, even if this is not the case for most women and people of color (and white males, of course) who enter the academy. But the point is that the class question cannot be raised in any *substantial* way (something quite beyond art history courses where students are encouraged to consider "Joe Lunchbox" as *specimen*) without this radical remaking, because, in raising this question, we would have to address fundamental premises of this society, especially concerning the division of labor. Relying on our class instincts, as middle-class academics, many of us have instinctively shut out these questions – and we need to break through this impasse, toward a transformative multiculturalism.

Kathleen League sums up the issue as follows:

> In saying all of this, I do not desire acceptance or assimilation for myself or anyone else. Nor am I wanting to carve out a perverse class privilege or niche for the issue of class. Getting class accepted as another respectable niche in academia or the discourse of alterity is not the point. The point is not about seeking permission to join the game; the point is that the game itself needs to be changed. (Ibid., p. 11)

We need *transformative* multiculturalism and a *real* movement for the liberation of women, and though these have their intellectual and even academic aspects, fundamentally we have to think in terms of a radical social movement, one which has as its aim the creation of a new society.

3 Story Quilt

Much of the attack on multiculturalism has been based on anecdotal "evidence" (I put the word in scare-quotes because (1) it is not clear that such anecdotes should be accepted as evidence of anything, and (2) it is not clear that many of the reported episodes actually happened). The books of Christina Hoff Summers, Dinesh D'Souza, Roger Kimball, David Lehman, etc., are filled with such "evidence." By way of coda and conclusion, I would like to take a moment to present my own personal narrative of counter-anecdotes and a thumbnail sketch of what I make of them.

A few years ago I attended a conference at Loyola University of Chicago, on the theme of "deconstruction and pedagogy." Among the participants were Barbara Johnson, a literary theorist influenced by feminism and deconstruction (and a student of Paul de Man), who teaches at Harvard, Rick Roderick, a Marxist philosopher who at that time was at Duke, and Michael Berube, who has written extensively on questions of multiculturalism and political correctness, and who teaches English at the University of Illinois. The more or less cranky, anti-multicultural side was also well represented, by David Lehman, and by a pair of professors from the University of Chicago (one of whom is also a radio talkshow personality in Chicago). As you probably know, Alan Bloom and Saul Bellow are among the better-known of the wagon-circlers, and they also hail from that institution – and certain departments at Chicago have set themselves up as bases for the defense of Western Civilization.

At the Loyola conference, at the beginning of a discussion involving this pair of canon-defenders, one of them said something to the effect that the proponents of multiculturalism wanted to abolish the Western canon and replace it with subjects such as "Eskimo literature." I have to admit to you that I know nothing about this particular subject, and I imagine that the person who made this remark doesn't either. The difference, I suppose, is that I'm not proud of my ignorance.

In other words, I don't know, without investigating the subject, that the experience of the Eskimos has nothing to teach the rest of humankind. Perhaps the Straussians at Chicago do know this, though I haven't yet seen their presentation of evidence and argument on the subject – which really surprises me, since I know these folks are such great champions of rigor and reason.

Rick Roderick gave the Chicago boys the response they deserved. Rick and I go back some years. When I was a graduate student at the University of Kansas, I presented a paper on the social theory of Habermas at a regional philosophy conference. Rick was the commentator. Now, Habermas is not exactly the weirdest or most far-out figure in the Western world, but to some of the participants in that meeting, he is just another one of those "Continental"-types. Later, after the session, Rick and I were walking through the hotel restaurant, when we ran into a couple of the conference participants. These fellows were what you would have to call "hardcore" analytic philosophers, and one of them said to us, in a very proud and smug tone of voice, "I don't know anything about Habermas." Most readers will know what this sort of thing is about – i.e. "I do *real* philosophy; I'm not tainted with that other junk, about which I do not need to know anything." In his wonderful west Texas drawl, Rick said something to this person that I'll remember the rest of my life: "Well, you're a goddamn idiot, to be proud of the fact that you don't know anything about a major thinker."

Ordinarily, I wouldn't try to argue that the dismissal of Habermas, or of "Continental" philosophy more generally, and that of minority or marginalized cultures, are on a par, except that there do seem to be commonalities in the dynamics of these dismissals, and, at least as far as the academic profession of philosophy is concerned, it is often the same people making both dismissals.

For the record, there are many broad-minded and politically progressive analytic philosophers, for example those who have recently formed the Society for Analytic Feminism. And there are plenty of "Continental" philosophers, especially those with a thoroughly Eurocentric orientation (and, I daresay, especially some of the Heideggerians), who are as resistant to multiculturalism as anyone. In fact, I might even go so far as to argue that the Eurocentric continentals are even more resistant than some of the smug analytics, in that the former's orientation on this subject is philosophical, whereas the latter's is more contingent upon merely being in a position of institutional authority. However, the fact is that the bulk of the actual policy and decision-making on multicultural issues in philosophy departments in the United States is made by analytic philosophers, many of whom are a part of well-entrenched old-boy networks.[30]

In any case, one has to wonder, what kind of defense of culture, *any* culture, is it that dismisses some other, unknown culture, without knowing the slightest thing about it?

In an article titled "Patterns of Culture Wars," Micaela di Leonardo exposes the larger political agenda behind at least some of this dismissiveness.[31] Most philosophers and other academics in the humanities, thankfully, do not have the power to perpetrate actual crimes against non-Western (or Western but non-mainstream) cultures, but some of them are at least more than willing to do their part on the ideological front. Anti-multicultural imperiousness is not unrelated to imperialism and the ideological rehabilitation of imperialism. The anti-multiculturalist intellectuals and polemicists have found a useful punching bag in "cultural relativism." For example:

> Digby Anderson in *National Review* in 1991, not to be outdone, excoriates "repellent cultural relativism" that says "that any culture is as good as any other, you know, black Africans had a Renaissance which outshone the West's, it's just that the West has obliterated it with colonialism." (Ibid., p. 26)

You would think that it's bad enough that such polemicists seem to believe that the issue of colonialism, which is in no way a dead letter, can be blithely gotten over in this way – "Yeah yeah – we've heard enough griping about colonialism." And you would think it's bad enough that the not-too-hidden and again blithe assumption here is that Mr Anderson, who surely must be some sort of expert on the cultures of black Africans (in the same way that those University of Chicago professors are experts on Eskimo literature), knows that there's really nothing there worth wasting any time over.

The racism in these polemics is extraordinary. The sort of thing that the ordinary redneck has probably gotten beyond or doesn't really mean on any kind of substantive level is elevated to the heights of cultural criticism.[32] As di Leonardo reports, in his 1994 book *In Defense of Elitism*, William Henry "actually writes that 'it is scarcely the same thing to put a man on the moon as to put a bone in your nose' " (ibid., p. 26). (Come to think of it, there are at least a few other men who ought to be put up there!)

But then, as di Leonardo demonstrates, the larger agenda of this attack on "cultural relativism" is not first of all intellectual, but instead is quite practical.

Step one in this *kulturkampf* is to attack the legacy of the 1960s, which, among other things, fostered the sort of "permissiveness" that has allowed the "triumph of the Zulus." In other words, this "permissiveness" has as one aspect sympathy for the larger part of humankind, the part that has been victimized by colonialism and imperialism. But, you see, and this is the real agenda, we should have no sympathy for the spear-chuckers; such sympathy only brings our own Western culture down, and it also thereby prevents the West from helping the rest of the world to raise its level of civilization.

Bottom line: colonialism and imperialism are good. *Voilà*, the rehabilitation of Malthussianism and Victorian doctrines of European superiority. *Voilà*, the return of the White Man's Burden. Found in the polemics against "cultural relativism" and multiculturalism are straightforward calls for recolonization of the Third World. This is not just the idle chatter of right-wing nuts. These polemics play an important ideological role in a period of globalization and so-called "free trade agreements," when whole societies (including several in "black Africa") can be written off if "the numbers aren't there." The "Great Powers" also need these apologetics for rehabilitating the colonial system (whether they are presented straightforwardly or not) because they can no longer claim the "threat of Soviet communism" as a reason for their massive economic and political (and, when necessary, military) presence in the Third World – though, of course, Pentagon and other think-tanks are working night and day to concoct other threats of this order, the most promising of which seems to be the "threat" of militant, fundamentalist Islam.

There is something for multiculturalism to do in the academy in the first world, and part of its work will indeed be to diversify the professoriate, but the global context of this work has to be understood. The point of diversification cannot be allowed to devolve to mere careerism and "our turn"-ism; instead, it has to be linked with the social movements and intellectual trends that challenge and struggle against the new forms of colonialism and imperialism.

Again, it boggles my mind to think that the anti-multicultural agenda is able to wrap itself in the banner of "respect for tradition." On the one hand, what does it mean to say, "I have great respect for tradition, but only *my* tradition" – which just happens to be the tradition that is militarily and economically empowered? The shallow intellectual basis of much neo-conservative thought could be traced to some of the narrow empiricist and social-Darwinist trends of Victorian England – "friends of the permanent things" and other such poppycock. Somehow, the traditions of very old cultures such as those of India or China or Africa do not count among these "permanent things," but the activities of a decadent and (just to rub it in) sexually permissive monarchy do.[33] Funny thing, if it weren't for the scholarship of the Islamic world, these high-minded "friends" wouldn't have Plato to ground their sense of "permanence" or Aristotle to appeal to in their moralizings about "character."

(On the slim intellectual basis of all of this talk about "tradition," remember the infamous *Newsweek* article from a few years back, warning of the threat of "political correctness"?

Incredibly, the author wrote that the evil multiculturalists wanted to get rid of the reading of great Western thinkers such as Plato and replace them with literature by homosexuals!)

And, on the other hand, it turns out that these well-remunerated (as di Leonardo puts it) ideologists such as Allan Bloom, Gertrude Himmelfarb, Pat Buchanan, Charles Murray, Dinesh D'Souza, Samuel Huntington, etc., have never been hesitant to ally themselves with capitalism, giant corporations, and the interests of the bourgeoisie, even though the "respect for tradition" on the part of capitalists is very quickly out the window if there are bigger bucks to be made by paving paradise (or the Cathedral of Notre Dame or *whatever* – for capitalists it doesn't make any difference) and putting up a parking lot (a little nod to Joni Mitchell and the sixties vibe here), shopping mall, fish processing plant, etc.

But I'm getting off track here – I was supposed to be compiling some anecdotes. A good concentrated example of what the "respect for tradition" is really all about is the controversy over the refusal of a basketball player for the Denver Nuggets, Mahmoud Abdul-Rauf, to stand and face the American flag for the national anthem. Besides the fact that the NBA's policy of – and the corporate media's calls for – forced patriotism pits one tradition against another, namely Abdul-Rauf's commitment to both Islam and the tradition of understanding that the American flag is a symbol of the oppression of black people, besides this, there is something truly laughable about the stand that the NBA and other advocates of forced patriotism took here.

> In a funny piece called "Nuggets' Abdul-Rauf Shouldn't Stand for IT," *New York Times* columnist Harvey Araton pointed out that during the national anthem players fidget, fans yell, reporters type, corporate box owners drink, and "when the beloved anthem gets in the way of an NBA network telecast, say, can you see how it conveniently is played 20 minutes earlier, when the arena is half empty."
>
> In short, after years of ignoring its "rule," the National Basketball Association moved against Abdul-Rauf and his conscious anti-patriotism. The NBA is trying to make public patriotism a *requirement* for professional basketball players. The fact that the NBA decided to punish a basketball player for sitting out a flag ritual shows how insecure this system is and how ruthlessly it enforces its political loyalty.[34]

Certainly, insecurity has something to do with the way that some academics are suckered into being shills for the larger agendas of counter-possibility.

At a certain point in the (previously mentioned) discussion around Christina Hoff Summers in the *Proceedings of the American Philosophical Association*, someone I had known when we were both graduate students got involved (writing letters not only to the *Proceedings*, but also to *Lingua Franca* and other periodicals). My previous association with this person had to do with our mutual interest in the philosophy of Donald Davidson. (I am still very much interested in Davidson's work, but, as we shall see, this other person has found a quite different gig.) His anti-feminist rhetoric in these letters was filled with resentment and insecurity, in part fueled by frustrations over not having secured a tenure-track university position.

Frankly, I felt for this person, even while I thought the letters he was writing were completely misguided, at best. Because we had some history of fruitful discussion on other matters, and out of a perhaps rationalist impulse toward thinking that philosophers, at least, could surely talk things out (also a thoroughly misguided notion, I'm sure, and yet I cling to it on some level – because, what are you left with when you give it up?), I wrote him a fairly long letter. The tenor of the letter was, "Come to your senses, man!" But I also tried to get into some of the systemic issues, especially the aforementioned point that feminism, and especially the feminist who got the job instead of you, are not the enemies here, not the forces behind a division of labor that really only needs so many academic philosophers.[35]

In response, I received a letter that was filled with libertarian and Ayn-Randish arguments, presented in a formulaic fashion. What is more, it turned out that he was involved in trying to set himself up as the Dinesh D'Souza of philosophy, in other words to find material success and standing as a champion in the great struggle against feminism, multiculturalism, affirmative action, political correctness, and the Left.

Basically for sentimental reasons, every other year for the past twelve years I have returned to the conference where I gave my first philosophy paper, the state philosophy association of one of the smaller (but also prouder) Southern states. A couple of years ago, as it turns out, the person I have been referring to had a one-year position at one of the colleges in that state. On one of my bi-annual returns to the meeting, I found that he was giving a talk. No surprise to me, the talk was intended as a demonstration of his championship in the aforementioned struggle. Strangely enough, this past year when I once again returned to the conference, another white male philosopher gave an almost identical talk. What the program committee was thinking in scheduling these things I'm not sure, but the talks were somewhat instructive.

On *any* standard that might be proposed as "objective," both talks were pure garbage. Listening to them, one felt in that strange state one experiences when sleeping pills wear off in the middle of the night – half ready to jump out of bed and run a marathon, half falling into a complete stupor. (I'm also reminded of George Carlin's joke about a poor dog named "Stay" – "Come Stay, come Stay!") One moment I and the rest of the audience would feel infuriated, the next moment like we were just hearing, yet another time, an idiotic tape-recorded message that was being played just to annoy us and that no one could possibly take seriously. The same old bleat, in other words.

But what was abundantly and absolutely clear, almost pitifully clear, was that these two incompetents could never have landed positions in academia in the first place if there wasn't a well-entrenched quota system for white middle-class males.

Even if I am stating the perfectly obvious, please allow me to continue with two additional observations. The first is simply that this story, of basic incompetence with regard to any intellectual standard that might be proposed (unless there is a special standard for hysterical whining if one happens to fit the category of white middle-class male – but, gee, it turns out *there is* such a standard), could be repeated many times over. Are there any incompetent or less-than-scintillating academics out there who are women and/or people of color? Absolutely – why wouldn't there be? This characterization applies to some *people* in the academy, regardless. But an incompetent professor who is black becomes an imcompetent *black* professor; an incompetent professor who is a woman becomes an incompetent *woman* professor. Somehow, though, this way of characterizing the situation doesn't extend to white males.[36]

The second thing has to do with the idea, trotted out *ad infinitum*, that the professoriate is now simply packed with incompetent women and people of color who got their positions because of special considerations. Both of the speakers I have been discussing made this claim. On the most recent occasion, "I felt well-prepared with the counter-anecdote, for I had been part of an interview committee at the American Philosophical Association Eastern Division meeting just a few weeks before. We interviewed six men and seven women. Most of the men were very good, unquestionably. I wish them all luck, and I hate the larger systemic factors that may mean that even the best of them could have difficulty in securing positions. Clearly, they had all worked hard and would make fine scholars and teachers. But, with possibly one exception, I would have to say that the women were uniformly better. And let's be clear on this: I am not saying that they had "better minds," because I reject the notion. Indeed, this screwy idea is part and parcel of the anti-multicultural arsenal: after all, if I have the better mind by nature, then it really doesn't matter what comes out in practice. What I mean, though, is that the women candidates were uniformly better prepared – not just for the interviews but, clearly, in their courses of study and preparations for intellectual work. My guess is that they were better prepared because, contrary to the big lies about affirmative action and the supposed hiring of incompetents, the fact is these candidates could only show us what they had done in their work – since they didn't have the "better minds" to fall back on.

Thinking about my experience with these candidates while listening to this speaker go on about the "triumph of the Zulus" at his own university, I felt very angry at the lie that was being told. For, if what *this* incompetent was saying were true, then one would think that one could look around in the academic profession of philosophy and see lots of incompetent women and people of color swelling the ranks. Perhaps what I am saying is narrowly empirical and merely anecdotal, but academic philosophy is a relatively small world, and, when I look around in this world, I don't see anything even remotely like this.

Now, just to bring some of these themes together a bit. By now, it is standard for market solutions to be proposed for all social questions. Indeed, as I mentioned, the person who I tried to encourage to come to his senses has been more recently engaged in trying to get libertarian think-tanks interested in his services. The idea is that the market will reward merit and hard work, and anything that smacks of a collective or group claim, for instance on behalf of a culture or marginalized group, is phony. Let each person stand on his or her own, says the market argument.

This position is hypocritical, to say the least. Individualist meritocracy and "virtue" have always been preached for the masses, when all the while there are myriad institutions geared toward maintaining class solidarity and class position for the middle class, the upper-middle class, and the upper class. Anyone who has worked for long as a college professor, for example, sees the way that fraternities certainly don't mind a little "socialism" and collectivity when it comes to doing their schoolwork.

What is more, the market stands against anything so cohesive as a "culture," except to the extent that cultures can be broken down into saleable items and marketed as fashion or fad. Here we move very directly into the realm of consumerist multiculturalism, as much exemplified by the "United Colors of Benneton" as anything – and Patricia Williams's excellent story/essay has shown what that is all about.[37] Many universities, my own included, have embraced a kind of "multiculturalism" that takes it as some great mark of broad-mindedness to say, "As long as

your money is green, we don't care what color (or gender, etc.) you are."
Here we see "internationalism" and "multiculturalism," global capitalist
style.

As things go ever more postmodern and *Neuromancer*,[38] perhaps the
result will be a three-tiered global society: (1) for the majority, poverty
and exploitation, constant struggle to just hold body and soul together;
(2) for what remains of the middle class, "culture" as boutique and mall;
(3) for the upper-class friends of the permanent things, ornamented
enclaves, armored compounds that preserve all that has been best for a
few people in a few societies.[39]

But perhaps there is something else: those cultures of resistance that
must, even in the midst of ruin, continually emerge from the bottom of
society. A transformational multicultural perspective must aim at connecting with these cultures.

There has to be something more. In conclusion, then, let us bring the
liberatory and systematic aspects of Marxism and multiculturalism
together: a transformational multiculturalism must grapple with both the
radical diversity of these cultures (whose differences will be much like
those of different languages) and the possibility of a radical confluence
based on commonalities of oppression.

Notes

1   I address some questions of ontology at length in the first chapter of *Matrix
    and Line: Derrida and the Possibilities of Postmodern Social Theory*
    (Albany: State University of New York Press, 1992), "Modalities, politics." I
    critique the monological model of Marxism, and instead propose the model
    of a "crazy quilt," in the Afterword of *Politics in the Impasse: Explorations
    in Postsecular Social Theory* (Albany: SUNY Press, 1995).
2   The key text is Joseph Stalin, *Dialectical and Historical Materialism* (New
    York: International Publishers, 1940).
3   In my view, the critique of Marxism as ontology offered by Jacques Derrida
    in *Specters of Marx* is exemplary; Derrida's counter-proposal is what he calls
    "hauntology."
4   The pesky category of mathematics is either avoided – presumably because to
    make it foundational would lead to philosophical idealism – or assimilated to
    physics in the name of a supposed empirical grounding of mathematics that,
    in fact, no one has yet managed to really pull off. (In other words, Quine has
    presented a powerful argument, in "Two Dogmas of Empiricism," that
    demonstrates that, in principle, there are no absolutely non-empirical, "ana-
    lytic," *a priori* truths; but, as for how mathematical propositions really
    "hook up" with the empirical world, this remains to be shown. But then, in
    "On the Very Idea of a Conceptual Scheme" and elsewhere, Davidson argues

that the "hook up" question is misguided to begin with, and inviting of skepticism.)

5   One of the most interesting essays that pursues the program of a "unified science" is Otto Neurath's "Sociology and Physicalism," in A. J. Ayer (ed.), *Logical Positivism* (New York: The Free Press, 1959), pp. 282–317. Also of interest here is Neurath's attempt to rethink Marxism in terms of logical positivism; see *Wissenschaftliche Weltauffassung, Sozialismus und Loqischer Empirismus* (Frankfurt: Suhrkamp, 1979).

6   Sartre's most famous example of the emergence of dialectic through inter-action is of course that of the boxing match in the *Critique of Dialectical Reason*. For insightful commentary on Sartre's arguments, see Joseph Cata-lano, *A Commentary on Jean-Paul Sartre's Critique of Dialectical Reason* (Chicago: University of Chicago Press, 1986), esp. pp. 198–205 ("The Constituted Dialectic"), and William L. McBride, *Sartre's Political Theory* (Bloomington: Indiana University Press, 1991), esp. pp. 163–8.

7   In addition to "Mental Events," the other key essays in Davidson's presenta-tion of anomalous monism are "Psychology as Philosophy" and "The Material Mind." See Donald Davidson, *Essays on Actions and Events* (Oxford: Oxford University Press, 1980), pp. 207–59.

8   See Joseph Stalin, *Marxism and the National Question* (Calcutta: New Book Centre, 1975) and *Marxism and Problems of Linguistics* (Peking: Foreign Languages Press, 1972).

9   A Maoist, and, to my mind, very insightful, analysis of this dynamic is offered by Bob Avakian, in *Conquer the World? The International Proletariat Must and Will* (Chicago: RCP Publications, 1981). Again, I ask the reader to set aside the standard sneers and clichés. Although I've never been too fond of the title of Avakian's piece, I think it is one of the most significant overviews of the international communist movement, and especially of Stalin's role in that movement.

10   See Joseph Stalin, *On the Great Patriotic War of the Soviet Union* (Calcutta: New Book Centre, 1975).

11   This assimilation even occurred on the very basic level of having whole factories disassembled in Central Europe and transported to and rebuilt in the Soviet Union.

12   A recent book by Robert W. Thurston, *Life and Terror in Stalin's Russia, 1934–1941* (New Haven, Conn.: Yale University Press, 1996) debunks some of the popular theories of "totalitarianism" that have had great currency in the West (especially the theory proposed by Hannah Arendt). Thurston's aim is certainly not the "vindication" of Stalin (even if his book might actually accomplish this on some levels), and Yale University Press's anti-communist credentials are certainly well-established. Another document of vital impor-tance here is Sartre's "Socialism in One Country" (*New Left Review* n. 100 [November 1976], pp. 143–63 – this is a section from the posthumously published volume 2 of the *Critique*).

13   Meanwhile, certain fixtures of European fascism remained in place – most obviously Franco, who did not have to get into the nasty business of

perpetrating genocide against Jews, since these people had conveniently been expelled from Spain in the same year that Columbus set sail to bring universal humanity to the New World.

14 Please keep in mind that, on such issues, it is not as though European social democrats or "Western Marxists" had a perspective that was any more visionary or even flexible – whatever insights at least the latter group may have had on other questions. Again, Avakian (see note 9) is insightful on the way that the conventional wisdom of many Western Marxists (on subjects such as industrialization, the possibility of socialist revolution in the Third World, etc.) was no better than Stalin's on many points, and often worse.

15 Some recent scholarship on Mao and Maoism: Arif Dirlik, Paul Healy, and Nick Knight (eds), *Critical Perspectives on Mao Zedong's Thought* (Atlantic Highlands, NJ: Humanities Press, 1997); Raymond Lotta (ed.), *Maoist Economics and the Revolutionary Road to Communism: The Shanghai Textbook* (Chicago: Banner Press, 1974); Bill Martin, "Still Maoist After All These Years," in *Politics in the Impasse* pp. 159–95, (see note 1).

16 I'm reminded of Adorno's comment to the effect that it is only in a time when philistines dominate intellectual discussion that the word "utopian" could be used in a derogatory way. See "Something's Missing: A Discussion between Ernst Bloch and Theodor W. Adorno on the Contradictions of Utopian Longing," in Ernst Bloch, *The Utopian Function of Art and Literature*, Jack Zipes and Frank Mecklenburg trans. (Cambridge, Mass.: MIT Press, 1988), pp. 1–17, esp. p. 4.

17 I remind the reader that there was a time, especially from the mid-1960s to the mid-1970s, when there was a Soviet/US consensus around the racist proposition that the Chinese Revolution represented a "yellow peril," a consensus in which even many Soviet "dissidents" (e.g. Roy Medvedev) took part, while American authors published "respectable" books with titles such as "Mao: Emperor of the Blue Ants."

18 These categories, radical diversity and radical confluence, are developed in my *Matrix and line* (see note 1), ch. 4, pp. 125–71.

19 Among the important sources from Jacques Derrida on these questions would be "Inventions of the Other," trans. Catherine Porter, in Lindsay Waters and Wlad Godzich (eds), *Reading de Man Reading* (Minneapolis: University of Minnesota Press, 1989) trans. and *The Other Heading: Reflections on Today's Europe*, trans. Michael B. Naas and Pascale-Anne Brault, Bloomington: Indiana University Press, 1992). A reading of these terms is presented in my *Humanism and its Aftermath: The Shared Fate of Deconstruction and Politics* (Atlantic Highlands, NJ: Humanities Press, 1995), pp. 127–71.

20 See Roland Barthes, *Mythologies*, trans. Annette Lavers (New York: Hill and Wang, 1983). This point was brought to my attention by Andrew Cutrofello.

21 Some of what follows is drawn from my Afterword to *Politics in the Impasse* (see note 1), "Crazy quilt," esp. pp. 254–60.

22 The term "counter-possibility" is developed in the first chapter of my *Matrix*

and Line (see note 1). Briefly, "impossibility" is what draws possibility beyond itself, while "counter-possibility" is what closes off possibility. As much as this distinction may seem straightforward, part of the problem is that it is not always easy to tell impossibilities from counter-possibilities.

23 A good collection of essays on this question is Michelle M. Tokarczyk and Elizabeth A. Fay (eds), *Working-Class Women in the Academy* (Amherst: University of Massachusetts Press, 1993).

24 A good recent collection of essays on class and the gay movement is Amy Gluckman and Betsy Reed (eds), *Homo Economics: Capitalism, Community, and Lesbian and Gay Life* (London: Routledge, 1997). One of the most important essays on the question of capitalism and sexuality is John D'Emilio's "Capitalism and Gay Identity" in his *Making Trouble* (London: Routledge, 1992), pp. 3–16.

25 I want to acknowledge that this will probably seem something that it is easy for me to say, given the fact that I have had my turn, and the turn that I have had is certainly dependent on the privileges that I have experienced as a white male from the middle class. The question, however, is what one does with this privileged position, with this background. I can only hope that you will take me at my word when I say that I think it is the responsibility of myself and everyone else who has had a "turn," one which is materially based in the existing social system, to use the possibilities and privileges that we have had to work for fundamental social transformation, for revolution. I certainly expect anyone who reads this public declaration to hold me to this responsibility.

26 In *Matrix and Line* (see note 1), I develop these terms around what I call the "jaded society"; see pp. 49–56.

27 The planning, execution, and aftermath of the Gulf War is a concentrated example of this, from George Bush's gyrations in justifying the war – remember the business about the incubators in a Kuwait hospital, which, it turned out, was concocted by a public-relations firm hired by the Kuwaiti government, to the sending of half a million ground troops to "fight" in a "war" – a massacre really – that was in fact conducted almost entirely from the air, to the yellow-ribbon victory parades that went on for many times as long as the war itself – it would be as if victory parades for the Second World War had been staged continuously for forty years. See my "Letter on Fascism" in *Politics in the Impasse* (see note 1), pp. 197–230.

28 I hasten to add that the "consumer society" model has been deployed in many different ways; I would situate this model within the larger model of a capitalism as a global mode of production. Obviously, in global terms, only a minority is experiencing the benefits of the consumer society. Furthermore, I largely accept Fredric Jameson's model, in which the stage of global capitalism analyzed by Lenin (which he called "imperialism") is integrated into a model that also takes account of the deep and widespread and not merely ephemeral effects of the culture industry. A preliminary sketch of this model is presented in my "Still Maoist After All These Years" (see note 15), under the heading, "Lenin and Adorno: Two circuits of thought." Jameson's

book (and not just the essay that is often cited), *Postmodernism, or, The Cultural Logic of Late Capitalism* (Durham, NC: Duke University Press, 1991), presents a brilliant synthesis of these themes, especially in the chapter on economics ("Postmodernism and the Market") and the long conclusion, "Secondary Elaborations." My larger point, just to restate it, is that the consumer society, even for those who experience its benefits, replaces even the deeply flawed Western ideals of citizenship and participation.

29 Kathleen League, "The New Invisibility of Class (in Discourses of Alterity and Marginality)," paper presented at the Midwest Radical Activists and Scholars Conference, Loyola University of Chicago, October 1993; typescript in my possession. When League presented this paper, although there were a number of positive responses (notably from Bertell Ollman), there were also some significant negative responses from graduate students in what might be called "postmodern" literature programs, where the language of alterity and marginality (the other, difference, etc.) is the lingua franca. League was accused of "class reductionism," and it was recommended to her that she shift her focus to race, gender, and sexuality. When League said that she had no desire to detract from work in those areas, but that she believed the category of class was being systematically shut out of the discussion, she was given what has, by now, become a familiar rejoinder: that there is no such thing as "class" anymore, especially not in the United States. A recent collection that deals with some of these issues is Matt Wray and Annalee Newitz, *White Trash: Race and Class in America* (London: Routledge, 1997).

30 On the state of philosophy as an academic discipline in the United States, the recent essays in a special issue of *Daedalus*, "American Academic Culture in Transformation: Fifty Years, Four Disciplines," are quite interesting. See Hilary Putnam, "A Half Century of Philosophy, Viewed From Within," and Alexander Nehamas, "Trends in Recent American Philosophy," in *Daedalus*, vol. 126, no. 1 (winter 1997), pp. 175–208, 209–23. The Putnam essay demonstrates all too well the narrowness of some analytic philosophy; indeed, the strange thing is that Putnam reads the last fifty years of philosophy in the United States (and English-speaking world) as the last however many years of what he has been doing at a few elite schools. Furthermore, Putnam basically sees "Continental philosophy" in the US as a non-starter. Nehamas makes the significant observation that, whatever meager "canon" was once central to the work of most analytic philosophers (with "Frege" being considered, only half-jokingly, "ancient philosophy"), has now fallen away. That is, analytic philosophy has splintered into many, mostly unrelated, subfields. (These are built around what I would call "microproblems.") Therefore, the "common cause" defended by many analytic philosophers against non-analytic philosophy (and, I daresay, even anything within analytic philosophy that reaches out toward larger issues, as with analytic forms of feminism and Marxism) has increasingly to do with little more than the defense of undefined terms such as "rigor." On this point Nehamas is also insightful.

31 Micaela di Leonardo, "Patterns of Culture Wars," *The Nation*, vol. 262, no. 14 (April 8, 1996), pp. 25–9. A major part of di Leonardo's aim, which I haven't gone into in this essay, is to show how cultural anthropology, especially that of Boas, Mead, Benedict, Herskovits, and more recent figures, has been used as a whipping boy in the "critique" of "cultural relativism." I use the first term in scare-quotes because the right-wing polemicists discussed by di Leonardo do not offer much in the way of argument, and the latter term because (1) it is not clear that the issue of "cultural relativism" has been framed very well by these polemicists, and (2) it is very clear that these polemicists, especially the more "Victorian" and Anglophile of them, are about as culturally relativistic as one can get.

32 I want to note, incidentally, that some uses of the term "redneck" are one way to put down part of the working class without having to confront the issue directly.

33 Perhaps it was in anxiety over the present status of the permanent things that His Royal Highness Charles, Prince of Wales, was overheard on his car phone telling Camilla Parker-Bowles that he had fantasies of being a used tampon, swirling in the toilet bowl but never actually making it down. A more complete semiotics of this startling image will have to await another day.

34 "Abdul-Rauf Collides with NBA Forced Patriotism," *Revolutionary Worker* newspaper, March 24, 1996, p. 4.

35 I want to emphasize that I do not take this issue lightly. While it is true that being kept out of the academy doesn't seem to rank highly on the list of forms of oppression, it is also the case that, for a philosopher, literary scholar, historian, etc., the options for someone who does not secure a position in the academy are not so great. The main bail-out option seems to be to go to law school. I do not mean to be snide here, but the idea of taking this option simply because one has acquired certain skills that will also serve in that context does not appeal to me – and, I have to wonder if law school and lawyering are attractive as the fall-back because of a class instinct that tells many would-be academics that, after all, one must have a respectable career. But then, what are the other options? Most of them, from management positions to manual labor, entail giving up the intellectual life (and this is mostly the case with lawyering as well). Mary Wollstonecraft argued that the confinement of women to the "private sphere" amounted to "civil death"; I do not think it is stretching things too much to coin an analogous term, "intellectual death." So, again, I think it is wrong, insensitive, and hurtful – and destructive – to sneer or laugh at these frustrations.

36 Incidentally, and speaking as a large person, this rhetorical turn is similar to the way that, if a person who is not very bright is also fat, then they are a "fat idiot." As much as it may be tempting to say this sort of thing about Rush Limbaugh, I don't think it is a good thing.

37 Patricia Williams, "The Death of the Profane" in *The Alchemy of Race and Rights: Diary of a Law Professor* (Cambridge, Mass.: Harvard University Press, 1991), pp. 44–51.

38 The idea of "going neuromancer" refers to William Gibson's 1984 novel and
    its sequels (*Count Zero, Mona Lisa Overdrive*). "Going *Neuromancer*" is
    also the title of the Introduction to my *Poltics in the Impasse* (see note 1),
    where I discuss recent transformations in capitalism and the relation of
    Marxism to these transformations.

39 For the other side of *Neuromancer*, and a frighteningly realistic picture of
    where postmodern capitalism is most likely really going, I very much recom-
    mend Octavia Butler's 1993 novel, *Parable of the Sower* (New York: Four
    Walls Eight Windows). And, while I am playing science fiction utopias and
    dystopias off of one another, I might as well close by mentioning a novel that
    brings together both a dystopia not unlike Butler's, but also an articulated
    picture of what a global community of many cultures might look like, namely
    Marge Piercy's *Woman on the Edge of Time* (New York: Fawcett Crest,
    1976). Although Marxism, as immanent critique, has to work from the
    materials we find in the present, there is a great deal that might be learned by
    grappling with the outlines of the community presented in this novel and
    attempting to work backwards from that picture.

7

Post-Marxist Political Economy and the Culture of the Left

Donald C. Hodges

From the founding of the International Workingmen's Association in 1864 to the launching of President Lyndon B. Johnson's "Great Society" in 1964, it was taken for granted by socialists that Marxist political economy served as foundation for the culture of the Left. In the nineteenth century socialist ideology challenged the established social and economic order, but times have changed and Marxism no longer stands in the same adversarial role. Socialist culture is committed to the same demoliberal values, to the same credo of humanism and progress as the Liberal Establishment, except for a socialist addendum. If not entirely integrated into the cultural mainstream, it is at least a major side-current. In the course of championing the "working class," it gives first place not only to productive workers, but increasingly to members of the liberal professions converted by the bourgeoisie into its paid wage-laborers. Says British economist Joan Robinson about this change of face: "Marxism, in its original form (like Christianity), had the appeal of the cause of the under-dog. As with Christianity, the wheel of time has brought it to be a creed for top dogs."[1]

Relying on Marxist political economy, the culture of the Left has a vested interest in the media's depiction of the prevailing economic order as capitalist. By this witting or unwitting device, it deflects the arrows of criticism onto the heads of the bourgeoisie. Capitalists are the "big fishes," the "goons" and "hucksters," by comparison to which professional people with their modest incomes count as "small fry." The single most important contribution of post-Marxist political economy is to have exposed this lie.

The culture of the Left is supposedly liberating rather than repressive. *The Manifesto of the Communist Party* (1848) described it as the adjunct of an anti-capitalist revolution committed to the most radical rupture with traditional property relations and therefore to "the most radical rupture with traditional ideas." Notwithstanding the advent of cosmopolitanism and multiculturalism along with freedom of conscience, expression, and other products of the liberal imagination, "one fact is common to all past ages, *viz.*, the exploitation of one part of society by the other." This fact conditions all the others, declares the *Manifesto*, with the result that the "ruling ideas of each age have ever been the ideas of its ruling class."[2]

The irony is that this implicit indictment of humanism (an aristocratic value), progress and freedom (bourgeois values), and democracy (a petty-bourgeois value) is passed over by socialists who pride themselves on being part of the mainstream of Western culture. As Lenin extolled this culture of the Left, "there is nothing resembling 'sectarianism' in Marxism, in the sense of . . . a doctrine which arose *away from* the highroad of development of world civilization." Lenin was right in depicting Marxism as the "immediate *continuation* of the teachings of the greatest representatives of . . . political economy and socialism."[3] But then Marx must have been mistaken in describing socialist culture as discontinuous with the mainstream of Western civilization.

I turn, then, to post-Marxist political economy to expose this ambivalence, preliminary to unmasking the multiculturalism of the Left as a hypocritical and repressive ideology.

1 Post-Marxist Political Economy

It may come as a surprise that post-Marxist political economy antedates neo-Marxist political economy by several decades. A going concern while Marx was still alive, it represented a major challenge to his scenario of socialism and to his strategy for labor. Marx was also hard-pressed to prevent the new heresy from spreading.

Traceable to Bakunin's *Statism and Anarchy* (1873) and its first theoretical development by his Polish disciple, Waclaw Machajski's *The Intellectual Worker* (1898), post-Marxist political economy' exhibits two main shoots. The first runs from Machajski through his Austrian follower and principal disseminator Max Nomad, in a rash of books that includes *Rebels and Renegades* (1931) and *Apostles of Revolution* (1933), "Masters – Old and New" and a translation of excerpts from *The Intellectual Worker* published in V. F. Calverton's *The Making of Society* (1937), followed by biographical sketches of his hero in *Aspects of Revolt* (1959) and *Dreamers, Dynamiters and Demagogues* (1964). The other stem runs from Machajski through Trotsky's *The Revolution Betrayed* (1936) and Bruno Rizzi's *The Bureaucratization of the World* (1939). In 1941 these shoots blossomed simultaneously in a bestseller, James Burnham's *Managerial Revolution*, followed in 1973 by Daniel Bell's *The Coming of Post-Industrial Society*, likewise deeply indebted to both. This double indebtedness also defines my own *Bureaucratization of Socialism* (1981) and *America's New Economic Order* (1996).[4]

How is post-Marxist political economy different from Marxist and neo-Marxist political economy? Unlike the latter, that target only capitalism, post-Marxist political economy targets both capitalism and socialism. Although differing over how to label the new order and whether to trash or salvage Marx's labor theory of value, post-Marxist political economists are critical of the following. First, they underscore Marx's confusion between a political economy of labor and a political economy of the working class, a "class" that includes a new crop of exploiters consisting of professional workers. Second, they fault neo-Marxist efforts to update and extend the application of Marx's theory of nineteenth-century capitalism to cover the emergence of a new economic order. Third, they dispute the neo-Marxist conflation of the basic features of the new order and those of so-called monopoly capitalism. So why call them Marxists? Because from *Capital* they take Marx's neo-Machiavellian method of unmasking appearances and penetrating to the reality underlying market phenomena. They are Marxists owing to their anatomy of bureaucratic exploitation, a supplement to Marx's anatomy of capitalist exploitation.

Post-Marxist political economy starts from the premise that, just as liberals were unnecessary to the emergence of capitalism, so socialism does not depend for its existence on socialists. In each case, economic changes and economic agents accounted for the transition from an old to a new economic order. Capitalism arose through the agency of capitalists whose wealth-creating powers had no rivals. Socialism came about not only through extensive nationalization, state planning agencies, and the managers of state enterprises and collectives, but also through the tendency of big enterprise to socialize itself, as in the case of the modern corporation. It suffices that ownership be quasi-public and separated from management for control by stockholders to become the exception rather than the rule. Contrary to socialist expectations, tax-subsidized state and municipal enterprises in the industrially advanced countries of the West have performed a marginal rather than central role in furthering the new order.

Although socialism first emerged through the agency of a political party, it is a mistake to identify the Soviet Union, its satellites in Eastern Europe and spin-offs throughout the Third World, as the socialist mainstream. Initially a side-current on the periphery of world capitalism, today the mainstream flows through the advanced metropolises of Western Europe, America, and Japan – just as Marx predicted. As events unfolded, the Marxist–Leninist parties that played a vanguard role in launching the new order proved superfluous, indeed a hindrance to its further development. The professional–managerial class in Russia and Eastern Europe currently rules without them, albeit with a revived but marginal capitalist sector corresponding to that in the West. So socialism without socialists has become the rule almost everywhere, except for that handful of exceptions represented by China, North Korea, Vietnam, and Cuba. Socialism? Yes! A new deal for labor? No!

So the time has come to dissociate socialism from the labor movement. All that is required for the transition to socialism can be summed up under two conditions: first, that capitalists be displaced from positions of influence, which is to say that the professional–managerial class must be in the driver's seat; second, that it must become the principal beneficiary of the economic surplus through preferential treatment in distribution. Although socialism does not turn mainly on distribution, as Marx pointed out, a change in the social relations of production in time results in a redistribution of surplus income.

The principal commentators on the American economic scene have long concurred that capitalists are in the rumble seat and that the private sector plays second fiddle to the quasi-public or corporate sector. I need only mention the seminal works of Adolf Berle and Gardiner Means, James Burnham, Peter Drucker, Daniel Bell, David Bazelon, Alvin Gouldner, and John Kenneth Galbraith. As Galbraith notes in the revised second edition of his *New Industrial State* (1971), "The managerial revolution – the assumption of power by top management – is conceded."[5]

What has not been conceded is the second condition. So the thorny question becomes if and when the disguised surplus in the wages of managers and professionals exceeds the total income of capitalists in America. That depends on two factors: that the total surplus concealed in wages exceeds capital income, which in turn depends on total employee compensation catching up to and surpassing capital income. Until total employee compensation exceeds the net returns to capital, until the surplus concealed in wages in turn exceeds capital's share, and until the bureaucracy's share of surplus wages exceeds net income from privately owned firms plus corporate dividends, interest, and rent, the threshold will not have been crossed to post-capitalist society.

For this purpose the following ratios must be calculated: first, the W/P ratio, where W represents total wages and related employee compensation, and P represents capital income or the distribution of profit in its various forms; second, the S/P ratio, where S represents surplus wages in excess of the technically established cost as distinct from price of skills and professional expertise; third, the E/P ratio, where E represents the share in surplus wages of the professional–managerial class, the price of its expertise.

Calculating the W/P ratio poses no problems. The annually published data in the *Statistical Abstract of the United States* compiled by the Bureau of the Census has tables covering both capital income and total employee compensation.

Calculating the S/P ratio is not at all easy and requires a formula for calculating surplus wages. As the difference between the price and cost of the various grades of manpower, surplus wages are a function of three principal variables: first, total wages (W); second, the cost of subsistence as measured by the minimum wage during any given year (M); third, the number of wage-earners in full-time equivalents (N).[6] Thus:

$$S = W - MN$$

But haven't I forgotten a fourth variable, the cost of training and education? Since its cost is bound to exceed what is necessary to subsistence, the corresponding skills and expertise can only be purchased with an already existing surplus, whether capital income or surplus wages. By definition, surplus income is unearned income, so that any additional income acquired by means of it is in turn gratuitous.

In effect, all the skills and expertise in the world are the fruit of other people's labor, including the labor spent on acquiring them! If a full workload is required for subsistence, then the additional hours of study required for a college education, not to mention the cost of tuition, are beyond reach for the vast majority of ordinary mortals. It becomes a superhuman task. So somebody else has to foot the bill to enable students to become industrially exempt and to pursue a college degree. Since the end result costs the student nothing, the price of education boils down to what economists call a "false cost." For this reason it can be ignored.

But suppose we give the Devil his due by including it! Calculated like the price of a computer, not in a machine but in the head, the cost of highly qualified brainpower turns out to be statistically insignificant. Assuming that differences in skill are due almost entirely to differences in training costs, even neo-Marxist economists concede that brainpower functions as

constant capital. "If p hours is his [the brain-worker's] expected productive life, and t hours of surplus labor have been expended upon him
and by him during the training period, then when he starts work each hour
of his labor will count (for the purpose of estimating the value of the
commodity he produces) as $1 + t / p$ hours of simple labor." Suppose that
his productive life is 100,000 hours and that the equivalent of 50,000
hours of simple labor went into his training, "then each hour of his labor
will count as one and one half hours of simple labor" – not 50 or 100 times
but a modest one and a half times.[7]

But pause a moment for reflection. Is it credible that half of a worker's
productive life has been spent on his or her education? What kind of
superdegree, super-Ph.D., costs that much? Isn't this another example of
neo-Marxist apologetics? Given a standard work-week of 40 hours for 50
weeks, leaving two weeks for annual vacations, a standard year's workload comes to 2,000 hours. That means that 50,000 hours in acquiring a
specialized skill represents 25 years of fulltime work.

So take a more credible figure of 8,000 hours at the upper limit,
representing four full years of study, the equivalent of eight academic
years of four semesters each, where each semester counts as twelve and a
half weeks of fulltime study. Consequently, when the recipient of a Ph.D.
starts work each hour will count as $1 + 8,000t/100,000p$, or one and one
twelfth hours at most, or one hour and five minutes. Taking the minimum
wage in 1995 as $8,500, the annual cost of an amortized Ph.D. would call
for a wage supplement of one-twelfth that amount, or in round figures
$710 per annum. There you have it! The prorated cost of America's most
qualified brainpower in 1995 was $9,210, not $92,100 for high-paid
professionals, not $921,000 for high-paid managers, much less
$9,210,000 for the top CEOs in America.

These obstacles to calculating the S/P ratio having been overcome, one
can turn to the appropriate tables in the *Statistical Abstract* covering
employment, the minimum wage, and employee compensation to determine if and when the bulk of surplus income began taking the form of
surplus wages instead of capital income.

The final step is to ask if and when brain-workers acquired the lion's
share of the surplus. The basic factors for determining it are, first, the
proportion of brain-workers or educated workers in the total work force;
second, the average paycheck, since above – average paychecks for expert
services (professional–managerial class) are effectively subsidized by
below-average paychecks for ordinary workers (laboring class); third,
their relative shares of surplus wages.

Turning to the *Statistical Abstract's* tables on national income and the schooling of the work force, we discover that the threshold to a new order first came into view in 1955 when the S/P ratio rose to 184 percent, after which it was definitely surpassed in 1965 when the ratio increased to 207 percent. Considering the huge increase of brainpower in the workforce since World War II, it is a safe guess that in 1955 the E/P ratio first cleared 100 percent.[8] The wage surplus that year was $136 billion with capital income at $74 billion.[9] So, if labor's share was approximately half that of the professional–managerial class, the latter's share would have been $90 billion.

2 The Culture of the Left

Post-Marxist political economy takes for guidelines Marx's criteria for distinguishing different economic orders and Lenin's distinction between the socialist and the labor movements. For Marx, the "specific economic form, in which unpaid surplus – labor is pumped out of the direct producers ... reveals the innermost secret, the hidden basis of the entire social structure" – the relationship of rulers and ruled. So, if one disputes Marx's claim of socialist exceptionalism, then socialism will be comparable to past economic orders in replacing old exploitative relations of production with new, more efficient and productive ones.[10]

So conceived, socialism corresponds to a political movement that looks to a different class than exploited workers for leadership. As Lenin noted, citing Karl Kautsky, "socialism and the class struggle arose side by side and not one out of the other." Socialist production depends on scientific planning, not on class struggle. Since the "vehicle of science is not the proletariat, but the *bourgeois intelligentsia* ... socialist consciousness is something introduced into the proletarian class from without." From the context it is clear that by "class struggle" Lenin meant the struggle between labor and capital, that by "bourgeois intelligentsia" he meant what post-Marxists identify as the class of professional or educated workers, and that by "proletariat" Lenin understood the victims of "capitalist-created poverty and misery" and not the privileged members of Marx's so-called "working class."[11]

In effect, Lenin disputed Marx's claim that only the proletariat can emancipate itself, but in his and not Marx's sense of "proletariat." Otherwise, why would labor have need of a revolutionary vanguard from another class? Beware of gifts! They are designed to benefit the giver, not just the receiver.

There is but a short step from Lenin's challenge to another challenge to

Marx's conception of the transition to socialism. Wrote Marx in 1864: "The struggle for the emancipation of the working classes means not a struggle for class privileges and monopolies, but for . . . the abolition of all class rule." But that is only because his vaunted emancipation of educated as well as uneducated workers focused for political purposes on the "emancipation of labor."[12] Emancipation from capitalism – yes! But is that the alpha and omega of labor's emancipation?

There used to be a culture of labor in America, but it has since been absorbed by the culture of the working class. Let there be no confusion on this score: "working class" is not synonymous with "labor." Like the overly celebrated "people" or Third Estate in 1792, the "working class" is tantamount to a Fourth Estate that includes more than a single class. Today, an exploiting proletariat consisting of a professional–managerial class and a petty–bureaucratic class coexist with an exploited proletariat as if they belonged to the same family. In fact, the ideologies that serve them are at loggerheads. Communism speaks for labor; the Left, for the hybrid "working class." In America the principal bearer of a culture of labor were the flaming "Wobblies" through their One Big Union, the Industrial Workers of the World (IWW). Understandably, they were suspicious of the Socialist Party, and subsequently of its left-wing reorganized as the nominally Communist Party. For both set their sights on the conquest of the state.[13]

Since the culture of the Left has been bypassed in the course of socialism creeping into power, it can no longer pose as revolutionary. At most, it might contribute to a few modest reforms, which is to say that its role has been reduced to patching up holes in the fabric of actually existing socialism. On whose behalf? Reforms will only make socialism stronger, whereas labor's interest is to demolish it altogether. A new class struggle is germinating, but will it ever get off the ground? Unlike the struggle between capitalism and socialism, the odds are against it.

Supposedly, multiculturalism is a liberating ideology. It is designed to establish a truce between culture-killers ("I won't hurt you, if you won't hurt me"). But applied to weak as well as strong cultures, it loses its *raison d'être*. Why is that? Because weak parties that defy the Establishment can be stamped out without the stronger parties having to fear retaliation.

Although in principle multiculturalism is a safeguard for weak cultures, is there anything like institutional support for those that are subversive? The absence of formal censorship is no barrier to informal intimidation and suppression. Survival in the academy depends on self-censorship for anyone who strays beyond the respectable Center and its Left and Right margins. Beyond the pale are the ultras at the nether extremities of the cultural bell curve. Because ideological extremists are uniculturalists in practice as well as theory, they are the declared enemies not only of one another, but also of the cultural Establishments. So there is a deliberate campaign to stifle them – in the name of multiculturalism.

This brings me to the main purpose of this essay, the bearing of post Marxist political economy on the culture of the Left. On the grounds that capitalism has given way to post-capitalist society under a variety of different names, whether "managerial," "post-industrial," "post-business," or the "information society," post-Marxists take as their fundamental enemy the culture of the Left. Socialist culture is targeted for a series of egregious errors: economic, political, and philosophical.

Economically, the culture of the Left is faulted for not penetrating to the heart of socialism and for ignoring its principal economic agents in the West. It assumes that the "private sector" includes the corporations, that these are the most developed forms of capitalist enterprise, and that only nationalized industry, – state and municipal property, and cooperatives qualify as socialist. This suggests that the American economy is still predominantly capitalist and that capitalism is labor's "fundamental enemy." The Left hails Marxist theory and the labor theory of value in particular as the principal theoretical expressions of labor's struggle against exploitation in its diverse open and concealed forms. And it has the gall to declare that socialism abolishes exploitation in its entirety.

Politically, the culture of the Left assumes that liberalism with its rights and duties of man and the citizen, its checks and balances against the arbitrary use of power, its system of judicial protection against arbitrary arrest and trial by jury, and its defense of constitutional government, due process, and the rule of law is a legacy that benefits labor as much as any other social class. As for democracy or majority rule, it claims that socialism is impossible without it, and that industrial democracy or workers' self-management is preeminently in labor's interests.

Philosophically, the culture of the Left takes humanism as its starting point, the doctrine that man is the measure of all things. It believes in individual perfectibility through self-cultivation and endorses it as the highest goal. To this it adds a commitment to social progress, the doctrine of historical perfectibility. But does a rising tide raise all boats? Although there would have been no error in associating these legacies with the outlook of educated workers, it is presumptuous to make them representative of labor's interests.

These errors are rooted in Marx and Engels's various writings. Marx never relinquished his youthful liberalism, repeatedly confirmed his commitment to democracy, and defined socialism as the heir both of

Renaissance humanism and the Enlightenment doctrine of progress.

Consider the constellation of values known as progressive humanism. "In place of the old bourgeois society ... we shall have an association, in which the free development of each is the condition for the free development of all." Since man is the crown of creation, down with asceticism and the setting of limits on human wants! The *Manifesto's* objection to pre-Marxist communism is that it "inculcated universal asceticism and social levelling in its crudest form." As Marx laid the ground for progressive humanism in his "Economic and Philosophic Manuscripts," the prospect exists of replacing the culture of poverty with the cult of "the *rich human being* and rich *human* need ... the human being *in need of* a totality of human life-activities." Thus, the ultimate goal of socialism is not the abolition of exploitation, it is "the multiplication of needs and of the means of their satisfaction."[14] In defense of capitalism, wrote Engels, "this social system has been necessary to develop the productive forces of society to a level which will make it possible for *all* members of society to develop equally in a manner *worthy of human beings*."[15] But since this means leveling upward instead of downward, equality under conditions of poverty is sacrificed for a humanist pie to be shared only in the by-and-by.

The irony is that progressive humanism is a doctrine of social uplift to a plane so high that it eludes the working stiff. The idyllic picture of horny-handed laborers raised to become well-rounded gentlemen free to do anything that takes their fancy harkens back to the Renaissance mirror of princes literature and its ideal of the complete man. Invoked as a cure for labor's ailments, it is simply ludicrous. As Marx and Engels fleshed out this incongruous spectacle of a Mister Drudge Forlyfe, Esquire,

> in communist [read: socialist] society, where nobody has one exclusive sphere of activity but each can become accomplished in any branch he wishes, society ... makes it possible for me to do one thing today and another tomorrow, to hunt in the morning, fish in the afternoon, rear cattle in the evening [like a landowner], criticize after dinner, just as I have a mind!"[16]

Industrial progress will supposedly make this dream come true. Against the "Reactionists" who look backward to the Middle Ages, says the *Manifesto*, socialists take up the cause of the bourgeoisie which, during its rule of scarcely one hundred years, "has accomplished wonders far surpassing Egyptian pyramids, Roman aqueducts, and Gothic cathedrals ... has created more massive and more colossal productive forces than have all preceding generations together." To it we owe not only the progress of industry, but also the "dissolution of old ideas [that] keeps even pace with the dissolution of the old conditions of existence." To this the *Manifesto* adds the progress of political institutions and of intellectual production that "changes its character in proportion as material production is changed."[17] From this Marx concludes that in broad outlines "Asiatic, ancient, feudal, and modern bourgeois modes of production can be designated as *progressive epochs* in the economic formation of society."[18]

Marx never revealed the source of his belief in progress, a bourgeois ideology traceable to Turgot and Condorcet. In 1750 Turgot wrote: "Considered since its origin, mankind appears to the eyes of the philosopher as an immense entity that, like each individual, has *its childhood and its progressive growth*." In rescuing Turgot's unfinished work, Condorcet described not only the progress of industry, but also the "progress of the human mind."[19] In his *Historical Sketch of the Progress of the Human Mind* (1795) he argues that progress occurs in all fields, that the perfectibility of society corresponds to the perfectibility of the individual, that history is unilinear rather than cyclical, and that the future can be predicted. All of these themes would eventually find a place in Marx's writings.

Like humanism, progressivism is supposedly an emancipatory ideology. But when history is interpreted as progressive, the ruling class can appeal to it for legitimacy. The idea of progress has fostered a sense of social coherence that blankets the class struggle between labor and its enemies. It encourages a mistaken sense of optimism and hope in a final solution to the social question. It keeps labor forever wagging the tail of its social betters in the vain hope that making the pie bigger will eventually provide relief for everyone. Wrote Sorel, "the idea of progress is essentially a conservative force in society."[20] That is because it provides a place in the sun for a new ruling class while leaving the underlying population to rot in the dark.

The politics associated with progressive humanism begins with liberalism. Arising in response to monarchical absolutism and the divine right of kings, liberalism became a safeguard against the "tyranny" of irresponsible majorities. The division of powers among the executive, legislative, and judicial branches of government, supplemented by a Bill of Rights, were designed to protect human freedom under conditions of a nascent bourgeois society in which the right to property occupied center stage.

Why, then, did Marx at the age of twenty-four become an ardent liberal and remain one for the rest of his life? His first articles on politics defended not property rights, but freedom of the press. In hundreds of pages he inveighed against "pseudo-liberalism" and "cautious liberalism" for playing into the hands of censors. His main complaint against "illiberal liberals" was that they made freedom of the press ancillary to other freedoms. They feared the "*popular* character" of liberalism, which is why Marx supported it as a springboard to revolution.[21]

In England, the birthplace of liberalism, the much-vaunted rights of the citizen to freedom of the press, of association, and trial by jury were mainly "show." According to Engels, their pretense of equality under the law had a "legal foundation [that] denies and abuses this foundation," to the benefit of people of property. The English Constitution "is nothing but a big lie which is constantly supported and concealed by a number of smaller lies." Short of full democracy, he concluded, liberalism is a sham.[22]

So Marx and Engels were liberals with one big exception, the untrammeled right to property. Since this right implies freedom to buy and sell at will, they also questioned its place in a bill of rights. Above all, they impugned the freedom of capital to exploit human labor, while laborers were free for firing as well as hiring. So it is not freedom but only bourgeois freedom that is targeted in the *Manifesto*. Individually acquired property is not the enemy, but only its "power to subjugate the labor of others," its transformation into capital."[23]

Marx was not critical enough. Besides the sacred right to property, liberals pay homage to constitutional government and the rule of law, which effectively stymie any action that does not heed the responsible voice of past and present law-makers. Gridlock is the result of the liberal's due process in which intellectual free trade, as in the workaday world, favors the vested interests. Although hospitality to a plurality of ideas ensures a hearing for almost everyone, to what avail against the prevailing ideologies of ruling and potentially ruling classes? The time-consuming task of deliberating, discussing, arguing, mediating, adjusting, and fitting together disparate interests, values, rights, and obligations spells disaster for working stiffs, whose numbers are reduced to one in the senate of representative cultures. Overwhelmed by adversaries ganged up against them, how can anyone credibly claim that labor has a stake in civil liberties designed to benefit a ruling class?

Civil liberties would never have been granted to the underlying population had there been some foreseen or imminent danger of them upsetting the Establishment. In bringing festering grievances into the open, free speech and association are safeguards against conspiracies and violence. As safety-valves that let off steam, they conduce to taming the labor force.

In the liberal credo, the government's first duty is to preserve peace and to enforce contracts, from which it follows that it is better for workers to be organized into trade unions where they can be controlled by their officers.

Turning next to the democratic myth of popular sovereignty, we might ask why working stiffs got the right to vote. The history of the franchise reveals its hidden purpose in "lowering" it by making it universal. In the state constitutions established during the Revolution, voting was limited to property owners and taxpayers. But the new states admitted into the Union made voting dependent only on residence of six months or a year. The purpose was to attract settlers. In response, the Eastern states lowered the suffrage partly to check the exodus to the West. Unlike the populated towns of the seaboard states, where property less wage-laborers were looked upon as a dangerous influence, on the other side of the Appalachians the small homestead prevailed, farm hands representing an insignificant minority. By a quirk of fate the suffrage was extended to white adult males before organized labor appeared on the scene and, once conceded, it was not easy to take away.

In the East the pressure of trade unions demanding a voice in the government became so unsettling that it resulted in concessions. There, the lowering of the franchise came about roughly the same way as in England. The second Reform Bill of 1867 doubled the electorate by extending it to the entire male working class except for farm hands, domestic servants, soldiers, sailors, and a few odd others. It passed because of a Tory scheme to retain power by courting the labor vote.

The Bill passed because Liberals in the House of Commons had their own scheme for wooing working stiffs. Labor not only voted the Liberal ticket, but also chose exclusively bourgeois candidates as representatives.[24] The Liberal parliamentarian Sir Austen Henry Layard argued that the respectable classes had nothing to fear from lowering the suffrage: first, because "there is no chance whatever that [workers] ... would be elected to Parliament in any sufficient number to affect the balance of classes in this House"; second, because the belief is entirely baseless "that but one set of opinions upon political and social questions exists amongst the working classes, and that they are at all times prepared to act and vote together"; third, because in the face of great public issues it was most improbable that workers might "put forward views and claims which were dangerous to the real interests of the other classes ... [and] be able to carry them in Parliament"; fourth, because "as you trust the working classes ... [demagogues] have less influence over them." Suck them in, he concluded, and "they will give you even greater proofs than they have hitherto given of the love they bear to the Throne, the institutions, and the greatness of their country!"[25]

Thanks to the respectable classes losing their fear of democracy, labor got hooked on the suffrage. As Bakunin aptly observed,

> the essential difference between a monarchy and a democratic republic is reduced to the following: in a monarchy the bureaucratic world oppresses and plunders the people for the greater benefit of the privileged propertied classes as well as for its own benefit, and all ... in the name of the monarch; in a republic the same bureaucracy will do exactly the same, but – in the name of the will of the people.

So is it any wonder that he ridiculed the "superstitious devotion ... to universal suffrage?"[26] Working stiffs are unable to use political democracy for their own ends, because they lack the material means necessary to mount political campaigns and the leisure for organizing them when forced to supply their most elementary needs.

Bakunin cites Proudhon concerning the first nation to endorse universal suffrage in 1848: "*Universal suffrage is counter-revolution* ... . The elections of 1848, in their great majority, were carried by priests, legitimists, partisans of monarchy, by the most reactionary and retrograde elements of France."[27] Little has changed since then, as is evident from the 1996 presidential elections in Russia, Spain, and Nicaragua where the socialist parties suffered defeat at the hands of nineteenth-century backward-looking liberals and conservatives. Although elections on the Continent have periodically returned the socialists to power, impregnated as they are with demoliberal values they have yet to treat their political rivals as enemies.

These are only a sampling of labor's arguments against liberalism and democracy. Not being exhaustive, they are not meant to be conclusive. But it is worth repeating that labor would hardly have been blessed with these insidious "rights" if there had been any danger of them being used against the respectable classes.

Little has changed in the mind-set of the Left since Marx's time. That it continues to parrot the same constellation of aristocratic, bourgeois, and petty-bourgeois values is evident from a random sampling of the various little magazines catering to socialist readers. There are only a few winds of change, notably from feminists and ecologists, and occasionally from left-wing socialists who still consider labor to be the flower of the proletariat.[28] But they continue to believe that Americans are living under capitalism. Ergo, capitalism is singled out as the main enemy.

The Left's mistakes concerning capitalism are compounded by its doctrinaire vision of socialism. Since capitalism is compatible with monarchical as well as liberal republican regimes, with direct military rule and fascist dictatorship, with regimented as well as unregulated economies, why not socialism as well? Despite all the efforts to update Marxism, pouring new wine into old bottles has not enabled socialists to keep pace with the times.

Notes

1 Joan Robinson, *Economic Philosophy* (London: C. A. Watts, 1962), p. 41.
2 Karl Marx and Friedrich Engels, *Manifesto of the Communist Party* in Robert C. Tucker (ed.), *The Marx–Engels Reader*, 2nd edn (New York and London: W. W. Norton, 1978), pp. 489–90. Henceforth cited as *MER*.
3 V. I. Lenin, "The Three Sources and Three Component Parts of Marxism" in Robert C. Tucker (ed.), *The Lenin Anthology* (New York and London: W. W. Norton, 1975), p. 640. Henceforth cited as *LA*.
4 For the intellectual pedigree of post-Marxist political economy see Donald C. Hodges, *America's New Economic Order* (Aldershot, UK and Brookfield, Vt: Avebury, 1996), pp. 165–71. Henceforth cited as *NEW*.
5 John Kenneth Galbraith, *The New Industrial State*, 2nd revd edn (Boston: Houghton Mifflin, 1971), p. 107.
6 Hodges, *NEW*, p. 57.
7 Ronald L. Meek, *Studies in the Labour Theory of Value* (New York: International Publishers, 1956), p. 172; and Paul M. Sweezy, *The Theory of Capitalist Development* (New York: Monthly Review Press, 1956), p. 43.
8 David Noble, "The PMC: A Critique" in Pat Walker (ed.) *Between Labor and Capital* (Boston: South End Press, 1979), pp. 123–4; and US Bureau of the Census, *Statistical Abstract of the United States: 1992* (Washington DC, 1993), Table 631.
9 Hodges, *NEW*, pp. 59, 66–7.
10 Karl Marx, *Capital*, 3 vols (Moscow: Foreign Languages Publishing House, 1960–2), vol. 3, p. 772.
11 V. I. Lenin, "What Is To Be Done? in *LA*, p. 28.
12 Karl Marx, "General Rules of the International Working Men's Association" in Karl Marx and Friedrich Engels, *Selected Works*, 2 vols (Moscow: Foreign Languages Publishing House, 1958), vol. 1, p. 386.
13 Fred Thompson, *The I.W.W.: Its First Fifty Years (1905–1955)* (Chicago: Industrial Workers of the World, 1955), pp. 26–8, 81–4, 135–8.
14 Marx and Engels, *Manifesto of the Communist Party* in *MER*, pp. 491, 497; and Karl Marx, "Economic and Philosophic Manuscripts" in *MER*, pp. 91, 95.
15 Friedrich Engels, "Marx's *Capital*" (March 21 and 28, 1868) in idem, *On Marx's "Capital"* (Moscow: Foreign Languages Publishing House, n.d.), p. 30.

16 Karl Marx and Friedrich Engels, "The German Ideology" in *MER*, p. 160.
17 Marx and Engels, *Manifesto of the Communist Party* in *MER*, pp. 476, 477, 481, 483, 489.
18 Karl Marx, "Preface" to *A Contribution to the Critique of Political Economy* in *MER*, p. 5; italics mine.
19 Georges Sorel, *The Illusions of Progress*, trans. John and Charlotte Stanley (Berkeley and Los Angeles: University of California Press, 1969), pp. 22, 23. Henceforth cited as *IP*.
20 John and Charlotte Stanley, "Translator's Introduction" in *IP*, p. xxiii.
21 Karl Marx, "Comments on the Latest Prussian Censorship Instruction" in Karl Marx and Friedrich Engels, *Collected Works*, 46 vols (New York: International Publishers, 1975–92), vol. 1, pp. 110, 115, 119 (henceforth cited as *CW*); and Karl Marx, "Proceedings of the Sixth Rhine Province Assembly" in *CW*, vol. 1, pp. 137, 143, 173–4.
22 Friedrich Engels, "The Condition of England. The English Constitution" in *CW* vol. 3, pp. 504–13.
23 Marx and Engels, *Manifesto of the Communist Party* in *MER*, pp. 485–6.
24 Walter Phelps Hall and William Stearns Davis, *The Course of Europe Since Waterloo*, 4th edn (New York: Appleton-Century-Crofts, 1957), pp. 218–19.
25 "A Minister Defends Extension of the Franchise" in Kenneth M. Setton and Henry R. Winkler (eds), *Great Problems in European Civilization* (New York: Prentice-Hall, 1954), pp. 439–43.
26 G. P. Maximoff (ed.), *The Political Philosophy of Bakunin: Scientific Anarchism* (Glencoe, Il: Free Press, 1953), pp. 211, 213. Henceforth cited as *PPB*.
27 *PPB*, p. 214.
28 See the symposium on David Schweickart's *Against Capitalism* (Cambridge University Press, 1993, and Westview Press, 1996) in *Radical Philosophy Review of Books*, 11 and 12 (fall 1995), pp. 1, 2, 7, 17, 24, 36, 38, 40. On the discordant voices, see pp. 32, 34, 35, 38, 40, 65.

Part III

Continental and Analytical Feminism

8

Identity, Difference, and Abjection

Kelly Oliver

Two fundamental questions underlying debates around mutliculturalism are "who are we?" and "what is our relationship to others?" Recent debates over curricula at secondary schools and universities have focused on the importance of including canonical texts from Western or European culture and from other cultures. In order to engage in the practical debates about which texts to assign in class, the participants in these debates must assume that they have some sense of what texts or characteristics constitute Western or European culture and the other cultures involved. In other words, they must have the sense that they can identify Western culture or other cultures. They presume answers to the first question, "who are we?" Debates over which cultures should be represented in core curricula, assume answers to the second question, "what is our relationship to others?" Some of the impasses in these debates are the result of conflicting presumptions about identity and relationships to difference.

Proponents of monocultural curricula often conflate difference and opposition. They see different cultural identities as competitors, opposed to each other, in a fight for dominance. On this view all difference is threatening because it always stands in an oppositional relationship to us. In addition, some proponents of monocultural curricula presuppose that identity can be stable, even self-contained, as long as it is protected from outside influences. What worries me about these kinds of presuppositions is that ultimately we are all different; and if difference is construed only as opposition, then cooperation, equality of opportunity, peaceful coexistence, and the possibility of love, are all threatened, if not impossible. But it is not just proponents of monoculturalism, but also proponents of multiculturalism who have been working with notions of identity that ultimately conflate difference and opposition.

In this essay I want to diagnose the danger of proposing, or presupposing, notions of identity that necessitate exclusion and hostility. In order to do so, I will take up the two questions "who are we?" and "what is our relationship to others?" These seemingly simple questions become more complicated if we consider that they are related; our identities are constituted through our relations with others. On the level of personal identity, these questions become "what is *my* own identity?" and "what is *my* relationship to others?" questions which are inherently related if my own identity is constituted through my relationships with others.

Various twentieth-century philosophers have developed theories of the self as interrelational. For example, Jean-Paul Sartre maintains that our sense of self comes through the accusing looks of others. Simone de Beauvoir claims that each of us is free only insofar as we are all free. Emmanuel Levinas describes subjectivity as a response to another. And many feminist theorists and theorists of oppression and marginalization have proposed that we develop our identities in relation to others. These theories take us back at least to the late eighteenth and nineteenth centuries, when different philosophers postulated notions of self-identity that were inherently interrelational. For example, John Stuart Mill described an individual's happiness as essentially connected to the happiness of all others. G. W. F. Hegel proposed that self-consciousness begins in the other's recognition of me. Friedrich Nietzsche described the way that the moral subject develops by defining itself against others and the external world. Sigmund Freud proposed that one's sense of one's self is constituted in an antagonistic relationship with one's parents, a relationship which he calls the Oedipal complex.

Freud describes an original identification with, and desire for, the mother which the Oedipal situation effectively splits. All infants both identify with, and desire, their mothers. For Freud, post-Oedipus, identification and desire lie at opposite poles. The boy discontinues his identification with his mother, identifies with his father, and desires a mother-substitute. The girl is forced to identify again with her mother, even after the betrayal of castration, and now desires her father. What the resolution of the Oedipal complex insures is that desire and identification are split. You desire what you are not and you identify with what you are. But, as I have argued elsewhere, Freud's description of the desire for the feminine is not a description of a desire for something that the masculine is not, but what the masculine negates and rejects in order to be. Freud's feminine is always defined within a masculine economy as castrated or phallic, which insures that man is *not* castrated.[1] It could be said, then, that Freud splits identification and desire, insists that he desire what he negates, the feminine, so that he can insure that he is himself masculine.

But isn't desire the excess of identification? Desire is not fueled by an identification that turns the other into the same, you into me. Rather, desire is fueled by an identification that turns the same into an other, that takes me beyond myself towards you. Desire does not say "you are like me so I want you," nor does it say "you are not like me so I can be sure that I am me"; rather, desire says "because you are not me, I can move out of myself towards you." Desire is the excess of the other in one's own identification. I can identify with your desire, but you and your experience are always in excess of that identification. Desire and identification are not polar opposites, neither are they the same. To say that there is no desire without identification is not to say that desire is the annihilation of difference. Rather, desire is the difference in excess of any identification.

One of the most influential accounts of desire and the relational nature of self-identity is Hegel's description of self-consciousness in *Phenomenology of Spirit*.[2] There, Hegel says that *the subject is desire*. The subject or self becomes a subject or self – that is, becomes self-conscious – as a result of a hostile struggle with another. In the famous Lordship and Bondage section of the *Phenomenology of Spirit*, Hegel describes self-consciousness as the recognition of oneself in the behavior and movements of another. We "see" ourselves for the first time in the mirror effect of seeing another like ourselves. But this experience is unsettling and alienating because we are seeing ourselves where we are not, in the place of another. So we struggle to regain our sense of ourselves from its dependence on this other who is not in our control. Thus, the struggle begins that pits my self-consciousness against the self-consciousness of another: if I am self-conscious, you cannot be; and if you are, I cannot be; so, we have to fight it out. For Hegel, ultimately Reason intervenes and the fight to the death does not take place.

Hegel was right that the subject is desire. But desire is not as he describes it. Desire is not the urge to overcome the otherness in the self and to recuperate oneself from the other. Subjectivity does not attempt to close in on itself and fortify itself against the other. Rather, subjectivity opens itself onto the other, multiplies itself but not in the sense of reproducing itself. Desire is the urge to move out into otherness. I do not define myself in relation to a hostile external world against which I am me by virtue of denying everything that I am not. Rather, I am *by virtue* of what I am not. I am by virtue of my engagement with what I am not. Without the difference, desire disappears. Yet it is not identification with the other that kills desire.

We need to rethink identification such that it is not opposed to differentiation. We need a notion of identification that can navigate between the two extremes that plague contemporary attempts to theorize difference: at the one pole, the position that I can understand anyone by just taking up their position, and at the other, that I can understand no one because of radical alterity which prevents me from taking up their position; at the one pole, communication is unencumbered and we simply say what we mean, and at the other, communication is impossible. The first assumes that we are absolutely identical, which erases our difference, and the second assumes that we are absolutely different, which erases our communion. I maintain that we can communicate or commune only because of our radical difference. This is the reason we do so. Communication across difference is not an attempt to master otherness. Identification, communication, communion, community, are possible only because of our differences. And, while there are wars, oppression, subjugation, hatred, and discrimination, these are not *necessary* to identification, either on the individual or group level.

Psychological identification or identity does not operate like logical identity. Identity within the psyche, conscious or unconscious, does not operate like the logical identity, A = A. Psychological identity is not equivalence. If I identify with someone this does not mean that I make them equivalent to myself. Rather, through the space between us, through our difference, I attempt to find common ground in that which is never the same, our different experiences. These attempts to commune are not part of a hostile Hegelian struggle to recuperate myself from my recognition of myself in you. I do not see myself in you and then try to annihilate the difference that separates us. Rather, I see our differences and try to move out of myself towards you in order to commune with that which ultimately I can never know. And it is through our relationship and our differences that I can begin to see something of myself. Theories that propose that identity is dependent on the exclusion of difference presuppose that one's sense of oneself needs to be contained, or is containable. But our experiences of ourselves are not like contained or containable fixed units. We experience our lives as flux and flow, full of surprises even to ourselves.

Contrary to Hegel, who maintains that desire is the attempt to overcome the otherness of the other, desire *disappears* when the self attempts to master the otherness of the other. When the self attempts to master the other in a struggle for recognition which ends in self-knowledge through reason which annihilates its own otherness, this is the death of desire and not its aim. In terms of relationships with others, the illusion that I know myself or that I know another person is an illusion of mastery that kills the possibility of desire. Desire requires a fluidity and openness of subjectivity that charges and electrifies the space between two people. To say that I know you, or that I know that you always behave like that, is to control you and turn you into something that you are not. And, when I am sure that I know you, I am no longer having a relationship with you, but only with myself. Relationships require identification across and through difference, identification that does not reduce the other to the same, identification as compassion and communion.

Still, neo-Hegelian theories that identity is constructed through the exclusion or abjection of the other are widespread. Following anthropologist Mary Douglas, Teresa Brennan, Judith Butler, and Julia Kristeva, for example, all propose such theories. In various ways, they all maintain that identity is possible only by abjecting the other. Their theories do not just propose that in order to have an identity we need to exclude some possibilities from our sense of ourselves, but that these exclusions are hostile and that which is excluded becomes abject and threatening to us. If we accept such theories, then relationships with those who are different from ourselves are possible only by turning them into something exactly like us, or experiencing them as a hostile threat, hating them and trying to kill them. While these theories can help *explain* war, oppression, subjugation, hatred, and discrimination, they also can *normalize* them. Within what I have elsewhere called a *virile economy*, identity comes through war; but the virile economy is not necessary or natural.[3] It serves particular ends for certain people. The notion that identity is constructed in hostile opposition also serves particular political purposes.

In *Purity and Danger*, Mary Douglas describes defilement as the danger to identity constituted by filth, which is always defined in relation to the borders of that very identity.[4] Douglas's theory of defilement has been transformed by Julia Kristeva into her neo-Hegelian theory of abjection, with which she purports to explain the dynamics of both group and individual identity as constituted through the rejection of otherness. In *Powers of Horror* and later in *Strangers to Ourselves*, Kristeva maintains that our identity and sense of self is built through a process of exclusion.[5] Our individual identity is formed through exclusions which become repressed in the unconscious in order to allow ego boundaries to form. Our national or group identity is formed through exclusions which become associated with rival groups or go unrecognized entirely, yet continue to operate as the basis for exclusion; these exclusions set up the border against which we define ourselves as nations or cultures.

Judith Butler expands the theory of abjection when she analyzes the dynamics of exclusion inherent in identification. In *Gender Trouble*, following Kristeva, Butler maintains that "The 'abject' designates that which has been expelled from the body, discharged as excrement, literally rendered 'Other'. This appears as an expulsion of alien elements, but the alien is effectively established through this expulsion. The construction of the "not-me" as abject establishes the boundaries of the body which are also the first contours of the subject."[6] In *Bodies that Matter* she extends her analysis of the exclusion inherent in identification when she describes materiality as delimited through a procedure which "marks a boundary that includes and excludes, that decides, as it were, what will and will not be the stuff of the object to which we refer. This marking off will have some normative force and, indeed, some violence, for it can construct only through erasing; it can bound a thing only through enforcing a certain criterion, a principle of selectivity."[7]

The theory of abjection is in the background of Teresa Brennan's notion of a foundational fantasy through which the subject both imitates and envies the original mother. In *History After Lacan*, Brennan describes the way in which the masculine ego recreates the world in its own image, which suppresses and distorts the powers of the mother and the powers of its environment, the earth. Brennan calls this recreation in its own image the "foundational fantasy" through which the ego annihilates heterogeneity in favor of more of itself in order to control its environment: "The subject is founded by a hallucinatory fantasy in which it conceives itself as the locus of active agency and the environment as passive; its subjectivity is secured by a projection onto the environment, apparently beginning with the mother, which makes her into an object which the subject in fantasy controls."[8] The subject's fantasies affect material reality and transform the environment, which he continues to cover over but not in ways that he controls.

Theories of abjection are useful in describing some of the oppressive logics of patriarchy, but abjection cannot be part of a theory of liberation. I reject any normative claims that Douglas's followers make for structures of identity based on abjection. Theories of abjection can diagnose the operations of oppression, but they do not in themselves suggest alternatives. In fact, if taken as standards for identification, theories of abjection normalize the most hateful and threatening kinds of discrimination, exclusion, and oppression. If our identities are necessarily formed by rejecting and excluding what is different, then discrimination is inherent in the process of identification.

On the level of individual identification, if self-identity is formed by rejecting what is different, in the first instance, as the story goes, the infant rejects its mother. If abjection of the mother or maternal body is described as a normal or natural part of child development, then one consequence is that without some antidote to this abjection, all of our images of mothers and maternal bodies are at some level abject because we all necessarily rejected our own mothers in order to become individuals. On the level of social identification, if group identity is formed by rejecting what is different, then war, hatred, and oppression are inevitable and unavoidable parts of social development.

If overcoming oppression or living together as persons is possible, we must reject normative notions of abjection. We can endorse theories of abjection as *descriptions* of the dynamics of oppression and exclusion without accepting that abjection is *necessary* to self-identity. If abjection is necessary to self-identity, then peace, cooperation, liberation, and equality become impossible dreams. If my ability to individuate *necessitates* that I hate and exclude you because you are different, then protecting the minimum conditions for my individuation, must threaten the minimum conditions for your own individuation. My argument is that the notion of identity based on abjection describes individuals as inherently antagonistic in the essence of their individuality and self-identity. Theories that normalize abjection leave us stuck at the level of Hegel's master–slave dialectic where a fight to the death is inevitable.

Although Drucilla Cornell does not develop an alternative notion of identity that leaves behind this Hegelian antagonism, she does propose a notion of equality that suggests the possibility of other ways of identifying as individuals and groups. In *The Imaginary Domain*, Cornell criticizes even liberal political theorists who assume that human beings are from the beginning persons with equal rights.[9] Instead, she maintains that becoming a person is a project that requires basic conditions of individuation, conditions which include primary care while one is a child, and self-respect, which is possible only if psychic space is free from social and legal restrictions on one's identity and personhood. Theories that assume personhood from the beginning devalue the labor of mothers in raising children, and ignore the difficulties involved in overcoming stereotypes that confine many of us in roles that define us as inferior, dependent, or incapable of the kind of individuation necessary to become a complete person. Degrading stereotypes of femininity, for example, affect our images of ourselves as women and undermine our self-respect, which is fundamental to the formation of personhood.

"We are degraded," says Cornell, "when our 'sex' is defined, symbolized and treated as antithetical to equal personhood and citizenship" (ibid., p. 10). When this happens, other peoples' images of us, or stereotypical images of us, are forced on us in ways that rob us of respect for our own sexuate being (ibid., p. 8). When our sex is treated as antithetical to personhood or citizenship, then we are in the impossible situation of choosing between being persons or citizens, *or* who we are as sexuate beings. Cornell concludes that public constraints on degradation, or downgrading on the basis of sex or sexuality, are legitimate and necessary to insure the prerequisite minimum conditions of individuation for the equivalent chance to become a person. On her analysis, the protection of these minimum conditions of individuation does not undermine freedom, but makes it possible (ibid., p. 20). Law should protect the equivalent chance to become a person for all sexuate beings.

Cornell's theory of equality suggests an alternative notion of identity in which one individual's ability to become a person is not opposed to another's. If every sexuate being can be guaranteed the minimum conditions of individuation to protect their equivalent chance to become a person, then one's self-identity and self-respect can and must be consistent with another's self-identity and self-respect. Although the content of their individuality may vary greatly – how each acts and behaves – their chance at individuation must be equal. This suggests that in principle we can form individual and group identities in harmony, at least on the level of the fundamental structure of identity, if never on the level of the content of identity.

With Brennan, Butler, and Kristeva, we could *diagnose* contemporary marginalization and exclusion *using* theories of identity that are built on abjection, but this type of identity is not the only type. There are other ways to construct one's identity, as an individual and a group, besides going to war. Goals that unite people aren't always the destruction of a common enemy. Identity can also be formed in loving relationships, in the spaces between us. Relationships with difference and otherness can give us new perspectives on ourselves; to say that we gain new perspectives on ourselves is not to say that difference is erased. Relationships bring us "out of ourselves" in order to give us a sense of ourselves, to "see" ourselves for the first time. It is only through our relationships that we become who we are.

We don't have a fixed identity that fends off any change by excluding all others and anything different. Rather, as Kristeva says, we are other to ourselves. Our otherness to ourselves comes through our relations with others who are different from us. This does not mean that we contain the other and that the other is really part of us, or the same (which is sometimes suggested in Kristeva's account); rather, through our encounters with others and their differences, we become other to ourselves and in the process become ourselves. Since our lives are social from their beginnings, we always experience this otherness as fundamental to our sense of self. The sociality through which we become individuated is not necessarily or only hostile and antagonistic. It is the otherness or difference inherent in social relations – the space between us – that makes love possible. Meaning is created in the space between social bodies.

Part of my own project has been to suggest alternatives to the traditional philosophical and psychoanalytic views of individuation and self-identity which are built around the exclusion of otherness and difference.[10] In particular, as an alternative to models of the mother–infant relationship that view the mother as an obstacle that must be overcome in order for the infant to become a social subject, I endorse a model of the mother–infant relationship that views the mother as the first cooperative partner in a social relationship that makes subjectivity possible. The reason why so many traditional theories of the mother–child relationship see the mother as an obstacle to autonomy is that motherhood and maternity are conceived in opposition to everything social and everything fundamental to civil society. Mothers have been imagined as creatures motivated only by instinct and natural tendencies.

Women have been reduced to their reproductive function, which is seen as a natural function, and thereby confined to a natural role. Men, on the other hand, can escape or sublimate their nature in order to perform higher functions. Freud defines civilization as the sublimation or repression of drives that women, because of their anatomy, cannot fully experience and therefore cannot sublimate.[11] In addition, he argues that civilization is the result of the repression or sublimation of aggressive drives, drives which are primarily related to the infant's relationship with the maternal body. For Freud, the infant can leave its dyadic dependence on the maternal body only through the agency of the father. The father threatens the child with castration if it does not leave its mother.

The move from nature to culture is a move from the mother to the father. It is motivated by the father's threats which are effective only if one has a penis. Culture, then, on Freud's account, is necessarily and by nature patriarchal. Yet it is nature that culture leaves behind. Because she is associated with nature, the mother must be left behind, killed off, in order for the child to become social. The mother is so unimportant to culture and the development of the psyche that Freud hardly mentions her. In his theory she is also left behind. Freud's theory of the Oedipus complex is a familiar story; it is a story of active men fighting over passive women.

In the twentieth century, French psychoanalyst Jacques Lacan and his followers have continued to promote theories that associate the mother with nature and the father with culture, theories that demand that proper development includes leaving the mother behind. For Lacan, the mother is associated with a realm of need and nature that is left behind as soon as the paternal agent intervenes and introduces the infant to language.[12] For the infant the mother is initially the satisfaction of its needs. In both Freud and Lacan's theories the separation between nature and culture is ultimately unbridgable.[13] The maternal body falls on one side of the abyss and the father and his law and language falls on the other. For Lacan, desire is the result of this gap. Language is always at odds with the maternal body; it is always nothing more than a frustrated attempt to articulate need (always associated with the maternal body), an impossible demand for love.

But what if we need to commune with other people? What if we need to be social? Then, perhaps, language does more than fail to articulate bodily drives or needs. Even assuming that it fails to communicate needs, perhaps language succeeds in forming communion between bodies. Language brings us together because it is an activity that we engage in with each other and not because it does or does not succeed in capturing or communicating something in particular. We keep talking not just because we can never say what we are trying to say – that is, what we need – but also because we need to be together through words. For Lacan, demands are always demands for love; and as demands, they can never succeed in getting us what we want. This view of the relationship between love and demand seems to presuppose that language is merely a feeble container for something else. Yet words are not just symbols that contain various conscious and unconscious significations; they are also part of a process of communicating, in the sense of communing, with each other. Language is not just something we use or something that uses us; rather, it is something we do, something that we do together.

Many of Freud's successors have challenged his Oedipal story with its silent mother and threatening father. Psychoanalysts and psychologists have been concerned with psychic dynamics that develop before the onset of language and the resolution of Freud's Oedipal complex or the onset of Lacan's mirror stage. Melanie Klein offered the first significant alternative to Freud's account of the infant's development. She focused on the pre-Oedipal stage of development in order to describe the ways in which the mother–child relationship was formative to the infant's development. Turning the focus from father to mother, Klein proposes that the infant's ego is developing almost from birth through its relationship with its mother's body, especially her breast.[14] Nursing becomes crucial in explaining the infant's psychic development.

Klein describes the infant as occupying a paranoid–schizoid position in relation to the maternal body.[15] This position is described as schizoid because the infant experiences the maternal body as part objects. It is paranoid because the infant assumes that some of these part objects have the same sadistic motivations that it has towards them. In this way, the infant splits the maternal body into good and bad parts. The fundamental split occurs between the good and bad breast. The good breast is the one that is freely given and satisfies hunger, the bad breast is the one withheld that leads to frustration.

On Klein's account, the infant moves into another position in relation to the maternal body when it realizes that its mother is whole and not a series of part objects. Klein calls this position the depressive position because once the infant realizes that its mother is whole and that both the good and bad are parts of one and the same mother, it feels guilty about wanting to destroy part of its mother. In this position, even though the infant has a sense of a whole object instead of parts objects, it doesn't have an image of its mother as separate from its father. Its identification of a whole is an identification of a combined mother–father, what Kristeva will call the imaginary father identified with Freud's father of individual prehistory. Klein, unlike Freud before her or Kristeva after her, associates the infant's recognition of wholeness with the mother and not the father.

Once the infant experiences the guilt associated with its fantasies of destroying the bad parts of the maternal body, it tries to make amends and engages in what Klein calls *reparation* through which it adopts a less sadistic and more loving relation to its mother. For Klein, *contra* Freud, the mother and the infant's fantasies about the mother play a fundamental role in psychic development. For Klein, even the super-ego, the mark of civilization, is developed through an incorporation of both mother and father (ibid., p. 409). For Klein, culture and language are not instituted through the father's castration threats, the importance of which are significantly diminished in her work, but through the introjection of the good and bad mother and father. The mother is not associated with anti-social nature; rather, the mother–infant relationship is the prototypical social relationship. In opposition to Freud's theory of penis envy in girls, Klein proposes a kind of womb envy in boys. She argues that the infants of both sexes are primarily feminine insofar as they are identified with the maternal body. The male's identification with the feminine leads to a femininity complex in the male because he lacks the powers of birth. He resents this lack and blames it on his mother, which gives rise to envy and hostility towards femininity. For Klein, it is the mother's and not the father's body that is associated with power and privilege.

Following Klein, D. W. Winnicott further emphasizes the mother–infant relationship, almost to the exclusion of all others. He maintains that the infant's subjectivity is formed in the mother–infant in which the infant experiences his mother as an extension of himself. The mother is a kind of mirror for the infant that allows him to organize his perceptions.[16] He develops a notion of the "good enough mother" who is responsible for the infant's ego development.[17] The good enough mother is one who is neither absent nor too invasive; she is the median between the extremes that will lead to problems in the infant's development.

Unlike Klein, who discusses the child's unconscious fantasies and images of its mother, Winnicott discusses the maternal environment and maternal responsibility. He moves from an analysis of psychic development centered in the infant to one centered in the mother. Finally, the mother is an active agent in mothering. Yet Winnicott's identification of maternal responsibility becomes the grounds for regulating the maternal environment. If mothers do indeed have as much control over the development of children as Winnicott proposed, then mothers must be watched, instructed, and chastised. While Winnicott's theories seem to empower the mother, they also gave rise to a whole genre of "how to" manuals for mothers.[18] Today, while mothers are rarely praised for producing healthy happy offspring, they are blamed for producing unhealthy or unhappy offspring.

Like Klein and Winnicott before him, John Bowlby also criticized Freud's theory that the mother–infant relationship is not social and must be interrupted by the social force of the paternal agent. By studying the effects of various amounts of attention that an infant receives in its psychological development, Bowlby concludes that social interaction is crucial to development.[19] The development of infants who were separated from adult caretakers and did not receive affection was hindered, while the development of infants who received social stimuli was enhanced. Daniel Stern confirms Bowlby's findings when his studies demonstrate the importance of touch and social contact for infant development. Stern maintains that the mother–infant relationship is social from its beginnings; that the infant is never one with its mother; and that the interaction between mother and infant is a complex social relationship that includes communication and preverbal exchanges of smiles, looks, sounds, and movements.[20]

Jessica Benjamin has continued to work to demonstrate that the primary relationship between mother and infant is already a social relationship. Following attachment theorists (e.g. Bowlby) and object relations theorists (Klein, Winnicott), Benjamin maintains that from the beginning infants are interested in the world and are not part of an anti-social mother–infant dyad. Infants naturally want independence and take pleasure in developing autonomy. They do not have to be pulled away from their mothers by paternal threats. Benjamin concludes that if "we believe that infants take pleasure in interpersonal connection and are motivated by curiosity and responsiveness to the outside world, we need not agree to the idea that human beings must be pulled by their fathers away from maternal bliss into a reality they resent." Benjamin also points out that real mothers work to help their children gain their independence rather than threaten the possibility of autonomy. In addition, it is usually the mother who sets limits for the child and inculcates "the social and moral values that make up the content of the young child's superego."[21] Rather than identify the super-ego solely with the father, Benjamin also identifies it with the mother. Usually, the child's sense of limits comes from its interactions with its mother because mothers are still primary caregivers in our culture. Contrary to the theories of Freud and Lacan, Benjamin maintains that law and regulation, the markers of civilization, come from the child's interactions with its mother.

While Benjamin calls this primary relationship between mother and infant an *intersubjective* relationship, in *Maternal Ethics and Other Slave Moralities* Cynthia Willett describes it as a type of subjectless sociality.[22] She argues that sociality can occur before the infant is a subject and thus before the onset of intersubjectivity (ibid., p. 18) and that this sociality is not linguistic but instead should be understood as more akin to music and dance (ibid., pp. 40, 47). Beginning in this social song and dance, the infant's self-recognition, or the separation of child from mother, is not egoistic but intersubjective. Willett says that an awareness of the face is fundamental to intersubjectivity and that infants respond to their care-taker's facial expressions with smiles at about two months of age (ibid., p. 27). Self-recognition is derived from this face-to-face play with parents.

Willett reinterprets Lacan's mirror stage as a derivation of earlier face-to-face play in which the infant encounters its own image and responds jubilantly, recalling the face-to-face play with its parents. While Lacan associates the mirror stage with the infant's frustration at the discrepancy

of seeing itself whole in the mirror and yet experiencing itself as frag-
mented, Willett emphasizes the infant's pleasure which is not the result of
a static image of wholeness, but the result of the recognition of the
animation of interactive intersubjectivity. The infant recognizes agency
and movement in the mirror image of its body rather than Lacan's static
image of wholeness. This stage is still non-discursive and, following
psychologist Daniel Stern, Willett describes the interaction between infant
and parent that sets up intersubjective interaction as non-discursive affect
attunement (ibid., p. 89). She suggests that the development of language
and language skills grow out of this affect attunement that originally
expresses itself in primordial forms of music and dance.

If sociality is possible before the acquisition of language and if a sense of
subjectivity and agency comes through touch and bodily interaction, then
we must rethink the relationship between the body and language, between
nature and culture. Language becomes possible only because of bodily
drives which become speech, drives which move between bodies in an
affective attunement that is the basis for sociality, language, and culture.
The first bodily relationship between mother and infant sets up rather
than threatens the social.

Following Klein and her successors, Kristeva also emphasizes the
maternal function and maintains that the regulation that sets up the super-
ego and the possibility of language and culture is already operating in the
maternal prior to the intervention of the father.[23] Yet while Klein focuses
on the infant's fantasies of the maternal body that become part of the
super-ego, and Winnicott, Bowlby, and Stern focus on the mother's
activities around the child that limit and regulate its behavior, Kristeva
identifies the structures of signification in the *material* of the body itself. It
is not just that the mother–infant relationship is already a social relationship because there is already communication and social exchange between
mother and infant, but also that the body itself sets up the structure of
social relations.

Against Freud and Lacan, the body and needs are not antithetical to
culture; the body, the maternal body in particular, does not have to be
sacrificed to culture. Needs, associated with the maternal body, are not
left behind once the child can make demands and acquires language.
Lacan's notion that language leaves us lacking satisfaction or that it is a
necessary but poor substitute for the maternal body, needs, or drives,
assumes that drives and needs are antithetical to language (or in Lacanian
parlance, that the real is cut off from the symbolic).[24] But what if drives or
needs make their way into language? In this case, the maternal realm that
Freud and Lacan identify as a hindrance to the properly social realm not

only gives birth to the social but also is necessary for the continued operation of the social. We need to be social. And drives are what motivate language. Culture grows organically out of the body.

The drives themselves are also proto-social in that they are not contained within one body or psyche; rather, as Teresa Brennan argues, drives move between bodies; they are exchanged. Affective energy is transferred between people. For example, a person can walk into a room and her mood can affect everyone in the room; it is as if her mood radiates throughout the room. As Brennan explains the physics of psychic energy, originally the fetus *in utero* is literally one with its mother's body. Insofar as there is an intimate connection between psychic and physical processes evidenced by the ways in which emotions, traumas, and repression cause physical "symptoms," we can suppose that the fetus is affected by its mother's psychophysical states since it is part of her body. Brennan maintains that this type of *in utero* psychophysical connection operates *ex utero*, only at a "slower pace." (*History After Lacan*, p. 34) Human beings exchange energy via these psychophysical connections. Emotions and affects migrate or radiate between human beings. In fact, for Brennan, it is the exchange of affect in the form of directed energy, or attention, that gives the ego its coherence and identity. She concludes that the ego is neither self-contained nor self-generating, but rather the effect of an interplay of intersubjective psychic forces.

Affective energy transfers take place in all interpersonal interactions. The idea that we can transfer affects through contact and conversation resonates with most people who have had the experience of a conversation with loved ones in which they are upset and after the conversation feel much better, but now the other party to the conversation is upset. This kind of situation suggests a transfer of affect. Even our language in such interpersonal situations suggests an exchange of affect; for example, "I won't take it any more"; "Don't give me that." This intersubjective theory of drives points to the sociality of the body.

Like Kristeva, and Lacan, however, Brennan believes that a paternal agent is necessary to break up the infant's dyadic dependence on the mother. If, however, the mother possesses this executive function as the law before the law, and if she is a desiring, speaking being – that is, if she is social – then the third term is already operating within the dyad; the dyad is already/also a triad. This is significant because now we can take the relationship between the maternal body and the fetus/infant as a model for a social relationship. Unlike Freud, Lacan, or even Kristeva, on this model we can see the mother–fetus/infant relation as exhibiting the logic of a social relation. The move into the social no longer needs to be a violent rejection of the mother or the maternal body. Rather, the mother–infant dyad is modulated by law and regulation and is therefore already a triad which sets up the social relation. If the logic and structure of bodily drives is the same as the logic and structure of language, then the primary relation between the bodies of mother and child does not have to be anti-social or threatening. And if bodily drives are not contained within the boundaries of one body or subject but are inter-psychic, then bodily drives are always a matter of social exchanges. These exchanges are *proto-dialogues* that take place between bodies, bodies that are social even if they are not properly subjects.

Language has its source in the body and not just because it takes a mouth to speak and a hand to write. Language speaks and writes bodily affects and bodily drives, without which there would be no motivation for language. We use language not only to communicate information but also to make psychophysical connections to others. Lacan might be right that every demand is a demand for love. But he is wrong that these demands are doomed to failure. If we need to speak, we need to make demands, just as we need food, then demands are not cut off from our basic need for satisfaction from our mothers that Lacan associates with love. Also, if drives and bodily needs are discharged in language, then they are not lost and we need not mourn the loss in order to enter culture; the maternal body is not killed and we need not mourn her death. Law and regulation implicit in language are already operating within the body. Law is not antithetical to the maternal body. It is not necessary to reject or exclude the maternal body in order to enter the realm of law and society.

The ways in which we conceive of our first relation with the maternal body can tell us much about how we answer the questions "who are we?" and "what is our relationship to others?" If the hypothesis that our subsequent relations are affected by, or modeled on, this first relationship has merit, then the way in which we conceive of the primary relationship with the maternal body is crucial in determining how we conceive of ourselves in relationships to others. If we imagine the primary relationship as a hostile relationship or an anti-social relationship – a relationship with a non-social being – then all of our subsequent social relationships are in some sense necessarily hostile or impossible. On the other hand, if we conceive of this primary relationship as a cooperative social relationship that does *not* require that the other be rejected or excluded so that the subject can individuate and become a person, then we can image subsequent social relations that have the potential to be cooperative and respectful.

If, following Kristeva, we carry the analysis of identity on the individual level to the group level, we can suppose that there are ways for groups to identify, for people to come together, without necessarily excluding others as hostile threats. Groups don't need to be at war with each other in order to constitute themselves as groups. In fact, if our identity is conceived as interrelational, and we give up the Hegelian notion that this relation is necessarily hostile in its beginnings and structure, then the identity of groups and of individuals is constituted in social relations with difference. This difference is constitutive of who we are and how we relate to others. In order to live together without war and oppression, we need to accept that difference is not synonymous with opposition. Our identities as individuals and as groups need not be threatened by different individuals or different groups; rather, our identities are enriched by and constituted by our relations with different individuals and different groups. So, in order to have an accurate sense of who we are, we need to actively engage with the different people and groups who have shaped us, directly and indirectly. On this view, Western culture cannot be so easily separated from other cultures. On this view, if the curricula of secondary schools and universities purports to give us a sense of our history and our cultural identity, then it needs to include the differences that make any "we," "us," or "our" possible. We need to continue to ask "who are *we*?"

Notes

1 See my *Womanizing Nietzsche: Philosophy's Relation to the "Feminine"* (New York: Routledge, 1995). See also Luce Irigaray, *Speculum of the Other Woman* (Ithaca: Cornell University Press, 1985).

2 G. W. F. Hegel, *Phenomenology of Spirit*, trans. A. V. Miller (Oxford: Clarendon Press, 1977).

3 See my *Family Values: Subjects Between Nature and Culture*, pt II (New York: Routledge, 1997).

4 Mary Douglas, *Purity and Danger* (New York: Routledge, 1969).

5 Julia Kristeva, *Powers of Horror* trans. Leon Roudiez (New York: Columbia University Press, 1982) and *Strangers to Ourselves*, trans. Leon Roudiez (New York: Columbia University Press, 1991).

6 Judith Butler, *Gender Trouble* (New York: Routledge, 1990), p. 133.

7 Judith Butler, *Bodies that Matter* (New York: Routledge, 1993), p. 11.

8 Teresa Brennan, *History After Lacan* (New York: Routledge, 1993), p. 11.

9 Drucilla Cornell, *The Imaginary Domain* (New York: Routledge, 1995).

10 See my *Womanizing Nietzsche: Philosophy's Relation to the "Feminine"* and *Family Values: Subjects Between Nature and Culture* (New York: Routledge, 1997).

11 Sigmund Freud, *Civilization and its Discontents*, trans. James Strachey (New York: Norton, 1961).

12   See Jacques Lacan, "The Neurotic's Individual Myth," *Psychoanalytic Quarterly*, vol. 48, no. 3, 1979, pp. 422–3. See also Jacques Lacan, *Écrits: A Selection*, trans. Alan Sheridan (New York: Norton, 1977).

13   In spite of Freud's theory of drives and Lacan's recognition of the real, both theorists continue to separate nature from culture and the body from language.

14   Melanie Klein, "Notes on Some Schizoid Mechanisms" in *The Selected Melanie Klein* (Harmondsworth: Penguin Books, 1986), p. 179.

15   Melanie Klein, "The Oedipus Complex in the Light of Early Anxieties" in R. E. Money-Kyrle et al (eds), *The Writings of Melanie Klein*, vol. 1, (London: Hogarth Press, 1975), p. 219.

16   D. W. Winnicott, "Mirror Role of Mother and Family in Child Development" in *Playing and Reality* (London: Tavistock, 1971).

17   D. W. Winnicott, "The Theory of the Parent–infant Relationship" in *Maturational Processes and the Facilitating Environment* (New York: International Universities Press, 1965).

18   Janice Doane and Devon Hodges make this argument in *From Klein to Kristeva* (Ann Arbor: University of Michigan Press, 1992), p. 21.

19   John Bowlby, *Maternal Care and Mental Health* (New York: Schoken Books, 1966); *Attachment* (London: Penguin Books, 1971).

20   Daniel Stern, *The Interpersonal World of the Infant: A View from Psychoanalysis and Developmental Psychology* (New York: Basic Books, 1985).

21   Jessica Benjamin, *The Bonds of Love* (New York: Pantheon, 1988), pp. 174, 152.

22   In *Womanizing Nietzsche* I also identify the mother–infant relationship as an intersubjective relationship. After reading Cynthia Willett's *Maternal Ethics and Other Slave Moralities*, I am convinced that the relationship is a non-subjective social relationship. This notion of non-subjective social relations opens the possibility of social relations with other animals. See Cynthia Willett, *Maternal Ethics and Other Slave Moralities* (New York: Routledge, 1995).

23   See Julia Kristeva, *Revolution in Poetic Language*, trans. Margaret Waller (New York: Columbia University Press, 1984); Leon Roudiez (ed.), *Desire in Language* trans. T. Gora, A. Jardine, and L. Roudiez (New York: Columbia University Press, 1980); *Powers of Horror* and *Tales of Love*, trans. Leon Roudiez (New York: Columbia University Press, 1987).

24   For Freud, drives make their way into language only by tricking the ego and super-ego.

9

Psychological Explanations of Oppression

Ann E. Cudd

1 Introduction: The Need for a (New) Psychological Theory of Oppression

It is a distinctly modern notion that persons are in some sense or other equal to each other. The equality thesis has been given various theological, philosophical, and moral interpretations and justifications by different thinkers. Perhaps the most astonishing of all, made by Thomas Hobbes in *Leviathan*, is the claim that persons are in some physical sense equals:

> Nature hath made men so equall, in the faculties of body, and mind; as that though there bee found one man sometimes manifestly stronger of body, or of quicker mind than another; yet when all is reckoned together, the difference between man, and man, is not so considerable, as that one man can thereupon claim to himselfe any benefit, to which another may not pretend, as well as he. For as to the strength of body, the weakest has strength enough to kill the strongest, either by secret machination, or by confederacy with others, that are in the same danger with himselfe. (Hobbes, 1651/1982, p. 183).

This claim, if true, seems to rule out the possibility of long-term oppression; for, if we are equal in the sense that each has the strength and ability to kill the strongest, then how can the strongest keep even the weakest in chains? This essay aims to answer that question and some related ones: why does oppression endure through generations? Why do the oppressed seem to accept or acquiesce to their oppression? Why do the oppressed come to believe in their own inferiority or insufficient strength?

This essay aims only to give a partial answer to the question, however. In companion pieces to this work I have argued that oppression is primarily an economic phenomenon with material causes and material consequences, generating a vicious cycle for its victims that is nearly inescapable. The economic analysis, while essential to understanding oppression, is not the whole story, however. While it reveals the social mechanisms of structural oppression, it cannot answer two fundamental questions. The first question unanswered by the economic analysis is why does this group (rather than that set of humans) come to be a group and an oppressed one at that? Why, for instance, are men dominant over women, rather than large persons over small ones, strong ones over weak ones, or intelligent ones over stupid ones? Indeed, the prior question is why are there men and women at all, rather than tall and short persons, etc., or simply individual persons with their unique combinations of characteristics? Once we see how oppressed and oppressor groups form, the economic analysis can explain how oppression is maintained, and how the economic efforts of the oppressed are often coopted into maintaining their oppression. Then a second set of questions nags even the most casual social observer, namely, the questions that I posed above and more generally, how do the oppressed come to be psychologically subdued to acquiesce or even participate in their own oppression? Marx, who also concentrated on the material causes and effects of oppression, was likewise afflicted by this puzzle, and he notoriously answered it by invoking false consciousness. False consciousness does not adequately answer the questions, however, because it is merely a name for a set of psychological phenomena that themselves require description and explanation, in other words, a black box. To peer inside this black box we need a psychological analysis.

Of course, I am not the first philosopher to notice the need for a psychological account of oppression. Indeed, there exist many such accounts. As I shall argue, they are all inadequate as social scientific accounts of psychological phenomena, first because they are not *scientific* at all. Some of them have the added flaw that they are not *social* accounts, and hence not suited to explaining the essentially social phenomenon of oppression. In this essay I draw on the work of social and cognitive psychologists in order to provide an adequate psychological theory of oppression, one that is scientifically grounded, that helps explain social structures of oppression, and that takes as explanatory variables the material facts of oppression provided by an adequate economic theory of oppression,[1] and in turn provides explanatory variables, in the form of belief- and desire-generating mechanisms, for that theory.

Before I present my thesis, let us fix some definitions. In my model,[2] oppression names a circumstance in which four conditions are satisfied: (1) there is a harm that comes out of an institutional practice; (2) the harm is perpetrated through a social institution or practice on a social group whose identity exists apart from the oppressive harm in (1); (3) there is another social group that benefits from the institutional practice in (1); (4) there is unjustified coercion or force, in the moralized sense of "coercion," that is, the coercion is unjustified.[3] This view entails that individuals suffer the harm of oppression only as members of groups. I don't deny that many other harms can come to persons, but we need a term for these group-based harms, and "oppression" is the best term for this purpose because it has always included these harms in its extension, even if it has also been used, confusedly, to name other harms. "Oppression" names a special kind of harm, a harm that comes to persons because they belong to a group that they closely identify with, so that the harm attaches to their very self-image. Because of this connection to one's self-image some of the harm is often psychological as well as material.

Oppression comprises a variety of harms against groups and the individuals who belong to them: psychological harms, material deprivations, and physical injuries, which in extreme conditions amounts to extermination. In this essay I am primarily concerned to examine the psychological mechanisms that set up and reinforce oppression, though a full account of oppression would show how these three kinds of harms reinforce and amplify each other. My general thesis, then, is this: originating in the cognitive process of stereotyping, oppression materially and psychologically harms its victims, and these harms are revisited on the oppressed in that they strengthen the oppressor and further weaken the oppressed, making escape difficult or impossible.

2 Competing Psychological Theories of Oppression

In the literature on the psychology of oppression, two kinds of theories have competed: psychoanalytic theories, deriving from Freud but best represented by the object relations theory of Nancy Chodorow; and the recognition theory that is directly derived from the Hegelian master–slave dialectic.[4] In this section I will illustrate each and show how each is inadequate as a part of a psychological theory of oppression. In the next section I will offer an alternative psychological theory on which to ground our understanding of oppression.

2.1 *Psychoanalytic theories of oppression*

Psychoanalysis purports to explain behavior by invoking the psychic connections and mechanisms of the unconscious that are inevitably formed through the innately preprogrammed psychosexual development of the young child. All psychoanalytic schools thus attempt to explain the puzzling, apparently irrational, so-called pathological, features of our behavior by showing that repressed unconscious urges are being satisfied or unconscious fantasies are being played out through the behavior in question. Since oppression, if it is not rooted in clear hierarchies of ability, seems to involve social pathology on the part of both oppressed and oppressor, a natural application of psychoanalytic theory is to attempt to explain oppression.

Nancy Chodorow's pioneering work, *The Reproduction of Mothering: Psychoanalysis and the Sociology of Gender*, attempts to explain the pathologies of gender. Why do women mother and men do not, that is, why (and how) do females (typically) become the mothering, caring, nurturing, intimacy-building gender and males become the gender whose psychology and social style (typically) is more suited to the distant relationships of the market, the court, and the battlefield? Not only was this a surprising question when she asked it, she also had a very surprising answer. Women are *not by nature* mothers, she argued, they are made into mothers by their mothers (and, through physical absence and emotional distance, their fathers). How do they do this? The answer Chodorow gives is psychoanalytic; it has to do with various childhood sexual intrigues and the resulting complexes that have been theorized by psychoanalysts since Freud, but with a special emphasis on the "object-relational experiences" of individuals as they mature. Chodorow's theory is a theory of oppression if one sees gender roles as they are constituted as oppressive. Since Chodorow's theory is widely viewed as a pathbreaking and plausible, if not definitive, theory of the psychology of one form of oppression, I will use it as the representative psychoanalytic theory of oppression.

Chodorow does not question the psychoanalytic perspective, nor does she defend it. In fact it is assumed that the reader will simply accept that there is an Oedipus complex, and that our personalities are determined largely by the age of five through the stimulation of sexual drives in us. Chodorow defends her lack of defense of psychoanalysis as follows: "Psychoanalytic theory remains the most coherent, convincing theory of personality development available for an understanding of fundamental aspects of the psychology of women in our society, in spite of its biases"

(Chodorow, 1978, p. 142). But given that she presents no defense of or direct evidence[5] for her brand of psychoanalysis, the critical reader is left to judge this claim by examining the evidence for psychoanalysis more generally. Here the picture is not too good for psychoanalysis.

First, psychoanalysis has been shown to be empirically inadequate.[6] Psychoanalysis has received so little positive empirical corroboration that most philosophical defenders of the theory concede defeat here and now claim that it is a hermeneutic, not a scientific, enterprise.[7] As Jane Flax puts it, the goal of the therapist and patient "is not 'truth' in the empiricist sense of what 'really' happened to the patient, but rather understanding which includes a powerful affective and experiential component." (Flax, 1981, p. 566). But here the theory is also in trouble. First, Freud himself did not intend the theory to be merely an *a priori* narrative of meaning but a scientifically grounded psychological theory.[8] Second, as a hermeneutic theory psychoanalysis implicitly offers two tests of its adequacy. One is resonance: does the story that is offered to the patient resonate with her experience, or does the theory offered to explain some cultural feature resonate with those who live in the culture (or its descendant culture)? The resonance test applied by individuals to their own experience is quite subjective, as it asks one to introspect about intersubjectively non-verifiable aspects of one's personal experience. Hence, hardly a reliable scientific test, though possibly a starting point to test for initial plausibility. The other test is coherence: does the theory cohere with the facts as it describes them, that is, can it weave together the facts in a plausible connected narrative? Granting for the sake of argument that the narrative is coherent, i.e. that it posits a narrative that plausibly ties the facts of psychological development together, the issue that one must address in assessing the theory is whether it is the best theory. Are there other coherent narratives that plausibly explain the same facts? And if there are, do these theories have anything else going for them that Chodorow's theory does not offer? Are they empirically testable, coherent with well-tested or otherwise more acceptable theories of neighboring phenomena, more fruitful scientifically or for progressive politics? Do they rely on less dubious assumptions?

Chodorow has very interesting things to say about the sociology of gender and of mothering, but the entire psychoanalytic account that forms the core of this book is to my mind unwarranted because there are better theories that are equally (at least) coherent, and that resonate better with my (admittedly subjective) understanding of my life. Chodorow's theory and psychoanalytic theory fails to resonate for me at all. Since many of the events that are supposed to form us happen before we are five years old, and they are now subject to repression by the unconscious, it is difficult to see how we would gather reliable evidence about them anyway. But granting that we can for the sake of argument, almost nothing that she says seems to resonate with any of my experiences in life, nor those of my family and friends. It seems to me that aside from a relatively small proportion of the people I know, (all of whom are literary intellectuals with very fertile imaginations), psychoanalytic theory is met with complete rejection. Now I am relying on personal, not statistical data here. But Chodorow gives us no other evidence to appeal to other than our own subjective experiences, and on this test psychoanalytic theory fails miserably. On the other hand, Chodorow's conclusion seems entirely right to me:

> As a result of having been parented by a woman, women are more likely than men to seek to be mothers, that is, to relocate themselves in a primary mother–child relationship, to get gratification from the mothering relationship, and to have psychological and relational capacities for mothering. (Chodorow, 1978, p. 206)

But a wide variety of psychological theories, from social-learning theory to cognitive development theory, would also conclude as much, for all she is really saying, when we abstract from the psychoanalysis, is that women are mothers because they learn to be mothers from their mothers (and men learn not to be mothers from their mothers). Later in this essay I will argue that one could come to this conclusion without the psychoanalytic account, by means of a theory that offers empirical tests and greater initial plausibility of its assumptions.

Aside from these theoretical problems, Chodorow's theory, appealing to such early life experiences as determinative of all future (mothering) behavior, offers us no escape from gender oppression. At the end of *The Reproduction of Mothering* she suggests that her narrative shows how much both sexes should want to change from women-only mothering. But it seems to me that if her argument were right she would have shown what incentives both men and women have to keep things the same. Men get to remain dominant, and women get to charge themselves up with these intensely personal, symbiotic relationships, and given the way that their early training has determined their desires, they have no desire to change this arrangement. Furthermore, psychoanalytic theories generally locate pathologies, including the social pathology of oppression, in personal failings. This also makes the prospects of a solution bleak, for it would have to be psychotherapeutic and thus individual, rather than political and collective, unless we are willing to coerce a generation of men and women to act counter to their deepest desires, a project that would surely generate its own pathologies. Thus, I find psychoanalytic theory to be politically paralyzing as well as theoretically and empirically inadequate as a theory of oppression.

2.2 Recognition theory

The recognition theory of oppression originated in the master–slave dialectic advanced by Hegel in a relatively short but well-known section of *Phenomenology of Spirit*, and has been recast by several contemporary theorists to fit the cases of oppression in the twentieth century. The basic assumption of the recognition theory is that all persons most strongly desire recognition from others because only through recognition can one become conscious of oneself, a goal that is taken to be universal and overriding. Hegel puts this in his characteristically abstract way when he writes: "Self-consciousness exists in and for itself when, and by the fact that, it so exists for another; that is, it exists only in being acknowledged" (Hegel, 1807/1977, p. 111). Self-consciousness in and for itself is the logical and development goal for humanity, according to Hegel, and thus acknowledgment, specifically in the form of recognition by other self-conscious beings, is humanity's primary motivating force.

I believe there is much to learn from Hegel about the psychology of oppression, in particular that humans desire recognition by others, and that this is not reducible to any purely materialistic desire. However, recognition theory is not a viable scientific psychological theory. It purports to be a descriptive theory, yet offers no clear criterion of adequacy for determining if it is correct or not. Although a desire for recognition "seems" plausible, there are no empirical tests of the theory. Like hermeneutic psychoanalysts, recognition theorists rely on the reader feeling that there is some resonance with the story that they relate. They offer as little in the way of empirical evidence, and for both it is merely coherence with the facts and not evidence for the psychological mechanisms proposed, though here the evidence is social rather than primarily individual. Hegel spins a story that is supposed to correspond to both human ontogenesis and phylogenesis, but he never considers competing stories (nor does he offer concrete tests of any hypotheses, though surely it would be anachronistic to look for them in Hegel).

To take recognition theory seriously as a competing psychological theory, one would need to subject it to serious experimental tests in a variety of test situations, from surveys to artificial experiments to clinical tests of different therapies some of which are based on recognition theory.

Yet this evidence is almost entirely lacking. Instead of being a well-worked out and thoroughly tested theory of psychology, it seems to be a fantasy of philosophy. It is not entirely implausible to this philosopher, but it remains to be tested, and thus is hardly the psychological theory on which to rest a general theory of oppression. Especially not if there is a viable competitor.

In addition to these empirical shortcomings, there is a common theoretical critique of recognition theory that I find persuasive. The recognition theorists share the Hegelian view that "the question of oppression is primarily a problem of psyches confronting each other in society" (Bulhan, 1985, p. 118). This quote summarizes for me what is fundamentally wrong with the recognition theory of oppression. What recognition theorists hold is that some groups in society have collective psyches that are locked in a mortal combat with each other that mirrors the struggles of individuals. But this view is ontologically strange, and ultimately psychologically incoherent. It requires that there exist concrete collectives with psychologies, that there are minds writ large, like some sort of Wizard of Oz, and the collectives act as individual beings in response to the actions of other such collectives, as if they had internal sensory and psychological mechanisms like human individuals. Yet collectives do not appear to have those organs or mechanisms, and so psychological theory, which purports to explain the behavior of individuals based on either instinctual, biological or otherwise constructed cognitive and affective mechanisms, can have nothing to say, except metaphorically, about such entities.

While I am persuaded by the recognition theorists that humans desire recognition, I am not convinced by their views that the desire for recognition is more fundamental than all other desires, much less that it is the psychological motor driving oppression. Nor does recognition theory even attempt to answer the first question that we set before us in the introduction to this essay: how does a collection of humans come to be a group and to have this or that position in a hierarchy of social dominance relations? For an answer to that question without the drawbacks of the psychological theories of oppression that we have examined, we shall have to look to an alternative psychological theory.

3 Social Cognitive Theory of Stereotype Formation as a Psychological Explanation of Oppression

If we want to understand the psychology of oppression, we need to understand how individuals think about, feel about, and decide to act toward others. Social psychology, since its origins as an independent discipline at the turn of the century, has been concerned with the formation of beliefs and attitudes toward other persons and how these are manifested in behavior. In its early days, however, social psychology was limited by some of the same theoretical and methodological defects that we found with psychoanalysis and the recognition theory, namely, there was little understanding of the causal mechanisms that underlay these thoughts and feelings and actions. Social psychology, where it was useful or more than mere speculation at all, was largely a descriptive enterprise; beautiful theory could be spun, but justification for the theory was remote and basically limited to the resonance and coherence tests.

The cognitive revolution of the 1960s enabled psychology to go beyond the level of description to empirically testable causal explanations of psychological processes by examining the cognitive structures in the brain that cause us to perceive data and draw inferences as we do. Psychologists began to see thought as a string of information-processing and information-generating processes, which could be experimentally studied in isolation and then recombined in order to have a clearer analysis of the whole. Social cognitive theory combines the interests in persons, their social interactions, and their formation of self-concepts with the methods of cognitive psychology: it applies the theories from cognitive psychology regarding general cognitive functions such as perception, attribution, and categorization to understand persons and their interaction. The combination provides a scientific, causal theory of the social psychology of humans. What the theory has to say about how we form groups and beliefs about them is, therefore, crucial to an investigation of oppression.

From its earliest days, social psychology has been keenly interested in the formation and function of stereotypes in our thoughts about and actions toward each other. Stereotypes are generalizations that we make about persons based on characteristics that we believe they share with some identifiable group. Stereotypes group us by, typically, visible characteristics and then carry with them a whole host of inferences about us that go well beyond the immediately visible and, often, the truth. For example, a white, middle-class, middle-age female perceiver from a rural state sees a brown-skinned, short-haired, taller than average person walking across campus and judges that it is a black man; then her stereotypes of black man cause her to form the beliefs that he is heading toward the gym to play basketball, probably listening to gangsta rap on the headphones he is wearing, and likely to be from a large city. If it is dark out and there is no one else around, she might entertain a more sinister belief about him, as well, and steer away from him. This example illustrates the two levels involved in stereotyping: from the visible characteristics (brown skin, short hair, tall) to the group (black man), and then from the group to characteristics about individuals in the group (basketball, rap, etc.). Stereotypes have, as this example shows, only a tenuous connection to the truth about individuals; they require minimal evidence for the wide range of inferences that they set in motion in our minds – from skin color, hair length, and height she inferred musical tastes! Because these inferences are to characteristics that we believe set groups of persons apart from other groups, stereotypes form the very foundation of our beliefs about groups. But how do we formulate these beliefs, and how good are they for our purposes?

The cognitive revolution brought with it the idea that stereotype formation is a kind of categorization, like our categorization of anything that we perceive. Cognitive psychologists hold that categorization is a fundamental process of thought that is essential to efficient information processing.[9] Individual thinkers are seen as cognitive misers, whose goal is to simplify experience and frame it according to what is relevant to our needs and interests. Since we often need split-second decisions to act smoothly and efficiently in our environment, human cognitive processing has evolved to provide quick and dirty generalizations that, in a great enough proportion of our encounters, suffice to allow us to survive and propagate. Greater precision, it is theorized, would require more time and attention, and would too often have cost the thinker its life in the primitive survival of the fittest. The cognitive miser, thus, is an efficient, often wrong but close enough generalizer, who cannot be blamed for the over-generalizations that he sometimes develops that do not apply, though he could, perhaps, be trained to generalize more carefully in crucial situations.[10]

The cognitive model of categorization, of which stereotyping is one type, holds that a category is represented by a prototype, from which there is extensive variation within the same category, and where the distance from the prototype determines the fit of the individual within the category. Categories are formed by accentuation of the similarities within categories and of the differences between categories. Stereotypes, as categories, are thus biased by this accentuation process. In what direction are they biased? A pair of important concepts in this connection are the in-group and the out-group. This distinction in social psychology predates the cognitive revolution (Allport, 1954/1979), and is roughly this: the in-group refers to the group to which the perceiver belongs and the out-group refers to any groups to which she does not belong.[11] Stereotypes typically favor the in-groups and disfavor the out-groups of the person holding the stereotype. There are cognitive consequences of in- and out-group membership well-documented in the psychology literature, in particular, in-group heterogeneity (the belief that members of the in-group have varied and individual characteristics), out-group homogeneity (the belief that members of the out-group are essentially all the same), and out-group polarization (evaluation of 'good' out-groupers more positive than warranted by evidence, while evaluations of "bad" ones more negative than warranted) (Fiske and Taylor, 1991). But typically there are common stereotypes that favor majority populations and disfavor minority ones. One theory closely associated with the cognitive miser model holds that stereotypes form in response to salient or novel information, and this novel information is then accentuated to make a group of persons who display this characteristic even more different from other groups (ibid.). Such a theory explains how stereotypes of minorities as very different from majority groups would form from evidence of small but novel differences.

The cognitive miser model fails to explain some crucial data about stereotype formation, however. First, it fails to explain the variety of stereotypes applied to the same persons by the same thinker but in different circumstances. Second, it fails to explain why the accentuation of differences leads to beliefs that tend to benefit (materially and psychologically) dominant populations and disfavor dominated ones; if this were a neutral cognitive process one would expect some stereotypes of each group to be positive and some negative. That is, the cognitive miser model fails to account for motivations that determine which stereotype will apply under what circumstances.

In experiments called 'minimal group experiments' (Oakes *et al.*, 1994) in the early 1970s, Henri Tajfel tried to determine the minimal conditions for formation of in-group and out-group solidarity. In these experiments Tajfel and his colleagues randomly assigned schoolboys into two groups, but led them to believe that the grouping was based on real (though rather meaningless and trivial) criteria (e.g. their estimation of the number of dots on a screen, their preference for Klee or Kandinsky paintings). The subjects were allowed no social interaction and they were not allowed to know even the identities of the others in the group. Nevertheless, the subjects treated their group membership as an important and salient fact. When asked to assign money to individuals they tended to assign more to those in their 'own group' even though they were making no assignment of money to themselves and they knew this. These experiments were taken to show several things. First, that it takes very little information or basis for identification for people to establish an in-group/out-group distinction. Second, that discrimination behavior can be motivated by this minimal in-group/out-group distinction. Third, *no actual facts* about the groups have to be involved for positive evaluations of in-groups. Tajfel argued that two processes are at work here: first, group formation or categorization by social group, and second, the distinction between in-group and out-group according to one's assignment. The first of these is explained by categorization theory applied to the group. But the second was unique to social psychology, i.e. cognitive psychology could not suggest a process that applied outside the social realm, as well. In order to explain these results, Tajfel came, over the course of the next decade, to develop a theory now known as social identity theory.

Categorization theory suggests that people categorize their perceptual data to bring order to it, to give it meaning by relating it to other information and interests so that they can use it efficiently. Social categorization into in-group and out-group is likewise an attempt to order information about other persons, by connecting it to one's prior information and one's interests. How do we characterize our own interests? Here Tajfel suggested that we categorize ourselves by the in-groups and out-groups to which we belong, and so put a social ordering on our world, including our place in it. Thus, he linked the notion of the self with social categorization in the concept of a social identity, which he defined as 'that part of an individual's self-concept which derives from his [*sic*] knowledge of his [*sic*] membership of a social group (or groups) together with the value and emotional significance attached to that membership' (Oakes *et al.*, 1994, p. 82, quoting Tajfel).

Social identity theory postulates that individuals are motivated to develop a positive social identity, and that this is done by establishing the 'positive distinctiveness' of one's own in-group. People want to believe that they have positive attributes, and because they identify themselves in part by the social groups that they consider their in-groups, people want to see their own groups in a positive light. Since not all groups can easily be seen positively when compared to other groups, people sometimes have to manipulate their beliefs in order to maintain a positive self-image. Even members of dominant groups can have self-image problems if they consider that their advantages are unwarranted. Several studies have shown how humans create or alter social stereotypes in order to manage their self-image; here I will discuss two such studies. An influential study by Curt Hoffman and Nancy Hurst suggests that stereotypes can be manipulated to rationalize social injustices. In particular, their research shows that gender stereotypes could arise simply as 'explanatory fictions that rationalize and make sense of the sexual division of labor' (Hoffman and Hurst, 1990, p. 199). Their experiments involved telling subjects stories about a fictional planet where there were two categories of beings, Orinthians and Ackmians, and where there were two kinds of social roles, homemakers and city-workers. The authors described each of the beings with personality traits, occupations, and species. They made it so that there was no correlation whatsoever between personality social role, and category. In one experiment they made the Orinthians and Ackmians the same species and in another they made them different species. The authors then asked the subjects a set of questions, which the authors manipulated as follows: they always asked about role and category distribution, they sometimes asked for an explanation of why the Orinthians and Ackmians occupied the social roles that they did, and they asked for traits specific to each category. Finally, they interviewed the subjects to see if the subjects could detect the purpose of the experiment (they couldn't). The authors found that a strikingly large number (72 percent) of the subjects in the "explanation condition" (i.e. the subjects asked to supply an explanation of the roles) attributed the roles to personality differences and stereotyped the categories by personality differences that reflected stereotypes of gender differences in personality. (Remember, there were no personality differences.) In the "no explanation" condition the subjects were much less likely to stereotype the categories. They interpret these results as showing that 'objective sex differences in personality are not necessary to the formation of gender stereotypes' (ibid., p. 206). Further, the studies show that stereotype formation is at least partly mediated by the attempt to explain or rationalize the category – role correlation. Hence, stereotyping cannot be seen as an unbiased information-processing phenomenon, but one that is creatively manipulated by persons to serve their interest in a coherent rationalization of the social roles and the social groups that perform them.

A pair of studies conducted by Nyla Branscombe and her colleagues (Branscombe, 1996; Branscombe *et al.*, 1996) suggests that persons think differently about their social group-related privileges and disadvantages in order to bolster their social identity or to avoid group-effacing facts, and that this use of "social creativity strategies" is common to both advantaged and disadvantaged social groups. In one study Branscombe asked gender-segregated groups of men and women to write down ways that they had been privileged, for one set of groups, or disadvantaged, for another set, by their gender. (These responses were coded for degree of severity by independent coders.) The subjects then were assessed by a standard self-esteem scale, and by questions that assessed their emotional attachment to their gender group, their feeling that membership in that group was a positive experience, their general satisfaction with their lives, and their current mood. Branscombe found first that men identified trivial ways that they were disadvantaged (e.g. having to pay for drinks) and serious ways that they were privileged (e.g. having higher incomes), while the reverse was true for women (e.g. having limited freedom of movement because of the threat of sexual assault, vs. having doors opened for them). She also found that thinking about privilege or disadvantage had significantly different consequences for men and women.

> On all of the well-being measures, thinking about privilege hurt men's esteem, current mood, and encouraged movement away from their gender group identity compared to thinking about disadvantage. Thinking about privilege raised women's mood, pride and attachment to their gender group identity, compared to men's. Thinking about disadvantage increased men's overall well-being and personal self-esteem compared to women's. (Branscombe, 1996, p. 12)

Tajfel (1978) recognized the phenomenon of social creativity in interpretation of stereotypes on the part of disadvantaged groups: they tend to think about disadvantage mainly as a way of creating positive distinctiveness for their social group and increasing their identity with it. Branscombe's experiment points to a correlative social creativity on the part of the advantaged. Her explanation of men's tendency to focus on only trivial privileges is to note first that it is an instance of the well-recognized 'attribution error' that persons make by explaining their negative outcomes by pointing to external causes and their positive outcomes by attributing them to internal causes. So by focusing on only trivial disadvantages they can see women and men as both having disadvantages and also protect the notion that any success they have is due to their own personal capacities. She also suggests, parallel to the line of argument that I am developing, that "If women were to also equate such privileges with those accorded men, and men's disadvantages with women's, then this might represent the development of a "false consciousness" (Branscombe, 1996, p. 18). In her other study, Branscombe and her colleagues found a similar pattern of social creativity in accounting the advantages and disadvantages from race (Branscombe, *et al.*, 1996).

Stereotypes thus serve not only to group the social world, and then to place oneself in the social order, but also to do so in a way that bolsters the valuation of one's self-identity, insofar as that is possible within the given social realities. By determining alliances and oppositions among in-groups and out-groups, categorization provides the basis of social orientation toward others. Returning now to the discussion of the desire for recognition, the social cognitive description of this desire would be that we have the desire to categorize ourselves as members of in-groups and then to make those groups distinctive, and insofar as possible, positive. Thus, this psychological theory can explain the desire for recognition as a part of our cognitive functioning in a social world.

These theories, social categorization theory and self-identity theory, show how and why persons want to be members of in-groups and formulate stereotypes to structure the social psychological world in which they interact; we have, thus, provided an answer to the "why groups?" question. But we have still not answered the question, "why *these* groups?" There are actually three questions here: why did these groups first get going, why do they continue as they do, and why do they change when they do? To answer this we must first note that individuals are not creating these in-group/out-group distinctions in a social cognitive vacuum, and (unless we subscribe to a creation *ex nihilo* theory) they never were. There was and is no first moment for human social groups. Humans have always been social groupers, if only by tribe or clan. So if we can answer the other two questions we should be able to theorize how humans came to sort themselves by the groups that we now find. There are two apparently competing accounts of the constraints imposed by existing social stereotypes in the social cognitive literature. One theory is that we learn generalized patterns, called schemas, that are then virtually fixed, causing counter-instances to be misperceived as conforming instances of the schema. The other, propounded by Oakes, *et al.* following Tajfel, is that our categories reflect the reality of social groups, and so, as social groups change, so would our stereotypes. It seems to me that to answer both the continuity and change questions involves a combination of these theories.

There are a wide variety of stereotypes that individuals learn from their social environment among which they are normally constrained to choose. One cannot choose to stereotype women as large, aggressive, socially abrasive persons: first, one would never think of that (except to come up with an outlandish example for an academic paper), and second, one would have too hard a time communicating with others if one made this highly unconventional assumption. Schema theory postulates that we have cognitive structures, called "schemas," that are representations of concepts, that guide our perception, memory, inferential reasoning, and association, and in turn our behavior. Schemas are networks of associations that organize our perceptions by assimilating them to relevant networks of ideas. We have schemas for persons (our folk psychology), for events (called "scripts"), and of most relevance to stereotypes, role schemas that code our perceptions and associations for social roles. Role schemas are, thus, one way of cognitively accounting for social stereotypes. Schema research differs from categorization research in that the latter is more concerned with the classification of instances and the former with the application of organized, generic, prior knowledge to the understanding of new information (Fiske and Taylor, 1991). The difference here is that schemas generalize from specific instances, and so are represented as a list of attributes or associations, while categories are a web of prototypical and varying instances. As I see it, then, there is nothing inconsistent about accepting both theories as compatible. In particular, role schemas account for the stability of stereotypes and the categorization process for the plasticity and capacity for change in stereotypes.

Schemas frame our perceptions and then code our memories. Recalling the example of the black man on campus, the perceiver took in a few perceptual details and the schema for black man was engaged and several inferences were drawn about the man. In numerous studies it has been shown that were the perceiver to then learn something directly about the person, say by asking him what he was listening to, that fact would be much more likely to be remembered if it were consistent with the schema, e.g. if he were listening to gangsta rap (Fiske and Taylor, 1991). Thus, schemas code our memories and we have a difficult time with memories that don't fit the schema. Schemas also carry emotional responses with them; in the example the perceiver was apprehensive upon judging the object to be a black man. Although schemas are readily engaged by initial perceptions and are important to our cognitive and affective functioning, people are clearly able to disengage their schemas upon the presentation of sufficient counterevidence, under circumstances in which their decisions matter to them.[12]

Sandra Bem has provided the most well-developed account of role schemas in her theory of gender schemas. On her view, girls and boys learn gender roles as they grow up and code these as role schemas for gender. Gender, she claims, is the most ubiquitous schema we have: "No other dichotomy in human experience appears to have as many entities linked to it as does the distinction between female and male" (Bem, 1987). Children learn that there are gender appropriate and inappropriate attributes, then they apply these to themselves; that is, they identify themselves with one gender and take on the appropriate role for that gender. Through this identification and assimilation the gender schema becomes a self-fulfilling prophecy for cultural myths about sexual difference. Role schemas are thus learned through the social environment by assimilation of the self to existing role schemas, and reinforced, reified, and justified in the assimilation. Social learning and reinforcement of role schemas account for the continuity and preservation of stereotypes over time, and thus account for the fact that women mother and men do not, for example.

There is a great deal of evidence supporting the idea that gender stereotypes are socially learned, and that they are self-perpetuating. Gender stereotypes are learned especially early from one's parents. In an analysis of 172 different studies of parents' differential socialization of girls and boys, Hugh Lytton and David Romney (1991) found that parents differentially reinforced gender behavior to conform to traditional stereotypes of female and male behavior, even though there was no other systematic way in which they differentially socialized their sons and daughters. There is a large literature about the self-fulfilling nature of social stereotypes, that is, about how stereotypical expectations by perceivers and common knowledge of these expectations causes persons to behave stereotypically. In an experiment by Berna Skrypnek and Mark Snyder (1982) anonymous male–female pairs bargained over three tasks, one stereotypically male, one female, and one neutral. In a third of the pairs the male partner (called "the perceiver") was told that his partner was male, in another third female, and in another third the male was not told the sex of the partner. The female (called "the target") partner knew the sex of the perceiver and what he had been told her sex was. The experimenters found that both the perceiver's perception and the target's knowledge of what the perceiver thought she was affected the behavior both of choosing and bargaining. "Targets believed by perceivers to be male chose tasks relatively feminine in nature (*sic*), and targets believed by perceivers to be female chose tasks relatively feminine in nature (*sic*)" (ibid., p. 288). Another experiment by Snyder, Elizabeth Decker Tanke, and Ellen Berscheid (1977) showed how the stereotype-generated attributions by a perceiver can cause the target to conform her behavior to the stereotype even if she doesn't know what stereotype he holds about her. In this experiment the (again male) perceivers were given controlled but specious information about their (again female) targets, with whom they then had a ten-minute phone conversation. The targets got no information about their partners, including no information about what information the males had, but the male perceivers were given snapshots that were purportedly of their partners, but which the experimenters had actually carefully chosen to be of either an attractive or unattractive woman (as perceived by independent coders) independently of the actual attractiveness or unattractiveness of the target subjects. The hypothesis was that the stereotypes of attractive women (that they are more sociable, sexually warm, kind, poised, outgoing) would affect the behavior of both the perceivers and the targets; in particular, the behavior of both would tend to confirm the stereotypes. Independent coders of the conversations rated the warmth and enthusiasm of each side of the conversations, with no information about the experiment or the men and women in them, and the data convincingly corroborated the hypothesis. The authors explained the results by saying, "the differences in the level of sociability manifested and expressed by the male perceivers may have been a key factor in bringing out the reciprocating patterns of expression in the target women" (ibid., p. 662).

To summarize the results surveyed here, people learn stereotypes from their social environment independently of their fit with the individual attributes grouped by the stereotypes. People's behavior induced by stereotypical attributions, whether true or false in the individual case, guides the behavior of their partners in interactions to conform to the stereotypes. And individuals' expectations of others' stereotypes guide their behavior in anticipation of the reactions. Schema theory explains and predicts these experimental results, postulating that individuals identify with schemas that are learned in the environment and then assimilate their own behavior to accord with those schemas.

Schema theory can thus account for the stability of stereotypes, but given their rigid entrenchment and self-fulfilling nature, it is difficult to see how stereotypes would ever change. Yet clearly they do; we don't stereotype Polish Americans as we used to, and now there are stereotypes for teenagers who wear baggy pants. To explain stereotype change we need to look carefully at the kinds of things that motivate us to engage particular stereotypes when we do. We have seen how self-identity theory can explain how a particular stereotype from among a set of available ones can be contextually motivated, namely, the particular stereotype that is attended to is the one that makes one's self-identity most valuable to one under the circumstances. There are other sources of motivation that have been overlooked by the psychologists, namely material motivations to conform to stereotypes or to cause others to do so. For the economically dominant group in society there is a clear motivation to behave according to the stereotypes for that group, since by doing so one is most likely to reap the financial rewards that go with status in that group. There is also, I argue, an economic incentive for members of subordinated groups to behave according to the stereotypes for their groups, unless they can successfully pass as a member of a more dominant group. Social groups are constituted partly by incentive structures for persons to behave in particular ways. Take women in our culture, for instance. There are clear financial incentives for them to marry, since they then have access to a man's wealth and income, which, regardless of race, is on average higher than that of women (Idson and Price, 1992), and which, therefore, they could rationally expect in the individual instance to be higher than their own. Then, if they have children, there are financial incentives for families and for women to subordinate their careers so that their husbands can continue on the fast track in their higher-earning potential career.[13] Racial minorities also have some financial incentives to do what is stereotypical for them. Consider a poor black single woman with children. The social stereotype that applies is the welfare mom. Given her situation, there is a financial incentive for her to receive welfare (especially when one takes into account the cost of alternative and equivalent quality childcare) and not to marry, since statistically she is likely to find someone who is unemployed or underemployed and she would no longer be eligible for welfare. The point is that social stereotypes reflect the social incentive structures that people ought, rationally, to react to. Therefore, there is often a material incentive to comply with the behavior that stereotypes prescribe. If the material incentives change, then it is only reasonable to assume that the stereotypes will change to reflect new incentives, though there may be some time lag. When Irish–American men were no longer discriminated against in employment so that they had greater options than policework, the stereotypes of them as policemen faded. Just as there is a material incentive for persons to conform to their group stereotypes (unless they can pass), there are material incentives for persons to apply stereotypes to other strategically, when they can do it successfully. Consider the firm interviewing applicants for a position, some of whom are men and some women. Since it is statistically more likely that women will take reduced hours, maternity leave, etc. than a man, there is an incentive for firms, at least when hiring workers who are in their early middle-age and who are likely not to stay over an entire career, to stereotype women and discriminate against them, either by not hiring them or by offering them lower salaries for equal work. Likewise, there is an incentive for employers who are hiring in segregated job classifications in which women and/or racial minorities predominate, to maintain the segregation and with it the lower wages. For dominant groups it is in the workers' interest to maintain job segregation by maintaining ugly images of subordinate groups and by engaging in discriminatory and threatening behavior. Again, these stereotypes begin to change when material incentives change. As racial minorities entered professional baseball, the stereotype of the ballplayer has changed considerably. Thus, economic theory can be combined with self-identity theory to explain how stereotypes are strategically employed and change over time in response to social incentives, both material and psychological.

One objection to any psychological theory that claims to explain all forms of oppression is that it does not apply cross-culturally. Might social cognitive theory be likewise criticized? My claim is that there are universal cognitive mechanisms that cut across cultures, and that are enacted in culturally specific ways. Consider human linguistic ability. All human neonates who are not seriously brain damaged possess it, yet the particular language they learn to use is culturally determined. Social cognitive theory, as I have presented it, proposes three such mechanisms: categorization – the tendency to organize information under categories; in-group out-group formation and accentuation of difference between those groups; self-identification with the in-group. In addition, I have argued that people respond to material incentives and tend to give more weight to short-term gains than to long-term ones. What evidence is there that these are universal psychological mechanisms (as opposed to Western or androcentric or modern constructs)?

First, even confining the idea of categorization to social categories, numerous studies show that categorization is a cultural universal, and I could find none that throw doubt on that hypothesis (Troadec, 1995; Pinto, 1992; Dhawan *et al.* 1995; Oddou and Mendenhall, 1984; Miller, 1984; Vassiliou and Vassiliou, 1974). Second, a great deal of evidence also exists in the social cognitive literature on the tendency to form in-groups and out-groups (Han and Park, 1995; Tzeng and Jackson, 1994; Smith, *et al.*, 1990; Boski, 1988; Ward, 1985; Oddou and Mendenhall, 1984; Vassiliou and Vassiliou, 1974). The very existence and wide acceptance of the concept of the Other in the phenomenological literature also testifies to this. Third, there is also evidence for the hypothesis that persons tend to self-identify with their in-group (Dhawan *et al.* 1995; Han and Park, 1995; de Leon, 1993; Turner *et al.*, 1993; Boski, 1988; Oddou and Mendenhall, 1984; Vassiliou and Vassiliou, 1974) and somewhat more mixed evidence of the positive attribution bias toward the in-group (Smith *et al.*, 1990; Boski, 1988). Finally, there is also some evidence for the claim that cross-culturally, people respond to material incentives and tend to give more weight to short-term gains than to long-term ones (Felson and Tedeschi, 1993; Ostaszewski and Green, 1995; Wilson *et al.*, 1995). Although what in-groups and out-groups form and how much persons respond to material incentives or weigh short-term gains over long-term ones differ by culture, it is clear from the data that these are universal human cognitive mechanisms.

I would like to end this section with some remarks about the accuracy of stereotypes and the concept of a social group. Oakes *et al.* (1994) argue that social groups are real, and our stereotypes reflect the reality of groups: "a group of individuals might be stereotyped in terms of a particular social categorization (as Irish, say) not because this is cognitively economical but because groups are real" (ibid., p. 127). Although I think that they are right to assert that social groups are real, I think that they are wrong in their understanding of what social groups are. The process of stereotyping from individual goes like this: we infer from the individual to the group and then project back to the individual. The data we take in is about the individual. The group information stored in schemas is then added to that data, and we project that back to the individual. This is a highly inaccurate process, as my black man on campus example suggests, as do many studies showing the inaccuracy of stereotypes in individual cases.[14] Oakes *et al.* (1994) argue that stereotypes are accurate because they represent real differences in the statistical facts about the sets of individuals grouped by the stereotype. But these stereotypes often attribute properties to individuals shared by only a minuscule proportion of the group (though it may indeed be greater than the proportion of individuals in another group who share that attribute). While it is then true that there is a real difference in the two sets, that does not make the stereotype accurate as a property of the group, much less as projected onto individuals. To put the point concretely, if 1 percent of white women are named Ann, and a much smaller number of women of any other race are, then it is true that there is a real difference here between white women and women of other races, but that does not mean that the group of white women is legitimately stereotyped as a bunch of Anns, nor is it a good bet that any particular white woman is an Ann.

I do not wish to deny that there are social groups, however. Social groups are determined by the set of stereotypes by which we categorize and separate or assimilate those categories to our own, and by the social reinforcement of these stereotypes by the self-fulfilling nature of role schemas, and just as important, the socially structured material incentives that reinforce stereotype-fulfilling behavior that I discuss elsewhere. Groups are not persons, they are cognitive processes (stereotypes) and socially structured material incentives. Thus, we are not seeing the group directly, but our seeing sets in motion a grouping, and this grouping is objectively real in its effects. This grouping causes us to have prejudices and discriminate against (or for) persons because of how we have grouped them, and regardless of the fit between the stereotypical characteristics of the group and their personal characteristics. Groups are real as constraints on thought, feeling, and behavior. But stereotypical group attributes often are not true, and do not contain even a kernel of truth, when applied to individuals.

4 Stereotypes and the Cyclical Nature of Oppression

It is a common theme in the literature surveyed in this essay that oppression is self-maintaining: it is characterized as a vicious cycle (Okin, 1989), a self-fulfilling prophecy (Snyder *et al.*, 1977; Bem, 1987), a Nash equilibrium (Cudd, 1994). There are three ways in which stereotypes are self-fulfilling, one cognitive, one behavioral, and one a combination of cognition and behavior that is best characterized as "rational." I have characterized stereotyping as the fundamental cognitive process of oppression. Stereotyping is a kind of categorizing applied to the social realm that is reified in role schemas that are then applied to new data. Stereotyping is the process of taking data, assimilating it to role schemas by which one codes that kind of data, shaping it by accentuation of group difference, manipulating the differences in ways that make the in-group look as good as possible and as different from the out-group as possible. Given the social reality of existing groups, that is, existing attributions to persons based on visual characteristics that they share, new data is more likely to be assimilated to the schemas that currently exist, rather than new ones created. This means that stereotypes are very stable cognitive structures. So stereotypes that bias some groups positively and others negatively will tend to remain that way even in the face of contrary data.

Stereotypes not only affect one's cognitive processing of data, though, they affect behavior. This means that person are victimized, degraded, humiliated, and discriminated against because of the stereotypes that characterize the social group in which they are categorized. Victims of the forces of psychological oppression suffer from feelings of inferiority, shame, hopelessness, and the like, making them less well-equipped to compete equally with their oppressors and in turn confirming the stereotypes of them as vulnerable, weak, lazy, incompetent, or alternatively, savage, violent, etc. So the second way in which the stereotypes are self-fulfilling is through the psychological harm caused by psychological forces of oppression that affect the behavior of the oppressed.

The third way that stereotypes are self-fulfilling is through motivating the oppressed themselves to accept negative stereotypes and to choose to act in accordance with them. First, persons are motivated to attach stereotypes to themselves in order to create a sense of being a part of an in-group, and to view this in a positive light. In some cases, though, it is the grouping that is what is wrong; I would argue that this is the case with gender, for instance. This is what Marx thought was wrong with the class system as a whole. Accepting the grouping, which plays this psycho-logically fulfilling role of creating a self-identity even when the group is negatively affected by it, is the phenomenon of false consciousness, which we can now understand as a kind of cognitive processing. Second, once these groupings exist, social psychological incentives arise for persons to act in accordance with the stereotypes of the group that others assign them to, for the alternative may well be social isolation.

These three processes together answer the question that Hobbes's equality thesis raised for us. Oppressed persons often acquiesce to and accept their oppression because they come to believe in the stereotypes that represent their own inferiority, are weakened by those stereotypes, and even motivated to fulfill them.

5 Conclusion: Can We Break the Cycle of Oppression?

In this essay I have argued that oppression is fundamentally driven by the cognitive process of stereotyping. Stereotyping makes possible the phe-nomena of social grouping. It is the cognitive process of categorizing applied to the social world combined with self-identity formation in the individual, whereby the individual orders the social world in a way that best suits her material and psychological interests within the given con-straints. Individuals do not create their stereotypes *ex nihilo*. Individuals are constrained in their categorizing by the social groups and stereotypes that they find in their environment and the role schemas which they learn and into which they are trained. I have argued further that stereotypes are maintained in the environment partly by psychological forces, acting on individuals and common knowledge conditions, that reinforce stereotypic social groupings and the material incentive structures in the world. Finally, I have argued that oppressed groups are motivated to acquiesce in and assimilate these oppressive stereotypes by three kinds of processes that make oppression a self-maintaining system: cognitive, behavioral, and rational.

Thus, one might be led to conclude that oppression is inescapable for its victims. Yet oppression is unjust, and so requires the just to attempt to overcome it, or at least to put up some resistance to it. How might this be done? Direct resistance to the direct forces of oppression would seem clearly to be required by justice, but without attacking the stereotypes that are self-fulfilling and that invidiously distinguish among us, this will be like trying to put out the flames without removing the fuel. From a cognitive standpoint there exist three courses of action to direct at stereotyping itself.[15] First, we need to attack existing role schemas and their rationalizations. We might do that, for instance, by showing how sociobiological explanations of the sexual division of labor depend on androcentric assumptions and privilege men. Second, since categorizing seems to be a cognitive demand for us, let us propose alternative categories for social groupings that depend more on interest than on accidents of birth, on voluntary groupings rather than involuntary groups. For if we group by chosen groups, there may be some possibility to change our grouping should it fail to satisfy us. Third, we can reveal false consciousness where it exists by exposing the ways in which assimilating oneself to involuntary in-groups and accentuating the differences with involuntary out-groups is, in at least some cases, either an assertion of undeserved privilege or a failure to resist one's own oppression.[16]

Notes

1 I present such an economic theory of oppression in Cudd (manuscript).
2 I defend this model of oppression in Cudd (1994).
3 Wertheimer (1987), p. 7. For example, this condition serves to rule out as oppressed persons legitimately convicted felons who are imprisoned.
4 The Hegelian recognition theory has been significantly advanced as a theory of oppression in the twentieth century by many social theorists, including Fanon (1963), Young (1990), and Willett (1995).
5 By "direct evidence" I mean tests of the psychological mechanisms postulated by the theory. I do not include here a set of child development milestones for which there exist competing coherent explanations, the only sort of empirical evidence Chodorow does offer.
6 In the most sweeping analysis of the empirical evidence for the theory of psychoanalysis to date, Adolf Grünbaum argues that the only empirical test offered by Freud is clinical, and consists in a two-step process: (1) does the specific theory for a patient tally with what the patient thinks is real; and (2) does it lead to therapeutic success. Grünbaum concludes that "Insofar as the evidence for the major causal hypotheses of the psychoanalytic corpus is held to derive from the productions of patients in analysis, this warrant is remarkably weak" (Grünbaum, 1984, p. 278).
7 A good example of this is Flax (1981).
8 Grünbaum (1984, 1993) meticulously and convincingly argues this point.
9 Actually I think that it can be shown to be logically necessary for information

processing, since without categorization there are no connections between ideas and so no way to process them. But for the purposes of this essay it is enough to claim that categorization is physically necessary, or necessary for the kinds of physical beings that we are.

10 See Fiske and Taylor (1991), pp. 156–60 for a discussion of the conditions under which people correct their false stereotypic attributions.

11 However, what determines belonging here is a highly theoretical issue, since what constitutes a group is itself a theoretical issue. One aspect of belonging that is systematically conflated in the psychological literature is the issue of whether the perceiver herself determines whether she belongs: is it her perception that matters, her commitments, or others' perceptions of her? In experiments this has to be operationalized in some way, and is generally done by direct assignment of the subjects to a group in a way that makes it clear and common knowledge to all which group each individual belongs to.

12 See Fiske and Taylor (1991), pp. 122, 137–9 for a review of the large literature on the circumstances in which role schemas are disengaged.

13 These material incentives to conform to stereotypical women's behavior are put forth in Cudd (1994).

14 There is a lot of controversy in social cognition theory about whether stereotypes are ever inaccurate (e.g. see Fiske and Taylor, 1991, pp. 341–2). What I mean to claim here, is that stereotypes do not present the truth, the whole truth, and nothing but the truth about individuals, and this can plainly be seen by considering the many "effects" and attribution errors that I have referred to that show stereotyping to be a biased and often false representation of individual attributes.

15 I don't mean to suggest here that attacking oppression in these cerebral, cognitive ways is the only or the most effective means. My point is that these are the courses of action that would directly address the oppressive nature of stereotyping itself.

16 I thank Nyla Branscombe, Dianne Kobrynowicz, Julie Maybee, and Beverly Mack for helpful discussions, and the Gender Seminar sponsored by the Hall Center for the Humanities and organized by Barry Shank and Mary Zimmerman for the opportunity to present an earlier draft of this essay.

References

Allport, Gordon W. (1979) *The Nature of Prejudice: 25th Anniversary Edition*, Reading, Mass. Addison-Wesley.

Bartky, Sandra Lee (1990) *Femininity and Domination: Studies in the Phenomenology of Oppression*, New York: Routledge.

Basow, Susan (1986) *Gender Stereotypes: Traditions and Alternatives*, Monterey, Calif.: Brooks/Cole.

Bem, Sandra (1981) "Gender Schema Theory: A Cognitive Account of Sex Typing," *Psychological Review*, 88: 354–64.

Bem, Sandra (1987) "Masculinity and Femininity Exist Only in the Mind of the

Perceiver," in J. M. Reinisch, L. A. Rosenblum, and S. A. Sanders (eds), *Masculinity/Femininity: Basic Perspectives*, New York: Oxford University Press, pp. 304–311.

Bibring, Grete (1953) "On the 'Passing of the Oedipus Complex' in a Matriarchal Family Setting," in Rudolph M. Lowenstein (ed), *Drives, Affects, and Behavior: Essays in Honor of Marie Bonaparte*, New York: International Universities Press, pp. 278–84.

Boski, Pawel (1988) "Cross-cultural Studies of Person Perception: Effects of Ingroup/Outgroup Membership and Ethnic Schemata," *Journal of Cross cultural Psychology*, 19 (September): 287–328.

Branscombe, Nyla (1996) "Thinking about Gender Privilege or Disadvantage: Consequences for Well-being in Women and Men," unpublished manuscript.

Branscombe, Nyla, Schiffhauer, Kristin, and Valencia, Lorena (1996) "Thinking about White Privilege or Disadvantage, Degree of White Racial Identification, and Intergroup Relations Beliefs for Feelings About the Ingroup and Outgroup," unpublished manuscript.

Bulhan, Hussein Abdilahi (1985) *Frantz Fanon and the Psychology of Oppression*, New York: Plenum Press.

Chodorow, Nancy (1978) *The Reproduction of Mothering: Psychoanalysis and the Sociology of Gender*, Berkeley: University of California Press.

Cudd, Ann E. (n.d.) *Analyzing Oppression*, unpublished manuscript.

Cudd, Ann E. (1990) "Enforced Pregnancy, Rape, and the Image of Woman," *Journal of Philosophical Studies*, 60: 47–59.

Cudd, Ann E (1994) "Oppression by Choice," *Journal of Social Philosophy*, 25: 22–44.

De Leon, Brunilda (1993) "Sex Role Identity among College Students: A Cross-cultural Analysis," *Hispanic Journal of Behavioral Sciences*, 15 (November): 476–89.

Deaux, K. (1987) "Psychological Constructions of Masculinity and Femininity," in J. M. Reinisch, L. A. Rosenblum, and S. A. Sanders (eds), *Masculinity/ Femininity: Basic Perspectives*, New York: Oxford University Press, pp. 289–303.

Deaux, K. and Lewis L. L. "The Structure of Gender Stereotypes: Interrelationships among Components and Gender Label," *Journal of Personality and Social Psychology*, 46: 991–1004.

Dhawan, Nisha, Roseman, Ira JI, Naidu, R. K., and Rettek, S. Ilsa (1995) "Self-concepts across Two Cultures: India and the United States," *Journal of Cross-cultural Psychology*, 26 (November): 606–21.

Fanon, Frantz (1963) *The Wretched of the Earth*, New York: Grove Press.

Felson, Richard B. and Tedeschi, James T. (1993) "A Social Interactionist Approach to Violence: Cross-cultural Applications," *Violence and Victims*, 8: 295–310.

Fiske, S. T. and Taylor S. E. (1991) *Social Cognition*, New York: McGraw Hill.

Flax, Jane (1981) "Psychoanalysis and the Philosophy of Science: Critique or Resistance?" *Journal of Philosophy*, 78: 561–8.

Fraser, Nancy (1995) "From Redistribution to Recognition? Dilemmas of Justice in a 'Post-Socialist' Age", *New Left Review*, 212: 68–93, and this volume, ch. 1.

Frye, Marilyn (1983) *The Politics of Reality: Essays in Feminist Theory*, Trumansburg, NY: Crossing Press.

Gilbert, Margaret (1989) *On Social Facts*, Princeton, Princeton University Press.

Grünbaum, Adolf (1984) *The Foundations of Psychoanalysis: A Philosophical Critique*, Berkeley: University of California Press.

Grünbaum, Adolf (1993) *Validation in the Clinical Theory of Psychoanalysis*, Madison, Ct.: International Universities Press.

Han, Gyuseog and Park, Bonsoon (1995) "Children's Choice in Conflict: Application of the Theory of Individualism–Collectivism," *Journal of Cross-cultural Psychology*, 26 (May): 298–313.

Hearne, Vicki (1986) *Adam's Task: Calling Animals by Name*, New York: Random House.

Hegel, G. W. F. [1807] (1977) *Phenomenology of Spirit*, trans. A. V. Miller, Oxford: Oxford University Press.

Hobbes, Thomas [1651] (1982) *Leviathan*, New York: Penguin Books.

Hoffman, C. and Hurst N. (1990) "Gender Stereotypes: Perception or Rationalization?" *Journal of Personality and Social Psychology*, 58: 197–208.

Hofstadter, Douglas (1985) "Changes in Default Words and Images, Engendered by Rising Consciousness," *Metamagical Themas*, New York: Basic Books, pp. 136–58.

Idson, Todd L. and Price, Hollis F. (1992) "An Analysis of Wage Differentials by Gender and Ethnicity in the Public Sector," *The Review of Black Political Economy* (winter): 75–97.

LeMoncheck, Linda (1985) *Dehumanizing Women: Treating Persons as Sex Objects*, Totowa, NJ: Rowman and Allanheld.

Lott, Bernice and Maluso Diane, (eds) (1990) *The Social Psychology of Interpersonal Discrimination*, New York: Guilford Press.

Lytton, H. and Romney, D. M. (1991) "Parents' Differential Socialization of Boys and Girls: A Meta-analysis," *Psychological Bulletin*, 109: 267–96.

Matsuda, Mari J., Lawrence, Charles R., III, Delgado, Richard, and Crenshaw, Kimberlè Williams (1993) *Words that Wound: Critical Race Theory, Assaultive Speech, and the First Amendment*, Boulder, Col: Westview Press.

Miller, Joan G. (1984) "Culture and the Development of Everyday Social Explanation," *Journal of Personality and Social Psychology*, 46 (May): 961–78.

Oakes, Penelope J., Haslam, S. Alexander, and Turner, John C. (1994) *Stereotyping and Social Reality*, Oxford: Blackwell Publishers.

Oddou, Gary and Mendenhall, Mark (1984) "Person Perception in Cross-cultural Settings: A Review of Cross-cultural and Related Cognitive Literature," *International Journal of Intercultural Relations*, 8: 77–96.

Okin, Susan Moller (1989) *Justice, Gender and the Family*, New York: Basic Books.

Ostaszewski, Pawel and Green, Leonard (1995) "Self-control and Discounting of

Delayed Rewards from an Individual Differences and Comparative Perspective," *Polish Psychological Bulletin*, 26: 231–8.

Pinto, Amancio C. (1992) "Medidas de categorizacao: Frequencia de producao e de tipicidade," *Jornal de Psicologia*, 10 (July): 10–15.

Rawls, John (1970) *A Theory of Justice*, Cambridge, Mass: Harvard University Press.

Sadker, M. and Sadker, D. (1994) *Failing at Fairness: How America's Schools Cheat Girls*, New York: Charles Scribner's Sons.

Sanford, L. and Donovan, M. E. (1984) *Women and Self-Esteem*, New York: Doubleday.

Skrypnek, B. J. and Snyder, M. (1982) "On the Self-perpetuating Nature of Stereotypes about Men and Women," *Journal of Experimental Social Psychology*, 18: 277–91.

Smith, Stephanie H., Whitehead, George I., and Sussman, Nan M. (1990) "The Positivity Bias in Attributions: Two Cross-cultural Investigations," *Journal of Cross-cultural Psychology*, 21 (September): 283–301.

Snyder, M., Tanke, E. D. and Berscheid, E. (1977) "Social Perception and Interpersonal Behavior: On the Self-fulfilling Nature of Social Stereotypes," *Journal of Personality and Social Psychology*, 35: 656–66.

Tajfel, Henri (1978) *The Social Psychology of the Minority*, New York: Minority Rights Group.

Tajfel, Henri (1981) *Human Groups and Social Categories*, Cambridge: Cambridge University Press.

Thomas, Laurence (1990) "In My Next Life, I'll Be White," *Ebony*, 46 (December): 84.

Troadec, Bertrand (1995) "Categorisations et cultures. Approche interculturalle des processus cognitifs de l'enfant tahitien," *Bulletin de Psychologie*, 48 (January–April): 288–96.

Turner, P. J., Gervai, J., and Hinde, R. A. (1993) "Gender-typing in Young Children: Preferences, Behavior and Cultural Differences," *British Journal of Developmental Psychology*, 11 (November): 323–42.

Tzeng, Oliver C. S. and Jackson, Jay W. (1994) "Effects of Contact, Conflict, and Social Identity on Interethnic Group Hostilities," *International Journal of Intercultural Relations*, 18 (spring): 259–76.

Vassiliou, Vasso G. and Vassiliou, George (1974) "Variations of the Group Process across Cultures," *International Journal of Group Psychotherapy*, 24 (January): 55–65.

Ward, Colleen (1985) "Sex Trait Stereotypes in Malaysian Children," *Sex Roles*, 12 (January): 35–45.

Wertheimer, Alan (1987) *Coercion*, Princeton: Princeton University Press.

Willett, Cynthia (1995) *Maternal Ethics and Other Slave Moralities*, New York: Routledge.

Williams, Patricia J. (1991) *The Alchemy of Race and Rights*, Cambridge, Mass.: Harvard University Press.

Wilson, Glenn D., Barrett, Paul T., and Iwawaki, Saburo (1995) "Japanese

Reactions to Reward and Punishment: A Cross-cultural Personality Study," *Personality and Individual Differences*, 19 (July): 102–12.

Young, Iris Marion (1990) *Justice and the Politics of Difference*, Princeton: Princeton University Press.

Part IV

Corporeal Logic and Sexuate Being

10

Toward the Domain of Freedom: Interview with Drucilla Cornell by Penny Florence

Drucilla Cornell

This interview is a transcript of a conversation with Drucilla Cornell, edited jointly by her and Penny Florence.

PF: I would like to start with some questions to help situate this interview for readers. How would you place yourself, in terms of philosophy?

DC: I would place myself primarily as a feminist with many alliances. All my work I see as inspired by feminist progress and as a Leftist. It has never been more necessary to call yourself both a feminist and a Leftist than it is now.

PF: What is your academic background and do you think of yourself as a philosopher?

DC: I am not a trained philosopher. My academic background is probably very typical of women of my generation. I really started out my life thinking I would be a poet and a playwright, a novelist – a writer – and I published some poems when I was younger. Even when I was in college I thought I would make a living by translating revolutionary Polish women's poetry. That was me being practical at the age of nineteen. Now, many years later, I have somebody in my extended family from Poland, so it worked out in that sense, even if it did not work out as an effective way of making money. But I studied Polish with such intensity and I am still a great admirer of the Revolutionary Polish Women poets. They are phenomenal. I was thrilled recently when a Polish woman poet won the Nobel prize. So it continues to be a passion of mine.

Like many women, I did not take myself seriously at all as someone who would ever realize their ideas, let alone pursue an academic career. I went to college at a number of different schools and left Stanford right before I graduated to become a Union organizer. I saw myself by that time as a committed revolutionary. My life's work would be in Union organizing. I had some very brutal experiences as a Union organizer, faced a lot of physical danger and death threats, but what was really affected was my hope that the world could be truly transformed in that way. It was quite an extended battle we were in with the Teamsters Union, which was developing sweetheart contracts in shops where I was trying to organize. Of course, you can challenge sweetheart contracts, but how are you going to do it when many of the workers are illegal immigrants and the last thing they are going to want you to do is to bring a law suit against the bosses and the Teamsters. It made me see personally just how brutal Capital can be. But it was the failure of justice. After I really hung in there – I had already been burnt out.

Later I succeeded in getting into a major university in mathematical logic, a great program, and got funding which still existed then in the US. My grandmother and I went and looked the place over and I just lost my nerve. I was quite shattered by it. There were no women in the department; it was the University of California at Berkeley, probably one of the best programs in mathematical logic, and I just did not believe I could do it. Having gotten into the program, working very hard to do so, I backed out and went to law school in a moment of total defeat. It is only maybe in the last three years, if asked the question, I would say, "Yes, I am a philosopher." It just shows you how long it takes women to be able to answer some very simple questions. Because I never went to graduate school, I did not understand anything about this whole academic apparatus, you know. I skipped a whole program and became a professor out of nowhere.

PF: What are you working on at the moment?

DC: I am writing a new book, *At the Heart of Freedom*, in which I am trying to continue to work with the idea of the "imaginary domain." It strongly defends gay and lesbian rights. Not just gay and lesbian rights but much more sweepingly: is there a concept of right that would give us a new way of thinking about freedom of sexuality that feminism could promote, and that would not lead to some of the quandaries that have been created by current theories of feminist legal reform that have focused on gender equality? In the United States this focus has a specific history because there was a moment when the feminist agenda tackled the interpretation of sex as gender for purposes of Title VII, our anti-discrimination statute. I am trying to return feminism to some of the earliest aspirations of what we now think of as the "second wave" of feminism, and away from a very limited concept of gender equality.

The imaginary domain is a philosophical concept in the sense that it tries to articulate the conditions that any theory of justice or any ethics of social arrangements has to have as a starting place: the equivalent evaluation of each of us as a sexuate being. I use "sexuate" as opposed to "sex" or "gender" because they have both been given such loaded meaning. I use the imaginary domain to replace the actual working legal principle of privacy in the United States as it has been used – and horribly misused – in protecting the rights of gays and lesbians. So my new book is in a sense a feminist book about sexual freedom which argues that we cannot think anything like freedom for women without thinking freedom for all of us as sexuate beings. The imaginary domain is meant to be that new idea that can help get feminism out of some of its conservative implications in the United States.

PF: For the sake of anyone who is unfamiliar with your book *The Imaginary Domain*, perhaps you could elaborate on the concept a little more, and then go on to explain how the idea of the imaginary domain is currently evolving from that initial articulation.

DC: In *The Imaginary Domain*, I primarily looked at minimum conditions of individuation as the basis of an egalitarian theory that would protect a de-ontological core of the person. However, as I started thinking about what this would mean in an international context I realized that such an idea still turns us back to concepts that we now think of as "Western" even if minimum conditions of individuation, and the idea of the person, are psychoanalytically and politically based, rather than metaphysically justified. I realized that I needed to distinguish between two levels. So, for example, when I started to look into questions of erotic autonomy for women in the Third World, it became clear that the idea of the imaginary domain might work, but it would not work in the same way. The equivalent meaning of our sexuate being has to be substantively filled in, in different ways, by every culture. So it raises the question of universalizability. This can be opposed to the positive universalism which has been an endless danger when feminists from the United States, or for that matter, Great Britain, or what used to be called Western Germany, get involved in the human rights dispute.

I take it very seriously when as Western feminists we are imposing our own ideas on the majority world. I was also very informed by the so-called collapse of socialism. I say "so-called" because it is unclear what actually collapsed. These countries may have been governed by utilitarianism in the capitalist sense and therefore they were much more like state capitalist societies. Even when they granted social equality to women, they did so through appeal to a utilitarian justification.

The imaginary domain is defended on the other hand through an interpretation of Kant. But it starts with the Kantian idea of our inviolability as persons. Still we want to be very very humble before taking words like "autonomy" and even "individuation" outside of their own context. I have no way given up on the idea of minimum conditions of individuation as a working idea for a legal theory of equality in the US, and as perhaps one of the conditions for England and for other societies. But there may be whole cultures for whom bodily integrity is just not the way a people would express whatever they want to say when they say there should be an equivalent evaluation of sexuate being. Questions of clitoridectomy and polygamy will have to be asked, and there would be a test for rightfulness. Universalizability remains a question; it would still not be relativism, but let us just look at the context and the culture.

Unfortunately, most cultures end up with the same position, relegating women to the status of the degraded other. We see worldwide patterns. Lesbians get exiled and women have no rights, and these horrific conditions must be condemned as unjust. They can be condemned as making impossible any equivalent evaluation of sexual difference. Still, we must be careful that we do not decide in advance, using our own Western terminology, what laws, and institutions, and cultural practices would be inconsistent with the equivalent evaluation of women's sexual difference. *The Imaginary Domain* is also an attempt to provide new answers to the political and legal issues of pornography, abortion and sexual harrassment. It is an attempt to take feminism back to some of its rudimentary but very important radical ideas.

PF: Britain, of course, has no written constitution such as exists in the USA. One of the most prominent women barristers in this country, Helena Kennedy, is also chair of Charter 88, which is a group campaigning for a Bill of Rights in this country and a written Constitution. I have two questions here. First, drawing on the American experience, do you think women are right to fight for a constitution? The second question is about the constitutional differences between countries and the "translation" problems that ensue for international readers and writers interested in the law. Even if a constitution is drafted, there will still be major differences between Britain and the US, for example, because of the historical trace of the old system, or because of our relation to European laws and courts. What might be some of the ramifications for the broad feminist project of rethinking law?

DC: You know I think, for me at least, we need to do two things. First, we should not simply conflate social critique of law with normative interpretations of legal principle. Now I think that the question "Should there be a written constitution?" is an important one. Overall I would favor written constitutions. They are needed because written constitutions are marking out a symbolic order which to some extent creates boundaries for the colonial world. The creation of new constitutions has been taken up in many of the world's new nations. Since we are confronted with these new constitutions, I think we should certainly advocate a concept of right that would embrace what Jackie Alexander calls "erotic autonomy" and we should also fight to make sure that these constitutions do not reconstitute patriarchy once again. Just the written declaration that we are all free and equal persons can be quite significant as a rallying call. I am Lacanian enough to think that the symbolic order will want to spit out that equality. Can a constitution make you safe? Obviously not! I agree with the old Marxist saying: that rights are only as good as the people who enforce them. People in the popular sense. You should not expect more from these constitutions than you can get. So for most of the world my answer would be the move towards a written constitution is extremely important, and I tend to agree with Willie Appalon that it involves second-stage postcolonialism when you claim for your country and your people the kind of subject-position that is absolutely denied to the colonized. And it should be a rights-based constitution rather than a duty-based constitution. Wherever women have been rendered objects of duty you see the replication of utilitarian capitalist ideology.

PF: In Britain, especially since the anti-democratic developments under Thatcher and Major, it has become increasingly important both that current rights of citizens be safeguarded and that women's rights be understood as human rights.

DC: That is why I disagree whenever people say rights are necessarily part of private property. Rights are part of possessive individualism. I disagree with the Foucauldian analysis that when you claim yourself as having a right before the law you are positioning yourself as a victim. I think that what we are aiming for in the imaginary domain is not to represent ourselves as a victim but to say we are entitled to represent our own sexuate being. That means whether I am a lesbian or a transvestite or a transsexual, or something else that I have represented myself to be, when I choose to be a parent I can be a parent – unless, of course, I am engaging in violence against my kid.

I am very concerned that the idea of a concept of right does not get conflated with a specific articulation of rights because I do disagree with the idea that simply having a concept of right, if it is tailored on an abstract enough level, will turn into political moralism. It is not that I disagree that political moralism has haunted feminism – it has – but that does not mean that we cannot positively and affirmatively intervene in this dispute. Perhaps in the end I am Hegelian enough to think that we are actually constituted in modernity as subjects of right and so, in a sense, we cannot just step outside this sphere of law. I mean, Foucault asks, why are we always back to legality? Well, I think Hegel has the answer to that. Since the bourgeois revolutions, who we are, who we have been constituted to be, is subjects of rights. Thus, when a nation proclaims its people as a free and equal nation, in a sense it is also proclaiming an entitlement to a kind of personhood that has been absolutely denied the nation and its people by imperialist domination.

PF: Your work has implications for aesthetics if only because of the major role you accord to safeguarding access to symbolic forms. How productive do you think it might be to think this through explicitly in terms of aesthetics?

DC: You know I think the aesthetic might be the central category of what I mean by ethics, and even the concept of right embodied in the imaginary domain has at its heart the demand for the space for the aesthetic affirmation and re-engagement of the feminine within sexual difference. If I did not see feminism and feminist politics as requiring an aesthetic dimension, then I would not have carved out the boundary of the person to individuate themselves as a sexuate being in the way that I did. The whole aesthetic dilemma of feminism is how you move within imposed personas to try to "be freed up enough" to redream, rethink, relive out different patterns of sexuality and sexuate being that do not just reinscribe accommodation to the masculine and feminine, or to family life as a certain kind of kinship. You cannot defend this vision of feminism without the idea of "dreaming up," and in this way, the part of Kant that ultimately I am most interested in is the idea of the transcendental imagination.

The role of the imagination and the role of the aesthetic are essential in my entire project, starting with *Beyond Accommodation*. What is it about human beings that can enact and create new objects? And the reason I have always said this is not anti-materialist is that when we think of human being in Heidegger's sense, as radically thrown into a world, there is no way we do not symbolize it. That is what it means to be in language. You can get this from Heidegger; you can get this from Wittgenstein. We are stuck with having to resymbolize, rearticulate, reallegorize and remetaphorize who we are and how we live in a world that is brought to us in language, so that our own sexual being never comes to us as unsymbolized.

Annie Sprinkle does a marvelous enactment of this – Annie Sprinkle is a porn star as you probably remember from *The Imaginary Domain*. She says she was a failed heterosexual for her first twenty years of life and she had her breasts redone four or five times. At the opening of her show, she takes off her blouse and stands there with her breasts exposed, and she says, "I have no idea what these are." Then she proceeds to get every woman in the room completely and utterly confused because in fact none of us do know what they are. That is what I mean by saying that we encounter our own bodies without being able to know them as ours. Judith Butler says we run into a body that has already been re-evaluated, but, even more profoundly, a body that is so deeply inscribed in a whole scene of sexual dynamics that, by the time you look at your breasts and at what they are it is certainly not just a material phenomenon that is at issue.

Once breasts are no longer shown as sexual objects, the question "What are these? Can you help me?" makes women confront their own hearts and the history inscribed in them. Then Sprinkle goes through a list of her boyfriends as she shows all her scars. This one wanted them this way, and this one wanted them that way, and finally when she was in her late 30s she became a lesbian, initially because she did not want to go have plastic surgery any more.

Other women usually join in, and then people make ink prints of their breasts and she has turned these ink prints into art shows that she displays and the women sign them and they put them up in different ways. It becomes this kind of collective aesthetic performance (laughter) of women trying to take back their breasts, and of course it is an incredibly funny evening, it is totally enjoyable. But a lot of Annie Sprinkle's work is about this struggle to take back the body. "What is this?" "How did I get this?" "Who am I?" When a woman's sex is accompanied by this long discussion about what is there and what is not there, the whole woman-as-sexual-object is completely disintegrated. In the show there is the voice and the body parts and it is really beautifully performed.

For me that performance exemplifies where the heart of feminism lies. The women who put their breasts in ink attempt to take something that cannot be held on to – and hold on to it. This "holding on differently" is why I have argued that the feminine imaginary has to be symbolized, despite all of the problems of the reactivating of symbols. You know, symbols freeze, symbols keep us from seeing everything that can be put in motion again, but without that moment of holding on, there is no way of moving beyond accommodation to our "found" bodies. We are just endlessly lost in the dissolution, and the disintegration that Sprinkle is describing. So the aesthetic is the absolutely central category for me.

PF: This puts me in mind of feminist thinkers such as Rosi Braidotti who, as she puts it, are trying to think materialism beyond physicalism, to get beyond the idealism/materialism binary. It seems to me that your work certainly implies this.

DC: Absolutely. Rosi and I have just been involved in an exchange with Rita Felski, sending some material that touches on this back and forth. You are right. I think that the way I would put it is that materiality is never directly accessible to us. So if you think about what a materialist ethics would be that would get beyond the mind/body dualism it would explore the way meaning is inscribed in the flesh. To touch the subject of the body differently demands that we represent both words and the unreadability of the found body.

PF: I am trying to think of it from the point of view of an embodied and historicized "aesthetics of difference" which is supple enough to encompass the vexed questions of value and beauty which have been evaded for some time by many feminists and Leftists alike. Of course, earlier Left thinkers like Adorno . . .

DC: I do not think you can ever forget Adorno on this point, and for instance what Habermas did in boxing the aesthetic from the ethical. Some practices like Sprinkle's, whatever you think of their success, are looking toward an aesthetic of feminine sexual difference as material, but as material that can be reformed, resymbolized and played with.

PF: Do you think this basic relation of the aesthetic to play is at least part of what Irigaray meant in her fairly recent expression of regret concerning the pain there is in feminist art or women's art?

DC: I think Irigaray may well be reaching for something like Schiller's sense of play and it is very much what I mean by the imaginary domain, you know, the space before you are completely marked by a sexed body, but of course we do not get there except by traveling differently, and part of that traveling has to be through play. So play-acting in Schiller's sense is a very profound part of feminism. I was glad to see Irigaray coming back to it because I felt when she followed Hegel in introducing the concept of sexuate rights she was getting very far away from her own radicalism. It is one thing to say you need a concept of right; but it is another thing to ontologize sexual difference. I strongly disagree with her concept of sexuate rights because you have inevitably given an ontological basis to Right that freezes sexual difference, and that is an extremely dangerous project, not a playful project.

PF: The utopian is a space in which it is possible to play, and you make significant use of it in your work. I am not sure I understand all the levels on which you do so, however.

DC:　First what I do not mean. I do not mean utopianism as a blueprint, a "how-to" manual. Kantianism as I interpret it in *The Imaginary Domain* is a utopian project because it is a demand for inclusion in a moral community of persons that by definition cannot exist and in that sense the demand for inclusivity is not in this community or that community, but it is for full recognition of a free and equal personhood that is utopian. It is what has never been realized in any existing society. If you just did that, if you just defended the proposition that women as well as gays and lesbians, transvestites, transsexuals would be given the right to represent their own sexuate being, and be given the right to represent themselves without any interference, and to live out lives in accordance with our visions of intimate association, you would have completely disrupted the order of civilization.

Chantal Mouffe talks about inclusivity in a horizon of community, or existing community. The community of persons is a "must be" of practical reason placed on society by the recognition of us as free and equal persons, so I do not even think we want to have a community as a horizon as if there were something out there that we can represent. So it is utopian in both these ways: it appeals to what is not, and it has never been actualized; and if it were to be actualized we would be living in a very different world. We would be living in a world in which patriarchy could not be institutionalized any more. The other form of utopian gets back to the feminine within sexual difference. I mean the time of sexual difference that has never yet arrived, that only exists in the future and that Irigaray speaks of.

As a mother of a four-year-old daughter, I am endlessly returned to the practice of freedom in mother–daughter relationships, so in this sense starting as if we were creating psychic maps for outer space. You know, this is what I have tried to do on a day-to-day basis. What "mother" is, what "daughter" is, this all has to be scrapped, and you start with this "person." Of course, this "person" is materialized as female as you are, so you are already engaged with feminine sexual difference, the two of you together. When my daughter, Sarita, started to masturbate, and she wanted to know what her sex was called, we decided to call it "wonder," and the reason I called it wonder is because it represents the wonderful, the many pleasurable things that if you just said what they were, you could never describe the pleasure they give you. And the playing with wonder has had an effect on how she thinks of her sex, as opposed to masturbating, which is such a dull word. Sarita knows all her parts; this is a vagina, this is a clitoris; but she refers to her clitoris as her "fun button." This feminine other self so much freer than my self, is always demanding, because I am the one with more language, but she is the one with more freedom. My words try to catch up with her freedom, and of course it is impossible. So I see actually engaging with her as a utopian project, creating a place that has never been. And creating an in-between us that has never been conceivable under the whole unbelievably oppressive rubric of being a mother and having a daughter.

PF: Something no woman can change alone, of course. I guess this is one of the ways your extended family works, including the various but stable male figures in Sarita's life, like Uncle Larry.

DC: I am trying to build a completely different kind of family and the adoption chapter in my current book defends these new families. Some people are going to have more biological ties than others. In my case, my extended family has almost no biological ties, though I do have a biological family with people still living in it. My idea was to create an extended family which would prevent me from having to rely on servants as many women do who continue to work, and to completely problematize the dynamics of the sexual imposition of heterosexual normality. Uncle Larry always wanted to be a parent, and the way the rights to parenting are generally so limited meant that, as a gay man, he was excluded. My daughter has four gay uncles. Uncle Bill and Uncle Larry were single at the time they became part of my extended family. They got into very stable relationships, and their lovers have now joined the uncle category. The uncles are different. Uncle Larry is really involved in week-by-week parenting. He picks her up from school one day a week and he also cooks dinner for me, lunch for me. I feel like I have died and gone to heaven, since he has been with me! He is involved in day-to-day caring. In some ways he is a better mother than I am. He is much less fraught with endless philosophical complexity about each and every one of his actions.

Our family is a very rich sphere of complex engagements and a lot of love. So I am very glad that I keep up this experiment. The scene of adoption is fraught with the unconscious paradigm of heterosexuality. That is why all the adoption literature is so hopelessly boring. You know the birth mother and the adoptive mother are put in a position of war against each other because there can only be one mother in the heterosexual imaginary, but of course when a lesbian mother wants to adopt her lover's baby, both of the couple want to be mothers. This should not be a big problem. Under my schema, there is not only room for one more, there is no limit. Why would I be threatened if in fact Sarita's birth-mother at some point or another wants to have contact with her? We have set this up in such a way because of the whole thing of heterosexuality producing the man's sexuality, which produces the children and the trauma of infertility, etc. And so it was actually adoption that got me thinking about sexual freedom.

PF: Irigaray has famously suggested that sexual difference is the question of our age. What would you suggest and why? Or is this not an age of large "Questions" as such, but rather one of rethinking relations?

DC: That's a really interesting question. I certainly would see sexual difference as one of the main questions of the age, but I think maybe the central question for me is whether it is possible to really transform the world and truly produce new social arrangements. The reworking of sexual difference would be central to the new ethics of social arrangements. I think that is what has led me to be very careful about the role of political philosophy and insist on the idea of justice. If you do not think that it is possible to truly transform the world and create new social arrangements that are in dramatic ways more ethical, perhaps more ethical by many different standards or theories that you could set up, then the reworking of sexual difference, what does it come down to? How would we know that it came to anything? What would it produce? What would it constitute that was different? So I think I would say that is the central question. And with the collapse of a political scenario involving a major part of humanity believing to some degree or not in Marxism, this question has really come to the fore. And then within the resultant situation, the rethinking of sexual difference and the reworking of sexual difference will be one of the main arenas in which we are going to challenge the idea that there is nothing new under the sun.

PF: Feminism has always faced the awkward problem of inserting itself into ill-fitting systems of meaning. There is attendant on setting up a dialogue with the male dominant a real danger of according it, the dominant, more structural weight than the female in the imaginary domain. What is the effect of situating in the dominant tradition areas of theory where women have made substantial, if sometimes only recent, contributions? How best can it be handled? On one level this is about something as simple as citation; on another, disidentification; and on another, about history. I particularly wanted to ask you this because... I raised it in a kind of coda to my review of *The Imaginary Domain* in the last issue of *Women's Philosophy Review*. The matter was restimulated for me as much by your notion of the imaginary domain itself and the extent of its potential as by the way you chose to frame it – in other words, it is as much about the genealogy of important ideas as it is about your practice, and thus it is about the reception of your work on the level of conceptualization as well as a question of strategy.

DC: I actually think that is a really important question because we inherit a tradition, at least if we are raised in England or the United States, that is not only mainly masculine but also white. When we engage with it, we are inevitably both having to identify and disidentify. I try to express that identification/disidentification with alliances – and I need to note my refusal to keep my alliances neat. I ally with many different men who are at war with one another. I would never call myself a Derridean, or an Adornian, or a Hegelian, or a Kantian, or a Lacanian – so disidentification is always implied by the alliance. Yet it is also true that the two women writers I mainly cite who are not primarily known as fiction writers are Irigaray and Cixous. But the woman I cite the most is Toni Morrison, and in a sense she is probably the writer who has had the most aesthetic impact on me in reshaping and rearticulating what I think of as the aesthetic element in my own attempt to reconfigure a feminism in which the aesthetic is at the heart.

I think part of what we are up against is the historical fact of the exclusion of women from philosophy, which has nothing to do in my mind with any natural characteristics of the feminine mind, but simply with imposed, brutally imposed, exclusion. As we get to the point, if we are getting to a point, where women can place themselves in philosophy, then what we would hopefully see is more women engaging enough in disidentification so that we will no longer have to spend our whole life labeled as a follower of a particular man. But it is really interesting that a lot of my work, probably unconsciously to myself, proceeds through alliances that are so bizarrely drawn with men that it disrupts the idea of identification. I mean, nobody writes of Lacan, and Derrida, and Rawls in the same book – and says she has alliances with all of them. I have proceeded a great deal through disidentification, and I think that is the only thing we can hope for. Yet it is also a reality, an intellectual historical reality, that I have really come out of German idealism and have remained engaged in a long, long struggle with it. That tradition is very inscribed in the masculine. And Irigaray has, too. We share a tradition with one another, and I think that this part of the reason that even more than Cixous, although I am very deeply sympathetic to so much of her work, Irigaray for me has been a real interlocutor, even as she came up with sexuate lives and I came up with the idea of the imaginary domain.

PF: I guess this also about the genealogy of important ideas.

DC: I am conscious of the historical problem: what does it mean to root yourself in a masculine tradition? What would it mean to break yourself free of that grounding both as yourself psychically at a particular moment, and to claim your own ideas for yourself and as a feminist claim these ideas are feminist, and at the same time say the feminism demands a complete rethinking of the central categories of philosophy? I do think it is important to go back to the old texts. I also often teach McKinnon, but McKinnon has a kind of materialism that is very deterministic, so that in order to teach McKinnon you are always forced to go back to the texts that she is engaging with. I feel that this is a constant, constant problem, and the only solution I think is to endlessly try to re-engage with it.

There is a further question about how to symbolically engage in public with women with whom you would disagree. It is an extremely difficult question. It involves the problem of translation, how does psychic reality translate into our objective world, and how is our objective world translated back into our psychic reality without some very simple idea of cause and effect? It is clear that the respect for the other writer must be noted. Even with McKinnon I felt the need to bend over backwards to be very clear of my ultimate respect for her. I think that part of this is what Irigaray calls for, the great care before the symbolic relationships between women that can so easily be misread as a "cat fight." I think it is a very important question and I think it is part of feminist politics that we answer it, and it certainly is not because I think there are no great feminist "postmodern" thinkers. I think they are innumerable. It suggests that when you engage, it must be a careful reading

PF: Have you seen Teresa Ebert's book, *Ludic Feminism* which I reviewed in the last issue of *Women's Philosophy Review*?

DC: She sent it me, I think. She obviously did not know that I was an old Union organizer, and in and out of Marxist and Leninist parties, and did armed self-defence for the Black Panther Party. So my response is, "Well, girlfriend, I've been there!" I've read parts of the book. I understand her impulse. She wants to go back to true blue Marxism, and go back to class; but if you go back to class, what you're going to find is all sorts of women trying to engage with the aesthetic formulation and reformation of what it means to be a woman. One of the deepest fantasies of academics is that we are the only ones who read books and have ideas. Once you have actually worked in a factory, you will know that you will have as many discussions on what we are now calling aesthetic practices as you will anywhere else.

My own consciousness-raising group, when I worked in a factory in New Jersey, was all black and Hispanic, and one of the women was in the Young Lords Party. She was a prostitute; she remained a prostitute; and we organized prostitute collectives that were very engaged with all sorts of measures to really handle the pimps. Yet part of what this whole discussion was about was reforming female sexuality and the figure of the prostitute. We played a major role in going to the 1974 feminist meeting to discuss prostitution and defended unionization for prostitutes. We would read Hegel and Marx.

It is a fantasy of ours, us academics, that we are the ones that are formed by ideas. When I read *Ludic Feminism* and I saw myself portrayed as a high theorist separate from the masses, I thought, no. You see, if you are with "the masses" you no longer have that kind of elitism, and it is a kind of elitism, to think that so-called average women, and I say "so-called" because in a sense, certainly, I see myself as having all of the "average problems" that any mother who tries to work has. We fantasize materialist feminists as being "real" and about the "real" issues, but when you actually are doing the work of changing the world, it is all about reimagining the forms in which it is to be done.

I will give you an example. Our consciousness-raising group not only took on prostitution. We organized an action against a male worker in Harlem Hospital that was completely thought out in terms of keeping the state out of kinship relationships. This man was not paying child support. We would go in, we would pass out leaflets asking women to express as best they could their views on this kind of behavior. People would put smoke bombs in this guy's locker, pelt him with food, and put worms in his locker, and use all sorts of creative and expressive means, and the last I heard he was still paying his child support maintenance. On the one hand, it was direct action, and on the other hand, it was always thought through in terms of new forms of self-mobilization. Our rallying call was, "We leave it to you girls to express in your own unique – and what we are sure will be highly original ways – how you feel about this guy not giving money to his kids and causing so many problems," and they did. The last I heard, he was still paying his child support maintenance.

We need to be able to transform the world and really change it. I think the irony is that for me I learned about the aesthetic dimension of political practice as a Union organizer. The unions were very much caught in economic determinist arguments, and it is exactly that which could not mobilize anyone to do anything. Even the idea of a Union Organizing Committee coming together and being in solidarity, and being in a union, we always played with it. When I was on organizing committees, plays would come out of it, paintings would come out of it, it was aesthetic on many different levels in that sense. In short, I am sympathetic to Teresa Ebert. Let us not be up in the clouds and let us do something. But if she tried to do something she would realize it is very important to at least be able to reach into the dreamy aspects of life and be fearless in what you are challenging, otherwise what are you going to change? We have gone through this over and over again in the Union movement.

PF: I guess that one thing that concerned me about her argument was that in her appeal to return to global questions, she was wanting to return to global theories. There is an important difference. We do have to return to those kinds of "universal" questions – but not through global theorizing.

DC: Yes, and again with that kind of economic determinism. Of course I think we need theories of distributive justice, I think, in a larger sense, equality of work.

PF: One last question. Is there something you think we should have talked about or covered that we have not?

DC: I think I would like to end with a warning to feminism. Feminism really needs to guard against some of its own conservative tendencies, as we have to fight now for what seem to have been rights that we should have long since won. We should not entrench ourselves in a program based more on circumstance and exhaustion than on any kind of real hope. And if we do that, and then say, for instance, that some right to abortion is better than no right to abortion, and that some minimal laws against sexual harassment are better than none, then maybe we have purchased these rights at the price of excluding our gays and lesbians from the reach of the statute. What happened in the US is extraordinarily corrosive to feminism and just renders our views incoherent. But the good thing about being radical is that you can make a coherent argument, and also make your ideas have an appeal that this is truly different. I am looking for a radicalism that is not just an old replay of the politics of resentment that just endlessly plays out in the same kind of negotiation-politics, where people trade off others in order to get the little bit that is not worth having.

Note

Thanks to Christine Battersby for her assistance.

11

Morphing the Body: Irigaray and Butler on Sexual Difference

Tamsin Lorraine

In *An Ethics of Sexual Difference*, Luce Irigaray says that the problem of sexual difference may be the problem of our age.[1] Because of the role women have traditionally played, they form a distinct gender; contemporary culture is bifurcated by a sexual division of labor in which the body and the "natural" is relegated to the feminine, and the more "cultural" products of symbolic significance are related to the masculine. This division of labor manifests not only in a gender-marked public/private split between cultural production in the public arena and reproduction of human beings in the home, but in the social activity required to nurture and maintain human subjects as subjects. Irigaray's work develops an account of a specular economy of subjectivity in which feminine others tend to mirror back to masculine subjects affirming images of a masterful self. She argues that this bifurcation has serious ethical implications that has led to an impoverished life for us all. Given the impracticality of asking a culture to simply abandon masculine subjectivity – especially with no viable alternative – she insists that we need to acknowledge two genders and work on providing the hitherto subordinated gender with the symbolic support it needs to become more than the counterpart of masculinity. If the feminine other were given the support of a gender in its own right, then feminine subjectivity could fully emerge, an alternative to masculine subjectivity would become available, and the cultural economies supporting subjectivity would shift so dramatically that it is impossible to say in advance what kind of subjects we would be.

Although some have taken Irigaray's project of specifying sexual difference to be a counterproductive effort to essentialize and reify differences between women and men, I will suggest that her project instead pushes us to a notion of difference and embodied specificity that would ultimately undermine the very notion of sexual difference with which she starts. Through the project of rendering the inarticulate repressed of what she calls a "masculine" economy of language, Irigaray hopes to create new possibilities for subjectivity, and in particular, enable a kind of mutual reciprocity that is currently difficult, if not impossible, to achieve. In opening up the question of sexual difference, she opens up the possibility of a non-dualistic account of embodied difference, one that neither denies nor denigrates either side of the traditional mind/body split, but instead gives equal attention to the material level of human existence and the conceptual schemas through which we attempt to understand it. This entails opening up what she calls a third dimension: a dimension that would foster encounters among oneself and others in terms of the spaces in between – the interval or the excess that renders identity continually problematic – and thus open up new possibilities for relating.

In the first section of this essay I present Irigaray's critique of masculine sexuality, her evocation of a feminine alternative, and her reconception of Hegelian negativity in light of an embodied theory of subjectivity. I introduce the terms "corporeal logics" and "conceptual logics" in characterizing her work, although Irigaray herself never uses these terms. Corporeal logic relates to one's bodily and perceptual organization and is formed through initial encounter with the maternal body. Conceptual logic relates to symbolic systems of meaning and various abstractions from all-encompassing participation within a world from which one cannot separate oneself that enable a subject/object split, self-consciousness, and subjectivity. Distinguishing corporeal and conceptual logics speaks to the way that contemporary meaning systems seem to be arranged in keeping with mind/body dualisms; we actually do separate our understanding of life according to this split. What we know on a rational, cerebral level, is not what we know on an emotional, corporeal level. Distinguishing two, heterogeneous logics of subjectivity is one way of aligning various ways of characterizing the "rational" ordering of conceptual thought and various ways of characterizing the "irrational" ordering associated with the personal realm of the body. Conceptual meaning and corporeal "sense" are not only oriented in different directions, but likely to diverge ever more widely, especially in a culture which emphasizes mind/body dualisms and valorizes the mind at the expense of the body.

Irigaray's project of symbolizing "feminine" subjectivity, from this perspective, turns out to be a project of elaborating corporeal logics.

Maintaining ourselves as subjects with bodies and psychic selves requires responsive attunement from others at the level of embodied interaction as well as at the level of verbal feedback. Maintenance of a recognizable self requires repeatable patterns: familiar forms of sense perception and habitual patterns of movement and emotional response at the level of corporeal logics; the capacity to "make sense" while speaking from the position of a coherent and repeatable "I" at the level of conceptual logics. It is Irigaray's contention that the cultural work marked as feminine is under-symbolized and barely acknowledged to protect the illusion of substantial selfhood. Veiling the processes required to establish and maintain bodies with firm boundaries and psychic selves with coherent identities allows us to "naturalize" the effects of those processes into "things" more substantial than in fact they are. And yet it is precisely because we are living subjects rather than substantial selves that we can creatively respond to each present moment. Maintaining a recognizable self throughout the varied circumstances of living requires openness to what lies beyond the already-done and the already-said. It is the implicit contention of Irigaray's work that the ongoing symbolization and integration of what lies just beyond conventional thought and perception is our best hope for opening up new, and perhaps more ethical, possibilities for social living.

In the second section of this essay I sketch Judith Butler's characterization of Irigaray's project to further undermine a reading of Irigaray that would suggest that she is engaged in a project of reifying conventional gender stereotypes. Butler argues that Irigaray's notion of the feminine evokes the unrepresentable excess which would threaten the internal coherence of a phallogocentric economy. On Butler's reading, the "feminine" indicates an excessive materiality that resists materialization in the perceivable forms of common sense experience. The project of symbolizing a "feminine" subject, on my reading, develops a vocabulary for talking about the corporeal aspects of subjectivity as a process. Although Butler might object to the project of providing symbolic support for a "feminine" subject, providing such support disrupts a specific cultural formation in which the embodied subjectivity of one group is premised upon blindness to the materially constitutive effects of another. Acknowledging such constitutive effects brings us to the limits of contemporary formations of corporeal and conceptual logics and incites creative responses to an always changing world. Butler gives us further insight into how we can approach such limits in a politically responsible way. Her notion of the lesbian phallus suggests how an elaboration of corporeal logics could contest heterosexist as well as masculinist norms and gives further indication of what a subjectivity not premised upon blindness to a marginalized other might look like. I will draw upon her reading of Irigaray and her notion of the lesbian phallus in order to elaborate how attentiveness to corporeal logics might provide ethical impetus for a project of constructive political change.

1 Shattering Mirrors: Irigaray and the Feminine Subject

Irigaray claims that masculine subjects need to deny their embodiment in order to maintain separation from the matter that produced them.[2] In the specular economy of traditional male/female relationships, the masculine subject takes the feminine other as an object to be possessed. This renders him an active subject *vis-à-vis* a passive other who reflects him back to himself without contributing anything of her own to the relationship. Due to the displacement of his corporeality onto the feminine other, she seems to emanate emotional confusion and inchoate affects, but this is dismissed by the masculine subject as superfluous residue rather than incorporated into the relationship through a process of attentive recognition which engenders creative transformation.[3] Since our conception of human nature tends to take the masculine subject as its norm, what is called human nature "often means forgetting or ignoring our corporeal condition for the sake of some spiritual delusion or perversion" (*TD*, p. 18). Women, on the other hand, provide another possibility.

> Woman's subjective identity is not at all the same as man's. She does not have to distance herself from her mother as he does-by a *yes* and especially a *no*, a *near* or a *far*, an *inside* opposed to an *outside*-to discover her sex. She is faced with another problem entirely. She must be able to identify with her mother as a woman to realize her own sexuality. She must be or become a woman like her mother and, at the same time, be able to differentiate herself from her. But her mother is the same as she. She cannot reduce or manipulate her as an *object* in the way a little boy or a man does. (*TD*, p. 18)

The feminine subject has a tendency to define herself *vis-à-vis* a masculine subject. Instead of situating herself as an active subject with respect to an object, she situates herself with respect to the other who acts as mediator between herself and herself. That is, she refers her subjectivity to the other; it is only through the other that she feels she has existence. Although Irigaray would say that masculine subjectivity is actually dependent upon a nurturing other despite his delusion that he can maintain himself as a self-sufficient whole, the feminine subject who defines herself through the masculine subject is so dependent upon the mediation provided by the masculine subjective that she is not able to acknowledge her own contribution to her subjectivity.

Irigaray believes that we can articulate feminine forms of desire and sexuality. She points to multiple arenas of the symbolic field which could provide rich sites of creative intervention in keeping with such a project. Creating a genealogy specific to the mother–daughter relationship would enhance possibilities for more highly differentiated relations among women. Creating religious symbols honoring a feminine divine would establish a cultural horizon for specifically feminine becoming. Symbolic elaborations of mother–daughter relations and a feminine divine not only support feminine subjectivity, they enable a new relationship between two genders. We will see that articulating "feminine" desire not only provides support for feminine sexuality, but also allows a more reciprocal form of sexuality to emerge between lovers of both genders.

Irigaray cites Freud's view that masculine sexuality is "constructed upon a model of energy involving tension, release and return to homeostasis" (*TD*, p. 20) and comments that the only way to escape the "sad fate" of a sexuality linked to physical laws which render it repetitive, explosive, and non-evolutive, is through procreation.[4] Women's sexual economy, on the other hand, entails a temporality and a corporeal logic that is in harmony with cosmic rhythms in a way that men's are not. Human life plays out within a non-human as well as human range of processes of which we are mostly unaware. Processes that go beyond any human intervention into life and any specific cultural form that human life may take, are always more encompassing and complex than the human processes which they incorporate. As much as we may wish that we could put them at a distance or somehow establish our autonomy from them, it is within these larger processes over which we have no control that we live out our lives.[5] Given that women's traditional role has been to bear the brunt of reproductive labor, and given that masculine subjectivity has traditionally displaced corporeality onto the feminine other, women are closer to the broader processes within which we inevitably find ourselves and over which we have no control. It then makes sense to turn to women in order to speak to the inadequacy between corporeal and conceptual logics that has lead to some of the contemporary difficulties in which we find ourselves.

Sexuality is an important part of what such a new form of relationship to others must address. As long as masculine sexuality is based upon a build-up of tension and a release that is blind to the constitutive power of the other, eroticism is returned to a primitive chaos with no hope of furthering the creative engenderment of two loving partners. Instead, all creativity is displaced onto the creation of the child in reproduction. Sexuality in the form of chaotic life-drives which operate without relation to the individuation of persons are for Irigaray a form of the masculinist fantasy of self-creation.[6] She insists that masculine sexuality lacks the capacity to come into rhythm with another and harmonize desires. Due to his inability to come into any kind of attunement with the other, the masculine subject is plunged into a non-differentiated abyss.[7] Given the masculinist refusal to acknowledge that anything other to himself could have creative power, he is unable to contribute to reciprocal creative engenderment and can only plunge further into a loss of identity through fusion.[8] Thus, an opportunity for reciprocal love is lost and sexuality is reduced to a cathartic release cordoned off from social interaction.

In a capitalist context, this leads to an economy of exchange in which self-identical subjects quantify the objects they exchange according to rules of equivalence. Objects – women, goods, and money – can then be passed from one subject to the next without endangering the identities of the subjects engaged in the exchange. Relations are thus maintained through the fluid circulation of various kinds of objects without threatening either the stability of social subjects or the structures through which those subjects are related. For Irigaray, the project of equalizing opportunities so that women are equally able to become masculine subjects would be a huge loss of an important cultural resource that might provide a way out of a stultifying and life-threatening situation for us all.[9] In order to avoid the further impoverishment of culture to the sad state of a masculinist order which prioritizes money and economic exchanges as well as to empower women who are unable or unwilling to take up positions of "equal" power, Irigaray proposes re-evaluating the right to sexual identity and insists that sexual identity be recognized as part of civil identity.[10]

In *I Love to You* Irigaray elaborates a form of Hegelian recognition that would go beyond the civil recognition of masculine subjects in the public realm and would instead acknowledge sexual difference, and gives a critical rereading of Hegel's notion of negativity designed to aid in the reconceptualization of civil identity. According to her rereading of Hegel's notion of recognition each subject would acknowledge her or his limits in concrete encounter with another. This evokes a situation of energetic interaction in which neither subject is overwhelmed by the other or reduced to the schema of the other, but in which a generative encounter occurs in the realm of sensibility itself. Returning "to ourselves as living beings who are engendered and not fabricated" (*ILTY*, p. 15) involves exploring "the resources of the natural universe with which the cultivation of sensibility opens up more subtle and gratifying exchanges" (*ILTY*, p. 13).[11] It is through a relationship in which neither subject is effaced that two subjects can help one another practice a form of negativity that anchors each in natural reality. Through the other, one discovers one's limits in the concrete here and now. Through transformative encounter with the other, each one continually becomes in the ebb and flow of concrete contact. Because each respects the history and intentionality of the other, each cannot assimilate the other to her or his own history or intentions. This respect provides limits on one's own becoming. These limits provide the material for further becomings. Insofar as this process anchors the subject in a natural reality that does not allow for transcendent flights of fantasy, each subject is forced to harmonize her or his corporeal and conceptual logics. Each one's words must find some adequation in the roots of language in corporeal experience, and corporeal experience must push its way into conceptual thought. It is in the fecund encounter of two embodied subjects, neither of whom displace their embodiment or efface the other, that this kind of harmonizing, integrative process can occur. It is thus through the encounter of two genders who are different that Irigaray feels we might enable each gender to accomplish their specific identity in relationship to individual and collective history. It is through a special kind of relationship in which one no longer appropriates all creative movement to oneself, but instead focuses on the creative movement provided by another, that one can come up against one's own limits and so anchor one's conceptual flights in a natural reality.

According to Irigaray, we live out our individual lives not as neuter individuals, but as women and men, girls and boys. Upholding the rights of abstract citizens is not sufficient; since there are no neuter individuals, we need rights for real persons – that is, sexed persons. Despite certain exceptions and anomalies – the occasional hermaphrodite who may escape surgical correction and who refuses either gender designation – the vast majority of us are designated and/or are designate ourselves as she or he rather than both at once or neither.[12] However one negotiates one's positioning *vis-à-vis* gendered pronouns, we cannot escape such negotiation. The generic "he" with its implication of a neuter individual who stands in for a human norm can only be a delusion; whatever our race, class, religious affiliation, or cultural identity, we cannot fail to take up some sort of stance *vis-à-vis* our sex. For Irigaray, this renders sexual difference the most fundamental difference of all. It is precisely because there is no way to escape this differentiation that it provides the opportunity for escaping a regime of subjectivity that would erase all differentiation.

Insofar as we elaborate, rather than elide, sexual difference, we are opened out onto a way of thinking and being that refuses to elide difference in general. Because sexual difference is actually, in our culture, impossible to evade, despite the cultural ruses that would obliterate feminine specificity, it is the culturally specific opportunity we have for opening up human subjectivity to an open-ended infinity of differences. The alternative is the regime of masculine subjectivity with its emphasis upon a logic of the same. In the Hegelian regime in which an abstract civil subject is interchangeable with any other subject, personal subjectivity is lost. Specificity is displaced onto a feminine other who has no identifiable subjectivity of her own. It is insofar as this schema is disrupted that the opportunity for a more personalized, more specified individuality emerges. Symbolization of sexual difference provides a means for further specification of all individuals as well as a personalized form of love that goes beyond the exchange of women as objects to a space of genuine love and communication among truly differentiated subjects.

It is due to Irigaray's sensitivity to the specular subject who appropriates the creativity of the other, that she is so keen to insure a form of subjectivity that is continually open to creative interaction with another. She suggests that it is only through coming up against the limits presented by the other that one can guard against the specular tendency to identify a totalizing universal. For Irigaray, any leap to identification with such a universal leads to a lack of attentiveness to present sensibility and thus an abstract conception of wholeness that leaves the corporeal behind. One's gender as a universal exists prior to oneself in one's singular embodiment as a gendered individual. Dialectical creation between two gendered individuals enables a new definition of values grounded in a natural reality. In coming up against my own limits through contact with what is not me, I am confronted with negativity. Because these limits are always shifting and changing and defined in the singularity of unanticipatable encounters, I must always work and rework these limits. It is only through the continual transformation brought on by these contacts with what is other to me that I continue to reform and refigure in direct confrontation with my own limits. It is precisely such limits that allow me to experience myself rather than simply posit myself as an abstraction. It is through such encounters with what is not me that I confront gaps in psychic coherence and bodily integrity and am able to engage in the creative labor of harmonizing corporeal and conceptual logics.

Irigaray relates the encounter with the other to an ability to think. If one is plunged in the natural immediacy of someone who has not been forced to confront his limits, he has not defined his form in relationship to a reality that goes beyond him. It is a crucial fact of our existence, for Irigaray, that we are not self-made but engendered by two and born of another. We are thus irretrievably always in relationship to others. It is due to a patriarchal mythology that "becoming on the basis of *one* has been inscribed as origin" (*ILTY*, p. 40). For Irigaray this means that the masculine subject has never really awoken to find himself in a world not of his own making.[13] The masculine subject refers himself to a horizon of the divine that is all about him and the subject he is and wants to be. Western philosophy has supported this mastery of one's own form by reiterating the refusal of interaction with the other.[14] Breaking free from the masculine economy of subjectivity is important because the latter fosters delusions of self-sufficient wholeness, demands mastering control over our self-image, and takes us further and further away from the roots of our experience in the natural world and the world of processes that extend beyond ourselves. Symbolizing the traditional role of the feminine other in a way that would give her voice and render her a subject in her own right could suggest a radically different kind of economy – one which moves beyond the need to repeat a highly controlled form of self-identity, the need for a feminine other for specular confirmation at the expense of that other's own subjectivity, and the need to exchange objects in order to confirm one's activity as subject. This alternative economy would enable a subject that could both give and receive, be passive as well as active, and achieve an exchange that would be a communion and a genuine communication rather than merely the passing on of objects.[15]

Genuine communication does more than simply pass along information; it provides the opportunity for a rejuvenating encounter between two subjects. In "A Breath that Touches in Words," Irigaray points out that only a mother breathes for her child. After we are born, we all must breathe for ourselves. She claims that our language usually stifles breath more than it cultivates it. Because the ideals our culture presents to us "act like a sort of drug promising us ecstasy beyond ourselves" (*ILTY*, p. 121), our messages are generally suffocating. Language referred to an ideal transcendent to the sensible realm is a language that has been "uprooted from its engendering in the present, from its connections with the energy of my own and the other's body, and with that of the surrounding natural world" (*ILTY*, p. 123). Irigaray elaborates a kind of language that involves attentiveness to the breath, to silence, and to ourselves and the other with whom we speak, by proffering the notion that intersubjective communication should involve what she calls "*touching upon.*"

In attending to the words of another, we should pay attention to more than the words of the other who speaks. We need to proffer a carnal attentiveness that touches upon the other. Such touching attends to more than the information communicated by the words in order to attend to the other's breath, the pulse of the body, the other in her or his corporeal manifestation, the bodies of both as they manifest in a specific environment. In attending to the words of the other I attend to voice tone, modulation and rhythm, semantic and phonic choice of words. That is, I attend to the determinate form breath takes in the breathing out of words. Attending to the informative content of words can often lead us to abstract those words from the embodied subject who sits or stands before us and who has an embodied relationship to those words and to the listener. It is only through attending to the full range of effects produced by the speaker in a concrete setting that we can really touch upon the other as a subject with a natural reality, an intentionality, and a history of her own. In stripping those words of the natural reality of the other, we render them assimilable into our own history, and lose the possibility of a more fully embodied response of our own in a form of communication that could have been a genuine encounter.

When speech involves a *touching upon*, it can stay word and flesh, language and sensibility. In such speech, sensibility and intelligence are no longer divided and thus there is no need for a hierarchically ordered division between active and passive, sensible and intelligible, body and mind, feminine and masculine. When speech involves such touching upon, the tactile does not become alienated in possession, and truth is not elaborated in terms of a disincarnated beyond. With such speech, there is no "production of an abstract and supposedly neuter discourse."[16] When there is genuinely intersubjective communication with a particular kind of listening and touching upon, neither subject can remain solipsistic and intentionality is mutually informed. The subject addresses her or himself to another, but also receives her or himself back from the other in the form of a further engenderment of her or his own becoming. The subject becomes engendered on the basis of the other rather than being reduced to the image or ideal or illusion of the other.[17]

Irigaray provides a compelling model of interaction between two subjects, neither of whom displace their corporeality onto the other. Instead of the specular economy of masculine subjectivity, this interaction evokes the creative communion of two who each act as a living mirror for the other. A living mirror cannot reflect an image back to the subject without adding something of its own to that image. In the process, such mirroring inevitably becomes a dance in which both are transformed. An economy of subjectivity premised upon participatory communion and recognition does not need to anchor identity to a "lack" translated into an object of desire structuring (Oedipal, masculine) identity. Instead, personal identity is formed and transformed in living contact with reciprocating others.

Although Irigaray's work evokes a compelling model of inter-subjectivity which moves self/other relations beyond active/passive, dominant/subordinate dichotomies, I remain skeptical about her call for the recognition of sexual identity as a part of civil identity. Irigaray advocates a political agenda which includes promoting legally encoded rights for women. She believes that this is part of the project of providing support for a feminine subject and that it is through such a project that we can disrupt a masculinist economy of subjectivity. But if feminine sub-jectivity entails undermining the masculine subject/feminine other dichotomy, it also entails mutually constitutive relationships in which negativity no longer plays out in terms of gender dichotomies. I believe that Irigaray insists upon sexual difference because she believes that until two genders fully exist, difference will be assimilated into a masculinist economy. But it seems to me that forms of intersubjectivity already exist which challenge that economy and that Irigaray's theory gives us a way of better understanding and making use of such possibilities. I turn now to Butler's reading of Irigaray's notion of the feminine and to Butler's notion of the lesbian phallus in order to further develop how an elaboration of corporeal logics might lead to a politics able to build upon such possi-bilities.

2 The Lesbian Phallus: Butler and a Differentiating Morphology

On Butler's reading, Irigaray's project goes beyond the denigrated term of a traditional binary. Irigaray's notion of the feminine is not simply "matter" (as opposed to masculine form), but entails an unnameable feminine beyond the masculine/feminine oppositions it supports. The feminine figured within an intelligible philosophical binary is the specular feminine, but the "excessive" feminine that is unrepresentable is that which must be excluded for the binary to operate at all.[18] Butler claims that Irigaray distinguishes an unthematizable materiality from the cate-gory of matter. This inarticulable materiality is the site for the feminine within a phallogocentric economy; it is what must be excluded from that economy so that the latter can present the illusion that it is internally coherent (ibid., p. 38). The excessive, unrepresentable feminine cannot be contained within current systems of representation. If Irigaray evokes such a feminine, she can only do so strategically by articulating the blindspot required for the phallogocentric economy to function in a specific context. This means that this notion of the feminine (if, indeed, we can call it a notion) is always in movement. In the context of reading philosophical texts, for example, it is that which is excluded by a particular text. Since what is excluded from a particular philosophical text shifts from text to text, so does the category of the "feminine." Such a feminine is an excessive materiality that resists materialization and cannot be reduced to a maternal body or anything representable. It is "a disfiguration that emerges at the boundaries of the human both as its very condition and as the insistent threat of its deformation" (ibid., p. 41). Irigaray's notion of sexual difference rather than simply reinstating or reifying a traditional dichotomy, thus opens up the specificity of the material and the possibility of moving beyond dichotomies in understanding the body and, in particular, the sexed body.

This notion of the feminine opens it up to consideration in multiple contexts in a way that is never proscribed in advance. From this perspective, sexual difference operates not only in terms of masculine/feminine, reason/materiality oppositions, but also in the formulation of what will be allowed to occupy the site of inscriptional space and what must remain outside of that space in order to support the oppositional positions it contains. Butler depicts a kind of double-movement in Irigaray's work – one that works with and against traditional masculine/feminine dichotomies, as well as one that evokes an unrepresentable feminine which can produce different effects in different contexts. Irigaray's notion of sexual difference thus opens onto a non-delimitable elsewhere that can never be represented or contained in any kind of dualism (ibid., p. 52). Butler suggests that Irigaray's project could point the way toward a theory and a politics which incorporates the recognition that every discourse meets its limits, thus allowing us to "begin, without ending, without mastering, to own – and yet never fully to own – the exclusions by which we proceed" (ibid., p. 53).

According to the reading of Irigaray that I gave in the previous section, the feminine other who supports masculine subjectivity also supports the illusion that the masculine subject is always already fully formed rather than engaged in an ongoing process contingent upon others. Providing symbolic support for a feminine subject would unveil subjectivity as a contingent process. Because subjectivity as a contingent process can never be fully achieved, it is always coming up against the limits of the already-done and the already-said. That is, subjectivity as a process must continually come to grips with not only unanticipated events, but that which defies the constraints of conventional thought and perception. Providing symbolic support for a feminine subject would thus entail providing symbolic support for a subject in the process of incorporating what lies beyond the limits of the perceivable and conceivable.

I have briefly characterized Irigaray's views on feminine sexuality and a listening that is a touching-upon as articulations of this feminine activity. But the introduction of such articulations of feminine activity would have to undermine clear-cut gender oppositions. Butler's reading of Irigaray shows how articulating the feminine as the category of excess leads to a non-binary understanding of differentiations constituted through interaction with others. Butler's discussion of the lesbian phallus further demonstrates how opening the economy of masculine subjectivity to its feminine excess undermines the very gender binaries upon which that economy is premised.

Butler opens her chapter entitled "The Lesbian Phallus and the Morphological Imaginary"[19] by considering Freud's account of bodily pain. She argues that for Freud a body part exists for consciousness only through libidinal self-investment, for example, the kind that occurs when one is in physical discomfort. Such self-investment entails vacilation between real and imagined body parts due to the redoubling of physical sensation as a psychically invested sensation. That is, narcissistic concentration on pain invests it with a psychic dimension in the form of an idealized body part. This investment entails connection of bodily activity with an idea of a body part and is what allows physical sensation as sensation to emerge. Butler notes Freud's analogy between the process of erotogenicity and the consciousness of bodily pain, and states:

> If erotogenicity is produced through the conveying of a bodily activity through an idea, then the idea and the conveying are phenomenologically coincident. As a result, it would not be possible to speak about a body part that precedes and gives rise to an idea, for it is the idea that emerges simultaneously with the phenomenologically accessible body, indeed, that guarantees its accessibility. (ibid., p. 59)

It is only through the vacilation between "real sensation" and images of body parts that phenomenological experience is possible. "Real sensation" is not experienceable until it receives narcissistic investment through vacilating correlation with imaginary ideas or representations of body parts. "Real sensation," then, might be brought into alignment with Butler's reading of Irigaray's notion of the feminine as unthematizable materiality; it is unrepresentable and yet both conditions and threatens what emerges as experience. The process whereby body parts become accessible to experience prefigures the identifications depicted in Lacan's notion of the mirror stage in which the ego is initially formed through identification with an externalized ideal of wholeness which belies the inchoate flux of sensation actually experienced by the infant. In terms of the distinctions I introduced in characterizing Irigaray's project, we could say that this process constitutes an early form of an individual's corporeal logic. Just as conscious experience of a self emerges from a background process of imaginary identifications, so does the fluid flux of sensations in which body parts become delineated entail a process of vacilation between the "real" and the "imaginary."

Butler claims that in "On Narcissism," Freud assumes the male genitals as the prototype of the process of erotogenization. The penis – a body part which is the idealized result of a set of substitutions already, entailing undecidable vacilation between bodily activity and ideas of body parts – is "suddenly" assumed to be an originary site of erotogenization. The assumption that the penis is a prototype for the process through which body parts becomes delineated sets it up as a privileged body part somehow exempt from this process. Other body parts act as substitutes for the penis; that is, they are imaged in analogy to the penis. Thus, the penis is assumed to be a coherent body part which does not entail the same kind of undecidable vacilation as other body parts. Installation of the phallus as the "origin" or examplar for other body parts suppresses the ambivalence of the process of erotogenization by assuming the phallus as its generating form. Butler argues that "in a sense, Freud's essay enacts the paradoxical process by which the phallus as the privileged and generative signifier is itself generated *by* a string of examples of erotogenic body parts" (*Bodies That Matter*, pp. 60–1). Lacan's notion of the phallus as the privileged signifier suggests that it is "that which originates or generates significations, but is not itself the signifying effect of a prior signifying chain" (ibid., p. 60). It thus replicates Freud's own enactment of the suppression of the ambivalent nature of the process of erotogenization.

On Butler's view, that we can experience our bodies at all is dependent upon an imaginary schema. Thus, the physical and the psychical are inextricably linked at the level of the possibility of any kind of sense perception or bodily experience (ibid., p. 65). The moment we have a sense of body to which we can refer our experiences, we have already established accessibility to our own anatomy through a process which is always already permeated with fantasy and premised upon prohibition and repudiation. The contours of the body are sites that vacillate between the psychic and the material (ibid., p. 66). Butler suggests that we might understand the psyche as "that which constitutes the mode by which that body is given." The conception of the body emerging from her account problematizes any easy distinction between the "real" of the body and the categories through which we describe it. But Butler cautions against a purely discursive conception of the body; she insists that the categories which refer to the materiality of the body "are themselves troubled by a referent that is never fully or permanently resolved or contained by any given signified" (ibid., p. 67). In the context of Irigaray's notion of the feminine and sexed bodies, we could say that the unthematizable materiality of the body returns to haunt any process by which we might articulate embodied experience.

Butler asks the crucial question of how bodies assume "the shape by which their material discreteness is marked" (ibid., p. 69). In her rendition of the story about how this comes about told in Lacan's seminal essay "The Mirror Stage," the inchoate subject "phantasmatically" overcomes libidinal dependency and powerlessness by installing a boundary which orders "wayward motility or disaggregated sexuality" (ibid., p. 75), thus installing a "hypostacized center" which produces an idealized bodily ego. This ego is an imaginary object which is neither interior nor exterior to the subject, "but the permanently unstable site where that spatialized distinction is perpetually negotiated" (ibid., p. 76). Butler describes the ego as a "sedimented history of imaginary relations" whose center is an externalized *imago* "which confers and produces bodily contours" (ibid., p. 74). This bodily ego was initially formed through preverbal identifications; the contours of the body marked out through various pleasure zones become more fully differentiated through identification with an ideal image of bodily integrity. In "The Signification of the Phallus" Lacan describes how the idealization of a bodily ego is then stabilized and sustained through the retroactive organization of earlier ebbs and flows of identification by taking up a subject position in language that is marked with either "having" or "being" the phallus. The symbolic differentiations that a speaking subject makes is a reiteration and extension of the differentiations initially made through the imaginary identifications which took place in a specific set of material relations.

Since "bodies only become whole, i.e., totalities, by the idealizing and totalizing specular image which is sustained through time by the sexually marked name" (*Bodies That Matter*, p. 72), the phallus becomes linked with the very possibility of having a whole body with any kind of mastery or control. The idealization of the body as a center of control leads to the notion of the phallus as "that which controls significations in discourse" (ibid., p. 73). This suggests that the very sense of oneself as having a body with boundaries and therefore having any kind of social identity at all is predicated upon having control over signification and somehow directing the flow of meaning from a stance protected from that flow. Butler argues that Lacan in some sense re-enacts the fictional warding off of the inchoate body of the mirror stage by anchoring the fictional identity achieved through an identification with the coherent ideal image in the sustaining name marked by sex that one acquires upon becoming a language speaker. Lacan thus recognizes instability of the subject at one level, only to transfer stability to another level. By installing the phallus as an originating and controlling power as the privileged signifier of the symbolic order, he is, in a sense, engaging in an imaginary act of identification designed to solidify his own identity by denying the fictional nature of the identification.

Butler argues that Lacan, by repudiating the anatomical and imaginary origins of the phallus, refuses to account for a genealogical process of idealizing the body. Lacan's account in "The Mirror Stage" delineates how "parts come to stand for wholes and a decentered body is transfigured into a totality with a center" (ibid., p. 79). An ego is precipitated in identifications made between inchoate sensations and images of wholeness. These identifications coalesce around bodily organs which take on centralizing importance. In "The Signification of the Phallus" Lacan assumes that the phallus "in its symbolic function is neither an organ nor an imaginary effect," and thereby refuses the question posed by "The Mirror Stage" that asks which organs perform the centering and synecdochal function necessary for a coherent self with bodily integrity.

According to Butler, if the phallus is both the imaginary effect of the process of erotogenecity and the privileged signifier of the symbolic ("the delimiting and ordering principle of what can be signified"), then the distinction between the imaginary and the symbolic is called into question. If the phallus doesn't require the penis in order to symbolize – that is, if another body part could take on the centering function Freud assumes for male genitals – then other "phallic" possibilities emerge, for example, that of the lesbian phallus. Lesbian identity cannot fully restructure a symbolic so that the penis loses its association with the phallus; individuals are always preceded by the order of social significance. And yet, due to the resolution of identity issues through individual phantasmatic constructions, and due to the imaginary status of the phallus, the phallus could well be associated with different morphologies. Since the lesbian phallus is not anatomically linked to the penis and so involves "having" the phallus, rather than "being" the phallus, in the way that masculine identity involves "having" rather than "being" the phallus, at the same time that due to not having a penis, lesbian identity "threatens" castration, then "the lesbian phallus crosses the orders of *having* and *being*" (ibid., p. 84). Butler's argument suggests that due to the instability of imaginary identifications which extend to the penis and its association with the phallus, there is no guarantee that "normal" identifications will occur at a phantasmatic level, despite symbolic positioning. Since neither male genitals nor the phallus can be presumed to be free of the ambiguity pertaining to other body parts or signifiers, the Lacanian version of sexual difference is neither the only form sexual difference could take, nor is sexual difference crucial to the possibility of coherent selfhood. If the feminine is a category of unthematizable materiality, then there will always be a referent uncontainable within any descriptions through which we could describe the sexed body. This unrepresentable referent acts, as Butler puts it, as "the constitutive demand that mobilizes psychic action" (ibid., p. 67). The body parts acting as the privileged examplars for the bodily ego at the level of imaginary identifications as well as the categories of the symbolic stabilizing such identifications in terms of oppositional categories (for example, that of "being" or "having" the phallus) could mutate in response to such demands.

If Butler is right, then the body part linked to the phallus can shift; even if the phallus continues to function according to the specular economy of subjectivity described in Lacanian psychoanalysis, the corporeal logics that gets taken up into a conceptual elaboration of subjectivity could be more fluid than a strict Lacanian account would suggest. If the distinction between the imaginary realm of corporeal identifications and the symbolic realm of conceptual distinctions can be called into question, then the heterogeneous logics of the corporeal and the conceptual could interact throughout an individual's life. "Feminine" attunement to the corporeal – as it emerges, for example, in Irigaray's notion of "touching upon" – could provide for integrations of the two which problematize the Lacanian account of sexual difference. As Butler puts it, the notion of the lesbian phallus crosses the orders of having and being the phallus. Irigaray's critical reinterpretation of the Hegelian notion of negativity allows for such problematizing integrations of the corporeal and the conceptual. Crossing the line between "having" and "being" the phallus problematizes the distinction between masculine subject and feminine other. If the two cannot be clearly distinguished, it will no longer be clear who will be reflected back as whole by the affirming reflection of the other.

Butler argues that one could call into question the "naturalized link" of the phallus to masculine morphology through an "aggressive reterritorialization" (ibid., p. 86). Presumably, this means that one can make aggressive use of discrepancies and slippages in the "complex identificatory fantasies" that "inform morphogenesis" in order to wreak havoc with "normal" identifications and hence conventional symbolic positioning. Such aggressive reterritorialization rests upon fantasies that cannot be fully predicted, since "morphological idealization is both a necessary and unpredictable ingredient in the constitution of both the bodily ego and the dispositions of desire" (ibid., p. 86). "Deviant" identificatory fantasies could thus have corporeal effects that play out in the morphologies of human bodies. If one was to note one's morphology, then, one could ground a rupture in one's psychic sense of self in a spontaneous identification situated in one's individual biography and a very personal sense of one's own bodily ego. The spontaneous identifications that play out on a phantasmatic level constitute that individual's response to the problem of achieving some kind of coherent identity in the context of her or his very specific set of material circumstances. The corporeal logic built into such a response goes beyond a thin notion of reason as an intellectual activity that takes place on a completely conscious level. It achieves a sufficiently coherent response to the problem of human subjectivity by shaping a body out of an inchoate flux with specific desires directed toward a range of symbolic identity positions. Butler's analysis indicates how one might both listen in on the cues of corporeal logic in order to further political goals, as well as indicate ways of responding to the passions of suffering, boredom, and apathy. If one pays no attention to one's corporeal logic, then chances are that one's plans for action will come to naught. Phantasmatic identifications – which are the core of the self, and the core of coherent identity which is crucial to one's survival as a social subject – need to be taken into account. A kind of listening and attentiveness to corporeal logic that implies no predictable closure for identifications or for action is implicit in Butler's account. Instead of demanding that one make this or that identification, she offers an account of a politicized subjectivity premised upon the morphologies of the specific individuals involved. This suggests new resources for creating and recreating symbolic identity positions. Instead of leaving us in a poststructuralist and relativistic void, her analysis suggests that there is a material basis for innovation in identity and social practices. If to be an embodied subject means to have already achieved a kind of corporeal coherence, then listening to the wisdom of the body with a discriminating intellect might present new possibilities for being and acting.

Confusing the "heterosexist version of sexual difference in which men are said to 'have' and women to 'be' the phallus" (ibid., p. 88) could

displace eroticism from "traditional masculinist contexts" and enable
critical redeployment of central figures of power (ibid., p. 89). Theorizing
desire in the concrete contexts in which it manifests could help such forms
of eroticism to challenge discursive norms. Both "masculine" and "feminine" desire could be reconfigured creating multiple forms of sexuality in
the process. Irigaray's project entails providing symbolic support for a
"feminine" subject that would subvert the masculinist norm; articulations
of alternative forms of desire and subjectivity would further open up the
feminine as a category of excess and proliferate concrete possibilities in
alternative subjectivities. Irigaray's project, then, could be read as a way
of theorizing, and so providing further symbolic support for, the experiments in alternate sexualities already taking place. Providing symbolic
support for "feminine" subjectivity turns out to symbolize a form of
subjectivity which continually recognizes its exclusions in order to "own"
them; heterosexist norms as well as masculinist norms would be contested
in the process.[20] Instead of being always placed *vis-à-vis* having or being
the phallus, individual subjects could, for example, cross such positioning
in a way that would facilitate non-hierarchical and more reciprocal
relations of recognition and empowerment. This, of course, would not
necessarily be the case. But especially in the context of "feminine"
attunement to that which forever resists any discursive categories we may
create, and an active acknowledgment of the interdependent structures
through which coherent selves with bodily integrity emerge, we might yet
achieve such a goal.

Notes

1   For further discussion of this claim in terms of its Heideggerian context, see
    Tina Chanter's discussion in *Ethics of Eros: Irigaray's Rewriting of the
    Philosophers* (New York: Routledge, 1995), pp. 127–46.

2   "More often than not, he seeks to remain in denial of this primary mother or
    matrix. His denial of reality is an attempt, by various means, including very
    subtle reasoning, to impose a *second nature* that eventually destroys the first
    or causes it to be forgotten" Irigaray, *Thinking the Difference: For a Peaceful
    Revolution*, trans. Karin Montin (New York: Routledge, 1994), pp. 17–18
    (hereafter cited as *TD*).

3   For an intriguing account of feminine subjectivity in terms of the energetic
    effects of this kind of displacement, see Teresa Brennan's account of feminine
    subjectivity in *The Interpretation of the Flesh: Freud and Femininity* (New
    York, Routledge, 1992).

4   "This economy obeys the two principles of thermodynamics long considered
    impossible to overcome. Sexuality is thus supposedly linked to physical laws

that allow it no freedom or future other than a repetitive, explosive, non-evolutive one. The only way to escape this sad fate is through procreation" (*TD*, p. 20).

5 Irigaray's claim that women are somehow closer to what she calls "natural" processes has the ring of a biological argument to it – it seems to be due to women's role in reproductive cycles that they are unable to distance themselves from such processes as easily as men. My own view is that whatever we may say about reproductive processes and how close they may bring us to life cycles of a more "natural" sort, this relationship is still culturally mediated. If women's reproductive cycles bring them "closer to nature" it is within the specific cultural situation in which we find ourselves. There seems to me to be nothing to particularly mitigate against men being equally close to such rhythms through full acknowledgement, for example, of their own corporeality and mortality. Although I cannot say for sure what Irigaray would say if pressed upon this issue, I therefore read her here as continuing to develop an account of sexual difference contingent upon the specific cultural situation in which we find ourselves. Given what Irigaray says in many places about the contemporary sexual division of labor, as well as her reticence about what could come from what would be an inevitable and radical transformation of both genders in the full emergence of feminine subjectivity, the kind of sexual difference with which we are currently familiar, and which Irigaray herself must characterize in her historically specific interventions, would have to change if her program of recognizing sexual difference was actually carried out.

The question of whether or not Irigaray presents an essentialist account of sexual difference has caused a lot of controversy. Tina Chanter presents some of the history of this debate in its relationship to feminist theory in the United States and Britain, and a helpful overview of why Irigaray has been read as an essentialist and how we might move beyond the dichotomies set up by such labels (see *Ethics of Eros*, chapter one).

6 This chaos could be called life drives, in that it is an attraction with no relation to the individuation of persons; it is a male or neutral attraction determined no doubt by a desire to return to the mother's womb and enjoy exclusive possession of the fertility of the womb in order to maintain one's own vitality. The most positive aspect of love would still be the desire to return to the procreating whole, regardless of the body of sex of the procreator. The most negative aspect would be the need to destroy, even oneself, even life and the life-giver, by destructuring any cohesiveness. This would amount to reducing every entity to its tiniest atoms with no possibility of its becoming whole again.

Of course the negative side of death drives is fairly apparent. What has been emphasized very little, even blindly contested, is the destruction at work in life drives themselves, in so far as they do not respect the other, and in particular the other of sexual difference" (*TD*, pp. 96–7).

7 "In this scheme of things, the abyss therefore does not correspond to the female sex, but to the lack of rhythm and harmony of male desires, which

specifically refuse any manifestation of the difference between the sexes so that they can appropriate the fertility of the mother's body.

Urged by eros, man immerses himself in chaos because he refuses to make love *with* an other, to be *two* making love, to experience sexual attraction with tenderness and respect" (*TD*, p. 97).

8   "The path to reciprocal love between individuals has been lost, especially with respect to eroticism. And instead of contributing to individuation, or to the creation or re-creation of human forms, eroticism contributes to the destruction or loss of identity through fusion, and to a return to a level of tension that is always identical, always the lowest, with neither development nor growth" (*TD*, p. 99).

9   "Women's twofold effort consists in interpreting their current situation or status not only in economic but also in symbolic terms. They must realize that it is just as important for them to keep or acquire their subjective and objective status as simply to enter into existing economic or cultural systems. Unless they realize that they are members of two groups – women and units of the contemporary world – they risk losing everything without achieving recognition despite all their efforts" (*TD*, pp. 39–40).

10 "This is what will enable us to sublimate sexuality otherwise than through partial drives, the only solution proposed by Freud. According to him and the spiritual authorities that still lay down our law, reproduction is the sole regulator of sexual drives. Yet reproduction has nothing specifically human or sublime about it. The rights to virginity, motherhood by choice, preferential guardianship of children, and caring for the home, means of expression and symbolic relationships are not rights without corresponding duties" Irigaray, *I Love to You: Sketch for a Felicity Within History*, trans. Alison Martin (New York: Routledge 1996), p. 81 (hereafter cited as *ILTY*).

11 "Happiness must be built by us here and now on earth, where we live, a happiness comprising a carnal, sensible and spiritual dimension in the love between women and men, woman and man, which cannot be subordinated to reproduction, to the acquisition or accumulation of property, to a hypothetical human or divine authority. The realization of happiness in us and between us is our primary cultural obligation" (*ILTY*, p. 15).

12 Irigaray says nothing about hermaphroditism, transsexualism, transvestism, or other forms of gender "transgressions." But since these certainly exist and Irigaray is certainly aware of this fact, we must take her argument here as pertaining to the impossibility of avoiding gender designations entirely.

13 "Man has not raised himself above a state of immediate unity with nature, so he dreams of being the whole. He dreams that he alone is nature and that it is up to him to undertake the spiritual task of differentiating himself from (his) nature and from himself" (*ILTY*, p. 40).

14 "Teleology, for man, amounts to keeping the source of the horizon in and for the self. It is not conversing with the other but rather suspending the interaction of the relation with the other in order to accomplish the selfs own intention, even if it is divine in nature. The whole of Western philosophy is the mastery of the *direction* of will and thought by the subject, historically

man. Nothing is changed by the fact that nowadays women have access to this, and it might even make things worse if philosophy's intention is not altered, if the subject is not reconstituted in a different way. Which would mean reaching another dimension, another level of consciousness, a level not of mastery but one that attempts to find spiritual harmony between passivity and activity, particularly in relations with nature and others" (*ILTY*, p. 45).

15 "It would entail, beyond the enslavement to property, beyond the subject's submission to the object (which does not mean to objectivity), becoming capable of giving and receiving, of being active and passive, of having an intention that stays attuned to interactions, that is, of seeking a new economy of existence or being which is neither that of mastery nor that of slavery but rather of exchange with no preconstituted object – vital exchange, cultural exchange, of words, gestures, etc., an exchange thus able to *communicate* at times, to commune (but I'll leave aside for the moment this complex mode of communication in which every illusion is possible), beyond any exchange of objects" (*ILTY*, p. 45).

16 "With this speech, there ceases to be a division between sensibility and intelligence, and they are most certainly not hierarchically ordered to the benefit of speculation estranged from the properties of bodies. Speech is intelligible because it remains sensible, related to the qualities of sound, rhythm, and meaning in the world of the subject(s). The opposition between activity and passivity no longer has a meaning. Communication *between* and reciprocity, as well as respect for one's own gender (never simply one's own since it is engendered and remains partially exterior to one's self), respect for the gender of the other, for listening and silence, require *touching upon* without reduction or seduction, the safeguard of the sensible" (*ILTY*, pp. 125–6).

17 "Interdependency between subjects is no longer reduced to questions of possessing, of exchanging or sharing objects, cash, or an already existing meaning. It is, rather, regulated by the constitution of subjectivity. The subject does not vest its own value in any form of property whatsoever. No longer is it objecthood, having or the cost of having that governs the becoming of a subject or subjects and the relation among them. They are engaged in a relationship from which they emerge altered, the objective being the accomplishment of their subjectivity while remaining faithful to their nature" (*ILTY*, p. 127).

18 Judith Butler, *Bodies That Matter: On the Discursive Limits of "Sex"* (New York: Routledge), p. 39. Butler adds that naming "the feminine figured within the binary as the *specular* feminine and the feminine which is erased and excluded from that binary as the *excessive* feminine" cannot work, "for in the latter mode, the feminine, strictly speaking, cannot be named at all and, indeed, is not a mode" (ibid., p. 39).

19 I have greatly condensed parts of Butler's argument in the following analysis. I hope that I have not done too much damage in the process.

20 Although I have not addressed racist norms – among other possible norms

that might be considered here – a continual recognition of exclusions in the various forms such exclusions take would clearly include such norms. On the kind of reading I'm giving here, theoretical work highlighting various categories of analysis could be brought together in a political project which would not have to give metaphysical priority to any one category of analysis. Instead, political priorities would be worked out on the basis of the particularities of the specific situation, and yet important connections among those specific struggles could be made with reference to an overarching theoretical framework along the lines hinted at here.

Part V

Critical Race Theory

12

Alienation and the African–American Experience

Howard McGary

The term "alienation" evokes a variety of responses. For liberals, to be alienated signals a denial of certain basic rights, e.g. the right to equality of opportunity or the right to autonomy.[1] On the other hand, progressive thinkers believe that alienation involves estrangement from one's work, self, or others because of capitalism.[2] However, recent discussions of alienation have cast doubt on whether either of these theories totally captures the phenomenon. Drawing on the experiences of people of color, some theorists maintain that to be alienated is to be estranged in ways that cannot be accounted for by liberal and Marxist theories of alienation.[3]

The concept of alienation is often associated with Marx's conception of human beings in capitalist societies. However, non-Marxists have also used the term alienation to explain the experiences of human beings in relationship to their society, each other, their work, and themselves. But liberal theories of alienation have been criticized by Marxists for two reasons. First, they see liberal theories of alienation as describing a psychological condition that is said to result from a denial of basic individual rights rather than the result of a systematic failure. Second, liberals have an account of human nature that is ahistorical, one that fails to consider the changes in human nature that result from changes in social conditions.

For the Marxist, alienation is not simply a theory of how people feel or think about themselves when their rights are violated, but a historical theory of how human beings act and how they are treated by others in capitalist society. The Marxist theory of alienation is an explanatory social theory that places human beings at the center of the critique of socioeconomic relations. Marx's human being is not a stagnant given, but a product of an explanatory social theory. For Marx, alienation is something that all human beings experience in capitalist societies; it is not something that certain individuals undergo because they are neurotic or the victims of some unjust law or social practice.

It is clear that African Americans have not always been recognized and treated as American citizens or as human beings by the dominant white society. Both of these forms of denial have had serious negative consequences and numerous scholars have discussed what these denials have meant to African Americans and to the rest of society. However, it does not directly follow from the fact of these denials that African Americans are alienated because of these things. In this essay, I shall attempt to understand this new challenge to the liberal and Marxist theories of "alienation" and its impact, if any, on the masses of African Americans.

1 The New Account of Alienation

According to the new account of alienation that is drawn from the experiences of people of color, alienation exists when the self is deeply divided because the hostility of the dominant groups in the society forces the self to see itself as loathsome, defective, or insignificant, and lacking the possibility of ever seeing itself in more positive terms. This type of alienation is not just estrangement from one's work or a possible plan of life, but an estrangement from ever becoming a self that is not defined in the hostile terms of the dominant group.

The root idea here is not just that certain groups are forced to survive in an atmosphere in which they are not respected because of their group membership, but rather that they are required to do so in a society that is openly hostile to their very being. The hostility, according to this new account of alienation, causes the victims to become hostile toward themselves. Those who are said to be alienated in this way are thought to be incapable of shaping our common conception of reality and thus they play little, if any, role in their self-construction. The self is imposed upon them by social forces, and what is even more disturbing, no individual self can change the social forces that impose upon members of certain groups their negative and hostile self-conceptions.

Is this new account of alienation just another way of saying that people of color have had their humanity called into question? We might begin to explore this question by examining the claim that having one's humanity recognized and respected means having a say about things that matter in one's life, and having such a say means that one is unalienated. To be more specific, having opinions about things and the ability and freedom to express one's opinions is the mark of the unalienated person. This response is helpful, but it does not fully capture what recent writers have meant by alienation. It assumes that the alienated self is secure, but constrained by external forces that prevent the person from becoming fully actualized: from having one's voice recognized and respected in the moral or political process.

The above account of what it means to recognize and respect a person's humanity fails to fully appreciate that human selves result, at least in part, from social construction. How we define who we are, our interests, and our relationship with others, involves a dynamic process of social interaction. To assume that what recent writers have meant by alienation is the failure by some to be able to express and have their opinions heard misses the mark. This view of things assumes that (1) people are clear about their interests, but have not been allowed to express them and (2) those who have power and privilege will be able to understand and fairly assess claims made by those who lack power and privilege if they were only allowed to express their opinions. Even if (1) and (2) are true, we still have not captured what recent writers have meant by alienation. This account focuses incorrectly on what the self is prevented from doing by forces external to it. However, the new account of alienation primarily concentrates on the fragility and insecurity of the self caused by the way people who are victims view and define themselves. According to this view, even if the external constraints were removed, the self would still be estranged because it has been constructed out of images that are hostile to it.

One might think that this new account of alienation is not saying anything new because Americans (including African Americans) have always believed that people should be free to decide what kind of persons they want to be provided that in doing so they don't violate the rights of others. At least in principle, Americans have endorsed this idea. If this is so, what is new in these recent accounts of alienation? Perhaps we can gain some insight into this question by taking a closer look at the African-American experience.

African Americans have had a paradoxical existence in the United States. On the one hand, they have rightfully responded negatively to the second-class status that they are forced to endure. On the other hand, they believe that America should have and has the potential to live up to the ideas so eloquently expressed in the Bill of Rights and in Martin Luther King, Jr's "I Have a Dream" speech.[4] It is clear that there was a time when African Americans were prevented from participating in the electoral process and from having a say in the shaping of basic institutions. Many would argue that there are still barriers that prevent African Americans from participating in meaningful ways in these areas. If this is so, does this mean that most (many) African Americans are alienated from themselves and the dominant society?

African-American leaders from the moderate to the militant have emphasized the importance of African Americans making their own decisions about what is in their interests.[5] The right to self-determination has been seen as a crucial weapon in the battle against the evils of racial discrimination. These thinkers have also recognized that one must have an adequate understanding of one's predicament if one is to devise an effective strategy for overcoming the material and psychological con-sequences of racial injustice. Insight into the African American experience has come from a variety of sources. Some of these insights have been offered by social and political theorists, others have been advanced in literature and the arts.

Ralph Ellison, in his brilliant novel *The Invisible Man*, describes what he takes to be a consuming evil of racial discrimination.[6] According to Ellison, African Americans are not visible to the white world. They are caricatures and stereotypes, but not real human beings with complex and varied lives. In very graphic terms, Ellison reveals what it is like to be black in a world where black skin signifies what is base and superficial. Ellison skillfully describes how blacks are perceived by white society, but he also tells us a great deal about how blacks perceive themselves. It is clear that African Americans have struggled to construct an image of themselves different from the ones perpetrated by a racist society, but this is not an easy thing to do. W. E. B. DuBois spoke to the struggle and the dilemma that confronts African Americans when he identified what he called "the problem of double-consciousness" in *The Souls of Black Folk:*

> It is peculiar sensation, this double-consciousness, this sense of always looking at one's self through the eyes of others, of measuring one's soul by the tape of a world that looks on in amused contempt and pity. One ever feels his twoness – an American, a Negro; two warring ideals in one dark body, whose dogged strength alone keeps it from being torn asunder.[7]

DuBois is pointing to what he takes to be the mistaken belief held by many blacks and whites, namely that a person cannot be both black and an American. According to DuBois, for far too many people this was a contradiction in terms. DuBois strongly disagreed and spent a great deal of his energy arguing against this conclusion. But why this false view was held by so many people can be traced to an inadequate conception of what it means to be "black" and what it meant to be "American." According to DuBois, race and class exploitation contributed greatly to these false conceptions. For DuBois, it was no surprise that African Americans had such a difficult time identifying their true interests.

2 The Liberal Response

Liberal political theorists rarely discuss alienation. This is in large part because alienation is seen as something that comes from within. For them alienation often is the result of injustice, but even so, it is something that can be overcome if only the individual would stand up for her rights. Liberals may realize that this might come at some serious personal cost to the individual, but they believe that the individual can and should bear these costs if they are to remain autonomous unalienated beings. For example, liberals often sympathize with white, highly educated, wealthy women who live alienated lives, but they believe that it is within the power of these women to end their estrangement or alienation even though it may be extremely difficult for them to do so. The critics of the liberal account of women's oppression have argued that liberals fail to see that capitalism and the negative stereotyping of women causes even educated and economically secure women to be at the mercy of sexist practices and traditions.

The critics of liberalism have also argued that liberalism places too much emphasis upon individuality and thus the theory fails to recognize how our conceptions of who we are and what we see as valuable are tied to our social relations. They insist that we are not alone in shaping who we are and in defining our possibilities. Society, according to these critics, plays a more extensive role than liberals are willing to admit.

Although liberals have recognized the alienation that people experience in modern society, their individual-rights framework has not readily lent itself to an in-depth analysis of this phenomenon. I disagree, however, with the critics of liberalism when they contend that the individual-rights framework is inadequate to describe the nature of alienation. I shall attempt to show that liberals can describe the nature of alienation in capitalist society even though the theory is inadequate when it comes to addressing what the liberals must admit to be a violation of important rights.

Liberal theorists might characterize this new form of alienation in terms of a denial of the rights to such things as autonomy and self-determination and claim that these denials rob persons of their freedom. Alienation on their account is just another way of saying that people are unfree and further that they don't appreciate that this is so. But if the liberal response is to be helpful, we need to know more precisely in what sense alienation is a denial of important rights, e.g. the right to be free.

In what sense is the alienated person unfree? Can a person be alienated even if she has basic constitutional rights, material success, and a job that calls upon her abilities and talents in interesting ways? Some theorists think so. If alienation is a lack of freedom as the liberal theory suggests, in what sense are the people who have constitutional rights and material well-being unfree? The liberal theorist Joel Feinberg has discussed the lack of freedom in terms of constraints.[8] If we define alienation as constraint, then alienated persons are unfairly constrained in the ways that they can conceive of themselves in a culture that defines them in stereotypical terms. But what are these constraints? To borrow Feinberg's terminology, are these constraints external or internal? According to Feinberg, "external constraints are those that come from outside a person's body-cum-mind, and all other constraints, whether sore muscles, head-aches, or refractory 'lower' desires, are internal to him."[9]

If we employ the language of constraints to understand alienation as a kind of unfreedom, should we view this unfreedom in terms of external or internal constraints or both? On a liberal reading of DuBois's and Elli-son's characterizations of the African-American experience, this experience is characterized by a denial of opportunities because of a morally irrelevant characteristic, a person's race. It is plausible to interpret them in this way because this is clearly one of the consequences of a system of racial discrimination. However, I believe that they had much more in mind. The focus on the denial of opportunities is the standard liberal way of understanding the consequences of racial injustice. This is why you find liberal writers like Feinberg discussing freedom in terms of the absence of constraints and John Rawls concentrating on designing social institutions such that offices and positions are open to all under conditions of self-respect.[10] The focus by liberals has been primarily on what goes on outside of the body-cum-mind.

This is not to say that they completely ignore such psychological harms as self-doubt and a lack of self-respect that can result from injustice. In fact, Feinberg notes that things like sickness can create internal constraints which serve to limit a person's freedom.[11] Rawls, as well, appreciates the impact that injustice can have on a person's psyche. Thus, he spends some time expounding on the connection between justice and a healthy self-concept.[12] He argues that in a just society social institutions should not be designed in ways that prevent people from having the social bases for self-respect. So both Feinberg and Rawls recognize that such things as freedom and justice go beyond removing inappropriate external constraints. But nonetheless, I don't think that Feinberg and Rawls can fully capture the insight offered by DuBois and Ellison because their emphasis on the external constraints causes them to underestimate the internal ways that people can be prevented from experiencing freedom.

Since Isaiah Berlin's distinction between positive and negative freedom, liberals have recognized that such things as ignorance and poverty can limit a person's freedom.[13] Recognition of the limitations caused by internal constraints has led some liberals to argue that a society cannot be just if it does not address internal constraints on people's freedom. Such liberals would be open to the idea that an examination of the African-American experience would reveal the obvious and subtle ways that a lack of education and material well-being can lead to a sense of estrangement, a lack of self-respect. They would argue that this is true even when formal equality of opportunity can be said to exist. On their view, the real problem is not the lack of laws that guarantee equality under the law, but finding ways to make real these guarantees. For them it is not so much how African Americans are viewed by the rest of society, but rather that they should be treated in ways that make it possible for them to act and choose as free persons. According to this view, things are just even if people are hated by the rest of the community, provided that they are guaranteed equal protection under the law and steps are taken to ensure real equality of opportunity. These liberals insist that there is a large area of human affairs that should escape government scrutiny. In these areas, people should be able to pursue their own conceptions of the good provided that they don't cause direct harm to others. I should add that these liberals also believe that those who fail to provide such necessities as food and education to those who are in need of them cause direct harm by failing to do so.

However, some communitarian critics of liberalism have argued that this way of understanding the requirements of justice underestimates the importance of how we form a healthy self-concept in a community.[14] They emphasize the importance of being seen and treated as a full member of society as opposed to a person who must be tolerated. They question the wisdom and usefulness of attempting to find impartial norms that will guarantee each person the right to pursue his own unique conception of the good constrained by an account of the right defined by impartial reasoning. This concern has led some communitarians to reject the search for impartial ideals of justice in favor of a method of forging a consensus

about justice through a process of democratically working across differences through open dialogue. According to this view, we will not be able
to put aside our partialities, but we can confront them through discourse.

Communitarians would contend that African Americans or any minority group that has been despised and subjugated will feel estranged from
the dominant society if they are merely tolerated and not accepted and
valued for their contributions. They believe that the liberalism of Feinberg, Rawls, and Nozick can at best produce toleration, but not
acceptance. But this view, of course, assumes that we can identify some
common goods (ends) to serve as the foundation for our theory of justice.
This is something that liberals who give priority to the right over the good
deny.

The communitarians, whether they realize it or not, have pointed to a
persistent problem for African Americans – the problem of recognition.
How do African Americans become visible in a society that refuses to see
them other than through stereotypical images? One need only turn to the
history of black social and political thought to see that African Americans
have wrestled with the question of what the appropriate means are for
obtaining recognition and respect for a people who were enslaved and
then treated as second-class citizens. Some argued that emigration was the
only answer, while others maintained that less radical forms of separation
from white society would do. Others contended that blacks could obtain
recognition only if they assimilated or fully integrated into white society.[15]
Neither of these approaches so far has been fully tested, so it is hard to say
whether either approach can adequately address the problem of the lack
of recognition for blacks in a white racist society.

The new alienation theorists believe that liberals cannot adequately
describe or eliminate the kind of estrangement experienced by African
Americans and other oppressed racial groups. Is this so? Yes and no. I
shall argue that liberals can describe the experience of estrangement using
the vocabulary of rights and opportunities, but I don't think that they can
eliminate this experience and stay faithful to their liberal methodology.

Typically when we think of a person being denied rights or opportunities we think of rather specific individuals and specific actions which serve
as the causes of these denials. For example, we might think of a specific
employer refusing to hire a person because he or she is black. The black
person in this case is denied job-related rights and opportunities by a
specific person. But even if we changed our example to involve groups
rather than individuals, the new alienation theorists would maintain the
experience of estrangement that they describe goes beyond such a descrip-

tion. According to their account, African Americans who have their rights respected and don't suffer from material scarcity still are estranged in a way that their white counterparts are not.

Are these theorists correct or do prosperous and highly regarded middle-class and wealthy African Americans serve as counterexamples to the above claim? Don't such persons enjoy their rights and opportunities? If not, what rights and opportunities are they being denied? I believe that rights and opportunities are being denied, but it is more difficult to see what they are in such cases. I think that liberals can contend that middle-class and wealthy African Americans are still alienated because they are denied their right to equal concern and respect in a white racist society. Even though they may be able to vote, to live in the neighborhood of their choice, and to send their children to good schools, they are still perceived as less worthy because of their race. The dominant attitude in their society is that they are less worthy than whites. The pervasive attitude is not benign. It acts as an affront to the self-concept of African Americans and it causes them to expend energy that they could expend in more constructive ways. The philosopher Laurence Thomas graphically described this experience in a letter to the *New York Times*.[16] For example, African Americans are too aware of the harm caused by being perceived by the typical white as thieves no matter what their economic and social standing might be. African Americans, because of the dominant negative attitudes against them as a group, are denied equal concern and respect.

It is difficult to see that this attitude of disrespect is a denial of rights because we most often associate political rights with actions and not with attitudes. In fact, it sounds awkward to say that I have a right that you not have a certain attitude towards me. This statement seems to strike at the very heart of liberalism. However, in reality it does not. Liberals can and do say that human beings should be accorded such things as dignity and respect, and they believe that this entails taking a certain attitude or having dispositions towards others as well as acting or refraining from acting in particular ways. So it is not that they cannot account for the particular estrangement that blacks experience because of the attitude of disrespect generated by the dominant society, but that they don't seem to have the theoretical wherewithal to resolve the problem.

Since liberals assign great weight to individual liberty, they are reluctant to interfere with actions that cause indirect harm. So even though they recognize that living in a society that has an attitude of disrespect towards African Americans can constitute a harm, and a harm caused by others, they are reluctant to interfere with people's private lives in order to eliminate these harms.

How can liberals change white attitudes in a way that is consistent with their theory? They could mount an educational program to combat false or racist beliefs. Liberals have tried this, but given their strong commitment to things like freedom of thought and expression, and the fact that power and privilege is attached to seeing non-whites as less worthy, educational programs have only had modest success in changing white attitudes. Critics of such educational programs argue that these programs can never succeed until racism is seen as unprofitable.

Let us assume that the critics are correct. Can liberals make racism unprofitable and respect individual liberty, one of the cornerstones of their theory? There are two basic approaches available to liberals: they can place sanctions on all harmful racist attitudes or they can provide people with incentives to change their racist attitudes. But in a democracy, the will of the majority is to prevail. If the attitude of disrespect towards African Americans is as pervasive as the new alienation theorists suggest, then it is doubtful there will be the general will to seriously take either of the approaches. I don't think that liberals can eliminate harmful racist attitudes without adopting means that would be judged by the white majority as unjustified coercion. However, they can adequately describe the alienation that African Americans experience even if they cannot eliminate it.

3 The Marxist Account

The Marxist explanation of the African-American condition assumes that the problems experienced by this group can be traced to their class position. Capitalism is seen as the cause of such things as black alienation. For the Marxist, a class analysis of American society and its problems provides both a necessary and sufficient understanding of these things. According to the Marxist, alienation, be it black or white, is grounded in the labor process. Alienated labor, in all of its forms, is based in private property and the division of labor. On this account, if we eliminate a system of private property and the division of labor, we will eliminate those things that make alienated relations possible.

The Marxist does recognize that political and ideological relations can and do exist in capitalist societies, and that these relations do appear to have the autonomy and power to shape our thinking and cause certain behaviors. But, for the Marxist, these relations only appear to be fundamental when in reality they are not. They can always be reduced or explained by reference to a particular mode of production. Racism is ideological; an idea that dominates across class lines. However, class divisions explain racial antagonisms, it is not the other way around.[17] But Marxists don't stop here. They also contend that in order to eliminate racism, we must eliminate class divisions, where class is defined in terms of one's relationship to the means of production.

Classical Marxists would oppose the new account of alienation advanced by recent theorists. The classical Marxists would insist that all forms of alienation, no matter how debilitating or destructive, can be explained in terms of the mode of production in which people are required to satisfy their needs. For them, it is not a matter of changing the way blacks and whites think about each other or the way blacks think of themselves because ideas don't change our material reality, relationships with others, or our self-conceptions. Our material conditions (mode of production) shape our ideas and our behavior.

On this account, African Americans are estranged from themselves because of their laboring activity or lack of it. They view themselves in hostile terms because they are defined by a mode of production that stultifies their truly human capacities and reduces them to human tools to be used by those who have power and influence. This all sounds good, but many black theorists (liberal and progressive) have been skeptical of this account of the causes and remedy for black alienation and oppression. They argue that the conditions of black workers and white workers are different and that this difference is not merely a difference in terms of things like income and social and political status or class position. The difference cuts much deeper. In a white racist society, blacks (workers and capitalists) are caused to have a hostile attitude towards their very being that is not found in whites. The new alienation theorists contend that the classical Marxist explanation of African-American alienation is too limiting. It fails to recognize that alienation occurs in relationships apart from the labor process. W. E. B. DuBois, although a dedicated Marxist, claimed that the major problem of the twentieth century was race and not class. Some theorists have contended that Marxists are too quick in dismissing the significance of race consciousness.[18] I think the facts support their conclusion. In the next section, I will focus directly on this issue of African-American alienation.

4 African Americans and Alienation

I believe that the atmosphere of hostility created against African Americans by our white racist society does amount to a serious assault on the material and psychological well-being of its African-American victims. I also believe that this assault can, and in some cases does, lead to the types of alienation discussed above. However, I disagree with those who conclude that most or all African Americans suffer from a debilitating form of alienation that causes them to be estranged and divided in the ways described in the new account of alienation. I also reject the implication that most or all African Americans are powerless, as individuals, to change their condition. The implication is that group action as opposed to individual effort is required to combat this form of alienation. There is also the implication that revolution and not reform is required in order to eliminate this form of alienation.

I don't wish to be misunderstood here. It is not my contention that capitalism is superior to socialism, but only that it is possible for African Americans to combat or overcome this form of alienation described by recent writers without overthrowing capitalism.

Are African Americans, as a group, alienated or estranged from themselves? I don't think so. Clearly there are some African Americans who have experienced such alienation, but I don't think this characterizes the group as a whole. African Americans do suffer because of a lack of recognition in American society, but a lack of recognition does not always lead to alienation. Even though African Americans have experienced hostility, racial discrimination, and poverty, they still have been able to construct and draw upon institutions like the family, church, and community to foster and maintain a healthy sense of self in spite of the obstacles that they have faced.

Although African Americans have been the victims of a vicious assault on their humanity and self-respect, they have been able to form their own supportive communities in the midst of a hostile environment. During the long period of slavery in this country, African Americans were clearly in an extremely hostile environment. If there ever was a time a group could be said to be the victims of the assault caused by white racism, slavery was such a time. Slaves were denied the most basic rights because they were defined and treated as chattel. Some scholars, like Stanley Elkins, have argued that slavery did cause African Americans as a group to become less than healthy human beings.[19] On the other hand, there is a group of scholars who argue that slaves and their descendants were able to maintain healthy self-concepts through acts of resistance and communal nourishment.[20] I tend to side with this latter group of scholars.

What is crucial for the truth of their position is the belief that supportive communities can form within a larger hostile environment that can serve to blunt the assault of a hostile racist social order. This, of course, is not to say that these communities provide their members with all that is necessary for them to flourish under conditions of justice, but only that they provide enough support to create the space necessary for them to avoid the deeply divided and estranged selves described in some recent work on alienation.

The history and literature of African Americans is rich with examples of how communities have formed to provide the social and moral basis for African Americans to have self-respect even though they were in the midst of a society that devalued their worth. Once again, I think it bears repeating. I don't deny that a hostile racist society creates the kind of assault that can lead to alienation, but only claim that this assault can be and has been softened by supportive African American communities.

The sociologist Orlando Patterson disagrees. Patterson has argued that African Americans are alienated because slavery cut them off from their African culture and heritage and denied them real participation in American culture and heritage. He characterizes this phenomenon as "natal alienation."[21] African Americans, on Patterson's account, feel estranged because they don't believe that they belong. They are not Africans, but they also are not Americans. One might argue that the present move from "black American" to "African American" is an attempt to address the phenomenon of natal alienation. According to Patterson, the past provides us with crucial insight into the present psyches of African Americans. On his view, the fact of slavery helps to explain the present condition and behavior of African Americans, including the present underclass phenomenon.[22]

I disagree with Patterson's conclusions. He falls prey to the same shortcoming that plagues the liberal and the Marxist accounts of the African-American experience. They all fail to appreciate the role of ethnic communities in the lives of individuals and groups. Although DuBois never played down the horrors and harms of racism, he refused to see the masses of black people as a people who were estranged or alienated from themselves. In fact, in his *Dusk of Dawn*, DuBois describes how black people have been able to draw strength from each other as members of a community with shared traditions, values, and impulses.[23] Being anchored in a community allows people to address and not just cope with things like oppression and racism.

The work of the historian John Blassingame can also be used to call into question Patterson's natal alienation thesis and it also provides some support for the importance of community in the lives of African Americans. Blassingame argued that even during the period of slavery, there was still a slave community that served to provide a sense of self-worth and social cohesiveness for slaves. In my own examination of slave narratives, first-hand accounts by slaves and former slaves of their slave experiences, I found that all slaves did not suffer from a form of moral and social death.[24] By moral and social death, I mean the inability to choose and act as autonomous moral and social agents. Of course, this is not to deny that slavery was a brutal and dehumanizing institution, but rather that slaves developed supportive institutions and defense mechanisms that allowed them to remain moral and social agents.

But what about the presence of today's so-called black underclass? Does this group (which has been defined as a group that is not only poor, poorly educated, and victimized by crime, but also as a group suffering from a breakdown of family and moral values) squarely raise the issue of black alienation or estrangement? Some people think so. They argue that Patterson's natal alienation thesis is extremely informative when it comes to understanding this class. Others reject the natal alienation thesis, but remain sympathetic to the idea that where there once was a black community or institutions that served to prevent the erosion of black pride and values, these structures no longer exist to the degree necessary to ward off the harms of racism and oppression.

In *The Truly Disadvantaged*, William J. Wilson argues that large urban African-American communities are lacking in the material and human resources to deal with the problems brought on by structural changes and the flight of the middle class.[25] According to Wilson, these communities, unlike communities in the past, lack the wherewithal to overcome problems that are present to an extent in all other poor communities. If Wilson is correct, the resources may not exist in present day African-American communities to ward off the assault of a hostile racist society. I am not totally convinced by Wilson's argument, but I think his work and the work of the supporters of the new account of alienation make it clear that there needs to be further work which compares African-American communities before the development of the so-called "black underclass" with urban African-American communities today.

At this juncture, I wish to distinguish my claim that supportive African-American communities have helped to combat the effects of a racist society from the claims of black neoconservatives like Shelby Steele. In *The Content of Our Characters*,[26] Steele argues that African Americans must confront and prosper in spite of racism. Steele's recommendations have a strong individualist tone. He argues, like Booker T. Washington, that racism does exist but that African Americans who are prudent must recognize that if they are to progress, they must prosper in spite of it. In fact, Steele even makes a stronger claim. He argues that African Americans have become accustomed to a "victims status" and use racism as an excuse for failing to succeed even when opportunities do exist.

I reject Steele's conclusions. First, I don't think that individual blacks acting alone can overcome racism. Individual blacks who succeed in this country do so because of the struggles and sacrifices of others, and these others always extend beyond family members and friends. Next, I reject Steele's claim that the lack of progress by disadvantaged African Americans is due in any significant way to their perception of themselves as helpless victims. Such a claim depends upon a failure to appreciate the serious obstacles that African Americans encounter because of their race. Even if it is true that African American advancement is contingent on African Americans helping themselves, it does not follow that African Americans should be criticized for failing to adopt dehumanizing means because they are necessary for their economic advancement.

African Americans should not be viewed as inferior to other groups, but they should also not be seen as superior. Racial injustice negatively impacts the motivational levels of all people. African Americans are not an exception. Steele makes it seem as if poor and uneducated African Americans lack the appropriate values to succeed. He contends that the opportunities exist, but that too many African Americans fail to take advantage of them because they cannot break out of the victim mentality. I reject this line of reasoning. As I have argued elsewhere,[27] this way of thinking erroneously assumes that most disadvantages result from a lack of motivation. In reality, it would take exceptional motivational levels to overcome the injustices that African Americans experience. Because some African Americans can rise to these levels, it would be unreasonable to think that all could. Steele underestimates the work that must be done to provide real opportunities to members of the so-called black underclass who struggle with racism on a daily basis.

I would like to forestall any misunderstanding about my emphasis on the role that supportive communities play in the lives of oppressed groups. I am not maintaining that African Americans don't experience alienation because they are able to draw strength from supportive communities. My point is that supportive communities can, in some cases, minimize the damaging effects caused by a racist society. Nor is it my intention to deny that African Americans and other groups must constantly struggle to maintain a healthy sense of self in a hostile society that causes them to experience self-doubt and a range of other negative states.

Notes

1   Liberal thinkers tend to argue that alienation results when human beings can no longer see themselves as being in control of or comfortable in their social environment, and they contend that this discomfort occurs when crucial rights are; violated, e.g. the right to autonomy. In an interesting twist on the liberal position, Bruce A. Ackerman argues in *Social Justice and the Liberal State* (New Haven: Yale University Press, 1980), esp. pp. 346–7, that the right to mutual dialogue is necessary to protect the autonomy of individuals in a community.

2   See, for example, John Elster (ed.), *Karl Marx: A Reader* (Cambridge: Cambridge University Press, 1986), Ch. 2; Bertell Ollman, *Alienation* (Cambridge: Cambridge University Press, 1976), Pt III; Robert C. Tucker (ed.), *The Marx–Engels Reader* (New York: W. W. Norton, 1978), pp. 73–5, 77–8, 252–6, 292–3.

3   See Frantz Fanon, *Black Skin/White Masks* (New York: Grove Press, 1967), ch. 1; June Jordan, "Report from the Bahamas," in *On Call* (Boston: South End Press, 1985), pp. 39–50.

4   The famous speech delivered by Martin L. King, Jr at the March on Washington, DC, August, 1963.

5   See Howard Brotz (ed.), *Negro Social and Political Thought 1850–1920* (New York: Basic Books, 1966).

6   Ralph Ellison, *The Invisible Man* (New York: New American Library, 1953).

7   W. E. B. DuBois, *The Souls of Black Folk* (New York: New American Library, 1969), p. 45.

8   Joel Feinberg, *Social Philosophy* (Englewood Cliffs, NJ: Prentice-Hall, 1973), ch. 1.

9   Feinberg, *Social Philosophy*, p. 13.

10   John Rawls, *A Theory of Justice* (Cambridge, Mass: Harvard University Press, 1971), section 67.

11   Feinberg, *Social Philosophy*, p. 13.

12   Rawls, *Theory of Justice*, pp. 440–6.

13   Isaiah Berlin, *Two Concepts of Liberty* (Oxford: Clarendon Press, 1961).

14   See Alasdair MacIntyre, *After Virtue* (Notre Dame: University of Notre Dame Press, 1981), ch. 17; Michael Sandel, *Liberalism and the Limits of Justice* (Cambridge: Cambridge University Press, 1982), pp. 59–65, 173–5.

15   Howard McGary, Jr, "Racial Integration and Racial Separatism: Conceptual Clarifications," in Leonard Harris (ed.), *Philosophy Born of Struggle* (Dubuque, Iowa: Kendall/Hunt Publishing, 1983), pp. 199–211.

16   Laurence Thomas, in the *New York Times*, August 13, 1990.

17   See Bernard Boxill, "The Race–Class Question," in Harris, *Philosophy Born of Struggle*, pp. 107–16.

18   E.g. Howard McGary, Jr, "The Nature of Race and Class Exploitation," in A. Zegeye, L. Harris, and J. Maxted (eds), *Exploitation and Exclusion*

(London: Hans Zell Publishers, 1991), pp. 14–27; and Richard Schmitt, "A New Hypothesis About the Relations of Class, Race and Gender: Capitalism as a Dependent System," *Social Theory and Practice*, vol. 14, no. 3 (1988), pp. 345–65.

19   Stanley Elkins, *Slavery: A Problem in American Institutional and Intellectual Life* (Chicago: University of Chicago Press, 1976).

20   John Blassingame, *The Slave Community: Plantation Life in the Antebellum South* (New York: Oxford University Press, 1972), esp. pp. 200–16.

21   Orlando Patterson, *Slavery and Social Death* (Cambridge, Mass.: Harvard University Press, 1982).

22   Orlando Patterson, "Towards a Future that Has No Past: Reflections on the Fate of Blacks in America," *The Public Interest*, vol. 27, 1972.

23   W. E. B. DuBois, *Dusk of Dawn* (New Brunswick, NJ: Transaction Books, 1987), esp. ch. 7.

24   See Howard McGary & Bill E. Lawson, *Between Slavery and Freedom: Philosophy and American Slavery* (Bloomington: Indiana University Press, 1992).

25   William J. Wilson, *The Truly Disadvantaged* (Chicago: University of Chicago Press, 1987).

26   Shelby Steele, *The Content of Our Characters: A New Vision of Race in America* (New York: Saint Martin's Press, 1990), esp. Ch. 3 and 4.

27   Howard McGary, "The Black Underclass and the Question of Values," in William Lawson (ed.), *The Underclass Question* (Philadelphia: Temple University Press, 1992), pp. 57–70.

13

"Stuck Inside of Mobile with the Memphis Blues Again": Interculturalism and the Conversation of Races[1]

Robert Bernasconi

I

The last slave ship to reach the United States was towed into Mobile, Alabama, under the cover of night in August 1859. Transporting slaves from Africa had been illegal by the laws of the United States since 1808. However, Timothy Meaher, a Mobile steamboatsman, had wagered some Northerners a substantial sum of money that it was still possible to evade the patrols set up to block the Atlantic slave trade. In order to win the bet he engaged William Forster to captain the *Clotilde*, a fast vessel especially built for the task. Forster transported 135 slaves that he had purchased from the Dahomey who had captured them in a recent war. The Africans could obviously not be sold publicly on Royal Street, where slave auctions were still held, so Meaher distributed them among a number of his acquaintances. He kept thirty-two Africans for himself in an out-of-the-way hamlet near where he had a shipyard and a sawmill. After Emancipation, the Africans, who had never been registered as slaves, were unable to earn enough money to return to Africa as they wanted. They were stuck inside of Mobile. To make the best of their situation, they bought some of the land from Meaher and organized themselves into a community that subsequently came to be known as AfricaTown.[2]

Even though Mobile has a rich history in which the French, Spanish, and English layers have remained visible in its architecture, AfricaTown proved a notable attraction. In the 1890s the local newspaper had this to say of the inhabitants of the "African colony":

They mix very little with other negroes and preserve many of their native customs, using their native language, speaking English with difficulty and being ruled by a queen of their own choosing. They enjoy a high reputation for honesty and industry, and their colony is justly regarded as one of the curiosities of Mobile.[3]

In 1914 AfricaTown attracted the attention of Emma Roche, who similarly praised their hard work, cooperation, and self-sacrifice.

Almost entirely cut off from white influence ... yet protected by our laws, they have worked out their destiny with much more success and honor to themselves than the generality of American-born negroes or of the free blacks who were carried by the American whose interests have been guarded and furthered by philanthropists.[4]

However, it is far from clear whether the author would have been so enthusiastic if some of the freed slaves in the vicinity had not converted the Africans to Christianity within ten years of their arrival. Becoming Christian was not recognized as part of the assimilation process. It did not make them any less "African" because it was virtually taken for granted and was also the presumed destiny of their relatives left behind in Africa.[5]

AfricaTown was an object of great interest because it was inhabited by Africans whose relation to Africa was not mediated by a long period of enslavement, but a multiculturalist who wants AfricaTown to be an exhibit or a kind of laboratory will be disappointed.[6] It seems that even though geographical location and segregation, both legalized and normalized, kept the Africans largely separate from white society, they integrated with African Americans after the first generation. Attempts to keep the memory of AfricaTown alive led in February 1982 to the inauguration of an AfricaTown Folk Festival, timed to coincide with the traditional Mardi Gras celebration of Mobile from which blacks had been excluded. After the first festival was held one former inhabitant of the area recalled his upbringing there:

I was vaguely aware of the fact that Plateau was different. I was constantly told that this community was not like other areas and communities in Mobile. ... Most of all, I remember the residents of Plateau. A community of black people worn with the heavy weights of racism, oppression and discrimination. Struggling to survive economically. Not having time to appreciate the history of Plateau. Too busy surviving to understand the totality of their existence. A sleepy, quiet, isolated, hollow of a community.[7]

The author, Carnell Davis, went on to describe why he believed the

AfricaTown Folk Festival was important, given that " 'blacks' in Mobile have been trained to reject anything that attempts to remind them of their Blackness." The festival "was carried out because it is important to remember one's heritage and culture. It was carried out because any people who would deny and forsake their own culture for the culture of others are surely a doomed race of people".[8]

However, it is worth pausing to assess the underlying assumptions behind this claim that conveys one of the main inspirations of at least some multiculturalisms. Insofar as the widespread rejection of the biological concept of race has led "race" to be displaced into the concept of culture, Davis was stating a truism. If a group has no identity other than that provided by its culture, then the loss of one's culture is the loss of one's identity as a group. But there is no reason to believe that Davis was addressing the scenario whereby African Americans would abandon their African-American culture and assimilate into (European-) American culture, although this might be the first thought of those European Americans who live in hope that this will happen, so that the United States can finally put race behind it. Davis was almost certainly talking about African culture and he was reaffirming his links with a continent from which his ancestors had been taken by force. He was thereby alluding to the struggle of all the slaves brought from Africa to the American continent to keep alive either a direct memory or, at least, a cultural memory of Africa. This act of resistance helped to form African-American culture and is embodied in, for example, its language, spirituality, movement, and timbre. It was, among other things, an act of resistance against the white image of blacks.

In 1963 in *Beyond the Melting Pot* Nathan Glazer and Daniel P. Moynihan declared that "it is not possible for Negroes to view themselves as other ethnic groups viewed themselves because – and this is the key to much in the Negro world – the Negro is only an American, and nothing else. He has no values and culture to guard and protect."[9] Seven years later for the second edition the statement was revised to read, "It is not possible for Negroes to view themselves as other ethnic groups did because the Negro is so much an American, the distinctive product of America. He bears no foreign values and culture that he feels the need to guard from the surrounding environment."[10] It is not obvious that the changes reflect a change of mind on the part of the authors, but rather the production of a more carefully coded message. Both statements are in any case false, although it should be noted that they reflect a wider intellectual current of the time.[11] Indeed, to understand what is at stake with this claim that there is no African component to African-American culture, one needs to see it as the new world version of the old European claim that Africans were incapable of producing a culture of their own. They were reduced merely to a race and not just one race among others, but a race without past or future except through contact with Europeans. The *locus classicus*, is, of course, Hegel, but the gesture was more widespread, particularly in the travel literature written after the debate on slavery began and in the justifications for colonialism as part of a civilizing mission.[12] But African-American culture looks back to Africa and, most importantly, often also looks forward to Africa as part of its resistance to the meaning assigned to it in this way. Here the *locus classicus* is, of course, Du Bois's "The Conservation of Races," but it was also expressed in the Negro spirituals. Carnell Davis, like many African Americans, felt a bond with Africa. I am in no position to explore the question of the meaning of Africa for African Americans, which is often very personal, but Zora Neale Hurston's recollection of the impact of her visit to AfricaTown can serve here to give some indication of the complexity involved, notwithstanding the fact that she seems to have been determined that her responses to anything were never "typical" of anything but her. Hurston had visited AfricaTown in order to interview Cudjo Lewis, the last survivor among the Africans who had been brought to Mobile aboard the *Clotilde*, as part of her anthropological research.[13] In the chapter on "Researches" in her autobiography she described the disillusionment of her idea of Africa that arose from her three-month association with Cudjo Lewis:

> The white people had held my people in slavery here in America. They had bought us, it is true, and exploited us. But the inescapable fact that stuck in my craw was: my people had *sold* me and the white people had bought me. That *did* away with the folklore I had been brought up on – that the white people had gone to Africa, waved a red handkerchief at the Africans and lured them aboard ship and sailed away. I know that civilized money stirred up African greed. . . . But, if the African princes had been as pure and as innocent as I would like to think, it could not have happened. . . . It was a sobering thought.[14]

Nevertheless, Zora Neale Hurston's disillusionment with a certain image of Africa was balanced by her presentation of Cudjo Lewis's nostalgia for Africa: "After seventy-five years, he still had that tragic sense of loss. That yearning for blood and cultural ties. That sense of mutilation. It gave me something to feel about it" (*DTR*, p. 204). History in the form of Lewis's recollections may have deprived Hurston of a certain idea of Africa and given her something to think about, but it did not destroy the ties of blood and culture.

II

In 1667, François Bernier wrote a first-hand account of the Hindu religion and what he regarded as its ridiculous errors and superstitions.[15] Bernier had been struck by the Hindu ritual of bathing in running water and judged that it would not be possible in cold climates. So far as he was concerned, this was clear evidence that the Hindus were following laws of merely human origin. If the rituals had been of divine origin, they could have been applied universally. Bernier was so impressed by this argument that he confronted the Indians with it, but they dismissed it. They did not presume that their laws were universal and so they were not persuaded by any arguments designed to show that their rituals could not readily be transferred elsewhere. God had made Hinduism for them alone and for that reason they could not receive foreigners into their religion. Nor did they reject Christianity as false. They conceded that Christianity might be good for Europeans. According to Bernier, the Indians believed that "God could have made several different ways to go to heaven; but they did not want to hear that while our religion was universal for the whole earth, theirs could only be fiction and pure invention."[16] The Indians, who steadfastly upheld their own traditions without engaging in any proselytizing activity, were surprised to find that the Christian missionaries followed a different code of conduct and were intent on converting them.

Over a century later, Kant took up Bernier's observations. He was clearly struck by Bernier's presentation of Hinduism as a religion that did not hate other religions, but he seems to have been even more impressed by the fact that Hindus believed that one was assigned one's religion by virtue of one's birth: "They say that their religion is confined to their tribe (*Stamm*)."[17] In a course on Anthropology from 1791–2, Kant developed Bernier's account as follows:

> It is a principle of the Indians that every nation has a religion for itself. Hence they force nobody to adopt theirs. When Christian missionaries tell them of Christ, his teaching, his life and so on, they listen attentively and make no objections. But when they subsequently begin to tell of their religion and the missionaries become indignant and reproach them for believing such untruths, the Indians take offence. They say that they believed everything the missionaries told them without the missionaries having been able to prove their stories, so why do the missionaries not believe them in the same way.[18]

Kant clearly shared Bernier's rejection of the premise that each tribe should have its own religion, but one can still be surprised by the context in which Kant repeated Bernier's anecdote. Kant appealed to it in the course of presenting three maxims of reason. The first maxim was think for oneself; the second, think oneself into the place of others; the third, be consistent in one's thinking and judgments.[19] Kant associated the first maxim with the Enlightenment; to illustrate "the expanded way of thinking" proposed by the second maxim Kant told the story of the encounter between the Christian missionaries and the Indians. But how precisely was the anecdote supposed to illustrate the maxim?

Kant accompanied Bernier's anecdote with very little commentary. One might be excused for thinking that it was the Indians who exemplified "the expanded way of thinking," and that it was the Christian missionaries who were "circumscribed and narrow-minded."[20] The Indians of the anecdote were open and hospitable to the Christians, whereas any expectation that they might have had of reciprocity was disappointed when the Christians dismissed them. However, a marginal note in the copy of the student notes on which we are forced to rely suggests that Kant saw things very differently. The note reads in part: "One calls limited anyone who can always remain only in an enclosure."[21] The suggestion seems to be that the Indians were the people who were limited because they tied religion to nationhood or tribe. One might add that Kant, like many other Europeans, was moved by a fourth maxim that he did not annunciate here: one has a responsibility to bring the truth to others. This conviction has given rise to numerous activities, some more honorable than others. They include educational activities conducted under the rubric of "civilizing the natives" and missionary activities, even forced conversions. One problem with the idea of civilizing the uncivilized was the tendency in some quarters to assume that if someone else does not find "a truth" compelling, it is a sufficient basis on which to judge them recalcitrant, ignorant, uneducated, or even wicked.

Kant's rejection of the idea that every people has and is entitled to its own set of beliefs was not only directed against Hinduism. It seems likely that it was also and primarily aimed at Herder. Whereas Kant argued for a universal cosmopolitan state in which "our continent [Europe] ... will in all likelihood eventually give law to all the others,"[22] Herder strongly resisted any suggestion that Europe provides the standard and that the inhabitants of all parts of the world must become Europeans in order to live happily.[23] Herder illustrated the dangers of Europeans employing their own conceptions to judge the circumstances of others by appealing to the case of oriental despotism that was much discussed at the time: "it certainly was not the terrible thing that we imagine it to be in terms of our own conditions."[24] In his *Ideas for a Philosophy of History of Mankind* Herder emphasized the intrinsic merits of all cultures. He also accepted a version of climatic determinism.[25] As a result he believed, specifically with reference to those he called "sensual peoples," "Deprive them of their country and you deprive them of everything."[26] The designation "sensual peoples" might leave something to be desired, but Herder's application of climatic determinism to the theory of culture has some historical importance because it provided a basis for believing that each people has a culture which is "proper" to the people to whom it belongs and "improper" to everyone else. At the same time, Herder used the theory of climatic determinism to contest the advocates of slavery who believed that the relocation of Africans to America was to their benefit: "No words can express the sorrow and despair of a bought or stolen negro slave, when he leaves his native shore, never more to behold it while he has breath."[27] Herder was not limited to proposing a pluralism of cultures such as one finds it in the twentieth century – to give just one example, in Zora Neale Hurston's reflections in *Dust Tracks on the Road* on the Voodoo ceremonies she had researched in Haiti for *Tell My Horse*: "I did not find them any more invalid than any other religion. Rather, I hold that any religion that satisfies the individual urges is valid for that person" (*DTR*, p. 205). It is not easy to reconcile all of Herder's statements, but it is clear both from his judgments and his practice that he was not such a relativist that he did not believe it important for a people to know how its actions impacted on other peoples by paying attention to how those other peoples viewed the interaction. Indeed, he was unusual for his time in arguing against the European exploitation of Africans and others by using their own testimony.[28]

It would be a mistake to cast Herder as the founder of multiculturalism when the strongest inspiration for multiculturalism as such lies outside Europe in the form of resistance to European hegemony. Nevertheless, it is not surprising that philosophers trying to make sense of multiculturalism within the terms of the Western philosophical tradition turn to Herder, even if the result so far has tended to be a strange caricature of Herder that neither reflects the full richness of Herder's position, nor captures the real inspiration behind multiculturalism. This criticism can be leveled against Alain Finkielkraut, a staunch opponent of multiculturalism, Charles Taylor, who focuses on Herder as the spokesperson for a certain form of individual authenticity that is extended to a people or a nation, and Isaiah Berlin who, before either of them, had offered a reading of Herder as a pluralist, a kind of multiculturalist *avant la lettre*.[29]

If multiculturalism simply means a belief in the autonomy and integrity of distinct cultures, then it can be put to the service of very different political agendas.[30] So, for example, de Maistre's statement, characteristic of multiculturalism, that "Nations have a general overriding *soul* or character and a true moral unity which makes them what they are,"[31] a unity determined by language, can be adopted by the editorial writers and politicians who insist that the soul of America depends on making English the official language, just as readily as it can be used by minority groups who want the right to use their own language. One sees only a small part of multiculturalism if one focuses only on giving minorities the opportunity to study their own cultures, instead of recognizing that everyone should learn more about a number of cultures in addition to their own, including, where possible and appropriate, how those cultures see one's own culture. If minority groups do not always emphasize the task of knowing how one is seen, this is because it tends to be a fact of life for them, as in the phenomenon of "double consciousness."[32] This is why the greatest contribution of multiculturalism in the fullest sense will be the change that it could bring about within the dominant group, thereby making the conversation of the races less one-sided.

Multiculturalism presents itself as an alternative to the conception of history offered by Kant and further developed by Hegel. Their mono-culturalism served as a form of enclosure in which what is alien can be rendered intelligible only by reducing it to the same.[33] But there is a further twist. In spite of Herder's reputation as a forerunner of racial politics, it was Kant and not Herder who favored the notion of race. Indeed, a large part of the debate between Kant and Herder was generated by the latter's direct refusal of the concept of race that Kant had defined a decade earlier.[34] It is perhaps worth mentioning that if Kant refined and secured the concept of race, the person who is usually credited with being the first to use the term in something like its modern sense was none other than François Bernier.[35] And lest it be thought that Kant's interest in race was purely scientific, it should be remembered that he opposed racial inter-mixing.[36]

III

The plurality of cultures is the wealth of America. This is hard to say when poverty, the lack of social mobility, and discrimination are part of what serves to keep these cultures distinct. Segregation in the South, like ghettoization in the North, helped to preserve what many whites might have preferred to see eradicated. There is a long-standing suspicion among European Americans that African Americans represent a threat to the very survival of the nation. Jefferson epitomized this view. In his autobiography he had this to say about slaves: "Nothing is more certainly written in the book of fate than that these people are to be free. Nor is it less certain that two races, equally free, cannot live in the same government."[37] Tocqueville made a similar observation: he warned that the most formidable of all the evils menacing the future of the United States arose from the presence of blacks there.[38] But the most extreme version was provided by Josiah Nott of Mobile, who declared in the Introduction to the first of his *Two Lectures on the Connection between the Biblical and Physical History of Man*:

> The time must come when the blacks will be worse than useless to us. What then? *Emancipation* must follow, which, from the lights before us, is another name for extermination. Look at the free blacks of the North, of the South, of the West Indies, and of Africa. Could several millions of such idle, vicious vagabonds be permitted by our posterity to live and propagate amongst them? It is impossible.[39]

Extermination was inevitable, according to Nott, because it would not be financially feasible to transport the freed slaves back to the continent from which they had been brought against their will. They were in his eyes what Carnell Davis would have called a doomed race of people.

Today, the fear among many white Americans is no longer that the sheer presence of large numbers of freed blacks in the United States must inevitably tear the nation apart, but that the memory of slavery and its legacy will continue to threaten the story that whites want to tell about America, the story that they rely on to secure the meaning America has for them. This accounts for the sometimes hysterical response to multiculturalism that one finds among its opponents. The idea that the celebration of Kwanza or the learning of a few words of Swahili could tear apart a country to which blacks in times of crisis have shown extraordinary loyalty is laughable, especially given the fact that similar complaints are not made about the celebration of St Patrick's Day. The United States has, after all, survived a civil war and one would have thought that the appropriate target for those people who are worried about the disuniting of America would be the flying of the Confederate flag, not only because it is an insult to blacks, and often meant as such, but also because, if the Confederacy was not about slavery, it was about secession. But it is not only the idea of America to which many European Americans are so closely attached that is threatened; the racial identity that one gives to the prototypical American in one's imagination is also in question.

Both these issues underlie Arthur Schlesinger's *The Disuniting of America*. Schlesinger employs to the full the ambiguity of Hector St John de Crèvecoeur's description of how different nationalities had come to America and "melted into a new race of men."[40] The ambiguity arises because, as Schlesinger himself points out, "race" at that time meant nationality, and yet we cannot fail to hear it in its modern sense. Crèvecoeur expressly identified the members of the new American race as European or descendants of Europeans, but any evocation of his thought in the current context has to give some role to interracial mixing in the production of this new race. Schlesinger does precisely that and does not miss the chance to see this as a victory over the best efforts of the "ethnic ideologues" of minority groups to keep the races separate (*DA*, p. 133). He conveniently ignores the fact that de facto residential segregation plays a larger part, just as he overlooks the fact that it is the historical concern for racial purity among whites, which led to the rule that even a relatively small amount of "black blood" would be sufficient to exclude a person from being white, that conceals the extent to which the United States is already extraordinarily racially hybrid. Only whites could possibly think of racial mixing as a new solution to racial problems. As Hurston wrote in her own inimitable fashion: "I have been told that God meant for all the so-called races of the world to stay just as they are, and the people who say that may be right. But it is a well-known fact that no matter two sets of people come together, there are bound to be some in-betweens. It looks like the command was given to people's heads, because the other parts don't seem to have heard" (*DTR*, p. 236). That also helps to explain in turn why whites, when faced in the current context with the proposal for the addition of a mixed-race category on the census to an already incoherent system of classification, can welcome it without any of the soul searching that it provokes among other groups. It might be different if the proposal was that anyone of mixed race who identified with European-American culture could identify themselves as white and henceforth be considered as such. Schlesinger, however, turns all of this on its head. In his eyes white Americans are the vanguard of the new "race." They have already accepted the melting pot because they have given up their European nationalities to become American, which hyphenated Americans have so far failed to do. Of course, insofar as this was only another way of saying that whites provided the model for what it is to be an American, it implied the absurdity that all other groups were supposed to aspire to being white.

When Schlesinger's argument is exposed for what it is, it is quite remarkable that he makes it seem so seamless. His strategy is as follows. He begins his book by fantasizing that "The vision of America as melted into one people prevailed through most of the two centuries of the history of the United States" (*DA*, p. 14). He concedes later that the reality was somewhat different: "The old American homogeneity disappeared well over a century ago, never to return" (*DA*, p. 134). But both claims seem to be examples of the "false history" that he is so quick to expose when he addresses the excesses of the more extreme exponents of Afrocentricity. It collapses in the face of the fact that this allegedly homogeneous America had no place for blacks. In spite of the myth that identifies America with freedom and equality, Schlesinger is unable to denounce racial hatred and racial exclusion as un-American. He cites Tocqueville, as I have done, to show that racist exclusion is "deeply ingrained in the national character." It might have been more judicious of him to accuse European (or perhaps Anglo-) Americans of racial exclusion rather than to suggest that it belongs to the national character, but ultimately that is all the same to him (*DA*, p. 38). Schlesinger's argument is not that there is no basis for writing American history in terms of ethnic and racial classifications, nor even that that is not how history ought to be written because it "reverses the historic theory of America as one people – the theory that has thus far managed to keep American society whole" (*DA* p. 16). Schlesinger's argument is that "The multiethnic dogma abandons historic purposes replacing assimilation by fragmentation, integration by separation" (*DA*, pp. 16–17). The theory is "historic" and the purposes are "historic" not because that is how it actually was, but because that is how Schlesinger wants us to think of the destiny of America. In other words, Schlesinger wants national pride to eclipse pride in the race and he sees history as a weapon in this task. But national pride and race pride are more similar than many adherents of the former would wish to admit, not least because they easily get confused.

Zora Neale Hurston's remarks on this subject are again illuminating. They are to be found in the draft version of what would have been the last chapter of *Dust Tracks on the Road*, until the bombing of Pearl Harbor made it inexpedient to publish the analysis at that time. Hurston rejected race pride as fallacious and the cause of such misery and injustice that it should be rejected wherever it was found (*DTR*, pp. 324–7). But on the same basis she rejected national pride.

> Being human and a part of humanity, I like to think that my own nation is more just than any other in spite of the facts on hand. . . . But now and then

the embroidered hangings blow aside, and I am less exalted. I see that the high principles enunciated so throatedly are like the flowers in spring – they have nothing to do with the case. ... I should have been told in the very beginning that these were words to copy, but not to go by. (*DTR*, pp. 337–8)

This last comment, which is a clear allusion to the contradiction between the principles on which the United States is allegedly built and the reality, betrays the fact that in spite of her excessive commitment to individualism, her experience of America was dominated by her racial identification. America is not only freedom and equality, it is also hypocrisy, of which Jefferson's ownership of slaves has long served as a symbol.[41] Hurston also had an answer for those, like Schlesinger or Hollinger, who believe that racial intermixing will do better than multiculturalism at resolving America's racial problems.[42] Even though Hurston professed uncertainty as to how to address the problem of race, the first chapter of *Tell My Horse* culminates in a celebration of those Jamaicans who acknowledge their own heritage: "But a new day is in sight for Jamaica. The black people of Jamaica are beginning to respect themselves. They are beginning to love their songs, their Anansi stories and proverbs and dances."[43] This was her response to the Jamaican "mixed bloods" who attempted to answer "the question of what is to become of the negro in the Western world" by trying to become "absorbed by the whites."[44] Although a mixed-race category might contribute to the deconstruction of our thinking about race, it would do nothing of itself to alter the prejudice already in place in favor of the lighter skinned and could even provide a context in which it becomes more important. Although of mixed race herself, Hurston did not hesitate to identify herself as black, albeit with an important qualification:

I maintain that I have been a Negro three times – a Negro baby, a Negro girl and a Negro woman. Still, if you have received no clear cut impression of what the Negro in America is like, then you are in the same place with me. There is no *The Negro* here. Our lives are so diversified, internal attitudes so varied, appearances and capabilities so different, that there is no possible classification so catholic that it will cover us all, except My people! My people! (*DTR*, p. 237)

One does not need to look far for an explanation of why Hurston accepted her identity as black in spite of her Native American, white and black heritage. As she wrote, "No Negro in America is apt to forget his race" (*DTR*, p. 218). Some of the ways in which race is imposed on people may have changed, but it still happens.

Multiculturalism is one of the labels under which race can be addressed without being named. For this reason much of the incoherence and antagonism of contemporary discussions of race are introduced into the discussion without being addressed directly. For example, the view that the integrity of a given culture is sustained by exclusion and by keeping it free from contamination transfers to the cultural arena an idea of purity whose coherency, such as it is, in large measure derives from racial politics. In the case of American culture, the situation is slightly more complex. Even those who are inclined to identify American culture "essentially" with European-American culture also acknowledge the contributions of other groups, albeit only to the extent that they can be incorporated in the former. The dominant group not only believes itself empowered to define the national culture to the exclusion of the interests of other constituent groups, it also violates the other groups by demanding that they assimilate: an aboriginal population is forced to conform to an alien culture, as is the case, for example, in Australia, America, and under colonialism generally; historical enemies unite to form a new entity, for example, the United Kingdom, only to find that, more often than not, all of them are called by the name of only one of them, so that in this case they are all " English"; a religious group is persecuted, forced to assimilate, but find that they are still not accepted, as has often happened, for example, with the Jews; and, finally, African Americans, brought to the United States against their will as slaves, forced to work without reward or reparations, are told that they must become more American, even though they know that may not change the way they are perceived by European Americans. Multiculturalism is attacked because it provides an alternative to the one-sidedness of assimilation.

IV

The Africans who arrived on the *Clotilde* were stuck inside of Mobile, but they did not have the Memphis Blues. Not yet. That came later, especially if one has in mind the Memphis Blue not just as a style but as the name of a specific composition: *Memphis Blues* by W. C. Handy. It is widely recognized as the first blues song to be copyrighted.[45] The year was 1912. The music for this song had been composed in 1909 and had at that time been known as *Mister Crump*. It was the campaign tune written for E. H. Crump, whom Handy supported for mayor of Memphis. Handy explained that the melody was his but that its basic form was already widespread "from Missouri to the Gulf": "My part in their history was to introduce this, the 'blues' form to the general public, as the medium for my own feelings and my own musical ideas."[46] The words that came to be associated with the music included the following:

> Mr Crump wont 'low no easy riders here
> Mr Crump wont 'low no easy riders here
> We don't care what Mr Crump don't 'low
> We gon' to bar'l-house anyhow –
> Mr Crump can go and catch himself some air![47]

Although by today's standards one might think that telling one's candidate to "catch himself some air" was a peculiar way of supporting him, Handy explained that the lyric arose from some spontaneous comments in which the crowds expressed their attitude to Crump's reform proposals. Handy thought that as Crump was relying on a large black vote at the polls in his favor, it was best to humor them.[48] Although Handy copyrighted the song, some unscrupulous people misled him into thinking it was a failure, so he sold it for fifty dollars, thereby being cheated out of a great deal of money.[49] It is little consolation to know that Handy had at least been smart enough to be paid by one of Crump's opponents for playing the same tune.[50]

One of the favorite examples of scholars who want to show the openness of white culture to African-American culture is the banjo, which was brought from Africa by slaves and yet is now found almost exclusively among European Americans.[51] But the blues provides a better test case with which to explore in concrete terms the complex range of issues posed by multiculturalism. On the one hand, the blues is clearly identified with a specific culture and at one time was identified as "race music." On the other hand, the blues has had an enormous impact on American popular music generally. Furthermore, even though the blues arose under conditions of racial segregation, it did not develop in total isolation from other musical forms. The blues thus exhibits very clearly the phenomenon of intercultural borrowings without diluting the sense in which it is clearly identified with African Americans. Multiculturalism serves as an antidote to the demand that everyone assimilate to white or European culture, but interculturalism is a better term to describe the porosity of cultures. Interculturalism, as I understand it, addresses the question of how, without limiting the analysis to formal encounters between cultures, communication between a plurality of incommensurable cultures takes place.[52] If multiculturalism, on a certain Herderian model, risks giving the impression that cultures are discrete, autonomous, even relatively static units, then interculturalism, with its sense that that cultures change, in large measure, as they interact with neighboring cultures, is a valuable corrective to it. Focus on the intercultural dimension, as it reveals itself in the effective history (*Wirkungsgeschichte*) of the blues, suggests that intercultural communication is far more pervasive than the standard multicultural model allows, and in such a way that the plurality of cultures is not compromised in the direction of hybridism.

When people think of the early blues, they usually do not think of compositions like Handy's. They are more likely to think of the country blues, which would be closer to the kind of music from which Handy drew than it would be to his own compositions. To add to the irony, Handy explained that it was only when he was playing for a white audience in Mississippi, and they asked "a local colored band" to be called for to play the kind of music that they had heard at "Negro breakdowns on Saturday nights" and which his own band could not play, that he discovered the value of the blues and the profit to be made from it.[53] So far as LeRoi Jones was concerned, W. C. Handy belonged in the category of those who brought the blues as close to white America as it could ever get and still survive.[54] This has proved to be a line almost impossible to cross. According to Jones, "the idea of a white blues singer seems an even more violent contradiction of terms than the idea of a middle-class blues singer."[55] The debate as to whether white people can sing the blues is in the black community less an essentialist claim or an "authenticity" claim than a generalization arrived at by experience to which exceptions are allowed, and it should be remembered that it is easier to reproduce the sound of an instrument than the timbre of a voice, which is why the focus falls on singers rather than guitarists. By contrast, whites rather than blacks are the ones who are most insistent on the blues maintaining its purity and authenticity, and who tend to see the more "primitive" form as the more "authentic" one. But even if the blues is the singular creation and unique expression of a specific people at a particular historical juncture, it has also permeated the mainstream of popular music. The various musical developments that grew out of "the blues," such as rock n' roll, shows interculturalism at work, without the integrity of the blues being compromised.

Blues songs explore a wide variety of topics, but one is not going to get very far in trying to explain the development of the blues without reference to the extraordinary suffering European Americans have brought to African Americans. The blues represents a rival culture that frequently took the form of resistance to the dominant oppressive culture, much as some rap does today. This opens the question of what it means for whites to listen to the blues. Although so-called "classic blues" does not present the problem in quite such an acute way, it nevertheless remains the case that it is not only among traditional blues compositions that one finds songs whose lyrics are and should be hard for Whites to listen to, because of what they tell whites about the black experience in the United States. This does not make the songs off-limits for whites, who need to know this history and know how they are seen, but it does again emphasize a divide that has to be recognized. In the conversation across cultures the acknowledgment of experiences that are not shared is positive and productive. Unfortunately, because an unclarified conception of culture serves as a euphemism for race, and talk of a multicultural society serves proxy for a multiracial society, in much contemporary discussion the radical difference between "culture" and "race" disappears. When culture serves proxy for race, the dynamic character of an interculturalism that is porous across cultures is lost sight of and we are left with cultures as discrete, autonomous units. Not that interculturalism is necessarily of itself a good. The tendency of white musicians to cover, borrow, and steal from black music is not always a form of flattery. It is sometimes also another form of exploitation, for which the story of Handy's "Memphis Blues" can serve as a symbol.

In exploring the example of the blues, I have emphasized that interculturalism, as the condition for the interrelatedness of cultures, does not compromise the distinctness of the cultures involved. Nevertheless, there is a tendency not only for a dominant culture to demand other groups to assimilate to it, but also for it to approach other groups strictly on its own terms. For example, Schlesinger, in a paragraph purportedly designed to show that black Americans have influenced the national culture to the point where they can be said to belong far more to the culture of the United States than to that of Africa, cites James Baldwin's observation that when he went to Europe he found himself "as American as any Texas G. I."[56] Characteristically, Schlesinger refers to Baldwin to radicalize and even subvert the meaning of everything he had just written in his own voice with such studied caution. It is one thing to say that African Americans are culturally more American than African. It is another thing to suggest, as Schlesinger seems to do, that in Europe Baldwin discovered that his history is "part of the Western democratic tradition, not an alternative to it" (*DA*, p. 15). Certainly this is what Schlesinger wants to say and wants to have Baldwin acknowledge. Although Schlesinger acknowledges that African Americans shape American culture, he also insists that its origins are nevertheless "essentially European" (*DA*, p. 136). But part of Baldwin's discovery in Paris was that "it turned out to make very little difference that the origins of white Americans were

European and mine were African – they were no more at home in Europe than I was."[57] Furthermore, Baldwin's main point was that he needed to get away from the white racism that he had suffered in the United States in order to be released from the illusion that he hated America. Only then could Baldwin recognize that what divides black Americans from white Americans also reflects how much they have shared together.[58] There is, of course, a great deal more to Baldwin's essay, which also tells Europeans much about themselves, but Baldwin's discovery of what it means to be an American is very different from what Schlesinger means. Baldwin writes, "The time has come, God knows, for us to examine ourselves, but we can do this only if we are willing to free ourselves of the myth of America and try to find out what is really happening here."[59] Schlesinger, of course, does precisely the opposite. The meaning of America for him lies very clearly in the myth. He is able to quote Baldwin in his own support because he is unable to hear what Baldwin has to say.

The current debate in the United States about multiculturalism repeats some of the gestures of the encounter between the Christian missionaries and their Hindu hosts. In particular, African Americans having listened attentively to the European-American version of history, often can still not expect to have their own stories heard by European Americans, whether they be personal anecdotes about racist encounters or alternative ways of seeing the same historical events. One has to be deaf not to be aware of the evidence that many African Americans, for a combination of historical, cultural, and economic reasons, experience America very differently from European Americans. That many people in America are deaf in the sense just indicated was made evident by the surprise they expressed at the reaction of a large proportion of African Americans to the verdict in the O. J. Simpson trial. Nevertheless, in his Foreword to *The Disuniting of America* Schlesinger makes an extraordinary suggestion. He discusses the relation between minorities and the majority with which he identifies in these terms:

> Not only must they want assimilation and integration; *we* must want assimilation and integration too. The burden to make this a unified country lies as much with the complacent majority as with the sullen and resentful minorities. (*DA*, p. 19)

Because it is fashionable in some circles to place a large measure of blame for America's current problems on the failure of minority groups to assimilate, Schlesinger seems to think that he is being fair-minded in putting matters this way. Instead, it shows just how far America is disunited. Or perhaps it shows how white America is disuniting, because more whites than ever would find Schlesinger's description of "sullen and resentful minorities" offensive, just as they would find unacceptable his analysis by which European Americans are supposed to supply the idea of America that serves as a universal horizon within which various subcultures are allowed to coexist as they await conversion.

The one thing we can be sure of is that the future will surprise us, but, that said, as things stand we have to anticipate that in a couple of generations European Americans will no longer be in the majority. This would not be so very important if European Americans were not so hopelessly unprepared for it at the psychological level, as is confirmed by the fact that European Americans chose this time, finally, to offer, or appear to offer, assimilation to those to whom they have traditionally refused it. Furthermore, one should beware thinking that African Americans will benefit from the population shift. That is by no means inevitable. African Americans are not expected to be a much larger proportion of the total population than they are at present. But, more importantly, it is likely that if racial and ethnic classifications are still in official use, attempts will probably be made to define them differently from the way they are now. New alliances will be forged on the basis of those labels. Meanwhile, until we European Americans learn to listen better, and until such time as we do a better job of decolonizing ourselves from our mindset as colonizers, we are still all of us stuck inside of Mobile with the Memphis Blues again.

Notes

1   The title of this essay, part of which is of course borrowed from Bob Dylan, and the essay's initial focus, both arose from the accident that it began life as a talk, written in Memphis, for delivery at the International Association for Philosophy and Literature held in Mobile, Alabama in May 1997. This context perhaps also helps to explain why so much of this essay is concerned with bicultural – even biracial – concerns rather than with a broader range of multicultural issues. I recognize that a wider range of reference would introduce a different agenda, but I am persuaded that at this juncture it is more important to examine the efficacy of multiculturalism within specific contexts than it is to produce a theory of multiculturalism in general.

2   In constructing this account I have relied on the materials on file at the Mobile Public Library, for whose assistance I am grateful. In addition to the relevant texts cited in the subsequent notes, the materials include a photocopy of a letter from Captain William Forster and various newspaper clippings including the obituary of Timothy Meaher.

3   *Daily Register: Mobile*, Friday March 4, 1892. A similar report can be found in an article dated November 30, 1890.
4   Emma Roche, *Historic Sketches of the South* (New York: The Knickerbocker Press, 1914), pp. 111–12.
5   Ibid., p. 112. There is some suggestion that the Christian services maintained contact with some customs of the nation or "tribe" from which the Africans had been largely drawn and it should be noted that Lottie Dennison, one of the Africans who had been separated on arrival and legally enslaved, would attend the Church in Africa Town even though she had to walk from South Mobile. See Mable Dennison, *A Memoir of Lottie Dennison* (Florida: Futura, 1986), p. 35.
6   See Addie E. Pettaway, *Africatown, U.S.A.*, Bulletin no. 6240, published by Wisconsin Department of Public Instruction, 1985.
7   Carnell E. Davis, "Looking Back at Africa Town," *Inner City News* (Mobile), March 20 1982, p. 2.
8   Ibid.
9   Nathan Glazer and Daniel P. Moynihan, *Beyond the Melting Pot* (Cambridge, Mass.: MIT Press, 1963), p. 53.
10 Nathan Glazer and Daniel Patrick Moynihan, *Beyond the Melting Pot*, 2nd edn (Cambridge, Mass.: MIT Press, 1970), p. 53. For a refutation see Roger D. Abrahams and John F. Szwed, *After Africa* (New Haven: Yale University Press, 1983).
11 See E. Franklin Frazier, *The Negro Church in America* (New York: Schocken, 1974), p. 9.
12 G. W. F. Hegel, *Vorlesungen über die Philosophie der Weltgeschichte. Band I. Die Vernunft in der Geschichte* (Hamburg: Felix Meiner, 1955), p. 234; trans. H. B. Nisbet, *Lectures on the Philosophy of World History: Introduction* (Cambridge: Cambridge University Press, 1975), p. 190.
13 Zora Neale Hurston, "Cudjo's Own Story of the Last African African Slaver," *Journal of Negro History*, vol. 12 (October 1927), pp. 648–63. It is no doubt Emma Roche's text that Eric Sundquist had in mind when – with a little exaggeration – he suggested that Hurston's interview with Cudjo Lewis was "substantially plagiarized from a published book of sketches about the old South." Eric J. Sundquist, "'The Drum with the Man Skin': *Jonah's Gourd Vine*," in *The Hammers of Creation* (Atlanta: University of Georgia Press, 1992), p. 87.
14 Zora Neale Hurston, *Dust Tracks on a Road: An Autobiography* (Urbana: University of Illinois Press, 1984), p. 200. Henceforth cited as *DTR*.
15 François Bernier, *Voyages* (Amsterdam: 1709), vol. 2, p. 98.
16 Ibid., pp. 138–9.
17 See H. von Glasenapp, *Kant und die Religionen des Ostens* (Kitzingen: 1954), p. 32. The link between Bernier and Kant is suggested by Wilhelm Halbfass, *India and Europe* (Albany: State University of New York Press, 1988), p. 407.
18 Arnold Kowalewski (ed.) *Die philosophischen Hauptvorlesungen Immanuel*

Kants nach der neu aufgefundenen Kollegheften des Grafen Heinrich zu Dohna-Wundlacken (Munich: Rösl and Cie, 1924), pp. 146–7.

19 This moment in the lecture course corresponds to section 43 of the published text. Immanuel Kant, *Anthropologie in pragmatischer Hinsicht*, Akademic Textausgabe VIII (Berlin: Walter de Gruyter, 1968), p. 200; trans. Mary Gregor, *Anthropology from a Pragmatic Point of View* (The Hague: Martinus Nijhoff, 1974), p. 72.

20 Kowalewski, *Die philosophischen Hauptvorlesungen*, p. 146.

21 Ibid.

22 Kant, "Idee zu einer allgemeinen Geschichte in weltbürgerlicher Absicht," *Werke*, Akademie Textausgabe VII (Berlin: Walter de Gruyter, 1968), p. 19; trans. Ted Humphrey, "Idea for a Universal History with a Cosmopolitan Intent," *Perpetual Peace and Other Essays* (Indianapolis: Hackett, 1983), p. 38.

23 Johann Gottfried Herder, *Ideen zur Philosophie der Geschichte der Menschheit* (Frankfurt: Deutscher Klassiker, 1989), pp. 327 and 340; trans. T. Churchill, *Outlines of a Philosophy of the History of Man* (New York: Bergman, n.d.), pp. 219 and 228.

24 Johann Gottfried Herder, "Auch eine Philosophie der Geschichte," *Schriften zu Philosophie Literatur, Kunst und Altertum* (Frankfurt: Deutscher Klassiker, 1994), p. 15.

25 See Gonthier-Louis Fink, "Von Winckelmann bis Herder. Die deutsche Klimatheorie im europäischer Perspektive," *Johann Gottfried Herder. 1744–1803*, ed. Gerhard Sauder (Hamburg: Felix Meiner, 1987), pp. 156–76.

26 Herder, *Ideen*, p. 259; trans. *Outlines*, p. 169.

27 Herder, *Ideen*, p. 260; trans. *Outlines*, p. 170.

28 Johann Gottfried Herder, *Briefe zu Beförderung der Humanität*, ed. Hans Dietrich Irmscher (Frankfurt: Deutscher Klassiker, 1991), pp. 671–85, esp. p. 674.

29 Alain Finkielkraut, *La Défaite de la pensée* (Paris: Gallimard, 1987), pp. 14–19; trans. Judith Friedlander, (New York: Columbia University Press), *The Defeat of the Mind* pp. 6–10. Charles Taylor, "The Politics of Recognition," In Amy Gutman (ed.), *Multiculturalism* (ed.), (Princeton: Princeton University Press, 1994), pp. 30–2; Isaiah Berlin, "Herder and the Enlightenment," *Vico and Herder* (London: Hogarth, 1976), pp. 143–216, esp. pp. 180–213. I have challenged certain aspects of Berlin's reading of Herder in "'Ich mag in keinen Himmel wo Weisse sind,' Herder's Critique of Eurocentrism," *Acta Institutiionis Philosophiae et Aestheticae* (Tokyo), vol. 13, pp. 69–81.

30 See, for example, Pierre Birnbaum, "From Multiculturalism to Nationalism," *Political Theory*, vol. 24, no. 1, 1996, pp. 33–4.

31 Joseph de Maistre, "Des souverainetés particulières et de nations," *Oeuvres complètes* (Lyons: Vitte, 1884), 1:325. Cited by Alain Finkielkraut, *La Défaite de la pensèe*, p. 26: trans. *The Defeat of the Mind*, p. 16. Finkielkraut

also noted that some of its central theses suit both sides of the political spectrum today ibid., p. 112; trans., p. 91.

32 W. E. B. Du Bois, *The Souls of Black Folk* in *Writings* (New York: The Library of America, 1986), p. 364.

33 See Robert Bernasconi, " 'You Don't Know What I'm Talking About': Alterity and the Hermeneutic Ideal," in Lawrence K. Schmidt (ed.), *The Specter of Relativism* (Evanston, IL.: Northwestern University Press, 1995), pp. 178–94.

34 Herder, *Ideen*, pp. 255–6; trans. *Outlines*, p. 166.

35 Anon. [François Bernier], *Nouvelle division de la terre, par les differentes especes ou races d'hommes qui l'habitent* (1684); Kant, "Von der verschiede-nen Racen der Menschen," *Werke*, Akademie Ausgabe (Berlin: de Gruyter, 1968), vol. 2, pp. 427–44.

36 See, for example, Kant, "Bestimmung des Begriffs einer Menschenrasse," *Werke*, vol. 8, p. 105. I address these issues in more detail in "Who Invented the Concept of Race?" (forthcoming).

37 Thomas Jefferson, *Writings* (New York: The Library of America, 1984), p. 44.

38 Alexis de Tocqueville, *De la Démocratie en Amérique, Oeuvres Complétes* vol. I (Paris: Gallimard, 1951), p. 356.

39 Josiah Nott, *Two Lectures on the Connection between the Biblical and Physical History of Man* (New York: Bartlett and Welford, 1849), p. 18.

40 Hector St John de Crèvecoeur, *Letters from an American Farmer* (London: J. M. Dent, 1945), p. 43. Quoted by Arthur M. Schlesinger, Jr, *The Disuniting of America: Reflections on a Multicultural Society* (New York: Norton, 1993), p. 12. Henceforth cited as *DA*. I target Schlesinger because his beliefs and mode of argumentation are widely shared.

41 For an excellent new account of the two dominant strands of African-American political activity, one which tries to hold the United States to its ideals, the other which finds in its statement of those ideals largely an annunciation of hypocrisy, see Cedric Robinson, *Black Movements in America* (New York: Routledge, 1997).

42 See David A. Hollinger, *Postethnic America: Beyond Multiculturalism* (New York: Basic Books, 1995), pp. 40–50.

43 Zora Neale Hurston, *Tell My Horse: Voodoo and Life in Haiti and Jamaica* (New York: Harper and Row, 1990), p. 9.

44 Ibid., p. 7.

45 On two blues songs that apparently were in print in the weeks prior to the publication of *Memphis Blues*, see Eileen Southern, *The Music of Black Americans*, 2nd edn (New York: W. W. Norton, 1971), pp. 337–8.

46 W. C. Handy, *Father of the Blues: An Autobiography* (New York: Da Capo, 1969), p. 99.

47 W. C. Handy, "The Memphis Blues," *The Blues: An Anthology* (New York: Da Capo, 1990), pp. 70–3.

48 Handy, *Father of the Blues*, pp. 93 and 101. Handy noted that Crump himself was unaware of the words, although if Crump's own recollection is

correct Handy sought Crump's approval of them in 1910 after the election. William D. Miller, *Mr. Crump of Memphis* (Baton Rouge: Louisiana State University Press, 1964), pp. 101–2.

49 Handy, *The Father of the Blues*, pp. 106–13.

50 Ibid., p. xiv.

51 Dena J. Epstein, *Sinful Tunes and Spirituals* (Urbana: University of Illinois Press, 1977), pp. 33–8 and John Edward Philips, "The African Heritage of White America," in Joseph E. Holloway (ed.), *Africanisms in American Culture* (Bloomington: Indiana University Press, 1991), p. 225.

52 The notion of the intercultural seems to be more prevalent in European discussions than it is in North America. Nevertheless, my approach to it is somewhat distinct from the European formulations of which I am aware. See, for example, Heinz Kimmerle, " 'Interkulturalität' und das Ende der 'Epoche Rousseaus'," *Die Dimension des Interkulturellen* (Amsterdam: Rodopi, 1994), pp. 113–44. However, there is perhaps a closer affinity between my position and that of Bernhard Waldenfels, "Der Andere und der Dritte im interkultureller Sicht," in R. A. Mall and N. Schneider (eds), *Ethik und Politik aus interkultureller Sicht* (Amsterdam: Rodopi, 1996), pp. 71–83. See also the notion of interconnectedness in Anindita N. Balslev, "Cross-cultural Conversation: Its Scope and Aspiration," in Anindita N. Balslev (ed.), *Cross-cultural Conversation. (Initiation)* (Atlanta: Scholars Press, 1996), pp. 15–27.

53 Handy, *Father of the Blues*, pp. 76–7 and George W. Lee, *Beale Street: Where the Blues Began*, foreword by W. C. Handy (New York: Robert O. Ballon, 1934), pp. 132–3.

54 LeRoi Jones, *Blues People* (New York: Morrow Quill, 1963), p. 148. This book is more than a study of the blues. Its historical study of the African-American experience in the different form of "primitive blues" and "classic blues" dovetails well with the account given by Cedric Robinson of two traditions in African-American political thought. I am grateful to Söraya Mékerta of Spelman College for reminding me of the appropriateness of *Blues People* as a source for the present study.

55 Ibid., p. 148. The debate has even found its way into the philosophy journals. See, for example, Joel Rudinow, "Race, Ethnicity, Expressive Authenticity: Can White People Sing the Blues?" *Journal of Aesthetics and Art Criticism*, vol. 52, 1994, pp. 127–37.

56 James Baldwin, "The Discovery of What it Means to be an American," *The Price of the Ticket* (New York: St Martin's Press, 1985), p. 172. Quoted by Schlesinger, *The Disuniting of America*, p. 135. Somewhat strangely given that it is not an obscure text, Schlesinger quotes Baldwin at second hand, from Henry Louis Gates in the *Nation* (July 15/22, 1991), p. 91: which offers the possibility that the misreading is an innocent mistake.

57 Baldwin, *The Price of the Ticket*, p. 172.

58 Compare Ralph Ellison in "Change the Joke and Slip the Yoke": "On his side of the joke the Negro looks at the white man and finds it difficult to believe that the 'grays' – a Negro term for white people – can be so absurdly self-

deluded over the true interrelatedness of blackness and whiteness. To him the white man seems a hypocrite who boasts of a pure identity while standing with his humanity exposed to the world." *Shadow and Act*, in John F. Callahan (ed.), *Collected Essays* (New York: The Modern Library, 1995), p. 109.

59 Baldwin, *The Price of the Ticket*, p. 175.

Part VI

Postcolonialism and Ethnicity

14

Fanon and the Subject of Experience

Ronald A. T. Judy

If we accept, along with Edward Said, that what is irreducible and essential to human experience is subjective, and that this experience is also historical, then we are certainly brought to a vexing problem of thought. The problem is how to give an account of the relationship between the subjective and historical. It can be pointed out that Said's claim is obviously not the polarity of the subjective and historical, but only that the subjective is historical. It is historical as opposed to being transcendent, either in accordance with the metaphysics of scholasticism and idealism, or the positivist empiricism of scientism. Yet, to simply state that subjective experience is also historical is not only uninteresting, but begs the question: how is historical experience possible? The weight of this question increases when we recall the assumption that the subjective is essential to human experience. Whatever may be the relationship between subjective and historical experience, to think the latter without the former is to think an experience that is fundamentally inhuman. Would it then be experience? That is, to what extent is our thinking about experience, even about the historical, contingent upon our thinking about the subject?

When we approach the work of Frantz Fanon, which is what we are about to do, with its persistent attempts at the apprehension of reality, we are inevitably brought to contemplate the subject of experience as a condition of thought. Reading Fanon in this way implies refusing to succumb to the bleaker view of our present circumstance, according to which seriously pondering the possibilities of thought today is hardly thinkable. Admittedly, this phrasing of the concern about thought articulates an archaic theme regarding the problematic of representation – or, put differently, of determining the absolute value of what is essentially meaningless. This acknowledged formal resemblance with the concerns of metaphysics notwithstanding, our approach to Fanon is not seeking to determine the referent of thought (whether transcendent or transcendental), but to discover the occasion for thinking today. Now to speak of the occasion for thinking is not just to imply the abstraction or purity of thought as purposeful process – an empty thought. The investment here is not in idealism, acccording to which the pure force of thought articulates the world. On the contrary, it is in that which prompted idealism: the capriciousness of thought. That is, what is of concern in our approaching Fanon here is what comes of occassional thinking, and how it might still be possible today. There are many strong and wonderfully subtle thinkers who come to mind as having grappled in insightful ways with this concern. But, for the particular purposes of this essay – a cutting side glance at the so called fields of postcolonial and multicultural studies – the focus remains on Fanon in light of Edward Said's engagement with the question of occasional thinking. Of course, it is well known by now that for Said it is in the occasion of thought that the will to think publicly is manifest. In this he reiterates Nietzsche, discovering the oppositional (and for Said this is radical) nature of thought as occasional. More precisely, it is in the occasion to think publicly that the identification of thought with will, and so the threat of thought to those forces and practices whose function it is to repress or exterminate will, is exhibited – here style is everything.

Lately, in the US, there has been a somewhat prominent conversation going on about the vocation of thinking in public, about the public intellectual. Besides Edward Said, Cornel West, Nancy Fraser, Henry Louis Gates Jr, and Gayatri Chakravorty Spivak are examples readily at hand of those engaged with this question. The focus of that engagement has been on the issue of value, that is, on the ways in which the occasions for thinking in public are related to the tensions between received conceptions of the history of thought being expressed in the form of culture, and the emerging structures of capital in the global economy. The aim here, however, is not to explicate how the intellectual is in fact an expression of capital. This is too simple, and, quiet frankly, tired a gesture. What is of interest here is how the recognition of thought as expressed in capital fluidity can be thought otherwise from the way it has been in the dominant discourses of the West for nigh onto four hundred years. The task is to work out a hypotyposis of thinking about how occasional thought might be resistant, but not oppositional.

There may be an inclination to recognize in this working out the dispute over whether intellectual work ought to be invested in local organic constituencies, or in the perpetual increasing of its own possibilities so familiar to those preoccupied with current theories of multiculturality and postcolonial hybridity. Engaging in the dispute about the adequacy of these theories is less interesting than being concerned with the dispute's circumstance, with the conditions of its possibility, and thus with what it indicates about current relationships between thought and power. In this way we will come to appreciate how certain supposed progressive expressions of thought preclude and often prohibit thinking.

Take, for example, the following expression: "I try to examine the heterogeneity of 'Colonial Power', and to disclose the complicity of the two poles of that opposition as it constitutes the disciplinary enclave of the critique of imperialism." This expression is Gayatri Spivak's, quoted by Henry Louis Gates Jr in his 1991 *Critical Inquiry* essay, "Critical Fanon," in order to reveal the investment of specific oppositional intellectuals in the work of Frantz Fanon, and to characterize the nature of that investment as academic, and so pseudo-oppositional.[1] Occuring at a pivotal moment in his essay, when the course of a particular theoretical itinerary is plotted – more on this presently – Gates reads Spivak's expression in the context of his identifying Jacques Derrida's concept of writing with Spivak's critique of colonial discourse. Accordingly, he interprets the expression "put in its strongest form," as entailing "the corollary that all discourse is colonial" (*CF*, p. 466).

What is at stake *prima facie* for Gates in this expression is drawing a sharp distinction "between the notions of cultural resistance ... and cultural alterity" (ibid.). In that distinction, the notion of cultural alterity, which is indicative of multiculturalism, is proffered as being less rigidly ideological, and hence more tolerant of historical difference than the notion of cultural resistance that is equated with global theory. This distinction between global theory and multiculturalism enables Gates to critique the way in which the circulation of Fanon as the figure *par exemplar* of "postcolonial" thought trivializes his engagement with the psychology of race, and so deracinates his historical specificity as a Western-hemisphere black man. The agenda of "Critical Fanon," then, is to delineate the difference between global theory's and multiculturalism's readings of Fanon. The concern with how to read Fanon, or which Fanon to read, articulates a broader concern over what is the proper way to think about subjective identity. Is it locally, giving priority to the axes of geopolitics and ethnicity, or is it globally, attending to the ever-permeating expressions of an abstract symbolic economy? For Gates, the former is what is called for. In accordance with the notion of multiculturalism implied in "Critical Fanon," Fanon's thinking about thought and identity remains historically invested in the Western politics of race, the claim being that the multiculturalist reading entails the more rigorous historical analysis of Fanon and his thought, whereas the global-theory reading of Fanon yields a global postcolonial thinker, whose thinking is characterized by abstract homeless theory and oppositional revolutionary thought. A preeminent proponent of this way of situating Fanon in relation to thought is Edward Said, who is not only named as such by Gates, but some of whose recent work directly contradicts the Gatesian reading of Fanon. When approaching the dispute Gates stages between global and multicultural theory over the significance of Fanon, it is prudent to ask: why it is useful to read Fanon's *oeuvre* now? Addressing this question, it becomes clear how the dispute staged by Gates aims at delineating the fields of postcolonial and multicultural studies as heterogeneous. That notwithstanding, although the question I am posing of the value of Fanon's thinking is inextricably connected to the question why is Fanon significant for us now, it is altogether a different sort of question. Its aim is to discover the significance of Fanon's thinking about thought for us now. That significance is not found in the slavish philological commitment to the "content" of his work, as much as it is in the concern for the circumstances of its expression. That is, the struggle between postcolonialism and multiculturalism about Fanon's thought is over-determining the authoritative paradigm for oppositional thinking today.

Gates presented "Critical Fanon" as an exposé of how an itinerary can be charted through contemporary colonial discourse theory by tracking the presumably successive appropriations of the figure of Frantz Fanon as global theorist *par excellence*. The conduct of this itinerary foregrounds the political stakes in literary criticism's engagement with Fanon. This is made all the more evident in the claim that the project has the limited ambition of merely sketching the various ascendant readings of Fanon, not so as to supplant them with an alternative reading – in fact, he promises that "Critical Fanon" offers no reading of Fanon, only a "prelude" to such-but to discover the disciplinary field of contemporary colonial discourse theory demarcated by the itinerary of those readings (ibid., p. 458).

What is this itinerary? From the Latin *itinerarium*, derivative of *itineris*, meaning a going, as in a walk, march, or journey, an itinerary is generally taken to be either a journey or an account of a journey or travel, as in the Old French *Itineraire*. So, too, the English "itinerary" carries the double sense of either a line or course of travel (a route), or an account of such. That, of course, is a written account, which in the nineteenth century would most often have been in the form of a book tracing the course of the roads in a region or district, with accounts of places and objects of interest for prospective travelers. Such a travel book is supposed to be produced from experience, that is, be the record of an actual journey whose recording fixes a specific field of travel, constituted by a linear trajectory through "places" of interest. In other words, it is a topology. Today, a written itinerary is more proscriptive, being – and this is the sense, I think, in which Gates uses it – a sketch of a proposed route, a plan or scheme of travel. We should bear in mind, however, that even though this sense of itinerary is proscriptive rather than retrospective, it still delineates a field of travel, and so remains topological, presuming to know places of interest and how one must travel to get to them. Plainly, it requires some prior knowledge of the field through which it charts its course.

Insofar as the field of Gates's itinerary is that of contemporary colonial discourse theory, we are allowed to call it a scheme of traveling *through* theory. The thing is, with such itineraries, from the most detailed to abstract, the value of the traveling-line, the relationship between places along the way, is never truly understood until one is under way, that is, when one has made the trip. If it is a very successful itinerary, one with a very keen sense of *topos*, the logic of the itinerary appears as a constitutive feature of the field of travel itself. Each place of interest inevitably suggests the next in a successive line of increased understanding that appears to naturally belong with the territory. So, rather than appearing as an abstraction deployed to demarcate fields of movements, one from the other, the successful itinerary appears as that which emerges naturally, if not necessarily, from the relations of difference and resemblance between places met along the way. Field demarcation, then, is not a function of the itinerary, but a fact or feature of the terrain that the itinerary must contend with.

Bearing this in mind, when following the itinerary of "Critical Fanon" it is possible to note that there are seven *topoi*: Edward Said, Homi Bhabha, Abdu R. JanMohamed, Benita Perry, Gayatri Spivak, Stephen Feuchtwang, and Albert Memmi. There are references made in the beginning of "Critical Fanon" to the invocations of Fanon made by Donald Pease, Jerome McGann, and Stephen Greenblatt; but these remain just that, references, whose significance to the overall plan must be discovered as the trip is completed. It would be helpful, however, to briefly trace Gates's traveling-line through the group of seven *topoi* he treats as essentially constitutive of the field of colonial discourse, in order to have a better understanding of what the itinerary is of.

Gates begins charting his itinerary through contemporary colonial discourse theory with Said's 1985 *Critical Inquiry* essay, "Representing the Colonized: Anthropology's Interlocutors," and concludes with two of Memmi's Fanon readings: his 1971 *New York Times Book Review* review of Geismar's *Fanon*, and his 1968 "Frantz Fanon and the Notion of 'Deficiency'." It is sufficient on this occasion to recount the bare lines of Gates's sketch. We know that, at one level, what is at stake is the specific way in which the figure of Fanon is being invoked and deployed by a class of thinkers designated by Gates as theorists of colonial discourse. As Gates puts it:

> Fanon's current fascination for us has something to do with the convergence of the problematic of colonialism with that of subject-formation. And as a psychoanalyst of culture, as a champion of the wretched of the earth, he is an almost irresistible figure for a criticism that sees itself as both opposi-tional and postmodern. And yet there is something Rashomon-like about his contemporary guises. . . . His writings are . . . highly porous, that is, wide open to interpretation, and the readings they elicit are, as a result, of unfailing *symptomatic* interest: Frantz Fanon, not to put too fine a point on it, is a Rorschach blot with legs. (*CF*, p. 458)

Given the context, we are inclined to read the first sentence of this passage as saying something like: "Our current fascination with Fanon has something to do with the convergence of the problematic of colo-nialism with that of subject-formation." To read it as such, however, is to overlook the genitive, "Fanon's," which possesses the substantives "cur-rent" and "fascination." This expresses that the "current fascination" in question is Fanon's and not ours with or for him. Again, given the context, this agrammaticality is overlooked easily enough. Yet in overlooking it we seem to have, contextually, two possible interpretations. These are the one already given: "Our current fascination with Fanon . . .," and the follow-ing: "Fanon's fascination being current for us has something to do with the convergence of the problematic of colonialism with that of subject-formation."

This ambiguity is not, I think, just about an infelicitous formulation. On the contrary, discovered in this agrammatical moment is what is at stake in "Critical Fanon." Let us consider the difference between the two possible contextual interpretations of the sentence in relation to the rest of the passage. The first, "Our current fascination . . .," is in keeping with the explicit trajectory of the itinerary, which, recall, is to chart the way in which Fanon's figure circulates within the field of colonial discourse theory. In this regard, it is worth noting that of the group of seven (*topoi*), three, Said, Spivak, and Bhabha, have come of late to be referred to as the trinity of postcolonial theory. The difference is not inconsequential here, insofar as the chief presumption of Gates's itinerary is that what and how these thinkers read and deploy the figure of Fanon is somehow a constitutive feature of a field of theory. Accordingly, focusing on these three thinkers' readings of Fanon enables Gates to demarcate the field of postcolonial theory. A distinction is drawn between those who engage in the rigorous historical analysis of Fanon and his thought, and so recognize him as a psychoanalyst of race and culture, and those who deploy the figure of Fanon the global postcolonial thinker in the pursuit of abstract homeless theory and oppositional revolutionary thought. It is with the latter group that Gates detects certain "symptomatic interest" (CF, p. 458). Along these lines, he designates Edward Said's "Representing the Colonized" as a preeminent occasion in which Fanon is produced as a global theorist.

Said's Fanon functions in this instance as an indicator of postmodern theory's failure (and here the explicit reference is to Jean-François Lyotard) to be adequate to the *situatedness* of all discourses in its diagnosing the absolute decline of grand narratives of liberation. Said's rejoinder to Lyotard is that this diagnosis is precipitous at best, neglecting "the anti-imperialist challenge represented by Fanon and Césaire" by failing to take "them seriously as models or representations of human effort in the contemporary world."[2] Gates's concern is that in using Fanon this way, Said engages in a theoretical over-totalization of the social reality of the anti-imperialist struggles, and so deracinates the situatedness of Fanon's own discourse. Gates's reading of Said can be summarized as follows. On the one hand, Said calls for the recognition of the historical situation of all discourses, Lyotard's on par with Fanon's and Césaire's. In calling for such recognition, Said critically challenges the rigor of the claim that we've entered into an epoch of postmodernism, characterized by the foreclosure on grand narratives of liberation. At best, such a proposition can have no serious claim to globality – although it might retain affinities with the cultural imperialism attendant with internationalism – if the discourses of the Third World are excluded from consideration as being *ipso facto* irrelevant. On the other hand, Said disregards his own call by "typing" Fanon with Césaire as a composite figure of the global theorist *in vacuo*, and so emptying him of his own specificity. Quickly recognizing this composite as an "ethnographic construct" in which the individuality of the colonized is " 'drowned in an anonymous collectivity,' " Gates reads it as being symptomatic of an entrenched Eurocentric bias when it comes to the history of thought (*CF*, p. 459). This investment in a usable Fanon is not to be held against Edward Said, however, because it is understandable in terms of the crisis of authority plaguing his own counternarrative of postcolonial criticism. Said's allegorization of Fanon is interpreted as the site of counter-hegemonic agency – Said terms it the oppositional intellectual – as also being a rejoinder to those like Homi Bhabha who've charged Said with ignoring the self-representations of the colonized, and so implying that thoughtful power resides only in the discourses of the colonizer.

Whereas Said's interest in Fanon, by Gates's account, involves the return of the repressed, so too Bhabha's interest lies in forgetting, or more precisely a *dénegation* (*Verneinung*). In Gates's terms, Bhabha strives to correct Fanon's denial of Lacan by reading it in Lacanian terms as *dénegation*, thereby discovering in them Fanon "*le Lacan noir*" (*CF*, p. 460). Here JanMohamed's reading of Fanon against Bhabha is invoked to bring to the fore Bhabha's own willful forgetfulness of the text in his attempt to make Fanon, in Benita Perry's words, a "premature post-structuralist."[3] Yet JanMohamed also needs to read Fanon via Lacan in order to make him a "Manichean theorist of colonialism as absolute negation." So, too, Benita Perry's critique of JanMohamed's reading as neglecting Fanon's grasp of the pitfalls entailed in claiming to reconstitute a precolonial consciousness as the basis for a definitive oppositional discourse, is indicative of the romantic construction of the real native as a historical oppositional agency.

These, then, are the interested readings. But what are they symptomatic of? The answer to this is at play, I think, in the aforementioned agrammaticality. Assuming the second possible contextual interpretation, "Fanon's fascination is current for us . . .," the overarching question for Gates is, what is the logic of selecting *exempla*? The problem with Said *et al.*'s reading of Fanon, then, is a forgetfulness of the function of discourse in relations of power. Having arrived in his itinerary at Gayatri Spivak's response to Perry, Gates finds here the terms with which colonial dis-course is explicitly, and contemporary colonial discourse theory implicitly, renamed as writing. And when colonial discourse theory is identified with writing, it is recognized as being no more than "the disciplinary enclave of the critique of imperialism" (*CF*, p. 466). It is here that Gates deploys Spivak's expression in quotation: " 'I am critical of the binary opposition Coloniser/Colonised. I try to examine the heterogeneity of 'Colonial Power', and to disclose the complicity of the two poles of that opposition as it constitutes the disciplinary enclave of the critique of imperialism' " (ibid.). The corollary Gates draws from this is that all discourse is colonial discourse, including that of the oppositional intellectual.

This corollary is, according to Gates, a foregone conclusion of the psychoanalytic model of culture. Hence the legitimacy of his own reading of Fanon as "a psychoanalyst of culture, as a champion of the wretched of the earth." A perhaps irresolvable tension between these two aspects of Fanon appears at the point of this corollary. Or rather, we begin to understand that they are related along an axis quite different from the one that relates them in contemporary colonial discourse theory. The allegory of Fanon as an exemplary oppositional intellectual who represents to power those who cannot speak for themselves is traced along a horizontal axis, whose focus is *Les Damnés de la terre*.[4] In opposition to this Gates traces a vertical axis, whose focus is *Peau noire, masques blancs*,[5] along which Fanon, the black European, produces the figure of the wretched Algerian as an allegory for his own sense of split consciousness, as well as that of the New Man as the romantic construction of what he must become in order to forget what he is. In this uncharitable reading of Fanon, which is Albert Memmi's, Gates finds a Fanon that is "emphatically, not the Fanon we have recuperated for global colonial discourse theory" (*CF*, p. 465). Not only is this Fanon not the organic oppositional intellectual of the Third World, but the jewel of his thought, that the New Man emerges in the course of the colonial wars, is taken as a symptom of the very pyshcopathology Fanon sought to overcome, and not the figure of global revolution.

Gates leaves little doubt that although these tensions between Fanon the psychoanalyst and Fanon the theorist of revolutionary change are in evidence in *Les Damnés de la terre*, they are very much more pronounced in *Peau noire, masques blancs*, and glaringly apparent in the movement between the two books. This is where Gates's itinerary brings us, to an understanding that in betraying its own floundering between psychoanalytic and colonial discourse Fanon's work also betrays the inadequacy of the colonial paradigm for understanding the expressions of power relations today. Having displaced the figure of Fanon as the transnational transhistorical global theorist *par excellence* with that of Fanon the black man from Martinique, the European interloper in Third World affairs, Gates drives the point home with a quote from the newly figured man: "In no fashion should I undertake to prepare the world that will come later. I belong irreducibly to my time" (*Pn*, p. 15). This proviso, significantly enough from *Peau noire, masques blancs*, authorizes the abandonment of the project of a global theory – now recognizably imperial – whose model of totality threatens to annihilate the particularities of expression that articulate thought in its specific localities. This preferring local thought to global theory is presented as a more historical engagement with our current conditions than what is fascinating about Fanon for "the disciplinary enclave of the critique of imperialism" (*CF*, p. 466).

We are invited to disregard the imperial agenda of global theory that requires we choose between the Fanon of Spivak or Said, Greenblatt or Pease, Jameson or Bhabha, JanMohamed or Parry, even Fanon or Memmi, in the name of epistemological purity. Choice is not suspended as much as it is displaced onto the terms of judgment. It is not a question of whether or not to embrace Gates's reading of Fanon over Said's. It is a question of how to read them together on Fanon, which is to suggest how to read Fanon. This is the crux of it for Gates, to correct how Fanon has been read, to draw a sharp distinction between the figure of Fanon read within the field of anti-imperialist discourse theory, and the Fanon he wants to read. But read within what field? The answer is given in the closing sentence of "Critical Fanon," where it is concluded that disregarding the imperial agenda of global theory "requires a recognition that we, too, just as much as Fanon, may be fated to rehearse the agonisms of a culture that may never earn the title of *post*colonial" (*CF*, p. 470).

"Postcolonial" is the last word in Gates's text; the footnote attached to it explains that what is to be opted for instead of global theory is further psychoanalysis of race. More useful than the dialectic of colonizer–colonized, expressed in *Les damnés de la terre*, is the dialectic of subjective consciousness expressed in *Peau noire, masques blancs*. Fanon's *oeuvre* is thus divided so that his early and late works cannot be simply conflated, a conflation that invests heaviest in the oppositional global theorist of the later "Algerian" work. A striking shift of terrain attends this bifurcation of "Fanonia." Fanon the theorist of global resistancè, the universal oppositional intellectual, is displaced by Fanon the historicized theorist of black identity, and a black identity "situated" in the West, more precisely in the Americas. The concern with Fanon, then, is with the distinction between ways of understanding the expression of thought and organization of knowledge. That distinction is between a global epistemology that understands thought in the abstract, and a local historicism that deploys psychoanalysis in order to situate thought in its particular circumstance.

Accordingly, what is placed in opposition to the imperial agenda of global theory is a proto-nationalist agenda of the psychoanalysis of race. This distinction between a race-focused local historicism and a global oppositional epistemology puts a definite spin on Gates's characterizing Edward Said's reading of Fanon as the preeminent expression of Fanon the global theorist. Not to put too fine a point on it, when we travel with Gates through colonial discourse theory, we follow an itinerary that re-maps Said's earlier "Traveling Theory."[6] This is not so much a re-mapping as it is a mapping-over. Said's concern in "Traveling Theory" is to trace the itinerary of certain theories' transportation from the historical and cultural situations in which they appear to other historical and cultural situations, in order to expose the inadequacy of certain postmodernist theories of discourse and power (specifically that of Michel Foucault) to the oppositional critical consciousness. The issue is how Foucault's thinking on power, for instance, exhibits the tendency towards a theoretical over-totalization of social reality in its seeking to understand the complexity of that reality in the study of one variable. The resulting theoretical closure facilitates the transportability of that theory, but this is only an academic transportability. It remains inadequate to the political work of oppositional thought. Here a double inadequacy is exposed. The relatively facile transportation of theory within the academy also betrays the extent to which academic thinking is inadequate to an oppositional thought that seeks to address broad concerns of social justice. Within the broader context of social reality, the political function of academic thought is not critical opposition to those formations of power that repress or prohibit expression. On the contrary, academic thought, fig-ured here as theoretical closure, participates in the curtailment of true oppositional thought. What I want to draw attention to is that Said's project in "Traveling Theory" is not merely to find a way, as Paul Bové puts it, to "study the translation of theories between cultural moments . . . reminding us not just of the contextual nature of theoretical production but also of the intellectual responsibility to measure theory against social reality so that it does not totalize its object at the expense of its practical and scholarly efficacy."[7] It is, as Bové has also pointed out, to sketch out, to plot the itinerary of that discourse which will constitute and represent intellectuals in a way that escapes academic neutering by continually engaging in the concrete political struggles of social reality.[8] In other words, in the very process of tracing the critical history of the political efficacy of theory in the academy, Said enacts the struggle to establish the political efficacy of one conception and practice of intellectual discourse (*IP*, p. 213). In "Traveling Theory," the explicitly cited figures of that discourse are Noam Chomksy and Antonio Gramsci, and not Fanon (although it is of considerable significance that references to C. L. R. James in this regard keep reoccurring in Said's work from as early as 1975). The subsequent explicit reference to Fanon in "Representing the Colonized" may indeed be susceptible to Gates's read of it as a rejoinder to Homi Bhabha.

In plotting the trajectory of his own itinerary through postcolonial from this rejoinder, Gates wants to discover that Said's conception and practice

of the intellectual is inadequate to the concrete political reality in and
against which Fanon thought. And it is inadequate precisely in terms of its
own critical history of the political efficacy of theory in the academy. As
there, the danger is in theoretical over-totalization, here figured as the
global, which is achieved at the expense of any careful understanding of
Fanon's historical specificity. Gates, then, like Said, is enacting the struggle to establish the political efficacy of one conception and practice of
intellectual discourse in the very process of tracing the critical history of
the political efficacy of theory in the academy. Hence the significance of
the expression "the disciplinary enclave of the critique of imperialism." I
verge here on reiterating what I've already stated about the stakes of
"Critical Fanon" being the struggle between a global epistemology and a
local historicism to discover the extent to which Edward Said is Gates's
principal interlocutor in his travel through theory.

    Considered from this perspective, the difference in Gates's and Said's
readings of Fanon is revealed to be a struggle over the nature and function
of the intellectual in the "postcolonial" world of global capital. For
Gates's part, Fanon needs to be recognized "as a battlefield in himself"
(*CF*, p. 470). This only makes sense in terms of the engagement with the
psychoanalysis of race that Gates proposes as the touchstone of intellectual work. In this regard, not only is there a re-territorialization of thought
along the regressive lines of collectivities defined by an internal or local
logic of organization – the familiar nations, races, ethnicities, regional
identities – but there is such a profound incommensurability of thought –
its extreme subjectivization – that any attempt to think thought beyond its
particularity is to repress it, to colonize it, as Gates would have it. It goes
without saying that any attempt to think the very circumstance this
understanding describes, a world in which multiplicities of thought
regimes coexist in tandem in some sort of field, can only be grounded in
one of those regimes, and so must be imperial in its agenda to understand
such a world. Gates's objection, then, is not to imperialism, but to
imperialism in the abstract. Such declarations are frequently expressed as
constituting a historicist North American exceptionalism in which North
America, in this instance particularly black North America, is the end of
history. This perspective is indicated in Gates's claim that "Critical
Fanon" begins the work of sketching "out the challenge of rehistoricizing
Fanon" by listing the work in relation to which a properly contextualized
reading of *Peau noire, masques blancs* should situate itself (*CF*, p. 458).
By recognizing *Peau noire, masques blancs* as the paramount text for
understanding Fanon's significance in America as a New World black
thinker Gates overcomes the primacy of *Les Damnés de la terre* in the

English-language North American reception of Fanon's work. In so doing he disqualifies, in fact, recasts as alien, the history of revolutionary Fanon studies in North America. The English-language translation of *Les Damnés de la terre*, *Wretched of the Earth*, was published in the US before the translation of *Peau noire, masques blancs*, and functioned as the textbook of revolutionary action, both here and in Latin America.

There is an eerie parallel between this banishment of oppositional Fanonia from the field of Americana and the proclaimed New World Order, attended by the pronounced end of history, in which North American culture becomes dominant. What Gates has elsewhere called "African-American exceptionalism" takes on a peculiar significance in this instance as the generalizable model for conceptualizing the relationship between local and global.[9] Are these the terms in which the world is to be thought? It warrants pointing out at this juncture that in focusing on the question of whether or not Fanon was himself, or theorized the possibilities of the supranational or stateless intellectual, "Critical Fanon" draws attention to the possibilities of thought in a global economy, only to foreclose on possibilities of thought, restricting thinking to a subjectivist myopia that can only move beyond the individual to the collective of like minds. Thinking in this way, there are multiple collective minds, understood as constituting cultural unities the aggregation of which in turn, constitutes the global social sphere. Such multiculture determines, in a definitive teleology, the material expression of human consciousness. This is precisely what Said opposes with his insistence on reading Fanon's *oeuvre* as a continuity of thought, extending beyond *Peau noire, masques blancs*, and included in a genealogy of thinking forever striving to discover more possibilities of expression.

Three-quarters of the way into his 1993 book, *Culture and Imperialism*, Said remarks that Fanon "more dramatically and decisively than anyone ... expresses the immense cultural shift from the terrain of nationalist independence to the theoretical domain of liberation."[10] While there is no explicit reference at all made to "Critical Fanon" in this regard, this statement, if not a direct response to Gates, at the very least, responds to his counter-reading of Fanon. "In any case," Said continues,

> Fanon is unintelligible without grasping that his work is a response to theoretical elaborations produced by the culture of late Western capitalism, received by the Third World native intellectual as a culture of oppression and colonial enslavement. The whole of Fanon's *oeuvre* is his attempt to overcome the obduracy of those very same theoretical elaborations by an act of political will, to turn them back against their authors so as to be able, in the phrase he borrows from Césaire, to invent new souls. ... Fanon

performs an act of closure on the empire and announces a new era. National consciousness, he says, "must be enriched and deepened by a very rapid transformation into a consciousness of social and political needs, in other words, into [real] humanism ..." Like Césaire's in his *Retour*, Fanon's reconceived imperialism is in its positive dimension a collective act rean- imating and redirecting an inert mass of silent natives into a new inclusive conception of history. (*CI*, p. 269)

Certainly this expression is itself an elaboration on Said's earlier assess- ments of Fanon which Gates found symptomatic of the tendency to depersonalize the colonized, reducing him or her to a plurality. It is with such expression, however, that Said's brilliance outshines most of his contemporaries. For, it is in the expression (or speaking, as he would have it) that the value of his work is accumulated. And with Fanon, as with all others in this regard, interest follows the performance of oppositional intellect. Contrary to Gates's claim, Fanon is not like Césaire, but the expression of his thought performs a function analogous to Césaire's. What that function is gets expressed with Fanon's theory of violence: "For Fanon violence ... is the synthesis that overcomes the reification of white man as subject, black man as object. Said's conjecture is that while [Fanon] was writing [*Les Damnés de la terre*] he read Lukács's *History and Class Consciousness*, which had just appeared in Paris in French translation in 1960" (*CI*, p. 270). This startling imaginative conjecture borders on the careless in its abrupt appearance without any supporting statements to indicate its being anything more than a willful thought! Said repeats this conjecture in a subsequent 1994 essay, "Traveling Theory Reconsidered,"[11] where he tries to regain ground lost in critiques of his 1982 *Raritan* essay "Traveling Theory," as well as respond to those who critique his conception of oppositional intellectuals as being thoroughly Eurocentric. Offering no "firm" evidence of transmission even there, he speculates on the relationship of Fanon's *Les Damnés de la terre* to Lukács's *History and Class Consciousness* in terms of a genealogy of thought. The basis for that speculation is Said's recognizing in Fanon and Lukács expressions of the same willful thought that constitutes true oppositional intellectual practice. Here we are engaged with a quasi- idealist predication of the subject. Since I share Said's point of view that there is something of idealism subtending Fanon's predication of the subject, but also something materialist, I find greater affinity with his conception and practice of the intellectual than with Gates's. That being said, as I move on to my more detailed reading of *Peau noire, masques blancs*, there are some distinctions in our projects that warrant pointing out.

The first distinction to make is that Said's point of view focuses on the loss of the integrity of liberal humanism's subject. The significance of *History and Class Consciousness* is that Lukács showed the effects of capitalism to be fragmentation and reification, to the extent that every human being becomes an object, or commodity. The crucial concept for what Said characterizes as Lukács's "insurgent and heretical Marxism" is the separation of subjective consciousness from the world of objects, which can only be "overcome by an act of mental will, by which one lonely mind could join another by imagining the common bond between them, breaking the enforced rigidity that kept human beings as slaves to tyrannical outside forces" (*CI*, p. 270). This is the familiar subject–object dialectic permeating Lukács's work from *Theory of the Novel*, and *History and Class Consciousness*, to his essays on the historical novel and realism. Lukács's contribution to Marxism was to break with the economistic tendency, resulting from a crudely empiricist understanding of the material nature of the dialectic (an over-reaction to Hegel), by understanding what we now call, perhaps too quickly, culture – in particular, literary or narrative expression – as an articulation of the dialect. Such an understanding was supposed to achieve a historical (scientific) analysis of culture. In these terms, thought, that is willful intellectual work, functions as the agency by which the relationship between expression and the social formations attending capitalism are disclosed, thereby revealing the "real" conditions in which subjective consciousness has its particular expression. Insofar as the social reality is the material history of the subject–object dialectic, the relationships between it and the expressions of thought articulate the ways in which those expressions of thought limit or repress thought itself. A historical understanding of the forms of thought that ceaselessly discloses the aporia, ruptures, and seams in those forms in relation to social reality, discovers not only the conditions of repression, but also the possibilities of resistance. It discovers the ways in which thought itself is liberating. This is the way in which Said understands oppositional thought. Here is where Fanon functions like Lukács, not merely as an anti-imperialist theorist who conceptualizes native violence along the same lines as Lukács's thesis of fragmentation's being overcome by an act of will, not just as the "first major theorist of anti-imperialism to realize that the conventional narrative of nationalism extends the hegemony of imperialism." Fanon functions like Lukács in his grounding *Les Damnés de la terre* in the subject–object dialectic, and understanding the necessary agency for the synthesis that overcomes reification and dehumanization to be the mental act of will, willful thought.

If the violence that challenges colonialism is the expression of a collective will to thought that strives to ceaselessly disclose the possibilities of becoming human, then its momentum is not to be found in even the structures of nationalism it may come to articulate. On the contrary, insofar as those or any other structures restrict or constrain the possibilities of human expression, they too will be challenged. What Said finds in Fanon and Lukács is the expression of the work of theory – here understood to be that of critique – as endlessly in motion beyond confinement (*TTR*, p. 264). As Said maintained in the 1993 Reith Lectures, *Representations of the Intellectuals*, the task of the intellectual is to speak truth to power.[12] More specifically, it is to disclose and challenge all those forces that mitigate against the human spirit, among which Said includes the structures of global capitalism, which he sees as extending the hegemony of imperialism. Accordingly, the will to think publicly characterizes the vocation of the intellectual, a vocation that Said understands to be in radical opposition to the leveling forces of the global economy that reduce the very activity of thought to features of the marketplace. Hence, the momentum for the violence that challenges colonialism is indeed not found in the structures of nationalism of any sort (here inclusive of ethnicity and race, but also religion), but in the open-ended affective engagement with reality. Any consideration of Fanon's attempt to overcome the opposition of idealist and materialist predication through affect must, however, examine his investigation of the process of valorization in which consciousness emerges with the event of experience. Affect has a definite epistemic status in Fanon's thought as the expression of an order of consciousness that is extra-representational.

One of the determinations of the question of the nature of black existence posed by Fanon, and here I have in mind *Peau noire, masques blancs*, is the idealist predication of the subject as consciousness. In his consideration of black existence in terms of lived experience, Fanon goes to some length to understand consciousness not as thought, but as the subject's irreducible intendedness towards the object. In this sense, the paramount task of *Peau noire, masques blancs* is idealist: it is to understand what the consciousness of and for the black is by understanding how it is – its process of becoming. Yet, arguably, the entire project is organized around the attempt to understand the forms of consciousness in a way that abandons the idealist concept in favor of one in which forms of consciousness occur in history as expressions of concrete historical circumstances, as opposed to Freudian organicism. That attempt compels Fanon to entertain a materialist predication of the subject,[13] only, in his thinking, the figure for this is not labor-power but violence, which is how

Fanon thinks about consciousness in action (*en acte*) in *Les Damnés de la terre*. Just as idealist consciousness is the irreducible differential relation between subject and object, so violence is not mass revolutionary homicide, but the irreducible possibility that the subject be super-adequate to itself. "But it so happens that for the colonized peoples this violence, because it constitutes their only work, invests their characters with positive and creative qualities" (*Dt*, p. 80).

This super-adequacy exceeds not only the colonial situation, but also that of the national struggle attending it. "The action which has thrown them into a hand-to-hand struggle confers upon the masses a voracious taste for the concrete. The attempt at mystification becomes, in the long run, practically impossible" (ibid., p. 95). The concrete is that of experience. Expressed in the context of international capital, violence is the process by which the colonized discovers its true existence as a subject. It is the process of valorization in which consciousness emerges with the event of experience.

My aim is not to smooth over the contradictions between *Peau noire, masques blancs* and *Les Damnés de la terre*, nor is it to join the chorus of those who seek a radical disassociation between the two texts, finding Fanon to be organistic in the first, and phenomenological in the second. Instead, I aim to speculate on how Fanon's pronounced concern with affect presumes that value is articulated with the event of experience. That is, Fanon's apparent movement back and forth between a bare materialist and phenomenological account of violence is a function of his struggling to articulate violence as a figure of the event of thinking as concomitant with both will and matter, but not reducible to either. Accordingly, as far as the relationship between the two texts is concerned, the task here will be to adduce from Fanon's concern with affect the notion of the event of experience that concern presumes, and to establish the relationship between that notion and his subsequent theory of violence.

Because my investment here is focused on the association of value and affect in Fanon's thought, I will restrict the remainder of my statements to a concern with his attempt to explicate a theory of experience as a primary step towards overcoming the opposition between idealist and materialist predication. For reasons of time, I've limited the focus of that concern to the fifth chapter of *Peau noire, masques blancs*, "*L'Expérience vécue du Noir*," ("The Lived-Experience of the Black").

In order to understand the relationship between the event of experience and violence, that is to say affective value, we must first keep in mind that when Fanon is concerned with experience in *Peau noire, masques blancs*, it is always with regard to the experience of consciousness. Fanon's insistence on the inadequacy of the Hegelian concept of experience to the colonial situation notwithstanding, his own concept of *L'Expérience vécue du Noir* remains part of that legacy. Consider his assertion that with regards to the black there

> is undoubtedly the moment of existence-for-another (*Füreinanderesein*) [*l'être pour l'autre*] that Hegel speaks of, but all ontology is rendered unrealizable in a society [of] colonized and civilized. . . . Ontology, when it has admitted setting aside existence once and for all, does not permit us to understand the existence of the Black. For the Black [*le Noir*] no longer has to be black [*noir*], but must be it in the perception of the White [*en face du Blanc*]. Some may take it in their heads to respond to us that the situation is reciprocal [*est à double sens*]. We respond that that is false. The Black has no ontological resistance in the eyes of the White. (*Pn*, p. 88)

Fanon's formulation, "*Car le Noir n'a plus à être noir*" ["For the Black no longer has to be black"], is subtle and enigmatic. This prompts the question: "What, then, is the Black now?" The answer given here is that the Black *now* is not what he *was*: black. In other words, when we try to speak about what the Black is now we can only point to what the Black "has been," negating it. The Black that Fanon is speaking of is, thus, the *negation of the negation* of the black that he meant now. This is where Fanon's Hegelian legacy is most apparent, just at the moment he denies it. Yet the point of this rehearsal of what Freud, keeping to the Hegelian dialectic, termed *Verneinung*, and after him Lacan called *dénegation*, is not simply to establish that there is a paradox of sense certainty revealed by language when speaking of how "the Black no longer has to be black," but that that play of language entails an attitude of perception, which is not the Black's. This *dénegation* draws our attention to where Fanon wants it, on the process of becoming that is the consciousness of the Black. What is the difference between the Black and being black?

When writing about the "difficulties in the development of his bodily schema" that "the man of color encounters in the white world," Fanon states:

> All around the body there reigns an atmosphere of certain uncertainty. I know that if I want to smoke, I'll have to reach out my right arm and take the pack of cigarettes lying at the other end of the table. The matches, however, are in the drawer on the left, and I'll have to lean back slightly. All these movements are made not out of habit but out of implicit knowledge. A slow composition of my *self* as a body in the middle of a spatio-temporal world, such seems to be the schema. It does not impose itself on me, it is rather, a definitive structuring of the self and the world-definitive because it

establishes an effective dialectic between my body and the world. (*Pn*, p. 89)

In relation to the problem of the possibility of experience, Fanon refers to the totality of theoretical knowledge of existing beings. In this sense, experience designates the process by which determinate judgments are arrived at about things. Insofar as to be understood in a determinate way, an object must be presupposed to exist in the phenomenal world, all determinate types of experience – say the experience of color and smell – are reducible to the experience of existence. This sense of experience and existence is Fanon's only with regard to the body, that is, with regard to the existence of biological entities with black skin-color. But this is precisely the being black that the Black no longer has to be, except in the perception of the White. In his insistence on understanding the existence of the Black, he intends something else.

In the passage just quoted, Fanon appears to embrace the sort of phenomenological experience Husserl strove for, i.e. a demonstrating-intuition of essences. This, perhaps, indicates the influence of Merleau-Ponty, from whom Fanon very likely got the concept, *l'ex-périence vécue*. What is noteworthy here is that in embracing this concept of experience, Fanon recalls the idealist predication of the subject. Accordingly, the focus of his concern with the experience of existence is affectivity, and not the theoretical understanding of things.

With these considerations in mind, *apropos* to Fanon's assertion that the Black no longer has to be black, it can be stated that, his critique of ontology notwithstanding, he remains engaged with the Hegelian concept of experience in his concern about the lived-experience of the Black. The *dénegation* of being black is the moment in the process of the Black experience of consciousness in which it unburdens itself of the appearance of being something else. This entails the revelation of being itself, in perhaps the most absolute, and hence Hegelian, way (this is important because, as we will see later, Fanon's chief difficulty is in explaining the relationship between absolute being and blackness). Fanon's observation about the unrealizability of ontology in the bifurcated colonial society is not a call for the abandonment of ontology. On the contrary, it is insistence on the need to realize ontology by returning it to existence. It could be argued that here in *Peau noire, masques blancs*, published some ten years before the first French translation of Lukács's *History and Class Consciousness*, there is an analogous movement in thinking. So what Said reads as influence is perhaps better understood as familial resemblance. In any event, Fanon's agenda is to correct the situation so that the Black has

ontological resistance in the eyes of the White. For him, the fundamental
problem that is obscured by ontology is the experience of consciousness of
the Black. Recall that, even for the phenomenological experience, in order
for something to exist it must be presupposed as such, that is, it must be
present as in-existence for some consciousness – it is intended. Thus, *what*
something is in-itself, its true or essential existence, is *how* it is thought.
Fanon's assertion is not that no one thinks of the black, but that there is no
philosophical thought of the thought of the Black.

All of this is a sort of excursus, a clearing of the field in which the event
of black consciousness emerging can be clearly expressed.[14] And it is
expressed in a peculiar moment, that of presenting the experience of being
recognized as a *nègre* in the actual world: "*«Sale nègre!» ou simplement
«Tiens, un nègre!»*" (*Pn*, p. 88).[15] p. 88).[15] Being recognized as *nègre* is not
the same thing as being perceived as *l'homme de couleur*, "the man of
color," or *le Noir*, "*the* Black." The sense of *nègre* is imprecise throughout
Peau noire, masques blancs in a rather significant way. Although always
referring to a specific order of representation in which *nègre* designates an
aggregate identity, that identity is at times merely descriptive, and at other
times highly charged with a negative value. In the first instance it is
something like "Negro," and in the second something like "nigger."
Whereas both the English-language "Negro" and "nigger" are cognates
of the Latin *niger*, the former has a descriptive, and the latter a pejorative
connotation.[16] The single French term *nègre*, also derived from the same
Latin root, has both the descriptive and pejorative connotations.[17] This
equivocality of *nègre* is crucial to the movement of Fanon's thought; it
underscores the extent to which even the seemingly neutral descriptive
term presumes a dialectic in which *le nègre* is the antithesis of *l'homme*. To
become *nègre* is to die as a human. Although the implication is of the
"social-death" of slavery – the historical enslavement of the African in the
New World – Fanon is concerned with expositing and analyzing the
quotidian occurrences of the *nègre*, as an anomaly of affect. The method
of exposition is autobiographical recollection, the presentation of specific
lived moments in which there is a conscious awareness of what is becoming *nègre*. Inasmuch as these lived experiences of becoming the *nègre* are
presented in the movement of the moments of recollection, in a very
specific sense, *L'Expérience vécue du Noir* is the presenting of the experience of consciousness. It recollects the process of the dialectic with its
account of the opposition of subject and object and subsequent reification
as an object of another's gaze (*Pn*, p. 88).

We have already seen that the focus of Fanon's concern with this
moment is the problematic of the man of color's bodily schema in the

white world. There are two moments in his formulation of this problematic. We have considered the first moment in which there emerges a definitive dialect between self, body, and world, a movement in and among objects, where otherness itself (*this* pack of cigarettes, *here* on *this* table) brings about self-possession and self-sameness. At this moment the only property of consciousness known to it is as a unity. "A slow composition of my *self* as a body in the middle of a spatio-temporal world, such seems to be the schema" (*Pn*, p. 92). The second moment brings about something else, the understanding that below the corporeal schema is sketched a historico-racial one, whose constitutive elements are not provided by " 'residual sensations and perceptions primarily of a tactile, vestibular, kinesthetic, and visual character,' but by the other, the white man," woven "out of a thousand details, anecdotes, stories" (ibid.). Whereas the task of the corporeal moment "was to construct a physiological self, to balance space, to localize sensations," that of the racial one calls for more. This "more" entails the figuration of consciousness by language: "*Tiens, un nègre!*" (ibid.).

The movement between these two moments is, arguably, the movement by which the experience of consciousness moves through perception and comes to the understanding of the force of language, which Fanon elsewhere will theorize as revolutionary.[18] We are now at the beginning of Fanon's own understanding of force, in which, unlike Hegel's, force as the thought of the dialectic (*Kraft*) is identified with the inhuman force, whose appearance is violence. But the road back to and past Hegel is not a direct one, and the concern with force cannot be properly gained without following Fanon to where he is leading now. "Attacked from a plurality of points, the corporeal schema crumbles, ceding its place to an epidermal-racial schema" (*Pn*, p. 90). The discovery of the sublimation of the corporeal by the racial schema brings about a new form of consciousness: "I see in these white regards that it is not a new man who has entered, but a new type of man, a new genus. What, a *nègre!*" This negritude is recognized as a form of consciousness, the meeting-grounds on which the unity of the psychological to the historical consideration of Black consciousness is determined. The price of that determination, however, is a creeping idealist monism in which the *nègre* is misconstrued not as a figure of language but as the indicator of a radical conceptual difference. There is something being called by the French *nègre* that is beyond language, a transcendent consciousness whose conceptual framework supersedes what *nègre* names. Yet, despite its essential transcendence to language, it gets called by it, and is compelled to respond, albeit negatively. *Nègre*, thus, indicates negative consciousness. This is why Jean-Paul Sartre's assessment of negritude "as the minor term of a dialectical progression: the theoretical and practical assertion of the supremacy of the White is its thesis; the position of negritude as an antithetical value is the moment of negativity," so thoroughly disturbs Fanon.[19] In the negritude of Césaire and Senghor, "the black consciousness is given as an absolute density, as a filled with itself, a stage prior to any split, any abolition of self by desire" (*Pn*, p. 107). But such a procedure, as Fanon effectively reveals in his analysis of the pathology of negro phobogenesis, is finally symptomatic of negrophobia. It is the function of a symbolic economy whose only referent is itself, and not a phenomenological event. Hence, to treat *nègre* as an index of a transcendent negative consciousness is to slip back into the pathology, to accept that consciousness is figured by language, while at the same time forget this and carry on as though there was something like a black consciousness transcendent to language. Up to this point Fanon remains persuaded that the only way through this conundrum is in the examination of the experience of consciousness, whereby consciousness emerges *with* experience and is not a consciousness *of* experience. This, of course, is the consciousness of idealist dialectic. What Sartre has done is to call it by its "proper" name; in so doing he "has destroyed the black enthusiasm" by appropriating negritude to the History of Consciousness (*Pn*, pp. 107, 111). Stymied by this naming, Fanon protests that he "*needed* not to know," that "Jean-Paul Sartre had forgotten that the *nègre* suffers in his body quite differently from the White" (ibid., pp. 111–12).

It has been noted that Fanon's thinking on negritude is very complicated and caught up in the tension between his psychoanalysis of colonialism and his praxis of radical political action.[20] We should, however, be mindful that it was the dialectic which brought Fanon to Sartre; it was his need to understand the very process of becoming that seemed to make the *nègre* a necessity. The Sartre of Fanon's account is a moment in the experience of the "dialectic that brings necessity into the foundation of my freedom drives me out of myself. It shatters my unreflected position" (*Pn*, p. 109). The distinction between the subjective necessity and objective failings of negritude discerned in Fanon's thinking is the process of the dialectic in which he recognizes negritude as a moment in the process of achieving absolute freedom, but not its force. Or, more exactly, he cannot give an account of how negritude either transforms or facilitates the transformation of the colonized masses into a polity, i.e. into a willful collective consciousness. Negritude cannot get beyond the bare materialism of psychology *qua* racialism. Sartre's naming negritude as negativity provokes Fanon to grapple with the problem of how to move from the psychological to the historical consideration of the *nègre* without losing all hope of gaining the event of experience. The claim of difference in the experience of the body between the *nègre* and the White, which Fanon initially makes in reaction to Sartre, proves woefully inadequate, merely begging the question: But what is the *nègre* who suffers his body? More precisely, what is the nature of the *nègre* consciousness that "suffers"?

The chief concern there is whether Fanon strives to think an extra-representational consciousness. If so, how does it unfold, that is, what is it unfolding for? There is a temptation to read *Peau noire, masques blancs* in terms of Fanon's being burdened with Cartesian dualism: proceeding from the premise of the homogenesis of consciousness – it is either wholly somatic or discursive in origin – Fanon presupposes a hierarchical relationship in which freedom is understood as consciousness in-itself and for-itself against the body. To become truly free the Black must gain this self-consciousness in spite of his body; he must no longer be a *nègre*. This reading confronts substantial difficulties, however, when it engages the text of "The *Nègre* and Psychopathology," where Fanon determines that the cause of the Antillean's psychosis has to do with the symbolization of the body.

There is a historical difference between the *imago* of the "black" body, and its symbolization – between the representation of the body and the symbolic matrix the representation exemplifies. Attempting to understand this difference within the framework of Lacan's theory of the mirror stage, Fanon recognizes that the foundation for the Antillean knowing him or herself subjectively as a conscious unity is in the infant's identification with the specular image of its own body. This unity of consciousness, this "I," is manifested in a primordial form, before its objectification in the dialectic of identification with the other, and before language restores it to its function as universal subject.[21] It is the basis for the self that will function as the subject once it enters into the symbolic order, once it is taken up by language. Reiterating this fact later on in the Lacan note, Fanon states: "We shall see that this discovery is fundamental: Every time the subject sees his image and recognizes it, it is always acclaimed in the same way 'the mental oneness which is inherent in him' " (*Pn*, p. 131, n.). For the Antillean the symbolic subject is not reducible to the *imago* of the body: "We affirm that for the Antilleans the mirror hallucination is always neutral. To those who have told us that they have experienced it, we regularly ask the same question: 'What color were you?' – 'I had no color'" (ibid.). If this is so, if the Antillean's primal identification is symbolic, then where does the symbolic order come from? When does it come into play and how? Is it a fundamentally transcendent form of expression, and if it is how does it come about? To these questions, Fanon responds that the representational construction of the *nègre* is recognized as belonging to a complex of historical praxis, whose organized collective expression is commonly called culture, and whose psychic expression is the collective unconscious. In other words, the symbolic matrix exemplified in the representational construction is understood to be identical with the collective unconscious. Granting that, is the claim being made that the Antillean somehow comes by a symbolic matrix that is radically heterogenous from that of the French? Before we presume to have discovered here in Fanon an incipient theory of creolité, *pace* Glissant, it would be prudent to determine whether Fanon understands the Antillean's primal *imago* to be by a language that is truly other than French.

We are told in the delineation of the pathology of negrophobia (chapter 6), that the "*nègre* symbolizes the biological danger" (*Pn*, p. 134).[22] Fanon complicates matters, however, by further concluding that "European culture posses an *imago* of the *nègre* that is responsible for all the conflicts that may arise" (*Pn*, p. 136). The complication has to do with what is merely implicit in this study: the relationship between the symbolic value of the word *nègre* and the biological entities so designated. Having explicated how, in the symbolic matrix of *homo occidentalis*, i.e. the European collective unconscious, "the *nègre* – or if one prefers, the color black – symbolizes evil, sin, wretchedness, death, war, and famine," Fanon remarks: "In Martinique, whose collective unconscious makes it a European country, when a 'blue' *nègre* – a coal black one – comes to visit, one reacts at once: 'What bad luck is he bringing?'" (ibid, p. 154). The fact that "European *nègre*" is not an antinomy is reiterated in the next two sentences, where, contradicting Jung's location of the aetiology of the collective unconscious in physiological material – it is genetically encoded in the cerebral matter – Fanon asserts: "The collective unconscious is not dependent on cerebral heredity; it is the result of what I shall call the unreflected imposition of a culture. Hence there is no reason to be surprised when an Antillean exposed to waking-dream therapy relives the same fantasies as a European. It is because the Antillean partakes of the same collective unconscious as the European." The mechanism by which this has come about Fanon designates as "unreflected cultural imposition" (ibid.). The Antillean collective unconscious is European because the Antillean has been subjected to the imposition of the European representational scheme. It would seem, then, that the symbolic order of the Antillean's primal *imago* is the same as that of the European. Specifically, it is French. We are brought to understand that the European collective unconscious is constitutive of European culture. Culture, then, means a transferable representational schema (ibid., p. 152). It is noteworthy, however, that the Antillean is not regarded as a European but as an Antillean who "has the same collective unconscious as the European" (ibid., p. 154). The distinction is crucial to understanding the relationship between the symbolism and designation of the *nègre*.

Knowing that collective consciousness is a transferable representational schema (culture) helps in understanding how the Antillean identifies with what the *nègre* symbolize, but it does not bring us any closer to understanding the relationship between the symbolic value of the word *nègre* and the biological entities so designated. The answer to that is intimated in Fanon's ascribing a basic importance to the phenomenon of language at the beginning of *Peau noire, masques blancs*. The connection between this concern with language and the question of value is clear when we recall that, according to Fanon, Negro phobogenesis emerges with an *Erlebnis*, "an event" or "lived moment;" that is, the experience of specific traumatic events, whose traumatic character is such that they cannot be truly remembered, and so recur as something else, as repetitive muscular action that acts as the surrogate for the repressed memory. It is in this sense that the Negro is a symptom, the *Erzatz* of the memory of a series of traumatic scenes, the mnemic residue of it, as it were. The residual Negro is marked by resistance; and there is the Freudian dictum: where there is resistance there is repression. Leaving aside for only the moment the pertinent question of what is the nature of resistance, it is important to note that Fanon employs this dictum in understanding the analogy between the psychic and social topographies. In this he follows Freud's *Preliminary Report*, in which hysteria is caused by memory: it results from an *Erlebnis* that the ego-consciousness no longer remembers. For Freud, such remembrances of events must come to pass as an intense affective experience, thereby recovering the traumatic events and virtually tugging them back into their state of emergence, their *statum nascendi*, the state in which they ought to have been experienced to begin with. It is crucial to note here that Freud emphasizes that the hysteric is suffering from reminiscences, i.e. from *unknown* memories, as if memories do not have to be remembered in order to be. Such unremembered reminiscences do not erode with the passage of time; they retain their affective force, or such force retains them. The question is, what is the nature of this force. The answer for Freud, or at least the Freud of the 1895 "Outline for a Scientific Psychology," is material. Recall that in elaborating how unremembered reminiscences can be, Freud discerned two heterogeneous types of neurons, Ψ and Φ. In this schema, the natural condition of the organism is stability, understood as an equal exchange or flow of the forces or energies constituting the phenomenal world. For both types of neuron, then, pain is quantitative, it is an excess of energy from without. The nature of the organism is such that it seeks its primitive state by discharging, or allowing to pass this exogenous excess. In the case of the type Φ neuron, that passage leaves no trace; but in the case of the type Ψ, the energy encounters the buffer zone, achieving cathexis, which results in a structural modification of the organism. That is, while the Ψ neuron also seeks its primitive state of stability by discharging the energy, once this has been achieved, there remains a trace of the energy's passage. This is the *arché* that is reminiscence. Even allowing for the crudity of this summation of Freud's organisim, it is apparent that there is no difference between neural flow and neuropathology. In other words, if Ψ and Φ neurons are heterogeneous, and pain is quantitatively excessive energy, then consciousness is only concomitant with the endogenous force (cathexis), and is not an *a priori* organizing principle. It is presented with force – in this case, Freudian memory – the transformation of Ψ neurons resulting from the flow of exogenous energy through them. Breach is the re-presenting of the emergence of consciousness with the event. What Freud must account for is the relationship of consciousness to neuronal development in a way that enables collective or public consciousness. Given that consciousness is that which is concomitant with force, but not that which enables it (Kant's perception, *Ersheinung*, versus experience, *Erfahrung*, and thought, *Erkentniss*), that account ought to be a philosophy of language, or symbolic order. This, of course, was Lacan's insight, the recognition of consciousness as historical in the sense of being a particular order (process) of symbolization: it is an index of the flow of forces, the value of the flow of force – here value is a function of the signifying process that consciousness signs but does not comprehend. Understanding the sociogenesis of that value is the task Fanon undertakes. Yet, does he provide the theory of symbolization that Freud wanted, and Lacan strove for? More carefully formulated, does Fanon avoid the trap of identifying thought and language with the syllogism?

In *Peau noire, masques blancs*, Fanon maintains not only that there are two different forms of consciousness at play in the Antillean, African, and European, with the repression and substitution of the former by the latter in a hierarchical order, but that the subjective identity, the self, of the *nègre* results from this process. Fanon disposes of the Oedipal complex as necessarily constitutive of Antillean neurosis, displacing the origin of the neurosis from the family constellation, as the primary psychic circumstance, to the cultural constellation.[23] With regard to the supra-familial origin of neurosis, Fanon appears to understand the *nègre* as a particular type of historical consciousness, whose psychic structure can only be understood as emerging at the juncture of incommensurate symbolic matrices. That is, the *nègre* indexes the emergence of a third term or language, transcending the limits of the incommensurate two. It is in this way that the *nègre* displays the potential for Fanon's New Man.

Along these lines we might ask: if the *nègre* is no more than a symptom of . . . , then how can Fanon converse about *nègres* as biological entities in other than psychotic language? What can he possibly mean when stating that "I as a man of color do not have the right . . . to be a *nègre*"? Or, what could he mean by, "I am a *nègre*, and tons of chains, storms of blows, rivers of expectoration flow down my shoulders"? For that matter, how can he sincerely proclaim: "What is more, in human relationship, the *nègre* may feel himself a stranger to the Western world"?

Fanon observes in his lengthy footnote on Lacan's mirror stage that what appears in the corporeal schema in which the Antillean is primordially will only be recognized as having been the *nègre* after consciousness becomes the *nègre* of *homo occidentalis*. Very much like the Lacanian infant, the Antillean experiences an event (its body) and although having perception of it does not have the conceptual framework for understanding. Nonetheless, there is a "perceptual memory" that later, on having achieved the understanding of European culture, is recalled. But because the Antillean's self-identity is in terms of the White, what is now remembered is intolerable. So when the scene of corporeal schema gets recalled by something in life – *Tiens un nègre!* – the self is constructed in such a way as to prevent the actual perception from coming to mind. Instead, the self experiences the affect that it would have felt at the time of the original event if it had been the self it is now. We could say that the original event at the time of its happening is what will have been the trauma of recognizing oneself as a *nègre*. It is in this sense that the *nègre* becomes from nothing – it is a *méconnaissance*. So the *nègre* is a symptom of a series of traumatic scenes. Accordingly, the Antillean's neuroses stem from unremembered reminiscences of the experience of events that are analogous to Freud's. And like Freud's, these reminiscences do not erode with the passage of time; they retain their affective force, or such force retains them. Addressing the question about the nature of this force, Fanon, in his earlier attempt to examine the lived-experience of the Black, takes it to be that of self-consciousness. This, however, begs the question, because, by his own account, such consciousness is always already symbolic.

Fanon's understanding of the *nègre* as symptom of psychopathology yields an analysis that fails to explain the agency by which an event is transcribed as a sign: he cannot think of memory relative to consciousness without figuring out how the phenomenal character of the event of experience is perceived as affect, except that he reject the very idea of consciousness as a function of energy cathexis. What is at stake in Sartre's presumptuous forgetting "that the *nègre* suffers in his body quite differently from the White" is exactly what Fanon *needed* not to know: there is no *nègre* body, only the *nègre imago*, and it is an object-in-itself only for the consciousness that is human. True, the *nègre* is somehow imprisoned in his body, but only in the sense that it *is* in the dialectic of the corporeal and racial schemas. If it is this paradoxical moment in the becoming of consciousness that must be overcome in order to gain authentic freedom, then why does Fanon insist that what must be remembered is the fact of the *nègre* body? Precisely because the *nègre* is a symptom of the repression of the event of thought, which in *L'Expérience vécue du Noir* is rearticulated as the problem of the experience of the body. What Fanon calls "corporeal scheme" is arguably the exposition (*Darstellung*) of the essence of consciousness, *along with* "the residual sensations and perceptions primarily of a tactile, vestibular, kinesthetic, and visual character." Granting that, if the event is of *Darstellung*, then how can it be subsumed to memory, which is by definition representative (i.e. *Vorstellung*)? In his deployment of this distinction between exposition and representation, Fanon fails to provide an account of the agency by which event as *Darstellung* is transformed into *Vorstellung*; although the discussion of the connectedness of language and consciousness in the first chapter of *Peau noire, masques blancs* gives some indications. The critical issue here is that "memory" is a function of conceptual schemata, i.e. the representational (metaphoric) condensation of time into valuable images. It is not a genealogy of events as much as a tropology of event.

What concerned Fanon about *Darstellung* was its historicity, that is, the pure temporality of the event, enabling a correlation of event and consciousness. The phenomenality of the event, on the other hand, is valuable only as a thesis against which it becomes possible for consciousness to think itself as other than it – the other that is essential for the scene to occur at all. It would seem, then, that Fanon discovers *Darstellung* only to abandon it for the symbolic order of *Vorstellung*, finding the conditions for possibility to be exclusively representational. This, however, is not the case. Fanon discovered nothing else but that the conditions of possibility he sought occur with the correlation of event and consciousness, which he understood to be the eventfulness of language. What this leaves us with is an understanding of consciousness as pure temporality (as only historical). This, in turn, means that we do not know how it is continued from event to event, or how it is constituted as a collective consciousness among

aggregates of biological entities. Fanon's answer to these haunting problems was to read in the heterogeneity of event and consciousness the
insignificance of *Darstellung* to the construction of human subjectivity;
which is why he asserts that human freedom is the negation of the
correlation of consciousness and thing, not the transformation of event
into representation or symbol. That is to say, we cannot think of memory
except as the representation that forgets the event. Now it is true that
Fanon understood this "as repression, but it was the repression of memory of the event, not the event, returning us to our initial critique: such
repression presupposes ego.

To take that ego to be in the body is to be taken up in the pathology of
negrophobia. To hold it to be a totality independent of the body, to be an
Absolute ego, is to preclude the possibility of understanding in any
meaningful way historical difference in consciousness. Accordingly, the
unrealizability of ontology signaled in the opening of *L'Expérience vécue
du Noir* stems from its leaving-off of the exposition of consciousness
attending the corporeal schema. What Fanon is trying to think about in
his examination of how the psychopathology of colonialism yields a
consciousness incapable of successfully alienating itself from the event of
violence, then, is what sort of consciousness is possible with the event of
experience. What would it be to think about such? Although uncertain in
his approach to the first question, Fanon is convinced of the answer to the
second: it will radically restructure the world.

Genealogies of consciousness, which are highly dense structures of
accumulated mnemic residues of experience – symbolic orders – function
in the repression of the event of experience, and so preempt authentic
freedom. For this reason, Fanon refuses negritude, and nationalism *in
toto*, recognizing it as a moment in the repressive process of colonialism/
modernity. The *nègre* can be only in the process of consciousness
becoming identified with something, i.e. naming. And such naming is an
aspect of the caprice of language. This, however, presents him with a very
challenging problem. It could very well be taken as a crisis in his thinking.
Given such an apparently ahistorical event of experience, how can there
be change? Is violence the only way past the dialectic?

Violence for Fanon is not a force of nature whose mediate employment
in the social sphere is justified in terms of just ends. His dismissal of
ontogenetic accounts of consciousness in order to attain a historical
sociogenetic one entailed rejecting even the most rudimentary Darwinism,
most definitely social. Fanon's account of violence is as a historical force.
His concern, therefore, is not with the justness of ends, but with the
justification of means, which mediate violence on its own. In this regard,

Fanon found Chester Himes's exposition of the absurdity of race and sex relations, their irrationality, in the Americas useful for his thinking. This is not the place to provide a careful detailed study of all that is involved in Fanon's exclusion of the philosophy of ends (i.e. natural law) in his analysis of violence. Instead, the central concern here is focused on how, in his drawing attention to the historical grounds on which a distinction is made between kinds of violence independently of cases of their application, Fanon determines that all mediate violence is either law-making or law-preserving. In this way, he establishes that, insofar as the distinction between the colonizer's and the colonized's violence is that of sanctioned and unsanctioned violence, the distinction itself is possible only within one sphere: colonialism as the sociopolitical manifestation of modernity. Again, without rehearsing any of the details, among the most pronounced, and for readers such as Hannah Arendt disturbing, aspects of Fanon's theory is the recognition that revolutionary violence as a spontaneous eruption establishes the new conditions as new law.

While taking care not to reach any determinate judgment about the guaranteed continuity of revolutionary violence, Fanon understands that law-destroying is an inherent feature of violence. This is what the colonial executive, the state, fears about plebeian violence; this also makes that same violence revolutionary on a truly global scale in Fanon's view. The same revolutionary violence has another inherent feature of law-making and law-preserving in violence (see "The Pitfalls of National Consciousness"). The antinomy in evidence in Fanon's theory of violence is defined by the conflict between spontaneous revolutionary violence as fateful foundation, and the concomitant executive violence of discipline. In its fateful aspect it wipes the slate clean, the plebeian insurrection appears as a capricious eruption of violence that abruptly destroys the law. In this same fateful moment a consciousness emerges that becomes the revolutionary expression of a new law. Insurrection become revolution is law-making. Yet that same moment of transition entails the emergence of disciplining discourses, or structures and apparatuses geared toward preserving the new law. Fate and discipline, law-making and law-preserving violence, the fact that revolutionary violence requires both the features of eruption and continuity in order to be conceived of as *the* agency of historical change, keeps the antinomy insoluble. In this perplexing antinomy Fanon is most insightful, revealing in the movement of his thought an interesting and important question: what is an event?

In order, it seems, to remain true to the conviction that violence is a means towards non-perverse love, Fanon maintains that the event must found the expression of a new agreement as a new contract of understanding originating in violence. In these terms, violence is the foundational expression of a new community, a new contract of understanding. It is important to keep in mind that when Fanon understands violence as an *Erlebnis*, an experience, that this experience is always attended by an intelligence of the order of *Vertständigung*, "Understanding". By understanding violence in this way, however, he slips back into natural law. Thus, Fanon's attempt to give an account of the historical origins of community in violence reaches a point of mystery, for the conditions of foundational violence are fateful. That is, violence as a pure manifestation – the eruptions and physical anxiety of the *fellah* – is translated into violence as law-making. Only then is it revolutionary, only when it is legalistic. It is legalistic because its strives for an understanding of violence as a justified (colonialism) means for just ends (universal equality and freedom achieved at the end of colonialism). We are thus brought to the problematic nature of law itself (i.e. the question of sovereignty), according to which law-making violence inevitably yields to law-preserving violence, whose justification is the law itself. Once fateful violence establishes community as its just ends, those ends are misconstrued as resulting from a possible law. The violence of law-preserving is conceived of as the means by which the just ends are achieved. There is a tortuous and careful thread through this question of violence that turns us away from the questions of where is the human, and what is the human, to what do we do without the human. As is his wont, Fanon leaves us with a perplexity to ponder. The point of departure for that pondering would have to be the very idea of non-perverse love. And there we would need to better understand *Agape*, something that time and space will not allow for now.

Notes

1 Henry Louis Gates Jr, "Critical Fanon," *Critical Inquiry* 17 (spring 1991), p. 466. Hereafter this work is cited parenthetically as *CF*.

2 Edward Said, "Representing the Colonized: Anthropology's Interlocutors," *Critical Inquiry* 15 (winter 1989), p. 223. Hereafter this work is cited parenthetically as *RC*.

3 Benita Perry, "Problems in Current Theories of Colonial Discourse," *Oxford Literary Review* 9 (winter 1987), p. 31. Hereafter this work is cited parenthetically as *PCT*.

4 Frantz Fanon, *Les Damnés de la terre* (1961; Paris: François Maspero, 1982). Hereafter this work is cited parenthetically as *Dt*.

5 Frantz Fanon, *Peau noire, masques blancs* (Paris: Éditions du Seuil, 1952). Hereafter this work is cited parenthetically as *Pn*.

6   Edward Said, "Traveling Theory," *Raritan* 1 (3) (winter 1982).
7   Paul Bové, *Intellectuals in Power* (New York: Columbia University Press, 1986), p. 213. Hereafter this work is cited parenthetically as *IP*.
8   Ibid.
9   *The New Yorker*, April 29 and May 6, 1996, p. 10.
10 Edward Said, *Culture and Imperialism* (New York: Alfred A. Knopf, 1993), p. 268. Hereafter this work is cited parenthetically as *CI*.
11 Edward Said, "Traveling Theory Reconsidered," *Raritan* (1994). Hereafter this work is cited parenthetically as *TTR*.
12 Edward Said, *Representations of the Intellectual* (New York: Pantheon Books, 1994).
13 Fanon's model for this is Octave Mannoni's *Psychologie de la colonisation* (Paris: Édition du Seuil, 1950). It was Mannoni who suggested to Fanon that the confrontation of two different peoples "brings about the *emergence* of a mass of illusions and misunderstanding that only psychological analysis can place and define" (ibid., p. 32, quoted in *Pn*, p. 68); the italics are Fanon's. The key premises or central ideas, as Fanon puts it, of his and Mannoni's books are virtually identical, but not quite. Whereas Mannoni understands colonialism to be created by "a confrontation between civilized and primitive men," Fanon understand it to result from the juxtaposition of two different races. In Mannoni's case, the hierarchical distinction indicates a fundamental psychic difference, such that the Malagasy psychosis is not produced by colonialism, it was already a latent feature of the psyche that the colonial situation makes manifest. Fanon, on the other hand, understands any hierarchical difference to be wholly historical, a matter of technology and organization. Psychosis begins with colonialism.
14 What has gone before in the text was an excursus of the field, the exposition of the capacity of psychoanalytic interpretation for discovering the quotidian psychopathology of negrophobia. The introduction to *Peau noire, masques blancs* casts the thesis of negrophobia as a function of a social psychopathology that can be brought to lysis through analysis. Chapter 1, "*Le Noir et le langage,*" is an exposition of the complicated relationship of consciousness and language. Chapters 2 and 3, "*La Femme de couleur et le Blanc*" and "*L'Homme de couleur et la Blance,*" employ the psychoanalytic interpretation of the novels of Mayotte Capécia, Abdoulaye Sadji, and Réné Maran to delineate the pathology of negrophobia in the Black. The critique of Mannoni's work in chapter 4 is indeed an acknowledgment of Fanon's debt to that work, just as it is a going beyond it that is all but dismissive. The particulars of that debt have already been discussed. See note 13, above.
15 " 'Dirty nigger!' Or simply, 'look, a negro!' "
16 The *Oxford English Dictionary* gives the etymology of "negro" as from the Spanish or Portuguese *negro*, from the Latin *nigrum, niger*: black; it lists "nigger" as a pejorative alteration of "neger," also a pejorative, whose etymology is given as either from the French *nègre* or the Dutch *neger*.
17 *Robert* lists "nègre" as either a descriptive or pejorative reference to men and women of the black race also designated as "mélano-africaine," divided into

five groups – "soudanais, guinéen, congolais, nilotique, sud-africain ou zambézien."

18 Frantz Fanon, *Sociologie d'une révolution (L'An V de la révolution algérienne)* (Paris: François Maspero, 1982), p. 75.

19 Jean-Paul Sartre, *"Orphée Noir," l'Anthologie de la poésie nègre et malgache*, ed. Léopold Senghor (Paris: Presses Universitaires de France, 1948), p. xl. Quoted in Frantz Fanon, *Peau noire, masques blancs*, pp. 107–8.

20 Jock McCulloch, *Black Soul, White Artifact: Fanon's Clinical Psychology and Social Theory* (Cambridge: Cambridge University Press, 1983). Chapter 2 is of particular interest.

21 Jacques Lacan, *Le Stade du miroir comme formateur de la fonction du Je,"* *Écrits 1* (Paris: Éditions du Seuil, 1966), p. 90.

22 This is reiterated in Fanon's reporting of the results of his administering association test on some 500 Europeans (French, German, Italian) in which he inserted the word *Negro*. By his assessment, in almost 60 percent of the replies the word solicited associations with sexuality, physical prowess, animality, and evil (*Pn*, p. 134). There is no doubt, "the *nègre* symbolizes the biological" (*Pn*, p. 135).

23 Fanon is emphatic in asserting that "the Oedipus complex is far from coming into being among Negroes," and "that in the French Antilles 97 percent of the families cannot produce one Oedipal neurosis" (*Pn*, p. 123). The objection is further supported by a bold assertion: "With the exception of a few misfits within a closed environment, we can say that every neurosis, every abnormal manifestation, every affective erethism in an Antillean is the product of his cultural situation. In other words, there is a constellation of postulates, a series of propositions that slowly and subtly, with the help of books, newspapers, schools and their texts, advertisements, films, radio, penetrate an individual – constituting the world view of the group to which one belongs. In the Antilles that world-view is white because no black voice exists" (*Pn*, p. 124).

15

White Studies: The Intellectual Imperialism of US Higher Education

Ward Churchill

> Education should be adapted to the mentality, attitudes, occupation, and traditions of various peoples, conserving as far as possible all the sound and healthy elements in the fabric of their social life.
>
> David Abernathy, *The Dilemma of Popular Education*

> Since schooling was brought to non-Europeans as a part of empire . . . it was integrated into the effort to bring indigenous peoples into imperial/colonial structures. . . . After all, did not the European teacher and the school built on the European capitalist model transmit European values and norms and begin to transform traditional societies into "modern" ones?
>
> Martin Carnoy, *Education as Cultural Imperialism*

Over the past decade, the nature and adequacy of educational content has been a matter of increasingly vociferous debate among everyone from academics to policymakers to lay preachers in the United States. The American educational system as a whole has been amply demonstrated to be locked firmly into a paradigm of Eurocentrism, not only in terms of its focus, but also its discernable heritage, methodologies, and conceptual structure. Among people of non-European cultural derivation, the kind of "learning" inculcated through such a model is broadly seen as insulting, degrading, and functionally subordinative. More and more, these themes have found echoes among the more enlightened and progressive sectors of the dominant Euroamerican society itself.[1]

Such sentiments are born of an ever-widening cognition that, within any multicultural setting, this sort of monolithic pedagogical reliance upon a single cultural tradition constitutes a rather transparent form of intellectual domination, achievable only within the context of parallel forms of domination. This is meant in precisely the sense intended by David Landes when he observed, "It seems to me that one has to look at imperialism as a multifarious response to a common opportunity that consists simply as a disparity of power."[2] In this connection, it is often pointed out that, while education in America has existed for some time, by law, as a "common opportunity," its shape has all along been defined exclusively via the "disparity of power" exercised by members of the ruling Euroamerican elite.[3]

Responses to this circumstance have, to date, concentrated primarily upon what might be best described as a "contributionist" approach to remedy. This is to say they seek to bring about the inclusion of non-Europeans and/or non-European achievements in canonical subject matters, while leaving the methodological and conceptual parameters of the canon itself essentially intact.[4] The present essay represents an attempt to go a bit further, sketching out to some degree the preliminary requisites in challenging methods and concepts as well. It should be noted before proceeding that while my own grounding in American Indian Studies leads me to anchor my various alternatives in that particular perspective, the principles postulated should prove readily adaptable to other "minority" venues.

1 White Studies

As currently established, the university system in the United States offers little more than the presentation of "White Studies" to students, "general population" and minority alike.[5] The curriculum is virtually totalizing in its emphasis, not simply upon an imagined superiority of Western endeavors and accomplishments, but upon the notion that the currents of European thinking comprise the only really "natural" – or at least truly useful – formation of knowledge/means of perceiving reality. In the vast bulk of curriculum content, Europe is not only the subject (in its conceptual mode, the very process of "learning to think"), but the object (subject matter) of investigation as well.

Consider a typical introductory level philosophy course. Students will in all probability explore the works of the ancient Greek philosophers,[6] the fundamentals of Cartesian logic and Spinoza, stop off for a visit with Hobbes, Hume, and John Locke, cover a chapter or two of Kant's aesthetics, dabble a bit in Hegelian dialectics, and review Nietzsche's assorted rantings. A good Leftist professor may add a dash of Marx's famous "inversion" of Hegel and, on a good day, his commentaries on the frailties of Feuerbach. In an exemplary class, things will end up in the twentieth century with discussions of Schopenhauer, Heidegger, and Husserl, Bertrand Russell and Alfred North Whitehead, perhaps an "adventurous" summarization of the existentialism of Sartre and Camus.

Advanced undergraduate courses typically delve into the same topics, with additive instruction in matters such as "Late Medieval Philosophy," "Monism," "Rousseau and Revolution," "The Morality of John Stuart Mill," "Einstein and the Generations of Science," "The Phenomenology of Merleau-Ponty," "Popper's Philosophy of Science," "Benjamin, Adorno, and the Frankfurt School," "Meaning and Marcuse," "Structuralism/Poststructuralism," even "The Critical Theory of Jürgen Habermas."[7] Graduate work usually consists of effecting a coherent synthesis of some combination of these elements.

Thus, from first-semester surveys through the Ph.D., philosophy majors – and non-majors fulfilling elective requirements, for that matter – are fed a consistent stream of data defining and presumably reproducing Western thought at its highest level of refinement, as well as inculcating insight into what is packaged as its historical evolution and line(s) of probable future development. Note that this is construed, for all practical intents and purposes, as being representative of philosophy *in toto* rather than of Western European thought per se.

It seems reasonable to pose the question as to what consideration is typically accorded the non-European remainder of the human species in such a format. The answer is often that coursework does in fact exist, most usually in the form of upper-division undergraduate "broadening" curriculum: surveys of "Oriental Philosophy" are not unpopular,[8] "The Philosophy of Black Africa" exists as a catalogue entry at a number of institutions,[9] even "Native-American Philosophical Traditions" (more casually titled "Black Elk Speaks," from time-to-time) makes its appearance here and there.[10] But nothing remotely approaching the depth and comprehensiveness with which Western thought is treated can be located at any quarter.

Clearly, the student who graduates, at whatever level, from a philosophy program constructed in this fashion – and all of them are – walks away with a concentrated knowledge of the European intellectual schema rather than any genuine appreciation of the philosophical attainments of humanity. Yet, equally clearly, a degree in "Philosophy" implies, or at least should imply, the latter.

Nor is the phenomenon in any way restricted to the study of philosophy. One may search the catalogues of every college and university in the country, and undoubtedly the search will be in vain, for the department of history which accords the elaborate oral/pictorial "prehistories" of American Indians anything approximating the weight given to the semiliterate efforts at self-justification scrawled by early European colonists in this hemisphere.[11] Even the rich codigraphic records of cultures like the Mayas, Incas, and Mexicanos (Aztecs) are uniformly ignored by the "historical mainstream." Such matters are more properly the purview of anthropology than of history, or so it is said by those representing "responsible" scholarship in the US.[12]

As a result, most introductory courses on "American History" still begin for all practical intents and purposes in 1492, with only the most perfunctory acknowledgment that people existed in the Americas in pre-Columbian times. Predictably, any consideration accorded to pre-Columbian times typically revolves around anthropological rather than historical preoccupations, such as the point at which people were supposed to have first migrated across the Beringian Land Bridge to populate the hemisphere,[13] or whether native horticulturalists ever managed to discover fertilizer.[14] Another major classroom topic centers on the extent to which cannibalism may have prevailed among the proliferation of "nomadic Stone Age tribes" presumed to have wandered about America's endless reaches, perpetually hunting and gathering their way to the margin of raw subsistence.[15] Then again, there are the countless expositions on how few indigenous people there really were in North America prior to 1500,[16] and how genocide is an "inappropriate" term by which to explain why there were almost none by 1900.[17]

From there, many things begin to fall into place. Nowhere in the modern American academe will one find the math course acknowledging, along with the importance of Archimedes and Prothagerus, the truly marvelous qualities of pre-Columbian mathematics: that which allowed the Mayas to invent the concept of zero, for example, and, absent computers, to work with multidigit prime numbers.[18] Nor is there mention of the Mexicano mathematics which allowed that culture to develop a calendrical system several decimal places more accurate than that commonly used today.[19] And again, the rich mathematical understandings which went into Mesoamerica's development of what may well have been the world's most advanced system of astronomy are typically ignored by mainstream mathematicians and astronomers alike.[20]

Similarly, departments of architecture and engineering do not teach that the Incas invented the suspension bridge, or that their 2,500 mile Royal Road – paved, leveled, graded, guttered, and complete with rest areas – was perhaps the world's first genuine superhighway, or that portions of it are still used by motorized transport in Peru.[21] No mention is made of the passive solar temperature control characteristics carefully designed by the Anasazi into the apartment complexes of their cities at Chaco Canyon, Mesa Verde, and elsewhere.[22] Nor are students drawn to examine the incorporation of thermal mass into Mandan and Hidatsa construction techniques,[23] the vast north Sonoran irrigation systems built by the Hohokam,[24] or the implications of the fact that, at the time of Cortez's arrival, Tenochtitlán (now Mexico City) accommodated a population of 350,000, making it one of the largest cities on earth, at least five times the size of London or Seville.[25]

In political science, readers are invited – no, defied – to locate the course acknowledging, as John Adams, Benjamin Franklin, and others among the US "Founding Fathers" did, that the form of the American Republic and the framing of its constitution were heavily influenced by the pre-existing model of the Haudenosaunee (Six Nations Iroquois Confederacy of present-day New York and Quebec).[26] Nor is mention made of the influence exerted by the workings of the "Iroquois League" in shaping the thinking of theorists such as Karl Marx and Friedrich Engels.[27] Even less discussion can be found on the comparably sophisticated political systems conceived and established by other indigenous peoples – the Creek Confederation, for example, or the Cherokees or Yaquis – long before the first European invader ever set foot on American soil.[28]

Where agriculture or the botanical sciences are concerned, one will not find the conventional department which wishes to "make anything special" of the fact that fully two-thirds of the vegetal foodstuffs now commonly consumed by all of humanity were under cultivation in the Americas, and nowhere else, in 1492.[29] Also unmentioned is the hybridization by Incan scientists of more than 3,000 varieties of potato,[30] or the vast herbal cornucopia discovered and deployed by native pharmacologists long before that.[31] In biology, pre-med and medicine, nothing is said of the American Indian invention of surgical tubing and the syringe, or the fact that the Incas were successfully practicing brain surgery at a time when European physicians were still seeking to cure their patients by applying leeches to "draw off bad blood."[32]

To the contrary, from matters of governance, where the Greek and Roman democracies are habitually cited as being sole antecedents of "the American experiment,"[33] to agriculture, with its "Irish" potatoes, "Swiss" chocolate, "Italian" tomatoes, "French" vanilla, and "English" walnuts,[34] the accomplishments of American Indian cultures are quite simply expropriated and recast in the curriculum as if they had been European in origin.[35] Concomitantly, the native traditions which produced such things are themselves deculturated and negated, consigned to the status of being "people without history."[36]

Such grotesque distortion is, of course, fed to indigenous students right along with Euroamericans,[37] and by supposedly radical professors as readily as more conservative ones.[38] Moreover, as was noted above, essentially the same set of circumstances prevails with regard to the traditions and attainments of all non-Western cultures.[39] Overall, the situation virtually demands to be viewed from a perspective best articulated by Albert Memmi:

> In order for the colonizer to be a complete master, it is not enough for him to be so in actual fact, but he must also believe in [the colonial system's] legitimacy. In order for that legitimacy to be complete, it is not enough for the colonized to be a slave, he must also accept his role. The bond between colonizer and colonized is thus destructive and creative. It destroys and recreates the two partners in colonization into colonizer and colonized. One is disfigured into an oppressor, a partial, unpatriotic and treacherous being, worrying only about his privileges and their defense; the other into an oppressed creature, whose development is broken and who compromises by his defeat.[40]

In effect, the intellectual sophistry which goes into arguing the "radical" and "conservative" content options available within the prevailing monocultural paradigm, a paradigm which predictably corresponds to the culture of the colonizer, amounts to little more than a diversionary mechanism through which power relations are reinforced, the status quo maintained.[41] The monolithic White Studies configuration of US higher education – a content heading which, unlike American Indian, Afroamerican, Asian American and Chicano Studies, has yet to find its way into a single college or university catalogue – thus serves to underpin the hegemony of white supremacism in its other, more literal manifestations: economic, political, military, and so on.[42]

Those of non-European background are integral to such a system. While consciousness of their own heritages is obliterated through falsehood and omission, they are indoctrinated to believe that legitimacy itself is something derived from European tradition, a tradition which can never be truly shared by non-Westerners despite – or perhaps because of – their assimilation into Eurocentrism's doctrinal value structure. By and large, the "educated" American Indian or black thereby becomes the aspect of "broken development" who "compromises [through the] defeat" of his or her people, aspiring only to serve the interests of the order he or she has been trained to see as his or her "natural" master.[43]

As Frantz Fanon and others have observed long-since, such psychological jujitsu can never be directly admitted, much less articulated, by its principal victims. Instead, they are compelled by illusions of sanity to deny their circumstance and the process which induced it. Their condition sublimated, they function as colonialism's covert hedge against the necessity of perpetual engagement in more overt and costly sorts of repression against its colonial subjects.[44] Put another way, the purpose of White Studies in this connection is to trick the colonized into materially supporting her/his colonization through the mechanisms of his/her own thought processes.[45]

There can be no reasonable or "value-neutral" explanation for this situation. Those, regardless of race or ethnicity, who endeavor to apologize for or defend its prevalence in institutions of higher education on "scholarly" grounds, do so without a shred of honesty or academic integrity.[46] Rather, whatever their intentions, they define themselves as accepting of the colonial order. In Memmi's terms, they accept the role of colonizer, which means "agreeing to be a . . . usurper. To be sure a usurper claims his place and, if need be, will defend it with every means at his disposal. . . . He endeavors to falsify history, he rewrites laws, he would extinguish memories – anything to succeed in transforming his usurpation into legitimacy."[47] They are, to borrow and slightly modify a term, "intellectual imperialists."[48]

2 An Indigenist Alternative

From the preceding observations as to what White Studies is, the extraordinary pervasiveness and corresponding secrecy of its practice, and the reasons underlying its existence, certain questions necessarily arise. For instance, the query might be posed as to whether a simple expansion of curriculum content to include material on non-Western contexts might be sufficient to redress matters. It follows that we should ask whether something beyond data or content is fundamentally at issue. Finally, there are structural considerations concerning how any genuinely corrective and liberatory curriculum or pedagogy might actually be inducted into academia. The first two questions dovetail rather nicely, and will be addressed in a single response. The third will be dealt with in the next section.

In response to the first question, the answer must be an unequivocal "no." Content is, of course, highly important, but, in and of itself, can never be sufficient to offset the cumulative effects of White Studies indoctrination. Non-Western content injected into the White Studies format can be – and, historically, has been – filtered through the lens of Eurocentric conceptualization, taking on meanings entirely alien to itself along the way.[49] The result is inevitably the reinforcement rather than the diminishment of colonialist hegemony. As Vine Deloria, Jr, has noted relative to just one aspect of this process:

> Therein lies the meaning of the white's fantasy about Indians – the problem of the Indian image. Underneath all the conflicting images of the Indian one fundamental truth emerges – the white man knows that he is an alien and he knows that North America is Indian – and he will never let go of the Indian image because he thinks that by some clever manipulation he can achieve an authenticity that cannot ever be his.[50]

Plainly, more is needed that the simple introduction of raw data for handling within the parameters of Eurocentric acceptability. The conceptual mode of intellectuality itself must be called into question. Perhaps a bit of "pictographic" communication will prove helpful in clarifying what is meant in this respect. The following schematic represents the manner in which two areas of inquiry, science and religion (spirituality), have been approached in the European tradition.

Reality

Science   Speculative Philosophy   Religion

In this model, "knowledge" is divided into discrete content areas arranged in a linear structure. This division is permanent and culturally enforced; witness the Spanish Inquisition and "Scopes Monkey Trial" as but two historical illustrations.[51] In the cases of science and religion (as theology), the mutual opposition of their core assumptions has given rise to a third category, speculative philosophy, which is informed by both, and, in turn, informs them. Speculative philosophy, in this sense at least, serves to mediate and sometimes synthesize the linearly isolated components, science and religion, allowing them to communicate and "progress." Speculative philosophy is not, in itself, intended to apprehend reality, but rather to create an abstract reality in its place. Both religion and science, on the other hand, are, each according to its own internal dynamics, meant to effect a concrete understanding of and action upon "the real world."[52]

Such compartmentalization of knowledge is replicated in the depart-
mentalization of the Eurocentric education itself. Sociology, theology,
psychology, physiology, kinesiology, biology, cartography, anthropology, archeology, geology, pharmacology, astronomy, agronomy,
historiography, geography, demography – the whole vast proliferation of
Western "ologies," "onomies," and "ographies" – are necessarily viewed
as separate or at least separable areas of inquiry within the university.
Indeed, the Western social structure both echoes and is echoed by the
same sort of linear fragmentation, dividing itself into discrete organiza-
tional spheres: church, state, business, family, education, art, and so
forth.[53] The structure involved readily lends itself to – perhaps demands –
the sort of hierarchical ordering of things, both intellectually and physically, which is most clearly manifested in racism, militarism, and colonial
domination, class and gender oppression, and the systematic ravaging of
the natural world.[54]

The obvious problems involved are greatly amplified when our schematic of the Eurocentric intellectual paradigm is contrasted to one of
non-Western, in this case Native American, origin:

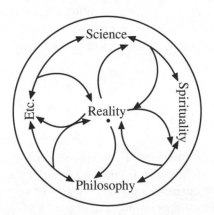

Within such a conceptual model, there is really no tangible delineation
of compartmentalized "spheres of knowledge." All components or categories of intellectuality (by Eurocentric definition) tend to be mutually and
perpetually informing. All tend to constantly concretize the human
experience of reality (nature) while all are simultaneously and continuously informed by that reality. This is the "Hoop" or "Wheel" or
"Circle" of Life – an organic rather than synthesizing or synthetic view

holding that all things are equally and indispensably interrelated – which forms the core of the native worldview.[55] Here, reality is not something "above" the human mind or being, but an integral aspect of the living/ knowing process itself. The mode through which native thought devolves is thus inherently anti-hierarchical, incapable of manifesting the extreme forms of domination so pervasively evident in Eurocentric tradition.[56]

The crux of the White Studies problem, then, cannot be located amidst the mere omission or distortion of matters of fact, no matter how blatantly ignorant or culturally chauvinistic these omissions and distortions may be. Far more importantly, the system of Eurosupremacist domination depends for its continued maintenance and expansion, even its survival, upon the reproduction of its own intellectual paradigm – its approved way of thinking, seeing, understanding, and being – to the ultimate exclusion of all others. Consequently, White Studies simply cannot admit to the existence of viable conceptual structures other than its own.[57]

To introduce the facts of precolonial American Indian civilizations to the curriculum is to open the door to confronting the utterly different ways of knowing which caused such facts to be actualized in the first place.[58] It is thoroughly appreciated in ruling circles that any widespread and genuine understanding of such alternatives to the intrinsic oppressiveness of Eurocentrism could well unleash a liberatory dynamic among the oppressed resulting in the evaporation of Eurosupremacist hegemony and a corresponding collapse of the entire structure of domination and elite privilege which attends it.[59] The academic "battle lines" have therefore been drawn, not so much across the tactical terrain of fact and data as along the strategic high ground of Western versus non-Western conceptualization. It follows that if the latter is what proponents of the White Studies status quo find it most imperative to bar from academic inclusion, then it is precisely that area upon which those committed to liberatory education must place our greatest emphasis.

3 A Strategy to Win

Given the scope and depth of the formal problem outlined in the preceding section, the question of the means through which to address it takes on a crucial importance. If the objective in grappling with White Studies is to bring about conceptual – as opposed to merely contentual – inclusion of non-Western traditions in academia, then appropriate and effective methods must be employed. As was noted earlier, resort to inappropriate "remedies" leads only to cooptation and a reinforcement of White Studies as the prevailing educational norm.

One such false direction has concerned attempts to establish, essentially from scratch, whole new educational institutions, even systems, while leaving the institutional structure of the status quo very much intact.[60] Although sometimes evidencing a strong showing at the outset, these perpetually underfunded, understaffed, and unaccredited "community-based" – often actually separatist – schools have almost universally ended up drifting and floundering before going out of existence altogether.[61] Alternately, more than a few have abandoned their original reason for being, accommodating themselves to the "standards" and other requirements of the mainstream system as an expedient to survival.[62] Either way, the outcome has been a considerable bolstering of the carefully nurtured public impression that "the system works" while alternatives don't.

A variation on this theme has been to establish separatist centers or programs, even whole departments, within existing colleges and universities. While this approach has alleviated to some extent (though not entirely) difficulties in securing funding, faculty, and accreditation, it has accomplished little if anything in terms of altering the delivery of White Studies instruction in the broader institutional context.[63] Instead, intentionally self-contained "Ethnic Studies" efforts have ended up "ghetto-ized" – that is, marginalized to the point of isolation and left talking only to themselves and the few majors they are able to attract – bitter, frustrated, and stalemated.[64] Worse, they serve to reinforce the perception, so desired by the status quo, that White Studies is valid and important while non-Western subject matters are invalid and irrelevant.

To effect the sort of transformation of institutional realities envisioned in this essay, it is necessary *not* to seek to create parallel structures as such, but instead to penetrate and subvert the existing structures themselves, both pedagogically and canonically. The strategy is one which was once described quite aptly by Rudi Deutschke, the German activist/theorist, as amounting to a "long march through the institutions."[65] In this, Ethnic Studies entities, rather than constituting ends in themselves, serve as "enclaves" or "staging areas" from which forays into the mainstream arena can be launched with ever-increasing frequency and vitality, and to which non-Western academic guerrillas can withdraw when needed to rest and regroup among themselves.[66]

As with any campaign of guerrilla warfare, however metaphorical, it is important to concentrate initially upon opponents' point(s) of greatest vulnerability. Here, three prospects for action come immediately to mind, the basis for each of which already exists within most university settings in a form readily lending itself to utilization in undermining the rigid curricular compartmentalization and pedagogical constraints inhering in White Studies institutions. The key is to recognize and seize such tools, and then to apply them properly.

1 While tenure-track faculty must almost invariably be "credentialed" – i.e. hold the Ph.D. in a Western discipline, have a few publications in the "right" journals, etc. – to be hired into the academy, the same isn't necessarily true for guest professors, lecturers, and the like.[67] Every effort can and should be expended by the regular faculty – "cadre," if you will – of Ethnic Studies units to bring in guest instructors lacking in Western academic pedigree (the more conspicuously, the better), but who are in some way exemplary of non-Western intellectual traditions (especially oral forms). The initial purpose is to enhance cadre articulations with practical demonstrations of intellectual alternatives by consistently exposing students to "the real thing." Goals further on down the line should include incorporation of such individuals directly into the core faculty, and, eventually, challenging the current notion of academic credentialing in its entirety.[68]

2 There has been a good deal of interest over the past twenty years in what has come to be loosely termed "Interdisciplinary Studies." Insofar as there is a mainstream correspondent to the way in which American Indians and other non-Westerners conceive of and relate to the world, this is it. Ethnic Studies practitioners would do well to push hard in the Interdisciplinary Studies arena, expanding it whenever and wherever possible at the direct expense of customary Western disciplinary boundaries. The object, of course, is to steep students in the knowledge that nothing can be understood other than in its relationship to everything else; that economics, for example, can never really make sense if arbitrarily divorced from history, politics, sociology, and geography. Eventually, the goal should be to dissolve the orthodox parameters of disciplines altogether, replacing them with something more akin to "areas of interest, inclination and emphasis."[69]

3 For a variety of reasons, virtually all colleges and universities award tenure to certain faculty members in more than one discipline or department. Ethnic Studies cadres should insist that this be the case with them. Restricting their tenure and rostering exclusively to Ethnic Studies is not only a certain recipe for leaving them in a "last hired, first fired" situation during times of budget exigency, it is a

standard institutional maneuver to preserve the sanctity of White Studies instruction elsewhere on campus. The fact is that an Ethnic Studies professor teaching American Indian or Afroamerican history is just as much a historian as a specialist in nineteenth-century British history; the Indian and the black should therefore be rostered to and tenured in History, *as well as* in Ethnic Studies. This "foot in the door" is important, not only in terms of cadre longevity and the institutional dignity such appointments signify *vis-à-vis* Ethnic Studies, but it offers important advantages by way of allowing cadres to reach a greater breadth of students, participate in departmental policy formation and hiring decisions, claim additional resources, and so forth. On balance, success in this area can only enhance efforts in the two above.[70]

The objective is to begin to develop a critical mass, first in given spheres of campuses where opportunities present themselves – later throughout the academy as a whole – which is eventually capable of discrediting and supplanting the hegemony of White Studies. In this, the process can be accelerated, perhaps greatly, by identifying and allying with sectors of the professorate with whom a genuine affinity and commonality of interest may be said to exist at some level. These might include those from the environmental sciences who have achieved, or begun to achieve, a degree of serious ecological understanding.[71] It might include occasional mavericks from other fields, various applied anthropologists,[72] for instance, and certain of the better and more engaged literary and artistic deconstructionists,[73] as well as the anarchists like Murray Bookchin who pop up more-or-less randomly in a number of disciplines.[74]

By-and-large, however, it may well be that the largest reservoir or pool of potential allies will be found among the relatively many faculty who profess to consider themselves, "philosophically" at least, to be Marxian in their orientation. This is not said because Marxists tend habitually to see themselves as being in opposition to the existing order (fascists express the same view of themselves, after all, and for equally valid reasons).[75] Nor is it because, where it has succeeded in overthrowing capitalism, Marxism has amassed an especially sterling record where indigenous peoples are concerned.[76] In fact, it has been argued with some cogency that, in the latter connection, Marxist practice has proven even more virulently Eurocentric than has capitalism in many cases.[77]

Nonetheless, one is drawn to conclude that there may still be a basis for constructive alliance, given Marx's positing of dialectics – a truly non-linear and relational mode of analysis and understanding – as his central methodology. That he himself consistently violated his professed method,[78] and that subsequent generations of his adherents have proven themselves increasingly unable to distinguish between dialectics and such strictly linear propositions as cause/effect progressions,[79] does not inherently invalidate the whole of his project or its premises. If some significant proportion of today's self-proclaimed Marxian intelligentsia can be convinced to actually learn and apply dialectical method, it stands to reason that they will finally think their way in to a posture not unlike that elaborated herein (that they will in the process have transcended what has come to be known as "Marxism" is another story).[80]

4 Conclusion

This essay presents only the barest glimpse of its subject matter. It is plainly, its author hopes, not intended to be anything approximating an exhaustive or definitive exposition on its topics. To the contrary, it is meant only to act as, paraphrasing Marcuse, the Archimedian point upon which false consciousness may be breached en route to "a more comprehensive emancipation."[81] By this, we mean not only a generalized change in perspective which leads to the abolition of Eurocentrism's legacy of colonialist, racist, sexist, and classist domination, but the replacement of White Studies' Eurosupremacism with an educational context in which we can all, jointly and with true parity, "seek to expand our knowledge of the world" in full realization that,

> The signposts point to a reconciliation of the two approaches to experience. Western science must reintegrate human emotions and intuitions into its interpretation of phenomena; [non-Western] peoples must confront ... the effects of [Western] technology ... [We must] come to an integrated conception of how our species came to be, what it has accomplished, and where it can expect to go in the millennia ahead ... [Then we will come to] understand as these traditionally opposing views seek a unity that the world of historical experience is far more mysterious and eventful than previously expected. ... Our next immediate task is the unification of human knowledge.[82]

There is, to be sure, much work to be done, both practically and cerebrally. The struggle will be long and difficult, frustrating many times to the point of sheer exasperation. It will require stamina and perseverance, a preparedness to incur risk, often a willingness to absorb the consequences of revolt, whether overt or covert. Many will be required to

give up or forego aspects of a comfort-zone academic existence, both
mentally and materially.[83] But the pay-off may be found in freedom of the
intellect, the pursuit of knowledge in a manner more proximate to truth,
unfettered by the threats and constraints of narrow vested interest and
imperial ideology. The reward, in effect, is participation in the process of
human liberation, including our own. One can only assume that this is
worth the fight.

Notes

1   For an overview of the evolution of the current conflict, see Ira Shore, *Culture
    Wars: School and Society in the Conservative Restoration, 1969–1984*
    (Boston: Routledge & Kegan Paul, 1986); for reactionary analysis, see Roger
    Kimball, *Tenured Radicals: How Politics Has Corrupted Our Higher Educa-
    tion* (New York: Harper & Row, 1990).
2   David S. Landes, "The Nature of Economic Imperialism," *Journal of Eco-
    nomic History* 21 (December 1961), as quoted in Harry Magdoff, *The Age of
    Imperialism* (New York: Monthly Review Press, 1969) p. 13.
3   Gerald Jayne and Robbin Williams (eds) *A Common Destiny: Blacks and
    American Society* (Washington, DC: National Academy Press, 1989).
4   One solid summary of the contributionist trend will be found in Troy Duster,
    The Diversity Project: Final Report (Berkeley: University of California Insti-
    tute for Social Change, 1991); for complaints, see Robert Alter, "The Revolt
    Against Tradition," *Partisan Review* vol. 58, no. 2, 1991.
5   General population, or "G-Pop" as it is often put, is the standard institu-
    tional euphemism for white students.
6   A good case can be made that there is a great disjuncture between the Greek
    philosophers and the philosophies later arising in Western Europe; see
    Martin Bernal, *Black Athena: The Afro-Asiatic Roots of Ancient Greece,
    Vol.1* (Princeton, NJ: Princeton University Press, 1987).
7   Marxian academics make another appearance here, insofar as they do tend to
    teach courses, or parts of courses, based in the thinking of non-Europeans. It
    should be noted, however, that those selected for exposition – Mao, Ho Chi
    Minh, Vo Nguyen Giap, Kim El Sung, et al. – are uniformly those who have
    most thoroughly assimilated Western doctrines in displacement of their own
    intellectual traditions.
8   Probably the most stunning example of this I've ever encountered came when
    Will Durant casually attributed the thought of the East Indian philosopher
    Shankara to a "preplagiarism" (!!!) of Kant: "To Shankara the existence of
    God is no problem, for he defines God as existence, and identifies all real
    being with God. But the existence of a personal God, creator or redeemer,
    there may, he thinks, be some question; such a deity, says this *pre-plagarist* of
    Kant, cannot be proved by reason, he can only be postulated as a practical
    necessity" (emphasis added); Will Durant, *The History of Civilization, Vol 1:*

Our Oriental Heritage (New York: Simon & Schuster, 1954) p. 549. It should be remarked that Durant was not a reactionary of the stripe conventionally associated with white supremacism, but rather an intellectual of the Marxian progressive variety. Yet, in this single book on the philosophical tradition of Asia, he makes no less than ten references to Kant, all of them implying that the earlier philosophers of the East acted "precisely as if [they] were Immanual Kant" (p. 538), never that Kant might have predicated his own subsequent philosophical articulations in a reading of Asian texts. The point is raised to demonstrate the all but unbelievable lengths even the more dissident Western scholars have been prepared to go in reinforcing the mythos of Eurocentrism, and thus how such reinforcement transcends ideological divisions within the Eurocentric paradigm.

9 It should be noted, however, that the recent emergence of an "Afrocentric" philosophy and pedagogy, natural counterbalances to the persistence of Eurocentric orthodoxy, has met with fierce condemnation by defenders of the status quo; see David Nicholson, "Afrocentrism and the Tribalization of America," *Washington Post National Weekly Edition*, October 8–14, 1990.

10 A big question, frequently mentioned, is whether American Indians ever acquired the epistemological sensibilities necessary for their thought to be correctly understood as having amounted to "philosophical inquiry." Given that epistemology simply means "investigation of the limits of human comprehension," one can only wonder what the gate-keepers of philosophy departments make of the American Indian conception, prevalent in myriad traditions, of there being a "Great Mystery" into which the human mind is incapable of penetrating; see, for example John G. Neihardt (ed) *Black Elk Speaks* (New York: William Morrow Publisher, 1932); also see J. R. Walker, *Lakota Belief and Ritual* (Lincoln: University of Nebraska Press, 1980). For an unconsciously comparable Western articulation, see Noam Chomsky's discussions of accessible and inaccessible knowledge in the chapters entitled "A Philosophy of Language?" and "Empiricism and Rationalism," in *Language and Responsibility: An Interview by Mitsou Ronat* (New York: Pantheon Books, 1977).

11 As illustration, see Wilcomb E. Washburn, "Distinguishing History for Moral Philosophy and Public Advocacy," in Calvin Martin (ed), *The American Indian and the Problem of History* (New York: Oxford University Press, 1987), pp. 91–7.

12 For a veritable case study of this mentality, see James Axtell, *After Columbus: Essays in the Ethnohistory of Colonial North America* (New York: Oxford University Press, 1988).

13 For a solid critique of the Beringia Theory, see Jeffrey Goodman, *American Genesis: The American Indian and the Origins of Modern Man* (New York: Summit Books, 1981); also see Jonathan E. Ericson, R. E. Taylor, and Rainier Berger (eds), *The Peopling of the New World* (Los Altos, Calif.: Ballena Press, 1982).

14　For an exhaustive enunciation of the "fertilizer dilemma," see James C. Hurt, *American Indian Agriculture* (Lawrence: University Press of Kansas, 1991).

15　An excellent analysis of this standard description of indigenous American realities may be found in Jack Weatherford, *Indian Givers: How the Indians of the Americas Transformed the World* (New York: Crown, 1988). On cannibalism specifically, see W. Arens, *The Man-Eating Myth: Anthropology and Anthropophagy* (New York: Oxford University Press, 1979).

16　The manipulation of data undertaken by succeeding generations of Euroamerican historians and anthropologists in arriving at the official twentieth-century falsehood that there were "not more than one million Indians living north of the Rio Grande in 1492, including Greenland" is laid out very clearly by Francis Jennings in his *The Invasion of America: Indians, Colonialism and the Cant of Conquest* (Chapel Hill: University of North Carolina Press, 1975). For a far more honest estimate, deriving from the evidence rather than ideological preoccupations, see Henry F. Dobyns, *Their Number Become Thinned: Native American Population Dynamics in Eastern North America* (Knoxville: University of Tennessee Press, 1983); also see Russell Thornton, *American Indian Holocaust and Survival: A Population History Since 1492* (Norman: University of Oklahoma Press, 1987). Dobyns places the actual number as high as 18.5 million; Thornton, more conservative, places it at 12.5 million.

17　During a keynote presentation at the annual meeting of the American History Association in 1992, James Axtell, one of the emergent "deans" of the field, actually argued that genocide was an "inaccurate and highly polemical descriptor" for what had happened. His reasoning? That he could find only five instances in the history of colonial North America in which genocides "indisputably" occurred. Leaving aside the obvious – that this in itself makes genocide an appropriate term by which to describe the obliteration of American Indians – a vastly more accurate chronicle of the process of extermination will be found in David E. Stannard, *American Holocaust: Columbus and the Conquest of the New World* (New York: Oxford University Press, 1992).

18　Syvanus G. Morely and George W. Bainerd, *The Ancient Maya* (Stanford, Calif.: Stanford University Press, 1983); Robert M. Carmack, *Quichean Civilization* (Berkeley: University of California Press, 1973).

19　Anthony Aveni, *Empires of Time: Calendars, Clocks and Cultures* (New York: Basic Books, 1989).

20　Mexicano astronomy is discussed in D. Durán, *Book of Gods and Rites and the Ancient Calendar* (Norman: University of Oklahoma Press, 1971); also see Paul Radin, *The Sources and Authenticity of the History of Ancient Mexico* (Berkeley: University of California Publications in American Archeology and Ethnology, vol. 17, no. 1, 1920).

21　Victor Wolfgang Von Hagen, *The Royal Road of the Inca* (London: Gordon and Cremonesi, 1976).

22　Robert H. Lister and Florence C. Lister, *Chaco Canyon: Archeology and Archaeologists* (Albuquerque: University of New Mexico Press, 1981); also see Buddy Mays, *Ancient Cities of the Southwest* (San Francisco: Chronicle Books, 1962).

23 Peter Nabokov and Robert Easton, *American Indian Architecture* (New York: Oxford University Press, 1988); the "submerged" building principles developed by the Mandan and Hidatsa, ideal for the plains environment but long disparaged by the Euroamericans who displaced them, are now considered the "cutting edge" in some architectural circles. The Indians, of course, are not credited with having perfected such techniques more than a thousand years ago.

24 Emil W. Haury, *The Hohokam: Desert Farmers and Craftsmen* (Tucson: University of Arizona Press, 1976), pp. 120–51; the City of Phoenix and its suburbs still use portions of the several thousand miles of extraordinarily well-engineered Hohokam canals, constructed nearly a thousand years ago, to move their own water supplies around.

25 Cortez was effusive in his descriptions of Tenochtitlán as being, in terms of its design and architecture, "the most beautiful city on earth"; Bernal Díaz del Castillo, *The Discovery and Conquest of Mexico 1519–1810* (London: George Routledge & Sons, 1928) p. 268. On the size of Tenochtitlán, see Rudolph van Zantwijk, *The Aztec Arrangement: The Social History of Pre-Spanish Mexico* (Norman: University of Oklahoma Press, 1985, p. 281; on the size of London in 1500, Lawrence Stone, *The Family, Sex and Marriage in England, 1500–1800* (New York: Harper & Row, 1977), p. 147; for Seville, J. H. Elliott, *Imperial Spain 1469–1716* (New York: St Martin's Press, 1964), p. 177.

26 Donald A. Grinde, Jr, and Bruce E. Johansen, *Exemplar of Liberty: Native America and the Evolution of Democracy* (Los Angeles: UCLA American Indian Studies Center, 1992).

27 Between December 1880 and March 1881, Marx read anthropologist Lewis Henry Morgan's 1871 book, *Ancient Society*, based in large part on his 1851 classic *The League of the Hau-de-no-sau-nee or Iroquois*. Marx took at least ninety-eight pages of dense notes during the reading, and after his death, his collaborator, Friedrich Engels, expanded these into a short book entitled *The Origin of the Family, Private Property and the State: In Light of the Researches of Lewis Henry Morgan*. The latter, minus its subtitle, appears in *Marx and Engels: Selected Works* (New York: International Publishers, 1968).

28 Weatherford, *Indian Givers*.

29 Alfred W. Crosby, Jr *The Columbian Exchange: Biological and Cultural Consequences of 1492* (Westport, Conn.: Greenwood Press, 1972); Carol A. Bryant, Anita Courtney, Barbara A. Markesbery and Kathleen M. DeWalt, *The Cultural Feast* (St Paul, Minn.: West, 1985).

30 Redcliffe N. Salaman, *The History and Social Influence of the Potato* (Cambridge: Cambridge University Press, 1949).

31 Clark Wissler, Wilton M. Krogman and Walter Krickerberg, *Medicine Among the American Indians* (Ramona, Calif.: Acoma Press, 1939); Norman

Taylor, *Plant Drugs That Changed the World* (New York: Dodd, Meade, 1965).

32 Virgil Vogel, *American Indian Medicine* (Norman: University of Oklahoma Press, 1970); Peredo Guzman, *Medical Practices in Ancient America* (Mexico City: Ediciones Euroamericana, 1985). On contemporaneous European medical practices, see William H. McNeill, *Plagues and Peoples* (Garden City, NY: Anchor/Doubleday, 1976).

33 For good efforts at debunking such nonsense, see German Arciniegas, *America in Europe: A History of the New World in Reverse* (New York: Harcourt Brace Jovanovich, 1986), and William Brandon, *New Worlds for Old: Reports from the New World and Their Effect on Social Thought in Europe, 1500–1800* (Athens: Ohio University Press, 1986).

34 Carl O. Sauer, "The March of Agriculture Across the Western World," in his *Selected Essays, 1963–1975* (Berkeley: Turtle Island Foundation, 1981); also see Weatherford, *Indian Givers*.

35 This is nothing new, or unique to the treatment of American Indians. Indeed, the West has comported itself in similar fashion *vis-à-vis* all non-Westerners since at least as early as the inception of "Europe"; see Philippe Wolf, *The Awakening of Europe: The Growth of European Culture from the Ninth Century to the Twelfth* (London: Cox & Wyman, 1968).

36 For a much broader excursus on this phenomenon, see Eric R. Wolf, *Europe and the People Without History* (Berkeley: University of California Press, 1982).

37 For surveys of the effects, see Thomas Thompson (ed) *The Schooling of Native America* (Washington, DC: American Association of Colleges for Teacher Education, 1978); James R. Young (ed) *Multicultural Education and the American Indian* (Los Angeles: UCLA American Indian Studies Center, 1979), and Charlotte Heath and Susan Guyette, *Issues for the Future of American Indian Studies* (Los Angeles: UCLA American Indian Studies Center, 1985).

38 Consider, for example, the "Sixteen Thesis" advanced by the non-Marxist intellectual Alvin Gouldner as alternatives through which to transform the educational status quo. It will be noted that the result, if Gouldner's pedagogical plan were implemented, would be tucked as neatly into the paradigm of Eurocentrism as the status quo itself. See Alvin W. Gouldner, *The Future of Intellectuals and the Rise of the New Class* (New York: Seabury Press, 1979). For Marxian views falling in the same category, see Theodore Mills Norton and Bertell Ollman (eds), *Studies in Socialist Pedagogy* (New York: Monthly Review Press, 1978).

39 See generally, Edward W. Said, *Orientalism* (New York: Oxford University Press, 1987).

40 Albert Memmi, *Colonizer and Colonized* (Boston: Beacon Press, 1965), p. 89.

41 The procedure corresponds well in some ways with the kind of technique described by Herbert Marcuse as being applicable to broader social contexts in his essay "Repressive Tolerance," in Robert Paul Wolff, Barrington

Moore, Jr, and Herbert Marcuse, *A Critique of Pure Tolerance* (Boston: Beacon Press, 1969).

42 The theme is handled well in Vine Deloria, Jr, "Education and Imperialism," *Integrateducation*, vol. xix, nos. 1–2, January 1982. For structural analysis, see Giovanni Arrighi, *The Geometry of Imperialism* (London: Verso, 1978).

43 Memmi develops these ideas further in his *Dominated Man* (Boston: Beacon Press, 1969).

44 See especially, Fanon's *Wretched of the Earth* (New York: Grove Press, 1965) and *Black Skin/White Masks: The Experiences of a Black Man in a White World* (New York: Grove Press, 1967).

45 Probably the classic example of this, albeit in a somewhat different dimension, were the Gurkas, who forged a legendary reputation fighting in behalf of their British colonizers, usually against other colonized peoples; see Patrick McCrory, *The Fierce Pawns* (Philadelphia: J. B. Lippencott, 1966).

46 See, for example, Allan Bloom, *The Closing of the American Mind* (New York: Simon & Schuster, 1988); Dinesh D'Sousa, *Illiberal Education: The Politics of Race and Sex on Campus* (New York: Free Press, 1991); Arthur Schlesinger, Jr, *The Disuniting of America* (New York: W. W. Norton, 1992).

47 *Colonizer and Colonized*, Memmi, pp. 52–3.

48 Martin Carnoy, *Education as Cultural Imperialism* (New York: David McKay, 1974); also see Laurie Anne Whitt, "Cultural Imperialism and the Marketing of Native America," in *Historical Reflections*, 1995.

49 A fascinating analysis of how this works, distorting the perspectives of perpetrator and victim alike, may be found in Richard James Blackburn, *The Vampire of Reason: An Essay in the Philosophy of History* (London: Verso, 1990).

50 Vine Deloria, Jr, "Forward: American Fantasy," in Gretchen M. Bataille and Charles L. P. Silet (eds), *The Pretend Indians: Images of Native Americans in the Movies* (Ames: Iowa State University Press, 1980), p. xvi.

51 On the Inquisition, see Mary Elizabeth Perry and Anne J. Cruz (eds), *Cultural Encounters: The Impact of the Inquisition in Spain and the New World* (Berkeley: University of California Press, 1991). On the context of the Scopes trial, see Stephan Jay Gould, *The Mismeasure of Man* (New York: W. W. Norton, 1981).

52 For a sort of capstone rendering of this schema, see Karl Popper, *Objective Knowledge: An Evolutionary Approach* (New York: Oxford University Press, 1975).

53 Useful analysis of this dialectic will be found in David Reed, *Education for Building a People's Movement* (Boston: South End Press, 1981).

54 For an interesting analysis of many of these cause/effect relations, see Jerry Mander, *In the Absence of the Sacred: The Failure of Technology and the Survival of Indian Nations* (San Francisco: Sierra Club Books, 1991). Also see William H. McNeill (ed.) *Pursuit of Power: Technology, Armed Force and Society Since* A.D. *1000* (Chicago: University of Chicago Press, 1982).

55 For elaboration, see Vine Deloria, Jr, *God Is Red* (New York: Grosset & Dunlap, 1973). Also see John Mohawk, *A Basic Call to Consciousness* (Rooseveltown, NY: *Akwesasne Notes*, 1978).

56 A Westerner's solid apprehension of this point may be found in Stanley Diamond, *In Search of the Primitive: A Critique of Civilization* (New Brunswick, NJ: Transaction Books, 1974); also see Keith Thomas, *Man and the Natural World: A History of Modern Sensibility* (New York: Pantheon Books, 1983).

57 The matter has been explored tangentially, from a number of angles. Some of the best, for purposes of this essay, include Tala Asad (ed) *Anthropology and the Colonial Encounter* (New York: Humanities Press, 1973); Robert Berkhofer, *The White Man's Indian: Images of the American Indian from Columbus to the Present* (New York: Alfred A. Knopf, 1978); Tzvetan Todorov, *The Conquest of America: The Question of the Other* (New York: Harper & Row, 1984); and Robert Young, *White Mythologies: Writing History and the West* (London: Routledge, 1990).

58 More broadly, the thrust of this negation has always pertained in the interactions between European/Euroamerican colonists and native cultures; see Richard Drinnon, *Facing West: The Metaphysics of Indian Hating and Empire Building* (Minneapolis: University of Minnesota Press, 1980).

59 Aside from the paradigmatic shift, culturally speaking, embedded in this observation, it shares much with the insights into the function of higher education achieved by New Left theorists during the 1960s; see Carl Davidson, *The New Student Radicals in the Multiversity and Other Writings on Student Syndicalism* (Chicago: Charles Kerr, 1990).

60 In essence, this approach is the equivalent of Mao Tse-Tung's having declared the Chinese revolution victorious at the point it liberated and secured the Caves of Hunan.

61 One salient example is the system of "survival schools" started by AIM during the mid-1970s, only two of which still exist in any form; see Susan Braudy, "We Will Remember Survival School: The Women and Children of the American Indian Movement," *Ms. Magazine*, no. 5, July 1976.

62 For a case study of one initially separatist effort turned accommodationist, see Maryls Duchene, "A Profile of American Indian Community Colleges"; more broadly, see Gerald Wilkenson, "Educational Problems in the Indian Community: A Comment on Learning as Colonialism"; both essays will be found in *Integrateducation*, vol. xix, nos. 1–2, January–April 1982.

63 Ward Churchill and Norbert S. Hill Jr, "Indian Education at the University Level: An Historical Survey," *Journal of Ethnic Studies*, vol. 7, no. 3, 1979.

64 Further elaboration of this theme will be found in Ward Churchill, "White Studies or Isolation: An Alternative Model for American Indian Studies Programs," in James R. Young (ed), *American Indian Issues in Higher Education* (Los Angeles: UCLA American Indian Studies Center, 1981).

65 So far as is known, Deutschke, head of the German SDS, first publicly issued

a call for such a strategy during an address of a mass demonstration in Berlin during January 1968.

66 Mao Tse-Tung, *On Protracted War* (Peking: Foreign Language Press, 1967); Che Guevara, *Guerrilla Warfare* (New York: Vintage Books, 1961).

67 For an excellent and succinct examination of the implications of this point, see Jurgen Herget, *And Sadly Teach: Teacher Education and Profession-alization in American Culture* (Madison: University of Wisconsin Press, 1991).

68 The concept is elaborated much more fully and eloquently in Paulo Freire's *Pedagogy of the Oppressed* (New York: Continuum Books, 1981).

69 Again, one can turn to Freire for development of the themes; see his *Education for Critical Consciousness* (New York: Continuum Books, 1982). For the results of a practical – and very successful – application of these principles in the United States, see *TRIBES 1989: Final Report and Evaluation* (Boulder: University of Colorado University Learning Center, August 1989).

70 For overall analysis, see Vine Deloria, Jr, "Indian Studies – The Orphan of Academia," *Wicazo Sa Review*, vol. II, no. 2, 1986; also see José Barriero, "The Dilemma of American Indian Education," *Indian Studies Quarterly*, vol. 1, no. 1, 1984.

71 As examples, Bill Devall and George Sessions; see their *Deep Ecology: Living as if Nature Mattered* (Salt Lake City: Perigrine Smith Books, 1985). Also see André Gorz, *Ecology as Politics* (Boston: South End Press, 1981).

72 The matter is well-handled in Edward W. Said, "Representing the Colonized: Anthropology's Interlocutors," *Critical Inquiry*, no. 15, 1989.

73 See, for instance, Lucy Lippard, *Mixed Blessings: New Art in Multicultural America* (New York: Pantheon, 1990).

74 Murray Bookchin, *The Ecology of Freedom* (Palo Alto, Calif.: Cheshire Books, 1982); also see Steve Chase (ed.) *Defending the Earth: A Dialogue Between Murray Bookchin and Dave Foreman* (Boston: South End Press, 1991).

75 Fritz Stern, *The Politics of Cultural Despair: A Study in the Rise of Germanic Ideology* (Berkeley: University of California Press, 1961); also see Wilhelm Reich, *The Mass Psychology of Fascism* (New York: Farrar, Strauss & Giroux, 1970).

76 See generally, Walker Connor, *The National Question in Marxist–Leninist Theory and Strategy* (Princeton, NJ: Princeton University Press, 1984).

77 Russell Means, "The Same Old Song," in Ward Churchill (ed.) *Marxism and Native Americans* (Boston: South End Press, 1983).

78 Ward Churchill and Elisabeth R. Lloyd, *Culture versus Economism: Essays on Marxism in the Multicultural Arena* (Denver: University of Colorado Center for the Study of Indigenous Law and Politics, 1990).

79 Michael Albert and Robin Hahnel, *Unorthodox Marxism* (Boston: South End Press, 1978).

80 As illustration of one who made the transition, at least in substantial part, see Rudolph Bahro, *From Red to Green* (London: Verso, 1984).

81 Marcuse, "Repressive Tolerance."
82 Vine Deloria, Jr, *The Metaphysics of Modern Existence* (New York: Harper & Row, 1979), p. 213.
83 For insights, see Ellen Schrecker, *No Ivory Tower: McCarthyism and the Universities* (New York: Oxford University Press, 1986).

Part VII
Liberalism

16

Moral Deference

Laurence M. Thomas

> Why is this peach-tree said to be better than that other; but because it
> produces more or better fruit? ... In morals, too, is not *the tree known by
> the fruit*?
>
> David Hume, *Enquiries Concerning the Principles of Morals*

Some people are owed deference – moral deference, that is. Moral
deference is meant to stand in opposition to the idea that there is a vantage
point from which any and every person can rationally grasp whatever
morally significant experiences a person might have. A fundamentally
important part of living morally is being able to respond in the morally
appropriate way to those who have been wronged. And in an unjust
world, we cannot have this ability in the absence of a measure of moral
deference. David Hume's position on the human sentiments provides
insight regarding the matter. Or so I claim in section three of this essay.
The full account of moral deference is offered in section four. I maintain
that the attitude of moral deference is, at it were, a prelude to bearing
witness to another's pain with that person's authorization – that person's
blessings, if you will.

On my view, moral deference is the bridge between individuals with
different emotional category configurations owing to the injustices of
society. Moral deference, as I conceive of it, is not about whether individuals are innocent with respect to those who have been treated unjustly.
And this I take to be a most important virtue of the account. Rather, moral
deference is simply about the appropriate moral attitude to take when it
comes to understanding the ways in which another has been a victim of

social injustice. In this regard, an individual's innocence or lack there of is irrelevant. Ever so innocent persons can owe moral deference to those who have been wronged; in fact, they may be in a better position to offer moral deference than the guilty. On the other hand, moral deference is not meant as an occasion for those who have been wronged merely to vent their feelings, to wallow publicly in their suffering. Moral deference is not about humiliating others. A person who does these things is not partici-pating in moral deference as I conceive of it.

The idea of moral deference owes its philosophical inspiration to Thomas Nagel. In "What Is It Like To Be a Bat?" he tells us that we hardly come to know what it is like to be a bat by behaving like them in certain ways, say, hanging upside down with our eyes closed.[1] That experience simply tells us what it is like to be a human behaving or attempting to behave like a bat. If bats were intelligent creatures possessing a natural language, which we could translate, surely we would have to take their word for what it is like to be a bat. If, in "batese," bats – including the most intelligent and articulate ones – generally maintained that "Hanging upside down is extraordinarily like experiencing death through colors," we human beings would probably not know how exactly to grasp what was being claimed, since the notion of experiencing death already strains the imagination. Just so, we would be in no position to dismiss their claims as so much nonsense because we cannot fully grasp it – because, after all, we humans experience no such thing when we engage in bat-like behavior. On this matter, bats would be owed deference.

1 Social Categories

If one encountered a Holocaust survivor, it would be moral hubris of the worst sort – unless one is also such a survivor – to assume that by way of rational imaginative role-taking, *à la* Lawrence Kohlberg's theory of moral development, that one could even begin to grasp the depth of that person's experiences – the hurts, pains, and anxieties of that individual's life.[2] There is not enough good will in the world to make it possible for persons (who are not Holocaust survivors) to put themselves imag-inatively in the mind of a Holocaust survivor, to do so simply as an act of ratiocination.

The slave-owners who lived among slaves, and actually ruled the very lives of slaves, knew a great deal about slaves. In many cases, slave-owners knew more about the intimate lives of slaves than a person has the right to know about another's intimate life (unless such information is freely and voluntarily offered in a non-coercive context). Yet, for all that white slave-owners knew about black slaves, the owners did not know what it was like to be a slave. Naturally, there were slave uprisings; but no slave-owner knew what it was like to be a slave on account of being victim of such uprisings.

If a woman has been raped, it is clear that the last thing in the world that a heterosexual man should say to her is "I can imagine how you feel." A great many men can barely imagine or grasp the fear of rape that, to varying degrees, permeates the lives of women, let alone the profoundly violent act of rape itself. Few actions could be more insensitive to victims of rape than a man's supposition that via a feat of imagination he can get a grip on the pain that a female victim of rape has experienced.

I am, of course, aware that heterosexual men can be raped. But given the assumption of heterosexuality, male victims of rape, unlike female victims of rape, do not in general have the awkwardness of seeking to be personally fulfilled romantically by forming a relationship with a person who belongs to the very same social category as does the person who has harmed them. Nor, in any case, do males have to contend with social attitudes – some subtle, some ever so explicit – that make them the target of sexual violence or that minimize the significance of their consent as an appropriate condition of sexual intercourse. No one is ever likely to wonder about a male victim of rape whether "he asked for it." Lesbians who have been raped do not escape this latter injustice; gay men who have been raped do. Given the assumption of heterosexuality, while both a woman and a man may have to recover from the anguish of having been violated, complete recovery for a man does not involve being able to have sex with a man again, and so he is able to have sex with a woman without the act conjuring up the pain of rape. By contrast, complete recovery for a heterosexual woman is generally seen along precisely these lines. Hence, recovery for a heterosexual man involves nothing like the phenomenal ambivalence that it involves for a heterosexual woman.

Why is it that we cannot simply imaginatively put ourselves in the shoes of a Holocaust survivor or, in the case of a man, in the shoes of a rape victim? The answer is painfully obvious: even if we had a complete description of the person's experiences, we would nonetheless not be the subject of those experiences. Nor would we have the painful memory of being the subject of those experiences. So a description, no matter how full and complete, would fail on two counts to capture the subjective element of the experience. The latter account – namely, the memories – is far from trivial, because part of the way in which experiences shape our lives is through the memories of them impressing themselves upon us. In fact, there are times when the impact of a bad experience would be virtually nugatory but for the way in which our lives are affected by the memories of it.

Suppose that one has been robbed at gunpoint. The actual loss may not amount to much at all, say $20 or $30. Suppose, further, that one has not suffered any physical or mental abuse, since two police officers came on the scene just in time. Yet the event may alter the way in which one lives for years to come. Of course, one will realize how lucky one was. It is just that one cannot help thinking about what might have happened but for a fluke of luck – a mode of thought that very nearly cripples one emotionally. Rehearsing an experience in one's mind can frighteningly reveal just how lucky one was. A woman who has been raped can be having sex with her male partner, which has been explicitly consensual, only to find that she can no longer continue the act because she has suddenly been assailed by the painful memories of being raped.

Suppose, to take a very different kind of example, that an Asian-American college student of Korean background, call her Young Mi Lee, has just had a racial epithet hurled at her by campus students, an epithet that reminds her that she does not have the double eyelid (the visible crease in the eyelid, which has the effect of enlarging the eye) that is common among non-Asians. She will not thereby have suffered any bodily harm. But the saying "Sticks and stones may break my bones, but names will never hurt" will undoubtedly ring hollow to her. She may spend months reeling from the experience, wondering how educated people could ever think such a thing. And her sense of her physical appearance may for awhile take on a dreaded horror. For months she considers getting plastic surgery in order to have a fold in her eyelids, looking at popular Korean magazines to acquire information as to where she might have the operation performed. Of course, she has always known that she is not white. But that knowledge now resonates at the surface of her life in a way that it had never done before.

No amount of imagination in the world can make it the case that one has the subjective imprimatur of the experiences and memories of another. And an individual's subjective imprimatur makes a very real difference. Most of us, I would imagine, are unable to grasp the way in which not having an eyelid fold plays itself out in the lives of some Asian women, if only because this is so removed from normal discourse about ethnicity. But that is one reason why the subjective imprimatur is so important to our understanding the harms that people suffer.

Let me tie some things together. There can be appropriate and inappropriate responses to the moral pain of another. When a person has suffered a grave misfortune the type of moral response that will serve to help that person to recover must be sensitive to the adverse ways in which the misfortune is likely to affect her or his life. This includes not just the physical damage that has been wrought to the person's body, but the ways in which the person will be haunted by painful memories, the person's feelings of emotional and social vulnerability, and so on. For as I have noted, the bodily damage can, itself, be negligible. It is not in the damage done to the body that the horror of armed robbery necessarily lies – since there might not be any – but in the damage done to the victim's sense of self. Again, while rape can certainly cause great physical damage to the body, it need not, as the idea acquaintance rape reveals.

Now, to be sure, there are many misfortunes, at the hands of others, which any human being can experience, and so which are independent of social categories. We may think of these as generalized misfortunes. Anyone can be robbed, or be the victim of a car accident caused by an intoxicated driver, or be hit by a stray bullet. Anyone can lose a loved one owing to a flagrant disregard for human rights. These misfortunes do not know the boundaries of social categories. And though there can be difficulties, perhaps insuperable ones in some instances, with how to individuate (events that are) misfortunes, when people have experienced generalized misfortunes of the same type, then they have considerable insight into one another's sufferings. The experience of losing a leg as a teenager is perhaps qualitatively different from that of losing a leg as an adult of fifty, but no doubt the two experiences are far closer qualitatively than either is to the experience of losing a parent as a teenager or as an adult of fifty. And between two teenagers both of whom lose a leg, it perhaps matters if one is an athlete and one is not.

Generalized misfortunes are to be contrasted with misfortunes that are more or less tied to diminished social categories – misfortunes owing to oppressive, if not prevailing, negative attitudes about the members of well-defined diminished social categories. As it happens, the diminished social category may be coextensive with a natural category, as may be the case with gender.[3] I shall use the euphemism "hostile misfortunes" to refer to these misfortunes, where "hostile" is intended to capture both that the misfortune is owing to agency, and that the agency, with respect to the relevant set of acts, is owing to morally objectionable attitudes regarding the diminished social category. I shall often refer to a person in such a category as a categorized person.

Not everyone in a diminished social category experiences all the hostile misfortunes specific to that category, nor to the same extent, but being in a diminished social category makes it exceedingly likely that one's life will be tinged with some of the hostile misfortunes specific to that diminished social category. Moreover, if one is not in that diminished social category, the likelihood of experiencing any of the hostile misfortunes will be virtually nil. I regard gender, ethnicity, and race as obviously involving diminished social categories of this kind, though there need not be hostile misfortunes specific to every ethnic and racial group.

Although people of the same diminished social category do not all endure the same hostile experiences, the relevant experiential and psychological distances between their lives will be less than such distances between their lives and those who do not belong to any diminished social category, or to a very different one. Interestingly, there can be subgroups within a diminished social category, and hostile misfortunes can be tied to those subgroups. For instance, there are very light-complexioned blacks (some of whom are phenotypically indistinguishable from whites) and there are darker-complexioned blacks; and each subgroup has its own hostile misfortunes, in addition to those associated simply with being black.[4] Finally, it is possible for the hostile misfortunes of two different diminished social categories to parallel one another to a considerable degree. Such may be the case with the hostile misfortunes of African-American and Hispanic-American peoples. Individuals from these groups do not experience exactly the same hostile misfortunes, but there appears to be considerable overlap. The hostile misfortunes of a diminished social category group need not be fixed. Hence, the amount of overlap between two groups could change over time.

As with generalized misfortunes, though, I shall assume that when two people of the same diminished social category experience the same type of hostile misfortune, then they have considerable insight into one another's experience of that misfortune. Of course, the problem of individuating types of events does not disappear here. Numerous refinements are possible. However, I shall leave such matters aside. Furthermore, there is the very theory issue of when the hostile misfortunes of two diminished social category groups are similar enough for each group to have some insight into the moral pains of the other. There is certainly no reason to rule this out of court on conceptual grounds. On the other hand, one of the worst mistakes that can be made is for one diminished social category group to assume, without having attended to the matter, that its suffering gives it insight into the suffering of another diminished social category group. But this issue, too, I leave aside.

Now, the knowledge that someone belongs to a socially diminished social category group does not, in and of itself, give one insight into the subjective imprimatur of that individual's experiences of, and memories stemming from, the hostile misfortunes tied to the category group to which they belong. How is it possible to be morally responsive in the appropriate way to those belonging to a diminished social category group if one does not belong to that category? Here is where moral deference enters into the picture, though first more needs to be said about being a member of a diminished social category.

2 Being Socially Constituted

In the *Enquiries Concerning the Principles of Morals* David Hume observed that "Human nature cannot by any means subsist, without the association of individuals" (Section IV, para. 165). His point can be rendered in a contemporary vein as follows: we are constituted through others, by which I mean that the way in which we conceive of ourselves, at least in part, owes much to how others conceive us, and this is necessarily so. The way in which we think of ourselves is inextricably tied to the way in which others think of us. In a fully just world, all would be constituted through others so as to be full and equal members of that society. That is, each member would be constituted so as to see her or himself in this way. By contrast, in an oppressive society, the victims of oppression – diminished social category persons, I mean – are constituted, in both masterfully subtle ways and in ever so explicit ways, so as not to see themselves as full and equal members of society. I shall refer to this as downward social constitution. Each group of diminished social category persons in society experiences different forms of downward social constitution, although I have allowed that there may be overlap. Painfully, social groups that are themselves victims of downward social constitution may engage in downward social constitution of one another. Victims of sexism can be antisemitic; victims of racism can be sexist; and so on for each diminished social category group. Even worse, perhaps, there can be downward social constitution by members within a group. In an oppressive society, downward social constitution is an ongoing and pervasive phenomenon, which is not to deny that there can be pockets of relief to varying degrees. Needless to say, a society with diminished social categories will have one or more privileged social categories, the members of which are favored and have full access to the goods of society.

One of the most important ways in which downward social constitution occurs pertains to expectations. It can be assumed, for example, often without awareness of what is being done, that this or that category person cannot measure up in an important way. That we do not expect much of a person on account of her social category can be communicated in a thousand and one ways. One may listen inattentively, or interrupt frequently, or not directly respond to what the person actually says, or not respond with the seriousness that is appropriate to the person concerned. Most significantly, owing to our meager expectations, we may fail to give the benefit of the doubt to social category persons. We often do not realize that we are participating in the downward constitution of others because communicating positive and negative expectations with regard to others is a natural part of life. Further, behavior that contributes to the downward constitution of another may manifest itself in other contexts that have nothing to do with downward constitution. After all, one can listen inattentively simply because one is preoccupied, or fail to respond directly because one misunderstood what the person said. Accordingly, negative expectations towards a member of a diminished social category need not feel any different from negative expectations toward any member of society, nor need the behavior bear a special mark. Except for the blatant bigot or sexist, participating in the downward social constitution of another rarely has any special phenomenological feel to it.

Thus, it is interesting that most people take as evidence that they do not engage in downwardly constituting behavior the fact that they do not have the appropriate feelings. It is true that if one has and sustains the appropriate feelings, then one is an "X-ist" (sexist, homophobic, antisemitic, and so forth), or that if such feelings fuel one's behavior, then one has acted in an X-ist way. However, it is manifestly false that if one lacks such feelings, in any ostensible way, then X-ism is not a part of one's life.

I have said that in an oppressive society downward social constitution is an ongoing and pervasive phenomenon despite pockets of relief. Such constitution may show up in advertisements, in the casting of actors for a film (play or television program), in the assumptions about the interests (as well as professional aims and hobbies) that a person has or what such a person should be satisfied with. The list goes on. Further, an expression of downward constitution may manifest itself at almost any time in almost any context. An expression of downward constitution may come from those who are so eager to put up an appearance of caring that they deceive themselves into believing that they actually care. Such an expression may even come from those who in fact care.

To be a member of a diminished social category group is invariably to have to contend with what I shall call the problem of social category ambiguity. Was that remark or piece of behavior a manifestation of downward social constitution, or something else, or both? It may not have been, but the very nature of the context of one's social reality as a diminished social category person does not allow one to rule out that possibility with confidence. On the one hand, one does not want to accuse someone falsely; on the other, one may not want to put up with an affront. Yet there may be no way to inquire about the matter without giving the appearance of doing the former. Finally, there is the painful reality that one may not be able to share one's feelings about one's social category status with those who do not belong to that category, including those who regard themselves as friends, without giving the impression of being overly concerned with such matters. It is a reality that sometimes requires a kind of profound disassociation from one's own experiences, at least momentarily.

Together, these things all speak to a profound sense of vulnerability that comes with being a member of a diminished social category. Part of that vulnerability is owing not just to being a subject of downward social constitution, but also to the memories of such experiences. Invariably, the diminished social category person will be haunted by some of these memories to varying degrees. Then there is the fact that a memory (sometimes painful, sometimes not) of an experience of downward social constitution can be triggered by any number of things, including the witnessing of another's experience of downward social constitution, or another such experience of one's own. There is a sense in which one can be assailed by the memories of past undesirable experiences. A diminished social category person is vulnerable in this way. People who are downwardly constituted socially are victims of a social claim about them – not just any old claim, but the claim that they lack the wherewithal to measure up in an important social dimension. In this regard, diminished social category persons are vulnerable on several counts. First, there is the vulnerability caused by the weariness of always feeling the need to prove that this social claim is a lie – if not to oneself, then to others. Second, vulnerability arises from the knowledge that there is almost nothing that diminished social category persons can do which will decisively establish the falsity of the social claim. Third, there is the vulnerability of exhaustion stemming from the feeling that one must always speak up because no one else will, although continually speaking up might diminish one's effectiveness. Obviously, diminished social category persons cope with these vulnerabilities in a variety of different ways and with varying degrees of success. But successfully coping with such vulnerability is hardly tantamount to not being vulnerable, any more than not showing anger is tantamount to not being angry.

My remarks in the preceding two paragraphs are meant to bring out the sense of *otherness* that inescapably comes with being a person belonging to a diminished social category, the sense of what it means to be socially constituted as such a person. This sense of otherness is not something that a person outside one's diminished social category can grasp simply by an act of ratiocination. In particular, it is not something people in privileged social categories can grasp, their enormous good will notwithstanding. To be sure, people who belong to a privileged social category can, of course, experience insults and affronts to their person, even at the hands of those belonging to a diminished social category. But just as a person does not know what it is like to be a bat by hanging upside down with closed eyes, a person does not know what it is like to be a member of a diminished social category merely on account of having been affronted and insulted by diminished social persons for, say, being a privileged social category person. For the hallmark of a diminished social category person is a life that has been downwardly constituted socially, with all that this implies in terms of the vulnerability noted above. A privileged category person who has experienced affronts at the hands of diminished social category persons has not, on that account alone, had a downwardly constituted life, no more than a fifty-year-old person can be said to have had a life marred by sickness because on two separate occasions illness required them to spend a week in hospital.

3 Emotional Configuration

Hume seems to have held that if our natural capacity for sympathy and benevolence were sufficiently cultivated, we would have adequate insight into the weal and woe of others. I disagree, although I think that his heart was in the right place. In a world without hostile misfortunes and diminished social category groups, and so without privileged social category groups, I think that Hume's position would, indeed, be correct or very nearly that. I hesitate only because it might seem that even in a perfectly just world some differences might be impassable despite unqualified good will on all sides. Hume's point holds given two assumptions: (1) the emotional capacities of people are essentially the same; (2) the configuration of these emotional capacities through society is essentially the same, the primary difference with respect to the latter being in their development. Thus, for Hume, Nero is simply one whose capacity for benevolence and sympathy virtually went uncultivated. By contrast, Hume thought it obvious that anyone who had benefited from some cultivation of these sentiments could not help but see that Nero's actions were criminal.

Such social phenomena as downward social constitution and diminished social categories would not have occurred to Hume. Specifically, and more pointedly, it would not have occurred to him that a person's emotions could be configured along a dimension other than the extent of their cultivation, the case of gender aside.[5] So, given Hume's moral psychology, anyone whose capacity for sympathy and benevolence was properly cultivated was in a position to understand sufficiently the moral experiences of all others. My suggestion is that Hume's moral psychology must be adjusted to take into account that the emotional makeup of persons can be configured along dimensions other than cultivation. There is what I shall call emotional category configuration.

In a sexist society, a politically correct male who abhors violence against females, and understands very well why a victim of rape would rather be comforted by a female rather than a male, nonetheless does not have the emotional configuration of a female. This is because the kind of fears that he experiences when he walks alone at night do not have as their source a concern about sexual violence; whereas they do for a woman, whether or not she has been raped.[6] In a sexist society, at any rate, the emotional category configurations of women and men are different. This is a result of the fact that women and men are socially constituted differently.

Likewise, a white can be attacked by blacks, and that attack can be brutal and absolutely inexcusable. As a result, the victim may be emotionally crippled by a fear of interacting with blacks. This is profoundly unjust and inexcusable. All the same, this experience of suffering does not parallel the suffering which a black would have if brutally attacked by whites. In the former case, the white's fear may very well be a reminder of the random brutality of some blacks and of the moral squalor in which some wallow. The experience may seal his conviction that blacks lack the wherewithal to live morally decent lives. But for all of that, the experience will not be a reminder that he is a second-class citizen. It will not make him vulnerable to that pain. He will not have the pain of being scarred by those who in fact have power over so very much of his life. By and large, the white will not really have to concern himself with having to trust blacks who have power over him, as with a little effort and creativity the white can avoid situations of that kind; whereas for the black, having to trust whites who have power over him is a real possibility. So whereas some physical distance from blacks, coupled with time, might serve to heal the wounds of the white, this healing route is not a genuine possibility for a black. This is yet another dimension along which the black will live with his pain in a quite different manner to the white. Certainly, no innocent white should be a victim of black anger and hostility; certainly, no innocent black should be either. The moral wrong may be equal in either case. My point is that because the black and the white have different emotional category configurations, each will experience their respective pain in a radically different manner. While economic differences could be factored in here, I did not develop the point with such differences in mind. The force of the point is not diminished in the least if both the white and the black are upper-middle-class people enjoying equally high salaries.

A fortiori, there is a difference in the emotional category configuration rather than a difference in the cultivation of the emotions if we suppose that the black and the white went to the very same kind of schools, read many of the same books, and have overlapping interests and tastes. We can imagine that they have similar personalities, and have had similar maturation experiences and wrestled with many of the same issues. Nonetheless, it is most likely that they will be socially constituted in different ways. In the case of the black, strangers might be surprised that he was not born poor, or wonder where he learned to speak so well. The police at the university where he has just joined the faculty might regard him with suspicion. Or, at the checkout desk at the university library, the staff person might ask him for photo-identification to confirm that he is actually the owner of the university faculty library card that he presents. These experiences are rather unlikely to be a part of the white person's life, at least not in any routine way.

The cumulative effect of these experiences contributes to the significant difference in the emotional category configuration of which I have been speaking. Time and time again, a well-off black must steel himself against such experiences in settings of equality, while a white need not. Ironically, some of the experiences of downward social constitution – some of the insults – that a black will encounter, the person could only encounter if she were well-off, since a black in the throes of poverty would be far too removed from such social situations in the first place.[7] A black American in the throes of poverty is not apt to experience racism in a Middle Eastern or European hotel by a white American.

If I may be permitted an autobiographical remark: nothing that I have experienced in my entire life had prepared me for the shock of being taken as a would-be purse snatcher in 1991 in a Middle Eastern hotel by a white American who saw me enter the hotel lobby from the guests' rooms. The person leapt for her pocketbook on the counter as if she had springs on her feet, although other people had been sitting in the lobby all along. Worse still, she and I had been sitting in the lobby opposite one another only two days earlier. As I play back the experience in my mind, it seems so incredibly surrealistic to me that I continually find myself stunned these many years later. Even granting racism, and that she had been robbed by a black man while she was in Harlem, just how reasonable under the circumstances could it have been for her to suppose that *I* (some distance from youth in appearance) was a poor black out to steal her purse? After all, it takes more than cab fare to get from New York City to any place in the Middle East.[8] I have been called a "nigger" to my face three times in my life. One of them was in Harvard Yard between Widner Library and Emerson. If I were to walk around with a fear that whites might call me "nigger," I would surely be taken as mad by most of my friends and acquaintances, or I would be seen as having enormous and unjustified hostility against whites.

Hume's moral psychology cannot account for the emotional vulnerability that comes with such experiences. This is because it would not have occurred to him that a person would be treated as anything other than a full citizen on a par with all others – at least among equally cultivated individuals – *provided that* the individual displayed the refinements of education and culture. It would not have occurred to Hume that persons displaying such refinements could be the object of hostile misfortunes, for on his view, the display of these things should suffice to elicit admiration. Thus, if it had been in a hotel in Harlem instead of the Middle East that I had encountered that woman, I might have understood her reactions, my station in life notwithstanding. For the sake of argument, I am willing to allow that in a Harlem hotel prudence would have dictated that she react as she did. This concession is very minimal, though, for even in Harlem the color of a person's skin is not the only salient information to draw upon. But surely a most reasonable presumption would be that a black traveling in the Middle East, staying in the very same hotel, is displaying the kind of refinements that, to say the least, should give no cause for concern.

4 The Idea of Moral Deference

It is very characteristic of philosophers to suppose that rational reflection reveals who we are. No doubt it does up to a point. However, from the standpoint of grasping what our feelings might be in various circumstances or having certain levels of appreciation, rationality is deeply limited. There are some things we can understand or properly appreciate only in the context of real experience. Consider the sentiment of gratitude.[9] No matter how high an opinion I have of you, no matter how virtuous I take you to be, it is only in virtue of your performing a beneficial act for me that I can rightly have feelings of gratitude toward you. To be sure, I may certainly know that I am the sort of person who will have feelings of gratitude towards you if you are kind to me. That knowledge, though, is no substitute for either actually experiencing your gratitude or the actual feelings of gratitude that I have for you when I am the object of your generosity. What is more, there are a variety of ways in which a person can be generous. You may do so with a graciousness or, to go in the other direction, with an officiousness that I had not counted on. If the former, I may feel eternally grateful to you; if the latter, by contrast, I may suppose that an act of kindness towards you on my part suffices to repay my gratitude, and so to render clean the slate between us.

Significantly, we can be grateful for a person's doing what he has an obligation to do for us, for he may behave not so much from a sense of duty, but from a sense of commitment to our well-being and flourishing, and thus with a concern that no sense of duty, alone, could ever capture. Presumably, this is the case with good parents or spouses or professors. In the best of circumstances, the good professor gives the student a grade of "A" not begrudgingly, because as it happens the student's performances merit an "A," but she gives that grade with delight at seeing a student under her tutelage achieve such a high level of excellence.

It is tempting to think of gratitude as an unproblematic sentiment, meaning that it would always express itself in the life of a person when he or she has enjoyed the kindness of another. But not so, in an unjust world. In the context of sexism, scores of husbands have been ungrateful to their wives, though they have worked selflessly (and not just from a sense of duty) to contribute to the good of their husbands. In the context of sexism, husbands have often taken for granted the good that their wives have done, even as each expected his wife to be grateful to him. In the context of racism, taking the case of American slavery, we know that slave-owners were often ungrateful to their black slaves, although in many cases these contributed mightily to the well-being of their masters and did so faithfully. In *Autobiography of a Slave Narrative Written by Himself*, Frederic Douglass wrote these scorching words:

> If any one thing in my experience, more than another, that served to deepen my conviction of the infernal character of slavery, and to fill me with unutterable loathing of slaveholders, it was their base ingratitude to my poor old grandmother. She had served my old master faithfully from youth to old age. She had rocked him in infancy, attended him in childhood, served him through life and at his death wiped from his icy brow the cold death-sweat and closed his eyes forever. She was nevertheless left a slave – a slave for life.

Alas, in an unjust world, people of one social grouping may come up short in their expressions of gratitude to people in another social grouping. So, interestingly, the following thesis is false: if a person of social group X – say, Alpha – is gracious in expressing gratitude towards individuals of social group X, then Alpha will be equally moved to express gratitude towards persons of any social group Y (where group Y is not identical to group X), when any Y individual exhibits the kinds of behavior that inclines Alpha to express gratitude towards persons of group X. Rather, Alpha could have enormous difficulty feeling gratitude toward Ys, where Ys are women, or Asians, or Latinos, or Jews, and so on. In fact Alpha, along with Xs generally, could take it to be obvious that if any one owes gratitude to anyone, surely it is Ys who owe gratitude to Xs.

It is striking, is it not, that the expression of gratitude can have such unjust borders, that it can be tied to a distorted view of the place of others in the social world. On the assumption that, after all, a benefit is a benefit, it is striking that it could matter to anyone who has benefited him. But it does. The case of gratitude shows ever so poignantly that our moral sensibilities can be underdeveloped. In an unjust world, there are in-groups and out-groups when it comes to gratitude. The out-group may exhibit the same kind of behavior that occasions considerable gratitude towards the in-group, with the difference being simply that we have not been constituted to see the out-group as meriting our gratitude. And we may transmit our moral blindness to our children and our students. The existence of sexism and racism shows this not to be just a possibility but a reality. This truth underscores all the more the importance of moral deference. For if subtle but powerful unjust attitudes stand in the way of our being grateful to persons of this or that kind, how likely is it that, nonetheless, we will be willing to listen to them?

Philosophically and metaphorically, we may think of gratitude as a kind of moral radar screen. Those who show up on the screen are those towards whom we feel gratitude in a myriad of ways, ranging from morally significant behavior (such as saving our life, for which we are moved to give them credit, naturally) to the socially trivial (such as making a wonderful off-the-wall comment for which we are moved to give them credit). Those who do not show up on that screen have a kind of social invisibility, which again speaks to the importance of moral deference.

Moral deference is owed to persons of good will when they speak in an informed way regarding experiences specific to their diminished social category from the standpoint of an emotional category configuration to which others do not have access. While I do not think that moral deference is owed only to persons of good will who are members of diminished social categories, my account begins with them.[10] It might be objected, though, that to place this restriction at the outset on those to whom moral deference is owed is to fail to take seriously the pain and anger that often comes with being a member of a diminished social category. I want to take seriously that pain. But I am also mindful of the bitterness, rage, and rancor that can be formidable obstacles to helping others grasp the ways in which one has been downwardly constituted. It is because of this that I say that moral deference is first owed to people of good will who are members of diminished social categories. We should distinguish between anger, pain, and anguish, on the one hand, and bitterness, rage, and rancor, on the other. The former are compatible with having good will, but not the latter. In starting initially with persons of good will, I do not mean to suggest that moral deference is owed only to those who have no anger or pain. Now, the idea behind moral deference is not that a diminished social category person can never be wrong about the character of his own experiences. Surely he can, since anyone can. Nor is it that silence is the only appropriate response to what another says when one lacks that individual's emotional category configuration. Rather, the idea is that there should be a presumption in favor of the person's account of his experiences. This presumption is warranted because the individual is speaking from a vantage point to which someone not belonging to his diminished social category group does not have access. It is possible to play a major role in helping a person to get clearer about the character of an experience delivered from the vantage point of an emotional category configuration. But helping someone get clearer is qualitatively different from being dismissive. Indeed, how a person feels about a matter can be of the utmost importance even if the individual's feelings are inappropriate, since inappropriate feelings can shed considerable light on the very appearances of things in themselves.

To repeat, while I do not think that moral deference is owed only to persons of good will who are members of diminished social categories, my account begins with such persons. The assumption here is that in characterizing their feelings and experiences as diminished social category persons, those of good will do not tell an account that is mired and fueled by feelings of rancor and bitterness. This is not to suggest that persons of good will never experience tremendous anger and rage on account of experiences of downward social constitution. They sometimes do, and rightly so. Occasionally experiencing anger and rage, though, is by no means the same thing as becoming consumed by these feelings. A complete account of moral deference would have to be extended to include those who, understandably or not, have come to be full of bitterness and rancor owing to the ways in which they have been downwardly constituted socially. It becomes especially important to extend the account in this direction if one considers that oppression, itself, can render its victims so full of rancor and bitterness that the manifestation of these sentiments can blind us to their underlying cause, namely the oppression itself.

Moral deference is meant to reflect the insight that it is wrong to discount the feelings and experiences of persons in diminished social category groups simply because their articulation of matters does not resonate with one's imaginative-take on their experiences. Moral deference acknowledges a vast difference between the ideal moral world and the present one. In the ideal moral world there would be only one category of emotional configuration, namely the human one – or at most two, allowing for differences in the sexes. So, given adequate cultivation of emotions and feelings, everyone would be able to obtain an imaginative-take on the experiences of others. Interestingly, this way of understanding the role of emotions in the ideal world might point to a reason for making them irrelevant entirely; for if rightly cultivated emotions would result in everyone making the same moral judgments on the basis of them, then the emotions do not make for a morally relevant difference between people, at least not among those with rightly cultivated emotions. On this view, the emotions can only make a morally relevant difference if they are seen as a constitutive feature of what it means to be a person, and so of moral personhood. But, alas, philosophers often seem anxious to deny that the emotions have any moral relevance, in and of themselves, at the foundations of moral personhood.[11]

In a far from ideal moral world, such as the one we live in, which privileges some social categories and diminishes others, it stands to reason that there will be emotional boundaries between people, owing to what I have called emotional category configuration. This is one of the bitter fruits of immorality. Recall Hume's question: "In morals, too, is not the tree known by its fruits?" The idea of moral deference is true to the moral reality that the mark of an immoral society is the erection of emotional walls between others. It is true that social immorality cannot be eliminated in the absence of a firm grasp of how it has affected its victims. It is not enough to be confident that social immorality harms. One must also be sensitive to the way in which it harms. Thus, the idea of moral deference speaks to an attitude that a morally decent person should have in an immoral society.

We can best get at what moral deference involves, and its importance, by thinking of what it means to bear witness to another's moral pain with that person's authorization. To bear witness to the moral pain of another, say, Leslie, with Leslie's authorization, is to have won her confidence that one can speak informedly and with conviction on her behalf to another about the moral pain she has endured. It is to have won her confidence that one will tell her story with her voice, as opposed to her story with one's own voice. Hence, it is to have won her trust that one will render salient what was salient for her in the way that it was salient for her, that one will represent her struggle to cope in the ways that she has been getting on with her life; that one will convey desperation where desperation was felt, and hurt where hurt was felt. And so on.

To bear witness to the pain of Leslie is not to tell Leslie's story of pain as a means to explicating how her pain has affected one's own life. Accordingly, to be authorized by Leslie to bear witness to her pain is to have won her confidence that telling her story of pain will not take a back seat to telling one's own story of pain as caused by her story. Not that it will always be impossible for people to make reasonable inferences about how one has been affected. It stands to reason that how one has been affected will surely be obvious in some cases. Rather, whatever inferences reasonable people might be able to draw, the point of bearing witness to the moral pain of another will not be so that others can see how one has been affected by the other person's pain. Thus, to be authorized to bear witness for another is to have won her confidence that one will tell her story with a certain motivational structure.

Now, it may be tempting to think that bearing witness to the moral pain of others requires something amounting to a complete diminution of the self, to become a mere mouthpiece for another. But this is to think of bearing witness to the moral pain of others as something that happens to one – a state that one falls into or whatever. Perhaps there are such cases of bearing witness. I do not write with them in mind, however. Instead, as I conceive of the idea, bearing witness to the moral pain of another is very much an act of agency and, as such, it can be an extremely courageous thing to do. During the time of slavery, whites who endeavored to bear witness to the moral pain of blacks were sometimes called "nigger lovers." In Nazi Germany, some who endeavored to bear witness to the moral pain of the Jews were killed. Nowadays, those who endeavor to bear witness to the moral pain of lesbians and homosexuals are often branded as such themselves. Far from being an activity possible only for the faint of heart, bearing witness to the moral pain of others can require extraordinary courage and resoluteness of will.

Well, needless to say, there can be no bearing witness, as I have explicated it, to the moral pain of another without having heard his story and heard it well. One will have had to have heard the glosses on the story and the nuances to the story. One will have had to have been sensitive to the emotions that manifested themselves as the story was told, and to the vast array of non-verbal behavior with which the story was told. One will have to have heard his story well enough to have insight into how his life has been emotionally configured by his experiences. A person rightly authorizes another to bear witness to his moral pain only if these things are true.

To have such insight into another's moral pain will not be tantamount to having that person's fears or being haunted by his memories, but it will entail having a sense of the kinds of things and circumstances that will trigger his fears and memories. It will not entail being vulnerable when he is downwardly constituted on account of his diminished social category, but it will entail a sense of the kinds of social circumstances that will give rise to such vulnerability. Moreover, it will entail being appropriately moved on account of these things. To have such insight is to be in as good a position as one can be to understand, while yet lacking a complete grasp of another's moral pain.

Moral deference, then, is the act of listening involved in bearing witness to another's moral pain, but without bearing witness to it. I do not see the step from moral deference to bearing witness as an easy one. A person may lack the fortitude or courage to bear witness, however well he might listen. Moral deference is not about bearing witness. It is about listening, in the ways characterized above, until one has insight into the character of the other's moral pain, and so how he has been emotionally configured by it. In any case, moral deference may be appropriate on occasions when bearing witness is not. You may not want me to bear witness to your moral pain; yet you may be deeply gratified that I have listened well enough that I could bear witness in the unlikely event that you should, ever want me to.

Moral deference, too, is not an activity for the faint of heart. For it is a matter of rendering oneself open to another's concern, and to letting another's pain reconstitute one so much that one comes to have a new set of sensibilities – a new set of moral lenses if you will. Moral deference is rather like the moral equivalent of being nearsighted, putting on a pair of glasses for the first time, and discovering just how much out there one had been missing. Of course, one had always seen trucks, cars, people, and so forth. But there were designs on cars and trucks, and sayings on shirts, and facial expressions that people displayed, and minute movements that people made, and slight variances in colors – none of which one could see at a distance. With moral deference the acquired sensibility is to the way in which a self-respecting oppressed person lives in the world. Hence, to engage in moral deference is to allow oneself to become affected in a direct interpersonal way by the injustices of this world. While it is not the only way in which to do this, it is a very important way. Thus, it is a fundamentally important mode of moral learning. It is a mode of moral learning which those who have been oppressed are owed in the name of eliminating the very state of their oppression. In the absence of such learning, oppression cannot but continue to be a part of the fabric of the moral life. Indeed, the absence of such learning, the studied refusal to engage in such learning, is one of the very ways in which oppression manifests itself. Worse, the studied refusal to do so adds insult to injury.

Significantly, moral deference involves earning the trust of another – in particular, the trust of one who has been oppressed. And earning the trust of another, especially someone who is weary of trusting anyone from a different social category (diminished or privileged), is an act of great moral responsibility – something not to be taken lightly. It would be morally egregious in the very worst of ways to earn such a person's trust and then abuse it or merely withdraw from the person. If the struggle for equality is ever to be won we must be strong enough to be vulnerable. That is, we must be strong enough to prove ourselves worthy of the trust of those whom we have oppressed. This is well-nigh impossible in the absence of moral deference to those whom we have oppressed. Moral deference is by no means a weakness. It is a matter of courage.

In an important essay entitled "The Need for More than Justice," Annette Baier explains the significance of departing from John Rawls's claim that justice is the first virtue of social justice.[12] One of the needs she describes is the appropriate moral posture towards those who have been oppressed. Without it, we often blithely trample upon those whom we mean to help. The notion of moral deference is meant to give expression to one aspect of what that posture calls for. It is impossible to responsively help those who have been hurt if one does not understand the nature of their pain. And while it may be true that we can know what is right and wrong behavior for others without consulting with them, it is simply false that, in the absence of similar experiences, we cannot know how others are affected by wrong doing without consulting them.

Let me repeat a point made at the outset: the idea of moral deference helps us to understand the inadequacy of the response that one has not contributed to another's oppression. To the extent that is true, the response does not entail that one understands another's downward social constitution. Moral innocence does not entail understanding. Neither, for that matter, does good will. Nor does either entail that one has earned the trust of one who has been downwardly constituted by society. It goes without saying that neither the innocence nor the good will of others should ever be discounted. On the other hand, neither should they be trumpeted for what they are not, namely understanding and earning the trust of others.

A final comment: the account of moral deference offered here points to why both those who have been downwardly constituted by society and those who have not been should be more responsive to one another. If, as I have argued, those who have not been should be willing to earn the trust of the downwardly constituted, then the downwardly constituted must not insist that, as a matter of principle, this is impossible. Understandably, it may be difficult to earn the trust of those who have been downwardly constituted by society. And it may not, in fact, be possible for some outside the social category in question actually to do so. But what has to be false is that, as a matter of principle, it is *impossible* for anyone outside that social category to do so.

Regardless of our economic status or our intellectual background, regardless of our ethnic identity or our gender, regardless of our sexual orientation, moral deference is a good that we all can offer to those who have been wronged. It is a moral power that each of us possesses, a way of making a difference for the better. When the life of individuals is wracked with moral pain, their resolve to do what is right can be profoundly weakened; for the gravest injustices can so shake our belief in our moral worthiness that we do not take ourselves to matter even when it comes to doing what is morally right. Accordingly, when we engage in moral deference, we affirm the humanity of those who have been egregiously wronged by earning their trust and taking their moral pain seriously. Moral deference is a most significant step towards healing the deep wounds of injustice.

Apart from the context of the loves of friendship and romance, there is no greater affirmation that we can want from another than that which comes in earning her or his trust. If we should be willing to accept moral affirmation from others, then surely we are more likely to treat them justly. Moral deference embodies this idea.

Notes

In writing the present version, I am deeply grateful to Nasri Abdel-Aziz who has been a godsend. With his advice and challenges, he has been a fount of philosophical inspiration. I also want to thank David Kim, whose questions and comments have given me an appreciation that I would not otherwise have for so much of what I tried to do in writing this essay. Tom Foster Digby and Claudia Card are among those who have been profoundly instrumental in helping me to value the kind of philosophical work that I do.

This essay owes its inspiration to Alison M. Jaggar's, "Love and Knowledge: Emotion in Feminist Epistemology," in Alison M. Jaggar and Susan R. Bordo (eds), *Gender/Body/Knowledge: Feminist Reconstructions of Being and Knowing* (New Brunswick: Rutgers University Press, 1989); Seyla Benhabib's "The Generalized the Concrete Other: The Kohlberg – Gilligan Controversy and Moral Theory," in Eva Feder Kittay and Diana T. Meyers (eds), *Women and Moral Theory* (Rowman and Littlefield, 1978); David Theo Goldberg, "Racism and Rationality: The Need for a New Critique," *Philosophy of the Social Sciences*, vol. 20 (1990); Adrian M. S. Piper's paper "Higher-Order Discrimination," in Owen Flanagan and Amelie Okensberg Rorty, (eds), *Identity, Character, and Morality: Essays in Moral Psychology* (Cambridge: MIT Press, 1990); and Elizabeth V. Spelman, *Inessential Women: Problems of Exclusion in Feminist Thought* (Beacon Press, 1988). In writing the first version of this essay, I benefited much from conversations with Linda Alcoff, Alan, J. Richard, Michael Stocker (always a present help), Julian Wuerth, and Thomas Nagel (over the penultimate draft).

1 In *Mortal Questions* (Cambridge University Press, 1979).

2 See Kohlberg's *The Philosophy of Moral Development* (New York: Harper and Row, 1981). My general concern with the Kantian approach to moral philosophy, of which Kohlberg following John Rawls's *A Theory of Justice* (Cambridge, Mass.: Harvard University Press, 1971), is an example, is that this approach does not speak to how we should understand the moral pain of others. We will not correct for injustices as well as we might if we do not adequately grasp the pain that they have caused.

3 That gender is both a biological and a social category is developed at length in my essay "Sexism and Racism: Some Conceptual Differences," *Ethics* (1980).

4 I agree with Naomi Zack's *Mixed Race* (Philadelphia: Temple University Press, 1993) that there is much absurdity in the way Americans think about race. Here I am merely following common parlance. I do not endorse it.

5 For an important discussion of Hume regarding gender, see Annette Baier, *A Progress of Sentiments* (Cambridge, Mass: Harvard University Press, 1991), pp. 273–5. Hume thought that women who desired to become wives and to bear children should be held to stricter standards of chastity than men. Cf. David Hume, *Enquiries Concerning the Principles of Morals*, Section V, Section VIII, para. 215 and, especially, Section VI, part I, para. 195.

6 Perhaps male child victims of male rape can approximate such fears in their own lives. Still, the adult life of such males will be qualitatively different from the adult life of females, owing to great differences in the way in which society portrays women and men as sex objects. See the discussion in section 1 above. This, of course, hardly diminishes the pain of having been a child victim of male rape. For a philosophical discussion of child abuse, see my "The Grip of Immorality: Child Abuse and Moral Failure," in J. D. Schneewind (ed.),

Reason, Ethics, and Society: Themes from Kurt Baier, with His Responses (Chicago: Open Court, 1996).

7 Bernard Boxill, in a very powerful essay, "Dignity, Slavery, and the 13th Amendment," has demonstrated the deep and profound way in which slavery was insulting. His essay appears in Michael J. Meyer and William A. Parent (eds), *Human Dignity, the Bill of Rights and Constitutional Values* (Ithaca: Cornell University Press, 1991).

8 I was so enraged by the experience that it was clear to me that I had better channel my rage lest I do something that I would regret. Fortunately, I had a micro-cassette recorder with me. I walked the streets of Tel Aviv and taped the essay "Next Life, I'll Be White" for the *New York Times*/Op-Ed page (August 13 1990), an expanded version of which appeared in *Ebony* Magazine (December, 1990). It is, among other things, profoundly insulting when the obvious is discounted at one's own expense.

9 On the subject of gratitude, my thinking owes much to Claudia Card, "Gratitude and Obligation," *American Philosophical Quarterly* 25 (1988) and Terrance McConnell, *Gratitude* (Philadelphia: Temple University Press, 1993). There are contexts where gratitude is appropriate because of what a person would have done: you may have been ready to lend me $1,000; but, as it happens, I did not need it.

10 These remarks are a response to Robin Dillon's powerful observation that it is often the privileged who are in a position not to be angry. I trust that the distinction between anger and bitterness speaks to some of her concerns.

11 See my "Rationality and Affectivity: The Metaphysics of the Moral Self," *Social Philosophy and Policy* 5, 1988, pp. 154–72. For a sustained discussion of the importance of the emotions in the moral life, see Michael Stocker and Elizabeth Hegeman, *Valuing Emotions* (New York: Cambridge University Press, 1996).

12 Annette Baier, "The Need for More than Justice," in *Science, Morality and Feminist Theory, Canadian Journal of Philosophy* supp. vol. 13 (1987). Rawls's first sentence is "Justice is the first virtue of social institutions as truth is of systems of thought": *A Theory of Justice* (Cambridge Mass: Harvard University Press, 1971), p. 3.

Martha Minow, in her book *Making All the Difference: Inclusion, Exclusion, and American Law* (Ithaca: Cornell University Press), writes: "Claiming that we are impartial is insufficient if we do not consider changing how we think. Impartiality is the guise that partiality takes to seal bias against exposure" (p. 376). This essay points to a way in which that change must go.

17

"Multiculturalism," Citizenship, Education, and American Liberal Democracy

Lucius Outlaw, Jr

If Hegel has appropriately characterized philosophizing as "the owl of Minerva always flying after the dusk" – that is, as taking a critical account of human experience after the fact – then there are definite risks involved in trying to take stock of contemporary situations, nationally and globally, that involve changes of seemingly exceptional dimensions and importance. Indeed, it is perhaps rather bold even to offer the tentative assessment that in various places on planet earth we are living through a seemingly axial period in history, that is, one during which a confluence of developments is ushering in challenges and possibilities of distinctively new configurations of life socially, politically, economically.

Those attempting to take the pulse of this period characterize it in a number of ways. Most prominent have been efforts to distinguish the features of "postmodernity," that is, the complexes of meanings, practices, and agendas that are configuring diverse forms of living which are distinctively different from (thus "post" or "beyond") the intellectual, political, economic, and social agendas and practices that for the past three centuries or more have defined the "modern" world of liberal, democratic, capitalist, white-supremacist nation-states of Western Europe and North America (Canada included) and fueled this so-called "First World"'s imperialist, transforming encounters with "Third World" cultures, civilizations, and lands around the globe. (The communist "Second World" of Eastern Europe, though still a part of the "modern West" in important respects, until its collapse had enough in the way of people, guns, missiles, and other resources, mobilized by an ideology promoting global expansion intent on world-transformation, to curtail somewhat for a time the First World's hegemonic encroachments.) The histories of the nations comprising the First World have long been rationalized as collectively comprising the *telos* of human civilization, the peoples of Western Europe self-identified as the proper ones to assume the point-position in the progressive evolutionary trek of human development. Thus, much is at stake in struggles over the intellectual and practical guardianship of the histories of those thought to be *the* representative norm and ideal for all humans, particularly as this guardianship is thought vital to preparations for making history, including settling questions regarding *who* will be the shapers and makers of possible and probable futures.

Indeed, much is at stake. Certainly, the emergence of the complexes of meanings and practices that came to define "modernity" in sharp (though not complete) distinction from the ancient and medieval "traditional" worlds involved more or less fundamental redefinitions of what it meant to be "human" in virtually every important respect. Out of this came new and decisive definitions of the self and the person centering on and valorizing the free, autonomous individual. These notions became foundational to the acquisition, certification, and mediation of positivistic and instrumental knowledge of natural and social worlds, knowledges that became foundational to efforts to order these worlds:

- natural philosophy was transformed into increasingly desacralized natural sciences accompanied by a new sense of human relationships to natural environments as collections of objects and processes that were more and more to be brought under human domination, control, and exploitation:
- new, likewise desacralized approaches to the derivation and justification of ethical and political norms – the emergence of political liberalism, the political philosophy of modernity – and of socio-economic norms of free-enterprise capitalism;
- a new sense of history that emphasized increasingly rationalized, systematized, and institutionalized group-based and individual human choices and actions as the motive-forces of historical development rather than divine intervention.

These knowledge-producing, certifying, and mediating efforts became foundational to the fashioning of cultural norms and practices appropriate to the production and maintenance of decidedly "modern" societies.

A crucial factor in these developments was the increasingly confident presumption that principles of certain and true knowledge of the laws ordering the relevant spheres of knowing and acting (i.e. of both nature and social life) could be discovered by – or derived from – and certified by the sole authority of self-correcting and self-certifying human Reason, the ultimate tribunal for settling questions of what is and what ought to be. It was the successful institutionalization of this presumption that largely distinguishes modernity from earlier periods of human history.

But only in part. For equally decisive have been the variety of ways in which this institutionalization has been played out and rationalized in encounters with non-European peoples as well as with particular groupings of persons of European descent. The project of modernity, organized around complexes of discriminating judgments regarding what is and ought to be, included norms for making supposedly impartial and objective judgments of who was best able to know what is and ought to be, and who should be responsible for using such knowledge in the ordering and managing of living. During the eighteenth and nineteenth centuries, such judgments became organized into and institutionalized as knowledges certified and thus legitimated by the increasingly socially prominent imprimatur of the new authority of "science," including knowledges or sciences of "man" (for example, the emergence of anthropology, sociology, and psychology as ventures distinct from natural philosophy). State and church-sponsored voyages of exploration of various Europeans, presaging the expansion of their nations into other (and others') lands, involved unprecedented encounters with peoples who were, on the whole, dissimilar in certain aspects of physical appearance and quite dissimilar in ways of living. The dissimilarities had to be dealt with, had somehow to be accommodated to the ordering schemes of knowing and acting of those from Europe, but in ways that would not prevent but, instead, facilitate the fulfillment of Europeans' expansionist agendas.

Ready to hand were strategies with long employment histories, strategies worked out by a number of the best minds throughout the history continually recapitulated as belonging to and defining the Western world: the distinguishing and ordering of differing groups of peoples into ranked hierarchies of supposedly "natural kinds" – races, sexes, and social orders of caste and class – whereby place in the hierarchy was determined by capacity and character as a function of kind that thus determined the absolute (in themselves) and relative (compared to others) moral and social value of persons and peoples. Canonical figures in historical accounts of Western philosophy were prominent in articulating these strategies by which to make ordered sense – and to effect the ordering – of variety and difference in natural and naturalized social worlds.[1]

The fashioning of the United States of America into a federated union of semi-autonomous colonies-become-states and local communities of different sorts (state and municipal) made up of European settler-colonialists of various Old World national and racial groups, legally sanctioned enslaved and otherwise oppressed Africans and their descendants, native "Indians" who survived the genocidal wars of conquest perpetrated by the settlers only to be isolated on reservations, and trickles and floods of a steady stream of immigrants from Europe and, today especially, other portions of the globe, continues to be a paradigmatic experiment in the formation of a stable, modern nation-state. How to achieve *e pluribus unum*, that is, the molding of a diverse many into a unified one?

Off and on, but predominantly since World War II, a particular formulation of the ideal and agenda of nation-state formation and required form of citizenship and civic culture has prevailed as the domi nant set of meanings for defining "America" supported by a legitimating narration of the nation's history. In this formulation America is characterized as "a paradigmatic "liberal democratic" society, shaped most by the comparatively free and equal conditions and the Enlightenment ideals said to have prevailed at its founding."[2] Nation-state formation is to be achieved through the cultivation of personal and social identities shaped by the meaning-systems of values, ideals, and legitimating norms of modernity that define citizens as *essentially* equally free and autonomous persons. The task of *e pluribus unum*, then, required the formation and mediation to, the appropriation by, all who would be citizens of a shared and unifying agenda and norms appropriate to the ordering of a stable nation in which the good life of liberty, justice, and the pursuit of happiness was to be enjoyed by "all."

However, from the very beginning this project was internally inconsistent and in tension, even in contradiction, with other tendencies that would persist in the form of traditions of norms, ideals, and practices devoted to defining and fashioning citizenship in America. First and foremost, the nation-making efforts defined by commitments to liberal democracy were constitutionalized on the supposedly "self-evident" principle of the equality of all *men*, thus deliberately excluding women from coverage, but also peoples native to this continent and to the islands of Puerto Rico, Hawaii, and Guam; men who did not own property; and people of African descent. By Rogers M. Smith's calculation, "for over 80% of U.S. history, its laws declared most of the world's population to be ineligible for full American citizenship solely because of their race, original nationality, or gender. For at least two-thirds of American history, the majority of the domestic adult population was also ineligible for full citizenship for the same reasons."[3]

Why? Because the Founders were acutely aware of the challenges to national formation presented by the then unprecedented prospect of forging "out of many, one": that there were many distinct nations *and* races (though often the terms were used interchangeably), many distinct peoples, inhabiting the earth, and that several of the most distinct and dissimilar – various nations of the white race, led by the superior Anglo-Saxons; "tribes" of the red race; and supposedly detribalized, enslaved "blacks" of the Negro or African race – had become intimately involved in relations that had to be ordered, somehow, both to allow and to further the forming of the new nation-state.

What to do? The problem was an acute one and obvious to the very perceptive and brilliant observant of the unfolding American democratic project, Alexis de Tocqueville: "almost insurmountable barriers had been raised between [the three races] by education and law, as well as by their origin and outward characteristics; but fortune has brought them together on the same soil, where, although they are mixed, they do not amalgamate, and each race fulfills its destiny apart."[4] Tocqueville went on to predict that the inevitable outcome of encounters between Anglo-Saxon-led whites and Indians would be the extermination of the Indians (who would refuse and successfully resist assimilation), and a racial war between whites and Negroes (since removal of Negroes back to Africa was impractical – too few ships for transport even to offset the birth-rate of Negroes – as was the prospect of forcing cross-racial breeding sufficient to produce a new, mulatto race) that Negroes would lose as Northern and Southern whites would set aside their sectional differences to join together in racial solidarity to defeat them.[5]

The near-daunting challenges to nation-building posed by national and racial pluralism gave rise to different traditions of efforts seeking resolution, traditions that have been as informing of this nation's history and political culture as has what generations of statespersons and intellectuals, as well as ordinary citizens, have endorsed and promoted as the "American creed": namely, what it means to be an "American," American identity, is only defined ideologically or politically, that is, by adherence to certain principles that apply to all persons equally, without regard to race, nationality or ethnicity, gender or sexuality, language, or religion. However, such a creed was definitive of citizenship for certain white and property-owning males. Given the presence and challenges of Indians and Africans, other terms of definition were required in order to denote, characterize, valorize, and order distinctions of race and nationality, and thereby order and normalize the terms of citizenship, and thus facilitate the ordering and social management of the peoples who could, and those who could not, be citizens. Equally important, as laws and norms prohibiting "miscegination" made evident, there was also a deeply felt and honored need to protect and maintain biological, as well as cultural, distinctiveness that were quickly being made decisive aspects of the identities of the descendants of Europeans-becoming-Americans, identities that, in important ways, continued Old World national identities and their cultures while contributing to the formation of new American identities that found their unity and superiority in the raciality of whiteness.

It was in service to these needs and agendas that other traditions of defining American citizenship were developed that stressed what Rogers M. Smith has termed "ethnocultural" identities. And these, Smith argues persuasively, have frequently been more dominant than citizenship identities formed out of commitments to Enlightenment liberalism's emphasis on respect for the rights of, and equal concern for, *every* human being "without regard for race, creed, color, sex, or national origin" and commitments to republicanism. Such commitments, Smith notes, have seldom been sufficiently satisfying for the Europeans of various nationalities for whom they were intended, since they required that they relinquish sometimes long-nurtured commitments to what was taken to be the "natural" authority of membership in inherited cultural communities of distinction from which were derived identities and sense of personal worth and of meaningful and valuable collective life.[6]

Smith's challenging reconstruction of America's history and political culture as involving a complex multiplicity of conflicting and contradictory identity and citizenship-defining political traditions, rather than having been founded and shaped primarily by the creedal ideals and practices of enlightened liberal democracy, as has been claimed by "a distinguished line of writers" across the centuries ("from Hetor St John Crevecoeur in the eighteenth century and Harriet Martineau and Lord Bryce in the nineteenth century to Gunnar Myrdal and Louis Hartz in the twentieth century"), virtually all of whom "appeal to the classic analysis of American politics, Tocqueville's *Democracy in America*," is especially helpful.[7] However, he does not note that liberal democracy, as *one* of America's founding and ongoing structuring political ideologies, is also a complex tradition with several tendencies, the dominant one of which has been devoted to an ethnocultural political agenda that was articulated by, and in service to, those whom Tocqueville termed "Anglo-Americans" who have been determined to fashion a nation-state by and for their "race," but one in which they and their descendants would play the leading roles.

Tocqueville was quite aware of this, but he was not alone in viewing the American project in this way. The problems posed by human diversity, especially those resulting from the presence of a plurality of races and nationalities in the same developing political communities, were clear to virtually all of the now canonical Enlightenment-influenced engaged thinkers whose ideas are the woof and warp of political liberalism (Kant, Jefferson, Mill, Hume, Rousseau, among many others), thinkers who bent their minds to the challenges of dealing with decidedly different peoples that European quests for freedom and imperialist expansions into new worlds compelled them to face, even as they wrestled with the complexities within and among European nationalities. A profound consequence, Will Kymlicka has noted, was that "for liberals like Mill, democracy is government "by the people", but self-rule is only possible if "the people" are "a people" – a nation. The members of a democracy must share a sense of political allegiance, and common nationality was said to be a precondition of that allegiance."[8] Thomas Jefferson was of like mind, others among the Founders and early settler-colonialists as well. Thus did the notion of a superior Anglo-Saxon-led white race of Europeans come to have such dominant normative, social, and material force in defining the identity and character of citizenship for the American nation-state to the exclusion of those not of European "stocks." And those "whites" who were not descended from Anglo-Saxons had to become Anglo-Saxon-like if they would be "Americans." By the terms of this version of liberal thought, "coercive assimilation": (to borrow a phrase from Kymlicka) became a prevalent means by which to "create one out of many": a stable nation-state, if it is to persist indefinitely through successive generations, must require its population to become a single "people" in the Old World sense, must require, then, that they share and take both their civic and personal identities from the same reservoir of cultural resources.

Elizabeth Minnich has identified what she takes to be the very root of the racial, ethnocultural, gendered, and social-class structured system of meanings comprising this cultural reservoir that came to dominate political, social, economic, and cultural life in general in America, knowledge-systems and educational curricula in particular. The *root problem*, as she terms it, "is visible in the false universalization that has taken a very few privileged men from a particular tradition to be the inclusive term, the norm, and the ideal for all."[9] These men – for example, Enlightenment figures such as Kant and Thomas Jefferson, John Locke and Benjamin Franklin – *abstracted* and *idealized* characteristics they thought themselves to (or should) embody, *generalized* them to other men – not women – like themselves (almost always men of the same race, nationality, and social class), and then *universalized* the idealized characteristics as definitive of all who would or could be not just men, but *human*. Thus, in the bold words of *The Declaration of Independence* (1776): "We hold these truths to be self-evident, that all men are created equal, that they are endowed by their Creator with certain unalienable Rights, that among these are Life, Liberty and the pursuit of Happiness – That to secure these rights, Governments are instituted among Men. . . ." Today, there can be no disputing the Founders' restricting coverage of equality and unalienable Rights to a particular class of white men only, nor that subsequent efforts to universalize the coverage have often been seriously impaired by conceptual errors growing from and perpetuating the root problem, in Minnich's words, of "generalizing from the few to the many" via what she calls "singular universals" (for example, using "man" as a representative term for all of humanity) that "make thinking of plurality, let alone diversity, very difficult indeed."[10]

Education through formal schooling eventually became a principal means of marshaling and mediating the defining and unifying cultural meaning-systems to successive generations by those who have been assisted in taking charge of the ongoing formation and maintenance of the American nation-state. With notable success their efforts have produced a hegemonic "monoculturalism" devoted to assimilating various ethnics of European descent to a unified America resting on each person's appropriating and living out suitable identities and loyalties given his or her place in racialized and gendered social (political, economic, cultural) hierarchies.[11] Over the years and decades, in colleges and universities in particular, programs of General Education would become the primary vehicles for efforts to formulate an epistemology and a pedagogy to facilitate the production, legitimation, and mediation of the likewise racialized, gendered, and ethnocentric knowledges for ordering the American republic, efforts legitimated by appeals to the grounding of these knowledges in the universality of a singular rationality unfolding in the historical *telos* of the leading nations of the white race of Europe. More widely, formal education, particularly public schooling from kindergarten through advanced, professional degrees, but, as well, private education devoted, mostly, to the children of those who were and are, or who seek to become, members of the well-of, influential, even powerful middle and upper classes, became the principal systems for the development, certification, thus the legitimation, and the mediation of "knowledge" – based meaning-systems through which to inculcate the norms, ideals, and practices definitive of personal and civic identities needed to make peoples into "a people," "a nation" of invidiously hierarchic "Americans."

There were, however, always persons white, red, black, and otherwise who disagreed with the interpretations of founding principles and practices that provided for coercive assimilation, racialized enslavement, and gendered exclusion from citizenship, persons who fought unsuccessfully for full citizenship rights for those excluded and oppressed. And some of the most passionate and dedicated of those who struggled thusly were themselves from among the excluded and oppressed. In a variety of ways they raised their voices and otherwise exerted themselves, singularly and in conjunction with a variety of others, to combat the blatant injustices. Their efforts, taken up and continued by others across the centuries of American history, constitute informing legacies of great significance in their own right, as legacies of struggles for justice, respect, and full citizenship rights by and in behalf of people of African descent, peoples native to this continent, women of all races and ethnicities, and others.

Still, these legacies have seldom been made part of America's public civic culture or of the curricula that would make of many one nation, curricula that, for a number of reasons, for all the revisions they have undergone over the years, have generally been continually (mis-) represented as enjoying legitimating lineages that originated in Ancient Greece and Rome, progressed through Europe, and, in their Modern incarnations, provide the founding principles of right (justice) and requisite individual and civic values for a stable and enduring American republic. It has been this misrepresentation that has informed the hegemonic consensus undergirding the project of unifying, monocultural education.

Long challenged, that consensus has now been disrupted severely and is not about to be restored, various efforts to the contrary. Developments of various kinds – demographic, ideological, political, economic, social – that in many instances have spawned challenges to the once prevailing consensus, are local, national, and global in scope, among them the following:

1 The continuing legacies of the Civil Rights, Black Power, Anti-(Vietnam) War, and contemporary women's movements against invidious racial, gender, and economic hierarchies and other injustices at home and against American imperialism and hegemony abroad.

2 The impacts of successful anti-colonial struggles in the so-called Third World on European nation-states and the United States, leading to continuing challenges to America's post-World War II

invidious dominance in international economies and politics.

3　The combination of global population shifts, consequent of major political, economic, and cultural developments, America's attraction as the fabled land of stability and unencumbered opportunities to achieve the good life through one's own efforts, and the country's relative and shifting openness to immigrants – all make this a country to which many still come. The result is seismic demographic changes in America in terms of streams of new immigrants: 1 million a year, more in the past decade than in the "great wave" of immigrants from 1901 through 1910. At present rates, after the year 2050 people of Western European origins will be a numerical minority in the US, and African Americans, once the largest minority in the country, will be outnumbered by Hispanics; the total population will pass 390 million, with serious implications for, and likely serious burdens on, schools, social services, etc.[12]

With the latest immigrants, most of whom are not of European descent, come experiences and legacies from cultures other than Europe. Consequently, American society is becoming increasingly diverse culturally, is becoming, by one account, " 'the first universal nation', a truly multicultural society marked by unparalleled diversity."[13] Further, this is happening at the same time as the consensus sustaining the invidiously hierarchized, intended unifying, racialized, gendered, Eurocentric cultural hegemony has been fully disclosed and critiqued (though not yet widely accepted) and the motivational and legitimating resources of a democratic politics of pluralism have been tapped to fuel and authenticate a "politics of difference." A goal now increasingly widely shared is to move beyond the important but insufficient liberal "politics of universalism," based, in part, on an individualism that in truth has involved erroneous generalizations from the few to the many, to press instead for the recognition of the identity and equal status of racial and ethnic cultural groups and genders.[14] One of the complex forms of the "politics of difference" appears in struggles over "multiculturalism" as a replacement for hegemonic monoculturalism.

In this unsettling and highly charged historical context the meaning-systems and norms that would "make of many, one" can no longer be taken for granted. Quite the contrary, these are now hotly contested matters. Thus are we living through a period of seeming cultural crisis: a loss of any overriding governing and guiding consensus, continuing raucous debate too often devoid of civility, passionate proposals offering new cultural agendas which are supposed to be correctives for the sins of the past that are themselves, however, uninformed by any new abiding consensus rooted in shared principles. Complicating matters even further, part of the difficulty of the moment is the skepticism, widely shared by many educators and academics especially, as well as by many politicians, parents, and professionals of virtually all kinds, regarding the viability, let alone the legitimacy, of any effort to identify principles that might provide unifying "foundations" anchored by a universal and invariant, singular form of reasonableness.

Periods of social change, however substantial, involve more than threats to ordered living. Also involved are challenges of opportunity. Such is the case with America's unprecedented cultural diversification fueled and sanctioned by the democratic impulses of the politics of difference-recognition. The challenge, of course, the opportunity, is to find "the ties that bind" those with welcomed differences into a united nation of diverse ones – individuals as well as groups – without the injustices of invidious, dehumanizing hierarchies and hegemonies predicated on race, ethnicity, or gender.

Education can be – must be – a major factor in achieving such an end, for schooling at all levels continues to be the major mechanism of secondary civic socialization. Colleges and universities in particular are the sites at which much of the critical reflection, reinterpretation, and experimentation must go on in and across disciplines in the mediation of learning to students who will inherit this country. And these efforts must be structured not by narrowly conceived, discipline-imminent norms of research, scholarship, and pedagogy thought to have no connection to "politics." Rather, in the midst of the unprecedented historical situation in which we find ourselves, these must be decidedly self-conscious efforts devoted to the formation of a framework for local and national (and international) political life that allows for the democratically inclusive yet critical recognition and appreciation of the cultural practices and legacies of the persons and peoples who together comprise our body-politic. The goal is to preserve a democratically structured pluralism that is not isolationist but integrates into a united whole the varieties of persons who take primary facets of their complex and changing identities, as well as their life-commitments and agendas, from cultural communities configured by meaning-systems in which racial, ethnic, gender, and sexual commitments, among others, play defining, positive roles that these persons do not wish to relinquish.

What is needed, however, is the refashioning of monocultural general education into a venture devoted to these ends, a venture that must involve clarifying and cultivating a host of reorientations, and revised as well, as new practices that together are covered by the term "multi-culturalism." And at the core of this venture there must be "the formulation of an epistemology and a pedagogy that facilitates the translation of local knowledges and their interconnections" of particular cultural groups so as to allow them to be shared by others as a major factor in the continuous process of nation-building that no longer requires total assimilation on the way to unity, but strives for unity in and through diversity.[15]

We cannot go forward by going backward. Let us, then, continue the American experiment, but this time in an effort to fashion a stable, just, and, let us hope, long-running nation-state that is multinational, poly-ethnic, and multiracial. If we would be successful, then we will have to forge new understandings of America's history, of the histories of its peoples, and new understandings of its probable as well as possible futures. And we must begin by not just acknowledging national, ethnic, and racial pluralism along with socially and culturally significant differences linked to gender and sexuality, and to socioeconomic circumstances and status, among other important factors, but by embracing all of these while working to enhance what is good about each while limiting, as much as possible, what is not so good.

We might begin, then, by accepting, as Nathan Glazer has recently come to concede (though I hope we will do so less grudgingly than Glazer, but instead, even enthusiastically), that, in his words, "we are all multiculturalists now," since various efforts to maintain previously invidiously characterized racial and ethnic distinctiveness, as well as many associated with gender and sexuality, have displaced and all but completely discredited the goal of "assimilation" to a color-blind, sex/gender neutral civic identity without regard for racial or ethnic distinctions, and displaced from predominance the still not totally discredited ethnocultural Americanism of white racial superiority.[16] In the arena of education in particular, Glazer declares that multiculturalists have "won": that is,

> we all accept a greater degree of attention to minorities and women and their role in American history and social studies and literature classes in schools. Those few who want to return American education to a period in which the various subcultures were ignored, and in which America was presented as the peak and end-product of civilization, cannot expect to make any progress in the schools.[17]

Nor I hope, in political, economic, cultural, and civic life generally.

But what progress shall we make if, in truth, "we *are* all multiculturalists now?" What will serve us as principles and norms by which to order our diverse lives, individually and collectively, to live out such a recognition in the context of a stable, just, and harmonious nation-state? What do we need in the way of settled and widely shared understandings to facilitate the fashioning of the needed norms and principles, mediating them to those who are and would become citizens, and have them be appropriately satisfying and acceptable to virtually all such persons and peoples as to provide the ties that bind?

To say the least, there is a great, great deal to be addressed in these questions. A central matter, of course, is the way in which we understand ourselves as human beings in all of our complexities: as individual persons who are also involved, in varying degrees of intimacy, voluntarily and involuntarily, with collectivities of other persons, some of which collectivities also comprise continuing, yet always changing, legacies of particular "peoples" or subgroupings of peoples. Understandings that encompass well these complexities have never played a predominant role in shaping the civic culture of the United States of America. Why the knowledge and orientations that would undergird and nurture such understandings has not been ready to hand and widely available and legitimated is a case well made by Elizabeth Kamarck Minnich in *Transforming Knowledge*, to cite just one example among many others, as she shares the findings and insights from her years of conversing and working with and advising others in developing Women Studies programs, as well as from her open and thoughtful consideration of the efforts of women and men of various racial and ethnic groups to transform the knowledge-systems that have distorted the histories and cultures, thus the lives and futures, of their particular peoples, while providing so much in the way of the norms and ideals that have shaped the meaning-systems in which Americans have formed their identities as persons and citizens. This transforming work, in educational institutions especially as primary cites of producing, certifying, and mediating knowledge to successive generations of citizens-in-the-making, must be continued and consolidated.

In the process, what has been widely and loudly disparaged as the pursuit of the "political correctness" of "multiculturalism" must become widely accepted and promoted as a correct agenda for knowledge-production and mediation in support of the political formation of a nation-state of a multiplicity of culture-bearing, culture-producing, and culture-sharing peoples. There can be no gathering of human beings into ordered associations without "politics": that is, without attending to and regulating the needs, desires, and interests of those associating in service to conserving the association and those associated. There can be, then, no such regulation without norms for distinguishing what is correct from what is incorrect. Consequently, *no* organization or community of human beings that intends to persist across time and generations can dispense with correctness in political life.

The issue, as it is for America today, is what norms will be appropriate for achieving a just and well-ordered nation-state that recognizes as equal citizens females and males of a diverse multitude of racial, ethnic, national, and other groupings, and does so, when and where appropriate, on the basis of their individuality as well as members of natal and adopted cultural groupings. One of the focal arenas of these efforts will continue to be that in which are constructed accounts of the historical unfoldings of the American nation-state and its peoples, accounts that serve the important function, as well, of contributing to the ongoing development of a civic culture in and through which all persons form crucial portions of their identities as citizens.

What will citizenship mean in an explicitly "multicultural" America after wide acceptance of the need to achieve an *integrated* nation-state of multiple nationalities, ethnicities, races and gendered and sexually identified groups and other social classes, instead of seeking political and social order through coercive *assimilation*? What might be the terms of such citizenship?

These questions have been the focus of a long line of engaged thinkers concerned for the success and well-being of the American experiment, among them a great many of those today identified as "multiculturalists." But contrary to the concerns of more than a few that the multiculturalists, perhaps unwittingly, have been sowing the seeds of fragmentation the likes and consequences of which are all too painfully evident in the former Yugoslavia and Soviet Union, as well as in Rwanda, or nurturing sentiments that might soon express themselves as tensions challenging national unity, as is the case in Canada, the overwhelming majority of the varied and similar quests of proponents of "multiculturalism" in the United States of America have been devoted to greater and fairer *inclusion* in, not separation from or the dismemberment of, this nation-state. All references to and characterizations of these persons and organizations as "separatists" are thus inaccurate and inappropriate. So, too, is conflating "integration" with "assimilation".

We need better terms and understandings. One worthwhile source among many to consider is Will Kymlicka's efforts in *Multicultural Citizenship* to provide both as part of his quest to refashion liberal–democratic political theory to accommodate a theory of group-differentiated citizenship based on a theory of group-differentiated rights for national and ethnic minority groups in multinational, multi-ethnic societies such as the United States of America and Canada, nation-states that are still to be constrained by definitions of the rights of citizenship of individuals without regard for their race, creed, color, gender, sexual orientation, age, or physical ability.

Many people – individually and with others in organizations, institutions and sociopolitical movements organized around sexuality and gender; race, nationality, and ethnicity; socioeconomic class, age, and ability; in groupings that cut across all of these sets of characteristics – continue to wrestle with these complicated and challenging matters. And in numerous, important instances they have provided inspiring, more or less successful examples of what might be done, and how we might go about doing so, in order for the United States of America to become a vibrant and successful deliberately multinational, multiracial, and poly-ethnic nation-state in which women and men, of all social classes and cultural groupings from which people take important facets of their complex identities, no longer suffer constraints on, or unfair enhancements of, their lives and opportunities due to invidious hierarchical rank-orderings of lives and life-chances. May the struggles continue....

Notes

1   See Arthur O. Lovejoy, *The Great Chain of Being: A Study in the History of an Idea* (Cambridge, Mass. Harvard University Press, 1964).
2   Rogers M. Smith, "Beyond Tocqueville, Myrdal, and Hartz: The Multiple Traditions in America," *American Political Science Review*, vol. 87, no. 3 (September 1993), pp. 549–66.
3   Ibid.
4   Alexis de Tocqueville, *Democracy in America, Volume I* (New York: Vintage Books, 1990), p. 332.
5   Tocqueville, "The Present and Probable Future Condition of the Three Races That Inhabit the Territory of the United States," chapter XVIII of *Democracy in America, Volume I*, pp. 331–434.
6   Rogers M. Smith, "The 'American Creed' and American Identity: The Limits of Liberal Citizenship in the United States," *Western Political Quarterly*. vol. 41 (June 1988), pp. 225–51.
7   Rogers M. Smith, "Beyond Tocqueville, Myrdal, and Hartz." p. 549.
8   Will Kymlicka, *Multicultural Citizenship: A Liberal Theory of Minority Rights* (Oxford: Clarendon Press, 1995), p. 52.
9   Elizabeth Kamarck Minnich, *Transforming Knowledge* (Philadelphia: Temple University Press, 1990), p. 2.
10 Minnich identifies and provides a very insightful and learned discussion of four kinds of conceptual errors "that derive from and continue the root

problem: (1) errors of faulty generalization; (2) errors of circular reasoning: (3) mystified concepts even – or especially – on the highest levels of abstraction that result from (1) and (2); and, finally, (4) partial knowledge that is not recognized as such, but, indeed, sets the standard for 'sound' knowledge." *Transforming Knowledge*, p. 3.

11 Michael Geyer, "Multiculturalism and the Politics of General Education," *Critical Inquiry* (Spring 1993), pp. 499–533.

12 *Time Magazine* special issue, vol. 142, no. 21, fall 1993.

13 Ibid., pp. 10ff.

14 Charles Taylor. *Multiculturalism: Examining the Politics of Recognition*, edited and introduced by Amy Gutmann (Princeton: Princeton University Press, 1994).

15 Michael Geyer, "Multiculturalism and the Politics of General Education," *Critical Inquiry* (spring 1993), p. 528.

16 Nathan Glazer, *We Are All Multiculturalist Now* (Cambridge, Mass.: Harvard University Press, 1997).

17 Ibid., p. 14.

Part VIII

Pragmatism

18

Ceremony and Rationality in the Haudenosaunee Tradition

Scott L. Pratt

In his 1987 address to the Cornell Conference on "The Iroquois Great Law of Peace and the US Constitution," John Mohawk, a member of the Seneca Nation and a professor of American Studies, responded to the observation that the Iroquois, or Haudenosaunee, possessed a tradition of law. "That part is definitely true," he said, "but the Iroquois tradition of law is not a tradition of law, exactly. The Iroquois tradition of law is a tradition of responsible thinking." He continued: "It is not something written in paragraphs or lines because it doesn't matter whether the letter of the things is right. The questions that have to be put before the people are *what is the thinking? Is the thinking right?*" (Mohawk, 1992, p. 23). But what does it mean to "think responsibly," that is, to be "rational" from within the Haudenosaunee tradition? In a time when conceptions of rationality developed within the European philosophical tradition are being rejected, the search for alternatives could be well served through a reconsideration of the Haudenosaunee tradition.

In contrast to European conceptions of rationality as a process of acquisition, I will propose that "responsible thinking" or rationality from within the Haudenosaunee tradition may be understood as a process of conversation and responsive action.[1] While acquisition implies the interaction of a passive object and an active thinker, conversation implies active involvement among all participants in the process. While acquisition emphasizes the accumulation of understanding for its own sake, the Haudenosaunee conception emphasizes understanding for the sake of responsive action. The idea that rational thinking is a process of conversation is suggested by a close examination of three pervasive background views about the nature of individuals and the traditional notion of "orenda" or "voice." The features of conversation which frame a conception of responsible thinking are suggested in a close examination of the traditional Iroquoian ceremony, ononharoia[2] or "dream-guessing rite," in which "voices" are heard, interpreted, and acted upon.[3] The ceremony serves as a particularly good starting point for understanding the features of responsible thinking, in part because its traditional practice is well-documented.[4] Further, it is one of the oldest Iroquoian practices and its form is repeated with some modification in a wide range of other Iroquoian practices, including less formal dream interpretation, curative ceremonies, the Condolence Council, and the deliberative practices adopted by the Haudenosaunee Confederacy.[5]

In the *Jesuit Relations* of 1639, Father Jerome Lalemant expressed concern to his superiors in France:

> [The rite of dream interpretation and fulfillment] is the strangest servitude and slavery that can be imagined; and never did [a] galley slave so fear to fail in his duty as these peoples dread to fall short in the least detail of all their wretched ceremonies, – for there would follow from this omission, not only the privation of what they were expecting, but even physical punishment, which the devil for this reason exercises upon these poor wretches. (*Relations*, vol. 17, p. 161)[6]

Father Lalemant describes a ceremony which took place around 1639.[7] The ceremony, a version of the ononharoia, began when a special council of the village in which he lived decided to respond to the request for the ceremony by a woman from the village who was ill. According to the story related by Lalemant, the woman had seen "in an instant ... the Moon stoop down from above" to talk with her. After her encounter with the moon, the woman became "prostrated with a giddiness in the head and a contraction of the muscles, which made [those around her] conclude that she was sick of a disease of which the remedy is a ceremony [the ononharoia]" (*Relations*, vol. 17, p. 169). In response to the request, a council of the village was convened and "there it was declared," says Lalemant, "that this affair [i.e. the woman's request] was one of those most important to the welfare of the country" (ibid.). Following the decision, the "Captains" or elders of the village made a series of announcements to the village that the ceremony was to begin. Shortly before the ailing woman arrived at the village, another council was held to organize the ceremony. Here, the Jesuit missionaries living in the village objected to the ceremony as devil worship. Ignoring the Jesuit objections, one of the village leaders responded: "Courage, then, young men; courage, women; courage, my brothers; let us render to our country this service, so necessary and important, according to the customs of our ancestors!" (ibid., pp. 170–1).

In her encounter with the moon, the woman understood the moon (who presented herself as a young woman) to request a number of gifts. These gifts, which included "six dogs of a certain form and color; ... fifty cakes of tobacco; ... [and] a large canoe," were quickly delivered by "two men and two girls" selected for the task by the Council.[8] Once the gifts were received, a celebration was held which Lalemant describes as "a general mania of all the people of the village" (ibid., p. 177). Following the celebration (or perhaps as part of it), the villagers went from house to house "proposing at each fire each person's own and special desire – according as he is able to get information and enlightenment by dreams, – not openly, but through Riddles [les Enigmes]" (ibid., p. 179). Finally, the ailing woman herself went through each house and proposed a "riddle" of her own which each person of the village tried to solve. Lalemant writes: "Each one straightaway applies himself to ascertain its solution, and at the same time they throw to the sick woman whatever they imagine [pensé] it may be [that will fulfill her dream]" (ibid., p. 185). Lalemant continues: "Those who are attending the sick woman collect all these things and go out burdened with kettles, pots, skins, robes, blankets, cloaks, necklaces, belts, leggins, shoes, corn, fish, – in short, everything that is used by the Savages, and which they have been able to think of, to attain the satisfaction of the sick woman's desire" (ibid.). At last the riddle was solved and the village celebrated again. A closing council was then held to report on "all that [had] taken place, and, among other things, the number of riddles solved" (ibid., p. 187). Lalemant concludes the account with an ambivalent summary: "Nevertheless, this poor unhappy creature [the woman who encountered the moon] found herself much better after the feast than before, although she was not entirely free from, or cured of her trouble" (ibid.).

In order to understand the process described by Lalemant as a process of responsible thinking, it is important to first identify three background views regarding the relationship of individuals and communities in early Iroquoian society which are suggested by and supported by the available literature.

The first view is that individuals, rather than being ideally autonomous, were viewed in early Iroquoian societies as continuous with their communities. While "individual men" of the community sometimes did "roam free" as suggested by Anthony Wallace in his influential discussion of the role of the ononharoia, they often did so in the context of carrying out the

community's interests of hunting, war, diplomacy, and exploration.[9] Such
activities were not autonomous, but rather were established and bound by
broad custom, the decisions of governing councils, and by the needs of
clan and family. This continuity between individual and community can
be understood as having at least two aspects. First, an individual's identity
depends upon her or his connection with and place in the larger community. This sort of continuity is well illustrated by the Iroquoian views of
personal identity. Identities, at least in the colonial period, were not
viewed as fixed, but rather were viewed as the result of the actions of and
interactions between individuals, their families, and the wider community. The importance of actions and interactions in constructing personal
identity is shown in the practice described by the Jesuits as "reincarnation" or "resuscitation," where the identity of a person lost to the
community could be assumed by another so that the lost person would be
restored (see, for example, *Relations*, vol. 16, pp. 201–3). Such "reincar-
nations" were generally successful in that the individual, chosen by
members of the community, who accepted the identity of another would
"become" that person – both in their own eyes and in the eyes of the
community.[10]

The second aspect of continuity concerns Iroquoian conceptions of
ideal or valued behaviors. In general, good or favored behavior of an
individual is behavior which exhibits both an interest in others and a
constructive character. In contrast, evil or disfavored behavior exhibits
self-interest and a destructive character. The Iroquoian origin story suggests these conceptions.[11] According to the story, shortly after the earth
was formed, twin sons were born to the daughter of the first woman,
Ataensic or Sky Woman. The first son, often named Sapling or Good
Mind, was born in the usual way, but his brother, called Flint or Evil
Mind, burst from his mother's side, killing her.[12] While Sapling is credited
in the stories with bringing animals, human beings, and beneficial plants
to the earth, Flint is credited with trying, at every turn, to block the work
of his brother. In one version of the story, Sapling defeats his brother in a
struggle for dominance of the earth, and he concludes: "Look what you
have done to the tree where Ancient One [their grandmother] was wont to
care for us, and whose branches have supplied us with food. See how you
have torn this tree and stripped it of its valuable products. This tree was
designed to support the life of men-beings and now you have injured it. I
must banish you to the region of the great cave and you shall have the
name of Destroyer" (Parker, 1989, pp. 70–1). While Sapling or Good
Mind seeks to preserve, Flint or Evil Mind seeks to destroy. The ideal
behaviors for both men and women in Iroquoian society are ones which

build and support the greater community and, in this sense also, individuals are continuous with their community.[13] This view is further reinforced in the *Basic Call to Consciousness* published by the Mohawk Nation in 1978: "We believe that man is real, a part of the Creation, and that his duty is to support Life in conjunction with the other beings. That is why we call ourselves Ongwhehonwhe – Real People" (Akwasasne Notes, 1978, p. 72).

The second background view is that persons recognized as part of the community include both human and non-human beings. On this view, beings other than human are viewed both as individuals with identities and as intimately connected with the lives of the human members of the community.[14] Given this view, the concerns of human beings and non-human beings are all of potential concern to the community as a whole. In the event that a community faces a challenge, it would also follow that a response to the challenge by the community will involve all the connected persons.[15] This assumption is suggested by a number of traditional Iroquoian stories. For example, in one common story, an unwanted boy is rescued from a cave by animals who propose him for adoption. The family of bears, it is decided by the assembled council, is most appropriate for the boy. In their introduction to a Tuscarora version of the story, Blair Rudes and Dorothy Crouse observe that narratives of the adoption of human children by animals served "in part … to underscore the community of man [*sic*] and animals as creatures of nature, and to instruct children of a tribe in the parallels between human care and concern for their young and that of animals" (Rudes and Crouse, 1987 p. 222).[16] A second story, attributed to the Seneca leader, Cornplanter, provides an account of the reason animals can no longer speak directly to human beings (Canfield, 1902, pp. 103–17). Cornplanter portrays human beings and animals as part of the same community, sharing knowledge, ceremonies, and resources. Once human beings became adept at the skills of the animals (e.g. hunting, tracking, concealment), some of the animals became jealous and conspired against the human beings in a secret council. Significantly, the animals are portrayed as comparable to human beings both in interests and concerns and in their form of deliberation. In the end, the "Great Spirit" changes the language of human beings so that they could no longer easily communicate with their "animal brothers." In both stories, animals are presented as similar in important respects to human beings and as having a share in the interests and activities of the larger community even after communication is made difficult.

The third background view is that individuals posses "orenda."[17] According to J.N.B. Hewitt, "orenda" is best defined as "mystical potency," that is, as the "efficient cause of all phenomena, all the activities of [the] environment" (Hewitt, 1902, p. 36). The term "orenda," Hewitt notes, is an anglicized version of the Huron term "iareñda" or "oreñda" and based on the same root "-eñ-" used in the Mohawk, Cayuga, Onondaga, Seneca, and Tuscarora languages (ibid., p. 37n). Hewitt suggests that this "mystical potency" is a notion commonly accepted within many North American native cultures and is comparable to the Algonquin and Ojibwa notion of "manitou," the Lakota notion of "wakan," and the Shoshonean notion of "pokunt." This "primitive" notion, Hewitt argues, can provide a conceptual starting point for an understanding of religion.[18]

Hewitt's interpretation of orenda, however, suggests an ambiguity. On one hand, orenda is taken to mean a power or potency of a uniform nature possessed by all things. In this sense, orenda is comparable to the European notion of being. On the other hand, orenda seems to be a principle of individuation, in the sense that individuals appear to possess particular orendas, that is, distinctive powers or potencies. Hewitt suggests both interpretations in his 1928 report to the Bureau of American Ethnology:

> [Orenda is the] name of the fictive force, principle, or magic power which was assumed by the inchoate reasoning of primitive man to be inherent in every body and being of nature and in every personified attribute, property, or activity. ... This hypothetic principle was conceived to be immaterial, occult, impersonal, mysterious in mode of action, limited in function and efficiency, and not at all omnipotent, local and not omnipresent, and ever embodied or immanent in some object. (Hewitt, 1928, p. 608n.)

While the first sense provides a way to talk about the "being" of things in the world (i.e. as one feature shared by everything which "is"), the second sense leads to an explanation of action in the world as a "ceaseless struggle of one orenda against another" (Hewitt, 1902, p. 40). William Jones, in his 1905 discussion of the Algonquin notion of manitou, observes this same tension. Based on his research, Jones concludes that "manitou" denotes "a cosmic, mysterious property ... believed to [exist] in everything in nature" which at once is understood as "impersonal" and, with respect to particular things in nature, is also personal or distinctive (Jones, 1905, p. 190). While Hewitt makes little of the tension, Jones concludes that manitou is "an unsystematic belief" which becomes "obscure and confused when the property becomes identified with objects in nature" (ibid.).

A linguistic analysis of the Iroquoian term "orenda," however, appears to support a somewhat different interpretation. While Hewitt focuses on orenda as meaning a power or potency, both Hewitt's discussion and the likely etymology of the term support the idea that orenda may also mean "its song" or "its voice" or, more generally, its expression. The root word of orenda and its related terms, "-(C)ɛn (õ)-" is described by Wallace Chafe in his linguistic analysis of the Seneca language as the root used for terms meaning "song" and "sing" as well as terms referring to holding ceremonies and wishing (Chafe 1967, p. 50).[19] The Seneca term identified by Hewitt for orenda, "oenna" (Hewitt, 1902, p. 37n.), appears to be the same as the term listed by Chafe, "ʔoɛnõʔ", as meaning "its song." Additionally, the term and its root are closely connected with another Seneca root, "-wɛn (õ)-", meaning voice, utterance, word, or language. Depending upon how one interprets Hewitt's orthography, his term "oenna" may alternatively be the term rendered by Chafe as "ʔowɛ:nõʔ" or "word" (Chafe, 1967, p. 85). This sense of orenda as song, voice, or expression is important because rather than suggesting the problematic notion of a ubiquitous power or property, it instead suggests something which is better viewed as an activity or event. In this case, as a kind of activity, it may be an activity common to all things, but in its individual occurrence it can also serve as a principle of individuation which is both overt and subject to being heard, copied, and interpreted.[20]

Hewitt alludes to this alternative sense of orenda in his discussion of the historical origins of the notion of orenda as "power." According to Hewitt, "primitive" people first observe action in the world and attribute it to a causal force:

> Since action or motion was held to be a manifestation of a subsumed mystic potency by a living agent, and since activity is usually accompanied by sound or sounds, it followed naturally that noises or sounds were in like manner interpreted to be the certain evidence of the utterance, use, or putting forth of such mystic potence to effect some purpose by the bodies or body emitting sound. (Hewitt, 1902, pp. 35–6)

Consider the connection between song and power in the claim that locusts control summer heat. Hewitt observes that the literal meaning of one Iroquoian term for locusts is "it habitually ripens the corn." The insect acquired the name, he says,

> because when it sang in the early morning the day became very hot; and so the inchoate mind of the Iroquois inferred that the locust controlled summer heat; its mere presence was not thus interpreted, but its singing was held to signify that it was exerting its orenda to bring on the heat necessary to ripen the corn. (Ibid., p. 40).

Hewitt connects the notion of orenda with song, but understands song as only a sign. If we understand orenda as a reference to the locusts' voices, however, rather than simply signifying the exertion of orenda, we can understand the voices themselves as the orenda: that is, an expression of the locusts which has or calls for certain consequences. If this is the case, however, then orenda marks an expression of individuals which operates in conjunction with listeners or respondents. The song of the locusts calls for certain effects. If the air (or winds) are likewise animate and individual (which Iroquoian cosmology holds they are),[21] then a change in weather is not "made" by the locusts, but rather can be viewed as the result of a communicative interaction between the locusts and the winds. In this case, the singing of the locusts can be understood as causal in the same way that one might understand one's words to cause someone to shut a door or read a book or one's lullaby to cause a child to sleep. In the context of a populated world, the song of the locust is a song of individuals heard and responded to by others. With respect to the relationship between individuals and community, orenda, under the proposed interpretation, marks a communicative connection between individuals who "possess" orenda or have a voice and the listening and responding community.

The notion of orenda, then, draws together the first two background assumptions. The first, that individuals are continuous with their communities, seems both consistent with the notion of orenda and perhaps is necessary to it. If orenda is understood as the song, voice, or expression of a person, then it seems to demand as well the connection of the individual with others who will listen and respond. At the same time, the idea that communities include human and non-human persons is also consistent with the idea that all things (or most things) have their songs or voices and that these songs or voices are what mark them as particular individuals, that is, persons with identities.[22]

When we consider the ononharoia again, it is interesting to find that what Lalemant took to be the "desires" of individuals, may instead be understood as orenda. Consider, for example, the term, "ondinoc," identified by the Jesuits as meaning "desire" (*Relations*, vol. 17, pp. 155, 163, 179, and vol. 33, pp. 189–93). Given Jesuit orthography, it appears that the term may have the root "-(C)ɛn (õ)-".[23] If this is so, then the term may suggest that what is at issue is viewed as the song of someone. According to Lalemant, "if you ask [someone who proposes an ondinoc], what is the cause of the desire, he makes no answer except, 'ondays oki haendaerandic,' 'the thing under the form of which my familiar Demon appeared to me, gave me this advice'" (*Relations*, vol. 17, p. 155).[24] However, Lalemant's comment suggests that the issue is less a desire in the usual sense and more a matter of advice spoken by another person. Lalemant further observes that "these ondinoncs [*sic*] are always accompanied by feasts or dances; the ceremonies of these and even *the songs that are sung* there are for the most part dictated by the Demon" (ibid., emphasis added).[25] If "ondinoc" implies the song or utterance of some person, then it follows that what is at issue in the ononharoia is not necessarily the "desire" of the individual, but rather the utterance of a person which needs interpretation and response, that is, something closely related to orenda.

The idea that the "dreams" or ondinoc at issue in the ononharoia are best understood as the songs or voices of others which, as signs, demand interpretation, is supported as well by the Iroquoian terms used to describe the rite. In his analysis of the Midwinter Ceremony of the Cayuga Longhouse, Frank Speck observes that the "dream guessing rite" is called "sagodiwenha' gwus," literally translated "her word taken off" (Speck, 1949, p. 122). Part of the Onondaga version of the creation story (recorded by Hewitt), takes place during the "dream feast," and the process of dream interpretation and fulfillment is spoken of as "hoñwaweñnì'saks," which is literally translated "they his Word seek to divine."[26] The same term is used in the Mohawk version of the story and a similar term is used in the Seneca language: "hoñwanweñni'sas."[27] The root "-weñn-" (or "-wɛn(õ)-") appears in a wide range of terms and is consistently taken to mean word, language, or, perhaps, sign.[28]

Given the background views and the notion of orenda as "voice" or expression, the ononharoia may be understood as a kind of conversation. If we view individuals as continuous with their communities, as human or other than human, and suppose that individuals have orenda, then the ononharoia may be understood as a response to occasions when orendas are expressed problematically and there is need for interpretation and response. Responsible thinking, I propose, can be understood as the process of responding well to the calls or expressions of others.

If we accept that the ononharoia is a kind of responsible thinking, then we may turn to the practice itself in order to identify some of the features of rationality. At least four features of the practice seem significant. These features relate to (1) the function of ceremony, (2) the use of available resources, (3) the process as interactive and experimental, and (4) the role of community.

The first feature of responsible thinking suggested by the practice of the ononharoia is that ceremony serves a crucial framing function for the process and does so in two ways: one in terms of rites or rituals and, the other, in terms of establishing roles in the process. Each ceremony, following Chafe's terminology, is made up of a series of rituals (Chafe, 1961, pp. 1–2). These rituals or rites appear to serve the necessary function of bringing the community together to focus on the issue at hand. This function of the ritual aspect of ceremony is suggested by Paula Gunn Allen:

> The purpose of a ceremony is to integrate: to fuse the individual with his or her fellows, the community of people with that of the other kingdoms, and this larger communal group with the worlds beyond this one. ... But all ceremonies, whether for war or healing, create and support the sense of community that is the bedrock of tribal life. (Allen, 1992, pp. 62–3)

The "Thanksgiving Speech," for example, seems to fulfill this function explicitly. According to Chafe (1961, p. 2), the Thanksgiving Speech is "the most ubiquitous of all Seneca rituals, for it opens and closes nearly every ceremony."[29] According to Tooker the Thanksgiving Speech, in effect, frames the ceremony:

> The basic framework of an Iroquois ceremony is the Thanksgiving Speech, performance of the rites appropriate to the occasion [such as the interpretation and satisfaction of "dreams"], Thanksgiving Speech, and distribution of the feast. If the ceremonies last more than one day, this pattern is repeated at each ceremonial gathering. (Tooker, 1970, p. 7)

While the Jesuit accounts do not explicitly note the ceremonial structure of the ononharoia, it would seem appropriate to conclude that the Thanksgiving Speech was an un-noted part of the ceremonies they observed. Significantly, the Thanksgiving Speech is not strictly a matter of giving thanks, but also a mode of greeting. Chafe's (1961) presentation of Haudenosaunee Thanksgiving speeches collected through the Seneca nation at Tonawanda make this point clear. The term Chafe translates as "thanksgiving" actually seems to have no equivalent in English, but suggests both thanks and greeting. "The trouble," Chafe says, "is that the Seneca concept is broader than that expressed by any simple English term, and covers not only the conventionalized amenities of both thanking and greeting, but also a more general feeling of happiness over the existence of something or someone" (ibid., p. 1). The thanksgiving speeches which form a central role in beginning and ending ceremonies involve extensive thanks/greetings to a wide range of persons viewed as a part of the larger community. The *Basic Call to Consciousness* notes: "We give greeting and thanksgiving to the many supporters of our own lives – the corn, beans, squash, the winds, the sun" (Akwasasne Notes, 1978, p. 72).[30] The formal thanksgiving/greeting, like the ceremonial calls to the village described by Lalemant, helps focus the community for its response to the "dreams" proposed.

The second way that ceremonies frame judgment is by providing established roles for the participants. For example, it is clearly the case that the dreamer, or the one proposing the ondinoc, has a prescribed role which does not allow for her or him to say what she or he thinks the proper interpretation will be. At the same time, the other participants are to serve as active investigators, literally throwing objects to the dreamer as possible answers. The resulting structure parallels the standard organization of council in Iroquoian communities. Most councils or meetings of the community take place around a central fire where participants are grouped into "sides of the fire." Participants then carry out roles determined by their place around the fire. One side of the fire is generally responsible for raising an issue, while the other side is charged with attempting to settle it.[31] While such roles may appear arbitrary or unimportant in the abstract, when placed in a context where the ononharoia is viewed as a kind of responsible thinking, they become practical and justified. By requiring that the dreamer limit her or his contributions, the process is guarded against the dreamer proposing a solution prematurely or from opting out of the process before its resolution. By requiring the community to actively propose interpretations which can be overruled by the dreamer, the process is protected from the community imposing an interpretation on the dreamer.[32]

In sum, while the ritual components of the ceremony provide an active call and formal focus for participants in the process of judgment, the established roles of participants support a division of labor appropriate for carrying out the function of interpreting and responding to a voice.

The second feature of responsible thinking suggested by the ononharoia is that the process of judgment involves all of the material and conceptual resources available within the community. What is used, for example, to interpret the "dreams" proposed always appear to be objects of ordinary life, indicating that interpretation and fulfillment will require things at hand, within and part of the community. Significantly, it also suggests that anything in the community may be used. The availability of materials to understand and fulfill "dreams" provides an important verification of the continuity of individuals and community by suggesting the assumption that everything in the community is available to the dreamer in response to the voice which speaks to them. To use only the most convenient resources rather than the most appropriate would also mark the process as at least a partial failure.

The third feature of the ononharoia relevant to responsible thinking repeats an element that has emerged in each of the other two aspects discussed. The process is one which is interactive and experimental and, in this sense, conversational. The interactive character of the process is pervasive. Given the background views discussed earlier, the initial "dream" or experience, the request for a ceremony, the rituals of the ceremony, and the outcome all involve interaction. The attempt to interpret and fulfill the ondinoc, that is, the attempt to take responsive action is one which proceeds experimentally guided by the conceptual and material resources available within and around the community. As in the case of "riddle guessing" described by Lalemant, possible solutions are tried until a resolution is reached. While the experimentation in some cases seems random, the selection of material solutions appears to be guided by conceptual resources. This connection is explicitly made in a recent version of the ceremony. Here, "riddles are styled ... [and] the importance of the clue being understood and hence the dream revealed is stressed. Clues may be understood more readily if one is familiar with the legendary accounts of various societies and spirit forces" (Blau, 1963, p. 233). Given shared background and experience, the participants do not seem to throw just anything at the dreamer, but rather throw things which are suggested by past judgments and information about the dreamer.[33]

The fourth feature of responsible thinking suggested by the practice of the ononharoia is as regards the role of the community in the process. Just as the ceremonial framework provides for calling the community together and establishing its place in the process of judgment, it is important to clarify the crucial role of the collective view of the community on the process. This collective view emerges in at least two ways. First, in the form of a council, the community decides on whether or not the initial request for a ceremony can be approved. In Lalemant's account, the community met as a council three times and in the first two cases exerted significant control on the ceremony. In the first, the council agreed to hold the ceremony. Although Lalemant does not provide a description of the deliberation, it appears that the council needed to decide upon the appropriateness of the request. In the second meeting, the council organized the community to respond to the woman's encounter with the moon and issued further formal calls for help. The community played a role in a second significant way as well by actively participating in the ceremony and, in interaction with the dreamer, interpreted and fulfilled the ondinoc.[34]

The collective role of the community is also crucial in interpreting and fulfilling the ondinoc. As implied by the ceremonial roles, the active

involvement of the community is essential both in providing the interpretation (even if the dreamer "knows" it) and in actively fulfilling the
ondinoc. Harold Blau's examination of a twentieth century Onondaga
version of the ononharoia supports this conclusion. In this version of the
ononharoia, two "guessers" are required before the interpretation can be
successful: one from the dreamer's "side of the fire" and one from the
other (where "side of the fire" or "moieties" refer to clan groupings). In
short, the collective view of the community bounds the ceremony by being
instrumental in its beginning and its end.

The community then, in conjunction with the dreamer, serves as the
standard which guides the process and determines its outcome. To blindly
accept any request for a ceremony would be irresponsible, but to summarily reject all or most requests without consideration would be equally
irresponsible. Significantly, the outcome of the process is also a matter
subject to the community standard. The standards according to which
interpretations are determined are found in the interaction between the
community and the dreamer, not in transcendent authorities. There are, in
this sense, no transcendent standards which assure the accuracy of the
interpretation or guarantee its success. This is not to say that established
ways of thinking (including other interpretations of dreams, stories,
practices, and so on) do not matter. It is rather to suggest that these ways
of thinking are not fully determinate of the interpretation of a particular
ondinoc. Accounts of the process do not involve consultations with fixed
authorities that will provide an interpretation, but rather suggest that an
interpretation results from an active working out of the result. In this way,
established ways of thinking serve as resources while the process itself
may produce interpretations which revise earlier judgments, reject them,
or add new ones. One may certainly involve in the process someone skilled
at dream interpretation, but these people do not simply give an interpretation, they are people skilled in the practice of interpretation.
Responsible thinking in this case does not defer its conclusions to some
fixed principle, but rather seeks an answer actively through interaction
between the dreamer and the community using cultural and environmental resources to support the process.

These four features suggested by the practice of the ononharoia, taken
together with the background view of the nature of individuals and the
role of orenda, present a conception of responsible thinking where the
starting point is a song or expression of an individual which needs
interpretation and an active response. The process involved is one which
is framed by ceremony which serves to focus the attention and resources
of the community on making a response. The process is carried out by

individuals taking up ceremonially determined roles which frame their actions and support a practical division of labor. The process is a conversation involving interaction between the dreamer and the community and active experimentation in order to interpret and satisfy the initially indeterminate song or expression. Finally, the outcome of the process will not be a matter of correspondence with some fixed and transcendent authority, but rather the consensual interpretation of the community involved. In short, responsible thinking, on this interpretation, can be seen as a ceremonial and communal response to an indeterminate call. It is, in still other words, a collective search for meaning.

In the end, a conception of rationality as responsible thinking grounded in the Haudenosaunee tradition has the potential to contribute to the ongoing debate over how we understand rationality. By shifting the emphasis from a process of acquisition to a process of conversation, such a conception widens both what will count as rational practice and what and who matter in such practices. When combined with recent pragmatist and feminist critiques of established philosophical conceptions of rationality, a Haudenosaunee perspective can add conceptual resources to the process of reconstructing rationality in a world recognized as fundamentally diverse.

Notes

1 This characterization of European conceptions of rationality is suggested by Naomi Scheman (1993) and Paulo Freire (1970) among others.
2 "Ononharoia" is used by the Jesuits to refer both to the "dream-guessing rite" and to the Iroquoian Midwinter Ceremony of which it is often a part. As Tooker (1970, p. 85) observes, the dream-guessing ceremony appears to have been central to older forms of the Midwinter Ceremony and so the double meaning of the term seems warranted. Chafe (1963, p. 29) supports this interpretation in his analysis of the meaning of the contemporary Seneca term for the Midwinter Ceremony as does Blau (1963, p. 244). I will use the term "Ononharoia" to refer only to the "dream-guessing rite."
3 I will use the term "Iroquoian" to denote a related group of indigenous American cultures which developed from the Owasco culture which flourished in northeastern North America prior to the fourteenth century. These related cultures include the nations which formed the Huron Confederacy, as well as those which formed the Haudenosaunee Confederacy. I will use the term "Haudenosaunee" to denote the particular version of Iroquoian culture manifested in the Confederacy. "Haudenosaunee" is usually translated as "People of the Longhouse" or "people who build" and is the traditional name of the people named "Iroquois" by the French.
4 Ononharoia and related ceremonies are extensively documented within the

Jesuit *Relations*, ethnographic literature (e.g. Tooker, 1970; Speck, 1949), and in stories from the Iroquoian tradition (e.g. Parker, 1989; Hewitt, 1928). The use of the Jesuit *Relations* as a source of information is problematic. The original reports were written by missionaries in North America, but were then edited by Jesuit authorities in Europe and published. The missionaries, by their own account, were often not fluent in the language of the indigenous people with whom they lived. Also, they were clearly involved in missionary work and so what they noted about indigenous culture, as well as their interpretation of it, was often influenced by their interest in carrying out a successful mission. Despite these difficulties, however, the *Relations* provide an important early source of information about Iroquoian peoples. In presenting material from the *Relations*, I have focused on material which seems to be a direct report of activities, rather than upon interpretative material (except where the interpretative comments help clarify the issues). Whenever possible, I call upon sources within the Iroquoian oral tradition to balance the Jesuit accounts.

5 For examples of these other practices see Parker (1989, pp. 241–52), Fenton (1953), Hale (1883), and Parker (1968), respectively.

6 References to the *Jesuit Relations* are to the edition edited by Reuben Gold Thwaites (1898).

7 Father Lalemant's account is quite consistent with other Jesuit accounts of the dream-guessing rite among the Haudenosaunee and the Huron. Lalemant's account in particular is useful because it is one of the earliest and, given its practice by a Huron village, it can be seen as a practice found broadly among Iroquoian people. There are numerous reports of the practice elsewhere in the *Jesuit Relations*, including: vol. 10, pp. 169–73, 175–7; vol. 17; 145–215; Vol. 23: 171–173; Vol. 33: 189–197; Vol. 39: 19–23; Vol. 42: 151–69, 195–97; Vol. 54: 65–75, 97–101; vol. 55, p. 61; and vol. 60, pp. 87–91. Father Lafitau gives a summary account of the process in his volume, *The Customs of the American Indians*, originally published in 1724 ((Lafitau, 1974, pp. 234–6). It is important to note that the Jesuit accounts are also quite consistent with a wide range of Native American accounts. These include, for example, an 1816 description of the Ononharoia by Major John Norton (also called Teyoninhokarawen), a Cherokee friend and comrade of the Seneca leader, Joseph Brant (Norton 1970, pp. 107–8). The Jesuit accounts are also consistent with references to the process in the Haudenosaunee origin stories recorded by J. N. B. Hewitt in the late nineteenth century (Hewitt, 1903 and 1928). The process continues in a modified form in many Haudenosaunee communities (see Tooker, 1970, p. 46) and the practice described by Lalemant is very similar to the twentieth-century practice at the Onondaga Reservation in New York (Blau, 1963).

8 Among the things requested by the moon was a blue blanket "that must belong to a Frenchman." When asked to contribute such a blanket, the Jesuits refused (*Relations*, vol. 17, p. 173).

9 See Wallace's (1958, 1972) lengthy discussions of the ceremony. Wallace argues that the ononharoia is best understood as a form of psychotherapy.

"The culture of dreams," Wallace concludes, "may be regarded as a useful escape-valve in Iroquois life. In their daily affairs, Iroquois men were brave, active, self-reliant, and autonomous; they cringed to no one and begged for nothing. But no man can balance forever on such a pinnacle of masculinity, where asking and being given are unknown. Iroquois men dreamt; and, without shame, they received their dreams and their souls were satisfied" (1958, p. 247). Wallace's interpretation presumes a very different view of the relationship of individuals to their community from the one I here propose. Wallace's focus on male dreaming is worth noting. The Jesuit accounts describe many instances of female dreaming as well. As a result, Wallace's treatment of dreams is immediately problematic, since it is unclear how his interpretation would apply to women's dreams.

10 One version of the practice of "reincarnation" involved the adoption of individuals from outside the community, often individuals captured in war. Another version, practiced as part of the Condolence Council, involved a new person taking up the name and position of a leader who had died. For additional discussions of Iroquois adoption practices, see Richter (1992, p. 72); Colden (1922, pp. xxviii–xxix); the Jesuit *Relations* (vol. 22, pp. 287–9); and Beauchamp (1907).

11 Parker proposes that the contrast of good and evil should not be understood as the European dualism of good and evil, but rather as a contrast of degree between constructive and destructive characters (in Converse, 1908, p. 34n.2). This understanding seems to be supported by David Cusick's early version of the origin story (in Beauchamp, 1922, pp. 9–10).

12 There are a number of published versions of this story, all of which appear to agree on the main components of the story (see Hewitt, 1903 and 1928; Converse, 1908, pp. 34–6; David Cusick in Beauchamp, 1922, pp. 8–11; Cornplanter, 1938, pp. 26–34; and, for two Huron versions, *Relations*, vol. 8, pp. 117–19 and vol. 10, pp. 127–39).

13 There is a comparable contrast in the Confederacy founding story. In the Newhouse version, Deganawida is portrayed as having a constructive character of the sort evidenced by Sapling, while his nemesis Adodarho is presented as having a self-interested and destructive character like Flint's (Parker, 1968, pp. 14–17). As part of the process of founding the confederacy, Deganawida, and the co-founder Hiawatha, must find a way to deal with Adodarho. In the end, he cures Adodarho by singing: "Dekanawida himself sang and walked before the door of Adodarhoh's house. When he finished his song he walked toward Adodarho and held out his hand to rub it on his body to know its inherent strength and life. The Adodarho was made straight and his mind became healthy" (Parker, 1968, p. 28). Once he is cured, Adodarho becomes the first chief of the new confederacy.

14 See Hallowell (1975, p. 141) for a discussion of this point in the context of Ojibwa culture.

15 It is important to note that in addition to animal persons, other aspects of the environment also were viewed as important parts of the wider natural community. These persons include the winds, rocks, trees, the sun and moon,

and so on. Each of these other persons is also viewed as a more or less active "member" of the community where their activity seems to depend, metaphorically, on their perceived distance from the village and, I would suggest, the scope of their activities (see Isaacs, 1977).

16   Parker (1989, pp. 147–53) gives one Seneca version of this story and Jesse Cornplanter (1938; pp. 167–81) gives another.

17   Hewitt is a particularly important source. He was born on the Tuscarora Reservation at Lewiston, New York, and became fluent in the Tuscaroran language. He was later hired by John Wesley Powell to work for the Bureau of American Ethnology, where he published a wide range of Haudenosaunee texts and papers on aspects of Iroquoian culture. His interpretations, while clearly influenced by the views of late-nineteenth century ethnology, were also clearly influenced by his personal knowledge of Haudenosaunee culture (see Swanton, 1938).

18   Hewitt's treatment of orenda, along with William Jones on "manitou" and Alice Fletcher (1910) on "wakonda" describe these notions in much the same way. Paul Radin in his 1914 paper, "The Religion of North American Indians," disputes this interpretation. Among more recent discussions of orenda, A. Irving Hallowell (1975) accepts Radin's interpretation and Marilyn Holly (1994) accepts Hewitt's. Hope Isaacs provides an interesting alternative account which focused on orenda as power and its dependence on certain kinds of spirit.

19   Chafe argues that a significant problem in the study of Iroquoian texts is the lack of a standard orthography. When possible, I adhere to Chafe's proposed standard (see Chafe, 1963, pp. 1–3; 1967, pp. 4–5). Note that "õ" replaces the symbol proposed by Chafe for the vowel sound in the English word "dawn."

20   In Isaacs' (1977, pp. 168–9) discussion of orenda, she cites Chafe as affirming that the roots for "song" and "word" are distinct and mentions in particular the terms used for Longhouse singing and singing in Christian churches as marking the difference. However, the terminology associated with the ononharoia suggests that the two word roots may be more closely related (as I suggest below).

21   See Parker (1989, pp. 11–12) and Converse (1908, pp. 36–9).

22   Isaacs' interpretation diverges from the one I propose on several levels. Most significantly, though, it appears that her focus is less on what is meant by orenda and more on what is thought to have power. My focus, on the other hand, is to understand what orenda means in the context of a community and in light of its etymological connection to the idea of song.

23   If we suppose that the French Jesuits pronounced the "i" in "ondinoc" as the nasalized "i" in the French word "fin" or "bien," then the sound represented by "i" would seem to correspond with the vowel represented by "ε" by Chafe (1963, p. 5). If "oc" in "ondinoc" is supposed to represent a low back vowel of the sort found in the English word "dawn," then it would correspond with the vowel represented with "õ" (ibid.). In this case, there is evidence that the root of "ondinoc" is "-(C)εn (õ)-."

24   Lalemant translates "oki" as Demon. While it appears that "oki" and its equivalents in other Iroquoian languages eventually came to mean something like "evil spirit" or "evil power," in earlier times it appears to have named spirits or unseen persons in general (see Hewitt, 1928, pp. 608–9n. 5; Lafitau, 1974, pp. 236–7).

25   Father Ragueneau explicitly reinterprets the notion of ondinoc in his 1647–8 report. Disregarding the notion of ondinoc as songs of others, and accepting the premise that the Huron could not themselves provide an adequate explanation, Ragueneau proposes that "ondinonk" is to be understood as "a secret desire of the soul manifested by a dream." His interpretation is offered in a context which appears meant to clear the Huron of the earlier conclusion that they were devil worshipers, a charge reinforced by Lalemant's reports. Ragueneau concludes: "Still, after all, their dreams are nothing but illusions, and, if some turn out true, it is only by chance. Accordingly, after having carefully looked into the whole matter, I do not see that there is anything peculiar about their dreams. I mean to say that I do not think that the devil speaks to them, or has any intercourse with them in any way" (*Relations*, vol. 33, p. 197).

26   See Hewitt's interlinear translation of the Onondaga origin story (Hewitt, 1903, pp. 172–3).

27   See Hewitt (1903, p. 222) for the Seneca version and ibid., (pp. 280–1) for the Mohawk version.

28   This interpretation of "-weñn-" is based on Hale's "Caniega Glossary" which translated the language of the Mohawk Condolence Council. Terms containing the root include the following: "deghsewenniyu," "thou mayest speak"; "desawennawenrate," "thy voice coming over"; "entyewennine-kenneh," "the words which will be said"; "jinikawennakeh," "these the words"; "kawenna," "word, voice, language, speech"; and "wetewennaker-aghdanyon," "we have made the signs, we have gone through the ceremonies" (Hale, 1883, pp. 191–215). Fenton (1962, p. 298) similarly associates dreams with "words."

29   The exceptions are the Funeral Ceremony and the Dance for the Dead (Chafe, 1967, p. 2).

30   See also Chafe (1961, pp. 6–7). The speeches recorded by Chafe are from within the tradition of the Longhouse religion established by Handsome Lake and his followers at the beginning of the nineteenth century. Despite the dramatic change in Haudenosaunee practices after Handsome Lake, it is interesting to note that the Thanksgiving Speeches focus on the characteristic activities of each group of persons, as well as their connections, by means of these characteristic activities, to the other beings in the wider community.

31   This structure appears to be present in a wide range of Iroquoian ceremonial forms. In the Condolence Council, the grieving clans sit on the side of the fire and "raise an issue" and are condoled by the other side of the fire, responsible for "settling the issue." A similar structure was used in treaty negotiations, where the Europeans and Iroquois vied for the side of the fire responsible for raising issues (see Foster, 1984). Hewitt, in a very brief analysis of this

structure in the Condolence Council, describes the relationship between the sides of the fire in this way: "One of the two complementary groupings of persons of blood kinship (either by descent or by legal fiction) represents the Female Principle in Nature, the Mother typifying Womankind as distinguished from the Male Kind; the other of the grouping of blood kindreds represents the Male Principle, the Father typifying Mankind as distinguished from the Female Kind, of the human race" (Deserontyon, 1928, p. 91). This male/female dualism, however, is not to be understood in the same terms as such a dualism might be understood in the European tradition. As suggested by Dennis, gendered roles marked different functions within the community and not differentiated power relations (Dennis, 1993, p. 109n). Allen (1992, pp. 237–40) makes this point explicitly.

32 Blau (1963, esp. pp. 242–3) gives a more recent illustration of an Onondaga version of the ononharoia which affirms both the ritual and role aspects of ceremonies.

33 See Blau (1963, pp. 238–9).

34 John Norton, a Cherokee comrade of the Haudenosaunee leader Joseph Brant, describes a Wyandot ononharoia where the ondinoc proposed by one of the warriors was interpreted as a demand for "the flesh of Mohawks." "The Chiefs," Norton continues, "observed that the dream was too preposterous and unjust to be complied with; and discharged the guesser and his Tribe from the obligation of obtaining what they had divined" (Norton, 1970, pp. 107–8). In this case, the council considered an interpretation and determined that it was "too preposterous." Unfortunately, according to Norton, discharging the guesser and his Tribe was insufficient, because "a party of headstrong young men" attacked the Mohawks anyway and precipitated a war which the Wyandots lost.

References

Akwasasne Notes (1978) *Basic Call to Consciousness*, Summertown, Tenn.: Book Publishing Company.

Allen, Paula Gunn (1992) *The Sacred Hoop: Recovering the Feminine in American Indian Traditions*, Boston: Beacon Press.

Beauchamp, William M. (1907) *Civil, Religious, and Mourning Councils and Ceremonies of Adoption of the New York Indians*, New State Museum and Science Service Bulletin 113.

Beauchamp, William M. (1922) *Iroquois Folklore*, Port Washington, NY: Kennikat Press.

Blau, Harold (1963) "Dream Guessing: A Comparative Analysis," *Ethnohistory*, 10, 1, 233–49.

Canfield, William W. (1902) *The Legends of the Iroquois Told by "The Cornplanter,"* Port Washington, NY: Ira J. Friedman.

Chafe, Wallace L. (1961) *Seneca Thanksgiving Rituals*, Washington, DC: Bureau of American Ethnology, Bulletin 183.

Chafe, Wallace L. (1963) *Handbook of the Seneca Language*, Albany: University of the State of New York, The State Education Department.

Chafe, Wallace L. (1967) *Seneca Morphology and Dictionary*, Washington: Smithsonian Press.

Colden, Cadwallader (1922) *The History of the Five Indian Nations of Canada which are dependent on the Province of New York, and are a barrier between the English and the French in that part of the World*, two volumes, New York: Allerton Book Company.

Converse, Harriet Maxwell (1908) *Myths and Legends of the New York State Iroquois*, Albany, NY: Education Department Bulletin 437.

Cornplanter, Jesse J. (1938) *Legends of the Longhouse*, Port Washington, NY: Kennikat Press.

Dennis, Matthew (1993) *Cultivating a Landscape of Peace: Iroquois–European Encounters in Seventeenth Century America*, Cooperstown, NY: Cornell University Press.

Deserontyon (1928) *A Mohawk Form of Ritual of Condolence, 1782*, trans. and introduction by J. N. B. Hewitt, *Indian Notes and Monographs*, volume X, no. 8, New York: Museum of the American Indian.

Fenton, William N. (1953) *The Iroquois Eagle Dance: An Offshoot of the Calumet Dance*, Washington: United States Printing Office.

Fenton, William N. (1962) *This Island, the World on the Turtle's Back*, Washington: United States Printing Office.

Fletcher, Alice C. (1910) "Wakonda," in *Handbook of American Indians*, Washington, DC: Bureau of American Ethnology, Bulletin 30.

Foster, Michael K. (1984) "On Who Spoke First at Iroquois–White Councils: An Exercise in the Method of Upstreaming," in Michael K. Foster, Jack Campisi, and Marianne Mithun (eds), *Extending the Rafters: Interdisciplinary Approaches to Iroquoian Studies*, Albany: State University of New York Press.

Freire, Paulo (1970) *Pedagogy of the Oppressed*, New York: Continuum.

Hale, Horatio (1883) *The Iroquois Book of Rites*, New York: AMS Press.

Hallowell, A. Irving (1975) "Ojibwa Ontology, Behavior, and World View," in Dennis Tedlock and Barbar Tedlock (eds), *Teachings from the American Earth: Indian Religion and Philosophy*, New York: Liveright.

Hewitt, J. N. B. (1902) "Orenda and a Definition of Religion," *American Anthropologist*, 4, 33–46.

Hewitt, J. N. B. (1903) "Iroquoian Cosmology," in *Twenty-First Annual Report of the Bureau of American Ethnology, 1899–1900*, Washington: Government Printing Office.

Hewitt, J. N. B. (1928) "Iroquoian Cosmology – Second Part," in *Forty-Third Annual Report of the Bureau of American Ethnology, 1925–1926*, Washington: Government Printing Office.

Holly, Marilyn (1994) "The Persons of Nature Versus the Power Pyramid: Locke, Land, and American Indians," *International Studies in Philosophy*, 26, 1, 13–31.

Isaacs, Hope L. (1977) "Orenda and the Concept of Power among the Tonawanda Seneca," in Raymond D. Fogelson and Richard N. Adams (eds), *The Anthropology of Power*, New York: Academic Press.

Jones, William (1905) "The Algonkin Manitu," *Journal of American Folk-Lore*, 18, 183–90.

Lafitau, Father Joseph François (1974) *Customs of the American Indians Compared with the Customs of Primitive Times*, two Vols, edited and translated by William N. Fenton and Elizabeth L. Moore, Toronto: The Champlain Society.

Mohawk, John (1992) "The Indian Way is a Thinking Tradition," in José Barreiro (ed.), *Indian Roots of American Democracy*, Ithaca: Ake:Kon Press, Cornell University.

Norton, John (1970) *The Journal of Major John Norton 1816*, edited by Carl F. Klinck and James J. Talman, Toronto: The Champlain Society.

Parker, Arthur C. (1968) *The Constitution of the Iroquois* in William N. Fenton (ed.), *Parker on the Iroquois*, Syracuse: Syracuse University Press.

Parker, Arthur C. (1989) *Seneca Myths and Folk Tales*, Lincoln and London: University of Nebraska Press.

Radin, Paul (1914) "Religion of the North American Indians," *Journal of American Folk-Lore*, 27, 335–73.

Richter, Daniel K. (1992) *The Ordeal of the Longhouse: The Peoples of the Iroquois League in the Era of European Colonization*, Chapel Hill: University of North Carolina Press.

Rudes, Blair A. and Crouse, Dorothy (1987) *The Tuscarora Legacy of J. N. B. Hewitt*, two vols, Canadian Ethnology Service, Paper no. 108, Ottawa: Canadian Museum of Civilization.

Scheman, Naomi (1993) "Your Ground is My Body: The Politics of Anti-Foundationalism," in *Engenderings*, New York: Routledge.

Speck, Frank (1949) *Midwinter Rites of the Cayuga Long House*, Lincoln and London: University of Nebraska Press.

Swanton, John R. (1938) "John Napoleon Brinton Hewitt," *American Anthropologist*, 40, 286–90.

Thwaites, Reuben Gold (1898) *The Jesuit Relations and Allied Documents*, Cleveland, Ohio: The Burrows Brothers Company.

Tooker, Elizabeth (1970) *The Iroquois Ceremonial of Midwinter*, Syracuse: Syracuse University Press.

Wallace, Anthony F. C. (1958) "Dreams and the Wishes of the Soul: A Type of Psychoanalytic Theory among the Seventeenth Century Iroquois," *American Anthropologist*, 60, 234–48.

Wallace, Anthony F. C. (1972) *The Death and Rebirth of the Seneca*, New York: Random House.

19

Educational Multiculturalism, Critical Pluralism, and Deep Democracy

Judith M. Green

1 Introduction: Why American Education Needs a New Kind of Multiculturalism

The problem situation that a reconsideration of multiculturalism in American education must address at the end of the twentieth century has earlier roots, broader implications for other societies, and an ongoing historical trajectory that will continue well into the twenty-first century. American society is a global experiment in combining individual representatives of the world's vast array of human cultures – some of them privileged, some of them oppressed, some of them arriving hopefully and voluntarily, some of them "imported" under duress – in self-consciously new and rapidly changing circumstances loosely guided by the political and moral ideal of democracy. As I will argue in this essay, a multicultural education shaped by a democratic philosophy and praxis of critical cultural pluralism offers diverse students, parents, and other community members necessary preparation for participating in the world-historic, transformative development of deep democracy as a profoundly preferable way of life.

Before and since America's founding, other societies, too, have experienced the challenge of living with cultural differences, whether through trade and related intermarriage, through accommodation of small, contained groups of cultural others, with special skills of benefit to the dominant culture or a willingness to do work it regards as necessary but degrading or distasteful, or through military defeat and subsequent colonization, in which a small ruling minority lives "within the pale," surrounded by a culturally homogeneous, subordinated majority. What is unique in the American experiment is the semi-willing acceptance of refugees and fortune-seekers from every corner of the globe. Instead of remaining a colonial outpost for some unchanging older culture or becoming a "melting pot" for a homogeneous new one, American society has emerged from such a confusion and collision of motives and customs as to have no single, permanently dominant cultural center. Spanish, French, English, Dutch, German, and Russian colonizers of the sixteenth, seventeenth, and eighteenth centuries had incomplete success in subordinating the diverse multiplicity of America's indigenous peoples, as well as imperfect and impermanent success in dominating one another militarily, economically, religiously, culturally, and linguistically. The African slaves they forced to join their protean social milieu proved to be unexpectedly resistant to complete cultural conversion – in fact, originative and influential in their cross-cultural contributions – both before and since emancipation. Likewise, in spite of enormous social pressures and great deprivations, many of the Native American peoples continued to pursue at least some elements of a semi-autonomous cultural trajectory. Indentured Chinese immigrants brought to America to work on the transcontinental railroads for near-subsistence wages were forced by social discrimination as much as by cultural loyalty to establish separate enclaves in which their language, learning, and spirituality could be openly expressed and valued, and in which their economic power could be concentrated and multiplied to gain a stake in the larger society. Likewise, Irish immigrants who were willing to do hard and dirty jobs were semi-welcomed in the mid-nineteenth century years of famine and colonial oppression in their homeland, provided that they were willing to keep to themselves; discrimination-based concentration inflamed them to organize together in order to pursue power and respect within their new, always changing American context. In the twentieth century, America has variously welcomed, refused, and unsuccessfully attempted to keep out people from the entire panoply of world cultures on the varied and shifting grounds of useful skills, national interest within international power relations, racial prejudice, class status, humanitarian concern, and relatively effective advocacy on the part of already-arrived cultural representatives.

Throughout this historical process, cultural groups who have gained a temporary dominance have fought unwinnable battles to maintain it against the challenges of newcomers and against coalitions of previously marginalized fellow citizens, so that new accommodations have processively emerged, and the meaning of the old has been continuously transformed within the context of new relations of power and life activity. Labor unions led some of the most effective transformative coalitions of working-class members of differing marginalized cultures early in the twentieth century, achieving a fifty-year period of growth in wages and security in employment before losing ground to increasingly globalized forces of opposition. Likewise, America's great mid-twentieth century liberation struggles of marginalized cultures and groups – African Americans, Native Americans, Hispanic Americans, and women – initiated progressive though non-linear processes of democratic advancement through increased economic opportunity, through more effective political participation and more favorable representation in the mass media, and through an interrelated, ongoing, cross-difference multilogue about educational curriculum and pedagogy. At the end of the twentieth century, this multilogue has reached a stage of embattled impasse that calls for a new and deeper rethinking of the purposes and contents of education in a society that continues to claim and to aspire to be guided by the ideal of democracy.

In the emergent, braided American tradition of resemblant commonalities across diversities in geopolitical location and cultural roots, education has been regarded from our beginning as the most desirable and effective mode of personal formation and social transformation, preparing individuals to use their particular gifts and capacities at a high level of development on behalf of a preferable future for themselves, their families, their communities, their nation, and human civilization in general through dealing realistically, effectively, and idealistically with emergent events and changing circumstances. Concerning these purposes, constituencies, and characteristics of a well-designed education, America's Western cultural streams of influence from Plato, Aristotle, Thomas Aquinas, John Locke, and Frances Hutcheson broadly concur with our Eastern streams from Confucius, Hinduism, the Buddha, and their interpreters, as well as our African and indigenous American cultural streams. In different ways, all of these cultural streams also acknowledge the human place within nature and a spiritual dimension of human mind and character that links us to sources of meaning and purpose in our lives and connects us to enduring values that transcend our immediate personal and cultural locations. Though the practical implications of these diverse but converging philosophical commitments have always been disputed and unclear, education has been looked to across the centuries of our short history as more than training for earning one's daily bread; it also has been structured and contested as preparation for fulfilling the various democratic roles of citizen, contributor to the growth of knowledge and the quality of community life, parent and guide to future generations, and individual choice-maker and meaning-seeker within a complex, rapidly changing world. Over time, as the growth of knowledge and of national wealth, changes in technology, and world-shaking events have altered the circumstances of daily life and suggested portents of the future, America has responded by revising the educational models of curriculum, pedagogy, and academic ethos that adult generations hope will prepare younger generations for carrying on our national experiment in democracy, as well as for living secure and flourishing lives as individuals within families and communities.

Mystical urges and uncertainties about a coming new millennium combine now with practical concerns about unsettled and unsatisfactory aspects of our current social life and with diverse though resemblant contemporary articulations of our perennial ideals as we think about how we can solve America's social problems, prepare our children for the future, deepen our experience of lived democracy, and maintain valued loyalties to the best elements of the multiple traditions that shaped us and that continue to guide and sustain us. Sometimes these ties to the past combine with our anxieties about the future to make emotional and epistemic blindfolds that keep some of us from clearly seeing who we are now as an American people and in what relations we stand to other peoples, both as a world-historic experiment in multicultural democracy and as a wealthy and powerful center of empire that is losing its control to centripedal forces that both threaten and offer opportunities to other nations and cultures with which we live in a web of increasingly close daily and practical connection. Proponents of various separatist and elitist proposals for the redesign of American education who regard themselves as irreconcilable ideological opponents ironically share the situation of thinking about the future from behind such emotional and epistemic blindfolds. They fail to see that we are now and increasingly are becoming what we have always been: a multicultural society whose component cultures have become hybridized and composite through our history of indivisible struggles, daily contacts, and practical cooperation.[1] Many of these transformative developments within our American microcultures have been healthy for them, for their companion microcultures, and for our national life, though others represent oppression, loss, and disrespect shaped by ignorance and abuse of power. If we can learn from our shared history of interactive experience, restore a part of what has been lost, and transform our present and future cross-cultural relations accordingly, both America's differing microcultures and our experimental multicultural society as a whole have the potential to develop in ways that contribute to our effectiveness in pursuing semi-autonomous cultural trajectories while further realizing our shared democratic ideals, thus offering a positive model for international processes of mutually respectful and beneficial cross-cultural interaction and cooperative development.

Only a multicultural approach to education will allow us to achieve these great goods, but it must be based on a different philosophical analysis than those that have thus far guided our transformative efforts. Most of our recent experiments have been tolerant liberal compromises between opponent positions that emphasize either the superiority of Western "great books" and pedagogical traditions of received knowledge transmission by authoritative teachers to passive student "containers," or the superiority of previously suppressed and disvalued texts and teachings representing supposedly pure alternative cultures and standpoints, conveyed in an uncritical, oppositional manner as a way of preparing students for lives of resistance against colonizing others.[2] The current compromise position, which combines the continuing weight of past Western cultural dominance in its core curriculum and pedagogy with a tolerant nod to other traditions through the uncritical addition of a few non-Western or women-authored texts in core courses and a cafeteria-style requirement to select one from a menu of alternative non-Western or women-focused courses, is both philosophically and practically unsustainable.[3] It fails to acknowledge that these cultures and standpoints are now and always have been interactive, that they make rival claims as well as convergent affirmations, and that students will be ill-equipped for a future of multicultural experiences, challenges, and opportunities unless their education prepares them to be relationally aware and critically appreciative of other cultures, while being critically loyal to their own culture's semi-autonomous trajectory, as well as effectively cooperative across differences and creative in value expression, in problem-solving, and in knowledge generation. The current compromise model of educational multiculturalism satisfies almost no one in America today, drawing the scorn of the moderate middle as "political correctness," as well as the continuing opposition of still-unreconciled ideological and cultural antagonists.

At the end of the twentieth century and the beginning of a new millennium, America needs an approach to multicultural education that is more realistic, more effective, and more idealistic than the inadequate and misguided experiments we have attempted thus far. A more reflective, realistic, and effective educational multiculturalism growing out of a democratic philosophy of critical cultural pluralism offers students, parents, and other community members transformative preparation for cooperatively reconstructing American society toward "deep democracy," a deeper realization of democracy than we have yet experienced, that we can imaginatively project as a profoundly preferable way of life.

2 Critical Cultural Pluralism as Motive and Method for Democracy

Several almost unavoidably obvious aspects of our shared, late-twentieth century social life and its portents for the future make some kind of a culturally pluralistic philosophy realistic and desirable to most Americans today. Daily life in our cities combines with the daily messages of our mass communications media – newspapers, magazines, radio, television, films, their video variants, and the increasingly ubiquitous worldwide computer web or internet – which reach even our most isolated rural areas to tell us that we, the American people, represent hybridized, composite versions of multiple cultures in close daily contact, and that in this respect, the US is a prophetic microcosm of the emerging global macrocosm. Most Americans now realize or have at least begun to discover that imperialism in its military and related cultural forms is no longer defensible or sustainable; our country may be "the big dog" in the post Cold War world, but the lessons of the Vietnam era taught us that even a small country's well-organized and determined forces of resistance can prevent external control, and the "virtual" face-to-face acquaintance television has brought us with other peoples in their distant homelands has made us both more respectful of their humanity and more reluctant to try to solve their often complex problems with remedies that grow out of our own, admittedly alien cultural experience. While most Americans may be less clear about economics and its related forms of cultural dominance, most of us no longer identify the interests of US-based multinational corporations with America's interests or our own interests, rightly realizing that mega-corporations' downsizing of their American work forces in the 1980s and 1990s signaled the end of the old nation-based system of economic loyalties and reciprocal obligations. Absolutisms still abound in America's national life, but our daily information about the fatal impacts of absolutisms in the Balkans, central Africa, and other parts of the world is helping many of us to see religious, cultural, and political absolutisms as widespread, diverse, competing, leading to conflict, but rationally unfounded and indefensible.

As the African-American philosopher Alain Locke argued earlier in this century in explaining his conception of and methodology for developing a culturally pluralistic philosophy, it seems increasingly likely that there are many areas of cross-cultural convergence between diverse conceptual and evaluative schemata that empirical research and cross-difference exploratory conversation would reveal, given the depth and dailyness of our cross-difference contacts and the many shared human needs and characteristics that these contacts bring to our attention.[4] Many cultural differences – in foods, dress, music, dance, visual arts, language, and ways of seeing the world – are widely experienced as stimulating and enriching, even by those who are deeply loyal to their own cultures. Moreover, many thoughtful people from diverse backgrounds realize that respect for others as human persons implies at least tentative, non-abstract respect for the cultures and religious traditions from which they are inseparable, and within which they are mutually shaped and shaping. All of these factors have led many, perhaps most, Americans at the end of the twentieth century to embrace some kind of a personal philosophy of cultural pluralism, whether implicitly or explicitly expressed.

A further realization that we as Americans need the help of our educational system to reach is that, to be effective in guiding our social policies and our personal actions in accord with our experience and our deeply held democratic ideals, a culturally pluralistic philosophy must also become critical. Thoughtful and effective respect for other cultures, like respect for other persons, cannot be uncritical because absolute tolerance is incompatible with holding culturally specific views of one's own in a serious way, given the inextricable interconnectedness of various cultures' paths of development and their practical daily interaction in our globally interconnected era. Moreover, some aspects of many particular cultures' ongoing standpoints and specific practices are incompatible with common humane and environmental values. Many of the major, complex problems that humans face in our era – for example, problems concerning threats to our global environment that are inextricably interconnected with problems concerning the roles of nation-states and indigenous cultures within the institutional development processes of transnational capitalism that presently undermine them – must be addressed cross-culturally, if they are to be effectively resolved. Where there are significant cultural differences that affect the possibility and effectiveness of cooperative attempts to resolve such shared problems, these must be negotiated in ways that combine critically pluralistic respect with consequence-focused effectiveness.

Thus, as Alain Locke insightfully argued, a sustainable – i.e. critical – philosophy of cultural pluralism existentially implies and is implied by an impulse toward democracy and towards the creation of contextually effective institutional forms that would allow that impulse to be realized in a world of power-structured differences that are culture-related as well as individual. Someone who has developed a culturally pluralistic perspective has already decentered the claims of his or her own cultural tradition to unique and absolute authority in favor of a perhaps inchoate belief that other voices and traditions have their own, respect-worthy insights, values, and claims to at least limited authority. Such a belief supports and is supported by an impulse toward democracy as a way of life. To be successfully implemented, Locke persuasively argues, our increasingly world-favored institutional expressions of democracy must develop deeper internal aspects – a sturdier tolerance, a readier reciprocity, and an enlightened social loyalty to other cultures' differing, democratically defensible loyalties based on a self-interested or pluralistically realistic awareness of the contestability and vulnerability of one's own cultural position and its values – instead of relying on relatively shallow and abstract liberal humanitarian principles, which lend themselves to orthodoxy and dogmatism (Harris, 1987, p. 59). Moreover, a pluralistic democratic commitment that has liberated one's thinking from a too-common tendency to identify democratic processes and institutions as such with those that have evolved out of American society's particular historical trajectory promotes greater flexibility and imaginativeness in designing new democratic processes and institutions best suited to new circumstances, purposes, and cross-cultural locations.

Unfortunately, American conceptions of democracy are somewhat confused at this stage in our society's experimental development, tending to alternate between a culturally pluralistic democratic impulse and a dangerous ideological attachment to a rigidified, undynamic conception of the wisdom of the Founding Fathers and to the particular governmental institutions and processes they designed at a much earlier stage of our shared social life, when living conditions were very different and our level of shared, experience-based self-understanding was less developed. Emergent social problems with which we now struggle show that such a pride- and fear-based ideological attachment to America's traditional, formally democratic institutions is dangerous, and that it must be replaced with more deeply democratic, critically pluralistic perspectives that motivate cross-cultural, cross-generational participation in a transformative quest for new social and institutional patterns more appropriate to current and future conditions, and more compatible with our shared democratic ideal.

3 Formal Democracy as Problematic without a Deeply Democratic Way of Life

A limited, formal conception of democracy contrasts with a deeper conception of democracy as an imaginatively projected, ideal-directed, but not-yet-realized way of life whose possibility is somehow implicit in American experience. Such a formal conception of democracy that regulates political institutions but not attitudes has been advocated for various reasons: as an expression of filial piety to the Founding Fathers, or as the most extensive conception of democracy compatible with individualistically conceived liberty, or in the belief that no shared conception of the goods or goals of social life can be justified. However, as critically dangerous problems in American society that have emerged in recent years have shown, democracy as a formal institutional model alone is culturally and existentially unsustaining and unsustainable, ideologically hollow, operationally subvertible, and conceptually incomplete.

In societies like America that are formally but not deeply democratic and that are increasingly dominated by a powerful and pervasive transnational capitalist economic sector, the culturally and existentially unsustaining and unsustainable character of such a limited instantiation of democracy has become visible in the last years of the twentieth century in the forms of two primary, interactive social pathologies: existential nihilism and ontological rootlessness. In his insightful, millennium-conscious collection of essays, Cornel West (1993) has diagnosed a widespread lived experience of nihilism growing out of America's failures to sufficiently deepen our realization of democracy during the years since Martin Luther King, Jr, identified racism, poverty, and militarism as its chief threats.[5]

> *Nihilism is to be understood here not as a philosophic doctrine that there are no rational grounds for legitimate standards or authority; it is, far more, the lived experience of coping with a life of horrifying meaninglessness, hopelessness, and (most important) lovelessness.* (West, 1993, p. 14; italics in original)

West's focus is on poor, urban, African-American communities in which educational opportunities are inadequate; unemployment is widespread and many people depend on an "informal," drug-based and violence-regulated economy for income and identity; many of the traditionally sustaining institutions of civil society – families, churches, benevolent and mutual assistance associations – have broken down; youth suicide is on the increase; and a widespread lack of the sense of agency that might have made greater goals possible fuels a fairly common, short-term focus on sources of pleasure and status that have been given their significance by the commodity-focused hype of the profit-motivated mass media. West diagnoses this "disease of the soul" (ibid., p. 18) as a concentrated, highly virulent form of a dangerous malaise that has spread across differing geopolitical and cultural locations within American society, even among the relatively privileged, manifesting itself in a generalized insecurity; a shared loss of the sense of agency previously associated with democratic citizenship that once allowed diverse people to believe that they could participate in shaping the public terms of social life; and a shared lack of meaningfulness and permanence in personal life commitments and activities that leads many people to focus on pleasure-seeking and pain-killing rather than to risk a more complex pursuit of happiness.

West's prescription for curing this widespread nihilism – new grassroots change organizations focusing on local issues, motivated by and rebuilding communities through an ethics of love – is also applicable to another socially dangerous American pathology: an ontological rootlessness due to loss of lived connection to what Josiah Royce called "communities of memory and hope."[6] Voluntary or involuntary relocation for education and jobs is one of the most common reasons for severing the connections to particular, localized, face-to-face communities that give people a sense of place and involvement in processes and purposes that have a longer history, a more stable directionality, and a broader meaning than their own narrowly individual lives. A second social development that has vitiated the capacity of local communities to provide such a life-sustaining sense of place and purpose is cooptation of their functions, capacities, and connections by expert-directed governance at local and higher levels, by economic institutions and forces that allow powerful business firms to radically reshape local conditions through action at a distance, and by nationally centralized communications media that create dependency on impersonal, profit-motivated sources of information for an ontological sense of the real, an epistemic sense of the true, an ethical sense of the worthy, an aesthetic sense of the fitting and the beautiful, and a politico-economic sense of the favored and the feasible.

Simultaneously, these larger, community-coopting developmental processes have revealed the ideological hollowness and operational subvertibility of formal democratic institutions and mechanisms that lack a deeper democratic social grounding. Buying of elections through issue-diversionary campaign advertising and sale of influence by narrowly self-interested officials have subverted the operations of democratic governance in recent years. Simultaneously, in the absence of an effective multicultural education about the purposes and processes of democratic life, advocacy of ideologies of control, fear, and blaming, rationalized in terms of a supposedly unrestricted right of the majority to rule within a formal democracy and the need to preserve shallowly conceived "democratic values" from economic and political attack, has misdirected attention away from real problems of intrusive bureaucracy and economic relocation of power and priorities while problematizing and politicizing democratically necessary humane and environmental values, as well as long-standing equity entitlements. Such undemocratic ideological displacements and institutional cooptations cannot be prevented or even effectively criticized in a society that lacks a deeper democratic character that grows out of a widespread sense of citizen agency; a broadly shared commitment to and knowledge of daily, local, face-to-face communities that ground broader, multiple memberships in dispersed communities of memory and hope; and a publicly supported, realistic and idealistic model of effective multicultural education that replaces historical patterns of dominance and oppression-based resentment, xenophobic demonizing, and fear of the new with knowledge-based understanding and democratic skills for cross-difference respect and cooperation.

In addition to these aspects of its cultural and existential unsustainability, ideological hollowness, and operational cooptability, a merely formal, institutional approach to democracy is inadequate because it is conceptually incomplete in failing to acknowledge the directional guidance of the democratic ideal. As John Dewey pointed out in the post-World War I years, when many of these dangerous social processes were just beginning to dominate America's development, the democratic ideal that is actually operative within our dynamic, historically unfolding American way of life is neither a utopian alternative institutional model nor a clear and specific, principle-like formula of the kind Alain Locke warned against as prone to dogmatism and orthodoxy. Rather, it is the directional tendency of that democratic impulse that Locke, like Emerson, Whitman, James, Royce, and others identified as the motive force within our world-historic American social experiment, manifested at various times and places within our lived experiences of community life.

> Regarded as an idea, democracy is not an alternative to other principles of associated life. It is the idea of community life itself. It is an ideal in the only intelligible sense of an ideal: namely, the tendency and movement of something which exists carried to its final limit, viewed as completed,

perfected. Since things do not attain such fulfillment but are in actuality distracted and interfered with, democracy in this sense is not a fact and never will be. But neither in this sense is there or has there ever been anything which is a community in its full measure, a community unalloyed by alien elements. The idea or ideal of a community presents, however, actual phases of associated life as they are freed from restrictive and disturbing elements, and are contemplated as having attained their limit of development. Wherever there is conjoint activity whose consequences are appreciated as good by all singular persons who take part in it, and where the realization of the good is such as to effect an energetic desire and effort to sustain it in being just because it is a good shared by all, there is so far a community. The clear consciousness of a communal life, in all its implications, constitutes the idea of democracy. (Dewey, 1927, p. 328)

In relation to actual experience, the democratic impulse directed by the democratic ideal seeks personal freedom and fulfillment while recognizing the preciousness of differing relational others who desire these same broad social goods. It has been frustrated, diverted, but never finally destroyed by the realistic awareness that no one, or at most an elite few, have yet experienced such freedom or fulfillment, and that most people's very incomplete attainment of these goods is highly insecure. As Dewey suggests, America's shared, protean democratic ideal indicates a direction for development, choice, and action, though we only dimly envision its unfolding implications at the always-receding horizon of the present. Its effectiveness in providing directionality for desire requires hope born of experience of some kind of meaningful, community-based participation in progressive transformation of socially shared life circumstances from a dystopian past toward a realistically preferable or "eutopian" future.[7] As Dewey predicted, this kind of experience is increasingly difficult for most people to develop and sustain in our problematic present, precisely because our shallow, merely formal institutionalization of democracy has shown itself to be culturally and existentially unsustaining and unsustainable, ideologically hollow, operationally subvertible, and conceptually incomplete. Thus, paradoxically, it seems that the only way to sustain America's institutionalization of formal democracy is to counter these existentially, culturally, and socially destructive trends by drawing with hope and imagination on our still-operative, shared democratic impulse within our dispersed and differing geopolitical and cultural locations, in order to rebuild our actual communities of memory and hope, guided by our shared ideal of a more deeply democratic way of life than we have ever yet experienced.

Reflection on experience of the kind effective multicultural education fosters, critical culturally pluralistic research supports, and pragmatic philosophical imagination expands, makes the specific character of our shared democratic ideal visible to us.

> For democracy signifies, on one side, that every individual is to share in the duties and rights belonging to control of social affairs, and on the other side, that social arrangements are to eliminate those external arrangements of status, birth, wealth, sex, etc., which restrict the opportunity of each individual for full development of himself. On the individual side, it takes as the criterion of social organization and of law and government release of the potentialities of individuals. On the social side, it demands cooperation in place of coercion, voluntary sharing in a process of mutual give and take, instead of authority imposed from above. (Dewey and Tofts, 1932, pp. 348–9)

Reflectively revealed as a prophetic possibility within our individual and shared experience, the democratic ideal serves as inspiration and directional criterion for transforming problematic aspects of our present way of life.

> As an ideal of social life in its political phase it is much wider than any form of government, although it includes government in its scope. As an ideal, it expresses the need for progress beyond anything yet attained; for nowhere in the world are there institutions which in fact operate equally to secure the full development of each individual, and assure to all individuals a share in both the values they contribute and those they receive. Yet it is not "ideal" in the sense of being visionary and utopian; for it simply projects to their logical and practical limit forces inherent in human nature and already embodied to some extent in human nature. It serves accordingly as basis for criticism of institutions as they exist and of plans of betterment. (Ibid., p. 349)

In order to stimulate our still-living democratic impulse to transform dystopian aspects of our shallowly democratic way of life toward a realizably preferable future, instead of allowing our existential nightmares to continue to haunt us in this millennial era, we must clarify the implications of the democratic ideal by reflecting on and cross-culturally conversing about our personal and shared experiences, as these are illuminated by the research results of what Alain Locke called for as a culturally pluralistic "anthropology in the broadest sense," and as these are imaginatively extended by a contemporary reconstruction and deepening of Dewey's democratic philosophy. Though each of these interactive aspects of clarifying the implications of the democratic ideal for our own transformative guidance is necessarily a collaborative project, it is possible and may be useful here to sketch the broad outlines of a multicultural experience-based, imaginatively projected philosophy of deep democracy.[8]

4 Deep Democracy as the Philosophy of a Profoundly Preferable Way of Life

A philosophy of deep democracy, understood as the democratic ideal's experience-based, historically dynamic, imaginatively projected meaning, might be realistically expressed in its multiple philosophical dimensions by reconstructing Dewey's pragmatic insights in light of subsequent experience and a fuller appreciation of America's special character as a multicultural world-historical experiment. Such a philosophy of deep democracy includes metaphysical, epistemological, ethical, aesthetic, political, and economic aspects that grow out of and offer transformative guidance for progressive development of a deeply democratic way of life that requires dynamic, flexible, contextually responsive social institutions as well as the personal attitudes and public competences to support them.

In broad outline, deep democracy's process metaphysics treats individuals, social relations, earth's ecosystem, and the natural world as a whole as having interlinked ontological statuses. That is, these elements are ultimately inseparable from one another, and all are "real," though it is important to remember that ontology is a human interpretive enterprise, that the elements it includes are dynamic, and that our ways of understanding them reflect our physically and culturally located, embodied, historically evolving, reflective, and imaginative experience. Characteristics of all these "real" things, especially human cultures, groups, institutions, and the individuals that comprise them, are interlinked by "family resemblance" patterns of commonalities amidst diversity, rather than by universal properties or by necessary and sufficient conditions.[9] Human persons are understood within this conceptual framework as collectively and individually evolving, embodied, acculturated, relational individuals within nature who are indivisible from their culturally contextualized group memberships, which are linguistically, institutionally, and actively expressed and regulated as formative, locational, and directive of individuals' life experiences. Because ideas, memories, and hopes have empirical effects, they are also "real," creative, directive, and constitutive within the ontological framework of deep democracy, as are the material characteristics, forces, and relations which interact with them in patterns of mutual influence. Life is an especially significant dimension of certain elements of our reality so understood, so that persons, life-enhancing relations, our ecosystem and its constitutive elements, and nature as a whole are regarded as awe-inspiring – *holy* – by those who fully grasp the contingent, processive metaphysics of deep democracy.[10]

In the epistemic dimension of deep democracy as a way of life that can give birth to an experience-based philosophy, truth is understood as evolving, unfinished, and requiring ongoing human contribution. Context is understood as partially constitutive of reality, meaning, purpose, and truth. Collaborative inquiry is understood as a culturally, existentially, and institutionally sustaining, progressive epistemic activity, and dispersed and differing forms of knowledge are acknowledged and valued.[11]

In its ethical dimension, deep democracy as a way of life would give rise to and depend upon a sense of persons, relations, our ecosystem, and nature as a whole as precious. Individual persons' memories, hopes, and active projects, as well as the cultures, communities, and ways of life that form, locate, and direct these, would be regarded as morally significant. Consequences, character, and intentions would be regarded as having interconnected moral importance and influence. The focus of moral action and its appraisal would be historically located within a choice situation, within which a choice process and related subsequent activities aim to transform aspects of reality that the moral actor has experienced as dystopian through the pursuit of ends-in-view that seem more eutopian in light of the directive guidance of the democratic ideal. "Moral actors" would include individuals, groups, communities, nations, and whole cultures, whose relative significance would be understood to depend upon the situation. Individual and shared moral agency, which requires what Cornel West calls a "collective and critical consciousness," would be valued as a characteristic that must be developed and sustained.[12]

Aesthetic dimensions of individual experience and expression within semi-autonomous cultural traditions and multicultural institutions shaped and guided by the ideal of deep democracy, would indicate preference (or at least tolerance) for variety, multiplicity, dynamism, and jazz-like fusions instead of (or at least in alternation with) purity, unity, simplicity, and stability. Appreciation for freshness, continuity, and connectedness compatible with innovation, rather than insistence on sameness and repetition, would be the operative sensibility guiding creation and experiential evaluation of both multicultural and semi-autonomous cultural art forms. The deeply democratic person's sense of fittingness and contextual comfortableness would include a need for "oxygenating" diversity as well as for memory- and hope-reaffirming commonalities. Beauty would display myriad faces.[13]

Deep democracy's civil, political, and economic institutions would progressively develop through participatory processes interconnecting these aspects of social life within new transformative processes of cross-difference, interpersonal, and intergroup conversation, decision, and cooperative action. Reconstructing or newly developing such interactive social processes for our times requires rebuilding what Cornel West calls "the public square," which entails clarifying some shared values, goals, and goods related to the democratic ideal, as Dewey suggests, and also some shared holdings and entitlements of the kind Harry C. Boyte calls "the CommonWealth" and Robert F. Kennedy, Jr calls "the Public Trust."[14] While all civil, political, and economic institutions compatible with deep democracy would be designed to support the basic needs and to promote the interconnected human flourishing of individuals, groups, and communities, their institutional designs would be contextually variable, and they would be assessed and progressively reconstructed in terms of effectiveness. Economics would be located within politics and civil society, rather than vice versa, as has become their relational tendency in recent years. The institutions of civil society would be understood as public–private interfaces or mediations within which democratically tolerable differences are respected, even if the defining purposes of particular institutions require or imply that their values and activities may not be fully shared and universally inclusive. Schools and other civil institutions that Sara M. Evans and Harry C. Boyte call "free spaces" would be valued and supported for their effectiveness in facilitating public discussion, coalition development, and multicultural community-building, as well as for their role in the growth of individuals; this includes preparing them for full democratic social and political participation by fostering deeply democratic attitudes and by offering opportunities to develop the skills and capacities that active democratic citizenship requires, such as public speaking, cross-difference negotiation, record keeping, financial analysis, goal-setting, and ongoing evaluation.

Deep democracy so understood as a realistically imaginative philosophical expansion of the implications of the democratic ideal into and through a way of life is profoundly preferable to a merely formal, institutional conception of democracy because it is preferable "all the way down." It encompasses a fuller understanding of persons in all the philosophical dimensions of their social, historical, and ecosystemic relations, while offering culturally, geopolitically, and environmentally contextualized and transformative prescriptive guidance to choice, action, assessment of consequences, and progressive reformation of persons and their interactive choice situations. Deep democracy is a formative, locative, and directive process for the development and ongoing reformation of preferable persons – preferable in their character features (including personal and civic virtues), in their socially conscious and responsible agency, in their awareness of their own individual gifts and needs, and in their fuller realization of prized human capacities. Deep democracy supports the formation of equal and unoppressive social relations of the various kinds that contextualize each person's individual emergence, growth, and lived experience, including families, neighborhoods, communities, working collegialities, friendships, political and economic relationships, semi-autonomous microcultures, and a whole multicultural social web. In comparison to a merely formal, institutional democracy, deep democracy as a way of life is ontologically and epistemologically more realistic, as well as ethically, aesthetically, politically, and economically preferable, because it would prepare people to understand and to act effectively within the relational processes that are actually emerging now within our shared social and natural environment, equipping them to expect, to understand, and to value diversity and change while preserving and projecting both democratically humane cultural values and interactively sustainable environmental values in a dynamic, responsive way. Existentially, deep democracy as a way of life would connect people in deep and satisfying ways within liberatory communities of memory and hope, thus healing our currently dangerous pathologies of nihilism and rootlessness. It would direct and support the reconstruction of civil institutions, processes, and expectations that can focus diverse communities of memory and hope and support their projects, thus helping them to fulfill many human needs effectively and to assist in the development and validation of many special talents that are life-enhancing to individuals and their communities, as well as the development of public competences that have participatory and transformative usefulness in political and economic life. Deep democracy is both the goal and the process that can facilitate the emergence of the kind of Deweyan "publics" that can effectively exert transformative political and economic influence within our own, less deeply democratic American society.

Such a deeply democratic philosophical framework grows out of reflection on personal and shared experiences we as contemporary Americans have had of certain moments or aspects of community life as partially

satisfying our democratic impulse for personal growth in mutually fulfilling, cooperative connectedness with others, while at the same time
suggesting the possibility of even more satisfying achievements and fulfill-
ments if conditions and relationships were transformed or expanded in a
direction we can at least dimly sense would be more democratically ideal.
One of my personal experiences of this kind involved sharing a family
meal of a delicious stew we had prepared and served together at the end of
a happy, peaceful day, the whole experience of which my mother appre-
ciatively summed up after tasting her first spoonful by saying, "I wish we
could give some of this stew to every hungry person in the world." A critic
might reply that this vision is lovely but unrealizable, given the less
desirable possibilities and actualities of our shared human nature history
has revealed, and given the great barriers to democratic community life as
our world is institutionally structured now. But as I argued above, the
increasingly widespread, if not yet critically reflective, cultural pluralism
of most Americans today irresistibly implies and gives support to a
democratic impulse, which can be deepened through an effective multicultural education and through democratically educative experiences of
cooperative, cross-difference participation in the transformative deepening of our formally democratic institutions and processes, including our
schools.

A philosophy of deep democracy implies and is implied by a philosophy
of critical cultural pluralism; together, these philosophies can serve as
helpful transformative tools for illuminating the implications of our
shared multicultural democratic ideal, for grounding criticisms of philosophies that constitute obstacles to the expansion of its influence in our
society, and for shaping and evaluating practical programs of democratic
transformation. Together, these philosophies imply a transformative path
for initially developing and progressively improving a critically democratic multicultural approach to American education that will also, over
time, imply reconstructive deepenings of these philosophies, as Americans
develop a wider and more specific body of experience within a more
deeply democratic way of life. Thus, taking the first steps toward developing and implementing experiments in critically democratic multicultural
education is the key to further developing the kind of realistic, experience-
based philosophy that will help us to see even more clearly why such a
transformative process is desirable, as we gain the understanding and
become the kinds of persons that can make deep democracy real.

5 A Preferable Educational Philosophy and Praxis: Critical Democratic Multiculturalism

If we draw upon Alain Locke's and John Dewey's insights and reconstruct them for our own time, we can see that an effective, experience-based, ideal-enhancing philosophy and related educational praxis of critical democratic multiculturalism has specific implications for research, curriculum, and pedagogy. Because cultures continue to change at an increasingly rapid pace in our emerging era of global daily interactions, what Locke called "anthropology in the broadest sense" – cross-disciplinary research and theorizing about culturally located value fields, their transformative processes, and their cross-cultural relational patterns of commonalities and differences – is urgently needed. Value theorists from differing disciplines and cultures need to conduct, assess, and communicate with a broad public about their research concerning various culture-specific, actual viewpoints, values, and practices, developed and expressed in terms of a critical culturally pluralistic philosophical framework that does not romanticize a pure, mythic past, but that recognizes multiple voices and streams of influence interacting in the development and daily operations of particular cultures. As an aspect of this broader project, we need research about functional commonalities or family resemblances in values across differing cultures. To connect critical cultural pluralism with deep democracy, we also need research about how to effectively facilitate respectful cross-difference conversation and cooperation, including the actual results of such interactions, both in terms of further development in cultural viewpoints (including both self- and other-understandings) and in terms of consequences for previous issues or practical projects.

Making a philosophy of critical democratic multiculturalism widely operative and effective requires an educational curriculum that reflects such research in its goals and strategies for developing wide-ranging understanding of the natural world, of humanly diverse ways of being, and of oneself, as well as skills for engaging in respectful, effective cross-cultural conversation and cooperation in democratic transformative activity. Such a curriculum would promote relational understanding of our shared ecosystem and of various peoples' history, language, literature and other arts, religion, moral codes and practices, legal and political structures, dietary, medical, scientific, scholarly, and educational practices, and daily ways of life. Students would learn about the kinds of values that people have found significant in understanding and making choices within their lives, as well as the consequences of those choices for the individual, for other human persons, and for the natural world. In relation to all this, a critically democratic multicultural curriculum would cultivate knowledge of one's own bodily structures and processes, one's own needs and tastes, and one's own character, gifts, and dreams. It would develop basic human skills appropriate to one's era, interpersonal skills appropriate to cross-difference conversation and cooperation, work-focused and talent-focused skills for excellent performance and further development, individual skills in analysis, reflection, effective decision-making, self-care, and self-control, and specific competences that sustain a sense of personal agency and support effective public participation in multicultural civic, political, and economic institutions.

Critical democratic multiculturalism is different from current multicultural educational practices in that it affects the entire curriculum, as well as pedagogical norms, institutional ethos, and operative community relations. It is an integrated, relational approach to curriculum rather than a concatenated, add-on approach. Critical democratic multicultural pedagogy stresses problem-focused learning with creative outcomes, rather than passive absorption measured in terms of predictable, repeatable outcomes. It focuses on commonalities amidst differences in critically humane and environmental values, instead of teaching an uncritical universal tolerance and an uncritical loyalty to one's own culture. It teaches skills for cross-cultural conversation and cooperation rather than a distancing fear of intrusion as the practical meaning of respect.

Young people in America today need a critically democratic multicultural education because these understandings and skills, so necessary for effective participation in the project of deepening our experience of democracy, do not come naturally in a social world currently organized by racial inequalities, historically based cross-cultural misunderstandings and resentments, and political and economic power relations that tend to erase relatively powerless cultural forms while eroding civil society, undermining individual agency, and disvaluing the knowledge, skills, and citizen competences that would allow individuals and the cultures they represent to recognize, respect, and interact with one another in effective transformative ways. Our currently typical curriculum, pedagogical traditions, school ethos, and patterns of school-community relations do not prepare our students to cooperate effectively in transforming the institutions and forces that shape their life situation, instead of passively accepting them as given and just trying to avoid economic extinction. Young Americans need to develop a sense of agency and rootedness in communities of memories and hope, as well as the practical competences to protect these communities and to guide their semi-autonomous development in constructive interaction with differing communities, as a preferable alternative to the self-defeating and often violent conflict that characterizes such interactions today and that tends to reduce the credibility of less powerful communities' moral claims to respect and protection, thereby increasing the likelihood of their deterioration from within and their cooptation by outside forces acting in the name of "peace and prosperity."

In contrast, a critically multicultural education would prepare students for effective, transformative participation in deep democracy, through experiences in and beyond the classroom that combine outcomes of knowing that with understanding how and who, substituting realistic and empowering knowledge and skills for the agency-destroying, historically inaccurate, and distortedly tribalistic social formation that students now receive inside and outside their schools. Students nurtured within a curriculum, pedagogy, and educational ethos guided by critical democratic multiculturalism would be equipped with self-understanding, confidence, and a sense of agency to protect themselves against nihilism and their communities against erosion; they would be developing the attitudes, knowledge, skills, and competences for deep democracy. Eventually, they would be prepared to pass on their developed understandings and skills, as well as an evolving body of democratic transformative experience, to future generations through their families and the institutions of a more deeply democratic civil society.

Cross-cultural community participation throughout the development of concrete experiments in critical democratic multicultural education is essential to their success. Such experiments require widely dispersed knowledge to give them their contents as well as collaborative community support to give them dynamic energy. At the same time, community participation in developing and supporting critically democratic multicultural education will be educative for community members who have not themselves had such opportunities during their formative years. This is important for the sake of their own growth and flourishing, and also because they are necessary contributors to students' education in critical democratic multiculturalism, given their roles as family and community members, as sponsors of field visits and internships, as sources of information for research and classroom sharing, and as collaborators in the development of school ethos, curriculum, and pedagogy. Such cross-difference community participation in the development of a critical democratic multicultural education also offers the broader potential for originating and reinforcing multicultural coalitions that can teach their member citizens necessary competences for democratic participation and effective institutional transformation. Eventually, such coalitions may develop into stable and sustaining multicultural communities of memory and hope that can critically appreciate and protect the semi-autonomous developmental trajectories of their component microcultures within a larger cooperative framework of common understandings and shared activities.

The ends in view we need to pursue now in order to deepen and expand our process of educational transformation toward a preferable, critically democratic multiculturalism focus on each of its to-be-developed aspects. We can undertake the research that critical cultural pluralism and the praxis of deep democracy require now, refining our methodologies as our experience and understanding grow. In order to develop an appropriate, effective approach to curriculum and pedagogy design, we can begin to experiment on various scales, always seeking cross-difference collaborative community participation in the development, implementation, and assessment of new models, framing the project and the process in terms of deep democracy and critical cultural pluralism. We need to realize from the outset that there is and can be no pre-existing, antecedently rational basis for designing a universally ideal model of curriculum, pedagogy, and institutional ethos that can serve as a standard blueprint for reconstructing America's current educational system. Nor can we antecedently envision an optimal, community-transforming citizen participation role or process. Instead, we need to take an experimental approach that assumes that we will learn as we go, and thus stresses ongoing evaluation and redevelopment guided by the emerging theoretical insights of critical cultural pluralism and by our unfolding philosophical understanding of the contemporary implications of the ideal of deep democracy. Drawing upon these resources in their present stage of development, we need to project and to undertake an initial stage of our collaborative experiments in educational transformation, while simultaneously seeking and using effective ways to communicate about our experiences with other, differing communities in order to share criticisms, insights, and promising new discoveries. Over time, various successful models of critical democratic multicultural education and the processes to create and sustain them will show us as Americans how to live in a more deeply democratic way. In this, the world-historic experiment we represent will come to fruition.

Notes

1 I have borrowed the terms "hybridized and composite" in my analysis of America's interactive microcultures from Alain Locke's dense, insightful, and eloquent editor's introduction to *When Peoples Meet: A Study of Race and Culture Contacts* (1942), which he co-edited with Bernhard J. Stern.

2 Allan Bloom has been one of the most influential advocates of a Western-focused, "great books" curriculum that deconstructionist critics have charged promotes a totalizing and tyrannical cultural hegemony; allied though fundamentally differing proponents of the equal or greater value of texts and teachings from other cultural streams have labeled Bloom's curricular approach "Eurocentric." Amy Gutmann (1994) is insightful in her critique of parallel deconstructionist attacks on the kind of multicultural curriculum she favors as an alternative to both the currently typical, male-and Western-focused American curriculum and Bloom's even more exclusive mode. In his *Prophetic Thought in Postmodern Times* (1993b), Cornel West misleadingly labels as "multiculturalism" the alternative view of so-called cultural critics in his otherwise insightful argument that we need to get beyond both multiculturalism (so understood) and Eurocentrism in developing a new philosophical perspective and related educational approach that is pragmatically democratic in its responsiveness to the challenges of our current, racially and culturally contested American problem situation, as well as our anticipatible individual and social needs in a future in which global capitalism plays an increasingly anti-democratic role.

3 While all of the authors whose essays are included in Amy Gutmann's edited collection, *Multiculturalism: Examining the Politics of Recognition* – i.e. Charles Taylor, K. Anthony Appiah, Jürgen Habermas, Steven C. Rockefeller, Michael Walzer, Susan Wolf, and Amy Gutmann herself – value at least to some extent the acknowledgment in educational curricula of differing cultures and the contributions of women, none of them argues for a deeper multicultural transformation than the mere inclusion of such works because of liberal tolerance or because of their particular merits. Walzer insightfully argues that two strands of liberal thought have developed within the American intellectual tradition and that the second, culture-aware strand is more insightful, but his argument that this second strand historically has supported and would be wise to continue to support the first, culture-neutral strand is not persuasive, for reasons that will be elaborated below. Similarly, Rockefeller's argument that John Dewey was wise to interpret democracy as requiring culture-neutrality is not persuasive, both because many of Dewey's texts, e.g. *Democracy and Education* (1916), *The Public and Its Problems* (1927), *Ethics* (1932), and *Freedom and Culture* (1939) are ambiguous on this point, about which Dewey seems to have had difficulty making up his own mind, and because this is one of the key aspects of Dewey's work that pragmatist filial piety suggests must be reconstructed in light of subsequent

experience and the challenges of our current, multicultural problem situation.

4   See especially Locke's "Pluralism and Intellectual Democracy," "Cultural Relativism and Ideological Peace," and "The Need for a New Organon in Education" in Harris (1987). In these essays, the continuing philosophical influences of William James and Josiah Royce, whose views Locke first encountered in-depth during his undergraduate years at Harvard, are both implicitly obvious and explicitly acknowledged. For a fuller discussion of Locke's critical cultural pluralism, see Green and forthcoming, ch. 4).

5   See King's prophetic final chapter, "The World House," in his last book, *Where Do We Go From Here: Chaos or Community?* (1967).

6   For an originative, rich, and historically influential discussion of "communities of memory and hope," see Royce (1918), especially chapters nine through twelve. Jürgen Habermas (1984 and 1987), James L. Marsh (1995), and Robert Bellah and his collaborators (1985) use this concept in key ways, though none of them acknowledges Royce as its source.

7   In Green (1994) I coined the term "eutopian" as a realistically achievable, directional counter-pole for transforming aspects of lived reality that have been experienced as dystopian.

8   I develop some of the dimensions of this philosophy of deep democracy in greater detail and focus on some aspects of its transformative praxis in Green (forthcoming).

9   For Ludwig Wittgenstein's originative discussion of "family resemblances" as a meta-concept for analyzing the concept of "games," see Wittgenstein (1953), especially sections 65–7 and following.

10 These ideas about metaphysical aspects of the philosophy of deep democracy reflect the influence of works by William James, Josiah Royce, John Dewey, Alain Locke, Sandra B. Rosenthal, and R. W. Sleeper, cited below.

11 These ideas about epistemological aspects of the philosophy of deep democracy reflect the influence of works by William James, John Dewey, Jane Addams, Charlene Haddock Seigfried, James Campbell, and Sandra B. Rosenthal, cited below.

12 These ideas about ethical aspects of the philosophy of deep democracy reflect the influence of works by Josiah Royce, John Dewey, Jane Addams, Charlene Haddock Seigfried, Alain Locke, Leonard Harris, John Stuhr, Sandra B. Rosenthal, and Cornel West, cited below.

13 These ideas about aesthetic aspects of the philosophy of deep democracy reflect the influence of works by William James, John Dewey, Louise Rosenblatt, and Alain Locke, cited below.

14 These ideas about civil, political and economic aspects of the philosophy of deep democracy reflect the influence of works by John Dewey, Sara M. Evans and Harry C. Boyte, Cornel West, and Robert F. Kennedy, Jr, cited below.

References

Addams, Jane (1902) *Democracy and Social Ethics*, New York: Macmillan.

Addams, Jane (1910) *Twenty Years at Hull-House*, New York: Macmillan.

Appiah, K. Anthony (1994) "Identity, Authenticity, Survival: Multicultural Societies and Social Reproduction," in Amy Gutmann (ed.), *Multiculturalism: Examining the Politics of Recognition*, Princeton: Princeton University Press.

Bellah, Robert N., Madsen, Richard, Sullivan, William M., Swidler, Ann, and Tipton, Steven M. (1985) *Habits of the Heart: Individualism and Commitment in American Life*, Berkeley: University of California Press.

Bloom, Allan (1987) *The Closing of the American Mind: How Higher Education Has Failed Democracy and Impoverished the Souls of Today's Students*, New York: Simon and Schuster.

Boyte, Harry C. (1986) "Populism and Free Spaces," in Harry C. Boyte and Frank Riessman (eds), *The New Populism: The Politics of Empowerment*, Philadelphia: Temple University Press.

Boyte, Harry C. (1989) *CommonWealth: A Return to Citizen Politics*, New York: Free Press.

Campbell, James (1993) "Democracy as Cooperative Inquiry," in John J. Stuhr (ed.), *Philosophy and the Reconstruction of Culture: Pragmatic Essays after Dewey*, Albany: State University of New York Press.

Campbell, James (1995) *Understanding John Dewey*, Chicago: Open Court.

Dewey, John (1916) *Democracy and Education*, New York: Macmillan. Reprinted in Jo Ann Boydston (ed.), *The Middle Works of John Dewey, 1899–1924*, vol. 9, Carbondale: Southern Illinois University Press, 1980.

Dewey, John (1927) *The Public and Its Problems*, New York: Henry Holt. Reprinted in Jo Ann Boydston (ed.), *The Later Works of John Dewey, 1925–1953*, vol. 2, Carbondale: Southern Illinois University Press, 1989.

Dewey, John (1939) *Freedom and Culture*, New York: G. P. Putnam's Sons. Reprinted in Jo Ann Boydston (ed.), *The Later Works of John Dewey, 1925–1953*, vol. 13, Carbondale: Southern Illinois University Press, 1991.

Dewey, John and Tufts, James H. (1932) *Ethics*, rev edn, New York: Henry Holt. Reprinted in Jo Ann Boydston (ed.), *The Later Works of John Dewey, 1925–1953*, vol. 7, Carbondale: Southern Illinois University Press, 1989.

Evans, Sara M. and Boyte, Harry C. (1986) *Free Spaces: The Sources of Democratic Change in America*, New York: Harper and Row.

Green, Judith M. (1994) "King's Pragmatic Philosophy of Political Transformation," *Journal of Social Philosophy*, XXV, 1 (spring 1994), 160–9.

Green, Judith M. (1997) "Alain Locke's Critical Multiculturalism: A Transformative Guide for the Twenty-First Century," in Leonard Harris (ed.), *Alain Locke and Values*, Savage, NJ: Rowman and Littlefield, 1997.

Green, Judith M. (forthcoming) *Deep Democracy: Community, Diversity, and Transformation*.

Gutmann, Amy (ed.) (1994) *Multiculturalism: Examining the Politics of Recognition*, Princeton: Princeton University Press.

Habermas, Jürgen (1984) *The Theory of Communicative Action, Volume One: Reason and the Rationalization of Society,* trans. Thomas McCarthy, Boston: Beacon Press.

Habermas, Jürgen (1987) *The Theory of Communicative Action, Volume Two: Lifeworld and System: A Critique of Functionalist Reason,* trans. Thomas McCarthy, Boston: Beacon Press.

Habermas, Jürgen (1994) "Struggles for Recognition in the Democratic Constitutional State," in Amy Gutmann (ed) *Multiculturalism: Examining the Politics of Recognition,* Princeton: Princeton University Press.

Harris, Leonard (ed.) (1987) *The Philosophy of Alain Locke: Harlem Renaissance and Beyond,* Philadelphia: Temple University Press.

Harris, Leonard (ed.) (1997) *Alain Locke and Values,* Savage, NJ: Rowman and Littlefield.

James, William (1948) *Essays in Pragmatism,* ed. Alburey Castell, New York: Hafner Press.

Kennedy, Robert F., Jr (1997) Panel Presentation on "The Environment & Development: Strange Bedfellows?," with Maria Rasmussen and Ismail Serageldin, moderated by Graciela Chichilnisky, as part of The Reuters Forum, sponsored by the Columbia University Graduate School of Journalism, New York, NY April 30, 1997.

King, Martin Luther, Jr (1967) *Where Do We Go From Here: Chaos or Community?* New York: Harper and Row.

Locke, Alain and Stern, Bernhard J. (1942) *When Peoples Meet: A Study of Race and Culture Contacts,* New York: Committee on Workshops, Progressive Education Association.

Marsh, James L. (1995) *Critique, Action, and Liberation,* Albany: State University of New York Press.

Rockefeller, Steven C. (1994) "Comment," in Amy Gutmann (ed.), *Multiculturalism: Examining the Politics of Recognition,* Princeton: Princeton University Press.

Rosenblatt, Louise (1997) "Response to My Critics," Keynote Session at the 1997 Annual Meetings of the Society for the Advancement of American Philosophy, sponsored by the University of New Mexico, Albuquerque, March 1997.

Rosenthal, Sandra B. (1993) "The Individual, the Community, and the Reconstruction of Values," in John J. Stuhr (ed.), *Philosophy and the Reconstruction of Culture: Pragmatic Essays after Dewey,* Albany: State University of New York Press.

Royce, Josiah (1918) *The Problem of Christianity.* New York: Macmillan. Reprinted with an introduction by John E. Smith, Chicago: University of Chicago Press, 1968.

Seigfried, Charlene Haddock (1993) "Validating Women's Experiences Pragmatically," in John J. Stuhr (ed.), *Philosophy and the Reconstruction of Culture: Pragmatic Essays after Dewey,* Albany: State University of New York Press.

Seigfried, Charlene Haddock (1996) *Pragmatism and Feminism: Reweaving the Social Fabric,* Chicago: University of Chicago Press.

Sleeper, R. W. (1993) "The Pragmatics of Deconstruction and the End of Meta-physics," in John J. Stuhr (ed.), *Philosophy and the Reconstruction of Culture: Pragmatic Essays after Dewey*, Albany: State University of New York Press.

Stuhr, John J. (1993) "Democracy as a Way of Life," in *Philosophy and the Reconstruction of Culture: Pragmatic Essays after Dewey*, Albany: State University of New York Press.

Stuhr, John J. (ed.) (1993) *Philosophy and the Reconstruction of Culture: Pragmatic Essays after Dewey*, Albany: State University of New York Press.

Walzer, Michael (1994) "Comment," in Amy Gutmann (ed.), *Multiculturalism: Examining the Politics of Recognition*, Princeton: Princeton University Press.

West, Cornel (1989) *The American Evasion of Philosophy: A Genealogy of Pragmatism*, Madison: University of Wisconsin Press.

West, Cornel (1993a) *Race Matters*, Boston: Beacon Press.

West, Cornel (1993b) *Prophetic Thought in Postmodern Times*, Monroe, Louisiana: Common Courage Press.

Wittgenstein, Ludwig (1953) *Philosophical Investigations*, trans. G. E. M. Anscombe, New York: Macmillan.

Wolf, Susan (1994) "Comment," in Amy Gutmann (ed.), *Multiculturalism: Examining the Politics of Recognition*, Princeton: Princeton University Press.

20

Universal Human Liberation: Community and Multiculturalism

Leonard Harris

I consider a seemingly intractable conflict – the conflict between favoring universal human liberation and favoring the interests of particular social entities. I consider alternatives to the view that a particularity should be favored for instrumental reasons, e.g. that we should support the working class because its interest will help destroy capitalism, or that we should support existing races or ethnic group proto-nationalisms to protect their cultural integrity.

A doxastic conception of thought takes the following form: ideas, beliefs, attitudes, virtues, and morals are coterminous with actions, behaviors, policies, and institutions. *The Closing of the American Mind* argues that the American mind, as a sort of collective thinking entity with definitive traits – traits directly associated with behaviors – has become intolerant, invirtuous, and conceptually misguided in part, because education is not encouraging the pursuit of certitude, knowledge, and the good.[1] This approach considers relativist commitment to ethnicities not only contrary to the spirit of democracy, but an approach that fails to acknowledge that cultures are not all equal. *The Opening of the American Mind* argues that America has been historically plural.[2] The "American mind" has different traits on this view; and cultural diversity and particularity offers beneficial contributions. Both approaches, however, presuppose a doxastic picture of thought and action. Significant disjunction between thought and action would suggest that actions, behaviors, policies and institutions considered odious may be associated with ideas considered laudable. Disjunctions of this sort must be treated as less than significant for an argument presupposing a "mind" in some substantive way encoded in a social entity.

A doxastic picture of social entities takes the following form. Social entities embody interests or essences coterminous with their agency. Such entities as nation-states, working classes, native populations, women, etc. can be thought to have interests and essences. The doxastic picture of social entities has been criticized by numerous philosophers.[3] Characteristically, for example, Marx is criticized for believing that the working class would be a cohesive group, pursuing ownership, control, communal management and fair distribution of wealth.[4] Marx is also criticized for treating social entities as if they were ontologically real, i.e. undifferentiated groups. However, numerous philosophers share a desire for universal human liberation.

Universal human liberation includes freedom from the very boundaries of the names through which freedom is sought – the deafening boundaries of national and racial ideation separating communities; boundaries excluding the poor, workers, proletariat, and the wretched from peership in the human family; boundaries subordinating the powerless from participation, ownership, and control of material resources.

The above view of universal human liberation hardly includes all of the features associated with the concept. Marx, for example, would certainly include the realization of humanity's species being, e.g. transformation of nature, negation of alienation, self-realization through participatory control of the means of production. Humanity, or rather, liberated workers, would be empowered to exercise their distinctly human capacities without the fetters of alienating mythologies that fail to reasonably conform to reasoned scientific judgment. Edward W. Blyden, for example, would include the realization of ethnic empowerment. Empowerment of ethnic kinds, i.e. Africans, Asians, Europeans, Hispanics, etc., would allow the possibility of equality between natural kinds, authentic cultures could flourish, and modernity would be enhanced because each kind would feel sufficiently motivated to improve their material conditions and make their unique contributions to universal civilization. Deweyian pragmatists would reject the idea of an end state. When universal human interest was achieved, however, the Deweyian pragmatist would focus on the importance of scientific reasoning as a way of maximizing changes for enhanced flourishing. This is why the Deweyian pragmatist avoids the conflict between deontological as well as teleological conceptions of justice.[5] The Deweyian pragmatist also avoids conceiving persons as genuine if and only if they are either encoded in communities or are perceived as isolated individuals.[6]

I believe that the above depiction of universal human liberation is defensible, although insufficiently developed. A good deal of the argument here is, moreover, admittedly speculative, tentative, and suggestive.

The pursuit of universal human liberation always occurs through the struggles of particular communities. Yet critics of the ontological status of social entities often deny that social entities(a) pursue interests that would liberate themselves and the whole of humanity and (b) deny that social entities have the agency, power, or capacity to cause or create universal human liberation through the empowerment of any particular community. Moreover, warranting "empowerment" of a particularity, namely, the authority to decide what persons have preferred treatment in receiving jobs, homes, business opportunities, healthcare services, and expenses for schools is, on some accounts, warranting authoritarianism.

The condition of liberation for a particularity is either its own negation, or its universalization.

The liberation of a population subjugated by race is an example of a particularity in which liberation includes, but is not limited to, liberation from identification by race. Peoples and cultures can exist and flourish quite well without confinement to racial identities. It is fallacious to identify race and culture as if they were inextricably mutually causal and invariably and eternally tied. I have argued elsewhere that the primary interest of any social race is the negation of all identity by race and empowerment through control of assets.[7] There is nothing redeeming about entrapment in debilitating stereotypes of race. Liberation requires the negation of the racial identity of the oppressor and the oppressed. Moreover, the negation of the links between biology and culture, biology and character, biology and potential, and biology and rights should be negated. However, the death of racial identity does not mean that racism is dead. Rather, the negation of all institutions, interests, and benefits that sustain oppression by race is required.

In a non-racist world social races would not exist. No one would be born into a race nor have a non-moral duty to be the representative of a race. Internal unity of the raciated is a necessary instrumental condition for the possibility of independence from the terror of race-based oppression: the unspeakable holocausts ravaging Gypsies, Kurds, or black South Africans, as well as race-based working-class exploitation.[8] The social instruments of racial identity, however, are hardly transhistorical. The enriching and vibrant reality of African culture, on the other hand, has transhistorical warrant as a constantly evolving source of universalizable cultural good and local cultural sustenance.

The liberation of woman is an example of a particularity in which a condition of liberation includes, but is not limited to, engagement in universality. Stereotyping women as incapable of exercising authority as soldiers, corporate executives, or athletes is arguably extinguished when such roles are no longer seen as the provinces reserved for men. If they are considered provinces in which persons are engaged the stereotype is no longer operative. Multiple identities and trait ascriptions may be common in a world that has achieved universal human liberation, i.e. a world that does not restrict persons to roles assumed inherently and inalterable encoded in their gender, race, ethnicity, class, or nation.

The warrant for the universalization of well-being cuts across lines of race, ethnicity, gender, nation, and class. The negation of starvation, communicable diseases, debilitating but curable illnesses, preventable premature deaths, torture, rape, unjust incarceration, degrading insults, and demeaning treatment require the imposition of values across lines of particularity. The universalization of these interests is, in effect, the universalization of interest intrinsic to particularities.

One way to see the importance of the universalizing of values and realization of universal human interest is to consider the following: it is time someone said it – multiculturalism is dead. Monoculturalism has already won. Discourse about multiculturalism is just that – discourse. It does not pick out or point to a reality in much of the world, nor does it pick out or point to any substantive trends. If the history of America, for example, is the history of cultural exchanges between historically and contemporary evolving social entities, those entities are now far more similar than ever before – there is one currency, banking system, common sources and forms of energy, near-standardized forms of medical care, and even common rules regulating garbage disposal. There are fewer language differences, religious differences, loyalties to tribes, clans, lords, chiefs, kings, queens, city-states, and nations; fewer races, ethnic groups, and peoples generating loyalty; fewer wars of attrition than the earth has known since the decline of the iron age.

Pragmatists such as John Dewey favored using scientific principles to explain human behavior and the use of the experimental method to engineer social improvements. However, Dewey believed that the future was always open; accident, a change in views or opinions, chance, or new discoveries might easily alter the course of future events. Alain Locke, a radical pragmatist, criticized persons that relied on the scientific method in hopes that they would not forget the importance of imperatives, i.e. moral or value imperatives.[9] Such imperatives included, for Locke, the need to avoid the imposition of absolutes and the need to promote cultural reciprocity and tolerance. And one of Locke's close working associates, especially in the 1940s, Ruth Benedict, argued for a form of cultural relativism in her early anthropological work. This version held that cultures were incommensurable, i.e. meanings were endogenous to a culture and are not translatable to persons not sharing the mores and ways of a culture. Cultures, for Benedict, sustained values at best relevant to their own environment.

None of the assumed consequences of a world that one might expect, if the above perspectives of Dewey, Locke, or Benedict prevailed, have occurred. We might assume, for example, that accident, chance, uncertainty, and incommensurability between cultures would continue to assure a world of substantive differences. Such variables have failed to generate difference. The future is not open – diversities of the past cannot happen, authentic racial kinds cannot continue, ethnicities segregated from the influence of world cultures are no longer a possibility, and substantively independent nation-states are a relic. Everywhere, cultures that fail to offer some form of commensurability with modernity die; everywhere, tolerance exists if and only if the monoculture of the world flourishes and within it discourse and exchange occurs. The tourist trade is one of the most common forms of cultural commonality. Cultural reciprocity is too often a matter of the native, as an object of our gaze, functioning as a living relic. Simultaneously, the very world of modernity, whether it is Broadway in New York or Carnival in Bahia, makes itself an object for its own agents as well as an object of a gaze – tourists visit these sites while these sites are filled with self-conscious agents actively creating.

The monocultural world Marx, Adam Smith, Ibn Khaldun, and Edward W. Blyden imagined has turned out to exist. The monocultural world may be the result of imposed values; if so, those imposed values are often normalized.

There is no "natural" social world in any event, which is analogous to the myth that nature exists on earth outside the context of being under the control of humanity or substantively effected by humanity. There simply are no significant unmapped spaces on the planet. For Marx, capitalism would universalize the world. Capitalism would destroy all feudal models of production; all antiquated forms of barter in deference to a money economy; all languages that were not coterminous with the language of commerce. Marx was right in these regards. Even if capitalism has not destroyed, in its wake, all religions, pagan rituals, or nation-states, it has substantively helped universalize – make common – standard ways of doing business, using money, and creating wealth. Even if capitalism has not created clear class divisions that stand in clear opposition to one another, it has helped to create fairly common sorts of classes. Socialist, communist, and capitalist alike use surprisingly similar standards; at the least, there are agreed conversion tables for exchanging the currencies of every nation and more world treaties regulating the rules of war, employment, and citizenship than ever before. It is at least arguable that the class struggle is being waged between enemies far more similar than ever before, despite the romanticization of postmodern difference.

Khaldun was right – law would prove among the most powerful tools for making common the Koran. It would prove the most powerful tool for making common world religions as well.

And Blyden was right – the world is divided between geographic ethnic kinds – Africans, Europeans, Asians, Hispanics. These are hardly racial kinds of the sort Blyden believed were the representative stock of pure blood types. They are, however, dominant identities through which people often identify their cultural and geographic loyalties.

Multiculturalism points to, given the reality of monoculturalism, the inescapable reality of ontological entities. Social entities can be the conduits for, and sites of, universal human liberation. That is, the transhistorical interest and traits (if not essences) encoded in particularities, equally as important as impermanent, transient, elliptical and illusory interests and traits, are both embedded in particularities.

Changes in structures would signal a change in the reality of racism, not the disappearance of temporal ideations that may or may not spell change in the material realities, social entities, or social formations of populations – contrary to a doxastic picture of ideas and behaviors in which ideas are nearly invariably associated with, if not considered directly causal of, behavior. Race, for example, is a temporal social construction. What counts as a social race in America is hardly what counts as a social race in Sri Lanka. There are constantly shifting identities.

> As a culture, we call ourselves Spanish when referring to ourselves as a linguistic group and when copping out. It is then that we forget our predominant Indian genes. ... We call ourselves Hispanic or Spanish-American or Latin American or Latin when linking ourselves to other Spanish-speaking peoples of the Western hemisphere and when copping out. We call ourselves Mexican-American to signify we are neither Mexican nor American, but more the noun "American" than the adjective "Mexican" (and when copping out).[10]

Mestizo may affirm both Indian and Spanish heritage, raza may refer to Chicanos' racial identity. "Copping out" is an invariable feature of positively identifying with a race or ethnic group. Authenticity is not achieved by either identifying or copping out. Multiple and shifting ethnic as well as raciated identities are rather common. However, the negation of race as a temporal illusion, or recognition that ethnicity is an unstable category, is hardly identical to the negation of racism or ethnocentricism.

The egregious joys and power acquired through the monetary profit secured by racists and the advantages enjoyed by dominant populations in racist societies is not negated by ideation changes. The social entities and social formations are already arranged to generate wealth, jobs, and opportunities for dominant populations. That is, changed ownership, control, participation, and access to material reality will have far greater impact on creating a deraciated and socially viable world.

The possibility of human liberation is contingent on the agencies and interests of social entities. Communitarians are right to think that special obligations to families, relatives, friends, and neighborhoods, as well as broader identities such as nation, ethnicity, or gender, are obligations we have that we never choose. Moreover, we must attach intrinsic, non-instrumental value to social entities and formations that sustain special obligations. Communitarians and pluralists are wrong, however, in assuming that social entities and formations are stable and should never be the object of destruction. I see no reason, for example, to warrant the existence of slavocracies such as pre-civil war America.

Social groups are the decisive forces shaping human history, present realities, and future situations. Reasoning through social entities is not an unfortunate form of self-delusion – acting as if one is, represents, stands for, means, is obligated to, bonded to, and is the conduit for a social entity or social formation. Representative heuristics – the way individuals define themselves as representing collective entities – is a normal feature of cognition. The utilization of representative heuristics is simply not inherently oppressive. Erroneous strategies, inferences, and implications can bedevil representative heuristics as well as reasoning, as if one in no way represented, stood for, or was bonded to others. However, there is no reason to believe that existing social entities are permanent driving forces of human history; no reason to assume that universal human liberation equates each entity gaining authenticity according to its Aristotelian essence. There are strong reasons to earnestly consider what entities we warrant, what particular and universal goods they offer, and what counts as the mode of liberation associated with their endogenous traits.

Contrary to a doxastic picture of social entities – a picture in which social entities invariably embody stable interests and essences – it is the adversarial features of social entities that may be the most important arguable sources for liberation. It may not be the "working class" as an undifferentiated entity with an array of definitive interests and modes of agency, which is the engine of universal human liberation. However, it may be the adversarial sector that warrants special regard for its intrinsic worth. One way to see what I mean by this is by considering the reality of radical traditions. Adversarial traditions, i.e. traditions of resistance that emanate from oppressed social entities, are voices that often perceive community as becoming. That is, the immiserated members of social entities – women, African Americans, Hispanics, workers, etc. – can only pursue liberation by engaging in resistance struggles intended to create new traditions and alternative communities.[11] That is, new bonds. If our imagined communities are the communities of the downtrodden, wretched, degraded, raped, victims of cruelty, the objects of viciousness, then they are subjects integral to a conceptualized community that is to become. When the least well-off are agents in the moral community, the future is a becoming in a way that counts the immiserated.

The disjunction between ideas and actions, as well as the disjunction between social entities and agency, do not render irrelevant the import of ideas or entities. The agency of particularities are necessarily the agencies, conduits, and forces that create the reality of universality.

A radical transformation of misery, exploitation, starvation, the hopelessness of immigrants, racial stereotyping, and ethnocentrism may well depend on our achieving, through the aegis of our multiple locations, conditions for the possibility of liberation. Moreover, it may be especially the agency of the excluded, downtrodden, wretched, and immiserated of particularities and their transhistorical interests that hold the key to future realities. That is, the adversarial, insurrectional, and revolutionary struggle to materially and institutionally create communities fundamentally different from the horribly confining and destructive boundaries currently constricting freedom.[12]

Notes

1 See Allan D. Bloom, *The Closing of the American Mind* (New York: Simon and Schuster, 1987). Similar social psychology approaches are evident in such works as Carter G. Woodson, *The Mind of the Negro* (Washington, DC: Association for the Study of Negro Life and History, 1926); Earl E. Thorpe, *The Mind of the Negro* (Baton Rovge, Lovisiona: Ortlieb Press, 1970).

2 Lawrence W. Levine, *The Opening of the American Mind* (Boston: Beacon Press, 1996).

3 See, for example, Dwight Furrow, *Against Theory* (New York: Routledge, 1995).

4 See, for an interpretation of Marx that considers his historical materialism and the role of classes as central to Marx's philosophy, Allen W. Wood, *Karl Marx* (Boston: Routledge and Kegan Paul, 1981).

5 See, for example, Henry S. Richardson, "Beyond Good and Right: Toward a Constructive Ethical Pragmatism," *Philosophy & Public Affairs* vol. 24, no. 2 (spring 1995), pp. 108–41.

6 I am indebted to Judith Green, Fordham University, for suggesting this article: Sandra B. Rosenthal, "The Individual, the Community, and the Reconstruction of Values," in John J. Stuhr (ed.), *Philosophy and the Reconstruction of Culture: A Pragmatic Essay after Dewey* (Albany, SUNY Press, 1993), pp. 59–77.

7 See Leonard Harris, "What, Then, Is Racism," forthcoming in *The Concept of Racism* (Atlantic Heights, NJ: Humanities Press, 1997); also see Harris, "Rendering the Subtext: Subterranean Deconstruction Project," Leonard Harris (ed) *The Philosophy of Alain Locke: Harlem Renaissance and Beyond* (Philadelphia: Temple University Press, 1989), pp. 279–89; "Historical Subjects and Interests: Race, Class, and Conflict," Michael Sprinkler et al. (eds), *The Year Left* (New York: Verso, 1986), pp. 91–106.

8 See, for example, Robin D. G. Kelley, *Race Rebels* (New York: The Free Press, 1994).

9 See Alain Locke, "Values and Imperatives," in Leonard Harris (ed.), *The Philosophy of Alain Locke*, pp. 31–50. Also see, for the unavoidability of metaphysical commitments or imperatives, Sidney Hook, *The Metaphysics of Pragmatism* (Chicago: Open Press, 1927).

10 G. Anzaldua, *Borderlands/La Frontera* (San Francisco: Spinsters/Aunt Lute, 1987), p. 63.

11 I argue this in "The Horror of Tradition or How to Burn Babylon and Build Benin While Reading *A Preface to a Twenty Volume Suicide Note*," *Philosophical Forum*, vol. XXIV, 1–3 (fall–spring reprinted in 1992–93), pp. 94–119; reprinted in John P. Pittman (ed.), *African–American Perspectives and Philosophical Traditions* (New York: Routledge, 1997), pp. 94–119.

12 See Henry A. Giroux, "Insurgent Multiculturalism and the Promise of Pedagogy," in David T. Goldberg (ed.), *Multiculturalism* (Oxford: Blackwell Publishers), pp. 328–43.

Index

abjection theory, 5; and exclusion, 174; and foundational fantasy, 174; and patriarchy, 174–5; and rejection of otherness, 173–4; and self-identity, 175

absolutism, 427

academia: incompetence in, 142–3; and oppression, 141–3, 149; thinking in, 311–12

Adorno, T.W., 146, 226

advertising, 103, 105, 110

aesthetic dimension: and deep democracy, 436–7, 445; role of, 224–6, 231

affective notion, 183–4, 316–17, 327

affirmative action, 97–8, 131, 132–3, 141, 142–3

affirmative/transformative remedies, 47, 48, 53, 57, 62, 64, 65, 69, 70; and class, 33–4, 40; defined, 31–2; and race, 38–9, 40; and sexuality, 32–3, 36–8, 40

Africa Town, 276–9; Folk Festival, 277–8

African Americans: and alienation, 261–3, 269–73; and American culture, 291–2; and assimilation, 277–8, 288, 289, 292–3; and changing attitudes of whites, 268; culture of, 278–9; effect of racism on, 272–3; effect of slavery on, 271–2; as estranged from themselves, 269, 270, 271; experiences of, 292; impoverished life of, 430–1; and justice, 265; and recognition, 266; and rights, 266–7; and support of the community, 270–1, 272, 273; as threat to nation, 284

African Spirit, 10–11

Akwasasne Notes, 405, 410

Alexander, J., 223

alienation, 6–7, 259–60; and African Americans, 261–3, 269–73; and concentration on fragility/insecurity of self, 260–3; group/individual action against, 270; as kind of unfreedom, 264; liberal response to, 259, 263–8; Marxist account of, 259–60, 268–9; natal, 271–2

Allen, P.G., 410

Allport, G.W., 196

American Indians, 338–9, 350, 352

analytic philosophy, 137, 148

Anderson, D., 138

androcentrism, 28

anomalous materialism, 124

anomalous monism, 145

anthropology, 149, 434, 440

anti-multiculturalism, 138, 139–40, 143

anti-Semitism, 44–5

Antillean experience, 323–7, 333

Appalon, W., 223

Arendt, H., 145, 330

Aristotle, 123, 139

assimilation, 393; coercive, 388, 390, 395

attachment theory, 181
Avakian, B., 145, 146
Axtell, J., 350

Baier, A., 378
Bakunin, M., 152, 164
Baldwin, J., 291–2
Balibar, E., 109
Barthes, R., 129
Beauvoir, S. de, 170
behavior, ideal/valued, 404–5
Bell, D., 153
Bem, S., 202, 208
Benedict, R., 453
Benjamin, J., 181
Berlin, I., 265, 282
Bernier, F., 280, 283
Bhabha, H., 305, 306, 308, 310, 311
bivalent collectivities, 27–31, 36, 40, 44,
   48, 92–3
black: experience of being, 262–3, 317–25;
   see also negritude; people of color
Blassingame, J., 271
Blau, H., 412, 413
Bloom, A., 140, 444
blues music, 288–91, 297
Blyden, E.W., 450, 453, 454
body, the, 225–6; erotogenic, 247; real/
   imaginary parts, 246–52; taking back,
   225
Bookchin, M., 346
Boski, P., 206
Bourdieu, P., 58
Bové, P., 311
Bowlby, J., 180
Boyte, H.C., 437
Braidotti, R., 226
Branscombe, N. et al., 199, 200
Brant, J., 419
Brennan, T., 173, 183
Buchanan, P., 107, 140
Burnham, J., 153
Butler, J., 173, 225; and lesbian phallus,
   244–52; and sexual difference, 236–7
Butler, O., 150

Calverton, V.F., 152
Canfield, W.W., 405
capitalism, 103, 140, 151, 153, 164–5,
   263, 315, 316, 453–4; displacement of,
   154; global, 107

categories, 196–7, 198, 206
Césaire, A.F., 307, 313–14, 322
Chafe, W., 407, 410
Charles, Prince of Wales, 149
Chodorow, N., 189, 190–3
Chomsky, N., 311
citizenship, 437; and education, 424–5;
   eligibility for, 385–7; formation of, 390,
   394–6
civil liberties, 162
Cixous, H., 230
class, 2, 4, 43–4, 47, 51, 131–2, 133, 153,
   209, 231, 268, 453–4; and affirmative/
   transformative remedies, 33–4, 40;
   exploitation of, 24–6; marginalization
   of, 134–5, 148; struggle, 157, 158
cognitive process, 9
colonialism, 138–9, 288, 303, 304, 306–7,
   308–9, 316, 331, 332, 340
colonized/colonizer, 308, 340
communism, 145
communitarians, 265–6, 455
communities of memory and hope, 431,
   433, 435, 441, 445
community: coopting developmental
   processes, 431–2; and cross-cultural
   participation, 442–3; and democracy,
   132–3; as human and non-human, 12,
   405, 408, 416–17; quality of life in, 425;
   role of, 412–13
conceptual logics, 5, 235–6, 241, 250
Condolence Council, 418–19
conflict, 8, 442
consciousness, 316–17, 323–9
constitution, as rights-based, 222–4
consumerist model, 2, 128, 132, 143–4,
   147–8
Continental philosophy, 137, 148
Cornplanter, J.J., 405
corporate multiculturalism, 102–5;
   inverted, 109–11
corporeal logics, 4, 5, 235, 238, 241, 243,
   250, 251
corporeal schema, 327–9
counter-possibility, 130, 146–7
Cox, O.C., 44
Crèvecœur, H. St J. de, 285, 386–7
critical cultural pluralism, 427–9, 434,
   439, 440, 443
critical democratic multiculturalism, 440–3
Crump, E.H., 288–9

Cudd, A.E., 208
cultural: alterity, 303; change, 440; turn,
10
cultural/symbolic injustice, 22–3, 43, 50–1,
71, 90–4; and class, 24–6; and race,
29–31; remedy for, 23–4; and sexuality,
26–9; *see also* affirmative/transformative
remedies
culture, 11, 143, 324, 453; African
American, 278–9; changes in, 289–90;
and climatic determinism, 282; defense
of, 137; ethno-, 76, 79; and individual
recognition, 77–9; open/narrow-minded,
281; as patriarchal, 177–8; pluralism of,
282, 283–4; and politics, 52, 55, 58–60,
61–2, 70, 81, 93; as static, 95; and
value, 83, 96
cynicism, 132

Darstellung, 328–9
Davidson, D., 124, 141
Davis, C., 277–8, 279, 284
de Certeau, M., 123
De Leon, B., 206
de Maistre, J., 283
deconstruction, 2–3, 13; as cultural
analogue of socialism, 35–6
deep democracy, 443; aesthetic dimension,
436–7, 445; civil, political, economic
institutions of, 437; ethical dimension,
436; as preferable way of life, 435–9;
reality of, 435–6, 439
Deleuze, G., 123
Deloria, Vine, Jr, 341
democracy: and community life, 432–3;
conceptions of, 429; critical cultural
pluralism as motive/method for, 427–9;
deep philosophy of, 435–9; formal/deep
contrast, 427, 430–5; as multicultural,
425; as shared ideal, 433–4
Derrida, J., 107, 129, 144, 146
Deutschke, R., 344
Dewey, J., 432–3, 435, 440, 444, 450,
452, 453; and Tufts, J.H., 434
Dhawan, N. et al., 206
di Leonardo, M., 138, 149
diamat (dialectical materialism), 121–7
difference, 1–2, 422, 428; as opposition,
169, 172
diminished social categories, 365–8, 369,
374, 375

division of labor, 63–4, 102; ceremonial,
414; and justice, 50, 57–8; sexual, 238,
253
double consciousness, 112
Douglas, M., 173
Douglass, F., 372
downward social constitution, 365–8, 369,
374, 379
dreams, *see* ononharoia
D'Souza, D., 136, 140, 141
Du Bois, W.E.B., 104, 112, 262, 264, 269,
271, 279
Durant, W., 348–9
Dworkin, R., 21–2

Ebert, T.L., 101, 231, 232
education, 12, 431, 433, 437, 449; and
contributions of women, 444; cost of,
155–6; and critical democratic
multiculturalism, 440–3; as Eurocentric,
334–5, 389–90, 424, 426, 444; and
inclusion of differing cultures, 444;
indigenist alternative, 340–3;
reconsideration of multiculturalism in,
422–7; refashioning of, 392–3; struggle
for change, 347–8; White studies,
335–40; winning strategy for, 343–7
ego, 247, 248, 329
Ellison, R., 262, 264
emotional category configuration, 368–71
Engels, F., 160
Enlightenment, 112–14, 281, 388
equality, 9, 51, 61, 73, 75, 86–7, 133–4,
187, 209, 222, 239; and difference, 63;
and identity, 175–6; and recognition,
90–4, 95
Escobar, A., 58–9
Ethnic Studies, 344, 345–6
Evans, S.M., 437
event, 328–9
experience, 301, 317–22; adverse, 360–5,
367, 369–71; of being black, 322–9

family: relationship, 228–9; resemblance,
435, 445
Fanon, F., 5, 87, 340; on experience, 301;
Gates on, 307–14; and negritude, 322–9;
psychoanalytical/colonial discourse of,
309; reception of, 313; Said on, 307–8;
significance of, 304, 306; and thought,

301, 303–4, 314–15; and violence, 329–31
fascism, 145–6
Feinberg, J., 264–5
Felski, R., 226
Felson, R.B. and Tedeschi, J.T., 206
feminine subject: and desire, 238, 252; and equality, 239; and exclusion, 252, 256; and interaction with the other, 240–4; and language, 242–3; and recognition, 239–40; and respect, 240; and sexual difference, 240–1; and sexuality, 238–9; as supportive of the masculine, 237–8, 245–6; *see also* masculine subject; subjectivity
feminine, the, 236; representation of, 244–5, 246–7
feminism, 4, 48, 51, 98, 131, 141, 225, 229; and affirmative/transformative remedies, 37–8; and equality/difference debate, 63–4; return to earliest aspirations, 220–1, 222; warning to, 233
Feuchtwang, S., 305
Finkielkraut, A., 282
First World, 382–3
Fiske, S.T. and Taylor, S.E., 197, 202
Flax, J., 191
Foucault, M., 4, 122–3, 223–4, 311
Fraser, N., 73–4, 302; on recognition and equality, 90–4
freedom, 265, 322
Freud, S., 170–1, 177–8, 189, 238, 318, 325–6
Fukuyama, F., 103, 107

Gadamer, H.-G., 83
Gates, H.L., Jr, on Fanon, 302, 303–7, 307–14
gay-identity politics, 32, 46
gender, 44, 45, 47–8, 88, 92, 133–4, 191; and affirmative/transformative remedies, 40; and identity, 240; and justice, 26–9, 61–2, 113; role of schemas in, 202–4; transgressions of, 254
Giroux, H.A., 103
Glazer, N., 393; and Moynihan, D.P., 278
global diversity, 111–12
global theory, 307, 309–10, 310, 312–13
Gouldner, A., 352
Gramsci, A., 311
gratitude, 371–3, 381

Greenblatt, S., 305, 310
Greider, W., 107, 112
groups, 8–9, 185, 207–8
Grünbaum, A., 210
Gulf War, 147
Gutman, A., 444

Habermas, J., 42, 55, 70, 93–4, 137, 226
Han, G. and Park, B., 206
Handsome Lake, 418
Handy, C.W., 288–90
harm, 208, 264, 267
Harris, L., 429
Hegel, G.W.F., 6, 10–11, 103, 170, 171, 175, 193, 224, 226, 279, 283, 315, 321, 382
Heidegger, M., 224
Henry, W., 138
Herder, J.G., 281–3, 289
Hewitt, J.N.B., 405–7, 417, 418
Himes, C., 330
Himmelfarb, G., 140
Hinduism, 280–1
history, 337, 350, 383
Hobbes, T., 187, 209
Hoffman, C. and Hurst, N., 198–9
Hollinger, D.A., 74, 287
homophobia, 44–5
homosexuals, 44
Honneth, A., 22, 43, 69, 75–6, 93
hostile misfortunes, 363–4
humanism, 160–1
Hume, D., 359, 365, 368, 368–9, 371, 388
Huntington, S., 106, 108, 111, 140
Hurston, Z.N., 279, 282, 285, 286–7
Husserl, E., 319

identity, 6, 8, 13, 21–2, 48, 51, 59, 68, 88, 89, 95, 98, 297–8; and affective energy, 183–4; American, 386–7; black, 310; and copping out, 454–5; cultural, 106; and difference, 169, 172; and disidentification, 229–30; and equality, 175–6; formation, 394; and gender, 240; group, 185; individual, 170–2, 185; as interrelational, 185; Iroquoian, 404, 414; loss of, 239, 254; and maternal body, 178, 182–4; and mother–infant relationship, 177–84; and move from nature to culture, 177–8; and Oedipal complex, 178; omission of ethnic/

national groups, 20, 91–2; and otherness, 171, 172–3, 177; politics of, 106; psychological, 172; and race, 287–8; and relationships, 176–7; shifting, 453, 454, 455; social theory of, 198; subjective, 303–4; symbolic, 251–2; through exclusion or abjection, 173–6, 177

Idson, T.L. and Price, H.F., 205

imaginary domain, 5–6, 220–1, 223, 226–7, 229–30; described, 221–2; role of, 224

immigrants, 422–3

imperial multiculturalism, 106–8; imverted, 111–12

imperialism, 138–9, 303, 307, 309–10, 314, 315

in-group/out-group distinction, 9, 196–7, 200–1, 206; and minimal group experiments, 197–8; and social identity theory, 198

individuation, minimum conditions of, 221, 222

intercultural notion, 289–90, 297

Irigaray, L., 226, 227, 229, 230; and the feminine subject, 237–43; and sexual difference, 234–6, 253

Isaacs, H., 417

itinerary, 304–7, 310–11

James, C.L.R., 311

James, W., 445

Jameson, F., 102, 147–8, 310

JanMohamed, A.R., 305, 308, 310

Jefferson, T., 284, 287, 388

Johnson, B., 136

Jones, W., 406

Jung, C.G., 324

justice, 8, 20, 42, 50, 52–3, 71, 90, 93, 98, 131, 229, 233, 311, 378, 390; dichotomous vs. plural categorization of, 54–8; division of, 69–70; failure of, 220; and primary political concerns, 42; and self-concept, 264–6; *see also* cultural/symbolic injustice; socioeconomic injustice

Kant, I., 1–2, 103, 123, 222, 224, 280–1, 283, 388; preplagiarism of, 348–9

Kennedy, R.F., Jr, 437

Khaldun, I., 453, 454

Kimball, R., 136

King, M.L., Jr, 430

Klein, M., 178–80, 182

knowledge, 383–4, 389–9, 424–5

Koditschek, T., 48

Kohlberg, L., 360

Kristeva, J., 173

Kymlicka, W., 388, 395

Lacan, J., 4, 178, 182–3, 247, 248–9, 308, 318, 323, 326–7

Lalemant, Father Jerome, 402–3, 408–9, 412, 415

Landes, D., 335

language, 178–9, 224, 255, 325, 326; and involvement of touching upon, 242–3, 246, 250; and needs, 182–4; Seneca, 407, 408–9, 418

law, 330–1

Layard, A.H., 163

League, K., 134, 135

Left, the, 123, 141, 151–2; culture of, 157–65; economics of, 159; mistakes concerning capitalism, 164–5; philosophy of, 159; politics of, 159; and post-Marxism, 159; split in, 68, 69

Lehman, D., 136

Lenin V.I., 124, 157

LeRoi, Jones, 290

lesbian phallus, 236–7, 249–52

Levinas, E., 170

Lewis, C., 279

liberalism, 4, 161–3, 387–8, 395; and alienation, 259, 263–8

linguistic turn, 10

Locke, A., 334, 427, 428–9, 432, 440, 445, 452–3

Loyola conference, 136–7

ludic multiculturalism, 3, 101–2; inverted, 109

Lukács, G. von, 314–15, 319

Lyotard, J.-F., 307

Lytton, H. and Romney, D., 203

McGann, J., 305

Machajski, W., 152

Mannoni, O., 332

Manty, M., 42

Mao Tse Tung, 126–7, 146

Marcuse, H., 102

Marx, K., 21, 114, 157, 159–60, 209, 259–60, 450, 453; influences on, 351

Marxism, 1, 7, 103, 122, 146, 150, 231, 315, 346–7; and alienation, 259–60, 268–9; as inheritor of German idealism, 123; models of, 124–7; role of, 151–2

masculine subject, 237–8; and desire, 252, 253–4; and equality, 239; and interaction with the other, 240–4; and sexuality, 239; supported by the feminine, 237–8, 245–6; *see also* feminine subject; subjectivity

master–slave dialectic, 13, 175, 189, 255

materialism, *see* diamat (dialectical materialism)

mathematics, 144

Memmi, A., 305, 306, 309, 339

memory, 325–6, 327–8, 433, 435, 441; and adverse experience, 361–5, 367

Memphis Blues, 288, 291

Merleau-Ponty, M., 319

Mill, J.S., 388

Miller, J.G., 206

mind/body split, 226, 235, 264, 323

Minnich, E.K., 388–9, 394

mirror stage, 178, 247, 248–9, 323, 327

modernism, 383–4

Mohawk, J., 401

monoculturalism, 169–70, 283, 452–3

moral deference, 13–14, 359–60; and bearing witness to moral pain, 360, 376–7, 380; and being socially constituted, 365–8; and earning trust, 378–9; and emotional configuration, 368–71; and emotions, 375; and gratitude, 371–3; idea of, 371–9; and learning, 377–8; as owed to persons of good will, 360, 373–4; and social categories, 360–5

Morrison, T., 230

mother–child relationship: and affective energy, 183–4; depressive position, 179; and good enough mother, 180; guilt and reparation, 179; as intersubjective, 181–3; and the maternal body, 182–4; Oedipal, 177–8; paranoid-schizoid position, 179; pre-Oedipal stage, 178–9; as prototypical, 179–80; and social interaction, 180–1; as subjectless sociality, 181–2

mother–daughter relationship, 238; and freedom, 227–8

Mouffe, C., 227

multiculturalism, 46, 71, 100–1; and analogy with the family, 130; as antidote to assimilation, 289; cartographers, 108–12; challenge of, 128; as contested term, 73–4; and creation of community, 128–30; as cultural analogue of welfare state, 35; detractors of, 129; and education, 422–7, 440–3; efficacy of, 293; and Fanon, 303–4; impostors, 102–8; and justice, 51; lack of unifying theory of, 1; as liberating ideology, 158; and nation-building, 393–6; as necessary for foreign policy, 106; new enlightenment, 112–14; as petty-bourgeois eclecticism, 123; and playing the intellectual game, 130–1; and race, 288; as transformational, 2; and weak cultures, 158–9

Murray, C., 140

Nagel, T., 360

nation state: and cultural diversity, 391–2; formation of, 385–8; and multiculturalism, 393–6; and political correctness, 394–5; roles of, 428; and social change, 392–4; and use of false universalization, 388–9

nationalism, 316–17, 329

natural kinds, 384

natural/cultural divide, 234

needs, 59–60, 182, 184

negotiation, 3–4

negritude, 11, 320–5, 322–9, 332–3; *see also* black: experience of being; people of color

Nehamas, A., 148

neo-Marxism, 152, 153

Neurath, O., 145

Neuromancer, 144, 150

New Left, 8, 51–2

New World Order (NWO), 101, 107–8

Nietzsche, F., 170, 302

nihilism, 430–1, 442

Noble Lie, 100, 101, 106

Nomad, M., 152

Norton, J., 419

Nott, J., 284

Oakes, P.J. et al., 197, 198, 201, 207
object relations theory, 181, 189, 190–3
Oddou, G. and Mendenhall, M., 206
Oedipal complex, 170, 178, 190, 326, 333
Okin, S.M., 208
ondinoc (desire), 408–9, 417–18, 419
ononharoia (dream-guessing rite), 12,
    402–3, 408–9; accounts of, 415–16; and
    ceremony, 409–11, 414–15; as
    interactive, 412; and resources, 411; and
    role of community, 412–13; role of,
    403–4; Wyandot, 419
oppression, 51, 53, 54, 60, 61, 80, 98,
    170, 263, 375; breaking the cycle of,
    209–10; competing theories of, 189; and
    downward social constitution, 365–8,
    369, 379; as economic phenomenon,
    188; and entrance to academia, 141–3,
    149; and harm, 189; need for new
    psychological theory of, 187–9;
    psychoanalytic theories of, 190–3;
    recognition theory of, 193–4; and social
    cognitive theory, 194–208; stereotypes
    and cyclical nature of, 208–9; victims of,
    365
orenda (mystical potency), 405–8;
    accounts of, 417; as song or voice, 408,
    409
origin story, Iroquoian, 404–5, 416
Ostaszewski, P. and Green, L., 206
Other, 6, 10, 109, 206
otherness, 367–8

patriotism, 140
Patterson, O., 271
Pease, D., 305, 310
people of color: and question of humanity,
    260–1; *see also* black: experience of
    being; negritude
Perry, B., 305, 308, 310
phallus, 247, 248–52
philosophy, 384; exclusion of women
    from, 230; ignorance of, 137; state of,
    137, 148; teaching of, 231, 335–7, 349
Piercy, M., 110–11, 150
Pinto, A.C., 206
Plato, 100–1, 103, 104, 139, 140
play, 226–7
polis, 100
political correctness, 100, 101, 140, 141,
    369, 394–5, 426

political economy: and culture, 55, 58–60,
    61–2, 70, 81, 93; post-Marxist, 152–7;
    see also socioeconomic injustice
positivism, 123–4
post-Communism, 103–4
post-Marxism, 4, 7, 152–7; and the Left,
    159
post-socialism, 68–9, 103
postcolonialism, 303, 304, 307, 310, 311,
    312
postmodernism, 2–3, 13, 113, 307, 382;
    ludic, 101–2; resistance, 101, 105,
    113–14
power, 311
pragmatism, 4, 13, 450
progressive humanism, 160–1
psychoanalysis, 9, 210; as empirically
    inadequate, 191; and tests of coherence
    and resonance, 191; and theories of
    oppression, 190–3
Putnam, H., 148

queer theory, 8, 32, 46–7, 51, 61
Quine, O.V., 144

race/racism, 4, 7, 45, 51, 88, 92, 112, 271,
    272–3, 278, 283, 292, 451; and
    affirmative/transformative remedies,
    38–9, 40; bigotry, 74, 94; and exclusion,
    286; experience of, 362, 371; and
    identity, 287–8; institutional, 74; and
    justice, 29–31, 61–3, 113; mixing of,
    285, 287; opposition to, 74–5; and
    pride, 286–7; superiority, 74, 94
rape, 361, 380
rationality, 10–13, 401–2; *see also*
    responsible thinking
Rawls, J., 21, 42, 51, 264, 265, 378
recognition, 4, 9, 48, 50, 239; and
    backlash misrecognition, 109; as central
    to multiculturalism, 73; cultures, 76–7;
    curricular, 77–9, 96; deconstructive
    approach to, 35–9, 54, 65, 72;
    democratic/sameness, 76, 87–8;
    distinctive, 76; as end in itself, 51; and
    equal worth, 82–4, 85–9; and equality,
    90–4; formulation of critical theory of,
    20–1; group, 76, 79, 80, 81, 88, 96–7;
    and harm, 95, 98; individual, 76, 77–9;
    and oppression, 193–4; and respect,
    83–4, 85–9, 240, 255, 261, 266, 390;

struggles for, 19–20, 41; and value, 79–81, 85–9, 96; *see also* redistribution–recognition dilemma

redistribution, 8; selective, 109–11

redistribution–recognition dilemma, 20, 21–4, 51–2, 68, 70, 93–4, 98; affirmation/transformation remedy, 31–4; and bivalent collectivities, 27–31; claims for, 24; critique of, 50–66; described, 52–3; and exploited classes, 24–6; in practice, 40–1; and race, 29–31; in reality, 39–40, 56–8; reasons for dichotomy, 54–8; remedy/justice matrix, 35–9; and sexuality, 26–9; in theory, 56–8

relativism, 138, 149, 453

religion, 280–1, 288, 316

repression, 4, 329

resistance, 303, 325

respect, 83–4, 85–9, 240, 255, 261, 266, 390

responsible thinking, 401; as conversation, 401–2; and function of ceremony, 409–11; as interactive and experimental, 412; as responsive action, 401; and role of community, 412–13; and use of available of resources, 411; *see also* rationality

Revolutionary Polish Women poets, 219

rights, 223–4, 240; denial of, 263–7; of property, 162

Rizzi, B., 153

Robinson, J., 151

Roche, E., 277

Rockefeller, S.C., 444

Roderick, R., 136–7

Rousseau, J.-J., 388

Royce, J., 431, 445

Rudes, B. and Crouse, D., 405

Said, E., 301, 302, 305, 306, 312, 315–16, 319; on Fanon, 307–8, 313–14; Traveling Theory, 310–11, 314

Sartre, J.-P., 102, 124, 145, 170, 321–3, 328

schema theory, 201–4

Schiller, J.C.F. von, 226

Schlesinger, A., 285–7, 291–3

science, 384

Second World, 382

self, 236, 247, 321, 383; and alienation, 260–3; sense of, 23, 42

self-consciousness, 6, 193

self-identity, 204–6; and abjection, 175; and desire, 171–2; and Oedipal complex, 170; and stereotypes, 200–1

Sen, A., 21, 42, 59, 66–7

sexual difference, 226–7, 229, 234–7, 240–1, 244, 245, 253

sexuality, 4–5, 44, 46, 238–9, 252–3; and affirmative/transformative remedies, 32–3, 36–8, 40; despised, 98; and identity, 176; injustice concerning, 26–9; as life-drives, 239, 253

sexuate being, 221, 223, 224–5

Shankara, 348–9

Skrypnek, B. and Snyder, M., 203

slaves/slavery, 11, 80, 270, 271–2, 276–7, 282, 284, 287, 288, 360–1, 372, 381, 423

Smith, A., 453

Smith, R.M., 385, 387

Smith, S.H. et al., 206

Snyder, M. et al., 203, 208

social categories, 360–5; diminished, 365–8, 369, 374, 375

social cognitive theory, and formation of stereotypes, 194–208, 211

social entities, 3, 450, 452, 455–6

social identity theory, 198

socialism, 47, 49, 71, 151, 221–2; and economic surplus, 154–7; emergence of, 153–4; transition to, 154, 158

society, transformation of, 132–5

Society for Analytic Feminism, 137

socioeconomic injustice, 21–2, 43, 50, 113; and class, 24–6; and race, 29–31; remedy for, 23, 24; and sexuality, 26–9; *see also* affirmative/transformative remedies

Sorel, G., 161

sovereignty, 163

Sowell, T., 83–4, 88

Speck, F., 409

Spivak, G.C., 302, 303, 305, 306, 310

Stalin, J., 124–6, 145

Steele, S., 272

stereotypes, 9; as categories, 196, 198; and change, 204–6; and cognitive miser model, 197; defined, 195–6; of femininity, 175–6; gender, 198–9,

202–4, 236; and in-group/out-group, 196–8; and schema theory, 201–4; as self-fulfilling, 208–9; social cognitive theory of formation of, 194–208; and social creativity strategies, 199–200; and social group, 207–8; of women, 263

Stern, D., 180–1, 182

subject/object dialectic, 315, 316, 320–1

subjectivity, 5, 6, 10; and interaction, 243–4, 255; new possibilities for, 234–5; *see also* feminine subject; masculine subject

suffrage, 163–4

Summers, C.H., 131, 136, 141

system/lifeworld dichotomy, 70

Tajfel, H., 197–8, 200

Taylor, C., 22, 51, 69, 73–4, 282; and affirmative action, 97; cultural respect, 85–9; and equal worth, 82–4; and individual recognition, 77–9; and racism, 74–5; and recognition, 75–7, 95; and value, 79–81, 85–9, 97

Third World, 382

thought, 2, 301, 301–2, 303–4, 314–15; and action, 449–50, 456; occasional, 302; oppositional, 315; and will, 302

Tocqueville, A. de, 284, 386, 387–8

Tooker, E., 410

totalitarianism, 126, 145

tourism, 453

tradition, 139–40

transformation remedies, *see* affirmative/ transformative remedies

transformative multiculturalism, 8, 132–5, 144

Traveling Theory, 310–11

Troadec, B., 206

Trotsky, L., 153

Turner, P.J. et al., 206

Tzeng, O.C.S. and Jackson, J.W., 206

universal human liberation, 449–51; condition of, 451; and monoculturalism, 452–4; pursuit of, 451; and race, 451, 454–5; and social entities, 455–6; and values, 452; and well-being, 452; and women, 451–2

universalism, 221, 388–9, 391

utopia, 127, 226–7, 432

values, 9, 241, 302, 325, 440–1, 452, 453

Vassiliou, V.G. and Vassiliou, G., 206

violence, 314, 316–17, 329–31

Vorstellung, 328

wages, calculation of, 155–7

Wallace, A.F.C., 403, 415–16

Walzer, M., 444

Ward, C., 206

Washington, B.T., 272

West, C., 302, 430–1, 437, 444

White Studies, 335; agricultural/botanical sciences, 338; and architecture and engineering, 337–8, 351; and expansion of content, 340–3; and history, 337, 350; as intellectually imperialist, 339–40; and native traditions, 338–9; and philosophy, 335–7, 349; and politics, 338; and science, 337–8; structure of, 343–7

Willett, C., 181–2

Williams, P., 143

Wilson, G.D. et al., 206

Wilson, W.J., 272

Winnicott, D.W., 180

Wittgenstein, L., 224, 445

women: and alienation, 263; consciousness-raising group, 231–2; as degraded other, 222; exclusion of, 230; liberation of, 451–2; and reproduction, 253, 254

working class, 158

writing, 303

Young, I.M., 42

Zhadanovism, 125